"We are overwhelmed, we are self-absorbed, we feel melancholy emptiness — most of us and more often than we like. Yet we long for our lives to contribute to something truly great, something that transcends our individual selves. Here is an excellent tool that helps us reflect on how our lives acquire depth and weight, that offers guidance about who we should be and what we should do if we are to lead lives that truly matter."

> — Miroslav Volf
> Yale Divinity School

"An elegantly crafted anthology and a treasure trove for the soul. Nuggets of insight, a gem of a story, or a strand of meaningful argument will capture your eye, reshape your heart and mind, and strengthen your resolve to listen more attentively — in the good company of these many authors — to the haunting, healing, creative sense of calling that yields the gift we call *vocation* — a life of meaning, purpose, and significance. Claim this book for yourself — and several more copies for the people you love."

> — Sharon Daloz Parks
> author of *Leadership Can Be Taught*

"How can I earn a living while living a worthwhile life? *Leading Lives That Matter* includes some of the most insightful authors to write about this question in a contemporary (or timeless) idiom. . . . Highly recommended."

> — Mark U. Edwards Jr.
> St. Olaf College

"*Leading Lives That Matter* speaks directly to the universal desire and urgent need to know what one should do and who one should be. Its broad range of texts, each aptly chosen and engagingly introduced, arms readers with a richer, more deeply textured vocabulary for thinking about these matters and with stunning models and examples of lives wonderfully lived."

> — Leon and the late Amy Kass
> University of Chicago

"Humanizes the sometimes-daunting task of self-discovery and the work required to live a life of purpose."

> — *Congregations*

"We recommend *Leading Lives That Matter* to parents, pastors, Sunday school teachers, and small group leaders. The book is centered on a topic of perennial importance, and instead of purporting to tell us how to live meaningfully, it invites us to join a conversation in order to develop wisdom in living."

> — *Critique*

Edited by

Mark R. Schwehn and Dorothy C. Bass

LEADING
LIVES
THAT
MATTER

What We Should Do and Who We Should Be

Second Edition

WILLIAM B. EERDMANS PUBLISHING COMPANY
GRAND RAPIDS, MICHIGAN

Wm. B. Eerdmans Publishing Co.
4035 Park East Court SE, Grand Rapids, Michigan 49546
www.eerdmans.com

26 25 24 23 22 21 20   1 2 3 4 5 6 7

ISBN 978-0-8028-7714-7

Library of Congress Cataloging-in-Publication Data

Names: Schwehn, Mark R., 1945– editor. | Bass, Dorothy C., editor.
Title: Leading lives that matter : what we should do and who we should be /
    edited by Mark R. Schwehn and Dorothy C. Bass.
Description: Second edition. | Grand Rapids, Michigan : Wm. B. Eerdmans Publish-
    ing Co., 2020. | Includes bibliographical references and index. | Summary: "Compiles
    a wide range of texts-from fiction, social science, philosophy, and ancient poetry-
    related to questions that arise for those who are trying to decide what to do with their
    lives" — Provided by publisher.
Identifiers: LCCN 2019046699 | ISBN 9780802877147 (paperback)
Subjects: LCSH: Vocation — Christianity. | Vocation. | Work — Religious aspects — Chris-
    tianity. | Work — Religious aspects. | Meaning (Philosophy) — Religious aspects —
    Christianity. | Meaning (Philosophy) — Religious aspects.
Classification: LCC BT738.5 .L43 2020 | DDC 248.4 — dc23
LC record available at https://lccn.loc.gov/2019046699

To Kaethe, Martha, and John

CONTENTS

Preface to the Second Edition   xi
Preface to the First Edition   xv
Introduction   1

PROLOGUE   9

William James *What Makes a Life Significant?* 16
Vincent Harding *I Hear Them ... Calling* 31

VOCABULARIES   41

Authenticity

Charles Taylor *The Ethics of Authenticity* 59
Parker Palmer *Explorations in True Self* 65
Elizabeth Cady Stanton *Solitude of Self* 72
Thanissaro Bhikkhu *No-Self or Not-Self?* 76
Ajahn Karunadhammo *This Is Who I Am* 79

Virtue

Aristotle *Nicomachean Ethics* 83
Rebecca Konyndyk DeYoung *Glittering Vices* 86
Josef Pieper *On Love* 92
Natalia Ginzburg *The Little Virtues* 97
David Brooks *The Moral Bucket List* 102
Mencius *Sayings* 108
Hsun Tzu *Improving Yourself* 110
Edith Jones *Patience* 114

Exemplarity

Linda Zagzebski *Why Exemplarism?* 119
Dorothy Day *Therese* 129
Gordon Marino *The Greatest* 138
Madeline Miller *False Counsellor* 143

Vocation

Denise Levertov *Annunciation* 149
Lee Hardy *Work, Life, and Vocational Choice* 153
Gary D. Badcock *Choosing* 164
C. S. Lewis *Learning in War-Time* 171
Dietrich Bonhoeffer *The Place of Responsibility* 176
Frederick Buechner *Vocation* 180
Will Campbell *Vocation as Grace* 182
Chuang Tzu *Mastering Life* 184

QUESTIONS 187

1. *Must My Job Be the Primary Source of My Identity?* 189

Russell Muirhead *Democracy and the Value of Work* 195
Dorothy L. Sayers *Why Work?* 199
Gilbert Meilaender *Friendship and Vocation* 204
Robert Frost *Two Tramps in Mud Time* 208
Margaret Piercy *To Be of Use* 212
Stephen Dunn *The Last Hours* 214
Carl Dennis *A Roofer* 216
Kazuo Ishiguro *The Remains of the Day* 218

2. *To Whom and to What Should I Listen
   as I Decide What to Do for a Living?* 229

Will Weaver *The Undeclared Major* 235
Amy Tan *Two Kinds* 242
Tayeb Salih *A Handful of Dates* 253
Lois Lowry *The Giver* 258
Willa Cather *The Ancient People* 268
Albert Schweitzer *I Resolve to Become a Jungle Doctor* 277

Matt Damon and Ben Affleck *Good Will Hunting* 285
James Baldwin *Sonny's Blues* 294

3. *With Whom and for Whom Shall I Live?* 323

Alasdair MacIntyre *Vulnerability, Dependence, Animality* 333
Kate Daniels *Prayer for My Children* 336
Malcolm Gladwell *The Roseto Mystery* 338
The Book of Ruth 344
Jhumpa Lahiri *My Two Lives* 350
Toni Morrison *Recitatif* 353
Sullivan Ballou *A Letter to His Wife, 1861* 371
Samuel Wells *Rethinking Service* 374
Martin Luther King Jr. *The World House* 388

4. *Is a Balanced Life Possible and Preferable
to a Life Focused Primarily on Work?* 391

Abigail Zuger *Defining a Doctor* 400
Karen S. Sibert *Don't Quit This Day Job* 403
Jane Addams *Filial Relations* 407
William Butler Yeats *The Choice* 412
Homer *The Iliad* 413
Martha Nussbaum *Interviewed by Bill Moyers* 414
Heather Boushey *Finding Time* 419
Matt Bloom *The Illusive Search for Balance* 427
Wendell Berry *Manifesto: The Mad Farmer Liberation Front* 432
Abraham Joshua Heschel *The Sabbath* 435

5. *What Are My Obligations to Future Human and Other Life?* 441

Larry Rasmussen *A Love Letter from the Holocene
to the Anthropocene* 451
Rachel Carson *A Fable for Tomorrow* 457
Scott Russell Sanders *Sanctuary* 460
Camille T. Dungy *Writing Home* 470
Paul Laurence Dunbar *The Haunted Oak* 474
Wanda Coleman *Requiem for a Nest* 477
Anthony E. Walton *Carrion* 478
Natasha Trethewey *Carpenter Bee* 480

Winona LaDuke *Our Home on Earth* 482
Wangari Maathai *Nobel Peace Prize Lecture* 489
Pope Francis *Laudato Si'* 496
Genesis 1–3 507
Ursula K. LeGuin *She Unnames Them* 513
Acoma Creation Story 516
Denise Levertov *Beginners* 518

6. *How Shall I Tell the Story of My Life?*   521

Robert Frost *The Road Not Taken* 527
Mary Catherine Bateson *Composing a Life Story* 529
Julia Alvarez *First Muse* 537
Wendell Berry *Jayber Crow* 541
Alice Walker *Saving the Life That Is Your Own* 543
Dan P. McAdams *A Life Story Made in America* 549
Michael T. Kaufman *Robert McG. Thomas, 60,
    Chronicler of Unsung Lives* 558

EPILOGUE   563

Leo Tolstoy *The Death of Ivan Ilych* 570

Acknowledgments   619
Index   625

PREFACE TO THE SECOND EDITION

Our work on *Leading Lives That Matter* began over fifteen years ago, when we started to prepare what would become the first edition of this book. A majority of the texts from that edition also appear in this revised volume, and we continue here to pursue our original goal of stimulating thoughtful and substantive conversations about what we should do and who we should be, or the relationship between work and identity. We have also retained the basic structure of the first edition, which readers report has been a helpful one. The book's two longest parts emphasize basic considerations that we still think are crucial to engaging the issues the book explores. In "Vocabularies," pages 41–185 below, we examine the various words and images that people ordinarily use when discussing what makes lives matter; analyzing these sheds light on the unexamined assumptions that often shape how we think about and decide on important matters of work and identity. In "Questions," pages 187–562 below, we take up specific concerns that most people are likely to worry about when trying to make the kinds of decisions the book addresses.

While the overall structure remains, substantial changes have been made. More than half of the texts in this edition are new. In adding some texts and questions and deleting others, we have been guided by our own recent experiences as teachers and readers, but also, and more so, by the counsel and aid of numerous faculty members, students, and other thoughtful readers who have used the first edition in their classrooms or who have taken a strong interest in the project stemming from their own curiosity and experience. Thus this edition's strengths derive in large part from what we learned during several years of unplanned field testing. We feel fortunate, as editors, to have the opportunity to revise our earlier work in ways that will serve a new generation of readers.

Readers of both editions will notice three main areas of change. First, this edition includes a much more diverse set of perspectives. There are more texts by women writers, writers from religious traditions other than Christianity, and writers from communities of color. Second, numerous changes and additions to the readings representing the vocabularies of authenticity, virtue, and vocation increase the clarity and illumine the significance of each of these ways of thinking about lives that matter. In addition, we have added a fourth vocabulary, exemplarity, which we believe adds an important set of concepts to the conversation we aim to evoke. Third, we have trimmed or combined some selections in the second part of the book to make way for two new questions.

The two new questions, which give focus to chapters 3 and 5, were prompted by two crucial streams of commentary from readers, which clarified our own growing concern about issues whose urgency has become more evident in recent years. The first is, "With whom and for whom shall I live?" Lives that matter are not undertaken alone, in isolation, or without thought of others. Such lives take shape in communities. In this new chapter, nine new readings explore the social character of lives of meaning and significance, offering different perspectives and stirring questions about what this might, or might not, mean. The second new question invites readers to ask, "What are my obligations to future human and other life?" We hope this chapter will encourage thoughtful conversations about whether and how we might lead lives that matter on a planet that is in peril.

Both editions of *Leading Lives That Matter* have received generous support from Lilly Endowment Inc. Indeed, they arose from and continue to contribute to major efforts to encourage reflection on basic questions regarding the meaning and purpose of life, beginning two decades ago with a national Program on the Theological Exploration of Vocation (PTEV). The concept of vocation, construed within the Christian tradition as a calling, soon expanded its influence well beyond its religious origins even as it retained its dynamic concern for the relationship between what we do and who we are, that is, between our various kinds of work and our identities. Since the link between preparing for a livelihood and preparing for life practically defines the central preoccupation of college students, the first wave of Lilly grants was made to colleges and universities; there students and faculty created countless ways to infuse courses of study, chapel programs, academic advising practices, and faculty development programs addressing broad concerns organized under the concept of vocation.

Such exploration, as well as other inquiries that flowed from it, required resources like this book. As a result, the Endowment funded two complementary anthologies. *Callings: Twenty Centuries of Christian Wisdom about Vocation* (2005), edited by our late friend and colleague William Placher, gathers theological texts that trace the idea of vocation from the Bible into the late twentieth century. *Leading Lives That Matter*, which we edited and published a year later, includes texts from a wider range of fields, organized around contemporary concerns and questions rather than a historical sequence.

Discussions and publications about human identity, purpose, and significance have increased in number, breadth, and depth in subsequent years, as the initial PTEV initiative led, directly and indirectly, to a still-expanding array of networks and programs. NetVUE (Network for Vocation in Undergraduate Education) supports institutions of higher education in pursuing this interest, under the auspices of the Council of Independent Colleges. NetVUE members, led by David Cunningham of Hope College, have been important conversation partners for us. We owe special thanks to David and to numerous NetVUE faculty who have offered editorial suggestions and ideas for particular texts and questions. We especially benefited from long discussions with Lynn Hunnicut and Laree Winer of Pacific Lutheran University and with Jean-Marie Kauth and Christine Fletcher of Illinois Benedictine University. We have also profited from the several publications that NetVUE has developed, which are listed under "Resources and Research" at https://www.cic.edu/programs/NetVUE. We hope this edition of *Leading Lives That Matter* will likewise be useful to these communities, as well as to others engaged in the expanding conversation on vocation, such as the Communities of Calling Initiative, a national effort based at Collegeville Institute and supported by Lilly Endowment, which aims to help congregations become places of vocational discernment.

We wish to repeat our thanks to students from Christ College — the Honors College of Valparaiso University, St. Olaf College, Saint John's University, and the College of St. Benedict who helped us to develop the structure and identify some of the questions and texts for the first edition. All of them, as well as other colleagues who helped with that edition, are named in the 2006 preface. Communities of research and conversation that contributed important ideas to the present edition include the Seminar on Christian Practical Wisdom (Kathleen Cahalan, Bonnie Miller-McLemore, James Nieman, and Christian Sharen); the Fall 2018 cohort of Resident Scholars at the Collegeville Institute (Roohi Choudry, Jotipalo Bhikkhu, Craig Boyd, Kris Kvam, Kathleen Norris, Fr. Columba Stewart, OSB, James Hoffman, and Gretchen Van Dyke); and Valparaiso University faculty and staff (Joseph Goss, Cynthia Rutz, Nancy Scannell, Anna Stewart, John Ruff, Ed Uehling, Fred Niedner, Mel Piehl, and Gretchen Buggeln). Dan McAdams of Northwestern University and Larry Rasmussen of Union Theological Seminary (emeritus) offered invaluable advice about the new questions explored in this edition.

For indispensable hospitality and support, we wish to express special thanks to Don Ottenhoff, director of the Collegeville Institute; Kathleen Cahalan, professor at Saint John's University School of Theology and Seminary and director of the Collegeville Seminars and the Communities of Calling Initiative; and the staff members of these organizations.

We dedicate this book to our three children. When the first edition appeared, all three of them were either in the process of discerning their vocations or in the process of trying to find good places to live out their vocations in financially remunerative ways. Now all three are settled, each of them blessed with a spouse and two children. Back in 2006, they were young adults with neither spouses nor full-time jobs; now they have passed the conventional sociological markers of adulthood. Yet they would be the first to tell you, as they have told us, that they continue to wrestle with the questions explored in this volume. They are at one and the same time settled and unsettled, and they are therefore ideal readers of *Leading Lives That Matter*. But each of them has given us two far more precious gifts: Thisbe and Matteus (from Kaethe and her husband, Peder), Naomi and Will (from Martha and her husband, Sam), and Lydia and Mira (from John and his wife, Anna). We hope and pray that all six of these grandchildren will grow up to lead lives that matter.

Mark Schwehn and Dorothy Bass
Valparaiso, Indiana
July 1, 2019

PREFACE TO THE FIRST EDITION

On October 19, 2005, we sent the manuscript of this anthology to the publisher. This date was also the twentieth birthday of our twin son and daughter. As second-year students in a liberal arts college, they were immersed that fall semester in a wide range of academic and non-academic pursuits. Yet they were also beginning to tire of the excess of options and to ponder more seriously than ever before the choices that will give shape and focus to what they do and become in the years after college. As of this writing, they do not yet know (or at least have not yet told us) what they hope to do to earn a living. At the same time, after a similar period of questioning, their older sister has discovered and embraced her calling as a writer and teacher of poetry. As we write, however, she is still searching for full-time employment.

The comparatively prolonged struggles of these and many other young adults to find their way in and through the process of figuring out what to do to earn a living are an important sign of our times, for the fluidity that characterizes their lives is also becoming increasingly common in the lives of older Americans. In this age of rapid economic, social, and cultural change, people of all ages and social classes can, and often do, experience unexpected unemployment, as well as other forms of personal or geographic displacement. Thus many people today are asking hard questions about how to make a living and what their work has to do with their identity.

We have composed this book not only for our children and their contemporaries but also for the many others who are asking these questions during this time of rapid social, cultural, and economic change. Although contemporary people bring special urgency to this set of questions, human beings have been asking them — and offering answers — for many centuries, and some have probed the heart of what gives a human life its shape, meaning, and significance. We have tried to capture in this book some of the wisdom that has found its way into words, by gathering texts from literature, philosophy, and everyday life that we believe may help readers to ponder these questions and to answer them well.

A few years ago the leaders of Lilly Endowment, a private family foundation in Indianapolis, noted this set of concerns and resolved to encourage students, faculty, and staff members in higher education to consider more deeply the insights inherent in the concept of *vocation*, a theological idea that also enjoys wide public use. The result was the Program for the Theological Exploration of Vocation (PTEV), which has given rise to exciting experiments at scores of colleges and universities in the United States and Canada. *Leading Lives That Matter* owes its origin to the new and vital interest in vocation sparked by PTEV but now evident far beyond its boundaries. In response to requests for material that could be used in campus settings as well as among parents and alums, Craig Dykstra and Chris Coble of the Lilly Endowment and Kim Maphis Early, coordinator of PTEV, invited the two of us and Professor William C. Placher of Wabash College to develop two complementary anthologies. *Callings: Twenty Centuries of Christian Wisdom about Vocation*, edited by Placher and published in the fall of 2005, includes theological texts that trace the development of the Christian idea of vocation over two millennia of history. *Leading Lives That Matter*, the present volume, looks beyond the idea of vocation *per se*, includes texts from a wider range of fields, and takes its organization from contemporary concerns rather than historical sequence. Each of the two books can stand alone, but we hope many readers will choose to read them both. Study guides for these books, as well as many other resources designed to foster theological reflection on vocation, are available for free download at www.ptev.org.

While compiling this anthology we have been reminded again and again that the endeavor to understand "lives that matter," like the endeavor to live them, is a communal venture, requiring at every point many voices, hands, hearts, and minds. We are indebted to all those who have aided us in the preparation of *Leading Lives That Matter*. From the beginning, Kim Maphis Early, Chris Coble, and Craig Dykstra provided generous encouragement, support, and counsel. Special thanks to Bill Placher, who has been a wise counselor and a good friend throughout the process. Bill also administered the Lilly Endowment grant that supported this work.

During the spring of 2005 in Christ College, the honors college of Valparaiso University, the students in Mark's seminar "What Makes a Life Significant?" helped to discover and shape some of the texts and questions that appear in this book. Special thanks therefore go to Sarah Benczik, Jeffrey Biebighauser, Julia Colbert, Katherine Hovsepian, Mark Koschmann, Nicole Kranich, Thomas Pichel, Jason Reinking, Amanda Schappler, Kendra Schmidt, Theodore Schultz, Jamie Stewart, and Joy Woellhart.

In August of 2005, the following students from Valparaiso University, St. Olaf College, Saint John's University, and the College of Saint Benedict reviewed a draft of part of the manuscript: Jeffrey Biebighauser, Hannah Bolt, Shaina Crotteau, Ben Durheim, Stephanie Mueller, Mike Reading, Martha Schwehn, Krista Senden, and Sarah Werner. Thanks to their criticisms, many of the introductions to sections and to specific texts were shortened and improved.

Many colleagues have suggested texts for inclusion and offered helpful comments on the shape of this anthology, including John Barbour, Kathleen Sprows Cummings, Sara Danger, John Feaster, Susan Felch, Darrell Jodock, Amy Kass, DeAne Lagerquist, and Dan McAdams. We benefited from challenging conversation about the issues explored here in sessions, at meals, and on the porches and trails of Holden Village. Our colleagues at the Collegeville Institute for Ecumenical and Cultural Studies and its director, Don Ottenhoff, asked hard questions and provided good company as we were finishing the work. The librarians at Valparaiso University, Saint John's University, and the College of Saint Benedict were patient and helpful. We are especially grateful for the diligence and perseverance of those who helped us with permissions and manuscript preparation: Doretta Kurzinski, Leslie Kurzinski, Sister Dolores Schuh, CHM, and Sarah Werner.

John Steven Paul, for many years chair of the Valparaiso University Theater Department and now the Program Director of the Lilly Fellows Program in Humanities and the Arts, and Margaret Franson, Associate Dean of Christ College, are remarkable educators who work daily to help others discern what they should do and who they should be. They are also godparents to one of our children, generous friends and guides to all three, and dear and faithful friends to the two of us. They lead lives that matter to us, to our children, to their colleagues, and to hundreds of students and alumni of Valparaiso University. We dedicate this book to them with gratitude and affection.

Mark R. Schwehn
Dorothy C. Bass

INTRODUCTION

This book is designed for people who want to lead lives that matter. The selections gathered here have been chosen because they can help readers think with greater clarity and depth about just what that might mean. In creating this book, we have been thinking about young people who are pondering what to do with their lives, and also about older people who feel that their lives lack significance for themselves or others. Both groups, we believe, want to "make a difference" in the world, as our own students and friends put it. They desire, as we ourselves do, to lead lives that are meaningful but also significant, lives that manifest both personal integrity and social responsibility.

What We Do and Who We Are

In the United States, fundamental questions about our purpose in life tend to emerge most forcefully when we are wondering what work we should do to earn a living. As many foreign observers have noticed, ours is a very pragmatic culture. When we make new acquaintances, we ask them first about what they do, not about what they believe, or where they live, or what and whom they love. Those questions come later, if at all. Similarly, most of us are impatient to answer questions about work for ourselves. Our eagerness to act can even prevent us from slowing down long enough to think carefully about what work would truly be best for ourselves and others.

The fact that these questions are so prominent in our lives suggests that they are related to other concerns, even beyond our need to make money. Many of us assume that what we do to earn a living somehow emerges from who we really are, and we also suspect that what we do to earn a living will somehow shape who we will be. A person's thinking about what to do to earn a living, in other words, is entangled with her identity and how she understands it. A person's choice of livelihood is framed by a sense of who he is and what he hopes to become as a particular human being — that is, when one *has* a choice in the matter, as many people do not; more on this later.

Leading Lives That Matter seeks to address a pragmatic society in a way that shows serious regard for ultimate concerns. Thus it invites readers into a set of questions and documents that attend both to immediate practical issues about what work we will do and to underlying religious and philosophical issues about identity and purpose. More important, the readings are arranged in a way that seeks to overcome the division between these two kinds of concerns. The essays, poems, and stories included here explore fundamental issues of human life and its meaning and purpose, to be sure. But they are clustered in chapters that respond directly to the practical questions that Americans who find themselves at important turning points in their lives most frequently ask.

In a sense, then, this book both yields to and resists Americans' obsession with work. Because jobs are such a focus of concern for people in our culture, the anthology often considers other vitally important parts of lives that matter — love and friendship, family and community, leisure and play, study and worship — primarily in connection to paid employment. Yet many of the readings also challenge this way of thinking, leading us to wonder whether our jobs really are or should be such important indicators of meaning and significance. We will find ourselves asking again and again, "Do our jobs really define who we are? And if so, should they?"

Multiple Traditions

This book seeks to overcome another division as well. Popular media in the United States often feature events and stories that pit the religious against the secular, the pious and devout against the skeptical and irreverent. Much that happens in our common life warrants the prominence of these depictions. Nevertheless, over the course of Western history, worldly and religious life, the secular and the sacred, have often informed, enriched, deepened, and constructively corrected one another. In this anthology, the readings are arranged in a way that will encourage that same dynamic of mutual correction and enrichment. Sources from both of these streams are intermingled, because wisdom and understanding from both are essential if we hope to explore together what it means to lead lives that matter.

All the great religious traditions contain abundant wisdom about questions of what we should do and who we should be. In this anthology, most of the religious authors and texts come from the Christian tradition. However, texts from other religious traditions also appear at certain points, adding crucial insights to the issues under consideration. Ours are small steps toward expanding the treasury of wisdom on which contemporary readers can draw — an important project that is currently under way in higher education and other parts of American culture. We hope that other authors will continue to add resources from other traditions to contemporary conversations about the questions explored in this book.

A similar restriction applies to the secular writings. Although secular culture, like Christianity, includes multiple and sometimes discordant modes of thought and reflection, most of the authors and texts in this volume belong loosely to what the philosopher Jeffrey Stout has called the "tradition of democracy." Perhaps the dominant voice among the many secular voices that define our common life, the voice of democracy emphasizes notions of equality and self-determination. As we shall see, the Christian tradition and the democratic tradition sometimes clash. At other points, however, they inform one another so closely that they are hard to distinguish. In any event, we should take every opportunity in these frequently contentious times to promote conversation between people of religious conviction and those who do not share such conviction, in the pursuit of common questions and ideas like those that define what it means to lead a life that matters.

Fostering Conversations about Lives That Matter

The pragmatism and impatience that infuse American culture have helped in recent decades to create a large market for self-help books. And so we must say: Readers beware! This is not a self-help book that provides ready answers to the questions it explores! Instead, the book is designed to lead readers to know their own minds better by encountering the minds of others who have gone before them. To read this book is to become a pilgrim along life's way, traveling in the company of other pilgrims who have left behind them records of their own journeys or the journeys of others. And as those who have read Chaucer's *Canterbury Tales* know, pilgrims like to talk while they travel. Reading this book is therefore more like joining a conversation than it is like going to a consultant or therapist. We hope that the book will enable readers to join an ongoing conversation that reaches back to ancient Israel, China, and Greece. But beyond this, we hope that it will encourage actual conversations among living companions who share the book's questions and concerns, including companions who bring different beliefs and experiences. Such conversations not only help us to refine our opinions; they also help us to enlarge our moral imaginations.

Happily, there is reason to think that readers are ready and eager to enter the conversation. *Leading Lives That Matter* has arisen in a context where multiple conversations and concerns are already alive. One group of conversations and concerns belongs to the young men and women in colleges, universities, and professional schools, or in the years just after graduation, who are struggling with questions of what they should do to earn a living and what that may mean for who they will become. Those who have been fortunate enough to attend institutions of higher education have long had the opportunity and burden of deciding what work to pursue — a privilege denied to most people in the past and one still denied to many in the United States and around the world. Our system of higher education, however, does not consistently encourage students to explore the kinds of basic questions this anthology raises. The vast majority of those who attend colleges and universities do so primarily to prepare for jobs of one kind or another, not to gain greater clarity about who they are or to discover what is true about the worlds of nature and culture. To be sure, most postsecondary schools do require students to take "liberal education" courses, in which basic issues of meaning, significance, value, justice, identity, and purpose should be raised and explored. However, these questions are often considered in isolation from the main concern that led most students to attend college in the first place: preparing for a job. Because of this division, which is structured by educators, many students come to believe that courses in literature or philosophy or history or religion are just academic requirements to be "gotten out of the way" until the "real" and more practical subjects can be studied. Resisting these assumptions, we hope that the readings gathered here will help students and recent graduates to see the importance of questions about meaning and purpose and to include reflection on these questions in their thinking about what they hope to do and become.

Another group of conversations and concerns is taking place within higher education itself, as well as in the many fields of endeavor to which it is related. At colleges and universities, administrators and faculties are asking how values, religious convictions, and ideals of service should influence education and scholarship. Meanwhile, at some hospitals, doctors, nurses, and medical students are gathering to discuss literature and philosophy, in an effort to clarify and deepen their sense of the profound human issues at stake in their profession. Those in other professions are engaging in similar explorations. In many cases, an effort to envision the work they do in relation to the kinds of philosophical and religious questions addressed by the readings gathered in this book is at the heart of their concern.

Beyond these arenas, a larger public composed of serious-minded citizens is deeply interested in thinking together about how best to spend their lives in order to bring about a better world both for themselves and for others. The emergence of large numbers of reading groups that focus on challenging literature similar to the texts gathered in this anthology provides evidence of a widespread hunger for engagement with the issues surrounding what we should do and who we should be. Even popular culture has been exploring these issues in recent years. The enormous popularity of the Harry Potter books and films may well arise from their capacity to explore for a mass audience stories about vocation, duty, and hope. *Black Panther*, *Wonder Woman*, and other superhero films take up similar concerns, gaining immense popularity with a mass audience hungry for images of strenuous and significant lives.

Although it is too early to know whether such developments amount to "straws in the wind" or a reconfiguration of public discourse, many of the economic and cultural forces driving them will probably remain in place for the foreseeable future. Global capitalism continues to reshape the workforce, displacing people, widening the gap between rich and poor, and saddling many with burdens that impede their freedom, including crippling debt. The rising number of maladies that are at least to some degree culturally induced (anxiety, depression, drug and alcohol abuse) suggests that millions have come to feel a loss of significance and purpose. The pressures that two-career marriages and single-parent households place upon individuals, children, and institutions complicate established patterns of employment and belonging. Meanwhile, the notion that material prosperity brings genuine fulfillment is rarely questioned — even though millions of people have learned by experience that this equation is false.

How Can I Use This Book to Greatest Advantage?

This anthology seeks to make easily available to readers of all kinds some of the best thinking and writing done over the centuries about the very questions that most trouble human beings when they wonder about how to lead lives of substance and significance. But not all readers are the same. For some, the most important question is, With whom and for whom shall I live? For others, the most urgent matter before them is, Is a balanced life possible and preferable to a life focused primarily upon work? Still others are trying to sort out all the conflicting advice they are receiving; for them, the question is, To whom and to what shall I listen as I decide what to do for a living? For many who share increasing awareness of the environmental degradation overtaking our planet home, the crucial question is, What are my obligations to future human and other life? Meanwhile, many ask, Must my job be the primary source of my identity?

The longest section of this anthology is organized around exactly these concerns, ending with the summative question, How shall I tell the story of my life? Those readers who come to the book with a particular, well-defined question are welcome to turn directly to the chapter that addresses just that question. Understanding and learning from the readings in any one chapter do not depend in any major way upon an understanding of the readings in other chapters. Even so, the introductions to readings in a given chapter often refer to readings in other chapters. We hope that these references will lead readers to move beyond their first question to consider other issues, which will in all likelihood set their initial question in a helpful, wider context.

Other readers will prefer to ponder the big picture before they attend to the more immediate and practical matters explored in "Questions." These readers should turn to "Vocabularies," which addresses a broad and some-what abstract question: How should we think and talk about what makes a life meaningful and significant? This section of the book addresses a concern that is far more urgent than it might at first appear. Today many of us have difficulty articulating what we really think and believe about what makes a life choiceworthy. We may be reluctant to admit that we make judgments, or we may hold a number of views that are difficult to reconcile with one another, or we may just find it hard to express ourselves very clearly about what we really think and care about. The section entitled "Vocabularies" endeavors to help readers make better judgments about their own lives and the lives of others by exploring four distinct sets of terms and ideas that people have used over the centuries to speak about what makes a life choiceworthy and admirable. Most of us draw primarily upon one of these vocabularies today, though many of us find creative ways to combine them. The key terms or ideas in each of the four vocabularies suggest what each of them will emphasize: authenticity and individualism, virtue and character, exemplarity and admiration, and vocation and the divine.

Whether readers are initially drawn to "Vocabularies" or "Questions," we encourage all readers first to read the prologue. It begins, as does each chapter, with a brief essay by the editors that sets forth the key issues readers should consider. In the prologue, this essay is followed by two wonderful readings that explore the underlying question of what makes a life significant, raising issues we shall revisit throughout the book.

The epilogue consists of only one reading, but it is arguably the most important one in the book: *The Death of Ivan Ilych,* by Leo Tolstoy. Because this short novel raises in a vivid and complete way all the questions that the anthology addresses, it can serve readers in at least two ways. First, it can provide a rich opportunity to exercise some of the capacities for judgment that other readings in the anthology should strengthen and sharpen. And second, it can be itself a rich source of wisdom about what it means to lead a life that matters. Many readers will want to read this novel more than once, even perhaps both before and after they engage with the other treasures in this anthology. Engaging texts like *The Death of Ivan Ilych* in this way will be at one and the same time an exercise in liberal learning and an exercise in vocational preparation. Moreover, as we noted at the outset, the anthology as a whole is based upon the assumption that one cannot think very well or very long about practical matters without sustained attention to the fundamental questions that have preoccupied human beings from the time they first began to think and talk together. We cannot ponder our livelihoods without at one and the same time thinking about the shape, the meaning, and the significance of our entire lives. We cannot decide what we should do without considering who we are and what we might become.

PROLOGUE

What is the difference, if any, between a good life and a significant one? When we put this question to a group of college students, some argued that a good life is a matter of character, having to do with the kind of person you are. A significant life, on the other hand, is a consequential life, they thought, a life that influences a great number of people. A person does not have to be morally good to be significant or influential.

But does morality have no bearing on significance? For many of the students, a significant life must not just influence the world; it must influence the world for the better. Thus, Joseph Stalin, though he changed the lives of millions, did not lead a significant life, because the results of his often brutal and arbitrary actions were terrible, not beneficial, for humankind. Besides, Stalin was, so these students insisted, an ignoble human being, someone of bad character, perhaps mentally deranged, and therefore not worthy of admiration. A significant life must be admirable, *and* it must change the world for the better.

The students expressed other views, of course, but these were the two extremes. Students at one extreme thought significance was a purely quantitative measure: the more people influenced by someone, the more significant his or her life. Students at the other extreme thought it was mostly a qualitative matter: people must lead good lives and change the world substantially for the better in order to lead significant lives. Students at both extremes agreed that significance had *something* to do with "making a difference," but here again, matters quickly grew complex. Who could tell how many lives a high school teacher might influence? "A teacher touches eternity, for he never knows where his influence stops," the historian Henry Adams once declared. Perhaps significance cannot be measured after all, unless we arbitrarily say it pertains only to the number of people whose lives are changed for the better by a person during the course of his or her lifetime. Even so, measurements would be hard to make. How many lives did Dwight David Eisenhower change for the better during his lifetime, first as a general in the army during World War II, later as a two-term president of the United

States? And what if some of his influence was not positive? How would we figure his significance then?

Questions that forever elude precise answers are not for that reason trivial or "merely academic." On the contrary. Most of the students in this conversation were soon to graduate. They wanted to gain some clarity about what makes for a significant life, because most of them longed to make a difference in the world. Yet they hoped to do so in a way that would honor other aspirations as well. And they worried that endeavors to lead a good or virtuous life might sometimes conflict with efforts to lead a significant one.

William James and Vincent Harding, the authors of the two documents in this prologue, also worried about what they should do and who they should be, even though their lives developed in quite different cultural locations. William James, a white American, endured a long vocational crisis, extending almost ten years and spanning the most terrible war in United States history, the Civil War. A century later, Vincent Harding, an African American, found a vocation — or rather, several vocations — as he responded to the needs of a number of communities, and to his own yearnings, during another crucial period in US history, the Freedom Movement of the 1950s and beyond. James's essay presents the fruits of his questions and struggles; without specifically describing his own path, he summarizes what he came to believe about a significant life in a lecture to college students. In Harding's case, an article written for a book on vocation tells the story of the winding road he traveled — always in the company of others — as he figured out how his life could be significant. Together, these documents raise questions we will encounter throughout this book.

James eventually became one of America's most distinguished psychologists as well as one of its most influential philosophers. But his road to these achievements was not easy. He grew up in a large and accomplished family. His sister Alice was a troubled but very gifted writer. And his brother Henry became one of America's foremost novelists. His father and mother were by and large permissive and indulgent parents; they seldom interfered in their children's decisions about their careers. But Henry James Sr. made an exception in William's case. For as long as William could remember, he wanted to be an artist. His brother Henry remembered him "drawing, drawing, always drawing." But his father had other plans for William, insisting that he become a scientist.

Though the reasons for William's father's manipulation of his son's choice of career are far from clear, much of the evidence points to a motive that is not uncommon among parents. Henry James Sr. had once hoped to be a scientist himself, but he gave up the effort. Instead, he tried to arrange matters so that his son William might realize Henry Sr.'s own ambitions. He therefore removed William from the studio where he was learning to paint and transported him to Germany, where he exposed William to some of the most advanced scientific study in Europe at the time. Yielding to his father's wishes, William abandoned painting, a move he was to regret for at least ten years, and enrolled in the Lawrence Scientific School at Harvard in 1861.

The manifold conflicts between paternal expectations and William's own longings led to painful academic and psychological experiences. In today's parlance, we would say he was a college student who was constantly changing his major. He enrolled in chemistry, soon changed to comparative anatomy and physiology, then resolved to study medicine, then decided that he preferred research to medicine, then took a trip to the Amazon on a specimen-collecting expedition to see whether he might pursue a career in natural history, then took another trip to Germany, where his interests broadened to include literature and philosophy.

He had also gone to Germany to seek relief from a variety of physical and psychological symptoms — insomnia, digestive disorders, eye trouble, and acute back pains. But the various treatments he received had little positive effect. By the late 1860s, William James was deeply depressed, often unable to find the energy to work or to care about life. He grew to believe that his life was completely determined by physical and social forces beyond his control. On the verge of suicide, James happened to read works of poetry and philosophy that defended human freedom, and he came to believe that he was after all free to make his own choices. Or, as he put it, his first act of free will was to believe in free will, to believe "in my individual reality and creative power." James always believed that his vocational crisis was at one and the same time physical, psychological, philosophical, and spiritual. The essay included here shows traces of his own struggles, with its emphases upon freedom, ideals, individual energy and initiative, and the belief that people can make a difference in the world.

Although the birthplaces of William James and Vincent Harding are just a few miles apart, the two men inhabited very different parts of the United States. James was born in a wealthy neighborhood in Manhattan in 1842, and Harding was born in Harlem in 1931, during the Great Depression. Material things were far more abundant in the James household, but young Vincent prospered in the care of his mother, a single woman who worked as a domestic, and in the nurturing community of the church to which they belonged. Although every life is to some degree unknowable, Harding's own writings and what others have said about him suggest that he had a notably positive approach to life from childhood until his death in 2014. He would have been the first to point out that early support from others — especially his church community and teachers — contributed immensely to the lifelong success he would enjoy. After growing up in Harlem and the Bronx, he excelled at the City University of New York and the Columbia School of Journalism. Then — as happened to many young American men in the 1950s — he was drafted into the army, an experience that led him, ironically, to embrace the nonviolent approach to social change that would become central to his life-work. As a graduate student in American history in the late 1950s, he found his way into an interracial Mennonite church in Chicago and then traveled to Montgomery, Alabama, with some of the congregation's leaders. There he met Martin Luther King, who urged him to move south to join the struggle for freedom. With his wife, Rosemarie Freeney Harding, his strong partner in the decades of activism that would follow, he did. Based at Mennonite House in Atlanta, an integrated community center located just around the corner from Coretta and Martin King's own home, Harding became a member of King's inner circle and a crucial leader in the civil rights movement.

In the decades that followed, Harding worked hard to make sure that younger Americans would remember the lives of King, other women and men of the civil rights movement, and those who had fought for freedom in earlier generations. One of the several callings that drew Harding's energy was writing; in several books, including the award-winning *There Is a River: The Black Struggle for Freedom in America*, he put his expertise as a historian to work in recovering and articulating memories of resistance and hope for a more just future. After finishing his PhD at the University of Chicago, he taught at several schools, including Spelman, Temple, Penn, Morehouse, and the Iliff School of Theology, in Denver. He also continued to invite wider publics to remember the history of struggle and to build a constituency to carry it on in the present. For example, he served as the chief historical consultant for an influential 1987 PBS documentary series about the civil rights movement, *Eyes on the Prize*, and created two organizations designed to foster relationships between activist elders and rising leaders committed to strengthening democracy.

A great theme of Harding's life and work was *community* — and we include him in this prologue in part to lift up the importance of that theme for all who are wondering what they should do and who they should be. The selection below offers testimony to the support, and the important challenges, he received from other people during his formative years. Even when he left one community for another — for example, his childhood church for the Mennonites — he still expressed gratitude for the earlier community. Beyond and behind these specific gatherings, moreover, he sensed a transcendent community that he called "my people." A profound sense of connection to the past, and a deep conviction that there is much to be learned there, mattered deeply as he sought to place his own life in a larger frame of significance.

Both of the readings that follow point, in different ways, to the importance of community to lives that matter. In contrast to Harding, James's own vocational struggle often left him feeling isolated. Further, in the lecture below, James seems to model an approach that has an individual thinking through a problem on his own. Yet if you read closely, you will see James drawing on resources from the past, praising those who make sacrifices for the sake of others, urging students to respect and help those experiencing injustice in their own day, and holding up various examples of community for consideration and critique.

Harding's different (and stronger) emphasis on community came partly from his experience, but also from the religious ideal of "beloved community" that energized the civil rights movement. This movement represented one of the most vital intersections of the two traditions that largely inform this anthology and that we discussed briefly in the general introduction — democracy and Christianity. Both Harding and James present noteworthy examples of how these traditions come to bear on significant lives. Although James was deeply interested in religious concerns and believed that our lives are suspended within a larger universe of religious meaning and purpose, he was suspicious of institutionalized religion and was never a regular churchgoer. The lecture below says little of religion, but it does reflect democracy, especially in James's argument against rising inequities of wealth in his time. Harding, on the other hand, was deeply shaped by his life in the church, from his childhood in Harlem's Victory Tabernacle Seventh-Day Christian Church to his embrace of the Mennonite tradition and its practice of nonviolence; later he served for decades as a professor in a seminary of the United Methodist Church. That said, Harding did not rest easy with many aspects of institutional religion. Tellingly, his title at Iliff School of Theology, where he taught, was Professor of Religion and Social Transformation. Later in life, as religious violence and extremism grew more visible, he broadened his vision to speak of building "a multiracial, multiethnic, multireligious, democratic society." He believed that America was still a "developing society" when it came to these hopes, and he continued to be a source of wisdom and encouragement for those who joined together to pursue them.

In spite of their cultural differences, both of these thinkers raise important questions about what makes a life significant. And both offer, by example and in writing, encouragement that our lives can indeed matter.

William James

WHAT MAKES A LIFE SIGNIFICANT?

William James (1842–1910) was a renowned psychologist, philosopher, and popular lecturer. He is probably remembered most for his 1905 Gifford Lectures, published as *The Varieties of Religious Experience,* and for his *Pragmatism,* one of the foundational works in a distinctively American school of philosophy that he helped to establish, along with his contemporary Charles Sanders Peirce and his heir, John Dewey. The following essay, "What Makes a Life Significant?," exhibits his characteristically exploratory and accessible style, having originally been delivered as a lecture to college students.

In the essay, James first suggests that a significant life must overcome great resistance in a struggle against malevolent forces; such a life is led by only a few heroes or heroines, who attain immortal fame. Later, he revises that view to suggest that a significant life is possible for everyone, perhaps especially for those ordinary laborers who struggle daily to earn a living in ways that are often exemplary. Which of the two views seems more plausible to you? Later in the essay, James suggests that ideals are a large part, at least half, of what makes lives significant. Are some ideals more worthy of our life's devotion than others? Is there any way of distinguishing between admirable devotion to an ideal and dangerous fanaticism?

As an example of a struggle that incorporates ideals and that is large enough to engage human energies and efforts, James discusses the "labor question," the effort to provide fair wages and conditions for workers, which was very much alive during the period in which he wrote. Which issues, questions, or struggles are most worthy of human devotion and energy today?

... A few summers ago I spent a happy week at the famous Assembly Grounds on the borders of Chautauqua Lake [a center for the arts and education in upstate New York]. The moment one treads that sacred enclosure,

William James, "What Makes a Life Significant?," in *The Writings of William James*, ed. John McDermott (Chicago: University of Chicago Press, 1977), 645–60.

one feels one's self in an atmosphere of success. Sobriety and industry, intelligence and goodness, orderliness and ideality, prosperity and cheerfulness, pervade the air. It is a serious and studious picnic on a gigantic scale. Here you have a town of many thousands of inhabitants, beautifully laid out in the forest and drained, and equipped with means for satisfying all the necessary lower and most of the superfluous higher wants of man. You have a first-class college in full blast. You have magnificent music — a chorus of seven hundred voices, with possibly the most perfect open-air auditorium in the world. You have every sort of athletic exercise from sailing, rowing, swimming, bicycling, to the ball-field and the more artificial doings which the gymnasium affords. You have kindergartens and model secondary schools. You have general religious services and special club-houses for the several sects. You have perpetually running soda-water fountains, and daily popular lectures by distinguished men. You have the best of company, and yet no effort. You have no zymotic diseases, no poverty, no drunkenness, no crime, no police. You have culture, you have kindness, you have cheapness, you have equality, you have the best fruits of what mankind has fought and bled and striven for under the name of civilization for centuries. You have, in short, a foretaste of what human society might be, were it all in the light, with no suffering and no dark corners.

I went in curiosity for a day. I stayed for a week, held spell-bound by the charm and ease of everything, by the middle-class paradise, without a sin, without a victim, without a blot, without a tear.

And yet what was my own astonishment, on emerging into the dark and wicked world again, to catch myself quite unexpectedly and involuntarily saying: "Ouf! what a relief! Now for something primordial and savage, even though it were as bad as an Armenian massacre, to set the balance straight again. This order is too tame, this culture too second-rate, this goodness too uninspiring. This human drama without a villain or a pang; this community so refined that icecream soda-water is the utmost offering it can make to the brute animal in man; this city simmering in the tepid lakeside sun; this atrocious harmlessness of all things, — I cannot abide with them. Let me take my chances again in the big outside worldly wilderness with all its sins and sufferings. There are the heights and depths, the precipices and the steep ideals, the gleams of the awful and the infinite; and there is more hope and help a thousand times than in this dead level and quintessence of every mediocrity."

Such was the sudden right-about-face performed for me by my lawless fancy! There had been spread before me the realization — on a small, sample scale of course — of all the ideals for which our civilization has been striving: security, intelligence, humanity, and order; and here was the instinctive hostile reaction, not of the natural man, but of a so-called cultivated man upon such a Utopia. There seemed thus to be a self-contradiction and paradox somewhere, which I, as a professor drawing a full salary, was in duty bound to unravel and explain, if I could.

So I meditated. And, first of all, I asked myself what the thing was that was so lacking in this Sabbatical city, and the lack of which kept one forever falling short of the higher sort of contentment. And I soon recognized that it was the element that gives to the wicked outer world all its moral style, expressiveness and picturesqueness, — the element of precipitousness, so to call it, of strength and strenuousness, intensity and danger. What excites and interests the looker-on at life, what the romances and the statues celebrate and the grim civic monuments remind us of, is the everlasting battle of the powers of light with those of darkness; with heroism, reduced to its bare chance, yet ever and anon snatching victory from the jaws of death. But in this unspeakable Chautauqua there was no potentiality of death in sight anywhere, and no point of the compass visible from which danger might possibly appear. The ideal was so completely victorious already that no sign of any previous battle remained, the place just resting on its oars. But what our human emotions seem to require is the sight of the struggle going on. The moment the fruits are being merely eaten, things become ignoble. Sweat and effort, human nature strained to its uttermost and on the rack, yet getting through alive, and then turning its back on its success to pursue another more rare and arduous still — this is the sort of thing the presence of which inspires us, and the reality of which it seems to be the function of all the higher forms of literature and fine art to bring home to us and suggest. At Chautauqua there were no racks, even in the place's historical museum; and no sweat, except possibly the gentle moisture on the brow of some lecturer, or on the sides of some player in the ball-field.

Such absence of human nature *in extremis* anywhere seemed, then, a sufficient explanation for Chautauqua's flatness and lack of zest.

But was not this a paradox well calculated to fill one with dismay? It looks indeed, thought I, as if the romantic idealists with their pessimism about our civilization were, after all, quite right. An irremediable flatness is coming over the world. Bourgeoisie and mediocrity, church sociables and teachers' conventions, are taking the place of the old heights and depths and romantic chiaroscuro. And, to get human life in its wild intensity, we must in future turn more and more away from the actual, and forget it, if we can, in the romancer's or the poet's pages. The whole world, delightful and sinful as it may still appear for a moment to one just escaped from the Chautauquan enclosure, is nevertheless obeying more and more just those ideals that are sure to make of it in the end a mere Chautauqua Assembly on an enormous scale. *Was in Gesang soll leben muss im Leben untergehn.* ["That which should live in song must perish in life."] Even now, in our own country, correctness, fairness, and compromise for every small advantage are crowding out all other qualities. The higher heroisms and the old rare flavors are passing out of life.

With these thoughts in my mind, I was speeding with the train toward Buffalo, when, near that city, the sight of a workman doing something on the dizzy edge of a sky-scaling iron construction brought me to my senses very suddenly. And now I perceived, by a flash of insight, that I had been steeping myself in pure ancestral blindness, and looking at life with the eyes of a remote spectator. Wishing for heroism and the spectacle of human nature on the rack, I had never noticed the great fields of heroism lying round about me, I had failed to see it present and alive. I could only think of it as dead and embalmed, labelled and costumed, as it is in the pages of romance. And yet there it was before me in the daily lives of the laboring classes. Not in clanging fights and desperate marches only is heroism to be looked for, but on every railway bridge and fire-proof building that is going up to-day. On freight-trains, on the decks of vessels, in cattle-yards and mines, on lumber-rafts, among the firemen and the policemen, the demand for courage is incessant; and the supply never fails. There, every day of the year somewhere, is human nature *in extremis* for you. And wherever a scythe, an axe, a pick, or a shovel is wielded, you have it sweating and aching and with its powers of patient endurance racked to the utmost under the length of hours of the strain.

As I awoke to all this unidealized heroic life around me, the scales seemed to fall from my eyes; and a wave of sympathy greater than anything I had ever before felt with the common life of common men began to fill my soul. It began to seem as if virtue with horny hands and dirty skin were the only virtue genuine and vital enough to take account of. Every other virtue poses; none is absolutely unconscious and simple, and unexpectant of decoration or recognition, like this. These are our soldiers, thought I, these our sustainers, these the very parents of our life. Many years ago, when in Vienna, I had had a similar feeling of awe and reverence in looking at the peasant-women, in from the country on their business at the market for the day. Old hags many of them were, dried and brown and wrinkled, kerchiefed and short-petticoated, with thick wool stockings on their bony shanks, stumping through the glittering thoroughfares, looking neither to the right nor the left, bent on duty, envying nothing, humble-hearted, remote; — and yet at bottom, when you came to think of it, bearing the whole fabric of the splendors and corruptions of that city on their laborious backs. For where would any of it have been without their unremitting, unrewarded labor in the fields? And so with us: not to our generals and poets, I thought, but to the Italian and Hungarian laborers in the Subway, rather, ought the monuments of gratitude and reverence of a city like Boston to be reared.

If any of you have been readers of Tolstoï [Leo Tolstoy, the Russian author], you will see that I passed into a vein of feeling similar to his, with its abhorrence of all that conventionally passes for distinguished, and its exclusive deification of the bravery, patience, kindliness, and dumbness of the unconscious natural man.

Where now is *our* Tolstoï, I said, to bring the truth of all this home to our American bosoms, fill us with a better insight, and wean us away from that spurious literary romanticism on which our wretched culture — as it calls itself — is fed? Divinity lies all about us, and culture is too hide-bound to even suspect the fact. Could a Howells or a Kipling [prominent authors of the time] be enlisted in this mission? or are they still too deep in the ancestral blindness, and not humane enough for the inner joy and meaning of the laborer's existence to be really revealed? Must we wait for some one born and bred and living as a laborer himself, but who, by grace of Heaven, shall also find a literary voice?

And there I rested on that day, with a sense of widening of vision, and with what it is surely fair to call an increase of religious insight into life. In God's eyes the differences of social position, of intellect, of culture, of cleanliness, of dress, which different men exhibit, and all the other rarities and exceptions on which they so fantastically pin their pride, must be so small as practically quite to vanish; and all that should remain is the common fact that here we are, a countless multitude of vessels of life, each of us pent in to peculiar difficulties, with which we must severally struggle by using whatever of fortitude and goodness we can summon up. The exercise of the courage, patience, and kindness, must be the significant portion of the whole business; and the distinctions of position can only be a manner of diversifying the phenomenal surface upon which these underground virtues may manifest their effects. At this rate, the deepest human life is everywhere, is eternal. And, if any human attributes exist only in particular individuals, they must belong to the mere trapping and decoration of the surface-show.

Thus are men's lives levelled up as well as levelled down, — levelled up in their common inner meaning, levelled down in their outer gloriousness and show. Yet always, we must confess, this levelling insight tends to be obscured again; and always the ancestral blindness returns and wraps us up, so that we end once more by thinking that creation can be for no other purpose than to develop remarkable situations and conventional distinctions and merits. And then always some new leveller in the shape of a religious prophet has to arise — the Buddha, the Christ, or some Saint Francis, some Rousseau or Tolstoï — to redispel our blindness. Yet, little by little, there comes one stable gain; for the world does get more humane, and the religion of democracy tends toward permanent increase.

This, as I said, became for a time my conviction, and gave me great content. I have put the matter into the form of a personal reminiscence, so that I might lead you into it more directly and completely, and so save time. But now I am going to discuss the rest of it with you in a more impersonal way.

Tolstoï's levelling philosophy began long before he had the crisis of melancholy commemorated in that wonderful document of his entitled 'My Confession,' which led the way to his more specifically religious works. In his masterpiece 'War and Peace,' — assuredly the greatest of human novels, — the rôle of the spiritual hero is given to a poor little soldier named Karataïeff, so helpful, so cheerful, and so devout that, in spite of his ignorance and filthiness, the sight of him opens the heavens, which have been closed, to the mind of the principal character of the book; and his example evidently is meant by Tolstoï to let God into the world again for the reader. Poor little Karataïeff is taken prisoner by the French; and, when too exhausted by hardship and fever to march, is shot as other prisoners were in the famous retreat from Moscow. The last view one gets of him is his little figure leaning against a white birch-tree, and uncomplainingly awaiting the end.

"The more," writes Tolstoï in the work 'My Confession,' "the more I examined the life of these laboring folks, the more persuaded I became that they veritably have faith, and get from it alone the sense and the possibility of life. . . . Contrariwise to those of our own class, who protest against destiny and grow indignant at its rigor, these people receive maladies and misfortunes without revolt, without opposition, and with a firm and tranquil confidence that all had to be like that, could not be otherwise, and that it is all right so. . . . The more we live by our intellect, the less we understand the meaning of life. We see only a cruel jest in suffering and death, whereas these people live, suffer, and draw near to death with tranquillity, and oftener than not with joy. . . . There are enormous multitudes of them happy with the most perfect happiness, although deprived of what for us is the sole good of life. Those who understand life's meaning, and know how to live and die thus, are to be counted not by twos, threes, tens, but by hundreds, thousands, millions. They labor quietly, endure privations and pains, live and die, and throughout everything see the good without seeing the vanity. I had to love these people. The more I entered into their life, the more I loved them; and the more it became possible for me to live, too. It came about not only that the life of our society, of the learned and of the rich, disgusted me — more than that, it lost all semblance of meaning in my eyes. All our actions, our deliberations, our sciences, our arts, all appeared to me with a new significance. I understood that these things might be charming pastimes, but that one need seek in them no depth, whereas the life of the hard-working populace, of that multitude of human beings who really contribute to existence, appeared to me in its true light. I understood that there veritably is life, that the meaning which life there receives is the truth; and I accepted it."

In a similar way does [Robert Louis] Stevenson appeal to our piety toward the elemental virtue of mankind. "What a wonderful thing," he writes, "is this Man! How surprising are his attributes! Poor soul, here for so little, cast among so many hardships, savagely surrounded, savagely descended, irremediably condemned to prey upon his fellow-lives, — who should have blamed him, had he been of a piece with his destiny and a being merely barbarous? . . . [Yet] it matters not where we look, under what climate we observe him, in what stage of society, in what depth of ignorance, burdened with what erroneous morality; in ships at sea, a man inured to hardship and vile pleasures, his brightest hope a fiddle in a tavern, and a bedizened trull who sells herself to rob him, and he, for all that, simple, innocent, cheerful, kindly like a child, constant to toil, brave to drown, for others; . . . in the slums of cities, moving among indifferent millions to mechanical employments, without hope of change in the future, with scarce a pleasure in the present, and yet true to his virtues, honest up to his lights, kind to his neighbors, tempted perhaps in vain by the bright gin-palace, . . . often repaying the world's scorn with service, often standing firm upon a scruple; . . . everywhere some virtue cherished or affected, everywhere some decency of thought and courage, everywhere the ensign of man's ineffectual goodness, — ah! if I could show you this! If I could show you these men and women all the world over, in every stage of history, under every abuse of error, under every circumstance of failure, without hope, without help, without thanks, still obscurely fighting the lost fight of virtue, still clinging to some rag of honor, the poor jewel of their souls."

All this is as true as it is splendid, and terribly do we need our Tolstoïs and Stevensons to keep our sense for it alive. Yet you remember the Irishman who, when asked, "Is not one man as good as another?" replied, "Yes; and a great deal better, too!" Similarly (it seems to me) does Tolstoï overcorrect our social prejudices, when he makes his love of the peasant so exclusive, and hardens his heart toward the educated man as absolutely as he does. Grant that at Chautauqua there was little moral effort, little sweat or muscular strain in view. Still, deep down in the souls of the participants we may be sure that something of the sort was hid, some inner stress, some vital virtue not found wanting when required. And, after all, the question recurs, and forces itself upon us: Is it so certain that the surroundings and circumstances of the virtue do make so little difference in the importance of the result? Is the functional utility, the worth to the universe of a certain definite amount of courage, kindliness, and patience, no greater if the possessor of these virtues is in an educated situation, working out far-reaching tasks, than if he be an illiterate nobody, hewing wood and drawing water, just to keep himself alive? Tolstoï's philosophy, deeply enlightening though it certainly is, remains a false abstraction. It savors too much of that Oriental pessimism and nihilism of his, which declares the whole phenomenal world and its facts and their distinctions to be a cunning fraud.

A mere bare fraud is just what our Western common sense will never believe the phenomenal world to be. It admits fully that the inner joys and virtues are the *essential* part of life's business, but it is sure that *some* positive part is also played by the adjuncts of the show. If it is idiotic in romanticism to recognize the heroic only when it sees it labelled and dressed-up in books, it is really just as idiotic to see it only in the dirty boots and sweaty shirt of some one in the fields. It is with us really under every disguise: at Chautauqua; here in your college; in the stock-yards and on the freight-trains; and in the czar of Russia's court. But, instinctively, we make a combination of two things in judging the total significance of a human being. We feel it to be some sort of a product (if such a product only could be calculated) of his inner virtue *and* his outer place, — neither singly taken, but both conjoined. If the outer differences had no meaning for life, why indeed should all this immense variety of them exist? They *must* be significant elements of the world as well.

Just test Tolstoï's deification of the mere manual laborer by the facts. This is what Mr. Walter Wyckoff, after working as an unskilled laborer in the demolition of some buildings at West Point, writes of the spiritual condition of the class of men to which he temporarily chose to belong: —

"The salient features of our condition are plain enough. We are grown men, and are without a trade. In the labor-market we stand ready to sell to the highest bidder our mere muscular strength for so many hours each day. We are thus in the lowest grade of labor. And, selling our muscular strength in the open market for what it will bring, we sell it under peculiar conditions. It is all the capital that we have. We have no reserve means of subsistence, and cannot, therefore, stand off for a 'reserve price.' We sell under the necessity of satisfying imminent hunger. Broadly speaking, we must sell our labor or starve; and, as hunger is a matter of a few hours, and we have no other way of meeting this need, we must sell at once for what the market offers for our labor.

"Our employer is buying labor in a dear market, and he will certainly get from us as much work as he can at the price. The gang-boss is secured for this purpose, and thoroughly does he know his business. He has sole command of us. He never saw us before, and he will discharge us all when the debris is cleared away. In the mean time he must get from us, if he can, the utmost of physical labor which we, individually and collectively, are capable of. If he should drive some of us to exhaustion, and we should not be able to continue at work, he would not be the loser; for the market would soon supply him with others to take our places.

"We are ignorant men, but so much we clearly see, — that we have sold our labor where we could sell it dearest, and our employer has bought it where he could buy it cheapest. He has paid high, and he must get all the labor that he can; and, by a strong instinct which possesses us, we shall part with as little as we can. From work like ours there seems to us to have been eliminated every element which constitutes the nobility of labor. We feel no personal pride in its progress, and no community of interest with our employer. There is none of the joy of responsibility, none of the sense of achievement, only the dull monotony of grinding toil, with the longing for the signal to quit work, and for our wages at the end.

"And being what we are, the dregs of the labor-market, and having no certainty of permanent employment, and no organization among ourselves, we must expect to work under the watchful eye of a gang-boss, and be driven, like the wage-slaves that we are, through our tasks.

"All this is to tell us, in effect, that our lives are hard, barren, hopeless lives."

And such hard, barren, hopeless lives, surely, are not lives in which one ought to be willing permanently to remain. And why is this so? Is it because they are so dirty? Well, Nansen grew a great deal dirtier on his polar expedition; and we think none the worse of his life for that. Is it the insensibility? Our soldiers have to grow vastly more insensible, and we extol them to the skies. Is it the poverty? Poverty has been reckoned the crowning beauty of many a heroic career. Is it the slavery to a task, the loss of finer pleasures? Such slavery and loss are of the very essence of the higher fortitude, and are always counted to its credit, — read the records of missionary devotion all over the world. It is not any one of these things, then, taken by itself, — no, nor all of them together, — that make such a life undesirable. A man might in truth live like an unskilled laborer, and do the work of one, and yet count as one of the noblest of God's creatures. Quite possibly there were some such persons in the gang that our author describes; but the current of their souls ran underground; and he was too steeped in the ancestral blindness to discern it.

If there *were* any such morally exceptional individuals, however, what made them different from the rest? It can only have been this, — that their souls worked and endured in obedience to some inner *ideal,* while their comrades were not actuated by anything worthy of that name. These ideals of other lives are among those secrets that we can almost never penetrate, although something about the man may often tell us when they are there. In Mr. Wyckoff's own case we know exactly what the self-imposed ideal was. Partly he had stumped himself, as the boys say, to carry through a strenuous achievement; but mainly he wished to enlarge his sympathetic insight into fellow-lives. For this his sweat and toil acquire a certain heroic significance, and make us accord to him exceptional esteem. But it is easy to imagine his fellows with various other ideals. To say nothing of wives and babies, one may have been a convert of the Salvation Army, and had a nightingale singing of expiation and forgiveness in his heart all the while he labored. Or there might have been an apostle like Tolstoï himself, or his compatriot Bondareff, in the gang, voluntarily embracing labor as their religious mission. Class-loyalty was undoubtedly an ideal with many. And who knows how much of that higher manliness of poverty, of which Phillips Brooks [a prominent Episcopal minister] has spoken so penetratingly, was or was not present in that gang?

"A rugged, barren land," says Phillips Brooks, "is poverty to live in, — a land where I am thankful very often if I can get a berry or a root to eat. But living in it really, letting it bear witness to me of itself, not dishonoring it all the time by judging it after the standard of the other lands, gradually there come out its qualities. Behold! no land like this barren and naked land of poverty could show the moral geology of the world. See how the hard ribs

. . . stand out strong and solid. No life like poverty could so get one to the heart of things and make men know their meaning, could so let us feel life and the world with all the soft cushions stripped off and thrown away. . . . Poverty makes men come very near each other, and recognize each other's human hearts; and poverty, highest and best of all, demands and cries out for faith in God. . . . I know how superficial and unfeeling, how like mere mockery, words in praise of poverty may seem. . . . But I am sure that the poor man's dignity and freedom, his self-respect and energy, depend upon his cordial knowledge that his poverty is a true region and kind of life, with its own chances of character, its own springs of happiness and revelations of God. Let him resist the characterlessness which often goes with being poor. Let him insist on respecting the condition where he lives. Let him learn to love it, so that by and by, [if] he grows rich, he shall go out of the low door of the old familiar poverty with a true pang of regret, and with a true honor for the narrow home in which he has lived so long."

The barrenness and ignobleness of the more usual laborer's life consist in the fact that it is moved by no such ideal inner springs. The backache, the long hours, the danger, are patiently endured — for what? To gain a quid of tobacco, a glass of beer, a cup of coffee, a meal, and a bed, and to begin again the next day and shirk as much as one can. This really is why we raise no monument to the laborers in the Subway, even though they be our conscripts, and even though after a fashion our city is indeed based upon their patient hearts and enduring backs and shoulders. And this is why we do raise monuments to our soldiers, whose outward conditions were even brutaller still. The soldiers are supposed to have followed an ideal, and the laborers are supposed to have followed none.

You see, my friends, how the plot now thickens; and how strangely the complexities of this wonderful human nature of ours begin to develop under our hands. We have seen the blindness and deadness to each other which are our natural inheritance; and, in spite of them, we have been led to acknowledge an inner meaning which passeth show, and which may be present in the lives of others where we least descry it. And now we are led to say that such inner meaning can be *complete* and *valid for us also,* only when the inner joy, courage, and endurance are joined with an ideal.

But what, exactly, do we mean by an ideal? Can we give no definite account of such a word? To a certain extent we can. An ideal, for instance, must be something intellectually conceived, something of which we are not unconscious, if we have it; and it must carry with it that sort of outlook, uplift, and brightness that go with all intellectual facts. Secondly, there must be *novelty* in an ideal, — novelty at least for him whom the ideal grasps. Sodden routine is incompatible with ideality, although what is sodden routine for one person may be ideal novelty for another. This shows that there is nothing absolutely ideal: ideals are relative to the lives that entertain them. To keep out of the gutter is for us here no part of consciousness at all, yet for many of our brethren it is the most legitimately engrossing of ideals.

Now, taken nakedly, abstractly, and immediately, you see that mere ideals are the cheapest things in life. Everybody has them in some shape or other, personal or general, sound or mistaken, low or high; and the most worthless sentimentalists and dreamers, drunkards, shirks and verse-makers, who never show a grain of effort, courage, or endurance, possibly have them on the most copious scale. Education, enlarging as it does our horizon and perspective, is a means of multiplying our ideals, of bringing new ones into view. And your college professor, with a starched shirt and spectacles, would, if a stock of ideals were all alone by itself enough to render a life significant, be the most absolutely and deeply significant of men. Tolstoï would be completely blind in despising him for a prig, a pedant and a parody; and all our new insight into the divinity of muscular labor would be altogether off the track of truth.

But such consequences as this, you instinctively feel, are erroneous. The more ideals a man has, the more contemptible, on the whole, do you continue to deem him, if the matter ends there for him, and if none of the laboring man's virtues are called into action on his part, no courage shown, no privations undergone, no dirt or scars contracted in the attempt to get them realized. It is quite obvious that something more than the mere possession of ideals is required to make a life significant in any sense that claims the spectator's admiration. Inner joy, to be sure, it may *have,* with its ideals; but that is its own private sentimental matter. To extort from us, outsiders as we are, with our own ideals to look after, the tribute of our grudging recognition, it must back its ideal visions with what the laborers have, the sterner stuff of manly virtue; it must multiply their sentimental surface by the dimension of the active will, if we are to have *depth,* if we are to have anything cubical and solid in the way of character.

The significance of a human life for communicable and publicly recognizable purposes is thus the offspring of a marriage of two different parents, either of whom alone is barren. The ideals taken by themselves give no reality, the virtues by themselves no novelty. And let the orientalists and pessimists say what they will, the thing of deepest — or, at any rate, of comparatively deepest — significance in life does seem to be its character of *progress,* or that strange union of reality with ideal novelty which it continues from one moment to another to present. To recognize ideal novelty is the task of what we call intelligence. Not every one's intelligence can tell which novelties are ideal. For many the ideal thing will always seem to cling still to the older more familiar good. In this case character, though not significant totally, may be still significant pathetically. So, if we are to choose which is the more essential factor of human character, the fighting virtue or the intellectual breadth, we must side with Tolstoï, and choose that simple faithfulness to his light or darkness which any common unintellectual man can show.

But, with all this beating and tacking on my part, I fear you take me to be reaching a confused result. I seem to be just taking things up and dropping them again. First I took up Chautauqua, and dropped that; then Tolstoï and the heroism of common toil, and dropped them; finally, I took up ideals, and seem now almost dropping those. But please observe in what sense it is that I drop them. It is when they pretend *singly* to redeem life from insignificance. Culture and refinement all alone are not enough to do so. Ideal aspirations are not enough, when uncombined with pluck and will. But neither are pluck and will, dogged endurance and insensibility to danger enough, when taken all alone. There must be some sort of fusion, some chemical combination among these principles, for a life objectively and thoroughly significant to result.

Of course, this is a somewhat vague conclusion. But in a question of significance, of worth, like this, conclusions can never be precise. The answer of appreciation, of sentiment, is always a more or a less, a balance struck by sympathy, insight, and good will. But it is an answer, all the same, a real conclusion. And, in the course of getting it, it seems to me that our eyes have been opened to many important things. Some of you are, perhaps, more livingly aware than you were an hour ago of the depths of worth that lie around you, hid in alien lives. And, when you ask how much sympathy you ought to bestow, although the amount is, truly enough, a matter of ideal on your own part, yet in this notion of the combination of ideals with active virtues you have a rough standard for shaping your decision. In any case, your imagination is extended. You divine in the world about you matter for a little more humility on your own part, and tolerance, reverence, and love for others; and you gain a certain inner joyfulness at the increased importance of our common life. Such joyfulness is a religious inspiration and an element of spiritual health, and worth more than large amounts of that sort of technical and accurate information which we professors are supposed to be able to impart.

To show the sort of thing I mean by these words, I will just make one brief practical illustration, and then close.

We are suffering to-day in America from what is called the labor-question; and, when you go out into the world, you will each and all of you be caught up in its perplexities. I use the brief term labor-question to cover all sorts of anarchistic discontents and socialistic projects, and the conservative resistances which they provoke. So far as this conflict is unhealthy and regrettable, — and I think it is so only to a limited extent, — the unhealthiness consists solely in the fact that one-half of our fellow-countrymen remain entirely blind to the internal significance of the lives of the other half. They miss the joys and sorrows, they fail to feel the moral virtue, and they do not guess the presence of the intellectual ideals. They are at cross-purposes all along the line, regarding each other as they might regard a set of dangerously gesticulating automata, or, if they seek to get at the inner motivation, making the most horrible mistakes. Often all that the poor man can think of in the rich man is a cowardly greediness for safety, luxury, and effeminacy, and a boundless affectation. What he is, is not a human being, but a pocket-book, a bank-account. And a similar greediness, turned by disappointment into envy, is all that many rich men can see in the state of mind of the dissatisfied poor. And, if the rich man begins to do the sentimental act over the poor man, what senseless blunders does he make, pitying him for just those very duties and those very immunities which, rightly taken, are the condition of his most abiding and characteristic joys! Each, in short, ignores the fact that happiness and unhappiness and significance are a vital mystery; each pins them absolutely on some ridiculous feature of the external situation; and everybody remains outside of everybody else's sight.

Society has, with all this, undoubtedly got to pass toward some newer and better equilibrium, and the distribution of wealth has doubtless slowly got to change: such changes have always happened, and will happen to the end of time. But if, after all that I have said, any of you expect that they will make any *genuine vital difference* on a large scale, to the lives of our descendants, you will have missed the significance of my entire lecture. The solid meaning of life is always the same eternal thing, — the marriage, namely, of some unhabitual ideal, however special, with some fidelity, courage, and endurance; with some man's or woman's pains. — And, whatever or wherever life may be, there will always be the chance for that marriage to take place. Fitz-James Stephen wrote many years ago words to this effect more eloquent than any I can speak: "The 'Great Eastern,' or some of her successors," he said, "will perhaps defy the roll of the Atlantic, and cross the seas without allowing their passengers to feel that they have left the firm land. The voyage from the cradle to the grave may come to be performed with similar facility. Progress and science may perhaps enable untold millions to live and die without a care, without a pang, without an anxiety. They will have a pleasant passage and plenty of brilliant conversation. They will wonder that men ever believed at all in clanging fights and blazing towns and sinking ships and praying hands; and, when they come to the end of their course, they will go their way, and the place thereof will know them no more. But it seems unlikely that they will have such a knowledge of the great ocean on which they sail, with its storms and wrecks, its currents and icebergs, its huge waves and mighty winds, as those who battled with it for years together in the little craft, which, if they had few other merits, brought those who navigated them full into the presence of time and eternity, their maker and themselves, and forced them to have some definite view of their relations to them and to each other."

In this solid and tridimensional sense, so to call it, those philosophers are right who contend that the world is a standing thing, with no progress, no real history. The changing conditions of history touch only the surface of the show. The altered equilibriums and redistributions only diversify our opportunities and open chances to us for new ideals. But, with each new ideal that comes into life, the chance for a life based on some old ideal will vanish; and he would needs be a presumptuous calculator who should with confidence say that the total sum of significances is positively and absolutely greater at any one epoch than at any other of the world.

I am speaking broadly, I know, and omitting to consider certain qualifications in which I myself believe. But one can only make one point in one lecture, and I shall be well content if I have brought my point home to you this evening in even a slight degree. *There are compensations:* and no outward changes of condition in life can keep the nightingale of its eternal meaning from singing in all sorts of different men's hearts. That is the main fact to remember. If we could not only admit it with our lips, but really and truly believe it, how our convulsive insistencies, how our antipathies and dreads of each other, would soften down! If the poor and the rich could look at each other in this way, *sub specie æternitatis,* how gentle would grow their disputes! what tolerance and good humor, what willingness to live and let live, would come into the world!

Vincent Harding

I HEAR THEM . . . CALLING

Vincent Harding (1931–2014) was both a scholar-teacher and a leader of domestic and international movements for peace and justice. In this article, written fairly early in his career, Harding traces his own story, telling how he listened, across the years, to an ever-expanding chorus of voices that eventually summoned him into his work as a leader in the civil rights movement, a peace activist, a husband and father, and a historian. How does Harding's sense of the scope and needs of the community that is "calling" to him change over time?

This selection points ahead to some of the questions explored later in this book. For example, Harding's sense of the multiplicity of voices calling to him begins to make us wonder, "Is a balanced life possible and preferable to a life focused primarily on work?" (chap. 4) and "To whom and to what should I listen as I decide what to do for a living?" (chap. 2). Because of Harding's strong emphasis on the importance of communities in his discernment about the shape of his life, this selection could also be a centerpiece in chapter 3, "With whom and for whom shall I live?" We should also notice that here Harding is beginning to make sense of the many pieces of his life by creating from them a narrative, as several authors will recommend in chapter 6, "How shall I tell the story of my life?"

In his strong, repeated emphasis on the "callings" he heard and responded to during the first forty years of his life, Harding makes vivid use of the vocabulary of vocation. This essay was written for a book coedited by Will D. Campbell, whose own chapter in the same book ("Vocation as Grace") is included in the "Vocation" section of *Leading Lives That Matter* (see pp. 182–83 below).

Vincent Harding, "I Hear Them . . . Calling," in *Callings!*, ed. James Y. Holloway and Will D. Campbell (New York: Paulist, 1974), 57–69.

Callings are strange things. I think I've heard a fair number in my time, perhaps fewer than I was supposed to — or maybe it was more; I'm not certain now. Sometimes they proved to be nothing more than echoes bouncing off from other lives (lives I sometimes thought were mine) and passed on their way. Others puzzled me, and led me into ways I do not yet understand. Some I understand and fear. A few — perhaps more than I know — I have followed as far as they led; and some are still moving. Still moving, preparing to join themselves to the sounds of the new summons, and I suspect there are yet borders to cross.

Callings are strange things. The first I remember (or want to remember?) came through the Black believers who were my extended family in a Harlem congregation. I felt their loving, often demanding grip on my life at an early time — maybe 6 or 7 — and heard the call through all their voices and fiercely possessive hopes.

Up there on platforms and stages, at all the church programs, reciting the poems and Bible verses, I heard them set me apart: "He's going to be a preacher," that call said (really meaning, he is going to be *our* preacher, ours, to assure the continuance of our hopes beyond the borders of our lives), and it was a while before I understood that it was supposed to be *my* calling, that I should hear it and respond.

It took a while for that to happen, for I was hearing other calls as well — or thought I was, though I'm sure I didn't name them that — and was trying to move with them. Like the calling to be an athlete. (This was before Jackie Robinson, so I'm not sure where I thought that road would lead. Perhaps I simply thought that a man should be able to spend his life doing what he really liked, and I liked everything that had to do with balls and bats and running and jumping and falling and feeling the strength of bodies against each other. I liked them far more than the violin and then the piano lessons that my mother hoped in vain I'd like.) That lasted for a while, but I wasn't growing as tall as I thought an athlete ought to be — especially one who thought he was called to play first base, among other things — and I began to hear other calls.

Somehow I got involved with building model airplanes, partly, I suppose, because no one had bothered to mass produce television sets yet (and we probably wouldn't have been able to afford one) and partly because there were no brothers and sisters to share the sometimes lonely days with. That's when the call came to be an aeronautical engineer (whatever that is), and I hadn't found out that Black folks weren't supposed to be aeronautical engineers. What I did find out was that my mathematical skills weren't good enough to pass the test for the high school where all the really bright, aeronautical engineer–types were supposed to attend; so that call too was pressed aside. I think the model airplanes were pretty good, though.

Meanwhile, the loving, tightly gripping community was pressing me forward — not entirely against the sometimes showmanship of my will — into minor church offices, and other responsibilities. And I continued to be up in front at the programs (we, education-oriented folks that we were, mostly of West Indian heritage on the way from Africa, we called them *Lyceum* programs, following traditions of self-improvement deeply instilled in the African people of this country and elsewhere), reciting, only now it was a kind of quasi-acting we used to call Dramatic Reading. That was how I met James Weldon Johnson and Paul Lawrence Dunbar (not really knowing who I was meeting, not really hearing many things they were calling to me), and Walt Whitman and Alfred Lord Tennyson and a lot of even stranger people. Then on youth days I would periodically be the preacher, and that was enough to assure my extended family — and I think my mother too — that the call they heard was authentic, needing only the seasoning of time and the deepening of commitment, much seasoning and deepening — because I had some ways about me that they weren't quite sure were supposed to go with preaching in a Biblically-immersed community of saints.

But I hadn't stopped hearing the callings from other sources. In high school the teachers were the media, and I heard the call to high school teaching. Then one odd teacher told me I'd never pass the oral examination with such a wide space between my two front teeth. And high school teaching was put aside for a time.

Now, this thing with writing is part of the strangeness of the callings. I have not yet moved deeply enough into the chambers of the past to be certain about where and how it came. Perhaps the church community was the voice here too, encouraging my terrible poetry and acting as if my quarterly reports or my summaries and homilies on the Bible lessons were great documents (arousing, of course, certain contrary feelings among the younger members of my family-tribe at Victory Tabernacle Seventh Day Christian Church). That original voice is at least temporarily lost to me, but I know it existed, and if it was the community of believers, they likely did not know then that they had helped open me to one of the major tensions of my world of callings, a sometimes fierce stretching between writing and speaking, between writing and preaching, between scholarship and ministry in the midst of the people.

And by the time I got to college — somehow I think I always knew I had to go to college; and since there was absolutely no money for such a thing, I had to go to the only college I knew where you could at once attend without tuition and also have all the teachers and the loving tribe beam and say, "how wonderful, City College, that's a *hard* school to get into" — the loudest calling was towards writing, pressing me deeply into short story courses, journalism courses (finally majoring in History because there weren't enough writing courses), still experimenting with poetry, mostly devoted to working with the weekly campus newspaper, eventually becoming the inevitable FIRST NEGRO editor of that ancient institution of wisdom and scandal.

At City College, the calling towards writing meant another tension, pressed me towards a period of largely white friends and co-workers who vied with the ancestral community for my loyalties and my attention, led me into certain strange pathways which shut out voices I should have heard, led to great pain. But callings are strange things.

Some of the Tribe was likely worried when, after college, I went off to something else that wasn't really preaching, to graduate work in Journalism. (With all due respect to *their* worries, I was more worried about the Army then. That was a call I hoped to avoid for as long as possible.) Again the tensions of college were there, perhaps multiplied, as I was clearly being groomed for another FIRST NEGRO position. The serious and painful double voices were there, raising questions about the callings of the believers down the hill, through the park, in Harlem, and the callings which sometimes seemed so right and noble and GOOD FOR THE RACE up at City College and over at Morningside Heights — and the worlds were deeply in tension. Callings will sometimes do that.

When I finally had to answer the call of the draft board, it was 1953. Knowing of no movement, lacking courage and desire to go the path of a C.O., which I did know a bit about — but didn't really hear that call, perhaps didn't want to — I went in. I wanted desperately to be sent to Germany or Japan or even Korea, any place outside of this country — for "education," not from alienation, yet. By then I thought I had filtered out the central call among the callings, and prepared for the next FIRST NEGRO experience, at some liberal newspaper, my preference, of course, being the New York *Times.* So, my post-Army movement seemed fairly well established as I went in, hearing all the raucous sounds of death and animality which substitute for life in the Army, but determining to be a good soldier, perhaps even an officer, getting overseas somewhere.

But in the strangeness that has surrounded so much of my life (coming, I know now, from deep sounding sources in the surrounding ancestral company of saints), I also decided, perhaps for the first time, to try to listen consciously, with anticipation, for the callings. I think I wanted to see if I would hear confirmations of the voices which had come through the believers or the teachers, seeking some release from the tension, suspecting perhaps that I might be pressed across new borders, following, listening. And in a place I never expected, under circumstances I would not have chosen, a brother spoke and asked me if I had ever thought of teaching; and for reasons far too complex and too far away to speak of now, I knew that I had heard the voice, the calling for that time.

(Strange about the Army. It never sent me anywhere, except Fort Dix, N.J. and Fort Benjamin Harrison, Indiana — partly because I knew how to type and play handball. Strange, too, that time of listening. I ended up rejecting all my inclinations towards the good soldier, became a C.O. in my heart. Strange, too: I had decided to engage in a very serious and sustained study of the Bible, partly for the listening, partly to prove to my girlfriend that she ought to be a Seventh Day Adventist like me. I did not know that in those long wrestlings with text and spirit I would be engaging in a major step on my journey beyond the borders of the loving family-tribe of believers at Victory Tabernacle [but like all tribal partings, of course, *never* being able to leave them].)

It was strange about the call. I still had the words of the odd high school teacher in my mind, and decided that if I were going to teach it might be better to try college, where I assumed that spaces between teeth didn't count. But I knew nothing about graduate schools, and finally, when pressed to choose among the ones where I had been accepted, opened myself with fear and trembling to the voice of the tribe/community/church, and went to Chicago — two weeks after discharge from the Army — where I could be of assistance as interim, part-time pastor of a little mission congregation that Victory Tabernacle sponsored there. That made the graduate school acceptable, worldly as they knew it was. Now, I would be anchored in an extension of the tribe; so they thought the calls and prayers had finally drawn me out of the strange and various paths I had explored.

How do you explain it? Callings are strange things. In Chicago, for the first time — after having grown up in Harlem and the Bronx — strangely it was in Chicago that I finally heard and saw the Black urban condition in America. On the Southside, I heard its singing and its screams, saw its determination and its terror, sensed its freedom and its captivity. And while there was much I did not then understand about such calls, I knew this was calling me.

One day I shall try to understand and speak more fully of the painful calling which took me away from the little mission congregation — and ultimately away from my immediate (but not my ultimate) relationship to the tribe of my childhood and my youth. That calling is not fully clear to me yet, and even if it were, it is not yet time to speak of it. This much can be said: the move to an interracial congregation as a lay pastor of a team ministry seemed to allow me to hold the tension of Blackness and whiteness (it was, of course, a time when such things seemed most urgent), the tension of teaching and preaching, of study and ministry. But those are only superficial statements, and should be received as such for now.

Nor is it yet time to speak fully of the ultimately transforming call that led to marriage, a call far different than any I had known, a call I was in too many ways unprepared to understand in all the richness of its meanings and its summons. But I know it is a calling, mine.

Then, before graduate work had ended, the call of the Southern Freedom Movement became overwhelming, pressing aside almost every other voice. There was no escaping it. It possessed me during my first, exploring journey into the South (grasped me there sitting on Martin King's bed in Montgomery where he rested recovering from his stabbing). It came to Chicago in the body of the students and found me. While sit-ins and freedom-rides were still sweeping across the South, we left Chicago and went South, hearing, following a call.

We shall understand it better by and by, and also speak more clearly of it, that calling. Now let it suffice to say that it was then that all the fiercely gripping, special callings of the South began, calls of the Movement, of Southwest Georgia (home of my wife's parents, repository of so many memories of hope and fear), of all the stretching land upon which my people walked, and worked, and ran, and stood, and died. Then it began, all the callings of Birmingham and Tuskegee, of Montgomery and Mobile, of Jackson and Meridian, of Gulfport and Greenwood, of New Orleans and Charleston, of Hickory and Atlanta, of Ella Baker and Amzie Moore, of Ralph Abernathy and Bill Shields, of Bob Moses Parris and Annelle Ponder, of Jim and Diane, of Septima Clark and Slater King, of Clarence Jordan and Staughton Lynd — this was the beginning of new callings.

And when, after four years that encompassed a generation of struggle, when the Movement had passed its height, it was possible to hear strange callings through personal tragedy, and there were endings and beginnings again. Then finally the finishing of graduate work and the beginning of teaching — still with a space between the front two teeth.

There the latest callings began. From somewhere — had Buddha visited? — there was an urgent aching to understand the meaning of Vietnam, and on the 20th anniversary of Hiroshima, that need plunged me past the superficial surfaces of my knowing, brought me in touch with the meaning of that brutal tale, that heroic defense of life, and provided new impetus for my continuing movement away from this America, towards a radically transformed society.

Teaching, spaces and all. There the latest callings began. Teaching history I was called to understand how little I knew of history. Teaching Black students, I learned how little this Black student, this FIRST NEGRO, had been taught, especially about the truth of his own long pilgrimage, about his people's struggles against the powers of death, about their determined movement towards new life. And when I knew that, I began — as in the Army, only a different army now — to listen again, hearing some things that I had let slip by in the days of the Tribe, understanding things I had only seen in the Movement. I began to hear voices more loudly than ever before, and they will not be silent, for they are me.

I hear all the varied sounds of my homeland, all its human sounds, all its animals, its spirit-filled rivers and lakes, its waterfalls, its mountains, its grass and trees playing with the wind. I hear them all.

I hear all the screaming of my homeland, all the mournful pacing down to the slave baracoons, all the piercing, dying shouts, all the parting wailing sounds. I hear children, crying children, I hear men, I hear women, calling, now desiring only to be remembered, and vindicated. I hear them between the decks of the ships called *Jesus* and *St. John,* and *Liberty,* and *Justice.* I hear their whispers and then their bursting yells as they come on decks prepared to die, and, if necessary, to kill for their freedom. I hear them calling, falling on the decks, thrown, often leaping to their ending — but not ending — in the waters. I hear them singing as they go under the waves — free.

I hear my people. I hear them calling from Virginia to San Francisco, I hear their songs and their cries and their defiant shouts and their long silences through all the horrors called slavery. I hear them lost in the wilderness, I hear them moving, seeking the North Star, determined to make their way to freedom.

I hear them in preaching and praying, holding one another through hunger and parting, through torture and sickness, through childbirth and dying, I hear them calling.

I hear my people, lurching, flooding towards freedom during the Civil War, seizing their own liberty. I hear them fighting and falling, rising and hoping again. I hear them in all the halcyon hopeful first days of Reconstruction, in all the bloody years that followed, when hope was crushed by the force of white arms and the power of white betrayals.

I hear them, mourning, weeping, wailing, prostrate around the thousands of trees where brothers and sisters were hung and burned and mutilated beyond recognition by a savage people. I hear them vowing never to give in, never to turn back, to endure, to resist, to live, to go on. I hear their calling.

I hear them coming North, I hear them in the armies, I hear them in the mills, I hear them in the railroads, I hear them in the fires, I hear them in the waters, I hear Nat Turner and David Walker, I hear Douglass and Delaney, I hear Harriet and Sojourner, I hear Ida B. Wells and Bishop Turner, I hear Garvey and DuBois, I hear Bessie Smith. I hear them calling.

I hear them in depression, picking their way through garbage piles, sharing even that with one another. I hear them calling for Robeson, for Father, for Daddy, for Adam, for Solidarity, for help.

I hear them in war, dying for a land that will not protect them. I hear them coming beyond war to struggle for truth. I hear them in court. I hear them in the streets. I hear ladies walking in Montgomery. I hear Martin preaching in the churches, hear his footsteps on the road. I hear old folks singing in churches, standing before dogs. I hear students risking their lives, freezing in jail, singing while hungry, laughing when afraid, not being overcome. I hear them calling.

I hear my people marching, refusing to stop, refusing to be quiet, refusing to be satisfied, refusing to die.

I hear Malcolm, I hear Stokely, I hear Rap and Feather, I hear Ruby and Jim. I hear Jonathan. I hear Angela. I hear Attica. I hear dying Panthers and preachers. I hear living men and women. I hear them. I hear voices, and I know what it means.

Callings are a strange thing. I know what it means: I am a witness, in spite of myself, beyond myself, and their voices must be heard.

I am a witness (teacher, preacher, ranter, raver, dissident, resistant, radical, revolutionary, silent carrier), witness to their truth and power, pressed forward by the force of their being, by the integrity of their struggle, by the silent roaring of their voices. No turning back.

I know what it means: I am historian — now recognizing all the long ago callings — summoned to tell their story, for them, for myself, for our children. They shall not be forgotten.

It means I am now of them, deep calling unto deep. Their voice has entered so profoundly into me that I am flesh of their flesh, bone of their bone, song of their song, pain of their pain, hope of their hope. Forever lost to scholarly "objectivity," forever seared by the passion of their fiery movement, unwilling and unable to be detached from their struggle. Bound by cords of life and death and love — and intimations of the morning. Privileged, permitted, summoned to join them, their struggle is mine, and I am called forward into tomorrow, searching for the way to carry the struggle, to break the bonds, to build the new land of their hopes.

(Callings are strange things. They find you in the midst of your own family.)

I hear my mother, sighing, scrubbing all the floors in all the white homes, bearing with love and pain and anxious prayer the burden that I was/am. (I would like to hear my father, and one day I suspect I shall.) I know it means I am still son, hope, strength, promise for tomorrow, beyond all the pain and death.

I hear voices — of my children, Rachel Sojourner and Jonathan Du-Bois. I believe that ancient rivers of our people flow in them. I hear their voices, and I know what it means. It means I am called to be father, rock and strength, encourager for the struggles of tomorrow, baptizer in the rivers of their past.

I hear a voice, of my wife, Rosemarie. I know what it means. I am to be husband and man, strength and solace, lover and companion in the way, resting place and summons to joy in the morning.

Callings are strange things. I think I have heard many voices in many times and places, but it may be that I have heard only One.

VOCABULARIES

Authenticity

Virtue

Exemplarity

Vocation

B e Like Mike!" This imperative captioned a television commercial that was popular during the time Michael Jordan was indisputably the best basketball player on the planet. Years after Jordan's retirement, advertisers put forward other sports figures to admire and imitate: Serena Williams and Roger Federer in tennis, and the successor to Michael Jordan, LeBron James, in basketball. Some athletes seem to transcend time and remain inspirations for all ages, like baseball player Lou Gehrig or tennis sensation Althea Gibson or the boxer described below, Muhammad Ali. Of course, the "Be Like Mike" advertisement suggested that one could be like Michael Jordan simply by purchasing the Nike shoes he wore. This is rather like suggesting that one could be like Michelangelo by learning to speak Italian. Even so, on the basis of sales records, many people apparently did "buy" the idea that they would eventually be like Mike if only they wore his shoes.

We may nevertheless wonder whether the millions of people around the globe who actually did want to be like Mike wished merely to imitate his choice of footwear. Something more complicated was going on. A much deeper and more encouraging human aspiration explains the appeal of star athletes and the success of slogans such as "Be Like Mike." People wish they were as gifted and as disciplined as one of these greats in *some* area of life. They want to excel at something. They have hopes and dreams that are fed and informed by real or imagined models of what they would like to become.

A second implication of the fact that so many millions want to be like those they admire is even more important than the simple desire to excel. In some fields of human endeavor people still believe it is possible to recognize genuine excellence. They can say with great confidence, "Michael Jordan was a better basketball player than (to take a tough case) Magic Johnson." Basketball fans believe they can be as certain about their judgments of basketball playing as chemists believe they can be certain about judgments of whether a given compound is sugar or salt.

But are people as ready and able to judge the relative excellence of whole lives or overall character as they are to judge the exercise of particular skills? When it comes to assessing the relative goodness, worth, or significance of different people's lives, our culture seems both hesitant and confused. Hesitations arise primarily from the considerations we examined in the general introduction to this anthology: we are committed to various notions of human equality, all of which seem set against judgments of relative worth or merit that imply an objective order of worthiness or goodness. Confusions abound. How many of the people who admire Michael Jordan as a basketball player assume that excellence on the basketball court is the same thing as human excellence in general? Some today believe that excelling in any skill leads directly to an excellent life overall. Others act as though popularity and virtue were one and the same thing. They consult rock stars and movie actors for advice about politics and religion, apparently believing that mere fame evinces wisdom about everything that matters in human life. Many social observers think that the growth of such confusions in our culture has created a "cult of celebrity," the worshipful adulation of men and women whose only claim to honor and respect is popularity.

These confusions have created a somewhat desperate situation. We want to make good judgments about how we should live. We want to learn how to lead lives that really matter. But we do not know how to talk very well or think very well about these things. Strange as it may seem, we sometimes do not even know what we really think. We cannot even give voice to our opinions, much less correct them if they prove to be mistaken. Our growing inability to articulate the point and importance of our own lives may go far to explain why many feel that their lives do not really have a point or that they do not finally matter at all.

Some of our best philosophers and social critics have thought that our troubles do indeed stem from our loss of any consistent and coherent way of talking about the things that matter most deeply to us. Instead, we have several "vocabularies" that have developed over the years from sometimes conflicting ways of speaking and thinking. We cobble these words and ideas together to try to make sense of our lives and aspirations. So our confusions are built into this effort to think in several languages at the same time. It is like trying to speak French, Hindi, and English in the same sentence. No wonder we are confused!

Can we possibly attain greater clarity both about what we really think and about what really might be true? More important, can we make genuine progress in helping one another determine whether some lives might really be more worth living and admiring than others? Yes, we can. First, we need to become aware of the various languages or "vocabularies" we are already using to make sense of these things. Second, we need to decide which of these languages or which combination of them will actually help us to make good judgments about how we might lead lives that matter. Third and finally, we need to converse with others, like those represented in this volume, in order to test, clarify, and strengthen our own ideas.

The four groups of readings in this part of *Leading Lives That Matter* explore four different vocabularies — authenticity, virtue, exemplarity, and vocation — that people use today in their efforts to think and talk about the kind of life they most admire and would therefore most like to lead.

Authenticity
- Charles Taylor, *The Ethics of Authenticity*
- Parker Palmer, "Explorations in True Self"
- Elizabeth Cady Stanton, "Solitude of Self"
- Thanissaro Bhikkhu, "No-Self or Not-Self?"
- Ajahn Karunadhammo, "This Is Who I Am"

Virtue
- Aristotle, *Nicomachean Ethics*
- Rebecca Konyndyk DeYoung, *Glittering Vices*
- Josef Pieper, "On Love"
- Natalia Ginzburg, *The Little Virtues*
- David Brooks, "The Moral Bucket List"
- Mencius, *Sayings*
- Hsun Tzu, *Improving Yourself*
- Edith Jones, "Patience"

Exemplarity
- Linda Zagzebski, *Why Exemplarism?*
- Dorothy Day, *Therese*
- Gordon Marino, "The Greatest"
- Madeline Miller, "False Counsellor"

Vocation
- Denise Levertov, "Annunciation"
- Lee Hardy, "Work, Life, and Vocational Choice"
- Gary Badcock, "Choosing"
- C. S. Lewis, "Learning in War-Time"
- Dietrich Bonhoeffer, "The Place of Responsibility"
- Frederick Buechner, "Vocation"
- Will Campbell, "Vocation as Grace"
- Chuang Tzu, "Mastering Life"

Authenticity

The philosopher Charles Taylor, perhaps more than any contemporary voice, has tried to help us understand how and why most people today speak the way they do about what they should do and how they should live. He describes this way of talking as "the ethics of authenticity," named after the central value that gives this manner of thinking its distinctively modern character. Authenticity, for those who advocate this ethic, simply means being true to ourselves: we must look within ourselves to find what authorizes our choices and thereby determine what we should do and wish to become.

Does Taylor really capture the way most of us think? He claims that people in Western democracies value free choice above almost anything else. So we are sometimes prone to talk as though a way of living is good or significant simply because we have freely chosen it. We worry whether a choice we make is "really our choice" more than we worry whether what we choose is really choice-worthy. So we try to help each other "get in touch with ourselves." We want to be as sure as we can that our life choices are not made for us by someone else — parents, friends, peers, or teachers. And we are very uneasy about the idea that someone who has made a free choice might also have made a bad choice.

Is this the way you talk and think on your campus or in your workplace or around your dinner table? Do you feel awkward about criticizing someone else's life choices? Do you doubt that some free choices are better or worse than other ones? When you are asked to account for why a very gifted science student has decided to become a beach bum, do you defend him by saying that this is "just his thing"? Do you find yourself deciding against whatever others who are important to you recommend, just to show that your choices are really your own? If your answer to most of these questions is yes, you are probably manifesting what Taylor calls "soft relativism," a trivial form of the ethics of authenticity.

Taylor wants not simply to show us how we think and talk about what matters in life these days. He wants to help us see what assumptions are behind that particular way of talking and to show us how we came to talk the way we do. He also wants us to reflect critically on the way we talk. Do we really believe that all ways of living are equally choiceworthy, equally significant? And when we look into ourselves, do we find only one authentic voice, our own voice, or do we find many voices that together make up the selves that we are?

The pursuit of authenticity has provided therapy for some people. The well-known educator Parker Palmer has written extensively about his own struggles with depression. In the excerpt from his book *A Hidden Wholeness* included below, Palmer writes that his "journey toward an undivided life" in large part involved the recovery and affirmation of his authentic identity. In a chapter whose title nicely captures the cornerstone of the ethics of authenticity, "Explorations in True Self," Parker argues at some length that we are born with knowledge about who we truly and uniquely are but that over the course of time we lose that knowledge. The loss is both cognitively crippling and psychologically painful. The therapy for such divided and wounded selves includes disciplines and practices that enable us to get back in touch with our core selves, the "souls in perfect form" that were ours at birth.

In addition to its sometime therapeutic value for individuals, the ideal of authenticity has provided support for the aspirations of many marginalized groups in American history. Elizabeth Cady Stanton, speaking before a committee of the US Congress at the end of the nineteenth century, invoked ideals of the self, free choice, and individual self-determination to defend and advance the cause of women's rights. She argued then, following the logic that Taylor would describe a century later, that we are all sovereign, independent selves and that our relationships to others are secondary, often instrumental, to our personal choices and purposes. She also used another "vocabulary," however, in sketching the kind of character human beings need to have in order to live well and responsibly, suggesting that some "selves" might be more admirable than others and that some ways of living might be more choiceworthy than others.

Although people from around the world would find intelligible the other vocabularies discussed in this part of the book — virtue, exemplarity, and vocation — many world cultures would have difficulty with the idea of authenticity. As we note in the introduction to chapter 3, the notion of an isolated "self" as an independent center of action and identity would be incomprehensible to many of the world's people. Two readings written by Buddhist teachers, included below, demonstrate that the idea of discovering an authentic self is also very problematic from the vantage point of at least one great religious tradition. Thanissaro Bhikkhu, a Buddhist monk in the Thai Forest Tradition who has translated many classic texts of Buddhism and has written several books on Buddhist thought and practice, corrects the popular Western idea that Buddhism espouses a doctrine of "no-self." The Buddha refused to give a categorical answer to the question of whether or not there was such a thing as a "self." Nevertheless, the Buddhist tradition rejects altogether the project of seeking a true self, finding such ventures bound up with stress, suffering, and clinging. In the course of his meditation, "This Is Who I Am," another Buddhist monk in the Thai Forest Tradition, Ajahn Karunadhammo, advocates a daily "letting go" of all self-images based upon particular traits or even combinations of them. Through such a process, he says, "we can understand that we are not bound by the sense of *me, mine, myself* — the sense of entrapped solidity." For these two Buddhists at least, the quest for an undivided authentic self, unique to each person, is chimerical at best and spiritually dangerous at worst.

Virtue

Elizabeth Cady Stanton, in her talk to a congressional committee that highlighted the language of individualism and authenticity, had to use a somewhat different vocabulary as well. When we talk as though some choices really are better or worse than others and some people's lives and characters really are better or worse than those of other people, we too are using another vocabulary. That way of speaking does not include the idea of authenticity, but it does include words like "virtue," "excellence," "character," and "choiceworthiness," and it goes back at least as far as 400 BCE. The ancient Greek philosopher Aristotle, for example, believed that there is only one way of living that is best for all human beings. He tried to provide a sketch of such a life and to show us why, if we are thinking honestly and carefully, everyone should choose that way of life over others. He argued that such a life would have happiness as its end, but he meant something very different from what we mean by the word "happiness." For him, happiness was not a feeling; it was activity in accordance with virtue. Leading a life that mattered meant leading a life that exhibited a firm, admirable character. Like most of us, Aristotle admired people who lived honestly, courageously, justly, wisely, moderately, and generously. He also admired people who enjoyed some very good and enduring friendships.

We are not, in other words, as far from Aristotle as we may think, even though we do sometimes use slogans that he would have disdained, like "do your own thing." As much as we may pretend that it is bad to be "judgmental," we are always making judgments about other people. Are they trustworthy? Should we befriend them? Can we rely on them to help us in dangerous situations? Would we loan them money? Would we rather be like Jill or like Sarah? Our lives sometimes literally depend upon how well we make these judgments about others. Judgments about whether someone has good character always consist of two parts. First, we ask, what is this person really like? And second, is this person admirable?

Why do we make judgments even as we insist that it is not good to be judgmental? Or why do so many of us say that one way of living is as good as any other even as we privately believe no such thing? It may be that we lack confidence in the judgments we make, so we refuse to make any. Or perhaps we don't want to offend people, and we think most of our contemporaries would be offended by the idea that some people do lead more admirable lives than others. Whatever the case, we cannot think very long or very well about how to lead lives that matter without *some* of Aristotle's vocabulary of virtue.

Our vocabulary of virtue today will need more words than Aristotle provided. Though he wrote about many virtues and vices, Aristotle did not and could not include, for example, what later became known as the three primary or capital Christian virtues: faith, hope, and love. His greatest expositor and commentator, the thirteenth-century Dominican priest and scholar Thomas Aquinas, absorbed, extended, and sometimes amended Aristotle's vocabulary of virtue in his great *Summa Theologiae*. And even today, Christian ethicists like Rebecca Konyndyk DeYoung continue to develop a vocabulary of virtue and vice by building upon Aristotle and Aquinas.

DeYoung's introduction to her book *Glittering Vices* engages both classical and Christian virtue ethics, and it provides a clear and succinct account of the terminology of virtue ethics over the course of centuries in the West. As the title of her book suggests, she is interested primarily in showing why the capital vices, known in Western culture as the seven deadly sins, have seemed so appealing and seductive even as they are so lethal both to living well and to developing a good character. As she explores a wide range of philosophical and theological sources, she is careful to show the subtle differences between classical notions of vice and Christian and Jewish notions of sin. Nevertheless, she also shows how Christians and non-Christians enjoy a large common vocabulary of virtue and vice, character, habituation, and choiceworthiness.

They do not share, however, a full appreciation of the capital Christian virtues of faith, hope, and love, which Christian tradition says are infused by divine grace rather than cultivated through habit, as Aristotle's virtues were. (Thus, they are often called spiritual virtues to distinguish them from moral virtues.) And yet a virtue like *agapē* (the Greek word for the Christian virtue of love) is in important ways akin to both *eros* (Greek for romantic or erotic love) and *philia* (Greek for friendship). Both Greek and Latin are richer in their vocabularies for the virtue of love in its many forms than English is. Josef Pieper, a Thomist philosopher who wrote for broad audiences, insists in his account of Christian love that *agapē* or *caritas* (the Latin word for Christian love) is very similar to both *eros* and *philia* — sexual love and friendship — since Christian love takes these other two up into itself and finally perfects them.

The vocabulary of virtue is present today not only in the writings of philosophers and theologians but also in more popular essays, editorials, newspaper columns, films, television shows, novels, and short stories. "Character" has long been central to works of literature — plays and novels, for example. But the language of character has recently become more frequently used and more urgently articulated by thinkers who believe its vocabulary has been alarmingly eclipsed by the vocabulary of authenticity.

Two works included below illustrate concern about the apparent weakening of the ethic of virtue in the modern West. Both traverse the whole terrain of virtue — moral virtues, intellectual virtues, spiritual virtues — and draw from both religious and secular sources. The first comes from the title essay in *The Little Virtues,* a collection by a distinguished Italian writer who flourished during the middle of the last century, Natalia Ginzburg. This essay offers yet another way to classify the virtues and their relationship to one another — "big" and "little." More important, Ginzburg foregrounds a theme that was and remains important to all who emphasize the vocabulary of virtue in thinking about what we should do and who we should be: education, or moral formation. If virtue is so important, how does one become virtuous? In considering this matter, Ginzburg stands in a long line of compatriots, extending back at least as far as the great Roman statesman and philosopher Cicero.

Few widely read pundits have written as much or as well about character and virtue as David Brooks, a regular columnist for the *New York Times.* The column included below, "The Moral Bucket List," grew out of his book *The Road to Character.* One of Brooks's most memorable points is the distinction between the "résumé virtues," the skills and achievements we bring to the market, and the "eulogy virtues," the qualities of character remembered at our funerals. Like Ginzburg and most virtue ethicists, Brooks is concerned not only about what virtue is but also about how people attain it; people are not born virtuous, he believes, but rather are formed in ways that enable them to become virtuous.

Questions about how best to educate young men and women to cultivate virtue within them have hardly been confined to Western culture. We can say with some confidence that the concern for moral formation has been and remains truly global. A small sampling of Confucian philosophers who were writing around the same time as Plato and Aristotle will demonstrate this widespread, cross-cultural concern with the ethics of virtue. One selection comes from Hsun Tzu, who believed, unlike Confucius and his great successor Mencius, that human beings are born into a state of moral depravity that can be changed only through proper discipline, ritual observance, and self-conscious renunciation of natural impulses. This selection is preceded by a short excerpt from the sayings of Mencius, who was second only to Confucius in his influence on Chinese ethical thought. The analogy drawn is characteristic of how Mencius argued, and it also comports very well with the subject of the relationship between humanity and the rest of the natural world, which we shall explore in chapter 5. Over many centuries, the vocabulary of virtue has called forth from both Eastern and Western philosophers a host of stories, striking images, parables, aphorisms, and analogies.

The vocabulary of virtue was once so pervasive in Western culture that it captivated visual artists, musicians, and poets as much as it did philosophers, theologians, and educators. Literally hundreds of paintings from the medieval and Renaissance periods personified various virtues and then portrayed them in lavish detail and in various complicated arrangements relative to one another. Since we are confined to the written word here, we offer but one comparatively recent example of poetry that features the personification of one of the virtues perhaps most needed today — patience. The poem by Edith Wharton (nee Jones) should make us wonder whether the nature of the virtues is better captured through real or imagined people than through abstract philosophy.

Exemplarity

This very idea, that virtue is best understood and developed through a consideration of exemplary human beings, actual or fictional, is at the heart of a third ethical vocabulary, which is designated by the unwieldy word "exemplarity." Like the vocabulary of virtue, exemplarity traces its origin to Aristotle, who well understood the importance of imitation in the education of the young. Thus, as we will see in the excerpt from *Glittering Vices*, when Rebecca Konyndyk DeYoung asks her students to draw up their own lists of virtues they admire, they draw implicitly on "moral ideals, embodied in heroes or saints or cultural icons. . . . That is, we implicitly draw our lists from a mental picture of someone we admire as a model of moral excellence."

Though both the vocabulary of virtue and the vocabulary of exemplarity understand the importance of models, there are significant differences between the two ways of understanding what we should do and who we should be. The exemplarist bases and derives his ethics entirely on the exemplary motives and inclinations of admirable agents. Moreover, as the philosopher Linda Zagzebski argues in the selection from her book *Exemplarist Moral Theory*, the emotion of admiration — not careful moral reasoning based upon general principles or practices — is what enables us to detect genuine human excellence. Ethical reflection must be grounded in admiration, Zagzebski argues, and in what we find admirable in particular agents we hold in high regard. Since we can sometimes be mistaken in our admiration, we must learn to discipline and refine that emotion to strengthen it as a sure source and guide to good ethical behavior.

Although philosophers employ a great deal of theoretical language when explaining the concept of exemplarity, this vocabulary also incorporates a down-to-earth focus on particular, widely admired human beings, real or fictional. Exemplarist ethicists, unlike virtue ethicists, give sustained attention to classifying admirable people into distinct groups who are admired for different qualities. Zagzebski, for example, offers three major types — the hero, the saint, and the sage — and provides concrete character sketches of particular people who embody each of those types. Because of this, the exemplarist approach comes the closest of the four vocabularies to capturing how most people most of the time actually engage in ethical reflection. So often we find ourselves discussing the people we admire and hence seek to emulate, or arguing over whether certain people are really worthy of admiration and imitation. Growth in ethical discernment and in ethical behavior comes about as the result of learning how to choose better and better examples of whom to imitate.

Another way in which the vocabulary of exemplarity comes closer to everyday ethical reflection than the vocabulary of virtue involves the concept of virtue itself. For many if not most virtue ethicists, in order to be virtuous in one respect one needs to be virtuous in all respects. To be genuinely courageous, one must also be temperate, just, and prudent. I must not only stand firm in the face of danger, I must also know what causes are worthy of the risks I may be taking and what dangers are better to be avoided than faced. Critics of this view have argued that this concept of the "unity of the virtues" sets an impossibly high ethical standard. Almost no one would be virtuous on this account. The exemplarist, by contrast, believes that it is perfectly proper to admire someone for her courage even though she may be in certain ways intemperate. We admire the hero, the saint, and the sage for different reasons and for different qualities. And a hero who runs great risks and makes great sacrifices for the well-being of others is genuinely admirable even if he is, say, a negligent parent.

Although the vocabulary of exemplarity does seem true to our efforts to determine what we should do and who we should be, there are problems with it. The relationship between virtue itself and the capacity rightly to admire it in others is very difficult to state in a clear and accurate way. Exemplarists tend to emphasize the ways in which admiration can lead to virtuous behavior in admirers. However, quite often a person must already be virtuous in order to recognize virtue in others. For example, during the course of her book on Saint Therese of Lisieux, excerpted below, Dorothy Day tells of how she did not recognize Therese as someone worthy of deep admiration until after she herself had undergone certain kinds of ethical development. Worthiness may not be evident to those who are not morally astute.

Moreover, admiration is itself something that changes over time for most of us. Gordon Marino, a philosopher who is also a boxing trainer, reports that though he "originally hated" Muhammad Ali, he grew over the years to admire him deeply. The process of this growth in admiration, as Marino recounts it below in "The Greatest," was extremely complicated. And such accounts of changes in the emotion of admiration do not apply simply to individuals. In considering the hero of one of Homer's epics in her essay "False Counsellor," Madeline Miller shows how the same exemplary figure can seem appealing in one era and repulsive in the next. In other words, admiration is not an isolated emotional impulse; it is instead to some degree culturally conditioned and may change both for individuals and for entire societies over time.

In short, the vocabulary of exemplarity, like the other two vocabularies considered thus far, is not always precise and certain. Aristotle famously said that we should not expect the same degree of precision in ethics, which deals with flesh-and-blood human beings and with complicated and varied human actions, as we do in mathematics, which deals with timeless abstractions. Our fourth vocabulary, the language of vocation, is also both contested and imprecise. What better way to introduce it than with an example?

Vocation

For Christians, the vocabulary of vocation provides a way of thinking about how to live, both in terms of the different kinds of work they do and in terms of the overall character and point of their lives. Aristotle was not much interested in the various kinds of paid employment, since he believed that most forms of work were at best necessary and irksome, at worst slavish and degrading. Writing in the context of a slave society, Aristotle developed an ethics for a small percentage of the population, for free men. The arenas within which these men lived the life of virtue included the battlefield, the political assembly, and friendship among citizens. Charles Taylor notes that with the Protestant Reformation and its reformulation of the idea of Christian vocation, the primary arenas for human achievement broadened to include two other domains — the realm of production, or paid employment, and the realm of reproduction, or the family. Thus, for Christians and non-Christians alike, the idea of vocation provides a vocabulary for thinking about the relationship between what human beings do to earn a living and what kind of life human beings should live. And the idea is far less exclusive than Aristotle's account, since manual workers and those providing direct care for dependents — and, indeed, all human beings — are included.

"Vocation" comes from the Latin word *vocare*, which means "to call." So a synonym for a "vocation" is a "calling," something we have been summoned to do. The most memorable and instructive example of a call narrative in all of Christian literature and art is the angel Gabriel's announcement (annunciation) to Mary that she will bear the Messiah. The summons comes not to an elite free man but to a poor young woman. It comes within the confines of a home and family, not in a vast public arena. Denise Levertov's poem both dramatizes that summons and shows its larger implication for all of us as we respond — or not — to the summonses that come to us.

Poetry's power derives in part from its capacity to contain ambiguity. In more expository and analytical prose, Christian writers have often disagreed sharply about the concept of vocation. Martin Luther, the first of the Reformers to formulate a radically new understanding of the Christian idea of vocation, argued that any kind of regular and legitimate work in the world — manual labor, parenting, civic activity — could be a vocation so long as the Christian did that work out of love for God and in service to humankind. Most Protestant Christian writers on the subject of vocation ever since have agreed with Luther on this point. However, some writers, like the seventeenth-century Anglican divine William Perkins, argued that all Christians have two callings, a general calling to the Christian life and a particular calling to some kind of productive work. Others have insisted that we have only one Christian calling, not two, as Perkins believed. So, for example, the contemporary theologian Gary Badcock has argued that all Christians are called to share in Christ's mission of love and service to the world, but he does not believe that they should think of their specific jobs as callings. The contemporary philosopher Lee Hardy agrees with Luther in thinking that we have multiple callings as workers, children, neighbors, and citizens, but he also believes, like Perkins, that our primary, particular calling is our paid employment and that our problem is to discern and to help one another discern what kind of work we are really called by God to do.

Though students are not typically paid for being students, they should not for that reason assume that college or university life is a mere preparation for their various callings. Instead, while they are students, their calling, according to C. S. Lewis, is just that: being students. Lewis made this argument at a very perilous time, when the young men of Oxford felt called instead to the battlefields of World War II. For Lewis, that summons was more of a siren song, beguiling, even perhaps nobly beguiling, but nevertheless a misleading summons to those who were gifted in other ways and whose presence at universities like Oxford should have been conclusive evidence of that fact. They were called to study, Lewis insisted. Being a student was their vocation.

Dietrich Bonhoeffer, a Christian theologian active in Germany before and during World War II, thought the idea of vocation had been deeply misunderstood, especially by some fellow Lutherans who had used the concept as a way of vindicating the status quo and validating such institutions as marriage and wage labor as preferable to all other social or economic arrangements. Like Badcock, he stressed that Christians are first of all disciples wherever they might find themselves "stationed" in the world. Beyond this, Bonhoeffer also argued that God's call summons us into responsibility to and for our fellow human beings and all of creation. Thus Christians are constantly summoned to break through the sometimes rigid circumscriptions of their roles as parents, citizens, or professionals. The responsibilities of a doctor, for example, might at some time include defending medical science itself, not simply caring for the patients immediately before her.

The contemporary theologian and novelist Frederick Buechner has tried to formulate the substance of vocation in a way that is exact yet flexible enough to take account of an almost infinite variety of gifts and circumstances. His short formulation of the nature of vocation is perhaps the most widely quoted one today. And the Christian novelist and preacher Will Campbell has reminded us that vocation is often as much a communal as it is an individual enterprise.

Although the vocabulary of vocation has been for the most part distinctively Christian, we should not think that the interpenetration of work, moral virtue, and spiritual practice is uniquely Christian or even uniquely Western. Yet another Chinese philosopher, Chuang Tzu, in his brief sketch of the woodworker Ch'ing, shows how good work, good character, and religious ritual are often of a piece.

However much these writers disagree with one another, all of them can help us, Christian and non-Christian alike, to think carefully about the relationship between what we do to earn a living and the quality and significance of our lives overall.

VOCABULARIES

Authenticity

Virtue

Exemplarity

Vocation

Charles Taylor

THE ETHICS OF AUTHENTICITY

Charles Taylor is a Canadian philosopher who has written on a wide variety of subjects, especially on ethics and identity. His largest and most influential work, *A Secular Age* (2007), which was something of a sequel to his earlier *Sources of the Self* (1987), examines the historical and philosophical backgrounds to the ways in which we in modern Western societies have come to think about who we are and how we should live. The reading below is from a shorter work, *The Ethics of Authenticity,* which critically examines the distinctively modern way in which a large number of people in the West, perhaps a majority, speak and think about their own lives and the lives of others.

The selection begins in the third chapter, which is entitled "The Sources of Authenticity." How does Taylor's account help you to understand such frequently heard phrases as "do your own thing" and "deciding for myself"? It looks like American popular culture is constantly offering us images of people we should emulate, including star athletes and other celebrities. Yet, according to Taylor, moderns are reluctant to "find models to live by outside of ourselves." Is Taylor right, especially in view of the whole exemplarist moral vocabulary that is treated below? Is there some way to explain this apparent contradiction?

In part 4 of the excerpt below, Taylor tries to do something very important for the purposes of this entire anthology. He shows us why and how we must talk and reason with each other about perplexing questions. It is not enough merely to express ourselves and move on, agreeing to "accept all points of view." How does Taylor describe or propose that we go about helping one another to reach deeper truth about who we really are and how we should live?

Taylor says that questions of identity provide the indispensable background for questions about our desires and aspirations. Moreover, he argues that our identities were first formed, and continue to be formed, in dialogue

From Charles Taylor, *The Ethics of Authenticity* (Cambridge, MA: Harvard University Press, 1991), 25–35.

with others. When we listen to ourselves to try to discover what we should do and who we should be, we often find several voices speaking to us, not one. My self is not one voice struggling to be heard but a medley of voices that sometimes sing in unison, sometimes in discord. More important still, we continue to define and discover our identities in company with others. Identity formation is a collective project. Note that this whole matter of identity and community is treated more extensively in question 3, "With Whom and for Whom Shall I Live?"

The ethic of authenticity is something relatively new and peculiar to modern culture. Born at the end of the eighteenth century, it builds on earlier forms of individualism, such as the individualism of disengaged rationality, pioneered by Descartes, where the demand is that each person think self-responsibly for him- or herself, or the political individualism of Locke, which sought to make the person and his or her will prior to social obligation. But authenticity also has been in some respects in conflict with these earlier forms. It is a child of the Romantic period, which was critical of disengaged rationality and of an atomism that didn't recognize the ties of community.

One way of describing its development is to see its starting point in the eighteenth-century notion that human beings are endowed with a moral sense, an intuitive feeling for what is right and wrong. The original point of this doctrine was to combat a rival view, that knowing right and wrong was a matter of calculating consequences, in particular those concerned with divine reward and punishment. The notion was that understanding right and wrong was not a matter of dry calculation, but was anchored in our feelings. Morality has, in a sense, a voice within.

The notion of authenticity develops out of a displacement of the moral accent in this idea. On the original view, the inner voice is important because it tells us what is the right thing to do. Being in touch with our moral feelings would matter here, as a means to the end of acting rightly. What I'm calling the displacement of the moral accent comes about when being in touch takes on independent and crucial moral significance. It comes to be something we have to attain to be true and full human beings.

To see what is new in this, we have to see the analogy to earlier moral views, where being in touch with some source — God, say, or the Idea of the Good — was considered essential to full being. Only now the source we have to connect with is deep in us. This is part of the massive subjective turn of modern culture, a new form of inwardness, in which we come to think of ourselves as beings with inner depths. At first, this idea that the source is within doesn't exclude our being related to God or the Ideas; it can be considered our proper way to them. In a sense, it can be seen just as a continuation and intensification of the development inaugurated by Saint Augustine, who saw the road to God as passing through our own reflexive awareness of ourselves.

The first variants of this new view were theistic, or at least pantheist. This is illustrated by the most important philosophical writer who helped to bring about this change, Jean-Jacques Rousseau. I think Rousseau is important not because he inaugurated the change; rather I would argue that his great popularity comes in part from his articulating something that was already happening in the culture. Rousseau frequently presents the issue of morality as that of our following a voice of nature within us. This voice is most often drowned out by the passions induced by our dependence on others, of which the key one is "amour propre" or pride. Our moral salvation comes from recovering authentic moral contact with ourselves. Rousseau even gives a name to the intimate contact with oneself, more fundamental than any moral view, that is a source of joy and contentment: "le sentiment de l'existence." Rousseau also articulated a closely related idea in a most influential way. This is the notion of what I want to call self-determining freedom. It is the idea that I am free when I decide for myself what concerns me, rather than being shaped by external influences. It is a standard of freedom that obviously goes beyond what has been called negative liberty, where I am free to do what I want without interference by others because that is compatible with my being shaped and influenced by society and its laws of conformity. Self-determining freedom demands that I break the hold of all such external impositions, and decide for myself alone. . . .

But to return to the ideal of authenticity: it becomes crucially important because of a development that occurs after Rousseau and that I associate with Herder — once again its major early articulator rather than its originator. Herder put forward the idea that each of us has an original way of being human. Each person has his or her own "measure" is his way of putting it. This idea has entered very deep into modern consciousness. It is also new. Before the late eighteenth century no one thought that the differences between human beings had this kind of moral significance. There is a certain way of being human that is *my* way. I am called upon to live my life in this way, and not in imitation of anyone else's. But this gives a new importance to being true to myself. If I am not, I miss the point of my life, I miss what being human is for *me*.

This is the powerful moral ideal that has come down to us. It accords crucial moral importance to a kind of contact with myself, with my own inner nature, which it sees as in danger of being lost, partly through the pressures towards outward conformity, but also because in taking an instrumental stance to myself, I may have lost the capacity to listen to this inner voice. And then it greatly increases the importance of this self-contact by introducing the principle of originality: each of our voices has something of its own to say. Not only should I not fit my life to the demands of external conformity; I can't even find the model to live by outside myself. I can find it only within.

Being true to myself means being true to my own originality, and that is something only I can articulate and discover. In articulating it, I am also defining myself. I am realizing a potentiality that is properly my own. This is the background understanding to the modern ideal of authenticity, and to the goals of self-fulfillment or self-realization in which it is usually couched. This is the background that gives moral force to the culture of authenticity, including its most degraded, absurd, or trivialized forms. It is what gives sense to the idea of "doing your own thing" or "finding your own fulfillment."

Inescapable Horizons

This is a very rapid sketch of the origins of authenticity. I shall have to fill in more detail later. But for the moment it is enough to see what is involved in reasoning here. And so I want to take up the second controversial claim that I made at the end of the last section. Can one say anything in reason to people who are immersed in the contemporary culture of authenticity? Can you talk in reason to people who are deeply into soft relativism, or who seem to accept no allegiance higher than their own development — say, those who seem ready to throw away love, children, democratic solidarity, for the sake of some career advancement?

Well, how do we reason? Reasoning in moral matters is always reasoning with somebody. You have an interlocutor, and you start from where that person is, or with the actual difference between you; you don't reason from the ground up, as though you were talking to someone who recognized no moral demands whatever. A person who accepted no moral demands would be as impossible to argue with about right and wrong as would a person who refused to accept the world of perception around us be impossible to argue with about empirical matters.

But we are imagining discussing with people who are in the contemporary culture of authenticity. And that means that they are trying to shape their lives in the light of this ideal. We are not left with just the bare facts of their preferences. But if we start from the ideal, then we can ask: What are the conditions in human life of realizing an ideal of this kind? And what does the ideal properly understood call for? The two orders of questions interweave, or perhaps shade into each other. In the second, we are trying to define better what the ideal consists in. With the first, we want to bring out certain general features of human life that condition the fulfillment of this or any other ideal.

In what follows, I want to work out two lines of argument that can illustrate what is involved in this kind of questioning. The argument will be very sketchy, more in the nature of a suggestion of what a convincing demonstration might look like. The aim will be to give some plausibility to my second claim, that you can argue in reason about these matters, and hence to show that there is indeed a practical point in trying to understand better what authenticity consists in.

The general feature of human life that I want to evoke is its fundamentally *dialogical* character. We become full human agents, capable of understanding ourselves, and hence of defining an identity, through our acquisition of rich human languages of expression. For purposes of this discussion, I want to take "language" in a broad sense, covering not only the words we speak but also other modes of expression whereby we define ourselves, including the "languages" of art, of gesture, of love, and the like. But we are inducted into these in exchange with others. No one acquires the languages needed for self-definition on their own. We are introduced to them through exchanges with others who matter to us — what George Herbert Mead called "significant others." The genesis of the human mind is in this sense not "monological," not something each accomplishes on his or her own, but dialogical.

Moreover, this is not just a fact about *genesis*, which can be ignored later on. It's not just that we learn the languages in dialogue and then can go on to use them for our own purposes on our own. This describes our situation to some extent in our culture. We are expected to develop our own opinions, outlook, stances to things, to a considerable degree through solitary reflection. But this is not how things work with important issues, such as the definition of our identity. We define this always in dialogue with, sometimes in struggle against, the identities our significant others want to recognize in us. And even when we outgrow some of the latter — our parents, for instance —

and they disappear from our lives, the conversation with them continues within us as long as we live.

So the contribution of significant others, even when it occurs at the beginning of our lives, continues throughout. Some people might be following me up to here, but still want to hold on to some form of the monological ideal. True, we can never liberate ourselves completely from those whose love and care shaped us early in life, but we should strive to define ourselves on our own to the fullest degree possible, coming as best we can to understand and thus gain some control over the influence of our parents, and avoiding falling into any further such dependencies. We will need relationships to fulfill but not to define ourselves.

This is a common ideal, but I think it seriously underestimates the place of the dialogical in human life. It still wants to confine it as much as possible to the genesis. It forgets how our understanding of the good things in life can be transformed by our enjoying them in common with people we love, how some goods become accessible to us only through such common enjoyment. Because of this, it would take a great deal of effort, and probably many wrenching break-ups, to *prevent* our identity being formed by the people we love. Consider what we mean by "identity." It is "who" we are, "where we're coming from." As such it is the background against which our tastes and desires and opinions and aspirations make sense. If some of the things I value most are accessible to me only in relation to the person I love, then she becomes internal to my identity.

To some people this might seem a limitation, from which one might aspire to free oneself. This is one way of understanding the impulse behind the life of the hermit, or to take a case more familiar to our culture, the solitary artist. But from another perspective, we might see even this as aspiring to a certain kind of dialogicality. In the case of the hermit, the interlocutor is God. In the case of the solitary artist, the work itself is addressed to a future audience, perhaps still to be created by the work itself. The very form of a work of art shows its character as *addressed*. But however one feels about it, the making and sustaining of our identity, in the absence of a heroic effort to break out of ordinary existence, remains dialogical throughout our lives.

Parker Palmer

EXPLORATIONS IN TRUE SELF

Parker Palmer has had considerable influence among those college and university professors who wish to think deeply about their teaching. In books like *To Know as We Are Known* and *The Courage to Teach*, Palmer has invited faculty to take account of the spiritual and moral dimensions of pedagogy and to think about the relationship between their own self-knowledge and their work as teachers. Both in his writing about teaching and learning and in his broader cultural commentaries, Palmer has disclosed a great deal about his own struggle with depression. In the book excerpted below, *A Hidden Wholeness: The Journey toward an Undivided Life*, he elaborates the therapeutic effects of the quest for authenticity, the recovery and affirmation of an original, unique, and integrated self that we all once had but have sometimes lost along the way. Are you persuaded by Palmer's somewhat Rousseauian account of the self? Do you agree that we were "born with a seed of selfhood that contains the spiritual DNA of our uniqueness — an encoded birthright knowledge of who we are, why we are here, and how we are related to others"? Why or why not?

Spiritual DNA

When "true self" is the topic, children are the best source, because they live so close to their birthright gifts. So I begin this chapter with another reflection on childhood. But instead of revisiting my own youth, as I did in Chapter II, I want to look at someone else's early years from the vantage point of my mid-sixties.

When my first grandchild was born, I saw something in her that I had missed in my own children some twenty-five years earlier, when I was too young and self-absorbed to see anyone, including myself, very well. What

From Parker Palmer, *A Hidden Wholeness: The Journey toward an Undivided Life* (San Francisco: Jossey-Bass, 2004), 32–39.

I saw was clear and simple: my granddaughter arrived on earth as *this* kind of person, rather than *that*, or *that*, or *that*.

As an infant, for example, she was almost always calm and focused, quietly absorbing whatever was happening around her. She looked as if she "got" everything — enduring life's tragedies, enjoying its comedies, and patiently awaiting the day when she could comment on all of it. Today, with her verbal skills well honed, this description still fits the teenager who is one of my best friends and seems like an "old soul."

In my granddaughter I actually observed something I could once take only on faith: we are born with a seed of selfhood that contains the spiritual DNA of our uniqueness — an encoded birthright knowledge of who we are, why we are here, and how we are related to others.

We may abandon that knowledge as the years go by, but it never abandons us. I find it fascinating that the very old, who often forget a great deal, may recover vivid memories of childhood, of that time in their lives when they were most like themselves. They are brought back to their birthright nature by the abiding core of selfhood they carry within — a core made more visible, perhaps, by the way aging can strip away whatever is not truly us.

Philosophers haggle about what to call this core of our humanity, but I am no stickler for precision. Thomas Merton called it true self. Buddhists call it original nature or big self. Quakers call it the inner teacher or the inner light. Hasidic Jews call it a spark of the divine. Humanists call it identity and integrity. In popular parlance, people often call it soul. And thus far in this book, I have called it by most of these names!

What we name it matters little to me, since the origins, nature, and destiny of call-it-what-you-will are forever hidden from us, and no one can credibly claim to know its true name. But *that* we name it matters a great deal. For "it" is the objective, ontological reality of selfhood that keeps us from reducing ourselves, or each other, to biological mechanisms, psychological projections, sociological constructs, or raw material to be manufactured into whatever society needs — diminishments of our humanity that constantly threaten the quality of our lives.

"Nobody knows what the soul is," says the poet Mary Oliver, "it comes and goes / like the wind over the water." But just as we can name the functions of the wind, so we can name some of the functions of the soul without presuming to penetrate its mystery:

- The soul wants to keep us rooted in the ground of our own being, resisting the tendency of other faculties, like the intellect and ego, to uproot us from who we are.

- The soul wants to keep us connected to the community in which we find life, for it understands that relationships are necessary if we are to thrive.
- The soul wants to tell us the truth about ourselves, our world, and the relation between the two, whether that truth is easy or hard to hear.
- The soul wants to give us life and wants us to pass that gift along, to become life-givers in a world that deals too much death.

All of us arrive on earth with souls in perfect form. But from the moment of birth onward, the soul or true self is assailed by deforming forces from without and within: by racism, sexism, economic injustice, and other social cancers; by jealousy, resentment, self-doubt, fear, and other demons of the inner life.

Most of us can make a long list of the external enemies of the soul, in the absence of which we are sure we would be better people! Because we so quickly blame our problems on forces "out there," we need to see how often we conspire in our own deformation: for every external power bent on twisting us out of shape, there is a potential collaborator within us. When our impulse to tell the truth is thwarted by threats of punishment, it is because we value security over being truthful. When our impulse to side with the weak is thwarted by threats of lost social standing, it is because we value popularity over being a pariah.

The powers and principalities would hold less sway over our lives if we refused to collaborate with them. But refusal is risky, so we deny our own truth, take up lives of "self-impersonation," and betray our identities. And yet the soul persistently calls us back to our birthright form, back to lives that are grounded, connected, and whole.

Skepticism about True Self

"This is the first, wildest, and wisest thing I know," says Mary Oliver, "that the soul exists, and that it is built entirely out of attentiveness." But we live in a culture that discourages us from paying attention to the soul or true self — and when we fail to pay attention, we end up living soulless lives.

Two streams in our culture contribute to our inattention. One is secularism, which regards the human self as a social construct with no created core; the other is moralism, which regards all concern for self as "selfish." Secularism and moralism may sound contradictory, but they take us to the same place: a denial of true self. If we accept their distortions of reality, the journey toward an undivided life becomes a fool's errand, so it is important to understand why both assessments of our condition are wrong.

Secularism holds that we arrive in the world not as unique individuals but as malleable raw material that receives the imprint of the gender, class, and race into which we happen to be born. We have an inherited nature, of course, a set of potentials and limits received on our roll of genetic dice. But from a secular standpoint, it is nonsense to believe that we are born with an inviolable soul, an ontological identity, a core of created selfhood.

And yet even in the face of this cynicism, the idea of true self persists — not because of some theory but because of experiences we would not and could not have if true self were an illusion.

For example, things fall apart for someone we care about. He makes bad choices and falls into despair, and we cannot understand why. "This is not the person we know," we lament. "He is simply not himself." Or things come together for someone we care about. After years of self-alienation, she learns to love her own life. "She has come into her own," we exult. "She has finally discovered who she really is." We perceive true self in people we know and care about, and we constantly use that perception as a benchmark of their well-being.

Deeper still, we find evidence of true self in our own self-awareness, in experiences we would not have if biology, psychology, and sociology were the whole of who we are. I know I have a true self when I encounter a painful truth that my ego has tried hard to evade and am compelled by the inner teacher to confront it. I know I have a true self when my self-protective heart opens up and another person's joy or suffering fills me as if it were my own. I know I have a true self when desolation visits and I lose my taste for life and yet find within myself a life force that will not die.

But the strongest evidence for true self comes from seeing what happens when we try to live as if we did not have one, a lesson I learned on my journey with clinical depression. Depressions come from a variety of causes, of course. Some result from genetic bad luck or imbalanced brain chemistry and must be treated with drugs. But others result from burying true self so deep that life becomes one long, dark night of the soul. My depression was of that kind: it responded to drugs only temporarily, returning again and again until I embraced my own truth.

The notion that depression may result from defying one's truth has received indirect support from science. Rudolph Nesse, director of the Evolution and Human Adaptation Program at the University of Michigan, suggests that depression "may have developed . . . as [an evolutionary] response to situations in which a desired goal is unattainable," situations in which "one of life's paths peters out into the woods." Depression, Nesse argues, so thoroughly drains us of will and energy that we are unable to continue on a path that once seemed desirable but is — for us, at least — impassable. We must find another way, a way more suited to our nature, thus contributing to individual survival and the evolutionary success of species.

Since one of the soul's functions is to give us life and get us to pass it along — which is soul language, I suppose, for "evolutionary success" — I find it hard to distinguish here between a "biological adaptation" and an "uprising of the soul"! In fact, the metaphor Nesse chose to help explain his theory, the path that peters out into the woods, is most famously found in Dante, that master cartographer of the soul's domain: "Midway on our life's journey, I found myself / In dark woods, the right road lost."

In my own case, at any rate, depression was the soul's call to stop, turn around, go back, and look for a path I could negotiate. If one ignores that call and doggedly presses on, the depression that comes from getting crosswise with true self can yield something worse than melancholy and lassitude: a deep desire to end one's life.

Such was the case with me, and looking back, I understand why. When I was living my outer life at great remove from inner truth, I was not merely on the wrong path: I was killing my selfhood with every step I took. When one's life is a walking death, the step into literal death can seem very easy to take. Medication may offer temporary relief from depressions of this sort, but the real cure goes beyond drugs. We can reclaim our lives only by choosing to live divided no more. It is a choice so daunting — or so it seems in the midst of depression — that we are unlikely to make it until our pain becomes unbearable, the pain that comes from denying or defying true self.

Secularism denies true self by regarding us as raw material. *Moralism* — the pious partner in this odd couple — achieves the same end by translating "self" into "selfishness" and insisting that we banish the word from our vocabulary. The whole problem with our society, the moralists claim, is that too many people are out for themselves at the expense of everyone else. This New Age emphasis on self-fulfillment, this constant "cult of me," is the root cause of the fragmentation of community that we see all around us. Or so the moralists argue.

Deep caring about each other's fate does seem to be on the decline, but I do not believe that New Age narcissism is much to blame. The external causes of our moral indifference are a fragmented mass society that leaves us isolated and afraid, an economic system that puts the rights of capital before the rights of people, and a political process that makes citizens into ciphers.

These are the forces that allow, even encourage, unbridled competition, social irresponsibility, and the survival of the financially fittest. The executives who brought down major corporations by taking indecent sums off the top while wage earners of modest means lost their retirement accounts were clearly more influenced by capitalist amorality than by some New Age guru.

But before I go too far in assigning blame, let me name the real problem with the moralists' complaint: there is scant evidence for their claim that the "cult of me" reigns supreme in our land. I have traveled this country extensively and have met many people. Rarely have I met people with the overweening sense of self the moralists say we have, people who put themselves first as if they possessed the divine right of kings.

Instead, I have met too many people who suffer from an empty self. They have a bottomless pit where their identity should be — an inner void they try to fill with competitive success, consumerism, sexism, racism, or anything that might give them the illusion of being better than others. We embrace attitudes and practices such as these not because we regard ourselves as superior but because we have no sense of self at all. Putting others down becomes a path to identity, a path we would not need to walk if we knew who we were.

The moralists seem to believe that we are in a vicious circle where rising individualism and the self-centeredness inherent in it cause the decline of community — and the decline of community, in turn, gives rise to more individualism and self-centeredness. The reality is quite different, I think: as community is torn apart by various political and economic forces, more and more people suffer from the empty self syndrome.

A strong community helps people develop a sense of true self, for only in community can the self exercise and fulfill its nature: giving and taking, listening and speaking, being and doing. But when community unravels and we lose touch with one another, the self atrophies and we lose touch with ourselves as well. Lacking opportunities to be ourselves in a web of relationships, our sense of self disappears, leading to behaviors that further fragment our relationships and spread the epidemic of inner emptiness.

As I view our society through the lens of my journey with depression — an extreme form of the empty self syndrome, an experience of self-annihilation just short of death — I am convinced that the moralists have got it wrong: it is never "selfish" to name, claim, and nurture true self.

There *are* selfish acts, to be sure. But those acts arise from an empty self, as we try to fill our emptiness in ways that harm others — or in ways that harm us and bring grief to those who care about us. When we are rooted in true self, we can act in ways that are life-giving for us and all whose lives we touch. Whatever we do to care for true self is, in the long run, a gift to the world.

Elizabeth Cady Stanton

SOLITUDE OF SELF

The conviction that each individual possesses a unique self and deserves a degree of individual choice and autonomy is, as Taylor has shown, closely tied to the emergence of democratic philosophies and cultures during the era of the French and American revolutions and the Romantic period that followed. Much of the history of the United States could be told as the history of struggles to widen the democratic principles evident in its founding, for example, through the abolition of slavery, the expansion of suffrage to all male citizens, and the movement to attain women's rights. The following selection stands within this historic stream.

Elizabeth Cady Stanton (1815–1902), a founder and leader of the woman suffrage movement in the United States, delivered the following address before a Congressional committee in January 1892. Her long career in reform began in antislavery activity but focused on women's rights after the Seneca Falls Convention of 1848 issued its Declaration of the Rights of Woman, of which she was one of the authors. Gaining the right to vote was the most visible goal of the nineteenth-century women's movement, but this document suggests that far more was at stake for Stanton than political power. What elements of the ethics of authenticity do you see here? Do you think that the arguments Stanton makes on behalf of women's rights would apply as well to other social groups?

The point I wish plainly to bring before you on this occasion is the individuality of each human soul; our Protestant idea, the right of individual conscience and judgment — our republican idea, individual citizenship. In discussing the rights of woman, we are to consider, first, what belongs to

Elizabeth Cady Stanton, "Solitude of Self: An Address Delivered before the United States Congressional Committee on the Judiciary, Monday, January 18, 1892," in Elizabeth Cady Stanton and Susan B. Anthony, *Correspondence, Writings, Speeches*, ed. Ellen Carol Dubois (New York: Schocken Books, 1981), 247–50.

her as an individual, in a world of her own, the arbiter of her own destiny, an imaginary Robinson Crusoe with her woman Friday on a solitary island. Her rights under such circumstances are to use all her faculties for her own safety and happiness.

Secondly, if we consider her as a citizen, as a member of a great nation, she must have the same rights as all other members, according to the fundamental principles of our Government.

Thirdly, viewed as a woman, an equal factor in civilization, her rights and duties are still the same — individual happiness and development.

Fourthly, it is only the incidental relations of life, such as mother, wife, sister, daughter, that may involve some special duties and training. . . .

The isolation of every human soul and the necessity of self-dependence must give each individual the right to choose his own surroundings. The strongest reason for giving woman all the opportunities for higher education, for the full development of her faculties, forces of mind and body; for giving her the most enlarged freedom of thought and action; a complete emancipation from all forms of bondage, of custom, dependence, superstition; from all the crippling influences of fear, is the solitude and personal responsibility of her own individual life. The strongest reason why we ask for woman a voice in the government under which she lives; in the religion she is asked to believe; equality in social life, where she is the chief factor; a place in the trades and professions, where she may earn her bread, is because of her birthright to self-sovereignty; because, as an individual, she must rely on herself. No matter how much women prefer to lean, to be protected and supported, nor how much men desire to have them do so, they must make the voyage of life alone, and for safety in an emergency they must know something of the laws of navigation. To guide our own craft, we must be captain, pilot, engineer; with chart and compass stand at the wheel; watch the wind and waves and know when to take in the sail, and read the signs in the firmament over all. It matters not whether the solitary voyager is man or woman. . . .

To appreciate the importance of fitting every human soul for independent action, think for a moment of the immeasurable solitude of self. We come into the world alone, unlike all who have gone before us, we leave it alone, under circumstances peculiar to ourselves. No mortal ever has been, no mortal ever will be like the soul just launched on the sea of life. There can never again be just such a combination of prenatal influences; never again just such environments as make up the infancy, youth and manhood of this one. Nature never repeats herself, and the possibilities of one human soul will never be found in another. No one has ever found two blades of ribbon grass alike, and no one will ever find two human beings alike. Seeing, then, what must be the infinite diversity in human character, we can in a measure appreciate the loss to a nation when any large class of the people is uneducated and unrepresented in the government.

We ask for the complete development of every individual, first, for his own benefit and happiness. In fitting out an army, we give each soldier his own knapsack, arms, powder, his blanket, cup, knife, fork and spoon. We provide alike for all their individual necessities; then each man bears his own burden.

Again, we ask complete individual development for the general good; for the consensus of the competent on the whole round of human interests, on all questions of national life; and here each man must bear his share of the general burden. It is sad to see how soon friendless children are left to bear their own burdens, before they can analyze their feelings; before they can even tell their joys and sorrows, they are thrown on their own resources. The great lesson that nature seems to teach us at all ages is self-dependence, self-protection, self-support. . . .

The chief reason for opening to every soul the doors to the whole round of human duties and pleasures is the individual development thus attained, the resources thus provided under all circumstances to mitigate the solitude that at times must come to everyone. . . .

Inasmuch, then, as woman shares equally the joys and sorrows of time and eternity, is it not the height of presumption in man to propose to represent her at the ballot box and the throne of grace, to do her voting in the state, her praying in the church, and to assume the position of high priest at the family altar?

Nothing strengthens the judgment and quickens the conscience like individual responsibility. Nothing adds such dignity to character as the recognition of one's self-sovereignty; the right to an equal place, everywhere conceded — a place earned by personal merit, not an artificial attainment by inheritance, wealth, family and position. Seeing, then, that the responsibilities of life rest equally on man and woman, that their destiny is the same, they need the same preparation for time and eternity. The talk of sheltering woman from the fierce storms of life is the sheerest mockery, for they beat on her from every point of the compass, just as they do on man, and with more fatal results, for he has been trained to protect himself, to resist, and to conquer. Such are the facts in human experience, the responsibilities of individual sovereignty. Rich and poor, intelligent and ignorant, wise and foolish, virtuous and vicious, man and woman; it is ever the same, each soul must depend wholly on itself.

Whatever the theories may be of woman's dependence on man, in the supreme moments of her life, he cannot bear her burdens. Alone she goes to the gates of death to give life to every man that is born into the world. No one can share her fears, no one can mitigate her pangs; and if her sorrow is greater than she can bear, alone she passes beyond the gates into the vast unknown. From the mountain-tops of Judea long ago, a heavenly voice bade his disciples, "Bear ye one another's burdens"; but humanity has not yet risen to that point of self-sacrifice; and if ever so willing, how few the burdens are that one soul can bear for another! . . .

Thanissaro Bhikkhu

NO-SELF OR NOT-SELF?

Three of the four vocabularies we are exploring are global, in that people around the world (the vocabulary of vocation would entail mainly Christians around the world) would find them at least intelligible. The vocabulary of authenticity belongs primarily to the modern West, however. As the two following selections written by Buddhists demonstrate, the idea of a "true self" within each human being that needs to be recovered in order to live responsibly and well would make little or no sense to the millions of people who practice Buddhism. Thanissaro Bhikkhu has translated several of the fundamental texts of Theravada Buddhism, the oldest strain of the Buddhist tradition. He writes from a position of great knowledge and authority as an expositor of Buddhism. Can an ethic of authenticity as described by Taylor be in any way compatible with what Thanissaro Bhikkhu describes as Buddhist thinking about the self? Why or why not?

One of the first stumbling blocks in understanding Buddhism is the teaching on *anattā*, often translated as no-self. This teaching is a stumbling block for two reasons. First, the idea of there being no self doesn't fit well with other Buddhist teachings, such as the doctrine of karma and rebirth: If there's no self, what experiences the results of karma and takes rebirth? Second, it seems to negate the whole reason for the Buddha's teachings to begin with: If there's no self to benefit from the practice, then why bother?

Many books try to answer these questions, but if you look at the Pāli Canon you won't find them addressed at all. In fact, the one place where the Buddha was asked point-blank whether or not there was a self, he refused to answer. When later asked why, he said that to answer either yes, there is a self, or no, there isn't, would be to fall into extreme forms of wrong view that

From Thanissaro Bhikkhu, *Noble Strategy: Essays on the Buddhist Path* (1999), www
.dhammatalks.org/books/NobleStrategy/Section0014.html.

make the path of Buddhist practice impossible. Thus the question should be put aside.

To understand what his silence on this question says about the meaning of anattā, we first have to look at his teachings on how questions should be asked and answered, and how to interpret his answers.

The Buddha divided all questions into four classes: those that deserve a categorical (straight yes or no) answer; those that deserve an analytical answer, defining and qualifying the terms of the question; those that deserve a counter-question, putting the ball back in the questioner's court; and those that deserve to be put aside. The last class of question consists of those that don't lead to the end of suffering and stress. The first duty of a teacher, when asked a question, is to figure out which class the question belongs to, and then to respond in the appropriate way. You don't, for example, say yes or no to a question that should be put aside. If you are the person asking the question and you get an answer, you should then determine how far the answer should be interpreted. The Buddha said that there are two types of people who misrepresent him: those who draw inferences from statements that shouldn't have inferences drawn from them, and those who don't draw inferences from those that should.

These are the basic ground rules for interpreting the Buddha's teachings, but if we look at the way most writers treat the anattā doctrine, we find these ground rules ignored. Some writers try to qualify the no-self interpretation by saying that the Buddha denied the existence of an *eternal* self or a *separate* self, but this is to give an analytical answer to a question that the Buddha showed should be put aside. Others try to draw inferences from the few statements in the discourse that seem to imply that there is no self, but it seems safe to assume that if one forces those statements to give an answer to a question that should be put aside, one is drawing inferences where they shouldn't be drawn.

So, instead of answering "no" to the question of whether or not there is a self — interconnected or separate, eternal or not — the Buddha felt that the question was misguided to begin with. Why? No matter how you define the line between "self" and "other," the notion of self involves an element of self-identification and clinging, and thus suffering and stress. This holds as much for an interconnected self, which recognizes no "other," as it does for a separate self; if one identifies with all of nature, one is pained by every felled tree. It also holds for an entirely "other" universe, in which the sense of alienation and futility would become so debilitating as to make the quest for happiness — one's own or that of others — impossible. For these reasons, the Buddha advised paying no attention to such questions as "Do I exist?" or "Don't I exist?" for however you answer them, they lead to suffering and stress.

To avoid the suffering implicit in questions of "self" and "other," he offered an alternative way of dividing up experience: the four noble truths of stress, its cause, its cessation, and the path to its cessation. These truths aren't assertions; they're categories of experience. Rather than viewing these categories as pertaining to self or other, he said, we should recognize them simply for what they are, in and of themselves, as they are directly experienced, and then perform the duty appropriate to each. Stress should be comprehended, its cause abandoned, its cessation realized, and the path to its cessation developed.

These duties form the context in which the anattā doctrine is best understood. If you develop the path of virtue, concentration, and discernment to a state of calm well-being and use that calm state to look at experience in terms of the noble truths, the questions that occur to the mind are not "Is there a self? What is my self?" but rather "Does holding onto this particular phenomenon cause stress and suffering? Is it really me, myself, or mine? If it's stressful but not really me or mine, why hold on?" These last questions merit straightforward answers, as they then help you to comprehend stress and to chip away at the attachment and clinging — the residual sense of self-identification — that cause stress, until ultimately all traces of self-identification are gone and all that's left is limitless freedom.

In this sense, the anattā teaching is not a doctrine of no-self, but a not-self strategy for shedding suffering by letting go of its cause, leading to the highest, undying happiness. At that point, questions of self, no-self, and not-self fall aside. Once there's the experience of such total freedom, where would there be any concern about what's experiencing it, or about whether or not it's a self?

Ajahn Karunadhammo

THIS IS WHO I AM

At the Abhayagiri Buddhist monastery in Redwood Valley, California, one of the monks offers a brief *Dhamma* reflection at the morning meetings five days a week so that the other monks and the guests of the monastery have something to think about throughout the day. These reflections are delivered extemporaneously and later transcribed and sometimes, as in this case, collected. The text below is a transcription of a reflection from April 2013 and is valuable as a spontaneous expression of Buddhist consciousness on matters of the self. Parker Palmer would answer the question implicit here, Who am I?, by saying I am my authentic or true self. How does this monk answer the same question? Are there any grounds of agreement here between him and Palmer, who, after all, speaks of Buddhism approvingly in his chapter on the self?

Before the work meeting, a few of us were talking about different kinds of characteristics, traits, and qualities we each have and how easy it is to indulge in our personal attributes. Some people are good visualizers and can easily create certain kinds of images in their heads. Others can remember music. I was reflecting how easy it is to take those characteristics that are an integral part of each of us and pick them up in a way that makes us think that's who we are. Whether it's positive qualities or negative qualities, we come into the world with these attributes based on past actions and past habitual conditioning. Whatever they are, we easily identify with them and believe that's who we are: *I'm a person who has abilities in construction, carpentry, or computers. I'm a person who has a lot of anger, sensual desire, fear, or anxiety.* We take these different kinds of qualities we experience throughout our lives and personalize them, creating an image of ourselves in our own minds.

We do the same with other people. We see certain qualities, characteris-

From Ajahn Karunadhammo, "This Is Who I Am," in *Beginning Our Day*, vol. 1 (Redwood Valley, CA: Abhayagiri Buddhist Monastery, 2015), 206–7.

tics, or habits, so we identify a person as a particular type or someone who always has a certain characteristic. *He's an angry person. She's a person who has a lot of sensual desire.* Even if we're smart enough and know about Buddhist practice to the extent we don't really believe that's who we are, for the most part that's still how we operate. We continue to go through our daily activities, seeing the world of ourselves and the world outside through that perceptual lens of good and bad qualities. To counter this tendency, we persist in chipping away at that sense of solidity, that sense of permanent self.

Every time we find ourselves lamenting over an unskillful quality or habit we have or puffing ourselves up thinking we're exceptionally good in some area, it's important to keep reflecting, *Well, that's not really who I am.* These are just qualities that come from conditioning — sometimes through skillful attention, sometimes through unskillful attention — and they're essentially a conglomeration of images and ideas that have formed into the perception: *This is who I am.* Try to see them objectively as conditioned qualities and don't take ownership. By recognizing this constant change and flow of characteristics moving through consciousness we can see clearly that we are merely holding onto shadows. We can learn not to hold onto these characteristics so tightly and watch them arise and cease, realizing their conditioned nature. If we can see little bits and pieces of how these different characteristics are dependently arising based on causes and conditions, then that strong and limiting sense of self starts to slowly disintegrate. Through this process we can understand that we aren't bound by the sense of *me, mine, myself* — the sense of entrapped solidity. It's good to bring this up as a recollection moving throughout the day, letting go little by little, and not feeling so entangled by our images and perceptions.

VOCABULARIES

Authenticity

Virtue

Exemplarity

Vocation

Aristotle

NICOMACHEAN ETHICS

The lectures on the nature of human excellence delivered by the ancient Greek philosopher Aristotle were gathered together by his students under the title *Nicomachean Ethics*. Nicomachus was the name of Aristotle's father, and also of his son. Since Aristotle believed that the most important influence upon a person's character was good upbringing, the book was aptly named. Western thought about virtue, character, human excellence, and moral education — the vocabulary of virtue — sooner or later traces at least some of its inspiration and substance back to Aristotle.

Aristotle sought to give an account of what the good life should look like. In order to do this, he consulted the opinions of "the many" and "the wise," believing that popular wisdom and expert advice would both have much to contribute to such a project of inquiry. Aristotle's approach sets forth both his own views and the opinions of others — so those who read Aristotle must read actively if they are to understand the book rightly. In other words, we must place Aristotle's arguments in conversation with what we ourselves think, testing whether we really think as he thinks we do or as he thinks we should. And if we differ with him, as we sometimes might, we must be able to show why our own views are superior to his.

As he sifted and critically examined many opinions, Aristotle developed a sketch of human excellence that has been remarkably durable throughout many centuries. Why is a sketch, by contrast to a highly detailed picture, the best depiction of the good life for human beings, according to Aristotle? When he asks us readers to fill in the details, what kinds of details does he have in mind?

In the brief beginning section of the *Nicomachean Ethics* below, Aristotle argues that all human beings aim at happiness or well-being above every other good. Happiness was not, for Aristotle, a state of contentment or euphoria; it was rather an activity. Moreover, happiness was an activity in accor-

....

From Aristotle, *Nicomachean Ethics*, trans. Terence Irwin, 2nd ed. (Indianapolis: Hackett, 1999), 8–9.

dance with virtue, a life well performed, if you will. In order to convince us that happiness is just such an activity, Aristotle considers the proper function of a human being as a human being. Do you agree with his account?

Book I [Happiness — The Good for Man]

7 [An Account of the Human Good]

... §5 Now happiness, more than anything else, seems complete without qualification. For we always choose it because of itself, never because of something else. Honor, pleasure, understanding, and every virtue we certainly choose because of themselves, since we would choose each of them even if it had no further result; but we also choose them for the sake of happiness, supposing that through them we shall be happy. Happiness, by contrast, no one ever chooses for their sake, or for the sake of anything else at all. . . .

§8 Moreover, we think happiness is most choiceworthy of all goods, [since] it is not counted as one good among many. [If it were] counted as one among many, then, clearly, we think it would be more choiceworthy if the smallest of goods were added; for the good that is added becomes an extra quantity of goods, and the larger of two goods is always more choiceworthy. Happiness, then, is apparently something complete and self-sufficient, since it is the end of the things achievable in action.

§9 But presumably the remark that the best good is happiness is apparently something [generally] agreed, and we still need a clearer statement of what the best good is.

§10 Perhaps, then, we shall find this if we first grasp the function of a human being. For just as the good, i.e., [doing] well, for a flautist, a sculptor, and every craftsman, and, in general, for whatever has a function and [characteristic] action, seems to depend on its function, the same seems to be true for a human being, if a human being has some function.

§11 Then do the carpenter and the leather worker have their functions and actions, but has a human being no function? Is he by nature idle, without any function? Or, just as eye, hand, foot, and, in general, every [bodily] part apparently has its function, may we likewise ascribe to a human being some function apart from all of these?

§12 What, then, could this be? For living is apparently shared with plants, but what we are looking for is the special function of a human being; hence we should set aside the life of nutrition and growth. The life next in order is some sort of life of sense perception; but this too is apparently shared with horse, ox, and every animal.

§13 The remaining possibility, then, is some sort of life of action of the [part of the soul] that has reason. One [part] of it has reason as obeying reason; the other has it as itself having reason and thinking. Moreover, life is also spoken of in two ways [as capacity and as activity], and we must take [a human being's special function to be] life as activity, since this seems to be called life more fully.

§14 We have found, then, that the human function is activity of the soul in accord with reason or requiring reason. Now we say that the function of a [kind of thing] — of a harpist, for instance — is the same in kind as the function of an excellent individual of the kind — of an excellent harpist, for instance. And the same is true without qualification in every case, if we add to the function the superior achievement in accord with the virtue; for the function of a harpist is to play the harp, and the function of a good harpist is to play it well. Moreover, we take the human function to be a certain kind of life, and take this life to be activity and actions of the soul that involve reason; hence the function of the excellent man is to do this well and finely.

§15 Now each function is completed well by being completed in accord with the virtue proper [to that kind of thing]. And so the human good proves to be activity of the soul in accord with virtue, and indeed with the best and most complete virtue, if there are more virtues than one.

§16 Moreover, it must be in a complete life. For one swallow does not make a spring, nor does one day; nor, similarly, does one day or a short time make us blessed and happy. . . .

Rebecca Konyndyk DeYoung

GLITTERING VICES

This text and the next one are the work of philosophers who wrote many centuries after Aristotle. Nevertheless, both of them explicate and develop the kind of virtue ethics that began with Aristotle some twenty-five hundred years ago, though they do so by basing their own ideas upon the work of Thomas Aquinas, the great medieval Catholic expositor of Aristotle. The first philosopher, Rebecca Konyndyk DeYoung, is Protestant; the second, Josef Pieper, was Catholic. The heritage of virtue ethics from Aristotle through Aquinas is by the time of these writers generally Christian, not specifically Protestant or Catholic, and writers like DeYoung and Pieper have been shaped by the thinking of many secular ethicists as well. Virtue ethics is neither exclusively religious nor exclusively secular.

In the following selection from her book *Glittering Vices: A New Look at the Seven Deadly Sins and Their Remedies*, DeYoung offers a wonderfully clear and succinct account of virtue ethics; she considers what virtue and vice are, how human beings become virtuous or vicious, and the substantial overlap between Christian virtue ethics and its secular predecessors. You should wonder as you read whether DeYoung is accurately describing your own experiences and judgments. Did you become an honest person in the way she describes? Do you see the difference between doing a courageous deed and actually being courageous? What about her comparison between Jane and Joe? Do you, like DeYoung, admire Joe more than Jane, because Joe is never inclined to be unfaithful to his wife and so embodies the virtue of fidelity, in comparison with Jane, who resists temptations to be unfaithful but who is nevertheless always struggling with feelings for men other than her spouse?

From Rebecca Konyndyk DeYoung, *Glittering Vices: A New Look at the Seven Deadly Sins and Their Remedies* (Grand Rapids: Brazos, 2009), 13–18.

Vices and Virtues

In a book on the vices, we ought to be clear what a vice is. How are vices and virtues distinguished? How is a vice different from sin? Understanding these terms will give us a foundation to explore the tradition and its history in chapter 1, where we will answer questions such as: Where did the list of vices come from? What does it mean to call a set of them "capital vices" or "deadly sins"? Which ones should we single out as "capital," which as "deadly," and why? We begin here, however, with the concept of vice itself.

Although most references to the lists of seven use "vice" and "sin" in a roughly synonymous way, distinguishing the two turns out to be important. A vice (or its counterpart, a virtue), first of all, is a habit or a character trait. Unlike something we are born with — such as an outgoing personality or a predisposition to have high cholesterol levels — virtues and vices are acquired moral qualities. We can cultivate habits or break them down over time through our repeated actions, and thus we are ultimately responsible for our character.

By way of an analogy, think of a winter sledding party, in which a group of people head out to smooth a path through freshly fallen snow. The first sled goes down slowly, carving out a rut. Other sleds follow, over and over, down the same path, smoothing and packing down the snow. After many trips a well-worn groove develops, a path out of which it is hard to steer. The groove enables sleds to stay aligned and on course, gliding rapidly, smoothly, and easily on their way. Character traits are like that: the first run down, which required some effort and tough going, gradually becomes a smooth track that one glides down without further intentional steering. Of course, a rider can always stick out a boot and throw the sled off course, usually damaging the track as well. So too we can act out of character, even after being "in the groove" for a long time. In general, however, habits incline us swiftly, smoothly, and reliably toward certain types of action.

Virtues are "excellences" of character, habits or dispositions of character that help us live well as human beings. So, for example, having the virtue of courage enables us to stand firm in a good purpose in the midst of pain or difficulty, when someone without the virtue would run away or give up. A courageous friend stands up for us when our reputation is unfairly maligned, despite risk to his own personal or professional reputation; a courageous mother cares for her sick child through inconvenience, sleepless nights, and exposure to disease. Courage enables us to be faithful to other people and our commitments when the going gets rough and so enables the loving, trusting, and secure human relationships that are essential to a good human life.

Courageous individuals are still admirable people even when their good purposes are thwarted: when the friend's reputation becomes unfairly tarnished or when the sick child does not recover. We think it is better to be the sort of parent who suffers for and with her sick child than to be the sort of parent who can't handle sacrifice and leaves the hard work of caregiving to others. So virtue helps us both to live and act well *and* to be good people, as Aristotle once famously wrote. Similarly, the vices are corruptive and destructive habits. They undermine both our goodness of character and our living and acting well. In the chapters that follow, we will explain how wrath, lust, gluttony, and the rest have a corrosive effect on our lives — how they eat away at our ability to see things clearly, appreciate things as we ought, live in healthy relationships with others, and refrain from self-destructive patterns of behavior.

Virtues and vices are gradually internalized and become firm and settled through years of formation. Often we develop habits by imitating those around us or following their instruction. We may or may not be intentional about all of our habit formation. For example, most children develop habits by imitating their parents, and in this way both virtues and vices can "rub off," so to speak. Other times, habit formation is the cumulative effect of many small, casual choices, similar to developing a smoking habit. Someone who wants to quit smoking after many years, or break any habit, needs serious deliberation and self-discipline. Sometimes we have a crisis that brings a new perspective. We see ourselves as if for the first time and want to change. But to make good on that desire to change, we have to wrestle daily against a deeply ingrained habit — and wrestle, perhaps, for the rest of our lives.

Very simply, a virtue (or vice) is acquired through practice — repeated activity that increases our proficiency at the activity and gradually forms our character. Alasdair MacIntyre describes a child learning to play chess to illustrate the process of habit formation. Imagine, writes MacIntyre, that in hopes of teaching an uninterested seven-year-old to play chess, you offer the child candy — one piece to play, and another piece if the child wins the game. Motivated by his sweet tooth, the child agrees. At first, he plays for the candy alone. (And he will cheat to win, in order to get more candy.) But the more the child plays, the better at chess he gets. And the better at chess he gets, the more he enjoys the game, eventually coming to enjoy the game for itself. At this point in the process, he is no longer playing for the candy; now the child is playing because he enjoys chess and wants to play well. And he understands both the intrinsic value of the game and the way cheating will now rob him of that value. He has become a chess player. Moral formation in virtue works much the same way. We often need external incentives and sanctions to get us through the initial stages of the process, when our old, entrenched desires still pull us toward the opposite behavior. But with encouragement, discipline, and often a role model or mentor, practice can make things feel more natural and enjoyable as we gradually develop the internal values and desires corresponding to our outward behavior. Virtue often develops, that is, from the outside in. This is why, when we want to re-form our character from vice to virtue, we often need to practice and persevere in regular spiritual disciplines and formational practices for a lengthy period of time. There is no quick and easy substitute for daily repetition over the long haul. First we have to pull the sled out of the old rut, and then gradually build up a new track.

As with most human endeavors, we usually do not do this alone. Our parents, most obviously and deeply, contribute to our character formation, but so do friends, mentors, historical figures, and the community of saints past and present. If we marry, our spouse will shape our character, as will our teachers and the fictional characters we read about and find inspiring. Our coworkers influence our habit formation, and so do the friends with whom we spend the most time — which is why good parents care so much about their children's friends. When we make a new resolution or try to cultivate a new habit, having a community back us, or even a single partner with whom to practice or from whom to learn, can make all the difference.

In the end, both virtues and vices are habits that can eventually become "natural" to us. Philosophers describe the perfect achievement of virtue as yielding internal harmony and integrity. Compare, for example, the following two married persons: The first, let's call Jane. Although she resists them, Jane regularly struggles with sexual feelings for men other than her husband. The second, call him Joe, enjoys an ardent affection for his wife throughout the ups and downs of thirty years of marriage. Are they both faithful? In a technical sense, at least, yes. Jane successfully exercises self-control over her wayward desire. But only Joe embodies fidelity as a *virtue*. His faithfulness is deeply rooted in who he is. While we can give her moral credit for her efforts, Jane's faithfulness stays on the surface; it is the uncomfortable voice of conscience countering her adulterous inclinations and keeping her actions in check. By contrast, Joe's desires are in harmony with his considered judgment. Who wouldn't rather have a spouse with Joe's fidelity than Jane's self-control?

The ancient Greek philosopher Aristotle called this the difference between acting *according* to virtue — that is, according to an external standard which tells us what we ought to do whether we feel like it or not — and acting *from* the virtue — that is, from the internalized disposition which naturally yields its corresponding action. The person who acts *from* virtue performs actions that fit seamlessly with his or her inward character. Thus, the telltale sign of virtue is doing the right thing with a sense of peace and pleasure. What feels like "second nature" to you? These are the marks of your character.

Virtues and Virtuous Character

As the previous examples make clear, it is not enough merely to *want* to be virtuous, or to wish we had greater harmony between our motivation and our action. One can aspire to be a better person, or want not to be corrupt or weak, but not yet have a clear sense of how to achieve those goals. "Cultivate good character" is a useless prescription if we don't know what good character amounts to and how to cultivate it. We need to be able to pinpoint our shortcomings and set our sights on specific objectives. If cultivating virtue and avoiding vice is the key to moral formation, then we need to know first of all what the particular virtues and vices are.

When I ask my students and friends to list various virtues, they invariably name things like honesty, courage, kindness, loyalty, and fidelity; for the vices, the list usually includes qualities like cowardice, greed, and selfishness. A *Newsweek* article on character education came up with this list of virtues: "prudence, respect, loyalty, love, justice, courage, hope, honesty, compassion, fairness, and self-control." Answers like these are generally on the right track. Despite our distance from traditions of ethics that focus on the virtues and vices, we retain a sense of what should count. But why privilege one list of vices over another? What makes one list a random collection and another an ordered set?

Contemporary lists given by my students usually share an important feature with those of the Christian virtue tradition. The process of compiling lists of virtues and vices implicitly starts with thinking about moral ideals, embodied in heroes or saints or cultural icons (or villains). That is, we implicitly draw our lists from a mental picture of someone we admire (or despise) as a model of moral excellence (or corruption). Role models who embody a moral ideal are anchors for moral education into the virtues (or vices), since we learn and acquire character traits by observing and imitating role models. From this model or ideal, we can then analyze more specifically what we find admirable or dishonorable about that person's character. A United States Marine embodies honor, courage, and fidelity; an Olympic athlete embodies perseverance and hope; a family practice doctor embodies compassion and wisdom; saints such as Mother Teresa are a model of kindness and mercy; heroes such as Martin Luther King Jr. are a picture of steadfastness and courage.

The Christian tradition is also explicit about its role model, a picture of perfected human nature, the image of God redeemed and restored, the one to be emulated by all human beings. As Aquinas writes, "Our Savior the Lord Jesus Christ . . . showed unto us *in His own self* the way of truth." Christ's life and ministry model the virtues for us, and we must rely on the grace and power of the Holy Spirit to make progress in our imitation of him.

How do Christ's example and the work of grace affect a Christian view of virtues and vices? A Christian understanding of temperance, for example, will have to include not only moderating our desire for food, but also fasting and feasting. Likewise, the virtue of courage challenges us to endure suffering for the sake of love, relying on God's strength, even to the point of martyrdom — this in contrast to contemporary portraits that show us a brave individual charging the enemy alone with guns ablaze. Christ teaches us too how gentleness and humility ground righteous anger, enabling us both to turn over tables of injustice and to turn the other cheek.

The tradition eventually singled out seven virtues — three theological virtues (faith, hope, and love) and four cardinal virtues (practical wisdom, justice, courage, and temperance). These are the qualities of character that *everyone* who wants to become Christlike must seek to cultivate, whatever his or her culture or calling. At the same time, these virtues are the foundation of human perfection for all human beings. They are meant to comprise a holistic picture of the human person — that is, to cover every aspect of our nature, from our mind to our will to our emotions, and to direct them all toward God. According to the Christian tradition, everyone needs faith, hope, and love, as well as practical wisdom, justice, courage, and temperance in order to become all God intended him or her to be as a human being. Of course, courage can be manifested in different ways at different times — on a battlefield or a sickbed — but no one can hold firmly to the good in the face of pain and difficulty without it. Chastity, a part of temperance, can be fulfilled through marriage, celibacy, or seasons of singleness, but the married and the celibate alike are called to order sexual desire rightly. In a parallel way, the seven vices depict for us the traits of character to which we must die in order to live as people with Christlike character.

Josef Pieper

ON LOVE

The life of Josef Pieper (1904–1997) spanned almost the entire length of the last century, and his writings on a variety of subjects remain widely read today. Much of his most memorable and influential work was devoted to the vocabulary of virtue, and especially to the Christian virtues. The selection below, from his book *Faith, Hope, Love*, focuses on what Christians regard as the crown of the Christian virtues, *agapē* (as it is called in Greek) or *caritas* (as it is designated in Latin). English speakers today refer to the virtue as "charity." Notice that Pieper works throughout the selection to suggest that charity is in many ways closely akin to other kinds of love, such as friendship, infatuation, and affection. But he does not end there. Instead, he tries to identify what the Christian account of love adds to the other loves and what it offers everyone, not only Christians, in making sense of actual experience. Pieper uses as his opening exemplar of charity a woman who was his contemporary, Teresa of Calcutta (1910–1997), who won the Nobel Peace Prize in 1979 and was canonized as a saint in 2016. Do you agree with Pieper that we simply cannot understand Saint Teresa and countless others who exhibit a similar sense of compassion and mercy without recourse to the virtue of charity? Does Pieper finally argue that the virtue of charity is possible only for Christians, or does he wish to say that just as God's grace is universal, so is charity? Is the virtue very rare among people, or is it quite common? What does Pieper think? What does your experience suggest?

We shall keep our eyes fixed upon the phenomenon of love as we encounter it in our experience. The question is, however, whether we may not, by dint of including in our considerations something that belongs to the realm of belief, be able to clarify and interpret a fact of experience that would otherwise remain obscure and uncomprehended.

There is, for example, to pitch our discussion in concrete terms at once,

From Joseph Pieper, *Faith, Hope, Love* (San Francisco: Ignatius, 1997), 274–81.

the quite empirical contemporary phenomenon of Mother Teresa, the Yugoslav nun in Calcutta who has recently been receiving a considerable amount of publicity. She taught English literature in her order's high school for girls. One day she could no longer endure seeing, on her way to school, deathly ill and dying people lying in the street without receiving any humane aid. She therefore persuaded the city government to let her have an empty, neglected pilgrims' rest house and in it established her subsequently famous Hospital for the Dying. I have seen this shelter, which at the beginning was a most dismal place. Of course people die inside it likewise — but now they need no longer perish amidst the bustle of the streets. They feel something of the presence of a sympathetic person.

On the one hand, what can we call this work of mercy but a form of loving concern, nourished by the fundamental impulse of "It's good that you exist" and affecting the loving person not just on a supernatural or spiritual level detached from all natural emotions. Rather, it affects him through all the levels of his being. *On the other hand*, something new and fundamentally different is taking place here or, at any rate, something that cannot so easily be reduced to a common denominator with friendship, liking, fondness, being smitten — and so on.

I should like to try, step by step, to make this new element seem plausible, to show how it is something lying within man's potential or, more precisely, something that has been put within the scope of human feeling. The first step, without our knowing it, has already been taken. It consists in our reenacting, whenever we love, the primal affirmation that took place in the creation. But it would also be possible that — taking the second step — we "realize" deliberately this iterative aspect of our loving. When we find something we see good, glorious, wonderful (a tree; the structure of a diatom seen under the microscope; above all, of course, a human face, a friend, one's partner for the whole of life, but also one's own existence in the world) — when we see something good, I say, when we love something lovable, we might become aware of our actually taking up and continuing that universal approval of the creation by which all that has been created is "loved by God" and is therefore good. It would be a further step, beyond the mere recognition of this truth, to wish to observe it expressly, as if we were joining in with the Creator's affirmative and allying ourselves with it in a sort of identification — joining with the primordial act of affirmation and also with the "Actor." We might, in other words, for our part also love the "First Lover." Obviously that would change our own love for things and people, especially for those whom one loves more than all others; our own love, that is, would receive a wholly new and literally absolute confirmation. And the beloved, though still altogether incomparable, still someone personally and specially intended for us, would at the same time suddenly appear as one point of light in an infinite mesh of light.

Yet even after we had taken this step, we would still not have attained the stage of *caritas* and *agapē* in the strict sense. The true motives of that remarkable nun in Calcutta would not yet have come into view. Incidentally, when a reporter remarked to her in astonishment that he would not do "anything like that" if he were paid a thousand dollars a day for it, she is said to have replied, tersely and magnificently, "Neither would I." Anyone who seriously asked her, "Why are you doing this?" would probably receive the reply — if she did not choose to remain silent — "For the sake of Christ!" At this point Anders Nygren is undeniably right; love in the form of *agapē* is "the original basic conception of Christianity." It rests upon the certain faith that the event that in the language of theology is called "Incarnation" conferred upon man the gift of an immediate and real participation in God's creative power of affirmation. Or, as we might also put it: participation in the divine love, which is what creates the being as well as the goodness of the world in the first place. As a consequence of that, man can turn to another person in a way that otherwise he would be utterly incapable of doing and, while remaining altogether himself, can say to that other, "It's good that you are." And it is precisely this more intensive force of approval, operating from a wholly fresh basis, that is intended by the word *caritas* (*agapē*). But because like God's own love it is universal, at least in intention, excluding nothing and no one, we find we can use the word meaningfully without explicitly naming an object, saying, for example, that someone is "in love" (I Jn 4:18). Such love, no matter how "forlorn" it may seem, possesses that imperturbable nonirritability of which the New Testament speaks: "caritas non irritatur" (I Cor 13:5). Likewise other hyperboles, such as that in love a maximum of freedom is attained and that it gives the heart perfect peace, prove true only with regard to *caritas*.

It is really self-evident that the images hitherto employed of a succession of steps and stages do not quite accord with the radical newness and otherness of that participation in the creative love of God that has been given to man — what in the New Testament is called grace. Nevertheless, the great tradition of Christendom has always insisted that this new thing is indeed tied to what man is by nature and by virtue of creation with an inseparable, though almost indescribable, bond.

Above all, *caritas* in the Christian sense does not invalidate any of the love and affirmation we are able to feel on our own and frequently we do feel as a matter of course. Rather, *caritas* comprehends all the forms of human love. For, after all, it is our own natural, native will, kindled at the creation and by virtue of this very origin tempestuously demanding appeasement, that is now exalted to immediate participation in the will of the Creator himself — and therefore necessarily presupposed.

Anyone who considers and accepts this principle cannot find it surprising that the whole conception of *caritas* is dominated by felicity. If happiness is truly never anything but happiness in love, then the fruit of that highest form of love must be the utmost happiness, for which language offers such names as felicity, beatitude, bliss. Nor should this be in any way confused with "eudemonism." In the first place, *felicity* means not so much the subjective feeling of happiness as the objective, existential appeasement of the will by the *bonum universale*, by the quintessence of everything for which our whole being hungers and which we are capable of longing for in (only seemingly paradoxical) "selfless self-love." Moreover, *felicity*, as has already been said, cannot be defined positively at all in regard to its content; it is *bonum ineffabile*, toward which our love ultimately directs itself, a good that cannot be grasped in words.

At any rate, although we may find the fact startling and troublesome at first, the great teachers of Christendom always considered the concepts of *caritas* and felicity as very closely linked. "*Caritas* is not just any kind of love of God, but a love for God that loves him as the object and the author of happiness." And in the world, we are told, we can love in the mode of *caritas* only what is capable of sharing happiness, or beatitude, with us. This includes our bodies, into which happiness will "flood back"; but above all our fellowmen, insofar as they will be our companions in beatitude (or ought to be).

Of course it is possible to ask skeptically just what it means to love another as the possible companion of future beatitude. Would love of this sort alter matters at all? I think that, in fact, a great deal would be altered if we succeeded in regarding another person (whether friend, beloved, son, neighbor, adversary and rival or even an unknown who needed our help) truly as one destined like ourselves to share in the perfection of bliss, as our "socius in participatione beatudinis." That other person would then, in my view, simply enter into a new dimension of reality. Suddenly we would realize that "there are no ordinary people."

It is no accident that almost all the above has been written in the conditional tense, the *modus irrealis*. In fact, it happens very seldom, and only to a few persons, to see the extraordinariness of everyone ("wonderfully created and even more wonderfully re-created"), let alone to respond to it with the exclamation of love: It's wonderful that you are! This is, as we see, not so very far from the vocabulary of eros. And truly, if anyone has asked what in the world the mutual rapture of lovers has to do with the work of a nun who wishes to succor dying beggars — precisely this is the point at which the hidden common element becomes visible, as if seen through a tiny crack.

It also becomes immediately apparent that the act of *caritas* is not simply a farther step on the road of eros, and that what is involved is something different from mere "sublimation." It is true that *caritas* can be incorporated into the most commonplace forms of expression in men's dealings with their fellows. In fact, that is usually what will be done with it — so that possibly, to the uninitiated eye, there will be scarcely anything noticeable about its outward appearance to set it off from the usual conduct of people reasonably well-disposed toward one another. In other words, the natural forms of love are presupposed to be intact; and no special, solemnly sublime vocabulary is needed to describe the operations of *caritas*. Still, the classical statement of the relationship of grace and nature speaks not only of presupposition and intactness but also of the perfecting of what man by nature is and has. And when I said that the bond between eros and *caritas* exists but is almost inde-scribable, the difficulty of description in practice consists in this question: "What is the meaning of *perfecting*?" This is one of those concepts which probably can never be known and defined before it is experienced. It is sim-ply in the nature of the thing that the apprentice can have no specific idea of what the perfection of the mastery looks like from inside or of all that is going to be demanded of him. Perfection always includes transformation. And transformation necessarily means parting from what must be overcome and abandoned precisely for the sake of preserving identity in change.

"Perfection" in *caritas*, therefore, may very well mean that eros, in order to keep its original impulse and remain really love, above all in order to attain the "foreverness" that it naturally desires, must transform itself altogether, and that this transformation perhaps resembles passing through something akin to dying. Such thoughts are, at any rate, not unfamiliar to mankind's reflections on love. *Caritas*, in renewing and rejuvenating us, also brings us death in a certain sense: "Facit in nobis quamdam mortem," says Augustine. The same thing is conveyed by the familiar figure of speech that calls *caritas*, because it consumes everything and transforms everything into itself, a fire.

Thus it is much more than an innocuous piety when Christendom prays, "Kindle in us the fire of thy love."

Natalia Ginzburg

THE LITTLE VIRTUES

Natalia Ginzburg (1916–1991) was a prize-winning Italian writer in many genres. She wrote especially about family life and politics, and for a time she was a political activist in Italy. Her essay "The Little Virtues" redraws Aristotle's conceptual map of virtue and character by introducing the idea of "little virtues," like thrift and caution, in contrast to "big virtues," like generosity and courage. Though this may look like Aristotle's distinction between the four cardinal moral virtues of prudence, courage, temperance, and justice and secondary moral virtues like generosity, Ginzburg's scheme is really quite different. For her, the "big" virtues actually contain and inform the "little" ones. A prudent (big virtue) person may well be cautious (little virtue) in the sense that prudence contains and constrains caution. But caution does not contain prudence: all prudent people will be to some degree cautious, but not all cautious people will be prudent. Moreover, Ginzburg develops her discussion of the little and big virtues within the context of child rearing and education. Like Aristotle, Ginzburg is worried as much about how to cultivate virtue in others as she is about how best to define and understand virtue. She does not shrink back from questions of magnitude: there really are great human beings, who have big virtues, by contrast to lesser human beings, who have only little ones. And a great life is more admirable and, thus, more choiceworthy. Aristotle would agree, but for rather different reasons. Ginzburg, unlike Aristotle, thinks that generosity is a big virtue, and she spends more time discussing that virtue than any other. In today's consumer culture (a very different world from Aristotle's), generosity may well be the most important and the most difficult big virtue to cultivate. We should all wonder whether some times and places call for or need a particular virtue above others. Might the relative importance of the virtues depend upon context? Which virtues do you think are most important today? Why? What would be on your lists of big and little virtues?

....

From Natalia Ginzburg, *The Little Virtues* (New York: Arcade Publishing, 1985), 97–102, 107–8.

As far as the education of children is concerned I think they should be taught not the little virtues but the great ones. Not thrift but generosity and an indifference to money; not caution but courage and a contempt for danger; not shrewdness but frankness and a love of truth; not tact but love for one's neighbor and self-denial; not a desire for success but a desire to be and to know. . . .

Education is only a certain relationship which we establish between ourselves and our children, a certain climate in which feelings, instincts and thoughts can flourish. Now I believe that a climate which is completely pervaded by a respect for the little virtues will, insensibly, lead to cynicism or to a fear of life. In themselves the little virtues have nothing to do with cynicism or a fear of life, but taken together, and without the great virtues, they produce an atmosphere that leads to these consequences. Not that the little virtues are in themselves contemptible; but their value is of a complementary and not of a substantial kind; they cannot stand by themselves without the others, and by themselves and without the others they provide but meagre fare for human nature. By looking around himself a man can find out how to use the little virtues — moderately and when they are necessary — he can drink them in from the air, because the little virtues are of a kind that is common among men. But one cannot breathe in the great virtues from the surrounding air, and they should be the basis of our relationship with our children, the first foundation of their education. Besides, the great can also contain the little, but by the laws of nature there is no way that the little can contain the great. . . .

In these days, when a dialogue between parents and their children has become possible — possible though always difficult, always complicated by mutual prejudices, bashfulness, inhibitions — it is necessary that in this dialogue we show ourselves for what we are, imperfect, in the hope that our children will not resemble us but be stronger and better than us.

As we are all moved in one way or another by the problem of money, the first little virtue that it enters our head to teach our children is thrift. We give them a moneybox and explain to them what a fine thing it is to save money instead of spending it, so that after a few months there will be lots of money, a nice little hoard of it; and how good it is not to give in to the wish to spend money so that in the end we can buy something really special. We remember that when we were children we were given a similar moneybox; but we forget that money, and a liking for saving it, were much less horrible and disgusting things when we were children than they are today; because the more time passes the more disgusting money becomes. And so the moneybox is our first mistake. We have installed a little virtue into our system of education.

That innocent-looking moneybox made of earthenware, in the shape of a pear or an apple, stays month after month in our children's room and they become used to its presence; they become used to the money saved inside it, money which in the dark and in secret grows like a seed in the womb of the earth; they like the money, at first innocently, as we like anything — plants and little animals for example — that grows because we take care of it; and all the time they long for that expensive something they saw in a shop window and which they will be able to buy, as we have explained to them, with the money they have saved up. When at last the moneybox is smashed and the money is spent, the children feel lonely and disappointed; there is no longer any money in their room, saved in the belly of the apple, and there isn't even the rosy apple any more; instead there is something longed for from a shop window, something whose importance and price we made a great fuss about, but which, now that it is in their room, seems dull and plain and ordinary after so much waiting and so much money. The children do not blame money for this disappointment, but the object they have bought; because the money they have lost keeps all its alluring promise in their memories. The children ask for a new moneybox and for more money to save, and they give their thoughts and attention to money in a way that is harmful to them. They prefer money to things. It is not bad that they have suffered a disappointment; it is bad that they feel lonely without the company of money.

We should not teach them to save, we should accustom them to spending money. We should often give children a little money, small sums of no importance, and encourage them to spend it immediately and as they wish, to follow some momentary whim; the children will buy some small rubbishy toy which they will immediately forget as they will immediately forget money spent so quickly and thoughtlessly, and for which they have no liking. When they find the little rubbishy toy — which will soon break — in their hands they will be a bit disappointed but they will quickly forget the disappointment, the rubbishy toy and the money; in fact they will associate money with something momentary and silly, and they will think that money is silly, as it is right that they should think whilst they are children.

It is right that in the first years of their life children should live in ignorance of what money is. Sometimes this is impossible, if we are very poor; and sometimes it is difficult because we are very rich. All the same when we are very poor and money is strictly a matter of daily survival, a question of life or death, then it turns itself before the baby's eyes into food, coal or blankets so quickly that it is unable to harm his spirit. But if we are so-so, neither rich nor poor, it is not difficult to let a child live during its infancy unaware of what money is and unconcerned about it. And yet it is necessary, not too soon and not too late, to shatter this ignorance; and if we have economic difficulties it is necessary that our children, not too soon and not too late, become aware of this, just as it is right that they will at a certain point share our worries with us, the reasons for our happiness, our plans and everything that concerns the family's life together. And we should get them used to considering the family's money as something that belongs to us and to them equally, and not to us rather than to them; or on the other hand we can encourage them to be moderate and careful with the money they spend, and in this way the encouragement to be thrifty is no longer respect for a little virtue, it is not an abstract encouragement to respect something which is in itself not worth our respect, like money, rather it is a way of reminding the children that there isn't a lot of money in the house; it encourages them to think of themselves as adult and responsible for something that involves us as much as them, not something particularly beautiful or pleasant but serious, because it is connected with our daily needs. But not too soon and not too late; the secret of education lies in choosing the right time to do things.

Being moderate with oneself and generous with others; this is what is meant by having a just relationship with money, by being free as far as money is concerned. And there is no doubt that it is less difficult to educate a child so that he has such a sense of proportion, such a freedom, in a family in which money is earned and immediately spent, in which it flows like clear spring water and practically does not exist as money. . . .

What we must remember above all in the education of our children is that their love of life should never weaken. This love can take different forms, and sometimes a listless, solitary, bashful child is not lacking in a love of life, he is not overwhelmed by a fear of life, he is simply in a state of expectancy, intent on preparing himself for his vocation. And what is a human being's vocation but the highest expression of his love of life? And we so must wait, next to him, while his vocation awakens and takes shape. His behavior can be like that of a mole, or of a lizard that holds itself still and pretends to be dead but in reality it has detected the insect that is its prey and is watching its movements, and then suddenly springs forward. Next to him, but in silence and a little aloof from him, we must wait for this leap of his spirit. We should not demand anything; we should not ask or hope that he is a genius or an artist or a hero or a saint; and yet we must be ready for everything; our waiting and our patience must compass both the possibility of the highest and the most ordinary of fates.

A vocation, an ardent and exclusive passion for something in which there is no prospect of money, the consciousness of being able to do something better than others, and being able to love this thing more than anything else — this is the only, the unique way in which a rich child can completely escape being conditioned by money, so that he is free of its claims; so that he feels neither the pride nor the shame of wealth when he is with others. He will not even be conscious of what clothes he is wearing, or of the clothes around him, and tomorrow he will be equal to any privation because the one hunger and thirst within him will be his own passion which will have devoured everything futile and provisional and divested him of every habit learnt in childhood, and which alone will rule his spirit. A vocation is man's one true wealth and salvation.

David Brooks

THE MORAL BUCKET LIST

David Brooks has written about American politics and culture in several books, but he is probably best known for his regular and widely syndicated columns in the *New York Times* and for his Friday evening political commentary on National Public Radio and the *PBS NewsHour*. He frequently writes about character, virtue, and related subjects, such as the moral quality of our public life. In the column included here, "The Moral Bucket List," Brooks offers two lists of virtues, as Ginzburg did in the preceding selection. Their lists are quite different, however, since they were drawn for different purposes. Composing your own lists of what Brooks calls "résumé virtues" and "eulogy virtues," and comparing those lists to your lists of what Ginzburg calls the big and little virtues, may teach you a lot about what you find most admirable about people's characters and why you admire some people more than others. As we have already begun to notice, most people who use the vocabulary of virtue sooner or later speak about moral formation and education. What do Ginzburg, Brooks, and DeYoung share and where do they differ when it comes to moral education?

About once a month I run across a person who radiates an inner light. These people can be in any walk of life. They seem deeply good. They listen well. They make you feel funny and valued. You often catch them looking after other people and as they do so their laugh is musical and their manner is infused with gratitude. They are not thinking about what wonderful work they are doing. They are not thinking about themselves at all.

When I meet such a person it brightens my whole day. But I confess I often have a sadder thought: It occurs to me that I've achieved a decent level of career success, but I have not achieved that. I have not achieved that generosity of spirit, or that depth of character.

A few years ago I realized that I wanted to be a bit more like those people.

From David Brooks, "The Moral Bucket List," *New York Times*, April 11, 2015.

I realized that if I wanted to do that I was going to have to work harder to save my own soul. I was going to have to have the sort of moral adventures that produce that kind of goodness. I was going to have to be better at balancing my life.

It occurred to me that there were two sets of virtues, the résumé virtues and the eulogy virtues. The résumé virtues are the skills you bring to the marketplace. The eulogy virtues are the ones that are talked about at your funeral — whether you were kind, brave, honest or faithful. Were you capable of deep love?

We all know that the eulogy virtues are more important than the résumé ones. But our culture and our educational systems spend more time teaching the skills and strategies you need for career success than the qualities you need to radiate that sort of inner light. Many of us are clearer on how to build an external career than on how to build inner character.

But if you live for external achievement, years pass and the deepest parts of you go unexplored and unstructured. You lack a moral vocabulary. It is easy to slip into a self-satisfied moral mediocrity. You grade yourself on a forgiving curve. You figure as long as you are not obviously hurting anybody and people seem to like you, you must be O.K. But you live with an unconscious boredom, separated from the deepest meaning of life and the highest moral joys. Gradually, a humiliating gap opens between your actual self and your desired self, between you and those incandescent souls you sometimes meet.

So a few years ago I set out to discover how those deeply good people got that way. I didn't know if I could follow their road to character (I'm a pundit, more or less paid to appear smarter and better than I really am). But I at least wanted to know what the road looked like.

I came to the conclusion that wonderful people are made, not born — that the people I admired had achieved an unfakeable inner virtue, built slowly from specific moral and spiritual accomplishments.

If we wanted to be gimmicky, we could say these accomplishments amounted to a moral bucket list, the experiences one should have on the way toward the richest possible inner life. Here, quickly, are some of them:

The Humility Shift

We live in the culture of the Big Me. The meritocracy wants you to promote yourself. Social media wants you to broadcast a highlight reel of your life. Your parents and teachers were always telling you how wonderful you were.

But all the people I've ever deeply admired are profoundly honest about their own weaknesses. They have identified their core sin, whether it is selfishness, the desperate need for approval, cowardice, hardheartedness or whatever. They have traced how that core sin leads to the behavior that makes them feel ashamed. They have achieved a profound humility, which has best been defined as an intense self-awareness from a position of other-centeredness.

Self-Defeat

External success is achieved through competition with others. But character is built during the confrontation with your own weakness. Dwight Eisenhower, for example, realized early on that his core sin was his temper. He developed a moderate, cheerful exterior because he knew he needed to project optimism and confidence to lead. He did silly things to tame his anger. He took the names of the people he hated, wrote them down on slips of paper and tore them up and threw them in the garbage. Over a lifetime of self-confrontation, he developed a mature temperament. He made himself strong in his weakest places.

The Dependency Leap

Many people give away the book "Oh, the Places You'll Go!" as a graduation gift. This book suggests that life is an autonomous journey. We master certain skills and experience adventures and certain challenges on our way to individual success. This individualist worldview suggests that character is this little iron figure of willpower inside. But people on the road to character understand that no person can achieve self-mastery on his or her own. Individual will, reason and compassion are not strong enough to consistently defeat selfishness, pride and self-deception. We all need redemptive assistance from outside.

People on this road see life as a process of commitment making. Character is defined by how deeply rooted you are. Have you developed deep connections that hold you up in times of challenge and push you toward the good? In the realm of the intellect, a person of character has achieved a settled philosophy about fundamental things. In the realm of emotion, she is embedded in a web of unconditional loves. In the realm of action, she is committed to tasks that can't be completed in a single lifetime.

Energizing Love

Dorothy Day led a disorganized life when she was young: drinking, carousing, a suicide attempt or two, following her desires, unable to find direction. But the birth of her daughter changed her. She wrote of that birth, "If I had written the greatest book, composed the greatest symphony, painted the most beautiful painting or carved the most exquisite figure I could not have felt the exalted creator more than I did when they placed my child in my arms."

That kind of love decenters the self. It reminds you that your true riches are in another. Most of all, this love electrifies. It puts you in a state of need and makes it delightful to serve what you love. Day's love for her daughter spilled outward and upward. As she wrote, "No human creature could receive or contain so vast a flood of love and joy as I often felt after the birth of my child. With this came the need to worship, to adore."

She made unshakable commitments in all directions. She became a Catholic, started a radical newspaper, opened settlement houses for the poor and lived among the poor, embracing shared poverty as a way to build community, to not only do good, but be good. This gift of love overcame, sometimes, the natural self-centeredness all of us feel.

The Call Within The Call

We all go into professions for many reasons: money, status, security. But some people have experiences that turn a career into a calling. These experiences quiet the self. All that matters is living up to the standard of excellence inherent in their craft.

Frances Perkins was a young woman who was an activist for progressive causes at the start of the 20th century. She was polite and a bit genteel. But one day she stumbled across the Triangle Shirtwaist factory fire, and watched dozens of garment workers hurl themselves to their deaths rather than be burned alive. That experience shamed her moral sense and purified her ambition. It was her call within a call.

After that, she turned herself into an instrument for the cause of workers' rights. She was willing to work with anybody, compromise with anybody, push through hesitation. She even changed her appearance so she could become a more effective instrument for the movement. She became the first woman in a United States cabinet, under Franklin D. Roosevelt, and emerged as one of the great civic figures of the 20th century.

The Conscience Leap

In most lives there's a moment when people strip away all the branding and status symbols, all the prestige that goes with having gone to a certain school or been born into a certain family. They leap out beyond the utilitarian logic and crash through the barriers of their fears.

The novelist George Eliot (her real name was Mary Ann Evans) was a mess as a young woman, emotionally needy, falling for every man she met and being rejected. Finally, in her mid-30s she met a guy named George Lewes. Lewes was estranged from his wife, but legally he was married. If Eliot went with Lewes she would be labeled an adulterer by society. She'd lose her friends, be cut off by her family. It took her a week to decide, but she went with Lewes. "Light and easily broken ties are what I neither desire theoretically nor could live for practically. Women who are satisfied with such ties do not act as I have done," she wrote.

She chose well. Her character stabilized. Her capacity for empathetic understanding expanded. She lived in a state of steady, devoted love with Lewes, the kind of second love that comes after a person is older, scarred a bit and enmeshed in responsibilities. He served her and helped her become one of the greatest novelists of any age. Together they turned neediness into constancy.

Commencement speakers are always telling young people to follow their passions. Be true to yourself. This is a vision of life that begins with self and ends with self. But people on the road to inner light do not find their vocations by asking, what do I want from life? They ask, what is life asking of me? How can I match my intrinsic talent with one of the world's deep needs?

Their lives often follow a pattern of defeat, recognition, redemption. They have moments of pain and suffering. But they turn those moments into occasions of radical self-understanding — by keeping a journal or making art. As Paul Tillich put it, suffering introduces you to yourself and reminds you that you are not the person you thought you were.

The people on this road see the moments of suffering as pieces of a larger narrative. They are not really living for happiness, as it is conventionally defined. They see life as a moral drama and feel fulfilled only when they are enmeshed in a struggle on behalf of some ideal.

This is a philosophy for stumblers. The stumbler scuffs through life, a little off balance. But the stumbler faces her imperfect nature with unvarnished honesty, with the opposite of squeamishness. Recognizing her limitations, the stumbler at least has a serious foe to overcome and transcend. The stumbler has an outstretched arm, ready to receive and offer assistance. Her friends are there for deep conversation, comfort and advice.

External ambitions are never satisfied because there's always something more to achieve. But the stumblers occasionally experience moments of joy. There's joy in freely chosen obedience to organizations, ideas and people. There's joy in mutual stumbling. There's an aesthetic joy we feel when we see morally good action, when we run across someone who is quiet and humble and good, when we see that however old we are, there's lots to do ahead.

The stumbler doesn't build her life by being better than others, but by being better than she used to be. Unexpectedly, there are transcendent moments of deep tranquillity. For most of their lives their inner and outer ambitions are strong and in balance. But eventually, at moments of rare joy, career ambitions pause, the ego rests, the stumbler looks out at a picnic or dinner or a valley and is overwhelmed by a feeling of limitless gratitude, and an acceptance of the fact that life has treated her much better than she deserves.

Those are the people we want to be.

Mencius

SAYINGS

The Chinese philosopher Mencius has for centuries been regarded as one of the two most influential and authoritative voices of the Confucian tradition of Chinese philosophy, the other one being, of course, Confucius himself. Mencius, who was born about a century after Confucius died, did not study with him directly, as Aristotle had studied with Plato, but even so, he has long been revered as Confucius's successor. The two great Greek philosophers were in effect contemporaries of Confucius and Mencius, a fact that has encouraged many scholars to compare the vocabularies of virtue that originated in the East and the West between the sixth and fourth centuries BCE.

For our purposes, two aspects of Mencius's sayings, excerpted below, are especially important. First, like Aristotle, Mencius clearly believed that human beings are born with the capacity (the seeds) for virtue. But he also thought, like Aristotle, that these seeds needed to be properly cultivated. Do you think human beings are naturally good, as Parker Palmer does, or naturally evil, as Hsun Tzu (the next selection) does, or naturally capable of goodness or virtue with the proper formation? Second, note the nature-based analogy here and remember it when we consider our own relationship to the natural world in question 5, "What Are My Obligations to Future Human and Other Life?" Is there a sense in which our violation of the earth is also a violation of our own characters?

Book VI – Part A

8. Mencius said, "There was a time when the trees were luxuriant on the Ox Mountain. As it is on the outskirts of a great metropolis, the trees are constantly lopped by axes. Is it any wonder that they are no longer fine? With the respite they get in the day and in the night, and the moistening by

From *The Sayings of Mencius*, trans. James R. Ware (New York: New American Library, 1960), 135.

the rain and dew, there is certainly no lack of new shoots coming out, but then the cattle and sheep come to graze upon the mountain. That is why it is as bald as it is. People, seeing only its baldness, tend to think that it never had any trees. But can this possibly be the nature of a mountain? Can what is in man be completely lacking in moral inclinations? A man's letting go of his true heart is like the case of the trees and the axes. When the trees are lopped day after day, is it any wonder that they are no longer fine? If, in spite of the respite a man gets in the day and in the night and of the effect of the morning air on him, scarcely any of his likes and dislikes resemble those of other men, it is because what he does in the course of the day once again dissipates what he had gained. If this dissipation happens repeatedly, then the influence of the air in the night will no longer be able to preserve what was originally in him, and when that happens, the man is not far removed from an animal. Others, seeing his resemblance to an animal, will be led to think that he never had any native endowment. But can that be what a man is genuinely like? Hence, given the right nourishment there is nothing that will not grow, and deprived of it there is nothing that will not wither away. Confucius said, 'Hold on to it and it will remain; let go of it and it will disappear. One never knows the time it comes or goes, neither does one know the direction.' It is perhaps to the heart this refers."

Hsun Tzu

IMPROVING YOURSELF

Hsun Tzu was born late in the fourth century BCE; Mencius was still alive, but as far as we know, the two philosophers never met. Like Mencius and his Greek counterpart Aristotle, Hsun Tzu was very concerned about moral education. But unlike them, Hsun Tzu was convinced that human beings were born into a state of moral deformity. In that respect, Hsun Tzu is more like Jews and Christians than like his fellow Confucians. For our purposes here, we note how Hsun Tzu, very much like Aristotle, realizes that virtues lie somewhere between extremes. Courage lies in a mean between cowardice and rashness, both of which are vices. Thus, for Hsun Tzu, moral discipline involves correcting for extremes: "If you are too hasty and flippant, regulate the fault with restraint." Aristotle thought that the virtue of practical wisdom enabled people to find the mean between extremes. Hsun Tzu seems to believe that such an ability comes through ritual observance. How do you think that good judgment about what we should do and who we should be is formed within us? Are we born with this trait? Must we hope that we are part of a community whose practices and rituals can instill good judgment within us? Or do we find and obtain this capacity by learning from others whose example we seek to follow? Which of these alternatives would Hsun Tzu choose?

When you see good, then diligently examine your own behavior; when you see evil, then with sorrow look into yourself. When you find good in yourself, steadfastly approve it; when you find evil in yourself, hate it as something loathsome. He who comes to you with censure is your teacher; he who comes with approbation is your friend; but he who flatters you is your enemy. Therefore the gentleman honors his teacher, draws close to his

From Hsun Tzu, *Basic Writings*, trans. Burton Watson (New York: Columbia University Press, 1963), 24–28.

friends, but heartily hates his enemies. He loves good untiringly and can accept reprimand and take warning from it. Therefore, though he may have no particular wish to advance, how can he help but do so? The petty man is just the opposite. He behaves in an unruly way and yet hates to have others censure him; he does unworthy deeds and yet wants others to regard him as worthy. He has the heart of a tiger or a wild wolf, the actions of a beast, and yet resents it when others look upon him as an enemy. He draws close to those who flatter him and is distant with those who reprimand him; he laughs at upright men and treats as enemies those who are loyal. Therefore, though he certainly has no desire for ruin, how can he escape it? This is what is meant by the lines in the *Odes*:

> They league together, they slander;
> It fills me with sorrow.
> When advice is good
> They all oppose it.
> When advice is bad,
> They follow all together.

This is the way with impartial goodness: use it to control your temperament and nourish your life and you will live longer than P'eng Tsu; use it to improve and strengthen yourself and you may become equal to the sages Yao and Yü. It is appropriate when you are in a time of success; it is profitable when you are living in hardship. It is in fact what is meant by ritual. If all matters pertaining to temperament, will, and understanding proceed according to ritual, they will be ordered and successful; if not they will be perverse and violent or slovenly and rude. If matters pertaining to food and drink, dress, domicile, and living habits proceed according to ritual, they will be harmonious and well regulated; if not they will end in missteps, excesses, and sickness. If matters pertaining to deportment, attitude, manner of movement, and walk proceed according to ritual, they will be refined; if not they will be arrogant and uncouth, common and countrified. Therefore a man without ritual cannot live; an undertaking without ritual cannot come to completion; a state without ritual cannot attain peace. This is what is meant by the lines in the *Odes*:

> Their rites and ceremonies are entirely according to rule,
> Their laughter and talk are entirely appropriate.

To make use of good to lead others is called education; to make use of good to achieve harmony with others is called amenity. To use what is not good to lead others is called betrayal; to use what is not good to achieve harmony with others is called sycophancy. To treat right as right and wrong as wrong is called wisdom; to treat right as wrong and wrong as right is called stupidity. To speak ill of good men is called slander; to do harm to good men is called brigandage. To call right right and wrong wrong is called honesty. To steal goods is called robbery; to act on the sly is called deceit; to go back on your word is called perfidy. To be without a fixed standard in your actions is called inconstancy. To cling to profit and cast aside righteousness is called the height of depravity. He who has heard much is called broad; he who has heard little is called shallow. He who has seen much is called practiced; he who has seen little is called uncouth. He who has difficulty advancing is called a laggard; he who forgets easily is called a leaky-brain. He whose actions are few and well principled is called orderly; he whose actions are many and disorderly is called chaotic.

This is the proper way to order the temperament and train the mind. If your temperament is too strong and stubborn, soften it with harmony. If your intellect is too deep and withdrawn, unify it with mild sincerity. If you are too courageous and fierce, correct the fault with orderly compliance. If you are too hasty and flippant, regulate the fault with restraint. If you are too constrained and petty, broaden yourself with liberality. If you are too low-minded, lethargic, and greedy, lift yourself up with high ambitions. If you are mediocre, dull, and diffuse, strip away your failings by means of teachers and friends. If you are indolent and heedless, awaken yourself with the thought of imminent disaster. If you are stupidly sincere and ploddingly honest, temper your character with rites and music. Of all the ways to order the temperament and train the mind, none is more direct than to follow ritual, none more vital than to find a teacher, none more godlike than to learn to love one thing alone. This is called the proper way to order the temperament and train the mind.

If your will is well disciplined, you may hold up your head before wealth and eminence; if you are rich in righteous ways, you may stand unmoved before kings and dukes. Look well inside yourself and you may look lightly upon outside things. This is what the old text means when it says, "The gentleman uses things; the petty man is used by things." Though it may mean labor for the body, if the mind finds peace in it, do it. Though there may be little profit in it, if there is much righteousness, do it. Rather than achieve success in the service of an unprincipled ruler, it is better to follow what is right in the service of an impoverished one. A good farmer does not give up plowing just because of flood or drought; a good merchant does not stop doing business just because of occasional losses; a gentleman does not neglect the Way just because of poverty and hardship.

If you are respectful in bearing and sincere in heart, if you abide by ritual principles and are kindly to others, then you may travel all over the world and, though you may choose to live among the barbarian tribes, everyone will honor you. If you are the first to undertake hard work and can leave ease and enjoyment to others, if you are honest and trustworthy, persevering, and meticulous in your job, then you can travel all over the world and, though you choose to live among the barbarians, everyone will want to employ you. But if your bearing is arrogant and your heart is deceitful, if you follow dark and injurious ways and are inconsistent and vile in feeling, then you may travel all over the world and, though you penetrate to every corner of it, there will be no one who does not despise you. If you are shiftless and evasive when it comes to hard work but keen and unrestrained in the pursuit of pleasure, if you are dishonest and insincere, concerned only with your own desires and unattentive to your work, then you may travel all over the world and, though you penetrate to every corner of it, there will be no one who does not reject you.

Edith Jones

PATIENCE

The poem below was published in the *Atlantic Monthly* in 1880. The poet, Edith Jones, later married; she is much better known by her married name, Edith Wharton. She became over the years one of the very best novelists of the twentieth century, known especially for works like *Ethan Frome*, *The House of Mirth*, and *The Age of Innocence*. "Patience" demonstrates a remarkable imagination, since the poem is able to personify a virtue that is often associated with old age, even though the writer wrote this when she was eighteen years old.

Here a careful reader can see how poetry, drawing on the art of personification, can capture the nuances of a moral virtue like patience much more effectively and economically than prose can. On the basis of this poem, do you think Patience is a young woman or an older one? Is this virtue characteristic of the young or of the old? Why should Patience be "Not beautiful to eyes profane"? The vocabulary of exemplarity in the next section will suggest that we can only become virtuous by imitating particular people who embody particular virtues. Does the poem suggest that we can only grasp the very nature of virtue through personifications?

Patience and I have traveled hand in hand
    So many days that I have grown to trace
    The lines of sad, sweet beauty in her face,
And all its veiled depths to understand.

Not beautiful is she to eyes profane;
    Silent and unrevealed her holy charms;
    But, like a mother's, her serene, strong arms
Uphold my footsteps on the path of pain.

....

Edith Jones, "Patience," *Atlantic Monthly*, April 1880.

I long to cry, — her soft voice whispers, "Nay!"
   I seek to fly, but she restrains my feet;
   In wisdom stern, yet in compassion sweet,
She guides my helpless wanderings, day by day.

O my Beloved, life's golden visions fade,
   And one by one life's phantom joys depart;
   They leave a sudden darkness in the heart,
And patience fills their empty place instead.

VOCABULARIES

Authenticity

Virtue

Exemplarity

Vocation

Linda Zagzebski

WHY EXEMPLARISM?

Linda Zagzebski is one of the foremost exponents of what has come to be called "exemplarist ethics." The vocabulary of exemplarity takes its somewhat awkward name from the supremely excellent human beings upon whom this ethic is based. Such people, who are called "exemplars," stir our admiration and inspire us to want to become more like them. We can succinctly distinguish between Aristotle's virtue vocabulary and Zagzebski's exemplarist vocabulary by saying that the former bases his ethical theory on what human beings most desire and the latter bases her ethical theory on what human beings most admire. These subjects of admiration, or moral exemplars, can be grouped into three categories — the hero, the saint, and the sage. Zagzebski offers an elaborated example of each in the selection below. Note that although all her examples are real people, she allows that fictional characters may also be exemplars.

Zagzebski excludes people like Michael Jordan, Serena Williams, and other athletes from consideration as exemplars, as well as geniuses like Mozart and Einstein. These exclusions are based on two principles: first, these examples of supreme excellence are not examples of supreme excellence that is specifically moral; and second, people cannot acquire an inborn talent in the way they can acquire, over a long period of cultivation, a moral virtue.

Although Zagzebski excludes the genius, she includes the sage, the man or woman of great practical wisdom, because people can, through practice, become more and more prudent. Zagzebski's example of a person who embodies the sage is Confucius, the great sixth-century BCE Chinese philosopher. Note that we have already encountered, in the section on virtue, texts by two of the most esteemed and influential sages in the tradition Confucius founded, Mencius and Hsun Tzu.

The crucial thesis of exemplarist ethics has two parts. First, we commonly detect moral excellence and are moved to emulate it through the emotion of

From Linda Zagzebski, *Exemplarist Moral Theory* (New York: Oxford University Press, 2017), 1–2, 65–66, 70–72, 80–82, 84–86.

admiration; and second, that particular emotion, unlike some others, is by and large trustworthy. However, as Zagzebski admits, it is not completely so. It can go wrong about who is and who is not worthy of moral admiration in a given case. As the other readings in this section on exemplarity will demonstrate, thoughtful people can and do recognize where, why, and how their emotion of admiration did go wrong — and, as a result, correct for their mistakes.

Can you make a list of people you admire and then distinguish between those you admire for their natural talents and those you admire for their acquired traits? Which persons that you once admired have you later come to feel differently about, perhaps even to the point of contempt? On what grounds did you change your feelings?

1. Introduction

In every era and in every culture there have been supremely admirable persons who show us the upper reaches of human capability, and in doing so, inspire us to expect more from ourselves. These are the people I am calling exemplars. Most exemplars are not exemplary in every respect, although the Christian saint comes close, assuming that a saint is someone who is both spiritually and morally exemplary. A different kind of exemplar is the hero, a person who takes great risks to achieve a moral end, often the end of helping others in distress. Heroes have dramatic moral accomplishments in character and in action, but they might not be praiseworthy in every respect.

There are also persons who are admirable for something non-moral. Geniuses and the athletically or artistically gifted are admirable for a talent, but while they are inspirational, we cannot imitate their talent. Such people do not express an ideal that others can adopt for themselves. But it is significant that talented people do not usually attract our admiration unless they have also developed their talent through determination and hard work, and those are qualities we can imitate.

There is also the category of the sage, or wise person, whose admirable features include both moral and intellectual excellences, and sometimes spiritual excellences. The sage is an important figure in Confucianism and Stoicism, and there are variations of the idea of the sage in Hinduism, Sufism, Buddhism, the Rabbinic literature, and Native American literature. Aristotle distinguished two kinds of wise persons: the *sophos*, or theoretically wise person, and the *phronimos*, or practically wise person. The latter can be used as a touchstone for moral decision making, whereas the former seeks goods above the human and is often useless in practical matters (*Nicomachean Ethics* [*NE*] 6 1141a 20–1141b 8). This division between two kinds of wisdom complicates the use of sage as an exemplar for the purposes of moral theory, but I do not mind beginning with a notion of an exemplar that is somewhat broader than the idea of the *moral* exemplar as recognized in contemporary Western discourse. I have no firm view on the limits of the moral anyway, and I think it is helpful to let the historical literature frame the discussion, recognizing that cultural and historical inclusiveness pushes us in the direction of broadening the domain of the moral. For readers who have a more restricted view of morality, it should be relatively easy to modify the theory I propose in this book to suit their point of view.

I will begin, then, with a notion of the exemplar that includes the saint, the hero, and the sage, but it will not include the genius. I assume that inborn talent is admirable, but in a sense that is non-moral even when the moral is broadly construed. I will, however, include the sage. Confucian ethics does not make sense without the sage, and I take it for granted that Confucian ethics is ethics.

Exemplars are not just good; they are supremely excellent. I said that they are supremely admirable. That is because I assume that there is something in us that detects the excellent, and that is the emotion of admiration. We identify the excellent with the admirable, and we detect the admirable by the experience of admiration. We can be mistaken in what we take to be admirable, and hence excellent, and that means that the emotion of admiration can be mistaken. It can mislead us. I will have more to say about admiration and its trustworthiness in Chapter 2, but I assume that the emotion of admiration is a universal human experience, and we recognize a connection between feeling admiration and seeing someone *as* admirable, as deserving of admiration. As we will see later, people sometimes resent the admirable, and this is one way in which judging that someone is admirable is not always associated with feeling admiration, but I believe that the emotion of admiration is the primary way we identify exemplars. . . .

2. Three Ways to Observe Exemplars

What I mean by exemplars are those persons whom we see, on close observation and with reflection, to be admirable in all or most of their acquired traits. I do not mean that exemplars must be admirable in the highest degree in every one of their acquired traits. It is highly unlikely that there is anyone like that. For instance, we know that some saints are so committed to their moral project that they become demanding of other people. They cannot see why others do not join their cause. There are also highly caring individuals who neglect their children. A harder kind of case is a person who is highly admirable for some trait, but is contemptible in some other respect, such as heroes who lack temperance or sexual restraint. These persons are exemplars of a certain trait — courage, compassion, justice, but they are not exemplars all things considered. They are still useful as exemplars in the sense I want for exemplarism, but since they are not exemplars without qualification, we need to keep the qualifications in mind in the way we use them for both theoretical and practical purposes. I believe, however, that there are persons who are admirable in most of their acquired traits. Whether there are such persons is something we can investigate by careful attention to people we admire in some way. Sometimes the more we observe someone, the less we admire her, but sometimes we admire her even more. We might have the good fortune to know individuals like that personally, but the primary cultural mode of transmitting observations about exemplars is through narratives.

I have identified three classes of exemplars for special treatment in this book: the hero, the saint, and the sage. In each category I focus on a particular person to exhibit the way the methodology of exemplarism can be applied. Although I think that all of the exemplars I discuss are admirable all things considered, each one is exemplary in a different way, and I believe that that is why it is important to separate the kinds of exemplars for investigation.

The exemplars I discuss are real persons, but I think that fictional exemplars are just as important. One of the advantages of fictional exemplars is that we get to see them in circumstances in which we would not be able to observe a person in real life, and we can have a window into their consciousness in a way that we rarely can do with actual persons. What exemplars do for us and our moral conceptions is largely irrelevant to their actual existence. For instance, it did not matter if Ajax was an actual person to be an exemplar for the ancient Greeks. Besides, there is often a fine line between an actual historical figure and the legend we have inherited. Surely that is the case with Confucius. The Confucius of the *Analects* is an exemplar whether or not the actual Confucius is accurately depicted in that work, and of course New Testament scholars debate the historical Jesus in the same way. . . .

3. Leopold Socha and the Holocaust Rescuers

3.1. The Story of Leopold Socha

On the last day of May 1943, the Nazis liquidated the Jewish ghetto in the Polish city of Lvov, now in Ukraine, which they had set up after the German invasion in 1941. During the day and all night long, Jews were shot, homes burned, and all surviving Jews were rounded up by the Germans and the Ukrainian militia and sent to their deaths in cattle trucks. A group of Jews with their families hid in the sewers beneath the city for fourteen months. They lived amid raw sewage and thousands of rats, in almost total darkness, battling dysentery, injury, and sometimes each other. They could not have survived without the aid of a Polish sewer inspector and former thief, Leopold Socha, who repeatedly risked his life to take care of them, using his ingenuity to bring them food, medicine, games, prayer books, candles for the Sabbath light, and providing them with crucial information about the outside world. Socha had the full cooperation of his wife and a friend and co-worker, Stefan Wroblewski, who helped Socha from the beginning. A journal was kept by Ignacy Chiger, a member of the group who hid in the sewers, and that journal, together with a book written by his daughter and interviews with other survivors, gives us a picture of the man from the perspective of the people he was helping.

At the beginning, Socha was paid to hide the Chigers and a few others, but the group grew on the night of the terror when it became obvious that all of them had to either go into the sewers or die. The survivors say that their relationship with Socha was the cornerstone of the ordeal and its success for ten of them. Chiger says that Socha liked to tell the story of seeing Paulina Chiger for the first time. "When I squeezed through the shaft, into the little cellar, you were sitting there with Krysia and Pawel under each arm. Like a mother kite and her chicks. It was at that moment, when you were sitting there with the children, at that moment I decided to save you."

For hundreds of years, Lvov had been a center for Western culture and commerce on the eastern edge of the Austro-Hungarian empire, and Socha had the vague anti-Semitic attitude of most of the Poles and Ukrainians in Lvov. In a short time his motive evolved from anti-Semitism to a desire to protect the Jews from the Nazis, making greater and greater personal sacrifices, motivated first by money, and then, after their money ran out,

out of care for them as individuals. He protected them from harms that had nothing to do with the Nazis. At some point he began to love them. When a man died, he and Wroblewski took great risks to give the man a proper burial. When a woman secretly gave birth to a baby, he ran out to find someone to care for the child, but sadly, when he returned with a plan, the mother had already smothered her infant, and they buried the baby. When hostility arose between Chiger and Weiss, the original leader of the group, Socha acted as keeper of the peace. When there was a violent storm and waters flooded the sewers, Socha ran into the sewer in a panic, terrified that the people had drowned, finding that the waters had stopped rising just as it reached their chins.

Ignacy Chiger became the leader of the group after Weiss attempted to escape and was shot. He says that Socha's relationship with him was based on mutual respect and trust. When Chiger gave Socha money, both men knew that Socha could have easily pocketed the money and then handed them over to the authorities and claimed a reward. No one ever thought he would do that. Socha liked to ask Chiger's advice about his own problems, and he told them accounts of his past life as a thief and his remorse over what he had done. He was a deeply religious man, and in speaking of his work to shelter the group, he told Chiger, "This is my mission. I have been called to do it, to atone."

The Russian army entered Lvov on July 26, 1944. Chiger's daughter, Krystyna, writes in her memoir that Socha had everything organized for them for their life after they left the sewers. He had found a building that could be divided into apartments, and prepared a home for each of the families with furnishings, clothes, and bedding. On July 28, 1944, the ten surviving Jews emerged from the sewers to the astonishment of a group of people who gathered to watch. Leopold Socha looked at the people and said proudly, "These are my Jews."

Socha died in the act of rescue, but it was not the rescue for which he thought he might die. On May 12, 1946, Leopold and his twelve-year-old daughter, Stefcia, were riding their bicycles through a narrow street when a Soviet army truck careened toward them directly in the path of Stefcia, who was riding ahead. Leopold desperately pedaled forward and knocked her safely out of the way, but was crushed to death by the truck.

In 1978 Leopold and Magdalena Socha were recognized as "Righteous among the Nations" by Yad Vashem. Stefan Wroblewski and his wife were given the same honor in 1981. . . .

4. Jean Vanier and the L'Arche Communities

4.1 The Story of Jean Vanier

In 1964, Jean Vanier, a philosophy professor and former naval officer, bought a small house in Trosly-Breuil, a village north of Paris, and invited two men with mental disabilities to make their home with him. He called their community L'Arche, after Noah's Ark. The aim of Vanier and the other volunteer "assistants" was to live in a community inspired by the Beatitudes and to create a family life for the mentally infirm. The communities multiplied, and quickly became an interfaith and intercultural movement. By 2008 there were more than 130 L'Arche communities on every continent of the globe, including sixteen in the United States.

Vanier was born in Geneva where his father was a distinguished soldier and later governor general of Canada. His family escaped Paris ahead of the advancing German army in World War II, and Vanier spend most of the war in an English naval academy, subsequently joining the Royal Navy and then the Royal Canadian Navy. In 1950 he resigned his commission, knowing that he needed to find another path. For a time Vanier studied for the priesthood in Quebec, but changed his mind and spent a few years searching, attempting to find the right kind of community. While he was in the navy, he had visited Friendship House in New York, a Catholic interracial apostolate founded in the early 1930s by Catherine de Hueck, and it touched him deeply. In Paris, while he pursued studies in philosophy and theology, he joined a small Christian community of students where everyone worked manually and prayed together. In 1962 Vanier earned his Ph.D. at the Institute Catholique de Paris with a dissertation on happiness in Aristotle. In 1963 his mentor and former philosophy professor, the saintly Père Thomas Philippe, inspired him to adopt a vocation to the intellectually disabled. Père Thomas was a scholar and a visionary whose mission focused on the "little" people, particularly people who had mental disabilities. When Vanier helped his friend refurbish a place to live and minister to these people, he felt a vocation to follow Père Thomas, yet he did not at first feel at ease with the mentally impaired. In January 1964, he went to the University of Toronto, where he had been invited to teach philosophy. At the end of the term he was offered a permanent position, but he decided to return to Europe and began visiting institutions for the mentally disabled. These places were horrifying, yet Vanier later said that he saw "something of God" in them that led him to decide that his true vocation was to bring about a gentle revolution:

> The idea of living together was there from day one, the idea of living happily together, of celebrating and laughing a lot, came very quickly and spontaneously. When the idea of the poor educating us came, I don't know exactly. The words of St. Vincent De Paul, "The poor are our masters," were always there, but when they became a reality is uncertain.

Vanier's religious vision was never clear at the beginning, and he probably did not realize that he was creating a new kind of community. All he knew was that he had made an irrevocable decision to live with two disabled men, Raphael and Philippe, for the rest of their lives or his. Gradually more people came and more communities were formed: a community for women, a community for both men and women, and eventually, they began welcoming people with more severe and multiple disabilities. Some of these people had such severe disabilities that they appeared to be beyond reach — for example, blind, autistic Claudia, who had never known love, and whose inner pain made her seem totally mad, screaming day and night, and spreading excrement on the walls. Vanier describes her transformation into a sweet, loving person under the guidance of her faithful caregiver, Nadine, and in story after story, we see the transformative power of those who can see the humanity in persons whom no one believed in and letting it blossom. The stories always include the transformative power on the caregiver as well — hence, the title of one of Vanier's most gripping books *Becoming Human*. Vanier's moral genius was in being able to create a revolutionary kind of human community, one that had never before been thought possible.

What the caregivers actually do is both extraordinarily simple and extraordinarily effective. More than forty years after L'Arche was founded, when it had spread to many countries, Kathleen Berken, an American woman assistant in a L'Arche community in Iowa, vividly described their daily life:

> I believe that we live as family despite roadblocks of anger, violence, and pain. Caring for our core members' needs while helping them be independent is staggering. We do most everything: cook; shop; bathe; brush teeth; wipe butts; handle expenses; drive them to medical appointments; spend weekends at Special Olympics; write letters; do paperwork; communicate with family, guardians, and case managers; accompany them to church; plan out-

ings; go to dances, the park, restaurants. But more, we hope to be friends. Yet hope can slam you in the face when, without warning, an angry core member threatens to kill you. That makes it challenging to be friends.

The mystery is that Kathleen Berken and the other L'Arche assistants can live as she describes, yet L'Arche keeps growing and the assistants keep coming, some staying for many years. Jean Vanier says at the end of his book, *Becoming Human* (1998), "We do not have to be saviors of the world! We are simply human beings, enfolded in weakness and in hope, called together to change our world one heart at a time." . . .

5. Confucius and Exemplars of Wisdom

5.1 The Sage and the Analects

Not all exemplars perform stunning acts of self-sacrifice or courage. Some are known for their wisdom. As I have said, I do not think that means that we have a concept of wisdom that we use to identify wise persons or sages. Rather, I think that in our natural moral development we learn what wisdom is by observing or reading about the persons who attract us in the way wise persons attract us. Wisdom is the quality that *that* person has. Unlike saints and heroes, we typically do not identify sages primarily by admirable overt acts, and we generally do not speak of "wise acts," although we might refer to "words of wisdom," and in retrospect, we may speak of "wise decisions." Wise persons may also attract our attention because they convey a sense of serenity and emotional tranquility, perhaps holiness. They have the harmony of soul that few of us have attained, and we can see that harmony in their outward demeanor. That was the case with Confucius.

Confucius is by far the earliest of the exemplars I mentioned in this book (b. 551 BC). Arguably he had the same pivotal role in the creation of Chinese philosophy that Socrates had for Western philosophy. Although Confucius himself showed no interest in building a theory in my sense of theory, Amy Olberding interprets the *Analects* within the framework of exemplarism, arguing that the moral theory of that work begins with identification of exemplary figures and careful observation of them, and then moves to increasingly refined and abstract moral concepts and rules derived from those observations. Confucius treats the Duke of Zhou as an exemplar, and Confucius's students treat Confucius as an exemplar. Olberding says,

"The reasoning of the *Analects* begins with people and ends in theory. Its governing imperative is that we ought to seek to be like our exemplars, and its generalized accounts of the virtues reflect efforts to assay, in an organized and careful fashion, what emulation of exemplars entails and requires."

I said at the beginning of this chapter that we are initially attracted to exemplars because of something easily observed about them, usually their acts, and we then seek to identify the psychological source of those acts. In the *Analects*, moral character is revealed in more than acts. A person's physical bearing, movement, and manner of speaking are expressions of his moral character, and Olberding suggests that the way Confucius looks and moves, and the style of his speech get considerable attention in the *Analects* because of the way they reveal his exemplarity. Other people admire the graceful and devoted way in which Confucius performs the *li*, or rituals which, Olberding says, "can be understood to formalize characteristic responses of exemplars into a code of behavior and demeanor keyed to recurrent patterns of circumstance." There is something striking in Confucius's sensitive performance of the *li* that makes him widely admired. There is a deep accord between his inclinations and the requirements of the *li*, yet because he has mastered it so perfectly, he can allow himself to improvise to great effect. Olberding proposes that Confucius was admired because his contemporaries and the readers of the *Analects* are able to see the way his motivations, emotions and behavior fit the circumstances. Moreover, Confucius is "uncommonly transparent" in the way he communicates the interior through the exterior. "His personal style . . . allows others to borrow a felt sense of his grace and ease in responding to the world as he finds it."

Dorothy Day

THERESE

Reading portions of Dorothy Day's biography of Saint Therese of Lisieux offers a rare opportunity to witness how someone's emotion of admiration can go wrong but later be corrected. As Dorothy Day recounts, she originally felt something very much like contempt for a young nun whom she later grew to admire so much that she wrote her biography, with the explicit goal of getting others to admire her too. Day demonstrates that admiration is a complex emotion, perhaps more a process than a simple feeling. Thus, Day's own moral growth helps to transform her original emotion of contempt to one of admiration. Further, the corrected emotion she comes to feel for Saint Therese of Lisieux inspires Day herself to greater levels of moral growth, strengthening her own moral witness to the world.

Both the author and the subject of the biography from which this selection is taken are by now widely admired, even venerated, as having lived lives of exceptional holiness. Dorothy Day (1897–1980) was a lifelong activist on behalf of peace and economic justice who converted to Catholicism shortly after the birth of her daughter. She would later found the Catholic Worker Movement and become an inspiring and influential advocate for social justice and compassion grounded in Catholic social thought and sustained by Catholic sacraments and prayer. Therese Martin, a French nun who died in 1897 at the age of twenty-four, led a far more secluded and outwardly uneventful life. Yet the "little way" of love and attentiveness she explored in her living and expressed in her writing became a strong influence on the spirituality of Day and millions of other believers.

Why do you think Day so admired "the Little Flower"? Do you consider Therese's life "extraordinary" or "ordinary"? How did Day correct her original emotion of contempt and transform it into admiration?

....

From Dorothy Day, *Therese* (Springfield, IL: Templegate Publishers, 1960), ix, xii, 70, 72, 106–7, 145–46, 161–67, and 173–74.

The first time I heard the name of St. Therese of the Child Jesus and of the Holy Face (to give her her whole title), also known as Therese of Lisieux, the Little Flower, was when I lay in the maternity ward of Bellevue Hospital in New York. Bellevue is the largest hospital in the world, and doctors from all over the world come there. If you are poor you can have free hospital care. At that time, if you could pay anything there was a flat rate for having a baby — thirty dollars for a ten days' stay, in a long ward with about sixty beds. I was so fortunate as to have a bed next to the window looking out over the East River, so that I could see the sun rise in the morning and light up the turgid water and make gay the little tugs and the long tankers that went by the window. When there was fog it seemed as though the world ended outside my window, and the sound of fog horns haunted the day and the night.

As a matter of fact, my world did end at the window those ten days that I was in the hospital, because I was supremely happy. If I had written the greatest book, composed the greatest symphony, painted the most beautiful painting, or carved the most exquisite figure, I could not have felt more the exalted creator than I did when they placed my child in my arms. To think that this thing of beauty, sighing gently in my arms, reaching her little mouth for my breast, clutching at me with her tiny beautiful hands, had come from my flesh, was my own child! Such a great feeling of happiness and joy filled me that I was hungry for Someone to thank, to love, even to worship, for so great a good that had been bestowed upon me. That tiny child was not enough to contain my love, nor could the father, though my heart was warm with love for both.

We were radicals and had no particular religious affiliations. If I was drawn to any "organized church," it was to the Catholic. I knew of such saints as St. Francis of Assisi and St. Augustine, and William James, in his *Varieties of Religious Experience*, had introduced me to St. Teresa of Avila, that well-traveled yet cloistered contemplative, with her vigorous writing and her sense of humor.

"What are you going to name your baby?" the girl in the next bed to mine asked me.

"Teresa," I told her. "Tamar Teresa. I have a dear friend whose husband is a Zionist, and she has a little girl named Tamar. It means little palm tree, in Hebrew."

"And Teresa is after the Little Flower?"

I had never heard of the Little Flower and she had never heard of Teresa of Avila. She was a Catholic, and although she didn't read much, she knew the outlines of the life of St. Therese of Lisieux. In her pocketbook, where she kept her powder and lipstick, tissues and rosary beads, money to buy candy and the *Daily News* when the boy made his rounds, she also had a medal of the Little Flower. "Here, I will give it to you for your baby," she said. "Pin it on her."

I was some years from being a Catholic and I shied away from this manifestation of superstition and charm-wearing. I wanted no such talisman. Besides, the baby might swallow it. The pin might come unloosed and pierce that tender flesh.

"But if you love someone, you want something around you to remind you of them," the girl protested. So I took the medal, and after hearing of St. Therese as the young novice mistress of a far-off convent of Lisieux in Normandy, who had died the year I was born, and whose sisters were still alive, I decided that although I would name my child after the older saint, the new one would be my own Teresa's novice mistress, to train her in the spiritual life. I knew that I wanted to have the child baptized a Catholic and I wanted both saints to be taking care of her. One was not enough.

The next time I heard of St. Therese of Lisieux was in 1928, a year after I had been baptized a Catholic. I was thirty years old. I had read the New Testament, the *Imitation of Christ*, St. Augustine, and had dipped into the writings of some of the saints William James had introduced me to. I had a daily missal, too, which presented a little biography of the saint of the day, commemorated in the Mass. I still knew nothing of modern saints. Perhaps, I thought, the days of saints had passed.

At that time I did not understand that we are all "called to be saints," as St. Paul puts it. Most people nowadays, if they were asked, would say diffidently that they do not profess to be saints, indeed they do not want to be saints. And yet the saint is the holy man, the "whole man," the integrated man. We all wish to be that, but in these days of stress and strain we are not developing our spiritual capacities as we should and most of us will admit that. We want to grow in love but we do not know how. Love is a science, a knowledge, and we lack it.

My confessor at the time was Father Zachary, an Augustinian Father of the Assumption, stationed at the Church of Our Lady of Guadalupe on West Fourteenth Street. He was preparing me for Confirmation, giving me a weekly evening of instruction.

One day Father Zachary said to me, "Here is a book that will do you good." He had already given me Challoner's *Meditations* and the St. Andrew Missal. The book he now handed me was *The Little White Flower: The Story of a Soul,* an unbound book which had a tan cover with a not too attractive picture of a young nun with a sweet insipid face, holding a crucifix and a huge bouquet of roses. I was by now familiar with the statues of this little Sister which were to be seen in every church. They always called her little, although it is said she was very tall, and completely emaciated when the last photographs of her were taken. She had a proud face, however, and her habit and cloak concealed how thin she was. She was very young and her writing seemed to me like that of a schoolgirl. I wasn't looking for anything so simple and felt slightly aggrieved at Father Zachary. Men, even priests, were very insulting to women, I thought, handing out what they felt suited their intelligence — in other words, pious pap.

I dutifully read *The Story of a Soul* and am ashamed to confess that I found it colorless, monotonous, too small in fact for my notice. What kind of a saint was this who felt that she had to practice heroic charity in eating what was put in front of her, in taking medicine, enduring cold and heat, restraint, enduring the society of mediocre souls, in following the strict regime of the convent of Carmelite nuns which she had joined at the age of fifteen? A splash of dirty water from the careless washing of a nun next to her in the laundry was mentioned as a "mortification," when the very root of the word meant death. And I was reading in my Daily Missal of saints stretched on the rack, burnt by flames, starving themselves in the desert, and so on.

Joan of Arc leading an army fitted more into my concept of a saint, familiar as I was with the history of labor with its martyrs in the service of their brothers. "Love of brothers is to lay down one's life on the barricades, in revolt against the hunger and injustice in the world," I told Father Zachary, trying to convert him to my point of view. Living as we were in a time of world revolution, when, as I felt, the people of the world were rising to make a better world for themselves, I wondered what this new saint had to offer. . . .

[Day's eventual admiration for Saint Therese leads her to write the latter's biography.]

My purpose in writing the book in the first place was to reach some of the 65,000 subscribers to the *Catholic Worker,* many of whom are not Catholic and not even "believers," to introduce them to a saint of our day. Many of them are familiar only with a St. Francis of Assisi or a St. Joan of Arc. Also I wrote to overcome the sense of futility in Catholics, men, women, and youths, married and single, who feel hopeless and useless, less than the dust, ineffectual, wasted, powerless. On the one hand Therese was "the little grain of sand" and on the other "her name was written in heaven"; she was beloved by her heavenly Father, she was the bride of Christ, she was little less than the angels. And so are we all.

* * *

Those were sunny years of childhood with delightful memories. Her father used to take the children to the pavilion where he kept his fishing tackle and books; he took them for walks on Sunday and then her mother was with them. She remembers the wheat fields studded with poppies and cornflowers and daisies. She loved, she said — she who was to wall herself in at the age of fifteen in a severely cloistered order — she loved "far distances, wide spaces and trees." Her whole soul was steeped in beauty and love, and her own happy nature made life all the more delightful. For four and a half years, the whole world was sunny for her.

And then came her mother's illness and death.

In Therese's world, she was faced with only three choices. She could look forward to marriage, or to living at home as a single woman and caring for her father, or to entering the convent. The atmosphere of this home was one of such liberty that the girls were always free to decide what they wanted, what they themselves thought was God's will for them. . . .

On the feast of Pentecost, Therese told her father of her desires. She did it in fear and trembling, at the close of the day, after they had come home from Vespers. Her father was sitting in the garden; it was sunset at the end of a most beautiful day. She had prayed to the Holy Spirit and to the Apostles to help her to speak, to ask her father's permission. After all, she was only fourteen.

The very words she uses in her autobiography show how important she considered her vocation, how out of the ordinary, not in the least like that of others. She felt herself to be, she wrote, "a child destined by God to be, by means of prayer and sacrifice, an apostle of apostles." Already once before, when out walking with her father, she had pointed to the large T made by the configuration of the stars and said childishly, "Look, my name is written in heaven." She felt her vocation to be a saint — and a special kind of saint for our times.

When she told her father, he wept at first. He tried to tell her she was too young to leave him, to take such a step into a harsh and rigorous life. But they continued to talk as they walked up and down the garden path, and her heart grew light with joy when she realized that he had consented. After they had walked for some time together, he stooped down to a little rock garden and picked a small white flower, which came out by the roots. Then he spoke to her of her sheltered life, and how God had chosen her, a little flower, preserving her in her fragility and obscurity. From then on she thought of herself as "a little white flower" — the name she first gave to her book. She took the flower and pressed it in her prayer book and since the roots had come up with the stem, she thought of herself as being transplanted to Carmel. Later, when the stem broke, she took it as a sign that she was going to die young, as she did.

Therese's habit was of coarse serge, her stockings of rough muslin, and on her feet she wore rope sandals. Her bed was made of three planks, covered by a thin pad and one woolen blanket. There was scarcity of food, inadequate bedding, no heat in the convent except for one small stove in one room. Prayer and penance! These are indeed spiritual works, spiritual weapons to save souls, penance for luxury when the destitute suffer, a work to increase the sum total of love and peace in the world.

Six or seven hours of prayer, a life of hard work in silence the rest of the time, two brief periods of recreation when there was permission to talk, sew, paint, or take up the "busy work" all women delight in. In addition to the works of the community, whether it was laundry, kitchen, dining room, sacristy, much of the work was done alone. When it came to the sewing, the fine embroidery done by the community, the tradition was to work in one's cell.

Much of the convent's physical work was carried on under very difficult circumstances. The Sisters, of course, had none of the machinery that makes today's household tasks relatively easy. There is a picture showing Celine and Therese bending over the stone washtubs, laughing together. But it was no laughing matter to stand outdoors during winter, rinsing the linen in cold water. Therese always tried to take the most difficult tasks, feeling that it was the part of charity to do so since she would be saving another Sister the hard labor. It was the same with the hot, steamy laundry in summer. When there was a choice of work, she took the hardest, not only as a penance but as an act of loving kindness, a practice in love. One could not love God without loving His household.

And whatever she did, she did with the utmost cheerfulness, always with a gentle smile, with briskness and alacrity. "She ran in the way of His commandments since He enlarged her heart," as the Psalmist writes. When she had other work and could not be present at recreation, the Sisters used to say that on those occasions there was little laughter. Therese was a mimic, could tell a story, always knew how to see the funny side of things in the little incidents that come up in convent life.

Her only reason for telling about the irritations encountered in her life with twenty others under obedience, was to show of what little things the practice of virtue is made up.

[During the long illness that led to her death,] to the community she gave every appearance of serenity and peace, and yet "in peace is my bitterness most bitter," she quotes. On another occasion she says, "Let us suffer, if need be, with bitterness." She, the realist, well knew that suffering of body and soul is not lofty and exalted, but mean and cruel, a reflection of the blackness of hell. It was not suffering for itself that she embraced. It was a means to an end; the very means used by Jesus Himself.

In order to hide this suffering from others, she wrote poems about the joys of faith, hope, and charity, and yet in the night of sense and soul that she was passing through, she felt none of these joys. She wanted her suffering to be hidden even from God, if that were possible, in order to atone for lack of faith in the world. She asked consolation from no one, not even from God. She had wanted martyrdom, and this heavy weight of despair is martyrdom.

She never complained, she went on with the work of the day in chapel and out of it, and said nothing. The rule calls for complete silence except during the two hours of recreation, one after the noonday meal, and the other after the evening collation. At these times she was merry, there was always a smile to disguise the deadly fatigue, and no mention was made of the fact that she was dying by inches.

The flies tormented her very much during the last hot summer. It must have been no little part of the suffering of Christ on the Cross, nailed and enduring the crawling of flies on His eyes, His wounds, His flesh. "They are my only enemies," Therese said when she was tormented by them. "God commanded us to forgive our enemies, and I am glad I have some occasion to do so. That is why I spare them."

"It is the way of spiritual childhood," she said in response to a question about her "little way." "It is the path of total abandonment and confidence. I would show them the little method I have found so perfectly successful and tell them there is but one thing to do on earth; to cast before Jesus the flowers of little sacrifices. That is what I have done and that is why I shall be so well received."

There has been so much discussion of the diminutive "little" which Therese used constantly that it is good to remember her words of explanation of August 6. "To be little . . . is . . . not to attribute to ourselves the virtues we practice, nor to believe ourselves capable of practicing virtue at all. It is rather to recognize the fact that God puts treasures of virtue into the hands of his little children to make use of them in time of need, but they remain always treasures of the good God. Finally, to be little means that we must never be discouraged over our faults, for children often fall but they are too small to harm themselves very much."

*   *   *

Therese Martin died on September 30, 1897. Only seventeen years later, when those who had been born in the same year with her were just forty-one years of age, the fame of her sanctity had so spread among the people that her cause was introduced at Rome. She was beatified on April 29, 1923, and canonized on May 17, 1925, an unusually rapid process for the Church in modern times.

So many books have been written about St. Therese, books of all kinds, too, so why, I ask myself again, have I written one more? There are popular lives, lives written for children, travelogue lives following her footsteps, lives for the extrovert, the introvert, the contemplative, the activist, the scholar, and the theologian.

Yet it was the "worker," the common man, who first spread her fame by word of mouth. It was the masses who first proclaimed her a saint. It was the "people."

What was there about her to make such an appeal? Perhaps because she was so much like the rest of us in her ordinariness. In her lifetime there are no miracles recounted; she was just good, good as the bread which the Normans bake in huge loaves. Good as the pale cider which takes the place of the wine of the rest of France, since Normandy is an apple country. "Small beer," one might say. She compares to the great saints as cider compares with wine, others might complain. But it is the world itself which has canonized her, it is the common people who have taken her to their hearts. And now the theologians are writing endlessly to explain how big she was, and not little, how mature and strong she was, not childlike and dependent. They are tired of hearing people couple her name with that of

Teresa of Avila, whom they call the "Great Teresa" as distinguished from the "Little Therese."

What did she do? She practiced the presence of God and she did all things — all the little things that make up our daily life and contact with others — for His honor and glory. She did not need much time to expound what she herself called her "little way." She wrote her story, and God did the rest. God and the people. God chose for the people to clamor for her canonization.

What stands out in her life? Her holiness, of course, and the holiness of her entire family. That is not an ordinary thing in this day of post-war materialism, delinquency, and all those other words which indicate how dissatisfied the West is with its economy of abundance while the East sits like Lazarus at the gate of Dives.

With governments becoming stronger and more centralized, the common man feels his ineffectiveness. When the whole world seems given over to preparedness for war and the show of force, the message of Therese is quite a different one.

Gordon Marino

THE GREATEST

This short essay by the philosopher and boxing enthusiast Gordon Marino offers yet another instance of corrected emotion, a movement from hatred and contempt to admiration. For our purposes, the case presents yet another complication of exemplarist ethics. Marino is writing about his growing admiration for an athlete, the kind of person admired more for natural talent than for acquired traits, the kind of person Zagzebski would exclude from her categories of exemplars because Muhammad Ali would not seem to be a moral exemplar. But is he or isn't he? Does Marino grow to admire Ali more because he comes to greater appreciation of his boxing prowess or because he enlarges his understanding of Ali to include moral traits as well as physical prowess? Do you think that people who are supremely excellent athletes but morally decent human beings should count as moral exemplars? Or must athletes and geniuses also excel morally in order to earn our admiration of them as exemplars?

Let us now praise famous men. Muhammad Ali is often touted for his courage outside the ring, for being a champion of justice, even when it cost him his livelihood. But let us not forget his matchless mettle in the ring. It could, after all, be argued that there is a relationship between physical and moral courage, that Ali's ability to endure punishing fights bulked up his capacity to take blows of a different kind for justice.

Heavyweight championship boxing is nuclear war in a twenty-foot ring. When Ali was coming up as a young fighter, the cynical cigar-chomping boxing scribes were sure that one good lick from Sonny Liston would button the "Louisville Lip." Ironically — and much to the detriment of his long-term health — no one could absorb punches better than Ali. Take, for a prime example, the ferocious back-and-forth between Ali and his archrival

Gordon Marino, "The Greatest: How Muhammad Ali Won Me Over," *Commonweal*, July 8, 2016, 8–9.

Joe Frazier in their 1975 "Thrilla in Manila." It was an oven-like 107 degrees, and considerably hotter under the klieg lights when the fighters toed the line. The battle, which ended with an Ali victory after the fourteenth round, was mind-boggling — first because of the sheer superhuman grit of the combatants but also because Ali and Frazier, by dint of their prowess and infinite resolve, managed to transform an event so brutal it almost made you feel guilty to watch into an exotic form of beauty.

For those of us who preach about the importance of commitment, Ali is an object lesson of someone who reached into the deepest parts of himself to achieve victory. In YouTube clips you can see the ledge that Ali pushed his body toward and over in his wars with Frazier, Norton, Foreman, and others.

His Achilles-like courage duly noted, let me confess that as a teenager with boxing aspirations I hated Muhammad Ali. Playful as he was, he had a vicious streak, especially with other black fighters who somehow threatened his center-stage status. I heard him disrespect Joe Louis and watched him torture and humiliate a hobbled Floyd Patterson in their 1965 fight. But Ali saved his real devils for my hero, the noble Joe Frazier. Before their fights — and even though Frazier had lent him money during the lean years when Ali was deprived of his boxing license — Ali sadistically taunted "The Smoke," saying he was too ugly and stupid to be champion. In the buildup to their final encounter, he started calling Frazier "the Gorilla," and even toted around a toy gorilla to yank out and smack around at media events. It stung Frazier and his family to the bone, so much so that in the moments before their epic fray, Frazier, a devout Christian, literally prayed to be forgiven for the murderous intentions he harbored toward Ali.

To be fair, Ali grew as a person after he grew out of boxing. Again and again over the years, he personally and sincerely apologized to Frazier and his family. Sadly, Joe was never able to pull the stingers out, and it seems as though he took his resentment with him to the grave in 2011.

But there were other less substantive reasons that Ali was glass in the gut for me. With his almost feminine good looks, his flitting about the ring, and his incessant jibber-jabber, he was at odds with the code of strong-and-silent masculinity that I instinctively revered. And for all I know of my cultural unconscious, maybe his flamboyant expressions of black pride chafed against the soft underbelly of my "liberal" self. But again, I didn't like him back then. When Frazier knocked him on his rump in the final stanza of their first fight, I almost jumped through the ceiling with joy. Maybe it took Ali's being defanged by illness, but I finally began to grasp the radiant beauty of this comet of a human being.

There are people with egos that dwarf those of the merely driven and highly ambitious. Muhammad Ali was one of them. Angelo Dundee once confided, "Even when he started out you couldn't tell Muhammad what to do. Even then, he had too big of an ego. So if I wanted to give him some instruction, I would compliment him. If I wanted him to bend his knees more when he was jabbing, I would wait until the end of the workout, slap him on the back and say, 'I loved the way you bent your knees today.' Afterwards Muhammad would smile and say, 'You liked that huh?'"

Unlike any braggart I have ever known, Ali had a self-love that was transferrable. While he beat up his opponents and pick-pocketed their confidence, he miraculously helped millions see a fresh set of possibilities in their bathroom mirrors.

Evander Holyfield once told me, "In my neighborhood, when I was just a boy, everyone was always telling me, 'You ain't gonna be nothing.' Then one day I heard Ali on television boasting about how he was the greatest and telling people 'you can do anything.' I was amazed. How could he talk that way? But then I thought, if he can do it, I can do it. He changed my life."

There are a few rare people who see themselves as the sun and the moon, but who are still somehow able to get outside their own orbit and care about others. For all his bluster about being the greatest and most beautiful, Ali was no narcissist: he noticed the people around him.

When I travelled to Louisville for the opening of the Ali Center in 2005, I met one person after another whose life had been pushed in a new direction by a fortuitous encounter with Ali. One fellow in his fifties told me that many years earlier he had given Ali a cookie. The champ, who had a sweet tooth, thought it was delicious and helped get the man started in what would become a thriving business. Howard Bingham, who would become one of Ali's lifelong friends, told me the tale of bumping into Ali in 1962 in Los Angeles. At the time, Bingham was a fledgling photographer. By giving him access, Ali catapulted him into a stellar career behind the lens. Over the course of the event, I heard many other testimonies from folks Ali had simply put his arms around at a difficult moment. Like a great cornerman, he gave them the fortitude to deal with the foe of a disease or a death in the family.

In his *Works of Love*, Søren Kierkegaard observed that we humans tend to identify need with weakness: the needier you are, the weaker you are. Then Kierkegaard reminds us that the need for God is the highest perfection. Likewise, we ungrateful bipeds heap praise upon the mighty men and women who overflow with strength and creativity; we are not as impressed with those possessed of an overabundance of love and need for others. That was Ali. He was blessed with a boundless affection for his fellow human beings. Even though he was arguably the most recognizable person on the planet, he always needed to immerse himself in crowds; he would wade into them, shaking hands, hugging and kissing babies like a presidential candidate, and bantering with fans. In our time, celebrities have become secular saints, but I don't know of anyone with the Hollywood halo whose boundaries with mere mortals were as tender and porous as Ali's. Sure, your Oscar-winning actor might donate a million dollars to a shelter for battered woman, but he is not likely to invite you to take a ride in his RV, hang out with you all day, and stay in touch for years.

One of my favorite tales about Ali comes from the author Davis Miller, who as a young man was a fanatical Ali devotee. After his retirement, Ali agreed to meet with Miller at his farm in Michigan. Naturally, Miller was star-struck, but Ali, who was a first-rate magician, knew how to put the rabbit of nervousness back in the hat. Within an hour or so the two were hanging around like old pals, slap-boxing and going out to McDonalds together. But now and again, Miller would remember who he was with. At one point, he excused himself to use the bathroom. After he closed the door, Ali quietly padded over and held the door handle so that Miller couldn't get out — all the while knowing that Miller was too bedazzled by the champ to start yelling for help.

Ali's sense of humor was as deep as his boxing talent. Years ago, he was being interviewed by a cadre of renowned reporters who saw him as a minor deity but at the same time felt something bordering on pity about his Parkinson's. They sat down at a table for a bite to eat and Ali, in the middle of the conversation, pretended as though he were slowly drifting off to sleep. There was an awkward couple of moments when the media pros scratched their heads and looked at each other as if to say "What do we do now?" Seconds later Ali, still seemingly asleep, started throwing punches. The reporters pulled back, embarrassed and trying to figure out how to respond. Then Ali seemed to slip back into a quiet sleep only to erupt with another flurry a few seconds later. No doubt Ali recognized that the guys with the notebooks saw him as punchy. About a minute later, he leapt up wide-eyed and with a beaming gotcha smile.

But what about all those dark years when Ali slowly closed up in the clam shell of Parkinson's? Looking back, Dundee, his cornerman for twenty-plus years sighed, "Even when he got afflicted by Parkinson's, I believed in my heart that he would beat it. That's the kind of faith he built up inside of you because he was such a remarkable human being." But Parkinson's was not something Ali or anyone else could rope-a-dope. Was it worth it? He was frequently asked whether he would do it all over again, knowing the illness those hurricane blows would eventually lead to. The answer was always the same: No regrets.

When I met the Great One at the opening of the Ali Center, he was already enveloped in the disease that would rob him of his divine wit and supernal gift of gab. That day there was a long line of adult fans waiting to have their photo taken with Ali as though he were Santa Claus. Sick and exhausted as he was, Ali wanted to accommodate everyone. At times, his once-beautiful countenance would contort and freeze in the grotesque shape of someone bolting up from a nightmare. It was a shot to the liver to see. For a moment, I could not help imagining that, for whatever bizarre inscrutable reason, the silver-tongued trickster — half-huckster, half-sage — was being played by the ultimate Trickster.

In his marvelous *The Tao of Ali*, Davis Miller recalled that when, near tears, he told Ali how sorry he was about his illness, Ali repeatedly assured him that this was just God's way of reminding Ali that he was just like everyone else.

Yes and no, God. Yes and no.

Madeline Miller

FALSE COUNSELLOR

The essay below describes changing estimations of Odysseus, the great hero of Homer's *Odyssey*. And along the way, the essay provides interesting challenges to those who might choose their moral exemplars from the world of fiction. For one thing, there are many different literary treatments of Odysseus, and some of them, like Sophocles's tragedy *Philoctetes*, portray him as a villain. Madeline Miller's own 2018 novel, *Circe*, offers yet another portrayal. In addition, Homer himself paints a very complex picture of his hero. The Odysseus of the *Odyssey* is, to be sure, resourceful and faithful, but he frequently blunders, and he is an inveterate liar. How much do such discrepancies matter? As Linda Zagzebski points out in her work on exemplarity, we need not and should not admire only those people who are supremely virtuous in all regards. Nevertheless, as Miller points out, "the ancient heroes have faults as large as their virtues." So is Odysseus really worthy of admiration, or isn't he?

Miller begins her essay by observing that Odysseus is much more appealing as a hero today than, say, Achilles, because we now prefer brains to brawn, resourcefulness to physical courage. To what extent is our admiration as much a cultural reflex as a private and highly personal emotion?

Wily Odysseus, much-enduring, man of many twists and turns. For nearly 3,000 years, we have admired Homer's brilliant, battered hero, and the story of his gruelling journey home from war. He has inspired countless storytellers, from Ovid, Joyce and Tennyson, to Derek Walcott, the Coen brothers and Margaret Atwood, yet still our interest in the prince of Ithaca is not exhausted. In fact, we seem to love the old dog-fox more than ever: in a recent BBC poll of the "100 Stories That Shaped the World," the *Odyssey* walked away with the number one spot (poor Achilles and the *Iliad* were stuck at number ten).

Perhaps it is no wonder: of all the ancient heroes, Odysseus is the one

....

Madeline Miller, "False Counsellor," *Times Literary Supplement*, October 10, 2018.

who seems most fitted to our modern sensibilities. In our world of desk jobs and degrees, we prefer brains to brawn, and Odysseus is the original brain. Most of us know we can't be Achilles, that god-like specimen of physical perfection, but we all like to think we could be clever Odysseus, beating the odds with our wits. Odysseus also appeals to postmodern cynicism. He isn't a creature of ideals like Achilles, but one of outcomes, a realist who understands war's necessities. On top of which, he is that most beloved narrative figure: an underdog. Beset on all sides by bloodthirsty monsters and wrathful gods, he prevails through improvisation and sheer grit. And last but never least there is his love for his family, particularly his loyal and brilliant wife Penelope. She and Odysseus are one of the closest things the ancient world offers to a modern mutual romance, two clever survivors who get their happy ending. Odysseus even turns down an eternity with the sexy goddess Calypso for Penelope's human imperfection.

Yet Odysseus hasn't always been so admired. The ancient authors were notably mixed in their portraits, often foregrounding his vices over his virtues. Sophocles made Odysseus the villain of his tragedy *Philoctetes*, depicting a callous, self-serving hypocrite who abandons a wounded war hero on a deserted island and only returns for him when his hand is forced. In the *Cypria*, a lost epic prequel to the *Iliad* and the *Odyssey*, he is a draft-dodger and oath-breaker who tries to weasel his way out of his sworn duty to the war effort. In the *Sack of Ilium*, another lost epic, he brutally kills the infant Astyanax, son of the Trojan prince Hector. The tragedian Euripides paints him as a heartless manipulator who plays an ugly role in enforcing the sacrificial murders of both the Trojan princess Polyxena and Agamemnon's daughter Iphigenia. Centuries later, even Dante piles on, placing Odysseus in the eighth circle of hell as a "false counsellor." By contrast, Achilles is in the second circle — his sin of lust is apparently preferable to Odysseus' abuse of power.

And then there's Homer himself. From Odysseus' very first appearance in the first line of the poem, it is clear that he is, as Emily Wilson translates in her terrific new *Odyssey*, "a complicated man" ("*andra . . . polytropon*"). In the *Iliad*, Homer presents him as a ruthlessly effective pragmatist. Odysseus and Diomedes catch a Trojan spy, who begs them for mercy. They allow him to think they have agreed, without actually promising anything. When he has coughed up the information they want, they dispatch him and head off to slaughter an army of sleeping Trojan allies. Meanwhile, in the *Odyssey*, one of the first things we learn about our hero is that he has detoured on his way home from Troy to visit a town renowned for its excellent poison. As a bowman, he wants to anoint the tips of his arrows with it. In the ancient heroic tradition, this was doubly dubious: poison was considered a dishonorable means of killing, and the bow was famously the weapon of the cowardly wife-stealing Paris.

Despite Odysseus' vaunted intelligence, Homer shows him making some truly bone-headed errors of judgment. We remember his clever escape from the cyclops' den, but what is less remembered is that it is his idea to explore Polyphemus' cave in the first place, looking for loot. His men want to steal a few provisions and run off. It is Odysseus who holds them there, in the hope that the giant will give him some particularly exciting gift of guest-friendship. We know the rest of the story: the cyclops comes home, traps the men inside, and eats several of them. Odysseus gets him drunk, introducing himself as "No one" before putting out the monster's eye. He and the remaining men are able to escape, clinging to the underside of the cyclops' sheep, but once they are safely back on their ships, Odysseus cannot resist gloating, shouting out his real name, and bringing down the rage of the cyclops' father, Poseidon, upon them.

Odysseus is often praised for being an excellent leader of men, single-handedly stopping the desertion of the Greek army in the *Iliad*. But the *Odyssey* shows another side: out of his twelve ships' worth of soldiers, only Odysseus himself makes it home. This is usually blamed on his men, who show a lack of discipline throughout. But the truth is that the majority of them are lost in an encounter with the fearsome Laestrygonians, a tribe of giant cannibals. Approaching the unknown shore, Odysseus conceals his own ship, while allowing his men to anchor theirs openly in the bay. When the Laestrygonians attack, only Odysseus and his personal crew are able to escape. The others — all of them — are killed. As Jonathan Shay witheringly points out in his book *Odysseus in America: Combat trauma and the trials of homecoming* (2002), this is a terrible breach of leadership. If Odysseus believed there was danger, why did he send his men into it, while saving himself? In today's world this decision would earn him a court-martial.

Then there's the question of Odysseus' honesty. Homer portrays him as an inveterate liar, who would rather fabricate than tell the truth. He even lies to his patron deity Athena, who sees through him, of course, and teases him: "You perverse man . . . your lying, artful words are dear to you through and through." But this quality was not universally amusing. In sharp contrast, Achilles tells us in the *Iliad* that "as hateful to me as the gates of death is the man who says one thing and hides another in his heart." (It's hard to think of a better description of Odysseus than that.) When the witch Circe tries to turn Odysseus and his men into pigs, we can assume it is because she thinks they are pirates. Her confusion is understandable: they offer deception and violence wherever they go.

Which brings us finally to Odysseus' rage. We are accustomed to thinking of Achilles as the angry one. His wrath is, after all, the first word of the *Iliad*. Yet Odysseus himself is often angry, wildly angry. In the *Iliad*, he beats the soldier Thersites for criticizing the army's leadership. In the *Odyssey*, he strikes his cousin Eurylochus for questioning him. His rage at the suitors who threaten his home and his wife feels earned, but after he slaughters them to the last man, it roars on unchecked, consuming all the men who helped them, all the female slaves who were obliged to sleep with them and even, had Athena not intervened, the fathers of the suitors. Achilles and Odysseus make wonderful foils for each other, but the truth is that they are nearly as alike as they are different: they are both deeply flawed men who share a fierce pride, a desire for glory, and an emotional intemperance that often wreaks havoc on those around them. They are humanized mostly by their love for their closest earthly companions: Patroclus in Achilles' case, and Penelope in Odysseus'.

None of this diminishes Odysseus as a character. Rather, his darkness is at the heart of what makes him such an enduring creation. It expands him, giving his character an unstable, kaleidoscopic quality which challenges us to examine and re-examine him. We use the word hero today to mean a moral exemplar, but the ancient heroes had faults as large as their virtues. Odysseus is interesting not only because of how he succeeds, but for how he fails, and why. Jonathan Shay, as a clinical psychiatrist who works with veterans of the Vietnam war, noted startling parallels between Odysseus' difficult journey back to Ithaca and the difficulties some returning veterans face: hypervigilance, damaged trust, alienation from family, even the lure of drugs and alcohol personified by the Lotus Eaters. It can be argued that some of Odysseus' struggles and self-sabotage may represent our earliest Western portrait of Post-Traumatic Stress Disorder. If we are interested solely in admiring Odysseus, or else making him a sort of lovable ancient Han Solo, then we risk missing these subtler resonances. If we invest him with his full history, however, Odysseus seems more modern than ever, a powerful, conflicted, possibly damaged man who could be the spiritual ancestor to Tony Soprano or Hilary Mantel's Cromwell. Homer's phrase, *andra . . . polytropon*, can also be translated as "a man of many sides." We shouldn't be afraid to appreciate them all.

VOCABULARIES

Authenticity

Virtue

Exemplarity

Vocation

Denise Levertov

ANNUNCIATION

Having considered in the preceding section the vocabulary of exemplarity, it seems altogether fitting to begin the present section on the vocabulary of vocation with the person Christians regard as the greatest exemplar of vocation, Mary, the mother of Jesus. Though the vocabulary of vocation has not inspired nearly as many great paintings as the vocabulary of virtue, the annunciation, the announcement by the angel Gabriel to Mary that she has been chosen to bear the Christ child, has inspired great paintings by many very different artists.

The annunciation, which is described in the Bible in Luke 1:26–38, has inspired great poetry as well. A poem by Denise Levertov (1923–1997) introduces this section. In an introduction to her religious poetry published in the year she died, Levertov remembered her own "slow movement from agnosticism to Christian faith, a movement incorporating much of doubt and questioning as well as of affirmation." How do doubt and affirmation appear, in different ways, in this poem? Is Mary seen here as an exemplar, and if so, what traits seem supremely excellent?

Consider the second part of the poem, beginning with "Aren't there annunciations / of one sort or another / in most lives?" Have you experienced an annunciation or a summons like the one described in the poem? How did you respond? How does the Mary of the poem respond to having been "Called to a destiny more momentous / than any in all Time . . ."? What can we learn from the poem about what a call is and how we should respond? Note that Mary had two virtues "fused" within her: compassion and intelligence. Does this come close to defining the Christian virtue of *caritas* as Pieper describes it in the reading above (see pp. 92–96)? Might our word "thoughtful," which can mean both considerate and intellectually profound, come close to capturing this virtue? Which virtue do you think the poet most admires in Mary?

Denise Levertov, "Annunciation," in *Selected Poems* (New York: New Directions, 2002), 162–64.

We know the scene: the room, variously furnished,
almost always a lectern, a book; always
the tall lily.
       Arrived on solemn grandeur of great wings,
the angelic ambassador, standing or hovering,
whom she acknowledges, a guest.

But we are told of meek obedience. No one mentions
courage.
       The engendering Spirit
did not enter her without consent.
           God waited.

She was free
to accept or to refuse, choice
integral to humanness.

              *   *   *

Aren't there annunciations
of one sort or another
in most lives?
       Some unwillingly
undertake great destinies,
enact them in sullen pride,
uncomprehending.
     More often
those moments
   when roads of light and storm
   open from darkness in a man or woman,
are turned away from
in dread, in a wave of weakness, in despair
and with relief.
Ordinary lives continue.
       God does not smite them.
But the gates close, the pathway vanishes.

              *   *   *

She had been a child who played, ate, slept
like any other child — but unlike others,
wept only for pity, laughed
in joy not triumph.
Compassion and intelligence
fused in her, indivisible.

Called to a destiny more momentous
than any in all of Time,
she did not quail,
            only asked
a simple, 'How can this be?'
and gravely, courteously,
took to heart the angel's reply,
the astounding ministry she was offered: .

to bear in her womb
Infinite weight and lightness; to carry
in hidden, finite inwardness,
nine months of Eternity; to contain
in slender vase of being,
the sum of power —
in narrow flesh,
the sum of light.
            Then bring to birth,
push out into air, a Man-child
needing, like any other,
milk and love —

but who was God.

This was the moment no one speaks of,
when she could still refuse.

A breath unbreathed,
            Spirit,
                        suspended,
                                    waiting.

*　*　*

She did not cry, 'I cannot. I am not worthy,'
Nor, 'I have not the strength.'
She did not submit with gritted teeth,
                              raging, coerced.
Bravest of all humans,
            consent illumined her.
The room filled with its light,
the lily glowed in it,
            and the iridescent wings.
Consent,
      courage unparalleled,
opened her utterly.

Lee Hardy

WORK, LIFE, AND VOCATIONAL CHOICE

In this selection, Lee Hardy, who has taught philosophy at Calvin University for more than thirty years, recounts his own somewhat prolonged struggle to find his vocation — not only, as he explains at the outset, the "general" calling to discipleship, but also the "particular" calling "to do certain kinds of things." While this distinction is characteristic of Hardy's Reformed tradition, notions of general and particular callings are not exclusive to Protestants; St. Teresa of Calcutta, who serves as an exemplar of *caritas* for Josef Pieper (see pp. 92–96 above), spoke frequently of her "call within the call," by which she meant her particular call to serve the poor within her more general call to the religious life as a nun. Hardy changed occupations several times before he discovered his calling as a philosopher. A life that included several changes of occupation would have been extremely rare when the Protestant idea of vocation was first developed in the sixteenth century, but in our own time, among relatively affluent people in Western, postindustrial societies, changing jobs several times is commonplace. What counsel does Hardy provide to enable us to live through times of vocational uncertainty and change with integrity and a sense of overall purpose?

Hardy suggests that without an understanding of and belief in God's providential care for the world, we are apt to think that our occupational roles are mere accidents and that our task is therefore to *create* a significant life from circumstances that are arbitrary and without intrinsic meaning. If, on the other hand, we believe that our own lives are part of a divine plan for the redemption and transformation of the world, our task is to *discover* our role in that plan. Hardy elsewhere states that there may not be only one thing we are called to do. Is our challenge then to discern what our occupational calling really is, or is it to accept and interpret whatever we find ourselves doing to earn a living as part of a larger, perhaps a divinely ordained, plan?

From Lee Hardy, *The Fabric of This World* (Grand Rapids: Eerdmans, 1990), 80–91.

How exactly does the Christian concept of work as a divine calling bear upon the problem of choosing a vocation? Before we answer this question, we would do well to make two preliminary observations. First, to those of us who are familiar with the language of the Bible, there is something odd about the phrase "choosing a vocation." For in the New Testament the primary, if not exclusive, meaning of the term "vocation" — or calling *(klēsis)* — pertains to the call of the gospel, pure and simple. We are called to repentance and to faith (Acts 2:38); we are called into fellowship with Jesus Christ (1 Cor. 1:9); we are called out of the darkness and into the light (1 Pet. 2:9); we are called to be holy (1 Pet. 1:15, 1 Cor. 1:2); indeed, we are called to be saints (Rom. 1:7). Here we are not being asked to choose from a variety of callings, to decide which one is "right" for us. Rather, one call goes out to all — the call of discipleship. For it is incumbent upon all Christians to follow Christ, and, in so doing, to become the kind of people God wants us to be. The call of the gospel is not to a particular occupation, but to sainthood.

Yet we are also as Christians commanded, and therefore called, to love and serve our neighbors with the gifts that God has given to us. Each one of us, writes St. Peter, "should use whatever gift he has received to serve others, faithfully administering God's grace in its various forms" (1 Pet. 4:10). For each of us has certain gifts, certain talents and abilities. Those gifts were not given that we might heap up fame and fortune for ourselves. Rather, the possession of those gifts places an obligation upon us to use them for the building up of the community of faith and the human community at large (Rom. 12:4–21). We are called, then, not only to be certain kinds of persons, but also to do certain kinds of things.

Because of this twofold character of God's call, the Puritans used to distinguish between the "general" and the "particular" calling. The general calling is the call to be a Christian, that is, to take on the virtues appropriate to followers of Christ, whatever one's station in life. St. Paul refers to these virtues as the "fruit" of the Spirit: love, joy, peace, patience, kindness, goodness, faithfulness, gentleness, and self-control (Gal. 5:22–23). It is not for us to pick and choose among these virtues. When it comes to being a Christian, the virtues come in one package. They are the fruition of the work of the Spirit in our lives.

The particular calling, on the other hand, is the call to a specific occupation — an occupation to which not all Christians are called. With respect to occupations within the church, St. Paul refers to such particular callings as the "gifts" of the Spirit: to be an apostle, a prophet, a teacher, a worker of miracles, an administrator, and the like (1 Cor. 12:28–31). Not all are called to be apostles, prophets, or teachers. For here the Spirit fits each member of the body of Christ differently for a specific work: we are not expected or able to do all things, but only the things which God has enabled and called us to do. In the discharge of our various particular callings we together build up the interdependent society of the saints, which finds its unity in Christ, the head of the church.

With the distinction between the general and the particular calling in mind, talk about "vocational choice" — in the sense of choosing a particular occupation in which we will exercise our gifts — is both biblically appropriate and religiously important. At certain junctures in our lives we are confronted with the need to identify our gifts and choose an occupation; and an occupation can provide us with the concrete opportunity to employ our gifts in the service of our neighbor, as God commanded us to do. This holds not only for the occupations within the church, but in society as well. For although the Bible concentrates on the spiritual gifts and their employment in the community of faith, the Christian tradition has generally extended the Biblical principle, confessing that our "natural" gifts also come from God and are to be employed for the benefit of the wider human community.

As a second preliminary observation, lest we move too quickly from the question of vocation to that of paid occupation, we ought to remind ourselves that vocation is the wider concept. One need not have a paid occupation in order to have a vocation. Indeed all of us have, at any one time, a number of vocations — and only one of them might be pursued as a paid occupation. To put it in Luther's language, at any given time we occupy a number of stations: parent, child, citizen, parishioner, and so on. Each one of these stations entails a specific vocation. As a parent it is my vocation to love, discipline, and care for my children; as a child it is my vocation to honor and obey my parents; as a citizen it is my vocation to participate in the political process and abide by the decisions and rulings of the government; as a parishioner it is my vocation to exercise my spiritual gifts for the edification of the body of Christ. I may not have a paid occupation. But that doesn't mean I have no calling in life.

Furthermore, it follows from the broad concept of vocation that we will always have a number of vocations as a result of certain social relations and historical circumstances which we ourselves have not chosen. I, for instance, was born in a modern nation-state known as the United States of America in the mid-twentieth century of white Anglo-Saxon Protestant parentage. I did not ask or choose to be so born. I just was. From the purely human perspective it seems almost accidental that I should be who I am. Could I not just as well have been a Chinese woman born during the Ming dynasty, or a Nicaraguan *campesino* born during the glory days of William Walker? Why was I born of this particular race and nationality, with this particular body and temperament? It's hard to say.

Existential philosophers of atheist persuasion have dwelt upon the apparently accidental nature of our identities, and refer to such as the brute "facticity" or "thrownness" of human existence. We find ourselves thrown into a particular situation with no apparent rhyme or reason, and our task as human beings is to appropriate our absurd circumstances into a meaningful life project which we ourselves freely choose.

But from a theistic point of view things look quite different. That I am who I am is not a result of chance, a mere cosmic accident. Rather it is the result of God's intention. There is a reason why I am who I am, although that reason may not be immediately apparent to me. I was placed here for a purpose, and that purpose is one which I am, in part, to discover, not invent. The facts about me are indicators of the divine intent for my life, indicators which are to be interpreted in the light of God's revealed Word. Perhaps, through no choice of my own, I inherit a vast family fortune and suddenly find myself wealthy to the point of embarrassment. An absurd event? No. A providential one in which I am to discern God's will for the shape and direction of my life. For the rich have at least one divine vocation just by virtue of being rich, namely, to use their money to benefit others. Many things about me I did not choose. But that does not mean that they are not meaningful, or that they have to be made meaningful through other choices that I make.

Even a vocation as a paid occupation may not be a matter of choice. In fact, for most people it never has been. Down through the ages and in many parts of the world today people did and do not have much choice in the kind of work they do. Their work was and is simply imposed upon them by circumstances beyond their control: the economic niche of the family into which they were born, or a combination of financial necessity and the existing job market. One is born a rice farmer or becomes a factory worker because that is the only line of work open at the time. "Today we consider it an imperfection of society for people to be fixed in their opportunities and jobs by class and birth," management theorist Peter Drucker observes, "where only yesterday this was the natural and apparently inescapable condition of mankind." Freedom of choice regarding occupation is a relatively novel social phenomenon. Those of us who are faced with such a choice are, historically speaking, a very small minority indeed.

It shouldn't come as a surprise, then, that guidelines for the responsible choice of an occupation have not been thoroughly worked out by the Christian community at large. The fact that in many parts of Christendom today work is still considered a secular matter, with little or no connection to religion, has not helped either.

But an initial attempt to formulate the principles of vocational choice was made by the Protestant reformers of the sixteenth and seventeenth centuries. They were, on the one hand, firmly convinced that all of life, even the life of everyday work, ought to be lived to the glory of God. On the other hand, they were aware that in their time people were being granted a greater measure of freedom in the choice of occupations. The rigid structures of medieval society were crumbling around them and social life was opening up, differentiating, and becoming more flexible. Higher education was no longer the prerogative of the aristocracy alone. As a direct result, an increasing number of people had access to an increasingly wider range of occupational options. Thus it was given to them to work out the principles of vocational choice in the light of the Word of God.

How did they go about this? Taking their initial bearings from the biblical witness together with a reflection upon the human condition, they began with a definition of work that went something like this: work is the social place where people can exercise the gifts that God has given them in the service of others. For God did not create us as self-sufficient individuals. We all have needs which we alone cannot meet. By necessity we live in communities of interdependent individuals. And we are to make use of what talents we do have to serve others as they, in turn, serve us. Together we build up society as a mutual support system.

With this concept of work, two practical items immediately arise: the gifts God has given me, and the exercise of those gifts for the sake of others. The first step then, in making a responsible choice of vocation, is ascertaining precisely which gifts God has bestowed upon me.

This in itself can be a difficult, painful, and protracted process. We were not born with job descriptions taped to our backs. Our vocational aptitudes have to be discovered in that process by which we come to know ourselves. But the road to self-knowledge can be a long one, and often we don't possess a clear idea of exactly what our talents are at the time we must make vocational decisions. If we are not sure what we are good at, it often pays to reflect upon our past experience with precisely that question in mind. What have I done, and done well? What kind of skills did I make use of? Planning, investigating, implementing, building, repairing, creating, writing, teaching, supervising? What kind of knowledge did I acquire? Knowledge about cars, computers, finance, administration, food, flowers, music, mathematics? What kind of objects did I work with? Numbers, words, people, mechanical things, living things, programs, institutions? In what capacity was I relating to others? As a team member, team leader, lone ranger, coach, manager, expert? Was I in a position with a lot of freedom and responsibility, or was I working in a highly structured situation, where my activity was thoroughly specified? With an autobiographical grasp of my talents I can begin, perhaps with some additional guidance, to see what kind of work I could do well.

Besides reflecting on past experience, remaining open to future experience is equally important. For self-knowledge is an open-ended process, a fact twentieth-century theologian Karl Barth underscored in his *Church Dogmatics:*

> In relation to the personal presuppositions which he himself brings, the action of man must be one which always and in all directions is open, eager to learn, capable of modification, perpetually ready, in obedience to the exclusively sovereign command of God, to allow itself to be orientated afresh and in very different ways from those which might have seemed possible and necessary on the basis of man's own ideas of his ability and capacity. In the last analysis man has no more knowledge of himself than mastery over himself. Again and again he must let himself be shown who he is. His faithfulness to himself, then, [consists] only in constant attention and openness to that which, as God claims him, will be continually disclosed to him as his true self, as the real aptitude which he has been given together with its limits, and then in the corresponding decision for perhaps a much more daring or possibly a much more humble action than that to which he has hitherto considered himself called.

Some experimentation, then, may be required in the process of career choice. If several occupational options lie before me, and they all look equally valid and interesting, rather than allowing myself to be paralyzed by the lack of a deciding factor, it would be better simply to choose one and pursue it. In the course of pursuing that occupation I will inevitably learn something I couldn't have known prior to its pursuit. I may become convinced that I had in fact made the right choice. On the other hand, I might find out in no uncertain terms that I made the "wrong" choice. Not to worry. I can still benefit from that. I have learned something about myself. And I can cross one occupational option off my list.

Besides, career decisions are rarely irrevocable. Most people nowadays go through four or five career changes in the course of a lifetime. When I was in high school I wanted to go into cinematography. I loved movies, and I wanted to make some. Instead I became an advertising artist. But later, while working in an art studio in the San Francisco Bay area, I found myself drawn into the discipline of philosophy. I needed to clarify certain issues in life. Today I am a professor of philosophy at a liberal arts college. And I suspect most people past their twenties have similarly crooked accounts of how they came to their present occupations. Career paths are rarely straight. Typically they are afflicted by detours, unmarked intersections, forced exits, blind alleys, and cul-de-sacs. When the philosophy majors I advise at Calvin College hesitate to go to graduate school because they are not sure if philosophy is their calling, I usually tell them that going to graduate school is the best way to find out if philosophy is their calling. We can't know everything before we act. An element of trial and error is unavoidable in the carving out of a niche for oneself in the world of work. Barth was entirely correct when he said that "a man can really learn to know his sphere of operation only as he sets to work in it."

Vocational counseling and testing can also help here. Not that the results of a vocational test are to count as the last word. The validity of the results depends upon how well the test was designed, how accurately and honestly you were able to answer the questions, and how carefully the results are interpreted. But a vocational test can at least do this: it can comfort you by confirming what you already thought you knew about yourself, but weren't sure; or it can challenge you by suggesting occupational possibilities you had never considered before.

An honest lack of self-knowledge is not the only problem in making a career choice. The sins of greed, pride, envy, and fear can enter into the picture too, clouding our vision of who we are and what we were cut out to do. We might have our eye on a certain career because of the salary. We approach our career as a means to untold riches and material delights. Or perhaps we find ourselves attracted to a certain career because of its social prestige. We want to prove to others — and perhaps to ourselves — that we are much more talented and capable than either thought. We treat our prospective career as a wand to wave before the crowds to command their respect, awe, and admiration. Or perhaps we are unhappy with the way God has made us, and we are envious of another person's gifts and accomplishments. In the course of our prospective career, we resolve to become just like her and excel where she has excelled. Our career becomes the tool of our covetousness. Or we begin by being aimed at certain careers due to family expectations about what we are going to do with our lives, and we are afraid to disappoint our parents. We live in fear of what others would think of us were we to strike out on our own. Our career becomes a place where we hide from others, and especially ourselves. On the basis of these and similarly errant motives, we can convince ourselves that we are qualified for certain careers, while what led us to choose those careers had very little to do with our particular gifts or the human needs around us.

Perhaps I have been raised in a community where intellectual prowess is held in high esteem. Perhaps other features of my upbringing led to an over-whelming psychological need to be highly esteemed by others. Or, I may have been raised in a community with a substantial anti-intellectual bias and, due to other features of my upbringing, I have an overwhelming psy-chological need to distinguish myself over against that community, thereby establishing my social independence. At any rate, on the basis of some sub-terranean motive of which I am not fully aware, I find myself quite naturally drawn in the direction of intellectual pursuits. When I get to college I might even boldly stage a direct assault on the very pinnacle of mental achieve-ment, surrounded by the chill, thin air of theoretical abstraction — I declare a philosophy major.

Thus I become convinced that in philosophy I have found my true calling. But have I? Has God really given me the appropriate intellectual gifts and a genuine zeal for the truth? Or am I just fooling myself? These are difficult questions to answer on the basis of private self-examination. The oppor-tunities for self-deception along these lines are almost limitless. Even if I received lousy grades in all my philosophy courses — enough to thoroughly discourage the average mortal — I could still convince myself that this failure was wholly due to the clumsy pedagogy of my professors, or their inabil-ity to detect the secret genius of my work. Resolute in purpose, I go on to graduate school against the advice of my mentors. No one will deny me the glory associated with my chosen field — and I proceed to make a total fool of myself trying to prove to everyone else that I am not a complete idiot.

Because of the innate human talent for self-deception, it is a good idea to seek the advice of others known for mature and balanced judgment. I may be convinced that God has especially called me to a particular occupation. But do others recognize in me the gifts I think I possess? Can my friends detect in the pattern of my life the passions, the interests, and the concerns I claim to have? Do my teachers take me to be mentally competent and personally well suited for the career of my own choosing? Their counsel may be encouraging. Or devastating. But it must be sought. Often I must seek the help of others if I am to be honest with myself before God.

It seems, then, that perceived social status combined with certain psychological needs can push people into occupations for which they are not at all qualified. But it can work the other way too. Low social status plus similar psychological needs can drive people away from an occupation for which they are eminently qualified. I may have formidable mechanical abilities and a genuine love for the automobile as an engineered system of intake and exhaust manifolds, regulators and alternators, camshafts and crankshafts. In the world of car repair, infested as it is by rip-off artists, I may be able to perform a genuine service to the community as a mechanic. But I chafe at the suggestion. After all, who wants to be a "grease monkey"? What would my parents think? My friends?

Finding our niche in life may not only require that we be honest with ourselves. It may also require a stiff dose of humility. Yet, as John Calvin said, "No task will be so sordid and base . . . that it will not shine and be reckoned very precious in God's sight." An occupation held to be of no account in the eyes of the world can nonetheless be important to God. The ranking of occupations in our society and in the kingdom of God are often two very different things. And it's important to keep the difference in mind. The garbage collector performs an infinitely more valuable social service than the advertising executive about to launch a campaign to convince the American homemaker that Pink Froth dish detergent is indispensable to gracious living. But the latter, for reasons difficult to fathom, enjoys more social status.

The first step, then, in responsible vocational choice is to identify the abilities and talents God has given us. Those talents and abilities, however, will probably not be unique. For that reason they will not, by themselves, lead a person to a unique job. That is especially true if we consider such things as the ability to grasp objects between the thumb and fingers. That ability is regularly exercised by the dentist, the electrician, and the surgeon — as well as the paperboy. Even rarer gifts, like a lightning-quick analytical mind, do not suggest only one profession. One could use such a mind in law, philosophy, or the CIA.

Although the absence of a unique gift may leave us in the lurch when it comes to choosing a specific career, we can take positive comfort in the fact that as generic human beings we already possess a wide range of abilities. And we can meaningfully put these ordinary abilities to use in a number of perfectly acceptable occupations. What is lost by way of unambiguous guidance is made up by flexibility. And we are thereby relieved of the frustrating and ultimately self-defeating quest for "the right job," as if there were only one per person. As a simple matter of fact, we are qualified to do a number of things. And a number of the things we are qualified to do would be good things to do.

Nonetheless, God can give us two other things that will narrow down the field considerably. First, he can give us a concern. Of course, we are all concerned about ourselves and how we will fare in this life. No special work of God is required for that. But if we can detect within a growing concern for others, then we can be sure God is at work within us. But not all of us will be concerned for others in the same way. Some may be concerned for their health. Others may be concerned for their emotional well-being, their spiritual condition, or the integrity of their natural or cultural environment. Once we become aware of the specific concern God has given us, we can go about cultivating the skills required to follow through on that concern effectively.

Furthermore, God may have endowed us with certain lively interests apart from any other-directed concerns — interests in mathematics, music, or microbiology. Those interests lead us to cultivate skills which we can in turn use in the service of others. For example, based on an innate love of literature, I might acquire the skills of appreciation and criticism that would later qualify me, as an English teacher, to introduce others to the wonders of the written word. Or I might become a writer myself, and proceed to open up God's world to others through the medium of language.

The assumption behind these recommendations is that discovering God's will for one's life is not so much a matter of seeking out miraculous signs and wonders as it is being attentive to who and where we are. It is not as if our abilities, concerns, and interests are just there, as an accident of nature, and then God has to intervene in some special way in order to make his will known to us in a completely unrelated manner. Rather, in making a career choice, we ought to take seriously the doctrine of divine providence: God himself gives us whatever legitimate abilities, concerns, and interests we in fact possess. These are his gifts, and for that very reason they can serve as indicators of his will for our lives. In coming to know ourselves and our situation, we come to know God's will. The Protestant theologian Emil Brunner claims, in fact, that "the idea of the Calling and of the Call is unintelligible apart from that of Divine Providence. The God who says to me here and now: 'Act where you are, as you are,' is not One who comes on the scene after all that has been done previously has been done without

His knowledge. Nothing can happen apart from Him. . . . To Him it is no accident that you are what you are here and now, an accident with which He must come to terms. He Himself places you where you are." Too often our search for God's will in our lives has been skewed by a highly secularized view of the world. We don't really believe that God is present and at work in the concrete events and circumstances of this world. Rather we think of Him as distant, removed, putting in only occasional appearances here on earth. If God speaks to us at all, he must speak to us in the freakish and miraculous, but not in the normal, everyday course of affairs.

At this point, however, we might step back and wonder if doing what God is calling us to do is always a matter of doing that for which we are best qualified. Certainly the Bible records numerous instances in which this was emphatically not the case. Are we developing a truly biblical approach to career choice? After all, a stuttering Moses was called by God to speak before Pharaoh; Jonah was instructed to call the city of Nineveh to repentance, a city he himself would have liked to see burn under God's judgment; and the personally unimpressive Paul was prevailed upon to present the gospel to the entire Gentile world. It seems unlikely that a modern vocational counseling agency would have directed these biblical characters to their respective tasks on the basis of their native interests and talents.

True. And the point is well taken. God does sometimes call people to do that for which they are outstandingly unqualified; and sometimes he calls people to do what they are entirely disinclined to do. But when he does that, it is because he is about to give a special demonstration of his power. That is, he is about to perform a miracle — which is, by definition, a departure from the normal course of affairs. As a rule people are to do that for which they are qualified. Of course, there are exceptions to the rule. And we must remain open to the possibility of an exception in our own case through prayer and awareness of God's leading hand.

Gary D. Badcock

CHOOSING

Gary Badcock is a Christian ethicist who wrote the book excerpted below in order to correct what he took to be unwarranted claims from writers like Lee Hardy. Like Hardy, Badcock addresses the whole matter of career choice from a theological point of view. Like Hardy, Badcock believes that issues of personal identity (who am I, and what sort of person should I become?) are closely related to decisions about what we should do to earn a living. Yet the conclusions of the two writers are different. "The will of God," says Badcock, "does not extend down to the details of career choice." He claims that this view is more "liberating" than a view like Hardy's, which does insist that God's will includes the details of our choices of careers. Do you think Badcock is right?

Both Hardy and Badcock include autobiographical material in their accounts of Christian vocation. Hardy tells us about the many occupations he actually held, whereas Badcock compares what he finally wound up doing with two other occupations he *might* have chosen. How are these two very different strategies of self-disclosure linked to the different accounts of vocation that the two men develop?

Individual people usually struggle with the question of career choice. The adolescent, encouraged, perhaps, by a fond parent, may well have a set view of what the future holds, but the transition to adulthood often brings into play serious doubts about formerly cherished ambitions. The young man who decides to marry, similarly, will inevitably reflect carefully on his choice of partner, but he will most likely be able to carry through with his commitment only in fear and trembling — sometimes quite literally at the altar on the "day of reckoning." Doubt is oftentimes a necessary ingredient in the quest for certainty, doubt that arises "out of the depths," *de profundis.*

From Gary D. Badcock, *The Way of Life: A Theology of Christian Vocation* (Grand Rapids: Eerdmans, 1998), 134–42.

Such considerations are prominent in a recent study by the Canadian philosopher James Horne, in which the relevance of mysticism to the question of career choice is highlighted. Horne notes that the typical experience of the mystic in the Christian tradition (among others) involves a path through darkness into light. The darkness is a necessary stage within the whole journey of spiritual development. Horne attempts to draw a parallel between such mystical experience and the psychological processes by which individuals make decisions concerning their future. There is, he suggests, much to be gained from such an analysis. The feeling of being "at sea," and even of lacking an integrated self-image and of wishing to have one, is common currency in many young people's experience. We cannot choose for the future without a sense of identity in the present and without a realistic sense of what we may become. Horne's treatment of mysticism and vocation allows us to understand this as a necessary part of the process by which such a decision is made — to give it a name, to "baptize" the apparent meaninglessness as something religiously and psychologically necessary. Yet the essential thing for those who wrestle with career choice in such an existential way is finally to transcend the darkness in such a way as to lay plans for the future, to have a project in life.

One must, of course, distinguish between what is theoretically possible and what is pragmatically possible, between the tentative decisions made at some earlier stage in life and what actually becomes possible on the basis of decisions already made. I may wish to work at such and such an occupation in some geographical area; in the event, I may be able to realize the first ambition, but not the second. I may even discover as life goes on that the second rather than the first ambition was closer to my heart. It may be that living "in exile" will be what pains me most about my circumstances as I mature; my children, for example, may thus grow up without knowing their grandparents. A sense of place, of location in the world, can be extremely important, whereas the working role assumed is less important. The potential variety of factors to consider is enormous, so much so that, in the final analysis, there is no escaping the conclusion that any career choice will inevitably be a risky venture, undertaken "in faith," or in a kind of faith, in relation to what is as yet unseen and unknown.

Vocation and Mission

For the Christian, however, the decisive consideration is that a life project must be capable of being integrated into the overall mission of Christ. Christ's mission is a mission of love, of self-giving service, and of obedience to God. My argument has been that the question, "What ought I to do?" really leads to another: "What kind of person ought I to be?" There is no clear answer to the first — insofar, at least, as it is a question concerned solely with career choice. However, much clearer answers can be given to the second question. I ought to be a person for whom love, service, and obedience to God are the major priorities. The Christian ethic is flexible insofar as it allows a multitude of possibilities by which one can fulfill such goals, but there is nevertheless an irreducible core concern within it, which can never be relinquished.

Let me illustrate this by outlining three possible paths that I might have taken in life. The first option requires some reference to my own family background. For centuries my ancestors have made a living from the sea. I also might have done so. I come from a region in which the fishing industry is a major source of wealth, and in which there were opportunities for a young man such as I was when I left school. Had I become a fisherman, my life would certainly have been very different from what it is today: I would, for example, most probably have remained a member of the local community within which I was born and grew up and thus maintained the link between my family and that place, a link that has lasted (until now) for some three centuries. The friends of youth would have remained the friends of adult life, and I would have been at hand for my aging parents. The commandment to honor one's father and mother would have been fulfilled in this way. I would also have been able to maintain contact with people and with a place that I love. No doubt there would have been opportunities to become involved locally in community and church work. I would have taken up a useful role in relation to the rest of society providing food for others. Had I married and raised a family, I could have shown love in that context; the monotony of early mornings and days at sea would have been offset by the knowledge that a family was cared for. My Christian faith would no doubt have remained simpler than it is now, for I would probably have read little theology, but this would not have been a great burden or hindrance to my fulfillment, which would have come in other ways. I am, in fact, attracted to such a life still, punctuated as it is by the rhythm of the seasons and based as it is on strong ties with the sea and the land.

Would any of this have been incompatible with sharing in the mission of Christ? I do not think so. Some of it would have been much more compatible with it than the path I finally took in life. For one surely owes a debt to one's own society and people, to those, for example, who provided an education, and to the Christian community that nurtured one's faith. The people whose lives might have been affected by my own were very much as real in that world as they are in my situation today. And for me, an especially important consideration is that my own father would not have died while I worked far away.

Another alternative was available. I might well have gone into business. Suppose, for the sake of argument, that the business had been successful and that I had gone on to build up a modest company which, after twenty years, employed twenty people and looked set to make me modestly wealthy. Would this have been compatible with the mission of Christ? The answer, I believe, is yes — especially in my home context. In resource-based economies, there is often insufficient secondary industry. The result is that there is much unemployment and sometimes surprising poverty. In such a context, the creation of wealth in business would have been more than self-service or worship at the altar of greed, even were such sins a factor in the whole story. For the creation of wealth can be the creation of new possibilities for an entire community, with prospects of work for young people and a prosperity that enables social as well as economic well-being. For a few people, at least, the cycle of welfare dependency might have been broken. Economic prospects can generate hope as well as wealth, sustaining communities and helping people to live a full life. And along the way, opportunities for service, for living in love within a family, or for participating constructively in the life of a Christian congregation would also have been present.

In the event, of course, I became a scholar. Contrary to my own expectation, which was that I would enter the Christian ministry and work with my own people in a pastoral way, I was drawn more and more deeply into academic issues and into an academic culture far from my original goals. It has been a surprising journey for me, going against my own plans at a number of crucial junctures. However, I find that the needs of my neighbor are much the same here as elsewhere, and that the so-called ivory tower of higher education has as much genuine reality in it as does any other sphere of life. As well as the usual grind that is the warp and woof of most occupations, ample opportunities for serving others and even for preaching and pastoral care arise. In the meantime, I have a wife and family, and within the home I am sustained and I help to sustain other human lives in dignity and in love.

Which of the three paths "ought" I to have taken? There is no clear answer to such a question, for there is no clear moral imperative governing the situation. In each case, the opportunity to participate in one way or another in the mission of Christ was open to me. I would go further, in fact, and say that it was *equally* open to me under any of the scenarios presented, for there is nothing especially saintly about my present work as a theologian, nothing intrinsic to it to lift it beyond the possibility of self-centeredness or faithlessness. The calling to be faithful and loving is one that extends to any and all walks of life and that cannot be identified with any one of them. And it is this calling to faithfulness and love with which Christian vocation is really concerned, the calling to follow the one who obeyed the Father to the end, who laid down his life for his friends — the one who, as such, was raised from the dead and exalted to the right hand of the Father.

The Way of Life

Psychological studies have demonstrated that people with a clear sense of direction are often also more integrated as persons. It is only what might be expected, though one has to add to this the qualification that some who *appear* to be most certain are also sometimes the most vulnerable should doubts about their chosen path ever arise. Nevertheless, there is a sense in which one constantly lives, and can only live, with a view to the future, to what one may become. Only thus can one be a full human being. The acorn becomes an oak, and in the same way the youth becomes an adult, while adulthood brings with it special opportunities and responsibilities; the adult, finally, grows old, enters into a period of retirement, and at last dies. Life itself is organic, being fundamentally characterized by growth and move-ment. Religious life is similar: one of the pervasive metaphors found within it is the "journey," the "pilgrimage," by which one travels along life's way into the light and love of God. Here as elsewhere, without such orientation to the future life itself would be inconceivable.

The philosopher Aristotle, who saw the entire universe in such develop-mental terms, once observed that we are likely to develop to our full poten-tial only if we have sight of our goal. Like archers who have a mark to aim at, it is obviously more likely that we will hit the target if we can actually see it than if we do not. Aristotle himself construed the goal of human life as hap-piness, by which he meant a general state of well-being corresponding to the fulfillment of various aspects of "natural" human potentiality, rather than a purely emotional state. He then went on to develop a moral philosophy of the virtues — that is, those qualities "by virtue of which" a person can attain to the human goal. Thus the human acorn becomes the adult oak. There is, I believe, a great deal of truth in this. A life is "full" to the extent that a person has reached a goal that is appropriate to a human being, and to this extent such a person will achieve "happiness" in the sense of well-being. What is entirely missing from Aristotle's account of the moral life, however, is any reference to the human relation to God as the context of such development. And at this point, I want to say, his position is badly flawed.

Jesus speaks of the human goal in two ways. The first is in terms of the great commandments. The human goal and the divine imperative here coalesce: "you shall love the Lord your God with all your heart . . . ; you shall love your neighbor as yourself" (Mark 12:30–31 par.). From the standpoint of the spiritual life, the human goal is succinctly summed up in these key statements. The second, and literally crucial way in which Jesus speaks of the goal of life is in terms of discipleship: "If any want to become my followers, let them deny themselves and take up their cross and follow me" (Mark 8:34 par.). According to this teaching, we find life by relinquishing it, by sacrificing our small goods to the overriding good of the gospel of the kingdom and for the sake of the name of Christ. I have chosen the title *The Way of Life* for this book with this in view: the "way of life," according to the Christian gospel, is a paradoxical "way" that involves self-denial and often leads through suffering. There is no other "way," in this sense, to our goal. Nevertheless, within this one "way" are a multiplicity of individual paths that we tread. But we navigate by means of the same signs, following the same rules, living one life of love and discipleship.

At the beginning of this book, I wrote of my own childish belief that God had a plan for each life, a plan that a given individual might miss if he or she was not attentive to God's call and obedient to his voice. As a youth, I took such a view. It was as if I were waiting for a bus, or a "streetcar named vocation"; if I became bored and decided to wander away from the street, it would pass me by: But is it really possible to miss the will of God in this way? I have found such a vision of the Christian vocation to be extremely unhelpful, and because I am convinced that there are many people (especially young people) who are similarly mistaken, I have sought to develop a different understanding of the Christian vocation. Christian vocation is not reducible to the acquisition of a career goal or to its realization in time. It is, rather, something relating to the great issues of the spiritual life. It has to do with what one lives "for" rather than with what one does.

Such an understanding, once developed, can liberate us from the tyranny of such notions as the one that some have vocations whereas others do not, from the idea that having a vocation is incompatible with being unemployed or retired, from despair over not being able to "hear" God's voice when looking into the future at turning points in life. The human vocation is to do the will of God and so to live life "abundantly" (John 10:10), but the will of God does not extend down to the details of career choice. And once this is realized, I believe, then it becomes possible for us to live more adventurously, more freely, breathing in an atmosphere of love rather than law, looking for *our own* way to share the good news of the gospel in daily life, whether in career choices or in business or in the ordinary transactions of the daily round. Here, new possibilities open for the creating of Christian lifestyle and modes of spirituality that reflect the generosity of God in Christ. For this, at heart, is the Christian's vocation.

C. S. Lewis

LEARNING IN WAR-TIME

Students in colleges and universities tend to regard their studies as a preparation for life rather than a part of life. Hence, it never occurs to them that being a student might be a calling or a vocation. Perhaps the most compelling case for regarding academic study as a vocation was made by C. S. Lewis under the most challenging and urgent of circumstances. The essay that follows should be required reading for all students entering college or university life.

Clive Staples Lewis (1898–1963) taught literature for many years at Oxford University in England. This selection is a sermon he delivered to students in a chapel service there on October 22, 1939. The Second World War had begun less than two months earlier. These students surely knew many classmates and relatives who had enlisted in the armed forces, and they must have felt that they should do so, too. At the beginning of the sermon, in fact, Lewis articulates the question on their minds: "Why should we — indeed how can we — continue to take an interest in these placid occupations when the lives of our friends and the liberties of Europe are in the balance?" They were questioning whether their daily lives as students had any significance during a time of historic struggle.

At this intense moment of national emergency and individual confusion, Lewis urged these students to "see the present calamity in a true perspective." Human beings always live on the precipice of calamity, he noted; and though war makes this reality more visible, the question of whether being a student can be justified is applicable even in peacetime, when students might also be asked why they "spend any fraction of the little time allowed them in this world on such comparative trivialities as literature or art, mathematics or biology." In the selection that follows, Lewis provides a justification for study, both in war and in peace, and encourages the students in front of him to embrace this as their calling at the present time.

....

C. S. Lewis, "Learning in War-Time," in *The Weight of Glory* (New York: HarperCollins, 1949 [2001]), 55–63.

Lewis himself had been a student at Oxford during the First World War. He left his studies, was commissioned as an officer at the age of nineteen, and was wounded in battle. He became a Christian several years later. Lewis is probably best known as the author of the *Chronicles of Narnia*, a seven-volume work of fiction for young people that features a number of stirring battles while also imparting a Christian vision of the world. Many of his more explicitly theological books, which are notable for making accessible a challenging ecumenical version of Christian faith, continue to be widely read as well.

What was it about Lewis's Christian view of life that led him to urge the students in his congregation to follow a course of action different from the one that he himself followed in an earlier war, before he became a Christian? If his arguments are sound here, could we ever justify abandoning our present pursuits for the sake of what we regard as "higher purposes"?

We are now in a position to answer the view that human culture is an inexcusable frivolity on the part of creatures loaded with such awful responsibilities as we. I reject at once an idea which lingers in the mind of some modern people that cultural activities are in their own right spiritual and meritorious — as though scholars and poets were intrinsically more pleasing to God than scavengers and bootblacks. I think it was Matthew Arnold who first used the English word *spiritual* in the sense of the German *geistlich,* and so inaugurated this most dangerous and most anti-Christian error. Let us clear it forever from our minds. The work of a Beethoven and the work of a charwoman become spiritual on precisely the same condition, that of being offered to God, of being done humbly "as to the Lord." This does not, of course, mean that it is for anyone a mere toss-up whether he should sweep rooms or compose symphonies. A mole must dig to the glory of God and a cock must crow. We are members of one body, but differentiated members, each with his own vocation. A man's upbringing, his talents, his circumstances, are usually a tolerable index of his vocation. If our parents have sent us to Oxford, if our country allows us to remain there, this is *prima facie* evidence that the life which we, at any rate, can best lead to the glory of God at present is the learned life. By leading that life to the glory of God I do not, of course, mean any attempt to make our intellectual inquiries work out to edifying conclusions. That would be, as Bacon says, to offer to the author of truth the unclean sacrifice of a lie. I mean the pursuit of knowledge and beauty, in a sense, for their own sake, but in a sense which does not exclude their being for God's sake. An appetite for these things exists in the human mind, and God makes no appetite in vain. We can therefore pursue knowledge as such, and beauty as such, in the sure confidence that by so doing we are either advancing to the vision of God ourselves or indirectly helping others to do so. Humility, no less than the appetite, encourages us to concentrate simply on the knowledge or the beauty, not too much concerning ourselves with their ultimate relevance to the vision of God. That relevance may not be intended for us but for our betters — for men who come after and find the spiritual significance of what we dug out in blind and humble obedience to our vocation. This is the teleo-logical argument that the existence of the impulse and the faculty prove that they must have a proper function in God's scheme — the argument by which Thomas Aquinas proves that sexuality would have existed even without the Fall. The soundness of the argument, as regards culture, is proved by experi-ence. The intellectual life is not the only road to God, nor the safest, but we find it to be a road, and it may be the appointed road for us. Of course, it will be so only so long as we keep the impulse pure and disinterested. That is the great difficulty. As the author of the *Theologia Germanica* says, we may come to love knowledge — our knowing — more than the thing known: to delight not in the exercise of our talents but in the fact that they are ours, or even in the reputation they bring us. Every success in the scholar's life increases this danger. If it becomes irresistible, he must give up his scholarly work. The time for plucking out the right eye has arrived.

That is the essential nature of the learned life as I see it. But it has in-direct values which are especially important today. If all the world were Christian, it might not matter if all the world were uneducated. But, as it is, a cultural life will exist outside the Church whether it exists inside or not. To be ignorant and simple now — not to be able to meet the enemies on their own ground — would be to throw down our weapons, and to betray our uneducated brethren who have, under God, no defense but us against the intellectual attacks of the heathen. Good philosophy must exist, if for no other reason, because bad philosophy needs to be answered. The cool intellect must work not only against cool intellect on the other side, but against the muddy heathen mysticisms which deny intellect altogether. Most of all, perhaps, we need intimate knowledge of the past. Not that the past has any magic about it, but because we cannot study the future, and yet need something to set against the present, to remind us that the basic assumptions have been quite different in different periods and that much which seems certain to the uneducated is merely temporary fashion. A man who has lived in many places is not likely to be deceived by the local errors of his native village; the scholar has lived in many times and is therefore in some degree immune from the great cataract of nonsense that pours from the press and the microphone of his own age.

The learned life then is, for some, a duty. At the moment it looks as if it were your duty. I am well aware that there may seem to be an almost comic discrepancy between the high issues we have been considering and the immediate task you may be set down to, such as Anglo-Saxon sound laws or chemical formulae. But there is a similar shock awaiting us in every vocation — a young priest finds himself involved in choir treats and a young subaltern in accounting for pots of jam. It is well that it should be so. It weeds out the vain, windy people and keeps in those who are both humble and tough. On that kind of difficulty we need waste no sympathy. But the peculiar difficulty imposed on you by the war is another matter, and of it I would again repeat what I have been saying in one form or another ever since I started — do not let your nerves and emotions lead you into thinking your predicament more abnormal than it really is. Perhaps it may be useful to mention the three mental exercises which may serve as defenses against the three enemies which war raises up against the scholar.

The first enemy is excitement — the tendency to think and feel about the war when we had intended to think about our work. The best defense is a recognition that in this, as in everything else, the war has not really raised up a new enemy but only aggravated an old one. There are always plenty of rivals to our work. We are always falling in love or quarrelling, looking for jobs or fearing to lose them, getting ill and recovering, following public affairs. If we let ourselves, we shall always be waiting for some distraction or other to end before we can really get down to our work. The only people who achieve much are those who want knowledge so badly that they seek it while the conditions are still unfavorable. Favorable conditions never come. There are, of course, moments when the pressure of the excitement is so great that only superhuman self-control could resist it. They come both in war and peace. We must do the best we can.

The second enemy is frustration — the feeling that we shall not have time to finish. If I say to you that no one has time to finish, that the longest human life leaves a man, in any branch of learning, a beginner, I shall seem to you to be saying something quite academic and theoretical. You would be surprised if you knew how soon one begins to feel the shortness of the tether, of how many things, even in middle life, we have to say "No time for that," "Too late now," and "Not for me." But Nature herself forbids you to share that experience. A more Christian attitude, which can be attained at any age, is that of leaving futurity in God's hands. We may as well, for God will certainly retain it whether we leave it to Him or not. Never, in peace or war, commit your virtue or your happiness to the future. Happy work is best done by the man who takes his long-term plans somewhat lightly and works from moment to moment "as to the Lord." It is only our *daily* bread that we are encouraged to ask for. The present is the only time in which any duty can be done or any grace received.

The third enemy is fear. War threatens us with death and pain. No man — and specially no Christian who remembers Gethsemane — need try to attain a stoic indifference about these things, but we can guard against the illusions of the imagination. We think of the streets of Warsaw and contrast the deaths there suffered with an abstraction called Life. But there is no question of death or life for any of us, only a question of this death or of that — of a machine gun bullet now or a cancer forty years later. What does war do to death? It certainly does not make it more frequent; 100 percent of us die, and the percentage cannot be increased. It puts several deaths earlier, but I hardly suppose that that is what we fear. Certainly when the moment comes, it will make little difference how many years we have behind us. Does it increase our chances of a painful death? I doubt it. As far as I can find out, what we call natural death is usually preceded by suffering, and a battlefield is one of the very few places where one has a reasonable prospect of dying with no pain at all. Does it decrease our chances of dying at peace with God? I cannot believe it. If active service does not persuade a man to prepare for death, what conceivable concatenation of circumstances would? Yet war does do something to death. It forces us to remember it. The only reason why the cancer at sixty or the paralysis at seventy-five do not bother us is that we forget them. War makes death real to us, and that would have been regarded as one of its blessings by most of the great Christians of the past. They thought it good for us to be always aware of our mortality. I am inclined to think they were right. All the animal life in us, all schemes of happiness that centered in this world, were always doomed to a final frustration. In ordinary times only a wise man can realize it. Now the stupidest of us knows. We see unmistakably the sort of universe in which we have all along been living, and must come to terms with it. If we had foolish un-Christian hopes about human culture, they are now shattered. If we thought we were building up a heaven on earth, if we looked for something that would turn the present world from a place of pilgrimage into a permanent city satisfying the soul of man, we are disillusioned, and not a moment too soon. But if we thought that for some souls, and at some times, the life of learning, humbly offered to God, was, in its own small way, one of the appointed approaches to the Divine reality and the Divine beauty which we hope to enjoy hereafter, we can think so still.

Dietrich Bonhoeffer

THE PLACE OF RESPONSIBILITY

Dietrich Bonhoeffer (1906–1945) was a German Lutheran pastor and theologian who was executed by the Nazis in the last days of World War II in Europe. He grew up in a very accomplished extended family, and he inherited from his parents a deep sense of social responsibility. During the course of his ministry in the 1930s, the Nazis relentlessly persecuted those churches and seminaries that were critical of their regime, including the Confessing Church seminary that Bonhoeffer headed in Finkenwalde. Because of his own public statements and affiliations, the Nazis withdrew his authorization for academic teaching in 1936, prohibited him from speaking publicly anywhere in the German Reich in 1940, and forbade him to write for publication in 1941.

The Nazis' suspicions of Bonhoeffer were not without foundation. As all avenues of more conventional protest and opposition were closed off, he became involved in a conspiracy to kill Hitler. He did so in full recognition that such an action was evil — a lesser evil, but an evil nonetheless. He wrote the many papers later assembled as his *Ethics* while the most intense military engagements of World War II were occurring, from 1941 through 1944, when he was himself most active in the conspiracy. For him, questions of vocation and responsibility were urgent matters of life and death. Did his calling as a pastor and theologian require him to attend first and last to his immediate, circumscribed duties to his parishioners and students, he wondered, or did it require something more of him?

Because Bonhoeffer's understanding of vocation was forged in the midst of a hideous regime that had incorporated almost all those "places" or "orders" in which human beings find themselves stationed — family, church, state, work — into an evil, totalitarian system, Bonhoeffer's account of vocation has a decidedly critical and countercultural edge to it. Like Lee Hardy, Bonhoeffer argues that we all are stationed in many places concurrently, but

....

From Dietrich Bonhoeffer, *Ethics*, Dietrich Bonhoeffer Works, vol. 6 (Minneapolis: Fortress, 2005), 290–93, 296–97.

he is much more alert than Hardy to how these places or orders can themselves be corrupted and how their various duties can and often do conflict with one another. Like Gary Badcock, Bonhoeffer insists that Christians are called above all things to a life of radical discipleship, but he is much more concerned than Badcock to specify what such discipleship actually means within our workplaces, families, churches, and polities.

For Bonhoeffer, radical obedience to Christ's call meant radical freedom to be fully responsible to and for others. Both because of his courage and because of the character of his witness, Bonhoeffer's account of Christian vocation has found wide admiration from both Christians and non-Christians. How might your own work and the character of your own relationships to others change if you were to adopt Bonhoeffer's view of vocation and responsibility?

In encounter with Jesus Christ, a person experiences God's call [*Ruf*], and in it the calling [*Berufung*] to a life in community with Jesus Christ. Human beings experience the divine grace that claims them. It is not human beings who seek out grace in its place, for God lives in unapproachable light (1 Tim. 6:16). Instead, grace seeks out and finds human beings in their place — the Word became flesh (John 1:14) — and claims them precisely there. It is a place that in every case and in every respect is burdened with sin and guilt, be it a royal throne, the home of a respected citizen, or a shanty of misery. It is a place of this world. This visitation by grace took place in Jesus Christ becoming human, and still occurs in the word about Jesus Christ that the Holy Spirit brings. The call reaches us as Gentile or Jew, slave or free, man or woman, married or unmarried. Right where they happen to be, human beings ought to hear the call and allow themselves to be claimed by it. It is not as if this would imply a justification of slavery, marriage, or singleness as such. Instead, those who are called may belong to God in one state or the other. Only by the call of grace heard in Jesus Christ, by which I am claimed, may I live justified before God as slave or free, married or single. From Christ's perspective this life is now my vocation; from my own perspective it is my responsibility.

... People do not fulfill the responsibility laid on them by faithfully performing their earthly vocational obligations as citizens, workers, and parents, but by hearing the call of Jesus Christ that, although it leads them also into earthly obligations, is never synonymous with these, but instead always transcends them as a reality standing before and behind them. Vocation in the New Testament sense is never a sanctioning of the worldly orders as such. Its Yes always includes at the same time the sharpest No, the sharpest protest against the world. Luther's return from the monastery into the world, into a "vocation," is, in the genuine spirit of the New Testament, the fiercest attack that has been launched and the hardest blow that has been struck against the world since the time of early Christianity. Now a stand against the world is taken *within* the world. Vocation is the place at which one responds to the call of Christ and thus lives responsibly. The task given to me by my vocation is thus limited; but my responsibility to the call of Jesus Christ knows no bounds. . . .

The question of the place and the limit of responsibility has led us to the concept of vocation. However, this answer is valid only where vocation is understood simultaneously in all its dimensions. The call of Jesus Christ is the call to belong to Christ completely; it is Christ's address and claim at the place at which this call encounters me; vocation comprises work with things and issues [*sachliche Arbeit*] as well as personal relations; it requires "a definite field of activity," though never as a value in itself but only in responsibility to Jesus Christ. By being related to Jesus Christ, the "definite field of activity" is set free from any isolation. The boundary of vocation has been broken open not only vertically, through Christ, but horizontally, with regard to the extent of responsibility. Let us say I am a medical doctor, for example. In dealing with a concrete case I serve not only my patient, but also the body of scientific knowledge, and thus science and knowledge of truth in general. Although in practice I render this service in my concrete situation — for example, at a patient's bedside — I nevertheless remain aware of my responsibility toward the whole, and only thus fulfill my vocation. In so doing, it may come to the point that in a particular case I must recognize and fulfill my concrete responsibility as a physician no longer only at a patient's bedside, but, for example, in taking a public stance against a measure that poses a threat to medical science, or human life, or science in general. Vocation is responsibility, and responsibility is the whole response of the whole person to reality as a whole. This is precisely why a myopic self-limitation to one's vocational obligation in the narrowest sense is out of the question; such a limitation would be irresponsibility. The nature of free responsibility rules out any legal regulation of when and to what extent human vocation and responsibility entail breaking out [*Durchbrechen*] of the "definite field of activity." This can happen only after seriously considering one's immediate vocational obligations, the dangers of encroaching on the responsibilities of others, and finally the total picture of the issue at hand. It will then be my free responsibility in response to the call of Jesus Christ that leads me in one direction or the other. Responsibility in a vocation follows the call of Christ alone. . . .

But now is it not the case that the law of God as revealed in the Decalogue, and the divine mandates of marriage, work, and government, establish an inviolable boundary for any responsible action in one's vocation? Would any transgressing [*Durchbrechung*] of this boundary not amount to insubordination against the revealed will of God? Here the recurring problem of law and freedom presents itself with ultimate urgency. It now threatens to introduce a contradiction into the will of God itself. Certainly no responsible activity is possible that does not consider with ultimate seriousness the boundary that God established in the law. Nevertheless, precisely as responsible action it will not separate this law from its giver. Only as the Redeemer in Jesus Christ will it be able to recognize the God by whose law the world is held in order; it will recognize Jesus Christ as the ultimate reality to whom it is responsible, and precisely through Christ it will be freed from the law for the responsible deed. For the sake of God and the neighbor, which means for Christ's sake, one may be freed from keeping the Sabbath holy, honoring one's parents, indeed from the entire divine law. It is a freedom that transgresses this law, but only in order to affirm it anew. The suspension of the law must only serve its true fulfillment. In war, for example, there is killing, lying, and seizing of property solely in order to reinstate the validity of life, truth, and property. Breaking the law must be *recognized* in all its gravity — "blessed are you if you know what you are doing; however, if you do not know what you are doing you are cursed and a transgressor of the law." Whether an action springs from responsibility or cynicism can become evident only in whether the objective guilt one incurs by breaking the law is recognized and borne, and whether by the very act of breaking it the law is truly sanctified. The will of God is thus sanctified in the deed that arises out of freedom. Precisely because we are dealing with a deed that arises from freedom, the one who acts is not torn apart by destructive conflict, but instead can with confidence and inner integrity do the unspeakable, namely, in the very act of breaking the law to sanctify it.

Frederick Buechner

VOCATION

Frederick Buechner is a contemporary novelist and theologian whose whose ability to condense complex issues into memorable aphorisms have made some of his theological formulations especially quotable. Indeed, his special gift for verbal economy may have encouraged him to produce a kind of dictionary of Christian theological terms in the book from which the selection below is taken, *Wishful Thinking: A Theological ABC*. The term that appears under the letter *V* in that volume is, of course, "vocation."

The conclusion of Buechner's short discussion of vocation is perhaps the most widely quoted formulation of vocation among contemporary American Christians. "The place God calls you to is the place where your deep gladness and the world's deep hunger meet." By "deep gladness," do you suppose that Buechner means "contentment," or does he mean the kind of joy that can be present even in the midst of suffering? Which of those two understandings would be more consonant with the ideas of vocation set forth by the other writers in this anthology?

[Vocation] comes from the Latin *vocare,* to call, and means the work a person is called to by God.

There are all different kinds of voices calling you to all different kinds of work, and the problem is to find out which is the voice of God rather than of Society, say, or the Superego, or Self-Interest.

By and large a good rule for finding out is this: The kind of work God usually calls you to is the kind of work (a) that you need most to do and (b) that the world most needs to have done. If you really get a kick out of your work, you've presumably met requirement (a), but if your work is writing cigarette ads, the chances are you've missed requirement (b). On the other hand, if your work is being a doctor in a leper colony, you have probably met

From Frederick Buechner, *Wishful Thinking: A Theological ABC* (New York: Harper & Row, 1973), 95.

requirement (b), but if most of the time you're bored and depressed by it, the chances are you have not only bypassed (a), but probably aren't helping your patients much either.

Neither the hair shirt nor the soft berth will do. The place God calls you to is the place where your deep gladness and the world's deep hunger meet.

Will Campbell

VOCATION AS GRACE

Will Campbell (1924–2013), who for most of his life lived on a farm in Tennessee, upset Christian complacencies for many years as a preacher, activist, essayist, and novelist. Like Bonhoeffer, Campbell believed that "when Christ calls a man, he bids him come and die." Campbell therefore had no patience for the idea of vocation as something that simply gives a spiritual gloss to what we have chosen to do for ourselves by ourselves in any case.

In the story below, Campbell challenges the conventional Christian notion that vocation is a purely individual matter. He suggests that our callings are best negotiated in community with others, through a process that leads us to discern not only our own gifts but also our own needs and weaknesses, not only the rich potential of the world but also its poverty. Campbell's story could just as easily have been included as one of the readings in question 3, "With Whom and for Whom Shall I Live?" Do you agree with Campbell in thinking that we cannot rightly hear our own call unless and until we recognize both others' dependence on us and our dependence on them?

Long before the process of my vocational self-examination (justification) began I once cornered and talked to a high wire artist in a small traveling circus. I asked him why he chose that particular way of making a living. The first few minutes were filled with circus romance — the thrill of hurling through space, feeling at the last instant that pasty flesh of two always welcomed hands pressing around the wrists, swinging you forward to the next set of pasty hands which in turn deliver you safely back to the starting platform; the joy of laughter and approval and applause in the eyes of "children of all ages," the clanking of train wheels moving you on to the next city; even the part about it being a comfortable life with good pay. But finally he said what I had not expected him to say. "Now you really want to know why I

Will D. Campbell, "Vocation as Grace," in *Callings!*, ed. James Y. Holloway and Will D. Campbell (New York: Paulist, 1974), 279–80.

go up there on that damned thing night after night after night?" I said I did. "Man, I would have quit it a long time ago. But my sister is up there. And my wife and my father are up there. My sister has more troubles than Job. My wife is a devil-may-care nut and my old man is getting older. If I wasn't up there, some bad night, man . . . smash!" His foot stomped the floor with a bone-cracking thud.

"H'mmm."

He started to walk away but I had one more question to ask and ran after him. "But why do *they* stay up there?" He looked like he didn't want to answer, wasn't going to answer. But then he did. Turning from the door of the boys' locker room in the county seat high school, with a brown craft cardboard box and heavy crayola sign: MEN'S COSTUMES above it for the evening's performance, he looked me up and down and then, as he disappeared, blurted it out: "Because I drink too much!"

Chuang Tzu

MASTERING LIFE

The short sketch below demonstrates beyond doubt that endeavors to understand one's work as bound up deeply with one's character and one's spiritual identity are not and never have been distinctively Christian or even
distinctively Western. This little story was written by a Chinese philosopher,
Chuang Tzu, whose dates of birth and death are uncertain but who may well
have been a contemporary of Mencius, a Confucian philosopher whose work
is included above. The sketch suggests that an artisan's moral or spiritual
condition may well affect the quality of the work that he or she produces.
Do you agree with this? Aristotle did not. Consider, for example, all the
works of visual art or literary art that you admire. Now consider the moral
quality of the painters or writers who created those works. Do you think the
moral quality of the work, the product, depends upon the moral quality of
the maker of that work?

Woodworker Ch'ing carved a piece of wood and made a bell stand, and when
it was finished, everyone who saw it marveled, for it seemed to be the work
of gods or spirits. When the marquis of Lu saw it, he asked, "What art is it
you have?"

Ch'ing replied, "I am only a craftsman — how would I have any art? There
is one thing, however. When I am going to make a bell stand, I never let it
wear out my energy. I always fast in order to still my mind. When I have
fasted for three days, I no longer have any thought of congratulations or
rewards, of titles or stipends. When I have fasted for five days, I no longer
have any thought of praise or blame, of skill or clumsiness. And when I have
fasted for seven days, I am so still that I forget I have four limbs and a form
and body. By that time, the ruler and his court no longer exist for me. My
skill is concentrated and all outside distractions fade away. After that, I go

From Chuang Tzu, *Basic Writings*, trans. Burton Watson (New York: Columbia University Press, 1964), 126–27.

into the mountain forest and examine the Heavenly nature of the trees. If I find one of superlative form, and I can see a bell stand there, I put my hand to the job of carving; if not, I let it go. This way I am simply matching up 'Heaven' with 'Heaven.' That's probably the reason that people wonder if the results were made by spirits."

QUESTIONS

Must my job be the primary source of my identity? To whom and to what should I listen as I decide what to do for a living? With whom and for whom shall I live? Is a balanced life possible and preferable to a life focused primarily on work? What are my obligations to future human and other life? How shall I tell the story of my life?

Must My Job Be the Primary Source of My Identity?

What question do college students most dread? Perhaps the one they get asked most often: "So, what are you going to *do* after you graduate?" Relatives have an irksome way of raising this question repeatedly. And adults of all ages are frequently subject to similar, abrupt interrogations about what they do to earn a living. Indeed, social observers have long noticed that in the United States people typically open a conversation with strangers by asking them what they *do,* a question that seems especially discomfiting to the unemployed or those working at a job they do not especially enjoy or respect.

These everyday queries are worth pondering, since they are not common everywhere. People in other countries find it offensive to be asked straightaway what they do to earn a living, rather like how we might feel if people began a conversation by asking us how much money we make. And even in this country, some people invite others to identify themselves by asking different questions. What tribe are you from? Tell me about your family, about your place of birth, or about how you came to be where you are now. In other words, there are many other ways in which people here and elsewhere begin to become acquainted with one another.

Why do questions about our jobs sometimes agitate us? Are we made uncomfortable by them only because we are unsure how to answer or unhappy with the answer we must give? We would probably not be embarrassed or irked by questions about where we plan to settle down or what kind of car we plan to buy, even if we didn't know the answers. Questions about what we *do,* however, can make us uncomfortable because we really do believe, even without realizing it, that our answers to them reveal something vitally important about who we are. Some people may not mind being asked — in fact, they may be quite eager to respond because they are proud of what they do and proud of what they believe that indicates about their overall character and standing in the world. But one way or another, for better or for worse, our sense of who we are and our sense of what we do for a living are deeply bound up with one another.

However, human beings have not always thought of their work as the most important thing about them. Such an exalted view of work is itself the result of complex social and economic changes that have been most pronounced in Western, capitalist countries over the last three or four hundred years. In earlier periods, and still today in much of the world, people regarded paid employment as necessary to gain sustenance and leisure, but not as a primary source of fulfillment and identity. And for the majority of people around the globe, making a living has involved and still does involve work that is onerous and sometimes dangerous. These historical and social realities have been ignored by many modern Americans in their thinking about what work to do.

The first two selections in this chapter explain why paid employment has become, for millions of US citizens, so vitally, even centrally, important to their sense of who they are, while the reading that follows these objects to seeing work as what defines people's identity.

- a selection from a book on work and democracy (Russell Muirhead)
- an essay arguing that we live in order to work (Dorothy Sayers)
- a selection from an ethicist's book on friendship (Gilbert Meilaender)

The readings by Russell Muirhead and Dorothy Sayers help us to think about the importance of the right kind of paid work in constituting a healthy society, personal well-being, and faithful Christian living. From the earliest years of American history, political life was closely tied to economic life; the right to vote, for example, was for a long time restricted to adult male property owners. This limitation of the franchise was based upon the seemingly unshakeable conviction that, to make wise political decisions, one had to be economically independent, not overly beholden to others for economic security. Holding property not only gave a man a stake in society; it also gave him a measure of freedom from the demands of others who might use their economic power over him to dictate his political preferences. Economic, social, and political identities were closely linked together in many ways, leading some historians to maintain that economic equality is a precondition for political equality — a claim that is still very much alive today.

The central importance of work in human life is as deeply embedded within Christian and Jewish stories of the beginnings of humankind as it is within secular accounts of the origins and social conditions of democracy. Dorothy Sayers argues that in and through our work we should be expressing our nature as beings who were created in the image of God. Sayers is not the only religious thinker who suggests that "in the beginning" human beings were made to labor and that their labor gave dignity, meaning, and purpose to their lives, but she goes further than most when she insists that we live in order to work. In the next selection, the Christian ethicist Gilbert Meilaender rejects her argument. After showing how certain interpretations of the Christian idea of "calling" have led to the mistaken notion that work is what gives meaning, purpose, and fulfillment to life, Meilaender lifts up instead the promise contained in Jewish and Christian Scriptures that *rest* is what God intends for God's people. We will read a selection that further develops this claim from a Jewish perspective in the chapter on the balanced life. In his account of the Sabbath (see pp. 435–40 below) Abraham Joshua Heschel agrees that God intended that human beings should labor, but he insists that we were finally made for rest, not for work.

All three of these selections acknowledge that work is important as a means of sustaining oneself and others economically. They diverge, however, on the question of how what we *do* matters when we consider who we *are*. One great difficulty with all the views that celebrate work and working men and women is perhaps best summed up by James Galvin in his novel *The Meadow*. "In the Depression a lot of people lost their lives," Galvin wrote, "if your life is what you do." Galvin was right. Unemployment during the Depression brought not only poverty; it also brought the despair that can accompany a loss of self. If we live to work, we may die if we have no work. If work is all that matters in life, then a life without work might not matter at all.

Two poems that consider why and how work matters in our lives follow:

- Robert Frost, "Two Tramps in Mud Time"
- Margaret Piercy, "To Be of Use"

Frost joins Sayers in wondering whether doing work primarily because we want or need the money degrades the intrinsic meaning and pleasure that labor brings to a human life. For the speaker in Frost's poem, working to live and living to work are in tension with one another. At issue is the relationship between work that is driven by the cash nexus of a capitalist economy and work that reflects God's intentions for how humankind should live — a relationship the poet suggests is not a harmonious one. By contrast, the poet Margaret Piercy emphasizes the "usefulness" of work. Her praise of the common work of the world suggests that she sees human labor as fitting both human identity and the needs of the world. While never denying how hard work can be, Piercy also seems to take delight in it.

The notion of "fitting" work developed by Russell Muirhead, the first author in this chapter, includes an awareness that those who work are often changed, in their character and view of the world, by the work they do. In other words, Muirhead thinks that what we do all day has a formative influence on who we become. The work we do "habituates and orients us in profound ways that over time impress a pattern on our emotional and intellectual life," he writes; "this is why for many work cannot be merely another of life's routines but is rather a key source of their identity." If Muirhead is right, as we editors believe he is, thinking about "who we should be" is a highly significant part of any sound reflection about "what we should do." Those who have the freedom to decide what kind of paid work they will do ought to include in their considerations what kind of person they hope to become.

Insight into the relationship between work and identity, in this sense, is evident in each of the three readings that conclude this chapter:

- a poem about a young man who rejects the life to which his job will likely lead him (Stephen Dunn)
- a poem that shows how a certain job has shaped someone's character (Carl Dennis)
- an excerpt from a novel about a butler (Kazuo Ishiguro)

In this chapter we meet only one person — the butler in the final reading — whose life is focused on work to the exclusion of every other part of life. Others, like most of us, experience more complexity. It is within this complexity that we need to figure out what is primary. Gilbert Meilaender suggests that it is possible to value our jobs without making them primary, that is, without allowing them to control who we are and will become. Taking this position seriously does not mean that our days would be free from the demands and rhythms of work. Instead, it means that we would be able to step back to consider the whole shape of our lives and relationships, and there to see other points of meaning, such as friendship. Other people gain similar perspective on the whole of life — and a way of preventing work from being primary — in religious practice, wilderness adventures, immersion in the arts, or other life-shaping activities.

And yet, since we do not live in an economic and cultural vacuum, almost none of us can evade the widespread assumption that the question of what it means to lead a life that matters should at least *begin* with the question of our livelihoods. Coming to understand *why* this is so is not the same thing, however, as coming to a conviction that it *should* be so. And alternatives do exist. Widespread yearning for a more encompassing sense of identity has led to two different projects embraced by people who are troubled by the encroachment of work on their lives and sense of self. One project is the one undertaken in the present chapter, namely, an effort to challenge the prevailing ideology of work even as we acknowledge its power and, to some extent, its cogency. The other project, explored in question 4, is the quest for a "balanced life," a life that makes room for sources of meaning and identity not derived from work.

Even in a context where such projects have great appeal, the character in this chapter whose identity is most thoroughly defined by his job — the butler in Kazuo Ishiguro's novel *The Remains of the Day* — has more to teach us than we might imagine. In the selection included here, the butler, Mr. Stevens, is thinking hard about what it means to engage in his particular line of work with genuine excellence. His thoughts are prompted in part by the fact that working as a butler in a wealthy house — work Stevens calls a "vocation" and a "profession" — is fading as Britain departs from traditionalism and falls in power after the Second World War. Even so, Stevens remembers his years of "service" with great pride and seeks to carry on in this position even in a changing world. In the course of his ruminations, many of the themes at issue in *Leading Lives That Matter* come into play. Indeed, all four vocabularies in which we typically discuss what makes a life meaningful and significant are vividly, if subtly, at play in this passage.

Consider, for example, the question of what quality is most essential to an excellent butler. The answer, Stevens determines, is "dignity," a virtue. Further, he argues that this virtue can be "acquired over many years of self-training and the careful absorbing of experience," a point often made by those who advance the vocabulary of virtue. Elsewhere in the passage, Stevens weighs the merits of various butlers he finds worthy of admiration. What is it, Stevens asks himself, that made Mr. Marshall and Mr. Lane such great butlers? He and other household staff spent hours in earnest conversation about this very point, he recalls. These staff members, of course, were using the vocabulary of exemplarity. In addition, especially in the rest of the novel, Stevens thinks long and hard about how his work has contributed to some larger historical good. Though he is mostly confident that it did, readers may be less so. Still, this concern shows that Stevens and Ishiguro also think in the vocabulary of vocation.

The novelist crafting Stevens's thoughts includes stories and language that may make readers uncomfortable about the persistent denial of self for the sake of the "excellent" and "dignified" service that Stevens and the butlers he admires sustained. Stevens does *not* use the vocabulary of authenticity! However, listening to Stevens is likely to stir up this vocabulary in our own minds, as Ishiguro's skillful creation of the thinking of the repressed butler prods readers to examine their own desire for self-expression. In the context of *Leading Lives That Matter*, this should also prod us to ask where and how self-expression fits, or not, in other workplaces. Even though this novel works by indirection, it may actually be one of the most serious considerations in literature of the relationship between authenticity and vocation.

As we continue to explore important questions about lives of meaning and significance, it will make sense to bring Stevens to mind again. He has given, with his life, a clear answer to one of our key questions: "With whom and for whom shall I live?" The answer is his employer — and through him, Stevens believes, England. We should notice that Stevens's "service" has been entirely "for" rather than "with" others, a distinction that will emerge in the selection by Samuel Wells in that chapter. We may also imagine Stevens pondering — or refusing to ponder — question 4, "Is a balanced life possible and preferable to a life focused primarily on work?" Yet the final question in this book may be the most difficult one for him. In a sense, it is the question that frames this entire novel: "How shall I tell the story of my life?"

The story of Ishiguro's fictional butler's life is primarily the story of his job — a job that shaped, and even overwhelmed, not only his hours and relationships but also his identity. In the readings that follow, we shall explore some of the cultural forces that make this outcome possible even in other lines of work, and also some alternative ways of understanding how the relationship between job and identity might be conceived.

Russell Muirhead

DEMOCRACY AND THE VALUE OF WORK

In this selection from the first chapter of his 2004 book *Just Work,* the Dartmouth political theorist Russell Muirhead explores the question of why work is so closely bound up with identity in democratic societies. Muirhead is writing from within what we have described as the tradition of democracy, and he is at the same time seeking to advance that tradition. He offers intimations of what makes for "just work" in a democracy in the form of several points that he later elaborates through careful argument during the course of his book.

Muirhead begins by reminding us of a theme that will run through many of the readings in this anthology: our freedom to forge an identity is constrained. Thus, though we can, within limits that differ from person to person, choose from a variety of roles the ones we wish to play in life, we ourselves did not create or select the roles themselves. Rather, the repertoire of roles set before us was created through long historical processes that we simply inherited. We must remember this when we consider the proper place of work in our lives.

Muirhead also challenges us to recognize that the relationship between who we are and what we do to earn a living is more complicated than it may at first seem. On the one hand, our character determines to a great degree our choice of occupation. But on the other hand, what we do to earn a living will determine to a great extent our character. Can you think of concrete ways in which, say, practicing law makes a lawyer into a certain kind of human being? Can you think of ways in which some of the jobs you have done have begun to shape you into a certain kind of human being?

Politics in the largest sense is about the lives individuals can choose under particular conditions, and the lives they are impelled to live or even choose

From Russell Muirhead, *Just Work* (Cambridge, MA: Harvard University Press, 2004), 26–29.

in a particular society and regime. These lives are composed of roles: parent, spouse, worker, to name a few. It matters that we choose these roles for ourselves. But the choices we make run only so deep, for the roles themselves exist independent of our choice. They come to us on a limited menu, one that is carried by social conventions and beliefs that in turn are sustained and buttressed by families, voluntary associations, traditions, and laws. From the perspective of consent, what matters most is that these roles are open to all, that no one is either forced into them or excluded from them. Thus we need to ensure that people have the freedom to choose among roles and to exit, when they wish, those they have assumed. But this does not exhaust the questions we ought to ask about such roles, even from a concern with justice. We ought to inquire, too, about the conditions of choice, the sorts of choices individuals are impelled to make under constraints, as well as the quality and variety of the options available for people to choose from.

This is especially so when it comes to work. As a descriptive matter and (if we reject a guaranteed minimum income as parasitic) as a normative matter, the working life is something that citizens necessarily share. The working life is *our* life. As we have seen, the necessity or obligatory character of work is in tension with the liberal ideal that citizens should be free (not only formally but effectively) to form and act from their own conception of the good. Yet work is one of the most common and inescapable constraints on our freedom. This raises a crucial question: can the regulative ideals that concern work be modeled entirely on the liberal values of freedom and equality? Or will they at times follow a different cue, one that more fully recognizes the reality that work itself is a kind of restraint, a sort of discipline?

Any full account of the justice of work would certainly need somehow to reconcile the work people do (and at some level *have* to do) with their freedom. It would take stock of how work might look if its form resulted solely from our choices. Yet since work as it appears in the world will reflect not only our freedom but also our need, since it does not and probably cannot reflect our choices precisely, it remains something to which we often need to attune or accommodate or even reconcile ourselves. The ideal of fitting work recognizes the constrained character of freedom. It acknowledges our freedom, since fitting work is work we might more likely endorse. At the same time, the concept of fit acknowledges that freedom in the world of work is always circumscribed. The category of fit thus allows for the possibility that even when work is good, it is something we have to make our peace with.

The ideal of fitting work also acknowledges the special kind of relationship that work involves. Along with family and religion, work remains one of the central activities constituting everyday life. Work is instrumental (we work to earn and spend), but is rarely only that: it is also formative. Devoting the bulk of our waking hours to a particular activity over many years has an effect on who we are, whether we like it or not. In a limited but crucial way, we are what we do ("What do you do?" is a kind of shorthand for "Who are you?"). In one sense, this reflects the way work positions us in a kind of hierarchy — both in the hierarchy of authority within organizations and in the larger social hierarchy represented by differences in income and wealth. If it is often inexplicit, it is no secret that some jobs are admired for their authority, command, glamour, compensation — in short, their prestige. And others are scorned. Our work makes manifest where we fall — or where we have climbed — in the social hierarchy. Yet we are also what we do in a more constitutive sense. What we do all day habituates and orients us in profound ways that over time impress a pattern on our emotional and intellectual life. Work might make us more compassionate or more stern, more decisive or more resentful, more deft or more argumentative. The way we spend the bulk of our waking energy can even come to inform our larger posture toward the world, depending on whether work prods us to experience the world as hostile or alien, compliant or beneficent. This is why for many work cannot be merely another of life's routines but is rather a key source of their identity.

The aspiration to work that fits us, as both individuals and as human beings, is one I locate in the public culture of American life, in the way many evaluate work. This aspiration, widely if not universally shared, in turn points to an ancient understanding of justice, where justice addresses what we as individuals morally deserve, and what we deserve depends on what fits us. Because it focuses on what we deserve, the justice of fit is distinct from Rawls's justice as fairness, which concerns what we would accept under impartial conditions. Yet if they are in tension with each other, they are not quite face-to-face rivals because they apply at different levels. Justice as fairness most directly addresses constitutional essentials, while the justice of fit concerns "middle level" regulative ideals that operate in civil society. Each might influence legislation, though in different ways. Justice as fairness, in its way, addresses legislation from above by offering a model of impartiality that legislators can follow when basic principles of justice are at stake. It is most relevant when legislation is directly and obviously coercive. Regulative ideals like justice as fit influence legislation from below, when legislators represent and advance the sort of ethical notions that their constituents endorse.

It is most relevant when legislation addresses not constitutional essentials but the circumstances of everyday life.

The regulative ideal of fit reflects the aspirations people bring to the world of work, as it also elucidates the common opinion that work somehow supports human dignity. What would be required of us to fit our work? What would be required of work? What is the difference between a good fit and a bad one? Are there some useful jobs that cannot be said to fit anyone very well? And if so, how should these be allocated? This book will engage these questions and others in a way that will be at times uncomfortable, for I do not presuppose that the familiar terms of equal opportunity and free choice exhaust the categories with which we might evaluate the world of work. Yet uncomfortable categories are necessary if we are to understand the sources of pride and disappointment (and the sense of dignity and justice) that our way of life contains.

Dorothy L. Sayers

WHY WORK?

Dorothy L. Sayers (1893–1957) was a British author and churchwoman who published plays, translations of medieval literature, a delightful series of detective novels, and theological essays like the one included here. It is said that she loved her work so much that writing filled almost all her waking hours. It is possible that the creative character of her own work had a strong influence on her thinking about work in general.

More than most other essays in this anthology, this one makes a powerful case for our identities being wholly determined by our occupations. Sayers argues that we live in order to work, suggesting that those who work merely in order to live have, by choice or necessity, distorted the meaning and significance of work in their lives. On what basis does she make such an argument? Is she writing in the language of authenticity, suggesting that our work must be an authentic expression of our true selves? Is she making the same kind of argument as Muirhead, suggesting that our work should fit our own personal preferences and skills and fit the needs of society as well? How does her argument, which she locates within the tradition of Christianity, compare to the other Christian readings in this book, such as those in the "vocation" section?

One of Sayers's other points also stands out as unusual: her argument that the first and perhaps the only obligation of Christians in their work is to "serve the work." She is probably right in thinking that Christian talk about work has overemphasized, often mindlessly, the idea of "service." So we should pay special attention to any effort to challenge conventional wisdom on this matter, while also wondering what form that service might take in the work we do as students or in the kinds of work that are emerging in the twenty-first-century economy.

From Dorothy L. Sayers, *Creed or Chaos?* (London: Methuen & Co., 1947), 47–64.

I have already, on a previous occasion, spoken at some length on the subject of work and vocation. What I urged then was a thorough-going revolution in our whole attitude to work. I asked that it should be looked upon — not as a necessary drudgery to be undergone for the purpose of making money, but as a way of life in which the nature of man should find its proper exercise and delight and so fulfil itself to the glory of God. That it should, in fact, be thought of as a creative activity undertaken for the love of the work itself; and that man, made in God's image, should make things, as God makes them, for the sake of doing well a thing that is well worth doing. . . .

What is the Christian understanding of work? . . . I should like to put before you two or three propositions arising out of the doctrinal position which I stated at the beginning: namely, that work is the natural exercise and function of man — the creature who is made in the image of his Creator. You will find that any one of them, if given in effect everyday practice, is so revolutionary (as compared with the habits of thinking into which we have fallen), as to make all political revolutions look like conformity.

The first, stated quite briefly, is that work is not, primarily, a thing one does to live, but the thing one lives to do. It is, or it should be, the full expression of the worker's faculties, the thing in which he finds spiritual, mental, and bodily satisfaction, and the medium in which he offers himself to God.

Now the consequences of this are not merely that the work should be performed under decent living and working conditions. That is a point we have begun to grasp, and it is a perfectly sound point. But we have tended to concentrate on it to the exclusion of other considerations far more revolutionary.

(a) There is, for instance, the question of profits and remuneration. We have all got it fixed in our heads that the proper end of work is to be paid for — to produce a return in profits or payment to the worker which fully or more than compensates the effort he puts into it. But if our proposition is true, this does not follow at all. So long as society provides the worker with a sufficient return in real wealth to enable him to carry on the work properly, then he has his reward. For his work is the measure of his life, and his satisfaction is found in the fulfilment of his own nature, and in contemplation of the perfection of his work. That, in practice, there is this satisfaction, is shown by the mere fact that a man will put loving labor into some hobby which can never bring him any economically adequate return. His satisfaction comes, in the god-like manner, from looking upon what he has made and finding it very good. He is no longer bargaining with his work, but serving it. It is only when work has to be looked on as a means to gain that it becomes hateful; for then, instead of a friend, it becomes an enemy from whom tolls and contributions have to be extracted. What most of us demand from society is that we should always get out of it a little more than the value of the labor we give to it. By this process, we persuade ourselves that society is always in our debt — a conviction that not only piles up actual financial burdens, but leaves us with a grudge against society.

(b) Here is the second consequence. At present we have no clear grasp of the principle that every man should do the work for which he is fitted by nature! The employer is obsessed by the notion that he must find cheap labor, and the worker by the notion that the best-paid job is the job for him. Only feebly, inadequately, and spasmodically do we ever attempt to tackle the problem from the other end, and inquire: What type of worker is suited to this type of work? People engaged in education see clearly that this is the right end to start from; but they are frustrated by economic pressure, and by the failure of parents on the one hand and employers on the other to grasp the fundamental importance of this approach. And that the trouble results far more from a failure of intelligence than from economic necessity is seen clearly under war conditions, when, though competitive economics are no longer a governing factor, the right men and women are still persistently thrust into the wrong jobs, through sheer inability on everybody's part to imagine a purely vocational approach to the business of fitting together the worker and his work.

(c) A third consequence is that, if we really believed this proposition and arranged our work and our standard of values accordingly, we should no longer think of work as something that we hastened to get through in order to enjoy our leisure; we should look on our leisure as the period of changed rhythm that refreshed us for the delightful purpose of getting on with our work. And, this being so, we should tolerate no regulations of any sort that prevented us from working as long and as well as our enjoyment of work demanded. We should resent any such restrictions as a monstrous interference with the liberty of the subject. How great an upheaval of our ideas that would mean I leave you to imagine. It would turn topsy-turvy all our notions about hours of work, rates of work, unfair competition, and all the rest of it. We should all find ourselves fighting, as now only artists and the members of certain professions fight, for precious time in which to get on with the job — instead of fighting for precious hours saved from the job.

(d) A fourth consequence is that we should fight tooth and nail, not for mere employment, but for the quality of the work that we had to do. We should clamor to be engaged on work that was worth doing, and in which we could take a pride. The worker would demand that the stuff he helped to turn out should be good stuff — he would no longer be content to take the cash and let the credit go. Like the shareholders in the brewery, he would feel a sense of personal responsibility, and clamor to know, and to control, what went into the beer he brewed. There would be protests and strikes — not only about pay and conditions, but about the quality of the work demanded and the honesty, beauty, and usefulness of the goods produced. The greatest insult which a commercial age has offered to the worker has been to rob him of all interest in the end product of the work and to force him to dedicate his life to making badly things which were not worth making.

This first proposition chiefly concerns the worker as such. My second proposition directly concerns Christians as such, and it is this: It is the business of the Church to recognize that the secular vocation, as such, is sacred. Christian people, and particularly perhaps the Christian clergy, must get it firmly into their heads that when a man or woman is called to a particular job of secular work, that is as true a vocation as though he or she were called to specifically religious work. The Church must concern herself not only with such questions as the just price and proper working conditions: she must concern herself with seeing that the work itself is such as a human being can perform without degradation — that no one is required by economic or any other considerations to devote himself to work that is contemptible, soul-destroying, or harmful. It is not right for her to acquiesce in the notion that a man's life is divided into the time he spends on his work and the time he spends in serving God. He must be able to serve God in his work, and the work itself must be accepted and respected as the medium of divine creation. . . .

The Church's approach to an intelligent carpenter is usually confined to exhorting him not to be drunk and disorderly in his leisure hours, and to come to church on Sundays. What the Church should be telling him is this: that the very first demand that his religion makes upon him is that he should make good tables. . . .

Let the Church remember this: that every maker and worker is called to serve God in his profession or trade — not outside it. The Apostles complained rightly when they said it was not meet [meant] they should leave the word of God and serve tables; their vocation was to preach the word. But the person whose vocation it is to prepare the meals beautifully might with equal justice protest: It is not meet for us to leave the service of our tables to preach the word. The official Church wastes time and energy, and, moreover, commits sacrilege, in demanding that secular workers should neglect their proper vocation in order to do Christian work — by which she means ecclesiastical work. The only Christian work is good work well done. Let the Church see to it that the workers are Christian people and do their work well, as to God: then all the work will be Christian work, whether it is Church embroidery, or sewage-farming. . . .

This brings me to my third proposition; and this may sound to you the most revolutionary of all. It is this: the worker's first duty is to *serve the work.* The popular "catch" phrase of to-day is that it is everybody's duty to serve the community. It is a well-sounding phrase, but there is a catch in it: It is the old catch about the two great commandments. "Love God — and your neighbor; on those two commandments hang all the Law and the Prophets." The catch in it, which nowadays the world has largely forgotten, is that the second commandment depends upon the first, and that without the first, it is a delusion and a snare. Much of our present trouble and disillusionment have come from putting the second commandment before the first. If we put our neighbour first, we are putting man above God, and that is what we have been doing ever since we began to worship humanity and make man the measure of all things. Whenever man is made the center of things, he becomes the storm-center of trouble — and that is precisely the catch about serving the community. It ought perhaps to make us suspicious of that phrase when we consider that it is the slogan of every commercial scoundrel and swindler who wants to make sharp business practice pass muster as social improvement. "Service" is the motto of the advertiser, of big business, and of fraudulent finance. . . .

There is, in fact, a paradox about working to serve the community, and it is this: that to aim directly at serving the community is to falsify the work; the only way to serve the community is to forget the community and serve the work.

Gilbert Meilaender

FRIENDSHIP AND VOCATION

In this selection from his book *Friendship*, Christian ethicist Gilbert Meilaender explores the theological turns that have led to the devaluation of
friendship in comparison to work. He argues that Protestant Christians, from
John Calvin and William Perkins to Dorothy Sayers (whose essay, which Meilaender quotes, immediately precedes this one), are responsible for "elevating
work to a central place in life." And he contrasts this Protestant Christian
view of life to the classical view of life in which work was regarded as irksome
and friendship was understood to be the primary source of human fulfillment.
Putting these views alongside one another, we realize that we are seeing not
merely two different kinds of love: love of work in service to many neighbors
who have been given to us (vocation) and reciprocal love of a few, carefully
chosen, human beings (friendship). Instead, we have two different views of
what should give to a human life its meaning and significance.

For Meilaender, as for many who have written on the subject before him,
friendship includes not only our close acquaintances but also our lifelong
partners — in short, all whom we have chosen to love in a reciprocal way.
Meilaender sets up his discussion of friendship in this broad sense — with all
its demands, pleasures, and rewards — as often being in some tension with the
demands, pleasures, and rewards of our work. Thus, he suggests, we cannot
really come fully to terms with the proper place of friendship in a life that
matters without at the same time coming to terms with the proper place of
our jobs, especially if we think of those jobs as vocations. This is a matter we
shall return to in question 4, where we shall consider whether it is possible
and preferable to lead a life that balances work with other parts of life.

Meilaender writes in the vocabulary of vocation, but he does so critically.
Do you think he has abandoned the Christian ideal of vocation? Do his views
prompt you to think differently about what it might mean to think of your
work in terms of vocation? What place do you imagine friendship having in
your own vision of a life of meaning and significance?

From Gilbert Meilaender, *Friendship: A Study in Theological Ethics* (Notre Dame, IN:
University of Notre Dame Press, 1981), 95–99.

To regard work as a calling is to suggest that we live to work, that our work is of central significance for our person. Still more, the calling gives to work a religious significance which it is not likely to acquire in any other way. Thus, Dorothy Sayers could suggest that work expresses something essential in human nature; for it is a natural function of human beings who are made in the image of their Creator. The worker gives full expression to an essential feature of our shared human nature. "His satisfaction comes, in the godlike manner, from looking upon what He has made and finding it very good." Sayers was no fool, of course, and she realized that it is not easy to say this about the work many, probably most, people spend their lives doing. But to realize that, and nevertheless keep on emphasizing the significance of work, is to risk obscuring something important. For the Greeks, friendship was clearly important for self-fulfillment. "No one," writes Aristotle, "would choose to live without friends, even if he had all other goods." In coming to know the friend as "another self," one came to know oneself as well and acquired a sense of one's personal significance. To suggest that we live to work — and to cloak this in the religious garb of the calling — is to try to have work play a similar role in our lives. It is to make work as central in our sense of who we are as friendship was for the Greeks.

It is crucial to see that when we take this step we have really distorted the significance of the calling as it was understood and developed by early Protestants like Perkins. The point of the calling was, quite simply, that it was appointed by God to serve neighbors. If along the way some self-fulfillment came as well, there was nothing wrong with that, but it was hardly the point of the calling. Our modern notion — into which even so independent a thinker as Sayers could be lured — that the point of work is to give meaning, purpose, and fulfillment to life is a degradation of the calling. It is a degradation against which we should have been guarded by both our experience and our theological tradition.

Our experience should surely have taught us that, although some people seem to find their work satisfying in itself, it is equally true that "work, for most people, has always been ugly, crippling, and dangerous." We may in good conscience recommend such work as service to the neighbor or even as an instrument of spiritual discipline, but it ought be cloaked in no other religious garb. When the system of vocations as we experience it today is described in terms which make work the locus of self-fulfillment, Christian ethics ought to object — on the empirical ground that this is far from true, and on the theological ground that vocation ought not make self-fulfillment central. When work as we know it emerges as the dominant idea in our lives — when we identify ourselves to others in terms of what we do for a living, work for which we are paid — and when we glorify such work in terms of self-fulfillment, it is time for Christian ethics to speak a good word for working simply in order to live. Perhaps we need to suggest today that it is quite permissible, even appropriate, simply to work in order to live and to seek one's fulfillment elsewhere — in personal bonds like friendship, for example.

Such a suggestion is likely to meet with disapproval from every side, and this disapproval is likely to use that magic word "alienation." Put most simply, "alienation" means that the worker has little sense of personal investment in his or her work. We work at one thing — live for another. The alienated worker, we are told, understands his work only instrumentally — as a means to having the wherewithal and the opportunity to pursue other ends and values. And, the argument continues, such an alienated worker — one who works only to live — can scarcely live a fully human existence. Self-fulfillment is impossible in such circumstances. We are by now so accustomed to taking this purported fact of alienation for granted that it comes as something of a shock to be told, as P. D. Anthony has recently argued, that "man can be regarded as alienated from his work only when he has been subjected to an ideology which requires him to be devoted to it." Yet, Anthony is quite correct. Alienation becomes possible only when, first, work has been given central place in human life, and, second, it is assumed that we are to gain a sense of personal fulfillment from our work. The idea of the calling contributed to the first of these; degradation of that idea to the second. The end of this road becomes apparent in Marxist thought, where alienation has been such a central concept. According to Marx, human beings "begin to distinguish themselves from animals as soon as they begin to *produce* their means of subsistence." The human being is a worker — and once that is made central, alienation becomes a possibility, indeed, a likelihood. As the place and importance of work in human life are exaggerated, the undesirable characteristics of work become more glaring and objectionable. It is possible to be alienated from our work only if we first imagine that we were to find in it a high degree of personal fulfillment. Whatever its defects, it is one of the virtues of capitalism that it must allow people simply to work for money and seek fulfillment elsewhere. Indeed, we might say with Anthony that "capitalism represents an imperfect stage in development towards the absolute transcendency of economic values and an associated ideology of work, the fullest development of which is represented in Marxism."

If our experience should have warned us against making work an essential feature of human nature and the locus of self-fulfillment, so ought our theological tradition. I have already noted that the idea of the calling, in its pure form, had little to do with achieving personal fulfillment. For Luther and Calvin one worked in order not to become a burden to others and because God had appointed for one this particular calling as service to one's neighbors. Even with those qualifications, however, it remains true that the calling may have given work greater centrality in life than it should have, and it is not surprising that coupled with exhortations to faithfulness in one's calling were vigorous attacks on idleness and begging. And in the modern world, work has certainly begun to have the status of an idol. In such circumstances we need to reassert other aspects of our theological tradition. Karl Barth, arguing that human beings, for the most part, work to live rather than live to work, directed a much needed polemic against the idol of work.

> It is of a piece with the rather feverish modern overestimation of work and of the process of production that particularly at the climax of the 19th century, and even more so in our own, it should be thought essential to man, or more precisely to the true nature of man, to have a vocation in this sense. On such a view it is forgotten that there are children and the sick and elderly and others for whom vocation in this sense can be only the object either of expectation and preparation or of recollection. It is also forgotten that there are the unemployed, though these are certainly not without a vocation. Finally, it is forgotten that there are innumerable active women who do not have this kind of vocation.

It is worth recalling that it was possible for biblical writers to speak of the promise of God for his people as *rest*. "So then, there remains a sabbath rest for the people of God; for whoever enters God's rest also ceases from his labors as God did from his" (Hebrews 4:9f.). And, indeed, that sabbath rest, as it even now recurs in the weekly cycle of Christian life, is already testimony to the fact that work offers no final fulfillment for human existence.

This is what we ought to have learned and what Christian ethics should call to mind: that work is not an essential feature of a human life, that the point of work is not our own fulfillment but service to others, that work has its limits and need not always make it impossible for us to fold our legs and have out our talk. The proper tone — which does not idolize work but which grants its necessity — was captured quite well by Calvin when he wrote of the calling: "each man will bear and swallow the discomforts, vexations, weariness, and anxieties in his way of life, when he has been persuaded that the burden was laid upon him by God."

Robert Frost

TWO TRAMPS IN MUD TIME

Robert Frost (1874–1963) may be the most famous and beloved American poet of the twentieth century. He used simple and easily accessible diction, combined with beguiling rhythms and rhyme schemes, to achieve remarkably complex effects and affects. The poem below may be the most searching twentieth-century poem about work, vocation, and avocation. It contains many contrasts, some of them in tension with one another, others complementing one another. Work and play, physical effort for enjoyment and physical effort for pay, avocation and vocation — these are just some of the contrasting pairs that need to be understood in order to appreciate the poem.

Sometimes the treatment of the main subject of the poem can best be understood obliquely, by thinking about something that does not at first appear central to it. Notice that the title includes a temporal reference, "mud time." Notice as well that the central part of the poem is taken up with characterizing the time of the day and the time of the year in great and telling detail. These temporal descriptions, showing how a day in April can feel, from one minute to the next, like winter or like spring, prepare us for understanding how the "same" physical activity, chopping wood, can be two very different things, perhaps both of them alternately, even both of them at one and the same time.

The interactions between the tramps and the speaker introduce two very different views of work and its proper place in a human life. The tramps are the title characters, and they work "for need," to earn a living. The speaker of the poem works "for love," for the sheer pleasure of physical exertion. The poem itself invites us to wonder which view of work is the better one and whether the two views can ever be brought together, and if so, how. This very complex drama between two views of work takes place within a cosmic framework. The poem begins with human origins expressed in a way

Robert Frost, "Two Tramps in Mud Time," in *A Further Range* (New York: Holt, 1936), 16–18.

that has a biblical resonance ("Out of the mud two strangers came") and concludes with references to heaven and the future. How important is this "frame" for understanding the way the whole poem works in its effort to educate our own imaginations about the proper place of work in our lives?

Out of the mud two strangers came
And caught me splitting wood in the yard.
And one of them put me off my aim
By hailing cheerily "Hit them hard!"
I knew pretty well why he dropped behind   5
And let the other go on a way.
I knew pretty well what he had in mind:
He wanted to take my job for pay.

Good blocks of oak it was I split,
As large around as the chopping block;   10
And every piece I squarely hit
Fell splinterless as a cloven rock.
The blows that a life of self-control
Spares to strike for the common good,
That day, giving a loose to my soul,   15
I spent on the unimportant wood.

The sun was warm but the wind was chill.
You know how it is with an April day
When the sun is out and the wind is still,
You're one month on in the middle of May.   20
But if you so much as dare to speak,
A cloud comes over the sunlit arch,
A wind comes off a frozen peak,
And you're two months back in the middle of March.

A bluebird comes tenderly up to alight   25
And fronts the wind to unruffle a plume,
His song so pitched as not to excite
A single flower as yet to bloom.
It is snowing a flake: and he half knew

Winter was only playing possum.   30
Except in color he isn't blue,
But he wouldn't advise a thing to blossom.

The water for which we may have to look
In summertime with a witching wand,
In every wheelrut's now a brook,   35
In every print of a hoof a pond.
Be glad of water, but don't forget
The lurking frost in the earth beneath
That will steal forth after the sun is set
And show on the water its crystal teeth.   40

The time when most I loved my task
These two must make me love it more
By coming with what they came to ask.
You'd think I never had felt before
The weight of an ax-head poised aloft,   45
The grip on earth of outspread feet,
The life of muscles rocking soft
And smooth and moist in vernal heat.

Out of the woods two hulking tramps
(From sleeping God knows where last night,   50
But not long since in the lumber camps).
They thought all chopping was theirs of right.
Men of the woods and lumberjacks,
They judged me by their appropriate tool.
Except as a fellow handled an ax   55
They had no way of knowing a fool.

Nothing on either side was said.
They knew they had but to stay their stay
And all their logic would fill my head:
As that I had no right to play   60
With what was another man's work for gain.
My right might be love but theirs was need.
And where the two exist in twain
Theirs was the better right — agreed.

But yield who will to their separation,   65
My object in living is to unite
My avocation and my vocation
As my two eyes make one in sight.
Only where love and need are one,
And the work is play for mortal stakes,   70
Is the deed ever really done
For Heaven and the future's sakes.

Margaret Piercy

TO BE OF USE

This poem by Marge Piercy, first published in 1973, is widely read and frequently anthologized. Perhaps it resonates because so many people feel that their work is not "of use," or because so many long for work that is "real," as the poem concludes. The title of the poem suggests that the meaning and significance of our work might best be understood in terms of its usefulness. However, the idea of usefulness begs a series of questions. Useful to whom? Useful for what? Consider how the poem answers these questions. How does Piercy understand usefulness, and why does she commend it to us?

The poem begins by portraying "the people I love" and their way of approaching work, and the poem's images seem at some points to suggest that how people work is as important as what they do. Do the images invite us to think of the people the speaker "loves best" as those whose work and identity merge or as those whose work and identity remain distinct?

Would it be fair to say that the workers Piercy admires are, as Sayers might say, "serving the work"? Do they "live to work"? What makes their work "real"?

In addition to writing poetry, Piercy has written several novels and books of essays.

> The people I love the best
> jump into work head first
> without dallying in the shallows
> and swim off with sure strokes almost out of sight.
> They seem to become natives of that element,
> the black sleek heads of seals
> bouncing like half-submerged balls.

Margaret Piercy, "To Be of Use," in *The Art of Blessing the Day: Poems with a Jewish Theme* (New York: Knopf, 1999), 73–74.

I love people who harness themselves, an ox to a heavy cart,
who pull like water buffalo, with massive patience,
who strain in the mud and the muck to move things forward,
who do what has to be done, again and again.

I want to be with people who submerge
in the task, who go into the fields to harvest
and work in a row and pass the bags along,
who are not parlor generals and field deserters
but move in a common rhythm
when the food must come in or the fire be put out.

The work of the world is common as mud.
Botched, it smears the hands, crumbles to dust.
But the thing worth doing well done
has a shape that satisfies, clean and evident.
Greek amphoras for wine or oil,
Hopi vases that held corn, are put in museums
but you know they were made to be used.
The pitcher cries for water to carry
and a person for work that is real.

Stephen Dunn

THE LAST HOURS

This poem reflects on a young man's decision whether to stay in a job that many in his society assume is a good one. The poet later wrote, "My first job out of college was writing in-house brochures for Nabisco in New York, and I kept getting promoted. I was in danger, literally, of becoming like the men who were around me." What does the poem's narrator see in his coworkers that he takes to be dangerous to him in some way? While Dunn's own experience may not have been exactly that of the poem's narrator, both Dunn's comment and the poem show awareness that the work someone does is likely to shape the person he becomes.

What does the poem tell us about the context within which the young man made his choice? Note the historical moment, his family connections, and the purpose of the company for which he works. How might these affect his ability to act? How do parallel factors in your own context liberate you, or not, to exert influence on what you will become? This question is worth asking even if, like the young man in the poem, you are unsure what you will do instead.

> There's some innocence left,
> and these are the last hours of an empty afternoon
> at the office, and there's the clock
> on the wall, and my friend Frank
> in the adjacent cubicle selling himself
> on the phone.
>   I'm twenty-five, on the shaky
> ladder up, my father's son, corporate,
> clean-shaven, and I know only what I don't want,
> which is almost everything I have.
>   A meeting ends.

Stephen Dunn, "The Last Hours," in *Different Hours* (New York: Norton, 2002), 55.

Men in serious suits, intelligent men
who've been thinking hard about marketing snacks,
move back now to their window offices, worried
or proud. The big boss, Horace,
had called them in to approve this, reject that —
the big boss, a first-name, how's-your-family
kind of assassin, who likes me.
    It's 1964.
The sixties haven't begun yet. Cuba is a larger name
than Vietnam. The Soviets are behind
everything that could be wrong. Where I sit
it's exactly nineteen minutes to five. My phone rings.
Horace would like me to stop in
before I leave. *Stop in.* Code words,
leisurely words, that mean *now.*
    Would I be willing
to take on this? Would X's office, who by the way
is no longer with us, be satisfactory?
About money, will this be enough?
I smile, I say yes and yes and yes,
but — I don't know from what calm place
this comes — I'm translating
his beneficence into a lifetime, a life
of selling snacks, talking snack strategy,
thinking snack thoughts.
    On the elevator down
it's a small knot, I'd like to say, of joy.
That's how I tell it now, here in the future,
the fear long gone.
By the time I reach the subway it's grown,
it's outsized, an attitude finally come round,
and I say it quietly to myself: *I quit,*
and keep saying it, knowing I will say it, sure
of nothing else but.

Carl Dennis

A ROOFER

Carl Dennis is a Pulitzer Prize–winning American poet who often writes about the daily lives of ordinary people in conversational language. In the book from which this poem comes, Dennis explores questions related to work, the belief that work gives life meaning, and the challenges of understanding work and doing it well.

    This poem provides a rich and subtle portrait of a man who has been deeply shaped by the work he does to make a living. What detailed images related to roofing are scattered throughout the poem? Where do these images apply specifically to the job of roofing, and where do they serve as metaphors for the way this man approaches other tasks and relationships? If you know the details of another trade or craft, try asking how the disciplines and habits associated with it might likewise shape a person's character. And also ponder this question in relationship to the kind of work most readers likely do today — what is called "knowledge" work, done at computers rather than on roofs or in other places requiring manual or mechanical dexterity. How does spending long working hours online shape us into people with a certain character? What capacities does such work develop, and what qualities does it impede?

> Down on the ground, it's hard for him to measure
> How well he's doing, whether he's liable, say,
> To be too quick when correcting his children
> Or too slow, too distant or too intrusive.
> And is honesty what he needs more of
> For his wife to be happier, or forbearance?
> But on the roof he knows exactly
> What the situation requires
> And how best to supply it,

Carl Dennis, "A Roofer," in *Callings* (New York: Penguin Books, 2010), 18–19.

Sustained as he is by the clear consensus
Of the ghosts of the great roofers of yesteryear,
Who nod their approval at work well done.

On the ground, as he walks from his job,
He has to be a witness to shoddy craftsmanship:
Potholes gaping again after a month or two,
Porches rebuilt last summer already listing.
And then the boarded windows of the bank
That gambled away the savings of the thrifty.
But on the roof the only work he observes
Is his own of yesterday and the day before.
Good work that inspires him once again
To set his shingles neatly in courses,
Each as secure as nails can make it.

How gently the morning light
Glances along the ladder
As it rises from the world of obscure beginnings
And obscure procedures to the luminous realm
Where the rows of shingles
Climb from drip edge to roof beam
With a logic that's irresistible.
As long as the light holds,
It's a pleasure to linger here
Where he can believe himself an agent of progress.
No need to rush. Already at hand
The last shingle the job requires
Waits to sit snug in its proper place.

Kazuo Ishiguro

THE REMAINS OF THE DAY

Stevens, an English butler who is the narrator and protagonist of Ishiguro's profound and moving novel, is someone for whom a job has definitely become the primary source of his identity. In fact, we learn in the course of the novel, Stevens's "vocation," as he considers it, has become the sole source of his identity. In the passage below, Stevens ponders a question that is therefore at the heart of both his vocation and his identity: What is a "great" butler?

Even as the world of great country houses comes to an end in the years after the Second World War, and with it a role for butlers like Stevens, this character clings to his belief that his work has given meaning and significance to his life. At the same time, the novelist also subtly conveys the questions and doubts that have crept into Stevens's mind, threatening to shatter his repressed existence. In this passage from early in the novel, Stevens has gone for a drive around the countryside at the suggestion of his new employer, an American who does not understand that this is not something butlers like Stevens typically do. Remember as you read that the voice you are hearing is Stevens's, created by Ishiguro to give us a singular, and poignant, glimpse into an insular world that is actually far less admirable than Stevens believes. For example, as this passage shows, both this world and the profession of butlering that belongs to it are exclusively "English," and infused with racial prejudice and nationalist aspirations.

Few people today can imagine having a job like the one at the heart of this novel. Yet the questions Stevens asks about his job could also be asked about other kinds of work. What virtue is necessary to doing a particular kind of work well? Where does a certain job fit in the social fabric that surrounds it? And, perhaps most important, who does one become after doing such a job over the years? Stevens and his father, also a butler, sound like extreme cases of formation — or deformation — by work. But if we look carefully, might we notice job-related character traits emerging also in those who do work that is more familiar to us? Think of your own profession, or a profession you

From Kazuo Ishiguro, *The Remains of the Day* (New York: Knopf, 1988), 33–44.

may enter, and ask, what makes a practitioner "great" rather than merely "competent"?

Ishiguro, who was born in Japan and raised in the United Kingdom, won the Nobel Prize in Literature in 2017.

If one looks at these persons we agree are "great" butlers, if one looks at, say, Mr. Marshall or Mr. Lane, it does seem to me that the factor which distinguishes them from those butlers who are merely extremely competent is most closely captured by this word "dignity."

Of course, this merely begs the further question: of what is "dignity" comprised? And it was on this point that the likes of Mr. Graham and I had some of our most interesting debates. Mr. Graham would always take the view that this "dignity" was something like a woman's beauty and it was thus pointless to attempt to analyze it. I, on the other hand, held the opinion that to draw such a parallel tended to demean the "dignity" of the likes of Mr. Marshall. Moreover, my main objection to Mr. Graham's analogy was the implication that this "dignity" was something one possessed or did not by a fluke of nature; and if one did not self-evidently have it, to strive after it would be as futile as an ugly woman trying to make herself beautiful. Now while I would accept that the majority of butlers may well discover ultimately that they do not have the capacity for it, I believe strongly that this "dignity" is something one can meaningfully strive for throughout one's career. Those "great" butlers like Mr. Marshall who have it, I am sure, acquired it over many years of self-training and the careful absorbing of experience. In my view, then, it was rather defeatist from a vocational standpoint to adopt a stance like Mr. Graham's.

In any case, for all Mr. Graham's skepticism, I can remember he and I spending many evenings trying to put our fingers on the constitution of this "dignity." We never came to any agreement, but I can say for my part that I developed fairly firm ideas of my own on the matter during the course of such discussions, and they are by and large the beliefs I still hold today. I would like, if I may, to try and say here what I think this "dignity" to be.

You will not dispute, I presume, that Mr. Marshall of Charleville House and Mr. Lane of Bridewood have been the two great butlers of recent times. Perhaps you might be persuaded that Mr. Henderson of Branbury Castle also falls into this rare category. But you may think me merely biased if I say that my own father could in many ways be considered to rank with such men, and that his career is the one I have always scrutinized for a definition of "dignity." Yet it is my firm conviction that at the peak of his career at Lough-borough House, my father was indeed the embodiment of "dignity."

I realize that if one looks at the matter objectively, one has to concede my father lacked various attributes one may normally expect in a great butler. But those same absent attributes, I would argue, are every time those of a superficial and decorative order, attributes that are attractive, no doubt, as icing on the cake, but are not pertaining to what is really essential. I refer to things such as good accent and command of language, general knowledge on wide-ranging topics such as falconing or newt-mating — attributes none of which my father could have boasted. Furthermore, it must be remembered that my father was a butler of an earlier generation who began his career at a time when such attributes were not considered proper, let alone desirable in a butler. The obsessions with eloquence and general knowledge would appear to be ones that emerged with our generation, probably in the wake of Mr. Marshall, when lesser men trying to emulate his greatness mistook the superficial for the essence. It is my view that our generation has been much too preoccupied with the "trimmings"; goodness knows how much time and energy has gone into the practicing of accent and command of language, how many hours spent studying encyclopedias and volumes of "Test Your Knowledge," when the time should have been spent mastering the basic fundamentals.

Though we must be careful not to attempt to deny the responsibility which ultimately lies with ourselves, it has to be said that certain employers have done much to encourage these sorts of trends. I am sorry to say this, but there would appear to have been a number of houses in recent times, some of the highest pedigree, which have tended to take a competitive at-titude towards each other and have not been above "showing off" to guests a butler's mastery of such trivial accomplishments. I have heard of various instances of a butler being displayed as a kind of performing monkey at a house party. In one regrettable case, which I myself witnessed, it had become an established sport in the house for guests to ring for the butler and put to him random questions of the order of, say, who had won the Derby in such and such a year, rather as one might to a Memory Man at the music hall.

My father, as I say, came of a generation mercifully free of such confu-sions of our professional values. And I would maintain that for all his limited command of English and his limited general knowledge, he not only knew all there was to know about how to run a house, he did in his prime come to acquire that "dignity in keeping with his position," as the Hayes Society puts it. If I try, then, to describe to you what I believe made my father thus distinguished, I may in this way convey my idea of what "dignity" is.

There was a certain story my father was fond of repeating over the years. I recall listening to him tell it to visitors when I was a child, and then later, when I was starting out as a footman under his supervision. I remember him relating it again the first time I returned to see him after gaining my first post as butler – to a Mr. and Mrs. Muggeridge in their relatively modest house in Allshot, Oxfordshire. Clearly the story meant much to him. My father's generation was not one accustomed to discussing and analyzing in the way ours is and I believe the telling and retelling of this story was as close as my father ever came to reflecting critically on the profession he practiced. As such, it gives a vital clue to his thinking.

The story was an apparently true one concerning a certain butler who had travelled with his employer to India and served there for many years maintaining amongst the native staff the same high standards he had commanded in England. One afternoon, evidently, this butler had entered the dining room to make sure all was well for dinner, when he noticed a tiger languishing beneath the dining table. The butler had left the dining room quietly, taking care to close the doors behind him, and proceeded calmly to the drawing room where his employer was taking tea with a number of visitors. There he attracted his employer's attention with a polite cough, then whispered in the latter's ear: "I'm very sorry, sir, but there appears to be a tiger in the dining room. Perhaps you will permit the twelve-bores to be used?"

And according to legend, a few minutes later, the employer and his guests heard three gun shots. When the butler reappeared in the drawing room some time afterwards to refresh the teapots, the employer had inquired if all was well.

"Perfectly fine, thank you, sir," had come the reply. "Dinner will be served at the usual time and I am pleased to say there will be no discernible traces left of the recent occurrence by that time."

This last phrase – "no discernible traces left of the recent occurrence by that time" – my father would repeat with a laugh and shake his head admiringly. He neither claimed to know the butler's name, nor anyone who had known him, but he would always insist the event occurred just as he told it. In any case, it is of little importance whether or not this story is true; the significant thing is, of course, what it reveals concerning my father's ideals. For when I look back over his career, I can see with hindsight that he must have striven throughout his years somehow to *become* that butler of his story.

And in my view, at the peak of his career, my father achieved his ambition. For although I am sure he never had the chance to encounter a tiger beneath the dining table, when I think over all that I know or have heard concerning him, I can think of at least several instances of his displaying in abundance that very quality he so admired in the butler of his story.

One such instance was related to me by Mr. David Charles, of Charles and Redding Company, who visited Darlington Hall from time to time during Lord Darlington's days. It was one evening when I happened to be valeting him, Mr. Charles told me he had come across my father some years earlier while a guest at Loughborough House — the home of Mr. John Silvers, the industrialist, where my father served for fifteen years at the height of his career. He had never been quite able to forget my father, Mr. Charles told me, owing to an incident that occurred during that visit.

One afternoon, Mr. Charles to his shame and regret had allowed himself to become inebriated in the company of two fellow guests — gentlemen I shall merely call Mr. Smith and Mr. Jones since they are likely to be still remembered in certain circles. After an hour or so of drinking, these two gentlemen decided they wished to go for an afternoon drive around the local villages — a motor car around this time still being something of a novelty. They persuaded Mr. Charles to accompany them, and since the chauffeur was on leave at that point, enlisted my father to drive the car.

Once they had set off, Mr. Smith and Mr. Jones, for all their being well into their middle years, proceeded to behave like schoolboys, singing coarse songs and making even coarser comments on all they saw from the window. Furthermore, these gentlemen had noticed on the local map three villages in the vicinity called Morphy, Saltash and Brigoon. Now I am not entirely sure these were the exact names, but the point was they reminded Mr. Smith and Mr. Jones of the music hall act, Murphy, Saltman and Brigid the Cat, of which you may have heard. Upon noticing this curious coincidence, the gentlemen then gained an ambition to visit the three villages in question — in honor, as it were, of the music hall artistes. According to Mr. Charles, my father had duly driven to one village and was on the point of entering a second when either Mr. Smith or Mr. Jones noticed the village was Brigoon — that is to say the third, not the second, name of the sequence. They demanded angrily that my father turn the car immediately so that the villages could be visited "in the correct order." It so happened that this entailed doubling back a considerable way of the route, but, so Mr. Charles assures me, my father accepted the request as though it were a perfectly reasonable one, and in general, continued to behave with immaculate courtesy.

But Mr. Smith's and Mr. Jones's attention had now been drawn to my father and no doubt rather bored with what the view outside had to offer, they proceeded to amuse themselves by shouting out unflattering remarks concerning my father's "mistake." Mr. Charles remembered marveling at how my father showed not one hint of discomfort or anger, but continued to drive with an expression balanced perfectly between personal dignity and readiness to oblige. My father's equanimity was not, however, allowed to last. For when they had wearied of hurling insults at my father's back, the two gentlemen began to discuss their host — that is to say, my father's employer, Mr. John Silvers. The remarks grew even more debased and treacherous so that Mr. Charles — at least so he claimed — was obliged to intervene with the suggestion that such talk was bad form. This view was contradicted with such energy that Mr. Charles, quite aside from worrying whether he would become the next focus of the gentlemen's attention, actually thought himself in danger of physical assault. But then suddenly, following a particularly heinous insinuation against his employer, my father brought the car to an abrupt halt. It was what happened next that had made such an indelible impression upon Mr. Charles.

The rear door of the car opened and my father was observed to be standing there, a few steps back from the vehicle, gazing steadily into the interior. As Mr. Charles described it, all three passengers seemed to be overcome as one by the realization of what an imposing physical force my father was. Indeed, he was a man of some six feet three inches, and his countenance, though reassuring while one knew he was intent on obliging, could seem extremely forbidding viewed in certain other contexts. According to Mr. Charles, my father did not display any obvious anger. He had, it seemed, merely opened the door. And yet there was something so powerfully rebuking and at the same time so unassailable about his figure looming over them that Mr. Charles's two drunken companions seemed to cower back like small boys caught by the farmer in the act of stealing apples.

My father had proceeded to stand there for some moments, saying nothing, merely holding open the door. Eventually, either Mr. Smith or Mr. Jones had remarked: "Are we not going on with the journey?"

My father did not reply, but continued to stand there silently, neither demanding disembarkation nor offering any clue as to his desires or intentions. I can well imagine how he must have looked that day, framed by the doorway of the vehicle, his dark, severe presence quite blotting out the effect of the gentle Hertfordshire scenery behind him. Those were, Mr. Charles recalls, strangely unnerving moments during which he too, despite not having participated in the preceding behavior, felt engulfed with guilt. The silence seemed to go on interminably, before either Mr. Smith or Mr. Jones found it in him to mutter: "I suppose we were talking a little out of turn there. It won't happen again."

A moment to consider this, then my father had closed the door gently, returned to the wheel and had proceeded to continue the tour of the three villages — a tour, Mr. Charles assured me, that was completed thereafter in near-silence.

Now that I have recalled this episode, another event from around that time in my father's career comes to mind which demonstrates perhaps even more impressively this special quality he came to possess. I should explain here that I am one of two brothers — and that my elder brother, Leonard, was killed during the Southern African War while I was still a boy. Naturally, my father would have felt this loss keenly; but to make matters worse, the usual comfort a father has in these situations — that is, the notion that his son gave his life gloriously for king and country — was sullied by the fact that my brother had perished in a particularly infamous maneuver. Not only was it alleged that the maneuver had been a most un-British attack on civilian Boer settlements, overwhelming evidence emerged that it had been irresponsibly commanded with several floutings of elementary military precautions, so that the men who had died — my brother among them — had died quite needlessly. In view of what I am about to relate, it would not be proper of me to identify the maneuver any more precisely, though you may well guess which one I am alluding to if I say that it caused something of an uproar at the time, adding significantly to the controversy the conflict as a whole was attracting. There had been calls for the removal, even the court-martialing, of the general concerned, but the army had defended the latter and he had been allowed to complete the campaign. What is less known is that at the close of the Southern African conflict, this same general had been discreetly retired, and he had then entered business, dealing in shipments from Southern Africa. I relate this because some ten years after the conflict, that is to say when the wounds of bereavement had only superficially healed, my father was called to Mr. John Silvers's study to be told that this very same personage — I will call him simply "the General" — was due to visit for a number of days to attend a house party, during which my father's employer hoped to lay the foundations of a lucrative business transaction. Mr. Silvers, however, had remembered the significance the visit would have for my father, and had thus called him in to offer him the option of taking several days' leave for the duration of the General's stay.

My father's feelings towards the General were, naturally, those of utmost loathing; but he realized too that his employer's present business aspirations hung on the smooth running of the house party — which with some eighteen or so people expected would be no trifling affair. My father thus replied to the effect that while he was most grateful that his feelings had been taken into account, Mr. Silvers could be assured that service would be provided to the usual standards.

As things turned out, my father's ordeal proved even worse than might have been predicted. For one thing, any hopes my father may have had that to meet the General in person would arouse a sense of respect or sympathy to leaven his feelings against him proved without foundation. The General was a portly, ugly man, his manners were not refined, and his talk was conspicuous for an eagerness to apply military similes to a very wide variety of matters. Worse was to come with the news that the gentleman had brought no valet, his usual man having fallen ill. This presented a delicate problem, another of the house guests being also without his valet, raising the question as to which guest should be allocated the butler as valet and who the footman. My father, appreciating his employer's position, volunteered immediately to take the General, and thus was obliged to suffer intimate proximity for four days with the man he detested. Meanwhile, the General, having no idea of my father's feeling, took full opportunity to relate anecdotes of his military accomplishments — as of course many military gentlemen are wont to do to their valets in the privacy of their rooms. Yet so well did my father hide his feelings, so professionally did he carry out his duties, that on his departure the General had actually complimented Mr. John Silvers on the excellence of his butler and had left an unusually large tip in appreciation — which my father without hesitation asked his employer to donate to a charity.

I hope you will agree that in these two instances I have cited from his career — both of which I have had corroborated and believe to be accurate — my father not only manifests, but comes close to being the personification itself, of what the Hayes Society terms "dignity in keeping with his position." If one considers the difference between my father at such moments and a figure such as Mr. Jack Neighbours even with the best of his technical flourishes, I believe one may begin to distinguish what it is that separates a "great" butler from a merely competent one. We may now understand better, too, why my father was so fond of the story of the butler who failed to panic on discovering a tiger under the dining table; it was because he knew instinctively that somewhere in this story lay the kernel of what true "dignity" is. And let me now posit this: "dignity" has to do crucially with a butler's ability not to abandon the professional being he inhabits. Lesser butlers will abandon their professional being for the private one at the least provocation. For such persons, being a butler is like playing some pantomime role; a small push, a slight stumble, and the façade will drop off to reveal the actor underneath. The great butlers are great by virtue of their ability to inhabit their professional role and inhabit it to the utmost; they will not be shaken out by external events, however surprising, alarming or vexing. They wear their professionalism as a decent gentleman will wear his suit: he will not let ruffians or circumstances tear it off him in the public gaze; he will discard it when, and only when, he wills to do so, and this will invariably be when he is entirely alone. It is, as I say, a matter of "dignity."

It is sometimes said that butlers only truly exist in England. Other countries, whatever title is actually used, have only manservants. I tend to believe this is true. Continentals are unable to be butlers because they are as a breed incapable of the emotional restraint which only the English race are capable of. Continentals — and by and large the Celts, as you will no doubt agree — are as a rule unable to control themselves in moments of strong emotion, and are thus unable to maintain a professional demeanor other than in the least challenging of situations. If I may return to my earlier metaphor — you will excuse my putting it so coarsely — they are like a man who will, at the slightest provocation, tear off his suit and his shirt and run about screaming. In a word, "dignity" is beyond such persons. We English have an important advantage over foreigners in this respect and it is for this reason that when you think of a great butler, he is bound, almost by definition, to be an Englishman.

Of course, you may retort, as did Mr. Graham whenever I expounded such a line during those enjoyable discussions by the fire, that if I am correct in what I am saying, one could recognize a great butler as such only after one had seen him perform under some severe test. And yet the truth is, we accept persons such as Mr. Marshall or Mr. Land to be great, though most of us cannot claim to have ever scrutinized them under such conditions. I have to admit Mr. Graham has a point here, but all I can say is that after one has been in the profession as long as one has, one is able to judge intuitively the depth of a man's professionalism without having to see it under pressure. Indeed, on the occasion one is fortunate enough to meet a great butler, far from experiencing any skeptical urge to demand a "test," one is at a loss to imagine any situation which could ever dislodge a professionalism borne with such authority. In fact, I am sure it was an apprehension of this sort, penetrating even the thick haze created by alcohol, which reduced my father's passengers into a shamed silence that Sunday afternoon many years ago. It is with such men as it is with the English landscape seen at its best as I did this morning: when one encounters them, one simply *knows* one is in the presence of greatness.

There will always be, I realize, those who would claim that any attempt to analyze greatness as I have been doing is quite futile. "You know when somebody's got it and you know when somebody hasn't," Mr. Graham's argument would always be. "Beyond that there's nothing much you can say." But I believe we have a duty not to be so defeatist in this matter. It is surely a professional responsibility for all of us to think deeply about these things so that each of us may better strive towards attaining "dignity" for ourselves.

To Whom and to What Should I Listen
as I Decide What to Do for a Living?

W hen you face a major decision, to whom do you turn for advice? Do
you turn to your friends? To your religious leader? To books? To
those appointed to be your "adviser" or "counselor" by your college, company, or health-care system? Or do you try to figure things out
on your own?

Throughout *Leading Lives That Matter* we have encountered people who
either sought to give advice or were the recipients of advice, welcome and
otherwise. William James, lecturing to his students, did not seek to guide
each one into a specific path. However, he did have strong convictions about
ideals and effort that he very much wanted to share with them all, in the
hope that they would make worthy and challenging life choices. We also
met Vincent Harding, not as the giver of advice but as its recipient, though
he identified what his communities were urging him to do not as advice but
as "callings." Harding's story should prompt those who are wondering what
to do to listen carefully — and should prompt those in a position to advise
others to be more alert to the distinctive gifts that belong to members of our
neighborhoods and communities of faith, so that we might become more
deliberate about calling a young Vincent Harding into the good work he
longs to do, to his own satisfaction and for the well-being of all.

There can be little doubt that other people matter immensely in the
choices we make. When we look within ourselves, we find a medley of voices
from important others in our lives — parents, grandparents, siblings, teachers,
pastors, and friends — that we have internalized. The philosopher Charles
Taylor, whose argument that contemporary people highly prize their distinctive individuality appears in the section on the vocabulary of authenticity (see
pp. 59–64 above), also argues that this same individuality is fashioned in a lifelong series of conversations with significant others. Moreover, he insists that
individual identity makes sense only when oriented to a horizon of meaning
that is more generally shared. If Taylor is right, even when we are not explicitly turning to others to help us decide what we should do and what kind of
person we want to become, we are still taking their voices into account.

Other people are not the only influences on our decision about earning a living. What we are good at also matters. And so does what we love. In many of the selections in this chapter, young people find themselves negotiating among these various forces.

Take the question of talent, for example. In our society, athletes and actors are the high-profile figures whose success is most often attributed to talent. Yet almost everyone who has what the philosopher Immanuel Kant called "fortunate natural aptitudes" is liable to face difficult choices about whether to base the pursuit of specific jobs on these aptitudes. As we shall see in one of the examples below, someone with exceptional mathematical ability might have to leave the place and community he loves if he is to work at a suitably challenging level and contribute his special insights to an important project. Should the fact that he has great talent override his other desires? Musicians face similar dilemmas: many are forced to spend years on the road, filling in in various orchestras or playing small venues all over the country until a permanent position is found or a big record contract is signed — something that never happens for many, in spite of their obvious talent and hard work. Similarly, many who have hoped to be professional baseball players have simply struck out, either because their talent was an infinitesimal and unpredictable bit short or because they pulled a muscle at just the wrong time. The convergence of desire, talent, and luck is rare, and only in exceptional cases is it possible to predict what an individual's success will be.

What and whom to listen to — our talents, our desires, our formal and informal advisers — can become an urgent question for those deciding what to do in life. The fact that we live in a society where what we do is seen as an important indicator of who we are raises the stakes considerably. And the likelihood of receiving different advice from different sources can make the prospect of listening to a range of voices seem only a path to further perplexity.

Those of us who are teachers often talk with students about what they should do in life. Most of the time we are reluctant to be too directive: we place high value on helping each individual make a decision she can claim as distinctively her own, as Charles Taylor would predict. Often, then, our task becomes one of helping a given student to identify and respond appropriately to the interaction of her abilities and desires with the many voices she has encountered and internalized over the years that might steer her in one direction or another. Among these might be voices that say no to certain aspirations because of prejudice based on gender, race, or class; voices that encourage ideals of service; voices that insist that money is the most important factor to consider; voices that point important decisions toward a horizon defined by religious faith.

To whom and to what should we listen? For those in the midst of making important choices, sorting out the character and worth of many influences is a crucial matter. This is true not only for students but also for those in times of transition later in life, for the voices in conversation with which our identities are formed will continue to be present all our lives long.

Every reading in this chapter focuses on an individual who must come to terms with forces such as these in deciding what to do in life. The mixture of fiction and autobiography in this chapter will allow us to share, in imagination, the experience of a variety of persons as they determine which voices to heed. The selections are:

- a short story by Will Weaver, "The Undeclared Major"
- a chapter entitled "Two Kinds," from *The Joy Luck Club,* a novel by Amy Tan
- a short story by Tayeb Salih, "A Handful of Dates"
- two chapters from Lois Lowry's young adult novel *The Giver*
- a selection from a novel by Willa Cather, *The Song of the Lark*
- an autobiographical essay by Albert Schweitzer, "I Resolve to Become a Jungle Doctor"
- two scenes from the screenplay of *Good Will Hunting*
- "Sonny's Blues," a short story by James Baldwin

For most of us, our parents are the earliest and strongest influence on what we do and who we become. The first two selections in this chapter are works of fiction, both written in the first person, which invite us into the imagination and thinking of two young people as they come to terms with the expectations of their parents. In "The Undeclared Major," twenty-year-old Walter Hansen comes home for a visit to his family's wheat farm in the Upper Midwest, deeply uncertain about how his parents will receive his decision not to major in a subject that will lead directly to a practical job in agriculture or business. It is evident that Walter's return home, even though only for a short visit, also draws him into internal conversation with a larger community — with uncles and cousins and townspeople, indeed, with all those who surrounded and nurtured him over the years. Walter's sense of the extent to which he belongs to and among these people expands during the course of the story. "The Undeclared Major" may well elicit thoughts in all of us about how much the approval of our families and communities of origin matters as we consider what we shall be. Would Walter, or would we, declare a different major, so to speak, if met with strong opposition from those among whom we grew up?

The next selection depicts a parent-child relationship that is more conflicted than the one Walter and his father enjoy. The title of this chapter in Tan's novel refers to a declaration the mother makes in condemnation of her daughter's efforts at independence. "Only two kinds of daughters," the mother shouts in Chinese. "Those who are obedient and those who follow their own mind." Most of the story focuses on a generational battle of wills that took place during the narrator's childhood. By the end, however, when she has become an adult and her mother has died, she can begin to perceive ways in which her mother's voice has become part of her own identity in spite of the struggles they experienced. This story may help us imagine ways of acknowledging our parents' influence even when we have resisted or opposed some of their wishes. In both stories the parents are making decisions about how forcefully to try to mold the lives of their children, even as the children figure out what to embrace from their parents' legacy.

In "A Handful of Dates," a story set in a village in Sudan, the narrator remembers a crucial moment in his childhood when the question of how he would receive his family's legacy first emerged for him. He was the favorite of his tall, bearded grandfather, a man of great prominence in the village, and as a child he imagined growing up to be like this man. In a series of encounters, the narrator glimpses a more complex view of his grandfather, his village, and his own aspirations. Although the story does not say what the narrator grew up to become, it does portray his initial questioning of the family-scripted path through life that was laid out before him. It also introduces other kinds of voices to which we can listen when deciding what we should do and who we should be — the voices of religious tradition and of conscience.

The question we are considering, of course, presumes that one may choose whose advice to follow or to ignore. In the fictional community depicted in Lois Lowry's novel *The Giver,* there is no space for this question or, indeed, for other difficult questions about life or work. There, a committee of adults simply assigns each young person an occupation at the age of twelve. The fact that the adults obviously attend with great care to the gifts and temperament of each child before making each assignment gives us something to admire, and assigning occupations also has the benefit of clarity and efficiency; readers who have experienced the paralysis of indecision might conclude that such a process could be in some ways a comfort. Most contemporary Americans would find the process described here unacceptable, of course. But might it nonetheless offer something of value for the way most of us determine the kind of work we choose?

In the next two readings, individuals seem to eschew the advice and assistance of others as they choose challenging life paths. In the selection from *The Song of the Lark*, the great American novelist Willa Cather tells how a burned-out singer, Thea Kronborg, finds her strength and her art renewed by opening herself to an ancient landscape and the people who once inhabited it. In a move that would be impossible for the students in the highly structured society depicted in *The Giver*, Thea makes a deliberate retreat in a place apart. In listening to voices that transcend her own immediate situation, she finds clarity about her own loves and purposes in life, and strength to pursue them. Such times of rest and reflection are often crucial to those discerning difficult choices.

Albert Schweitzer, the author of the next selection, changed his vocation several times during his life, often in the face of incomprehension and even opposition from family and friends. He made his own most important vocational decision during a busy and productive period of his life; at the age of thirty, he was already the president of a seminary, a successful musician, and a prominent scholar. Telling no one except one trusted friend, he spent years investigating the various ways he might instead pursue work that directly served others. The life-shaping guidance he was seeking finally appeared in a magazine article about the need for doctors in Africa. Later, after he sent a letter about his plans to his friends and relatives, they uniformly sought to dissuade him from this course. He chose to reject their counsel.

The final two selections take up the question of how strongly our own talents and desires should influence what we will do for a living. Both readings invite us to ponder the choices faced by young men from working-class urban backgrounds who possess remarkable gifts. For Will, the lead character in the movie *Good Will Hunting*, a mathematics genius from South Boston, deciding to accept a job that will use his immense talent means leaving his friends and neighborhood. For James Baldwin's Sonny, a musical genius from Harlem, finding work as a jazz pianist means entering a dangerous subculture that is also remote from the support he knew earlier in life. We meet Will in the midst of his decision; we see Sonny after his is made. In each case, we will want to ask what these characters should have done. Is doing work that draws fully on their remarkable talents the best path to a life that matters?

For many exceptionally gifted people, choosing *not* to cultivate their talents is simply unthinkable. For Sonny, the gift and the person seem to be one. In addition, strong currents in Western culture press in favor of the cultivation of talents, even in the face of the long odds against, say, artistic or athletic success. As some of the readings in this chapter make plain, it is widely presumed that talent is a strong indication of what kind of work we should pursue. Those who prefer to do something that leaves an outstanding talent undeveloped can be accused of "burying their treasure" (in a common interpretation of a biblical passage, Matthew 25:14–30). Talents are given, in this common judgment, to be used. Even this set of arguments leaves some questions open, however. Must talents be used to provide income? Could a gifted pianist not enjoy playing for her family and friends in the same way that the man in Robert Frost's poem "Two Tramps in Mud Time" enjoys chopping his own firewood?

These eight readings, when taken together, challenge each of us to listen with care to and for those voices we believe to be trustworthy, within and beyond ourselves. They also challenge those in a position to advise others, as almost all of us are at one time or another, to do so with care, compassion, and close attention to the needs, gifts, and circumstances of those who entrust us with their yearning to lead significant and fulfilling lives. The narrator of "Sonny's Blues" struggles with just this challenge, as an older brother to whom Sonny has turned for help in spite of the brother's difficulty in understanding Sonny's life choices. And the stories set on the Minnesota farm and in the California household explore other dimensions of this challenge as it arises between parents and children, no matter their age.

To whom and to what should I listen?, then, suggests a parallel question: How should I speak? In the readings that follow, some of the characters speak abysmally, but a few acquit themselves very well indeed.

Will Weaver

THE UNDECLARED MAJOR

From the very beginning of this story, we are in the presence of a young person who is thinking deeply about what he will do as his life's work and what the implications of his choice will be. As Walter returns to the land, family, and community where he was raised, he wonders how much he still belongs there and whether the people among whom he grew up will accept him as he grows in new directions. This story portrays — explicitly and in more subtle ways — the ties Walter actually has to this community. Notice how Walter's own sense of these ties changes over the course of the story.

The concern of this chapter of *Leading Lives That Matter* — "To Whom and to What Should I Listen as I Decide What to Do for a Living?" — is one Walter has worried about, because he has gone against what he imagines is the advice of his family, friends, and acquaintances. Have you or others you know done something similar? Do you admire Walter's apparent refusal to heed the counsel of those who know him best? Is it necessary to refuse such advice in order to "become ourselves"? Or does the story challenge this way of putting the question?

Will Weaver, who grew up on a farm in northern Minnesota, taught English for many years in the same region, at Bemidji State University.

In his gloomy periods Walter Hansen saw himself as one large contradiction. He was still twenty, yet his reddish hair was in full retreat from the white plain of his forehead. He had small and quick-moving blue eyes, eyes that tended skyward, eyes that noted every airplane that passed overhead; his hands and feet were great, heavy shovels. As Walter shambled between his classes at the University of Minnesota in Minneapolis, he sometimes caught unexpected sight of himself in a tall glass doorway or window. He always stopped to stare: there he was, the big farm kid with a small handful

Will Weaver, "The Undeclared Major," in *A Gravestone Made of Wheat* (New York: Simon & Schuster, 1989), 169–75.

of books. Walter Hansen, the only twenty-year-old Undeclared Major on the whole campus.

But even that wasn't true. Walter Hansen had declared a major some time ago; he just hadn't felt up to telling anyone what it was.

At present Walter sat in the last, backward-facing seat of the Greyhound bus, reading *The Collected Stories of John Cheever.* Occasionally he looked up to stare at the blue-tinted fields, which in their passing pulled him, mile by mile, toward home. Toward his twenty-first birthday this very weekend.

By the third hour of the trip Walter had a headache from reading. He put away Cheever and began to watch the passing farms. It was a sunny, wet April in central Minnesota. Farmers were trying to spread manure. Their tractors left black ruts in the yellow corn stubble, and once Walter saw two tractors chained together straining, the big rear wheels spinning, throwing clods in the air, as they tried to pull free a third spreader sunk to its hubs beneath an overenthusiastic load of dung.

At the end of the fourth hour Walter's hometown came onto the horizon. It was low and scattered, and soon began to flash by in the windows of the slowing bus like a family slide show that was putting to sleep even the projector operator. A junkyard with a line of shining hubcaps nailed on the fence. A combination deer farm and aquarium with its stuffed black bear wearing a yellow hula skirt, and wheels that stood by the front door. Then the tall and narrow white wooden houses. The square red brick buildings of Main Street, where the bus sighed to a stop at the Shell station. Ducking his head, Walter clambered down the bus steps and stood squinting in the sunlight.

Main Street was three blocks long. Its two-story buildings were fronted with painted tin awnings or cedar shake shingles to disguise the brick and make the buildings look lower and more modern. At the end of Main Street was the taller, dull gray tower of the feed mill. A yellow drift of cornmeal lay on its roof. A blue wheel of pigeons turned overhead. At the stoplight a '57 Chevy chirped its tires, accelerated rapidly for half a block, then braked sharply to turn down Main Street.

Which Walter planned to avoid. On Main Street he would have to speak to people. They would ask him things.

"Walt — so how's the rat race?"

"Walt — where does a person park down there?"

"So Walt, what was it you're going into again? Business? Engineering? Veterinary?"

Carrying his small suitcase, and looking neither left nor right, Walter slipped undetected across Main Street. He walked two blocks to the railroad crossing where he set out east.

The iron rails shone blue. Between the rails, tiny agates glinted red from their bed of gravel, and the flat, sun-warmed railroad ties exhaled a faint breath of creosote. On Walter's right, a robin dug for worms on the sunny south embankment; on the north side, the dirty remnant of a snowbank leaked water downhill. Walter stopped to poke at the snowbank with a stick. Beneath a black crust and mud and leaves, the snow was freshly white and sparkling — but destined, of course, to join the muddy pond water below. Walter thought about that. About destiny. He stood with the chill on his face from the old snowbank and the sun warm on his neck and back. There was a poem buried somewhere in that snowbank. Walter waited, but the first line would not visit him. He walked on.

Walter was soon out of town and into woods and fields. Arms outstretched, suitcase balanced atop his head, he walked one rail for twenty-two ties, certainly a record of some sort. Crows called. A redheaded woodpecker flopped from east to west across the rails. The bird was ridiculously heavy for the length of its wings, a fact which made Walter think of Natural Science, Biology, Veterinary Medicine and other majors with names as solid and normal as fork handles.

Animal Husbandry.

Technical Illustration.

Mechanical Engineering.

Ahead on Walter's left was a twenty-acre field of new oat seeding, brown in the low spots, dusty chartreuse on the higher crowns of the field.

Plant Science.

He could tell people he was developing new wheat strains for Third World countries, like Norman Borlaug.

He walked on, slower now, for around a slight bend he could see, a half mile ahead, the gray dome of his father's silo and the red shine of the dairy barn. He neared the corner post of the west field, where his father's land began. Half the field was gray, the other half was freshly black. He slowed further. A meadowlark called from a fence post. Walter stopped to pitch a rock at the bird.

Then he heard a tractor. From behind a broad swell in the field rose his father's blue cap, tan face, brown shirt, then the red snout of the Massey-Ferguson. The Massey pulled their green four-row corn planter. His father stood upright on the platform of the tractor. He stood that way to sight down the tractor's nose, to keep its front tires on the line scuffed in the dirt by the corn planter's marker on the previous round. Intermittently Walter's father swiveled his neck for a glance back at the planter. He looked, Walter knew, for the flap of a white rag tied around the main shaft; if the white flag waved, the main shaft turned, the planter plates revolved, pink kernels fell — Walter knew all that stuff.

He stopped walking. There were bushes along the fencerow, and he stooped to lower his profile, certain that his father hadn't seen him. First Walter wanted to go home, talk to his mother, have a cup of coffee. Two cups, maybe. A cinnamon roll. A bowl of bing cherries in sauce, with cream. Maybe one more splash of coffee. Then. Then he'd come back to the field to speak with his father.

Nearing the field's end, his father trailed back his right arm, found the cord, which he pulled at the same moment as he turned hard to left. Brakes croaked. Tripped, the marker arms rose, the Massey came hard around with its front wheels reaching for their new track, the planter straightened behind, the right arm with its shining disk fell, and his father, back to Walter, headed downfield.

Except that brakes croaked again and the tractor came to a stop. His father turned to Walter and held up a hand.

Walter waved once. He looked briefly behind him to the rails that led back toward town, then crossed the ditch and swung his suitcase over the barbed wire.

His father shut off the tractor. "Hey, Walt — " his father called.

Walter waved again.

His father waited by the corn planter. He smiled, his teeth white against the tan skin, the dust. Walter came up to him.

"Walt," his father said.

They stood there grinning at each other. They didn't shake hands. Growing up, Walter believed people shook hands only in the movies or on used-car lots. None of his relatives ever shook hands. Their greeting was to stand and grin at each other and raise their eyebrows up and down. At the university Walter and his circle of friends shook hands coming and going, European style.

"How's it going?" Walter said, touching his boot to the corn planter.

"She's rolling," his father said. "Got one disk that keeps dragging, but other than that."

People in Walter's family often did not complete their sentences.

"A disk dragging," Walter said.

"Yep," his father said. He squinted at Walter, looked down at his clean clothes. "What would you do for a stuck disk?" he asked.

"I'd take out the grease zerk and run a piece of wire in there. That failing, I'd take off the whole disk and soak it in a pan of diesel fuel overnight," Walter said.

Father and son grinned at each other.

His father took off his hat. His forehead was white, his hair coppery.

"So how's the rat race, son?"

"Not so bad," Walter said.

His father paused a moment. "Any . . . decisions yet?" his father said.

Walter swallowed. He looked off toward town. "About . . . a major, you mean?" Walter said.

His father waited.

"Well," Walter said. His mouth went dry. He swallowed twice. "Well," he said, "I think I'm going to major in English."

His father pursed his lips. He pulled off his work gloves one finger at a time. "English," he said.

"English," Walter nodded.

His father squinted. "Son, we already know English."

Walter stared. "Well, yessir, that's true. I mean, I'm going to study literature. Books. See how they're written. Maybe write one of my own some day."

His father rubbed his brown neck and stared downfield.

Two white sea gulls floated low over the fresh planting.

"So what do you think?" Walter said.

His father's forehead wrinkled and he turned back to Walter. "What could a person be, I mean with that kind of major? An English major," his father said, testing the phrase on his tongue and his lips.

"Be," Walter said. He fell silent. "Well, I don't know, I could be a . . . writer. A teacher maybe, though I don't think I want to teach. At least not for a while. I could be . . ." Then Walter's mind went blank. As blank and empty as the fields around him.

His father was silent. The meadowlark called again.

"I would just be myself, I guess," Walter said.

His father stared a moment at Walter. "Yourself, only smarter," he added.

"Yessir," Walter said quickly, "that's it."

His father squinted downfield at the gulls, then back at Walter. "Nobody talked you into this?"

Walter shook his head no.

"You like it when you're doing it?" his father asked. He glanced across his own field, at what he had planted.

Walter nodded.

His father looked back to Walter and thought another moment. "You think you can make a living at it?"

"Somehow," Walter said.

His father shrugged. "Then I can't see any trouble with it myself," he said. He glanced away, across the fields to the next closest set of barns and silos. "Your uncles, your grampa, they're another story, I suppose."

"They wouldn't have to know," Walter said quickly.

His father looked back to Walter and narrowed his eyes. "They ask me, I'll tell them," he said.

Walter smiled at his father. He started to take a step closer, but at that moment his father looked up at the sun. "We better keep rolling here," he said. He tossed his gloves to Walter. "Take her around once or twice while I eat my sandwich."

Walter climbed onto the tractor and brought up the RPMs. In another minute he was headed downfield. He stood upright on the platform and held tightly to the wheel. The leather gloves were still warm and damp from his father's hands. He sighted the Massey's radiator cap on the thin line in the dirt ahead, and held it there. Halfway downfield he remembered to check the planter flag; in one backward glance he saw his father in straight brown silhouette against the chartreuse band of the fencerow bushes, saw the stripe of fresh dirt unrolling behind, the green seed canisters, and below, the white flag waving. He let out a breath.

After two rounds, Walter began to relax. He began to feel the warm thermals from the engine, the cool breath of the earth below. Gulls hovered close over the tractor, their heads cocked earthward as they waited for the disks to turn up yellow cutworms. A red agate passed underneath and was covered by dirt. The corn planter rolled behind, and through the trip rope, a cotton cord gone smoothly black from grease and dusty gloves, Walter felt the shafts turning, the disks wheeling, the kernels dropping, the press wheel tamping the seed into four perfect rows.

Well, not entirely perfect rows.

Walter, by round four, had begun to think of other things. That whiteness beneath the old snowbank. The blue shine of the iron rails. The damp warmth of his father's gloves. The heavy, chocolate-layer birthday cake that he knew, as certain as he knew the sun would set tonight and rise tomorrow, his mother had hidden in the pantry. Of being twenty-one and the limitless destiny, the endless prospects before him, Walter Hansen, English Major.

As he thought about these and other things, the tractor and its planter drifted a foot to the right, then a foot to the left, centered itself, then drifted again. At field's end his father stood up. He began to wave at Walter first with one hand, then both. But Walter drove on, downfield, smiling slightly to himself, puzzling over why it was he so seldom came home.

Amy Tan

TWO KINDS

The first-person narrative below describes a conflict that is at once generational and cultural. The mother who expends every effort to shape her
daughter's identity and to evoke her gifts is Chinese; the daughter, partly as
the result of her mother's actions, is becoming increasingly American. The
narrator is Jing-Mei Woo, one of the main characters in Amy Tan's novel
The Joy Luck Club. Like Tan herself, these characters were born in America
to parents who had emigrated from China, though each responds differently
to her cultural heritage and context.

For most of us, the most formative influences in our lives, shaping both
who we become and what we wind up doing to earn a living, are our parents.
What does the narrator learn in the course of her conflicts with her mother?
What does she hope for and expect from her mother? Are these hopes and
expectations reasonable? Typical or unusual? Moderate or excessive? The
narrator's most important lesson in the story is something she learns, only
after her mother's death, in the act of playing once again the piano that had
been the occasion and the scene of a formidable test of wills. What is that
lesson? What can it teach us about how to learn from our parents without
being crushed by their influence?

My mother believed you could be anything you wanted to be in America.
You could open a restaurant. You could work for the government and get
good retirement. You could buy a house with almost no money down. You
could become rich. You could become instantly famous.

"Of course you can be prodigy, too," my mother told me when I was nine.
"You can be best anything. What does Auntie Lindo know? Her daughter,
she is only best tricky."

America was where all my mother's hopes lay. She had come here in 1949
after losing everything in China: her mother and father, her family home,

From Amy Tan, *The Joy Luck Club* (New York: Putnam's Sons, 1989), 132–44.

her first husband, and two daughters, twin baby girls. But she never looked back with regret. There were so many ways for things to get better.

We didn't immediately pick the right kind of prodigy. At first my mother thought I could be a Chinese Shirley Temple. We'd watch Shirley's old movies on TV as though they were training films. My mother would poke my arm and say, *"Ni kan"* — You watch. And I would see Shirley tapping her feet, or singing a sailor song, or pursing her lips into a very round O while saying, "Oh my goodness."

"Ni kan," said my mother as Shirley's eyes flooded with tears. "You already know how. Don't need talent for crying!"

Soon after my mother got this idea about Shirley Temple, she took me to a beauty training school in the Mission district and put me in the hands of a student who could barely hold the scissors without shaking. Instead of getting big fat curls, I emerged with an uneven mass of crinkly black fuzz. My mother dragged me off to the bathroom and tried to wet down my hair.

"You look like Negro Chinese," she lamented, as if I had done this on purpose.

The instructor of the beauty training school had to lop off these soggy clumps to make my hair even again. "Peter Pan is very popular these days," the instructor assured my mother. I now had hair the length of a boy's, with straight-across bangs that hung at a slant two inches above my eyebrows. I liked the haircut and it made me actually look forward to my future fame.

In fact, in the beginning, I was just as excited as my mother, maybe even more so. I pictured this prodigy part of me as many different images, trying each one on for size. I was a dainty ballerina girl standing by the curtains, waiting to hear the right music that would send me floating on my tiptoes. I was like the Christ child lifted out of the straw manger, crying with holy indignity. I was Cinderella stepping from her pumpkin carriage with sparkly cartoon music filling the air.

In all of my imaginings, I was filled with a sense that I would soon become *perfect.* My mother and father would adore me. I would be beyond reproach. I would never feel the need to sulk for anything.

But sometimes the prodigy in me became impatient. "If you don't hurry up and get me out of here, I'm disappearing for good," it warned. "And then you'll always be nothing."

Every night after dinner, my mother and I would sit at the Formica kitchen table. She would present new tests, taking her examples from stories of amazing children she had read in *Ripley's Believe It or Not,* or *Good House-keeping, Reader's Digest,* and a dozen other magazines she kept in a pile in our bathroom. My mother got these magazines from people whose houses she cleaned. And since she cleaned many houses each week, we had a great assortment. She would look through them all, searching for stories about remarkable children.

The first night she brought out a story about a three-year-old boy who knew the capitals of all the states and even most of the European countries. A teacher was quoted as saying the little boy could also pronounce the names of the foreign cities correctly.

"What's the capital of Finland?" my mother asked me, looking at the magazine story.

All I knew was the capital of California, because Sacramento was the name of the street we lived on in Chinatown. "Nairobi!" I guessed, saying the most foreign word I could think of. She checked to see if that was possibly one way to pronounce "Helsinki" before showing me the answer.

The tests got harder — multiplying numbers in my head, finding the queen of hearts in a deck of cards, trying to stand on my head without using my hands, predicting the daily temperatures in Los Angeles, New York, and London.

One night I had to look at a page from the Bible for three minutes and then report everything I could remember. "Now Jehoshaphat had riches and honor in abundance and . . . that's all I remember, Ma," I said.

And after seeing my mother's disappointed face once again, something inside of me began to die. I hated the tests, the raised hopes and failed expectations. Before going to bed that night, I looked in the mirror above the bathroom sink and when I saw only my face staring back — and that it would always be this ordinary face — I began to cry. Such a sad, ugly girl! I made high-pitched noises like a crazed animal, trying to scratch out the face in the mirror.

And then I saw what seemed to be the prodigy side of me because I had never seen that face before. I looked at my reflection, blinking so I could see more clearly. The girl staring back at me was angry, powerful. This girl and I were the same. I had new thoughts, willful thoughts, or rather thoughts filled with lots of won'ts. I won't let her change me, I promised myself. I won't be what I'm not.

So now on nights when my mother presented her tests, I performed listlessly, my head propped on one arm. I pretended to be bored. And I was. I got so bored I started counting the bellows of the foghorns out on the bay while my mother drilled me in other areas. The sound was comforting and reminded me of the cow jumping over the moon. And the next day, I played a game with myself, seeing if my mother would give up on me before eight bellows. After a while I usually counted only one, maybe two bellows at most. At last she was beginning to give up hope.

Two or three months had gone by without any mention of my being a prodigy again. And then one day my mother was watching *The Ed Sullivan Show* on TV. The TV was old and the sound kept shorting out. Every time my mother got halfway up from the sofa to adjust the set, the sound would go back on and Ed would be talking. As soon as she sat down, Ed would go silent again. She got up, the TV broke into loud piano music. She sat down. Silence. Up and down, back and forth, quiet and loud. It was like a stiff embraceless dance between her and the TV set. Finally she stood by the set with her hand on the sound dial.

She seemed entranced by the music, a little frenzied piano piece with this mesmerizing quality, sort of quick passages and then teasing lilting ones before it returned to the quick playful parts.

"Ni kan," my mother said, calling me over with hurried hand gestures, "Look here."

I could see why my mother was fascinated by the music. It was being pounded out by a little Chinese girl, about nine years old, with a Peter Pan haircut. The girl had the sauciness of a Shirley Temple. She was proudly modest like a proper Chinese child. And she also did this fancy sweep of a curtsy, so that the fluffy skirt of her white dress cascaded slowly to the floor like the petals of a large carnation.

In spite of these warning signs, I wasn't worried. Our family had no piano and we couldn't afford to buy one, let alone reams of sheet music and piano lessons. So I could be generous in my comments when my mother bad-mouthed the little girl on TV.

"Play note right, but doesn't sound good! No singing sound," complained my mother.

"What are you picking on her for?" I said carelessly. "She's pretty good. Maybe she's not the best, but she's trying hard."

I knew almost immediately I would be sorry I said that.

"Just like you," she said. "Not the best. Because you not trying." She gave a little huff as she let go of the sound dial and sat down on the sofa.

The little Chinese girl sat down also to play an encore of "Anitra's Dance" by Grieg. I remember the song, because later on I had to learn how to play it.

Three days after watching *The Ed Sullivan Show,* my mother told me what my schedule would be for piano lessons and piano practice. She had talked to Mr. Chong, who lived on the first floor of our apartment building. Mr. Chong was a retired piano teacher and my mother had traded housecleaning services for weekly lessons and a piano for me to practice on every day, two hours a day, from four until six.

When my mother told me this, I felt as though I had been sent to hell. I whined and then kicked my foot a little when I couldn't stand it anymore.

"Why don't you like me the way I am? I'm *not* a genius! I can't play the piano. And even if I could, I wouldn't go on TV if you paid me a million dollars!" I cried.

My mother slapped me. "Who ask you be genius?" she shouted. "Only ask you be your best. For you sake. You think I want you be genius? Hnnh! What for! Who ask you!"

"So ungrateful," I heard her mutter in Chinese. "If she had as much talent as she has temper, she would be famous now."

Mr. Chong, whom I secretly nicknamed Old Chong, was very strange, always tapping his fingers to the silent music of an invisible orchestra. He looked ancient in my eyes. He had lost most of the hair on top of his head and he wore thick glasses and had eyes that always looked tired and sleepy. But he must have been younger than I thought, since he lived with his mother and was not yet married.

I met Old Lady Chong once and that was enough. She had this peculiar smell like a baby that had done something in its pants. And her fingers felt like a dead person's, like an old peach I once found in the back of the refrigerator; the skin just slid off the meat when I picked it up.

I soon found out why Old Chong had retired from teaching piano. He was deaf. "Like Beethoven!" he shouted to me. "We're both listening only in our head!" And he would start to conduct his frantic silent sonatas.

Our lessons went like this. He would open the book and point to different things, explaining their purpose: "Key! Treble! Bass! No sharps or flats! So this is C major! Listen now and play after me!"

And then he would play the C scale a few times, a simple chord, and then, as if inspired by an old, unreachable itch, he gradually added more notes and running trills and a pounding bass until the music was really something quite grand.

I would play after him, the simple scale, the simple chord, and then I just played some nonsense that sounded like a cat running up and down on top of garbage cans. Old Chong smiled and applauded and then said, "Very good! But now you must learn to keep time!"

So that's how I discovered that Old Chong's eyes were too slow to keep up with the wrong notes I was playing. He went through the motions in half-time. To help me keep rhythm, he stood behind me, pushing down on my right shoulder for every beat. He balanced pennies on top of my wrists so I would keep them still as I slowly played scales and arpeggios. He had me curve my hand around an apple and keep that shape when playing chords. He marched stiffly to show me how to make each finger dance up and down, staccato like an obedient little soldier.

He taught me all these things, and that was how I also learned I could be lazy and get away with mistakes, lots of mistakes. If I hit the wrong notes because I hadn't practiced enough, I never corrected myself. I just kept playing in rhythm. And Old Chong kept conducting his own private reverie.

So maybe I never really gave myself a fair chance. I did pick up the basics pretty quickly, and I might have become a good pianist at that young age. But I was so determined not to try, not to be anybody different that I learned to play only the most ear-splitting preludes, the most discordant hymns.

Over the next year, I practiced like this, dutifully in my own way. And then one day I heard my mother and her friend Lindo Jong both talking in a loud bragging tone of voice so others could hear. It was after church, and I was leaning against the brick wall wearing a dress with stiff white petticoats. Auntie Lindo's daughter, Waverly, who was about my age, was standing farther down the wall about five feet away. We had grown up together and shared all the closeness of two sisters squabbling over crayons and dolls. In other words, for the most part, we hated each other. I thought she was snotty. Waverly Jong had gained a certain amount of fame as "Chinatown's Littlest Chinese Chess Champion."

"She bring home too many trophy," lamented Auntie Lindo that Sunday. "All day she play chess. All day I have no time do nothing but dust off her winnings." She threw a scolding look at Waverly, who pretended not to see her.

"You lucky you don't have this problem," said Auntie Lindo with a sigh to my mother.

And my mother squared her shoulders and bragged: "Our problem worser than yours. If we ask Jing-mei wash dish, she hear nothing but music. It's like you can't stop this natural talent."

And right then, I was determined to put a stop to her foolish pride.

A few weeks later, Old Chong and my mother conspired to have me play in a talent show which would be held in the church hall. By then, my parents had saved up enough to buy me a secondhand piano, a black Wurlitzer spinet with a scarred bench. It was the showpiece of our living room.

For the talent show, I was to play a piece called "Pleading Child" from Schumann's *Scenes from Childhood*. It was a simple, moody piece that sounded more difficult than it was. I was supposed to memorize the whole thing, playing the repeat parts twice to make the piece sound longer. But I dawdled over it, playing a few bars and then cheating, looking up to see what notes followed. I never really listened to what I was playing. I daydreamed about being somewhere else, about being someone else.

The part I liked to practice best was the fancy curtsy: right foot out, touch the rose on the carpet with a pointed foot, sweep to the side, left leg bends, look up and smile.

My parents invited all the couples from the Joy Luck Club to witness my debut. Auntie Lindo and Uncle Tin were there. Waverly and her two older brothers had also come. The first two rows were filled with children both younger and older than I was. The littlest ones got to go first. They recited simple nursery rhymes, squawked out tunes on miniature violins, twirled Hula Hoops, pranced in pink ballet tutus, and when they bowed or curtsied, the audience would sigh in unison, "Awww," and then clap enthusiastically.

When my turn came, I was very confident. I remember my childish excitement. It was as if I knew, without a doubt, that the prodigy side of me really did exist. I had no fear whatsoever, no nervousness. I remember thinking to myself, This is it! This is it! I looked out over the audience, at my mother's blank face, my father's yawn, Auntie Lindo's stiff-lipped smile, Waverly's sulky expression. I had on a white dress layered with sheets of lace, and a pink bow in my Peter Pan haircut. As I sat down I envisioned people jumping to their feet and Ed Sullivan rushing up to introduce me to everyone on TV.

And I started to play. It was so beautiful. I was so caught up in how lovely I looked that at first I didn't worry how I would sound. So it was a surprise to me when I hit the first wrong note and I realized something didn't sound quite right. And then I hit another and another followed that. A chill started at the top of my head and began to trickle down. Yet I couldn't stop playing, as though my hands were bewitched. I kept thinking my fingers would adjust themselves back, like a train switching to the right track. I played this strange jumble through two repeats, the sour notes staying with me all the way to the end.

When I stood up, I discovered my legs were shaking. Maybe I had just been nervous and the audience, like Old Chong, had seen me go through the right motions and had not heard anything wrong at all. I swept my right foot out, went down on my knee, looked up and smiled. The room was quiet, except for Old Chong, who was beaming and shouting, "Bravo! Bravo! Well done!" But then I saw my mother's face, her stricken face. The audience clapped weakly, and as I walked back to my chair, with my whole face quivering as I tried not to cry, I heard a little boy whisper loudly to his mother, "That was awful," and the mother whispered back, "Well, she certainly tried."

And now I realized how many people were in the audience, the whole world it seemed. I was aware of eyes burning into my back. I felt the shame of my mother and father as they sat stiffly throughout the rest of the show.

We could have escaped during intermission. Pride and some strange sense of honor must have anchored my parents to their chairs. And so we watched it all: the eighteen-year-old boy with a fake mustache who did a magic show and juggled flaming hoops while riding a unicycle. The breasted girl with white makeup who sang from *Madama Butterfly* and got honorable mention. And the eleven-year-old boy who won first prize playing a tricky violin song that sounded like a busy bee.

After the show, the Hsus, the Jongs, and the St. Clairs from the Joy Luck Club came up to my mother and father.

"Lots of talented kids," Auntie Lindo said vaguely, smiling broadly.

"That was somethin' else," said my father, and I wondered if he was referring to me in a humorous way, or whether he even remembered what I had done.

Waverly looked at me and shrugged her shoulders. "You aren't a genius like me," she said matter-of-factly. And if I hadn't felt so bad, I would have pulled her braids and punched her stomach.

But my mother's expression was what devastated me: a quiet, blank look that said she had lost everything. I felt the same way, and it seemed as if everybody were now coming up, like gawkers at the scene of an accident, to see what parts were actually missing. When we got on the bus to go home, my father was humming the busy-bee tune and my mother was silent. I kept thinking she wanted to wait until we got home before shouting at me. But when my father unlocked the door to our apartment, my mother walked in and then went to the back, into the bedroom. No accusations. No blame. And in a way, I felt disappointed. I had been waiting for her to start shouting, so I could shout back and cry and blame her for all my misery.

I assumed my talent-show fiasco meant I never had to play the piano again. But two days later, after school, my mother came out of the kitchen and saw me watching TV.

"Four clock," she reminded me as if it were any other day. I was stunned, as though she were asking me to go through the talent-show torture again. I wedged myself more tightly in front of the TV.

"Turn off TV," she called from the kitchen five minutes later. I didn't budge. And then I decided. I didn't have to do what my mother said anymore. I wasn't her slave. This wasn't China. I had listened to her before and look what happened. She was the stupid one.

She came out from the kitchen and stood in the arched entryway of the living room. "Four clock," she said once again, louder.

"I'm not going to play anymore," I said nonchalantly. "Why should I? I'm not a genius."

She walked over and stood in front of the TV. I saw her chest was heaving up and down in an angry way.

"No!" I said, and I now felt stronger, as if my true self had finally emerged. So this was what had been inside me all along.

"No! I won't!" I screamed.

She yanked me by the arm, pulled me off the floor, snapped off the TV. She was frighteningly strong, half pulling, half carrying me toward the piano as I kicked the throw rugs under my feet. She lifted me up and onto the hard bench. I was sobbing by now, looking at her bitterly. Her chest was heaving even more and her mouth was open, smiling crazily as if she were pleased I was crying.

"You want me to be someone that I'm not," I sobbed. "I'll never be the kind of daughter you want me to be!"

"Only two kinds of daughters," she shouted in Chinese. "Those who are obedient and those who follow their own mind! Only one kind of daughter can live in this house. Obedient daughter!"

"Then I wish I wasn't your daughter. I wish you weren't my mother," I shouted. As I said these things I got scared. It felt like worms and toads and slimy things crawling out of my chest, but it also felt good, as if this awful side of me had surfaced, at last.

"Too late change this," said my mother shrilly.

And I could sense her anger rising to its breaking point. I wanted to see it spill over. And that's when I remembered the babies she had lost in China, the ones we never talked about.

"Then I wish I'd never been born!" I shouted. "I wish I were dead! Like them."

It was as if I had said the magic words. Alakazam! — and her face went blank, her mouth closed, her arms went slack, and she backed out of the room, stunned, as if she were blowing away like a small brown leaf, thin, brittle, lifeless.

It was not the only disappointment my mother felt in me. In the years that followed, I failed her so many times, each time asserting my own will, my right to fall short of expectations. I didn't get straight As. I didn't become class president. I didn't get into Stanford. I dropped out of college.

For unlike my mother, I did not believe I could be anything I wanted to be. I could only be me.

And for all those years, we never talked about the disaster at the recital or my terrible accusations afterward at the piano bench. All that remained unchecked, like a betrayal that was now unspeakable. So I never found a way to ask her why she had hoped for something so large that failure was inevitable.

And even worse, I never asked her what frightened me the most: Why had she given up hope?

For after our struggle at the piano, she never mentioned my playing again. The lessons stopped. The lid to the piano was closed, shutting out the dust, my misery, and her dreams.

So she surprised me. A few years ago, she offered to give me the piano, for my thirtieth birthday. I had not played in all those years. I saw the offer as a sign of forgiveness, a tremendous burden removed.

"Are you sure?" I asked shyly. "I mean, won't you and Dad miss it?"

"No, this your piano," she said firmly. "Always your piano. You only one can play."

"Well, I probably can't play anymore," I said. "It's been years."

"You pick up fast," said my mother, as if she knew this was certain. "You have natural talent. You could been genius if you want to."

"No I couldn't."

"You just not trying," said my mother. And she was neither angry nor sad. She said it as if to announce a fact that could never be disproved. "Take it," she said.

But I didn't at first. It was enough that she had offered it to me. And after that, every time I saw it in my parents' living room, standing in front of the bay windows, it made me feel proud, as if it were a shiny trophy I had won back.

Last week I sent a tuner over to my parents' apartment and had the piano reconditioned, for purely sentimental reasons. My mother had died a few months before and I had been getting things in order for my father, a little bit at a time. I put the jewelry in special silk pouches. The sweaters she had knitted in yellow, pink, bright orange — all the colors I hated — I put those in moth-proof boxes. I found some old Chinese silk dresses, the kind with little slits up the sides. I rubbed the old silk against my skin, then wrapped them in tissue and decided to take them home with me.

After I had the piano tuned, I opened the lid and touched the keys. It sounded even richer than I remembered. Really, it was a very good piano. Inside the bench were the same exercise notes with handwritten scales, the same secondhand music books with their covers held together with yellow tape.

I opened up the Schumann book to the dark little piece I had played at the recital. It was on the left-hand side of the page, "Pleading Child." It looked more difficult than I remembered. I played a few bars, surprised at how easily the notes came back to me.

And for the first time, or so it seemed, I noticed the piece on the right-hand side. It was called "Perfectly Contented." I tried to play this one as well. It had a lighter melody but the same flowing rhythm and turned out to be quite easy. "Pleading Child" was shorter but slower; "Perfectly Contented" was longer, but faster. And after I played them both a few times, I realized they were two halves of the same song

Tayeb Salih

A HANDFUL OF DATES

Tayeb Salih (1929–2009) was one of the most distinguished writers in Arabic of the last century. Born in Sudan and educated there and in England, he spent most of his working life in London as a novelist, a broadcaster, and a columnist for the London-based Arabic-language newspaper *al Majalla*. During the last ten years of his life, he worked in Paris for UNESCO, serving as its representative in the Arab States of the Persian Gulf. The short story included here, "A Handful of Dates," was first published in 1964, two years before the publication of the novel for which he is best known, *Season of Migration to the North*.

The story features an older narrator remembering what it was like to begin forming his own judgments about other people and puzzling situations. To whom does he finally listen in his efforts to understand and judge his neighbor Masood and the situation in which Masood finds himself? His grandfather? The sacred book of his Muslim faith, the Koran, especially the chapter he is asked to recite? His own impressions, feelings, and intuitions? Are his feelings toward his grandfather and Masood warranted or unwarranted in the end? And what is the narrator's view of his own maturation at the end of the story? What is the significance of what befalls the handful of dates in the last surprising dramatic action of the narrative?

The boy's community expresses its benediction upon him both for his devotion to his grandfather and for his devotion to the Koran. Are these two influences on his young life equally worthy of obedience? Is it clear which source of authority — familial, religious, individual — is most worthy of regard in the world of this story, or is the story, like most of Salih's writings, ambiguous about this matter? Is one source of wisdom always the most trustworthy, or does trustworthiness depend upon context?

Tayeb Salih, "A Handful of Dates," in *Under African Skies: Modern African Stories*, ed. Charles R. Larson, trans. Denys Johnson Davies (New York: Farrar, Straus & Giroux, 1997), 86–90.

I must have been very young at the time. While I don't remember exactly how old I was, I do remember that when people saw me with my grandfather they would pat me on the head and give my cheek a pinch — things they didn't do to my grandfather. The strange thing was that I never used to go out with my father, rather it was my grandfather who would take me with him wherever he went, except for the mornings, when I would go to the mosque to learn the Koran. The mosque, the river, and the fields — these were the landmarks in our life. While most of the children of my age grumbled at having to go to the mosque to learn the Koran, I used to love it. The reason was, no doubt, that I was quick at learning by heart and the Sheikh always asked me to stand up and recite the *Chapter of the Merciful* whenever we had visitors, who would pat me on my head and cheek just as people did when they saw me with my grandfather.

Yes, I used to love the mosque, and I loved the river, too. Directly we finished our Koran reading in the morning I would throw down my wooden slate and dart off, quick as a genie, to my mother, hurriedly swallow down my breakfast, and run off for a plunge in the river. When tired of swimming about, I would sit on the bank and gaze at the strip of water that wound away eastwards, and hid behind a thick wood of acacia trees. I loved to give rein to my imagination and picture to myself a tribe of giants living behind that wood, a people tall and thin with white beards and sharp noses, like my grandfather. Before my grandfather ever replied to my many questions he would rub the tip of his nose with his forefinger; as for his beard, it was soft and luxuriant and as white as cotton wool — never in my life have I seen anything of a purer whiteness or greater beauty. My grandfather must also have been extremely tall, for I never saw anyone in the whole area address him without having to look up at him, nor did I see him enter a house without having to bend so low that I was put in mind of the way the river wound round behind the wood of acacia trees. I loved him and would imagine myself, when I grew to be a man, tall and slender like him, walking along with great strides.

I believe I was his favorite grandchild: no wonder, for my cousins were a stupid bunch and I — so they say — was an intelligent child. I used to know when my grandfather wanted me to laugh, when to be silent; also I would remember the times for his prayers and would bring him his prayer rug and fill the ewer for his ablutions without his having to ask me. When he had nothing else to do he enjoyed listening to me reciting to him from the Koran in a lilting voice, and I could tell from his face that he was moved.

One day I asked him about our neighbor Masood. I said to my grandfather: "I fancy you don't like our neighbor Masood?"

To which he answered, having rubbed the tip of his nose: "He's an indolent man and I don't like such people."

I said to him: "What's an indolent man?"

My grandfather lowered his head for a moment; then, looking across at the wide expanse of field, he said: "Do you see it stretching out from the edge of the desert up to the Nile bank? A hundred *feddans*. Do you see all those date palms? And those trees — *sant*, acacia, and *sayal*? All this fell into Masood's lap, was inherited by him from his father."

Taking advantage of the silence that had descended on my grandfather, I turned my gaze from him to the vast area defined by his words. "I don't care," I told myself, "who owns those date palms, those trees or this black cracked earth — all I know is that it's the arena for my dreams and my playground."

My grandfather then continued: "Yes, my boy, forty years ago all this belonged to Masood — two-thirds of it is now mine."

This was news to me, for I had imagined that the land had belonged to my grandfather ever since God's Creation.

"I didn't own a single *feddan* when I first set foot in this village. Masood was then the owner of all these riches. The position has changed now, though, and I think that before Allah calls me to Him I shall have bought the remaining third as well."

I do not know why it was I felt fear at my grandfather's words — and pity for our neighbor Masood. How I wished my grandfather wouldn't do what he'd said! I remembered Masood's singing, his beautiful voice and powerful laugh that resembled the gurgling of water. My grandfather never laughed.

I asked my grandfather why Masood had sold his land.

"Women," and from the way my grandfather pronounced the word I felt that "women" was something terrible. "Masood, my boy, was a much-married man. Each time he married he sold me a *feddan* or two." I made the quick calculation that Masood must have married some ninety women. Then I remembered his three wives, his shabby appearance, his lame donkey and its dilapidated saddle, his *galabia* with the torn sleeves. I had all but rid my mind of the thoughts that jostled in it when I saw the man approaching us, and my grandfather and I exchanged glances.

"We'll be harvesting the dates today," said Masood. "Don't you want to be there?"

I felt, though, that he did not really want my grandfather to attend. My grandfather, however, jumped to his feet and I saw that his eyes sparkled momentarily with an intense brightness. He pulled me by the hand and we went off to the harvesting of Masood's dates.

Someone brought my grandfather a stool covered with an oxhide, while I remained standing. There were a vast number of people there, but though I knew them all, I found myself for some reason watching Masood: aloof from that great gathering of people he stood as though it were no concern of his, despite the fact that the date palms to be harvested were his own. Sometimes his attention would be caught by the sound of a huge clump of dates crashing down from on high. Once he shouted up at the boy perched on the very summit of the date palm who had begun hacking at a clump with his long, sharp sickle: "Be careful you don't cut the heart of the palm."

No one paid any attention to what he said and the boy seated at the very summit of the date palm continued, quickly and energetically, to work away at the branch with his sickle till the clump of dates began to drop like something descending from the heavens.

I, however, had begun to think about Masood's phrase "the heart of the palm." I pictured the palm tree as something with feeling, something possessed of a heart that throbbed. I remembered Masood's remark to me when he had once seen me playing with the branch of a young palm tree: "Palm trees, my boy, like humans, experience joy and suffering." And I had felt an inward and unreasoned embarrassment.

When I again looked at the expanse of ground stretching before me I saw my young companions swarming like ants around the trunks of the palm trees, gathering up dates and eating most of them. The dates were collected into high mounds. I saw people coming along and weighing them into measuring bins and pouring them into sacks, of which I counted thirty. The crowd of people broke up, except for Hussein the merchant, Mousa the owner of the field next to ours on the east, and two men I'd never seen before.

I heard a low whistling sound and saw that my grandfather had fallen asleep. Then I noticed that Masood had not changed his stance, except that he had placed a stalk in his mouth and was munching at it like someone sated with food who doesn't know what to do with the mouthful he still has.

Suddenly my grandfather woke up, jumped to his feet, and walked toward the sacks of dates. He was followed by Hussein the merchant, Mousa the owner of the field next to ours, and the two strangers. I glanced at Masood and saw that he was making his way toward us with extreme slowness, like a man who wants to retreat but whose feet insist on going forward. They formed a circle around the sacks of dates and began examining them, some taking a date or two to eat. My grandfather gave me a fistful, which I began munching. I saw Masood filling the palms of both hands with dates and bringing them up close to his nose, then returning them.

Then I saw them dividing up the sacks between them. Hussein the merchant took ten; each of the strangers took five. Mousa the owner of the field next to ours on the eastern side took five, and my grandfather took five. Understanding nothing, I looked at Masood and saw that his eyes were darting to the left and right like two mice that have lost their way home.

"You're still fifty pounds in debt to me," said my grandfather to Masood. "We'll talk about it later."

Hussein called his assistants and they brought along donkeys, the two strangers produced camels, and the sacks of dates were loaded onto them. One of the donkeys let out a braying which set the camels frothing at the mouth and complaining noisily. I felt myself drawing close to Masood, felt my hand stretch out toward him as though I wanted to touch the hem of his garment. I heard him make a noise in his throat like the rasping of a lamb being slaughtered. For some unknown reason, I experienced a sharp sensation of pain in my chest.

I ran off into the distance. Hearing my grandfather call after me, I hesitated a little, then continued on my way. I felt at that moment that I hated him. Quickening my pace, it was as though I carried within me a secret I wanted to rid myself of. I reached the riverbank near the bend it made behind the wood of acacia trees. Then, without knowing why, I put my finger into my throat and spewed up the dates I'd eaten.

Lois Lowry

THE GIVER

The Giver, which falls into the category known as "young adult fiction," is popular among middle schoolers and older adults alike, for it probes ethical issues of enduring interest. It is set in a seemingly utopian, futuristic world organized in ways that are meant to remove pain and conflict from everyday life. Yet there are evidently a few cracks in the system; Jonas, the novel's protagonist, has begun to notice unusual things and to have some questions about the society in which he lives.

This selection describes an annual community ceremony in which young people are assigned to the work the adults believe will be most fitting for them. Clearly, the process leading up to this ceremony is proof that the adults have paid careful attention to the gifts of each child in the community as well as to the community's need for certain kinds of work to be done. Does this ceremony therefore embody Frederick Buechner's definition of vocation as the place where "the world's deep hunger" and a person's "deep gladness" meet (see p. 181 above)? And in what ways does the Assignments ceremony fulfill Russell Muirhead's proposal that everyone should have "fitting" work (see pp. 195–98 above)? How might Buechner and Muirhead criticize this fictional community's process of assigning individuals to specific occupations?

Chapter Seven

Now Jonas's group had taken a new place in the Auditorium, trading with the new Elevens, so that they sat in the very front, immediately before the stage.

They were arranged by their original numbers, the numbers they had been given at birth. The numbers were rarely used after the Naming. But each child knew his number, of course. Sometimes parents used them in irritation at a child's misbehavior, indicating that mischief made one unworthy

From Lois Lowry, *The Giver* (New York: Dell Laurel-Leaf, 1993), 50–64.

of a name. Jonas always chuckled when he heard a parent, exasperated, call sharply to a whining toddler, "That's *enough,* Twenty-three!"

Jonas was Nineteen. He had been the nineteenth new child born his year. It had meant that at his Naming, he had been already standing and bright-eyed, soon to walk and talk. It had given him a slight advantage the first year or two, a little more maturity than many of his groupmates who had been born in the later months of that year. But it evened out, as it always did, by Three.

After Three, the children progressed at much the same level, though by their first number one could always tell who was a few months older than others in his group. Technically, Jonas's full number was Eleven-nineteen, since there were other Nineteens, of course, in each age group. And today, now that the new Elevens had been advanced this morning, there were *two* Eleven-nineteens. At the midday break he had exchanged smiles with the new one, a shy female named Harriet.

But the duplication was only for these few hours. Very soon he would not be an Eleven but a Twelve, and age would no longer matter. He would be an adult, like his parents, though a new one and untrained still.

Asher was Four, and sat now in the row ahead of Jonas. He would receive his Assignment fourth.

Fiona, Eighteen, was on his left; on his other side sat Twenty, a male named Pierre whom Jonas didn't like much. Pierre was very serious, not much fun, and a worrier and tattletale, too. "Have you checked the rules, Jonas?" Pierre was always whispering solemnly. "I'm not sure that's within the rules." Usually it was some foolish thing that no one cared about — opening his tunic if it was a day with a breeze; taking a brief try on a friend's bicycle, just to experience the different feel of it.

The initial speech at the Ceremony of Twelve was made by the Chief Elder, the leader of the community who was elected every ten years. The speech was much the same each year: recollection of the time of childhood and the period of preparation, the coming responsibilities of adult life, the profound importance of Assignment, the seriousness of training to come.

Then the Chief Elder moved ahead in her speech.

"This is the time," she began, looking directly at them, "when we acknowledge differences. You Elevens have spent all your years till now learning to fit in, to standardize your behavior, to curb any impulse that might set you apart from the group.

"But today we honor your differences. They have determined your futures."

She began to describe this year's group and its variety of personalities, though she singled no one out by name. She mentioned that there was one who had singular skills at caretaking, another who loved newchildren, one with unusual scientific aptitude, and a fourth for whom physical labor was an obvious pleasure. Jonas shifted in his seat, trying to recognize each reference as one of his groupmates. The caretaking skills were no doubt those of Fiona, on his left; he remembered noticing the tenderness with which she had bathed the Old. Probably the one with scientific aptitude was Benjamin, the male who had devised new, important equipment for the Rehabilitation Center.

He heard nothing that he recognized as himself, Jonas.

Finally the Chief Elder paid tribute to the hard work of her committee, which had performed the observations so meticulously all year. The Committee of Elders stood and was acknowledged by applause. Jonas noticed Asher yawn slightly covering his mouth politely with his hand.

Then, at last, the Chief Elder called number One to the stage, and the Assignments began.

Each announcement was lengthy, accompanied by a speech directed at the new Twelve. Jonas tried to pay attention as One, smiling happily, received her Assignment as Fish Hatchery Attendant along with words of praise for her childhood spent doing many volunteer hours there, and her obvious interest in the important process of providing nourishment for the community.

Number One — her name was Madeline — returned, finally, amidst applause, to her seat, wearing the new badge that designated her Fish Hatchery Attendant. Jonas was certainly glad that *that* Assignment was taken; he wouldn't have wanted it. But he gave Madeline a smile of congratulation.

When Two, a female named Inger, received her Assignment as Birthmother, Jonas remembered that his mother had called it a job without honor. But he thought that the Committee had chosen well. Inger was a nice girl though somewhat lazy, and her body was strong. She would enjoy the three years of being pampered that would follow her brief training; she would give birth easily and well; and the task of Laborer that would follow would use her strength, keep her healthy, and impose self-discipline. Inger was smiling when she resumed her seat. Birthmother was an important job, if lacking in prestige.

Jonas noticed that Asher looked nervous. He kept turning his head and glancing back at Jonas until the group leader had to give him a silent chastisement, a motion to sit still and face forward.

Three, Isaac, was given an Assignment as Instructor of Sixes, which obviously pleased him and was well deserved. Now there were three Assignments gone, none of them ones that Jonas would have liked — not that he could have been a Birthmother, anyway, he realized with amusement. He tried to sort through the list in his mind, the possible Assignments that remained. But there were so many he gave it up; and anyway, now it was Asher's turn. He paid strict attention as his friend went to the stage and stood self-consciously beside the Chief Elder.

"All of us in the community know and enjoy Asher," the Chief Elder began. Asher grinned and scratched one leg with the other foot. The audience chuckled softly.

"When the committee began to consider Asher's Assignment," she went on, "there were some possibilities that were immediately discarded. Some that would clearly not have been right for Asher.

"For example," she said, smiling, "we did not consider for an instant designating Asher an Instructor of Threes."

The audience howled with laughter. Asher laughed, too, looking sheepish but pleased at the special attention. The Instructors of Threes were in charge of the acquisition of correct language.

"In fact," the Chief Elder continued, chuckling a little herself, "we even gave a little thought to some retroactive chastisement for the one who had been *Asher's* Instructor of Threes so long ago. At the meeting where Asher was discussed, we retold many of the stories that we all remembered from his days of language acquisition.

"Especially," she said, chuckling, "the difference between snack and smack. Remember, Asher?"

Asher nodded ruefully, and the audience laughed aloud. Jonas did, too. He remembered, though he had been only a Three at the time himself.

The punishment used for small children was a regulated system of smacks with the discipline wand: a thin, flexible weapon that stung painfully when it was wielded. The Childcare specialists were trained very carefully in the discipline methods: a quick smack across the hands for a bit of minor misbehavior; three sharper smacks on the bare legs for a second offense.

Poor Asher, who always talked too fast and mixed up words, even as a toddler. As a Three, eager for his juice and crackers at snacktime, he one day said "smack" instead of "snack" as he stood waiting in line for the morning treat.

Jonas remembered it clearly. He could still see little Asher, wiggling with impatience in the line. He remembered the cheerful voice calling out, "I want my smack!"

The other Threes, including Jonas, had laughed nervously. "Snack!" they

261

corrected. "You meant snack, Asher!" But the mistake had been made. And precision of language was one of the most important tasks of small children. Asher had asked for a smack.

The discipline wand, in the hand of the Childcare worker, whistled as it came down across Asher's hands. Asher whimpered, cringed, and corrected himself instantly. "Snack," he whispered.

But the next morning he had done it again. And again the following week. He couldn't seem to stop, though for each lapse the discipline wand came again, escalating to a series of painful lashes that left marks on Asher's legs. Eventually, for a period of time, Asher stopped talking altogether, when he was a Three.

"For a while," the Chief Elder said, relating the story, "we had a silent Asher! But he learned."

She turned to him with a smile. "When he began to talk again, it was with greater precision. And now his lapses are very few. His corrections and apologies are very prompt. And his good humor is unfailing." The audience murmured in agreement. Asher's cheerful disposition was well known throughout the community.

"Asher." She lifted her voice to make the official announcement. "We have given you the Assignment of Assistant Director of Recreation."

She clipped on his new badge as he stood beside her, beaming. Then he turned and left the stage as the audience cheered. When he had taken his seat again, the Chief Elder looked down at him and said the words that she had said now four times, and would say to each new Twelve. Somehow she gave it special meaning for each of them.

"Asher," she said, "thank you for your childhood."

The Assignments continued, and Jonas watched and listened, relieved now by the wonderful Assignment his best friend had been given. But he was more and more apprehensive as his own approached. Now the new Twelves in the row ahead had all received their badges. They were fingering them as they sat, and Jonas knew that each one was thinking about the training that lay ahead. For some — one studious male had been selected as Doctor, a female as Engineer, and another for Law and Justice — it would be years of hard work and study. Others, like Laborers and Birthmothers, would have a much shorter training period.

Eighteen, Fiona, on his left, was called. Jonas knew she must be nervous; but Fiona was a calm female. She had been sitting quietly, serenely, throughout the Ceremony.

Even the applause, though enthusiastic, seemed serene when Fiona was given the important Assignment of Caretaker of the Old. It was perfect for such a sensitive, gentle girl, and her smile was satisfied and pleased when she took her seat beside him again.

Jonas prepared himself to walk to the stage when the applause ended and the Chief Elder picked up the next folder and looked down to the group to call forward the next new Twelve. He was calm now that his turn had come. He took a deep breath and smoothed his hair with his hand.

"Twenty," he heard her voice say clearly. "Pierre." *She skipped me,* Jonas thought, stunned. Had he heard wrong? No. There was a sudden hush in the crowd, and he knew that the entire community realized that the Chief Elder had moved from Eighteen to Twenty, leaving a gap. On his right, Pierre, with a startled look, rose from his seat and moved to the stage.

A mistake. She made a mistake. But Jonas knew, even as he had the thought, that she hadn't. The Chief Elder made no mistakes. Not at the Ceremony of Twelve.

He felt dizzy, and couldn't focus his attention. He didn't hear what Assignment Pierre received, and was only dimly aware of the applause as the boy returned, wearing his new badge. Then: Twenty-one. Twenty-two.

The numbers continued in order. Jonas sat, dazed, as they moved into the Thirties and then the Forties, nearing the end. Each time, at each announcement, his heart jumped for a moment, and he thought wild thoughts. Perhaps now she would call his name. Could he have forgotten his own number? No. He had always been Nineteen. He was sitting in the seat marked Nineteen.

But she had *skipped* him. He saw the others in his group glance at him, embarrassed, and then avert their eyes quickly. He saw a worried look on the face of his group leader.

He hunched his shoulders and tried to make himself smaller in the seat. He wanted to disappear, to fade away, not to exist. He didn't dare to turn and find his parents in the crowd. He couldn't bear to see their faces darkened with shame.

Jonas bowed his head and searched through his mind. *What had he done wrong?*

Chapter Eight

The audience was clearly ill at ease. They applauded at the final Assignment; but the applause was piecemeal, no longer a crescendo of united enthusiasm. There were murmurs of confusion.

Jonas moved his hands together, clapping, but it was an automatic, meaningless gesture that he wasn't even aware of. His mind had shut out all of the earlier emotions: the anticipation, excitement, pride, and even the happy kinship with his friends. Now he felt only humiliation and terror.

The Chief Elder waited until the uneasy applause subsided. Then she spoke again.

"I know," she said in her vibrant, gracious voice, "that you are all concerned. That you feel I have made a mistake."

She smiled. The community, relieved from its discomfort very slightly by her benign statement, seemed to breathe more easily. It was very silent.

Jonas looked up.

"I have caused you anxiety," she said. "I apologize to my community." Her voice flowed over the assembled crowd.

"We accept your apology," they all uttered together.

"Jonas," she said, looking down at him, "I apologize to you in particular. I caused you anguish."

"I accept your apology," Jonas replied shakily.

"Please come to the stage now."

Earlier that day, dressing in his own dwelling, he had practiced the kind of jaunty, self-assured walk that he hoped he could make to the stage when his turn came. All of that was forgotten now. He simply willed himself to stand, to move his feet that felt weighted and clumsy, to go forward, up the steps and across the platform until he stood at her side.

Reassuringly she placed her arm across his tense shoulders.

"Jonas has not been assigned," she informed the crowd, and his heart sank.

Then she went on. "Jonas has been *selected*."

He blinked. What did that mean? He felt a collective, questioning stir from the audience. They, too, were puzzled.

In a firm, commanding voice she announced, "Jonas has been selected to be our next Receiver of Memory."

Then he heard the gasp — the sudden intake of breath, drawn sharply in astonishment, by each of the seated citizens. He saw their faces; the eyes widened in awe.

And still he did not understand.

"Such a selection is very, very rare," the Chief Elder told the audience. "Our community has only one Receiver. It is he who trains his successor.

"We have had our current Receiver for a very long time," she went on. Jonas followed her eyes and saw that she was looking at one of the Elders. The

264

Committee of Elders was sitting together in a group; and the Chief Elder's eyes were now on one who sat in the midst but seemed oddly separate from them. It was a man Jonas had never noticed before, a bearded man with pale eyes. He was watching Jonas intently.

"We failed in our last selection," the Chief Elder said solemnly. "It was ten years ago, when Jonas was just a toddler. I will not dwell on the experience because it causes us all terrible discomfort."

Jonas didn't know what she was referring to, but he could sense the discomfort of the audience. They shifted uneasily in their seats.

"We have not been hasty this time," she continued. "We could not afford another failure."

"Sometimes," she went on, speaking now in a lighter tone, relaxing the tension in the Auditorium, "we are not entirely certain about the Assignments, even after the most painstaking observations. Sometimes we worry that the one assigned might not develop, through training, every attribute necessary. Elevens are still children, after all. What we observe as playfulness and patience — the requirements to become Nurturer — could, with maturity, be revealed as simply foolishness and indolence. So we continue to observe during training, and to modify behavior when necessary.

"But the Receiver-in-training cannot be observed, cannot be modified. That is stated quite clearly in the rules. He is to be alone, apart, while he is prepared by the current Receiver for the job which is the most honored in our community."

Alone? Apart? Jonas listened with increasing unease.

"Therefore the selection must be sound. It must be a unanimous choice of the Committee. They can have no doubts, however fleeting. If, during the process, an Elder reports a dream of uncertainty, that dream has the power to set a candidate aside instantly.

"Jonas was identified as a possible Receiver many years ago. We have observed him meticulously. There were no dreams of uncertainty.

"He has shown all of the qualities that a Receiver must have."

With her hand still firmly on his shoulder, the Chief Elder listed the qualities.

"*Intelligence,*" she said. "We are all aware that Jonas has been a top student throughout his school days.

"*Integrity,*" she said next. "Jonas has, like all of us, committed minor transgressions." She smiled at him. "We expect that. We hoped, also, that he would present himself promptly for chastisement, and he has always done so.

"*Courage,*" she went on. "Only one of us here today has ever undergone the rigorous training required of a Receiver. He, of course, is the most important member of the Committee: the current Receiver. It was he who reminded us, again and again, of the courage required.

"Jonas," she said, turning to him, but speaking in a voice that the entire community could hear, "the training required of you involves pain. Physical pain."

He felt fear flutter within him.

"You have never experienced that. Yes, you have scraped your knees in falls from your bicycle. Yes, you crushed your finger in a door last year."

Jonas nodded, agreeing, as he recalled the incident, and its accompanying misery.

"But you will be faced, now," she explained gently, "with pain of a magnitude that none of us here can comprehend because it is beyond our experience. The Receiver himself was not able to describe it, only to remind us that you would be faced with it, that you would need immense courage. We cannot prepare you for that.

"But we feel certain that you are brave," she said to him.

He did not feel brave at all. Not now.

"The fourth essential attribute," the Chief Elder said, "is *wisdom*. Jonas has not yet acquired that. The acquisition of wisdom will come through his training.

"We are convinced that Jonas has the ability to acquire wisdom. That is what we looked for.

"Finally, The Receiver must have one more quality, and it is one which I can only name, but not describe. I do not understand it. You members of the community will not understand it, either. Perhaps Jonas will, because the current Receiver has told us that Jonas already has this quality. He calls it the Capacity to See Beyond."

The Chief Elder looked at Jonas with a question in her eyes. The audience watched him, too. They were silent.

For a moment he froze, consumed with despair. He *didn't* have it, the whatever-she-had-said. He didn't know what it was. Now was the moment when he would have to confess, to say, "No, I don't. I *can't*," and throw himself on their mercy, ask their forgiveness, to explain that he had been wrongly chosen, that he was not the right one at all.

But when he looked out across the crowd, the sea of faces, the thing happened again. The thing that had happened with the apple.

They *changed*.

He blinked, and it was gone. His shoulders straightened slightly. Briefly he felt a tiny sliver of sureness for the first time.

She was still watching him. They all were.

"I think it's true," he told the Chief Elder and the community. "I don't understand it yet. I don't know what it is. But sometimes I see something. And maybe it's beyond."

She took her arm from his shoulders.

"Jonas," she said, speaking not to him alone but to the entire community of which he was a part, "you will be trained to be our next Receiver of Memory. We thank you for your childhood."

Then she turned and left the stage, left him there alone, standing and facing the crowd, which began spontaneously the collective murmur of his name.

"Jonas." It was a whisper at first: hushed, barely audible. "Jonas. Jonas."

Then louder, faster. "JONAS. JONAS. JONAS."

With the chant, Jonas knew, the community was accepting him and his new role, giving him life, the way they had given it to the newchild Caleb. His heart swelled with gratitude and pride.

But at the same time he was filled with fear. He did not know what his selection meant. He did not know what he was to become.

Or what would become of him.

Willa Cather

THE ANCIENT PEOPLE

The novel from which this selection comes tells the story of Thea Kronborg, a woman born in a small town in the desert West who eventually goes on to a luminous international career as an opera singer. As this section of the novel begins, Thea is at a low point, having failed to attain the success of which she had dreamed. At a friend's suggestion, she goes on what we might today call a retreat, placing herself in a situation that allows her to view herself, the world, and her future in a different way. What are the sources of the renewed strength and confidence that Thea gradually attains? What does the place to which she has come for respite enable her to recover in herself and to understand about her own art?

These four chapters of *The Song of the Lark,* by the American novelist Willa Cather (1873–1947), belong to a section of the novel entitled "The Ancient People."

I

The San Francisco Mountain lies in Northern Arizona, above Flagstaff, and its blue slopes and snowy summit entice the eye for a hundred miles across the desert. About its base lie the pine forests of the Navajos, where the great red-trunked trees live out their peaceful centuries in that sparkling air. The *piñons* and scrub begin only where the forest ends, where the country breaks into open, stony clearings and the surface of the earth cracks into deep canyons. The great pines stand at a considerable distance from each other. Each tree grows alone, murmurs alone, thinks alone. They do not intrude upon each other. The Navajos are not much in the habit of giving or of asking help. Their language is not a communicative one, and they never attempt an interchange of personality in speech. Over their forests there is the same inexorable reserve. Each tree has its exalted power to bear.

....

From Willa Cather, *The Song of the Lark* (Boston: Houghton Mifflin, 1915), 295–308.

That was the first thing Thea Kronborg felt about the forest, as she drove through it one May morning in Henry Biltmer's democrat wagon — and it was the first great forest she had ever seen. She had got off the train at Flagstaff that morning, rolled off into the high, chill air when all the pines on the mountain were fired by sunrise, so that she seemed to fall from sleep directly into the forest.

Old Biltmer followed a faint wagon trail which ran southeast, and which, as they traveled, continually dipped lower, falling away from the high plateau on the slope of which Flagstaff sits. The white peak of the mountain, the snow gorges above the timber, now disappeared from time to time as the road dropped and dropped, and the forest closed behind the wagon. More than the mountain disappeared as the forest closed thus. Thea seemed to be taking very little through the wood with her. The personality of which she was so tired seemed to let go of her. The high, sparkling air drank it up like blotting-paper. It was lost in the thrilling blue of the new sky and the song of the thin wind in the *piñons*. The old, fretted lines which marked one off, which defined her, — made her Thea Kronborg, Bowers's accompanist, a soprano with a faulty middle voice, — were all erased.

So far she had failed. Her two years in Chicago had not resulted in anything. She had failed with Harsanyi, and she had made no great progress with her voice. She had come to believe that whatever Bowers had taught her was of secondary importance, and that in the essential things she had made no advance. Her student life closed behind her, like the forest, and she doubted whether she could go back to it if she tried. Probably she would teach music in little country towns all her life. Failure was not so tragic as she would have supposed; she was tired enough not to care.

She was getting back to the earliest sources of gladness that she could remember. She had loved the sun, and the brilliant solitudes of sand and sun, long before these other things had come along to fasten themselves upon her and torment her. That night, when she clambered into her big German feather bed, she felt completely released from the enslaving desire to get on in the world. Darkness had once again the sweet wonder that it had in childhood.

II

Thea's life at the Ottenburg ranch was simple and full of light, like the days themselves. She awoke every morning when the first fierce shafts of sunlight darted through the curtainless windows of her room at the ranch house.

After breakfast she took her lunch-basket and went down to the canyon. Usually she did not return until sunset.

Panther Canyon was like a thousand others — one of those abrupt fissures with which the earth in the Southwest is riddled; so abrupt that you might walk over the edge of any one of them on a dark night and never know what had happened to you. This canyon headed on the Ottenburg ranch, about a mile from the ranch house, and it was accessible only at its head. The canyon walls, for the first two hundred feet below the surface, were perpendicular cliffs, striped with even-running strata of rock. From there on to the bottom the sides were less abrupt, were shelving, and lightly fringed with *piñons* and dwarf cedars. The effect was that of a gentler canyon within a wilder one. The dead city lay at the point where the perpendicular outer wall ceased and the V-shaped inner gorge began. There a stratum of rock, softer than those above, had been hollowed out by the action of time until it was like a deep groove running along the sides of the canyon. In this hollow (like a great fold in the rock) the Ancient People had built their houses of yellowish stone and mortar. The over-hanging cliff above made a roof two hundred feet thick. The hard stratum below was an everlasting floor. The houses stood along in a row, like the buildings in a city block, or like a barracks.

In both walls of the canyon the same streak of soft rock had been washed out, and the long horizontal groove had been built up with houses. The dead city had thus two streets, one set in either cliff, facing each other across the ravine, with a river of blue air between them.

The canyon twisted and wound like a snake, and these two streets went on for four miles or more, interrupted by the abrupt turnings of the gorge, but beginning again within each turn. The canyon had a dozen of these false endings near its head. Beyond, the windings were larger and less perceptible, and it went on for a hundred miles, too narrow, precipitous, and terrible for man to follow it. The Cliff Dwellers liked wide canyons, where the great cliffs caught the sun. Panther Canyon had been deserted for hundreds of years when the first Spanish missionaries came into Arizona, but the masonry of the houses was still wonderfully firm; had crumbled only where a landslide or a rolling boulder had torn it.

All the houses in the canyon were clean with the cleanness of sun-baked, wind-swept places, and they all smelled of the tough little cedars that twisted themselves into the very doorways. One of these rock-rooms Thea took for her own. Fred had told her how to make it comfortable. The day after she came old Henry brought over on one of the pack-ponies a roll of Navajo blankets that belonged to Fred, and Thea lined her cave with them. The room was not more than eight by ten feet, and she could touch the stone roof with her finger-tips. This was her old idea: a nest in a high cliff, full of sun. All morning long the sun beat upon her cliff, while the ruins on the opposite side of the canyon were in shadow. In the afternoon, when she had the shade of two hundred feet of rock wall, the ruins on the other side of the gulf stood out in the blazing sunlight. Before her door ran the narrow, winding path that had been the street of the Ancient People. The yucca and niggerhead cactus grew everywhere. From her doorstep she looked out on the ocher-colored slope that ran down several hundred feet to the stream, and this hot rock was sparsely grown with dwarf trees. Their colors were so pale that the shadows of the little trees on the rock stood out sharper than the trees themselves. When Thea first came, the chokecherry bushes were in blossom, and the scent of them was almost sickeningly sweet after a shower. At the very bottom of the canyon, along the stream, there was a thread of bright, flickering, golden-green, — cottonwood seedlings. They made a living, chattering screen behind which she took her bath every morning.

Thea went down to the stream by the Indian water trail. She had found a bathing-pool with a sand bottom, where the creek was dammed by fallen trees. The climb back was long and steep, and when she reached her little house in the cliff she always felt fresh delight in its comfort and inaccessibility. By the time she got there, the woolly red-and-gray blankets were saturated with sunlight, and she sometimes fell asleep as soon as she stretched her body on their warm surfaces. She used to wonder at her own inactivity. She could lie there hour after hour in the sun and listen to the strident whir of the big locusts, and to the light, ironical laughter of the quaking asps. All her life she had been hurrying and sputtering, as if she had been born behind time and had been trying to catch up. Now, she reflected, as she drew herself out long upon the rugs, it was as if she were waiting for something to catch up with her. She had got to a place where she was out of the stream of meaningless activity and undirected effort.

Here she could lie for half a day undistracted, holding pleasant and incomplete conceptions in her mind — almost in her hands. They were scarcely clear enough to be called ideas. They had something to do with fragrance and color and sound, but almost nothing to do with words. She was singing very little now, but a song would go through her head all morning, as a spring keeps welling up, and it was like a pleasant sensation indefinitely prolonged. It was much more like a sensation than like an idea, or an act of remembering. Music had never come to her in that sensuous form before. It had always been a thing to be struggled with, had always brought anxiety and exaltation and chagrin — never content and indolence. Thea began to wonder whether people could not utterly lose the power to work, as they can lose their voice or their memory. She had always been a little drudge, hurrying from one task to another — as if it mattered! And now her power to think seemed converted into a power of sustained sensation. She could become a mere receptacle for heat, or become a color, like the bright lizards that darted about on the hot stones outside her door; or she could become a continuous repetition of sound, like the cicadas.

III

The faculty of observation was never highly developed in Thea Kronborg. A great deal escaped her eye as she passed through the world. But the things which were for her, she saw; she experienced them physically and remembered them as if they had once been a part of herself. The roses she used to see in the florists' shops in Chicago were merely roses. But when she thought of the moonflowers that grew over Mrs. Tellamantez's door, it was as if she had been that vine and had opened up in white flowers every night. There were memories of light on the sand hills, of masses of prickly-pear blossoms she had found in the desert in early childhood, of the late afternoon sun pouring through the grape leaves and the mint bed in Mrs. Kohler's garden, which she would never lose. These recollections were a part of her mind and personality. In Chicago she had got almost nothing that went into her subconscious self and took root there. But here, in Panther Canyon, there were again things which seemed destined for her.

Panther Canyon was the home of innumerable swallows. They built nests in the wall far above the hollow groove in which Thea's own rock chamber lay. They seldom ventured above the rim of the canyon, to the flat, wind-swept tableland. Their world was the blue air-river between the canyon walls. In that blue gulf the arrow-shaped birds swam all day long, with only an occasional movement of the wings. The only sad thing about them was their timidity; the way in which they lived their lives between the echoing cliffs and never dared to rise out of the shadow of the canyon walls. As they swam past her door, Thea often felt how easy it would be to dream one's life out in some cleft in the world.

From the ancient dwelling there came always a dignified, unobtrusive sadness; now stronger, now fainter, — like the aromatic smell which the dwarf cedars gave out in the sun, — but always present, a part of the air one breathed. At night, when Thea dreamed about the canyon, — or in the early morning when she hurried toward it, anticipating it, — her conception of it was of yellow rocks baking in sunlight, the swallows, the cedar smell, and that peculiar sadness — a voice out of the past, not very loud, that went on saying a few simple things to the solitude eternally.

Standing up in her lodge, Thea could with her thumb nail dislodge flakes of carbon from the rock roof — the cooking-smoke of the Ancient People. They were that near! A timid, nest-building folk, like the swallows. How often Thea remembered Ray Kennedy's moralizing about the cliff cities. He used to say that he never felt the hardness of the human struggle or the sadness of history as he felt it among those ruins. He used to say, too, that it made one feel an obligation to do one's best. On the first day that Thea climbed the water trail she began to have intuitions about the women who had worn the path, and who had spent so great a part of their lives going up and down it. She found herself trying to walk as they must have walked, with a feeling in her feet and knees and loins which she had never known before, — which must have come up to her out of the accustomed dust of that rocky trail. She could feel the weight of an Indian baby hanging to her back as she climbed.

The empty houses, among which she wandered in the afternoon, the blanketed one in which she lay all morning, were haunted by certain fears and desires; feelings about warmth and cold and water and physical strength. It seemed to Thea that a certain understanding of those old people came up to her out of the rock shelf on which she lay; that certain feelings were transmitted to her, suggestions that were simple, insistent, and monotonous, like the beating of Indian drums. They were not expressible in words, but seemed rather to translate themselves into attitudes of body, into degrees of muscular tension or relaxation; the naked strength of youth, sharp as the sun-shafts; the crouching timorousness of age, the sullenness of women who waited for their captors. At the first turning of the canyon there was a half-ruined tower of yellow masonry, a watch-tower upon which the young men used to entice eagles and snare them with nets. Sometimes for a whole morning Thea could see the coppery breast and shoulders of an Indian youth there against the sky; see him throw the net, and watch the struggle with the eagle.

Old Henry Biltmer, at the ranch, had been a great deal among the Pueblo Indians who are the descendants of the Cliff-Dwellers. After supper he used to sit and smoke his pipe by the kitchen stove and talk to Thea about them. He had never found any one before who was interested in his ruins. Every Sunday the old man prowled about in the canyon, and he had come to know a good deal more about it than he could account for. He had gathered up a whole chestful of Cliff-Dweller relics which he meant to take back to Germany with him some day. He taught Thea how to find things among the ruins: grinding-stones, and drills and needles made of turkey-bones. There were fragments of pottery everywhere. Old Henry explained to her that the Ancient People had developed masonry and pottery far beyond any other crafts. After they had made houses for themselves, the next thing was to house the precious water. He explained to her how all their customs and ceremonies and their religion went back to water. The men provided the food, but water was the care of the women. The stupid women carried water for most of their lives; the cleverer ones made the vessels to hold it. Their pottery was their most direct appeal to water, the envelope and sheath of the precious element itself. The strongest Indian need was expressed in those graceful jars, fashioned slowly by hand, without the aid of a wheel.

When Thea took her bath at the bottom of the canyon, in the sunny pool behind the screen of cottonwoods, she sometimes felt as if the water must have sovereign qualities, from having been the object of so much service and desire. That stream was the only living thing left of the drama that had been played out in the canyon centuries ago. In the rapid, restless heart of it, flowing swifter than the rest, there was a continuity of life that reached back into the old time. The glittering thread of current had a kind of lightly worn, loosely knit personality, graceful and laughing. Thea's bath came to have a ceremonial gravity. The atmosphere of the canyon was ritualistic.

One morning, as she was standing upright in the pool, splashing water between her shoulder-blades with a big sponge, something flashed through her mind that made her draw herself up and stand still until the water had quite dried upon her flushed skin. The stream and the broken pottery: what was any art but an effort to make a sheath, a mold in which to imprison for a moment the shining, elusive element which is life itself, — life hurrying past us and running away, too strong to stop, too sweet to lose? The Indian women had held it in their jars. In the sculpture she had seen in the Art Institute, it had been caught in a flash of arrested motion. In singing, one made a vessel of one's throat and nostrils and held it on one's breath, caught the stream in a scale of natural intervals.

IV

Thea had a superstitious feeling about the potsherds, and liked better to leave them in the dwellings where she found them. If she took a few bits back to her own lodge and hid them under the blankets, she did it guiltily, as if she were being watched. She was a guest in these houses, and ought to behave as such. Nearly every afternoon she went to the chambers which contained the most interesting fragments of pottery, sat and looked at them for a while. Some of them were beautifully decorated. This care, expended upon vessels that could not hold food or water any better for the additional labor put upon them, made her heart go out to those ancient potters. They had not only expressed their desire, but they had expressed it as beautifully as they could. Food, fire, water, and something else — even here, in this crack in the world, so far back in the night of the past! Down here at the beginning that painful thing was already stirring; the seed of sorrow, and of so much delight.

There were jars done in a delicate overlay, like pine cones; and there were many patterns in a low relief, like basket-work. Some of the pottery was decorated in color, red and brown, black and white, in graceful geometrical patterns. One day, on a fragment of a shallow bowl, she found a crested serpent's head, painted in red on terra-cotta. Again she found half a bowl with a broad band of white cliff-houses painted on a black ground. They were scarcely conventionalized at all; there they were in the black border, just as they stood in the rock before her. It brought her centuries nearer to these people to find that they saw their houses exactly as she saw them.

Yes, Ray Kennedy was right. All these things made one feel that one ought to do one's best, and help to fulfill some desire of the dust that slept there. A dream had been dreamed there long ago, in the night of ages, and the wind had whispered some promise to the sadness of the savage. In their own way, those people had felt the beginnings of what was to come. These potsherds were like fetters that bound one to a long chain of human endeavor.

Not only did the world seem older and richer to Thea now, but she herself seemed older. She had never been alone for so long before, or thought so much. Nothing had ever engrossed her so deeply as the daily contemplation of that line of pale-yellow houses tucked into the wrinkle of the cliff. Moonstone and Chicago had become vague. Here everything was simple and definite, as things had been in childhood. Her mind was like a ragbag into which she had been frantically thrusting whatever she could grab. And here she must throw this lumber away. The things that were really hers separated themselves from the rest. Her ideas were simplified, became sharper and clearer. She felt united and strong.

When Thea had been at the Ottenburg ranch for two months, she got a letter from Fred announcing that he "might be along at almost any time now." The letter came at night, and the next morning she took it down into the canyon with her. She was delighted that he was coming soon. She had never felt so grateful to any one, and she wanted to tell him everything that had happened to her since she had been there — more than had happened in all her life before. Certainly she liked Fred better than any one else in the world. There was Harsanyi, of course — but Harsanyi was always tired. Just now, and here, she wanted some one who had never been tired, who could catch an idea and run with it.

She was ashamed to think what an apprehensive drudge she must always have seemed to Fred, and she wondered why he had concerned himself about her at all. Perhaps she would never be so happy or so good-looking again, and she would like Fred to see her, for once, at her best. She had not been singing much, but she knew that her voice was more interesting than it had ever been before.

She had begun to understand that — with her, at least — voice was, first of all, vitality; a lightness in the body and a driving power in the blood. If she had that, she could sing. When she felt so keenly alive, lying on that insensible shelf of stone, when her body bounded like a rubber ball away from its hardness, then she could sing. This, too, she could explain to Fred. He would know what she meant.

Another week passed. Thea did the same things as before, felt the same influences, went over the same ideas; but there was a livelier movement in her thoughts, and a freshening of sensation, like the brightness which came over the underbrush after a shower. A persistent affirmation — or denial — was going on in her, like the tapping of the woodpecker in the one tall pine tree across the chasm. Musical phrases drove each other rapidly through her mind, and the song of the cicada was now too long and too sharp. Everything seemed suddenly to take the form of a desire for action.

It was while she was in this abstracted state, waiting for the clock to strike, that Thea at last made up her mind what she was going to try to do in the world, and that she was going to Germany to study without further loss of time. Only by the merest chance had she ever got to Panther Canyon. There was certainly no kindly Providence that directed one's life; and one's parents did not in the least care what became of one, so long as one did not misbehave and endanger their comfort. One's life was at the mercy of blind chance. She had better take it in her own hands and lose everything than meekly draw the plough under the rod of parental guidance. She had seen it when she was at home last summer, — the hostility of comfortable, self-satisfied people toward any serious effort. Even to her father it seemed indecorous. Whenever she spoke seriously, he looked apologetic. Yet she had clung fast to whatever was left of Moonstone in her mind. No more of that! The Cliff-Dwellers had lengthened her past. She had older and higher obligations.

Albert Schweitzer

I RESOLVE TO BECOME A JUNGLE DOCTOR

Albert Schweitzer (1875–1965) was an organist, organ-builder, philosopher, theologian, and, for many years, a doctor in equatorial Africa. An internationally famous lecturer and humanitarian, he wrote on subjects ranging from the music of J. S. Bach to biblical scholarship to world religions. Over time he developed a distinctive ethical and religious credo that he called simply "A Reverence for Life." In 1953, he was awarded the Nobel Peace Prize. His work below is chapter 9 from what he regarded as his most important work, the autobiographical *Out of My Life and Thought,* published in 1931. People of all ages and from many nations still find this telling of his own story both instructive and inspiring.

Young people who say they hope to become doctors or missionaries in a challenging and remote locale are often met with deep suspicion, today no less than in Schweitzer's time. Many people view such aspirations as stereotypically romantic or hopelessly idealistic or suspiciously paternalistic, even condescending. In this passage Schweitzer describes some of the arguments people made against his plans. Notice the reasons he gives for his decision, the steps he took in arriving at it, and the exchanges he had with those who criticized it. At what points do you agree or disagree with his critics? What do you make of the fact that Schweitzer almost always discouraged others from embarking on risky and exceptional ventures like the one he himself undertook?

On October 13, 1905, I dropped into a letter box on the avenue de la Grande Armée in Paris letters to my parents and to some of my closest friends telling them that at the beginning of the winter term I would embark on the study of medicine with the idea of later going out to equatorial Africa as a doctor. In one letter I submitted my resignation from the post of principal of the

From Albert Schweitzer, *Out of My Life and Thought: An Autobiography* (New York: Holt, 1944), 102–18.

Collegium Wilhelmitanum (the theological seminary of St. Thomas) because of the time my studies would require. The plan I hoped to realize had been in my mind for some time. Long ago in my student days I had thought about it. It struck me as inconceivable that I should be allowed to lead such a happy life while I saw so many people around me struggling with sorrow and suffering. Even at school I had felt stirred whenever I caught a glimpse of the miserable home surroundings of some of my classmates and compared them with the ideal conditions in which we children of the parsonage at Günsbach had lived. At the university, enjoying the good fortune of studying and even getting some results in scholarship and the arts, I could not help but think continually of others who were denied that good fortune by their material circumstances or their health.

One brilliant summer morning at Günsbach, during the Whitsuntide holidays — it was in 1896 — as I awoke, the thought came to me that I must not accept this good fortune as a matter of course, but must give something in return.

While outside the birds sang I reflected on this thought, and before I had gotten up I came to the conclusion that until I was thirty I could consider myself justified in devoting myself to scholarship and the arts, but after that I would devote myself directly to serving humanity. I had already tried many times to find the meaning that lay hidden in the saying of Jesus: "Whosoever would save his life shall lose it, and whosoever shall lose his life for My sake and the Gospel's shall save it." Now I had found the answer. I could now add outward to inward happiness.

What the character of my future activities would be was not yet clear to me. I left it to chance to guide me. Only one thing was certain, that it must be direct human service, however inconspicuous its sphere.

I naturally thought first of some activity in Europe. I formed a plan for taking charge of and educating abandoned or neglected children, then making them pledge to help children later on in a similar situation in the same way. When in 1903, as director of the theological seminary I moved into my roomy and sunny official quarters on the second floor of the College of St. Thomas, I was in a position to begin the experiment. I offered help now in one place, now in another, but always to no avail. The charters of the organizations that looked after destitute and abandoned children had made no provisions for accepting volunteers. For example, when the Strasbourg orphanage burned down, I offered to take in a few boys temporarily, but the superintendent did not even let me finish my sentence. I made similar attempts elsewhere also in vain.

For a time I thought I would someday devote myself to tramps and discharged convicts. To prepare myself for this I joined the Reverend Augustus Ernst at St. Thomas in an undertaking he had begun. Between one and two in the afternoon he remained at home ready to speak to anyone who came to him asking for help or a night's lodging. He did not, however, give the applicant money, nor did he make him wait until the information about his circumstances could be confirmed. Instead he would offer to look up the applicant in his home or shelter that very afternoon and verify the information he had been given about the situation. After this, he would give him all necessary assistance for as long as was needed. How many bicycle rides did we make into town or the suburbs, and quite often only to find that the applicant was unknown at the address he had given. In many cases, however, it provided an opportunity for giving appropriate help, with knowledge of the circumstances. I also had friends who kindly contributed money to this cause.

As a student, I had been active in social service as a member of the student association known as the Diaconate of St. Thomas, which held its meetings in the St. Thomas seminary. Each of us had a certain number of poor families assigned to him, which he was to visit every week, taking some aid and then reporting about their situation. The funds we thus distributed we collected from members of the old Strasbourg families who supported this undertaking, begun by earlier generations and now carried on by ourselves. Twice a year, if I remember correctly, each of us had to make a fixed number of financial appeals. For me, being shy and rather awkward in society, these visits were a torture. I believe that in this preparatory experience of soliciting funds, which I had to do much more of in later years, I sometimes showed myself extremely unskillful. However, I learned through them that soliciting with tact and restraint is better appreciated than any sort of aggressive approach, and also that correct soliciting methods include the friendly acceptance of refusal.

In our youthful inexperience we no doubt often failed, in spite of our best intentions, to use the money entrusted to us in the wisest way. The expectations of the givers were, however, fulfilled with respect to their purpose — that young men should devote themselves to serve the poor. For that reason I think with deep gratitude of those who met our efforts with so much understanding and generosity, and hope that many students may have the privilege of working as recruits in the struggle against poverty.

As I worried about the homeless and former convicts it became clear to me that they could only be effectively helped if many individuals devoted themselves to them. At the same time, however, I realized that in many cases individuals could only accomplish their tasks in collaboration with official organizations. But what I wanted was an absolutely personal and independent activity.

Although I was resolved to put my services at the disposal of some organization if it should become really necessary, I nonetheless never gave up the hope of finding an activity to which I could devote myself as an individual and as a wholly free agent. I have always considered it an ever renewed grace that I could fulfill this profound desire.

One morning in the autumn of 1904 I found on my writing table in the seminary one of the green-covered magazines in which the Paris Missionary Society (La Société Evangélique des Missions à Paris) reported on its activities every month. A Miss Scherdlin used to pass them on to me. She knew that in my youth I had been impressed by the letters from Mr. Casalis, one of the first missionaries of this society. My father had read them to us in his mission services.

Without paying much attention, I leafed through the magazine that had been put on my table the night before. As I was about to turn to my studies, I noticed an article with the headline "Les besoins de la Mission du Congo" ("The needs of the Congo Mission," in the *Journal des Missions Evangéliques*, June 1904). It was by Alfred Boegner, the president of the Paris Missionary Society, an Alsatian, who complained in it that the mission did not have enough people to carry on its work in the Gaboon, the northern province of the Congo colony. The writer expressed the hope that his appeal would bring some of those "on whom the Master's eyes already rested" to a decision to offer themselves for this urgent work. The article concluded: "Men and women who can reply simply to the Master's call, 'Lord, I am coming,' those are the people the Church needs." I finished my article and quietly began my work. My search was over.

I spent my thirtieth birthday a few months later like the man in the parable who, "desiring to build a tower, first calculates the cost of completion whether he has the means to complete it." The result was a resolve to realize my plan of direct human service in equatorial Africa.

Aside from one trustworthy friend, no one knew of my intention. When it became known through the letters I had sent from Paris, I had hard battles to fight with my relatives and friends. They reproached me more for not taking them into my confidence and discussing the decision with them than they did for the enterprise itself. With this secondary issue they tormented me beyond measure during those difficult weeks. That theological friends should outdo the others in their protests struck me as all the more absurd because they had no doubt all preached a fine sermon — perhaps a very fine one — that quoted Paul's declaration in his letter to the Galatians that he "did not confer with flesh or blood" before he knew what he would do for Jesus.

My relatives and friends reproached me for the folly of my enterprise. They said I was a man who was burying the talent entrusted to him and wanted to trade in false currency. I ought to leave work among Africans to those who would not thereby abandon gifts and achievements in scholarship and the arts. Widor, who loved me as a son, scolded me for acting like a general who, rifle in hand, insists on fighting in the firing line (there was no talk about trenches at that time). A lady who was filled with the modern spirit proved to me that I could do much more by lecturing on behalf of medical help for Africans than I could by the course of action I contemplated. The aphorism from Goethe's *Faust*, "In the beginning was the Deed," was now out of date, she said. "Today propaganda is the mother of events."

In the many adversarial debates I had to endure with people who passed for Christians, it amazed me to see them unable to perceive that the desire to serve the love preached by Jesus may sweep a man into a new course of life. They read in the New Testament that it can do so, and found it quite in order there.

I had assumed that familiarity with the sayings of Jesus would give a much better comprehension of what to popular logic is not rational. Several times, indeed, my appeal to the obedience that Jesus' command of love requires under certain circumstances earned me an accusation of conceit. How I suffered to see so many people assuming the right to tear open the doors and shutters of my inner self!

In general, neither allowing them to see that I was hurt nor letting them know the thought that had given birth to *my* resolution was of any use. They thought there must be something behind it all, and guessed at disappointment with the slow development of my career. For this there were no grounds at all, in that, even as a young man, I had received as much recognition as others usually get only after a whole life of toil and struggle. Unhappy love was another reason alleged for my decision.

The attitude of people who did not try to explore my feelings, but regarded me as a young man not quite right in the head and treated me with correspondingly affectionate ridicule, represented a real kindness.

I felt it to be quite natural in itself that family and friends should challenge the rationality of my plan. As one who demands that idealists should be sober in their views, I was aware that every venture down an untrodden path is a venture that looks sensible and likely to be successful only under unusual circumstances. In my own case I held the venture to be justified, because I had considered it for a long time and from every point of view, and I thought that I had good health, sound nerves, energy, practical common sense, toughness, prudence, very few wants, and everything else that might be necessary for the pursuit of my idea. I believed, further, that I had the inner fortitude to endure any eventual failure of my plan.

As a man of independent action, I have since that time been approached for my opinion and advice by many people who wanted to risk a similar venture. Only in comparatively few cases have I taken the responsibility of giving them encouragement. I often had to recognize that the need "to do something special" was born of a restless spirit. Such people wanted to dedicate themselves to larger tasks because those that lay nearest did not satisfy them. Often, too, it was evident that they were motivated by quite secondary considerations. Only a person who finds value in any kind of activity and who gives of himself with a full sense of service has the right to choose an exceptional task instead of following a common path. Only a person who feels his preference to be a matter of course, not something out of the ordinary, and who has no thought of heroism but only of a duty undertaken with sober enthusiasm, is capable of becoming the sort of spiritual pioneer the world needs. There are no heroes of action — only heroes of renunciation and suffering. Of these there are plenty. But few of them are known, and even they not to the crowd, but to the few. Carlyle's *On Heroes and Hero-Worship* is not a profound book.

The majority of those who feel the impulse and are actually capable of devoting their lives to independent action are compelled by circumstances to renounce that course. As a rule they have to provide for one or more dependents, or they have to stay with their profession in order to earn a living. Only a person who, thanks to his own efforts or the devotion of friends, is free from material needs can nowadays take the risk of undertaking such a personal task.

This was not so much the case in earlier times because anyone who gave up remunerative work could still hope to get through life somehow or other, but anyone thinking of doing such a thing in the difficult economic conditions of today runs the risk of coming to grief both materially and spiritually.

I know not only by what I have observed but also by experience that there are worthy and capable people who have had to renounce a course of independent action that would have been of great value to the world because of circumstances that made it impossible.

Those who are given the chance to embark on a life of independent action must accept their good fortune in a spirit of humility. They must often think of those who, though equally willing and capable, were not in a position to do the same. And as a rule, they must temper their own strong determination with humility. Almost always they must search and wait until they find a path that will permit the action they long to take. Fortunate are those who have received more years of creative work than years of searching and waiting. Fortunate those who succeed in giving themselves genuinely and completely.

These favored souls must also be humble so as not to get irritated by the resistance they encounter, but to accept it as inevitable. Anyone who proposes to do good must not expect people to roll any stones out of his way, and must calmly accept his lot even if they roll a few more into it. Only force that in the face of obstacles becomes stronger can win. Force that is used only to revolt wastes itself.

Of all the will toward the ideal in mankind only a small part can manifest itself in public action. All the rest of this force must be content with small and obscure deeds. The sum of these, however, is a thousand times stronger than the acts of those who receive wide public recognition. The latter, compared to the former, are like the foam on the waves of a deep ocean.

The hidden forces of goodness are alive in those who serve humanity as a secondary pursuit, those who cannot devote their full life to it. The lot of most people is to have a job, to earn their living, and to assume for themselves a place in society through some kind of nonfulfilling labor. They can give little or nothing of their human qualities. The problems arising from progressive specialization and mechanization of labor can only be partly resolved through the concessions society is willing to make in its economic planning. It is always essential that the individuals themselves not suffer their fate passively, but expend all their energies in affirming their own humanity through some spiritual engagement, even if the conditions are unfavorable.

One can save one's life as a human being, along with one's professional existence, if one seizes every opportunity, however unassuming, to act humanly toward those who need another human being. In this way we serve both the spiritual and the good. Nothing can keep us from this second job of direct human service. So many opportunities are missed because we let them pass by.

Everyone in his own environment must strive to practice true humanity toward others. The future of the world depends on it.

Great values are lost at every moment because we miss opportunities, but the values that are turned into will and action constitute a richness that must not be undervalued. Our humanity is by no means as materialistic as people claim so complacently.

Judging by what I have learned about men and women, I am convinced that far more idealistic aspiration exists than is ever evident. Just as the rivers we see are much less numerous than the underground streams, so the idealism that is visible is minor compared to what men and women carry in their hearts, unreleased or scarcely released. Mankind is waiting and longing for those who can accomplish the task of untying what is knotted and bringing the underground waters to the surface.

What to my friends seemed most irrational in my plan was that I wanted to go to Africa, not as a missionary, but as a doctor. Already thirty years of age, I would burden myself with long and laborious study. I never doubted for an instant that these studies would require an immense effort, and I anticipated the coming years with anxiety. But the reasons that made me determined to enter into the service I had chosen as a doctor weighed so heavily that other considerations were as dust in the balance and counted for nothing.

I wanted to be a doctor so that I might be able to work without having to talk. For years I had been giving of myself in words, and it was with joy that I had followed the calling of theological teacher and preacher. But this new form of activity would consist not in preaching the religion of love, but in practicing it. Medical knowledge would make it possible for me to carry out my intention in the best and most complete way, wherever the path of service might lead me.

Given my choice of equatorial Africa, acquiring this knowledge was especially appropriate because in the district to which I planned to go a doctor was, according to the missionaries' reports, the most urgent of all its needs. In their reports and magazines they always regretted that they could not provide help for the Africans who came in great physical pain. I was greatly motivated to study medicine and become, one day, the doctor whom these unhappy people needed. Whenever I was tempted to feel that the years I should have to sacrifice were too long, I reminded myself that Hamilcar and Hannibal had prepared for their march on Rome by their slow and tedious conquest of Spain.

There was still one more reason why it seemed to be my destiny to become a doctor. From what I knew of the Paris Missionary Society, I could not but feel very doubtful that they would accept me as a missionary.

Matt Damon and Ben Affleck

GOOD WILL HUNTING

The title of this 1997 film is a pun. On the one hand it refers to the title character, whose name is Will Hunting. On the other hand it implies that the film is about this character's hunt for something — for his vocation or, in a larger sense, for his identity — that he can accept with good will.

Will Hunting is a genius. He can work out problems in mathematics that baffle the professors who teach at MIT, where he works as a janitor. For complicated reasons that he does not himself fully understand, Will simultaneously hides and displays his prodigious ability by sneaking around the halls of the school at night and writing the solutions to complicated problems others cannot solve on chalkboards in the hallways. Will claims that he simply wants to be a manual laborer — a custodian or a bricklayer — instead of a code breaker for the government, the job he has been offered. As the scene unfolds between Will and Sean, his therapist, do you think Will really means what he says, or is he troubled by, or even afraid of, his own genius? Have you ever failed to develop a talent for fear of what might be expected or required of you if you did so?

The second series of exchanges in the screenplay takes place between Will and his friend Chuckie, both of whom are doing construction work. Chuckie thinks that he will be and probably should be a construction worker for his entire life. Like Sean, however, he recognizes Will's talent and hopes that Will will use it. Sometimes our teachers and friends can recognize and appreciate our talents more than we can. If several of our acquaintances urge us to pursue a particular vocation on the basis of our extraordinary aptitudes for that calling, are we obliged to follow their advice? Why or why not? In his exchange with Chuckie, Will suggests that he values place — the neighborhood and his friends — over career, desire over talent. Gary Badcock, in the section on the vocabulary of vocation, argued that it is often quite legitimate to prefer place over occupation, desire over talent. What do you think?

From Matt Damon and Ben Affleck, *Good Will Hunting: A Screenplay* (New York: Miramax Books, 1997), 125–34.

Damon and Affleck won an Academy Award for writing the screenplay for this film, in which they also starred as Will and Chuckie. Robin Williams played Sean, Will's therapist.

INT. SEAN'S OFFICE — NIGHT

Will sits across from Sean.

SEAN   So you might be working for Uncle Sam.

WILL   I don't know.

SEAN   Gerry says the meeting went well.

WILL   I guess.

SEAN   What did you think?

WILL   What did I think?

A beat. Will has obviously been stewing on this.

WILL   Say I'm working at N.S.A. Somebody puts a code on my desk, something nobody else can break. So I take a shot at it and maybe I break it. And I'm real happy with myself, 'cause I did my job well. But maybe that code was the location of some rebel army in North Africa or the Middle East. Once they have that location, they bomb the village where the rebels were hiding and fifteen hundred people I never had a problem with get killed.

(rapid fire)

Now the politicians are sayin' "send in the Marines to secure the area" 'cause they don't give a shit. It won't be their kid over there, gettin' shot. Just like it wasn't them when their number got called, 'cause they were pullin' a tour in the National Guard. It'll be some guy from Southie takin' shrapnel in the ass. And he comes home to find that the plant he used to work at got exported to the country he just got back from. And the guy who put the shrapnel in his ass got his old job, 'cause he'll work for fifteen cents a day and no bathroom breaks. Meanwhile my buddy from Southie realizes the only reason he was over there was so we could install a government that would sell us oil at a good price. And of course the oil companies used the skirmish to scare up oil prices so they could turn a quick buck. A cute, little ancillary benefit for them but it ain't helping my buddy at two-fifty a gallon. And naturally they're takin' their sweet time bringin' the oil back and maybe even took the liberty of hiring an alcoholic skipper who likes to drink martinis and play slalom with the icebergs and it ain't too long 'til he hits one, spills the oil, and kills all the sea life in the North Atlantic. So my buddy's out of work and he can't afford to drive, so he's got to walk to the job interviews, which sucks 'cause the shrapnel in his ass is givin' him chronic hemorrhoids. And meanwhile he's starvin' 'cause every time he tries to get a bite to eat the only blue plate special they're servin' is North Atlantic scrod with Quaker State.

A beat.

WILL   So what'd I think? I'm holdin' out for somethin' better. I figure I'll eliminate the middle man. Why not just shoot my buddy, take his job and give it to his sworn enemy, hike up gas prices, bomb a village, club a baby seal, hit the hash pipe and join the National Guard? Christ, I could be elected President.

SEAN   Do you think you're alone?

WILL   What?

SEAN   Do you have a soul mate?

WILL   Define that.

SEAN   Someone who challenges you in every way. Who takes you places, opens things up for you. A soul mate.

WILL   Yeah.

Sean waits.

WILL   Shakespeare, Neitzsche, Frost, O'Connor, Chaucer, Pope, Kant —

SEAN   They're all dead.

WILL   Not to me, they're not.

SEAN   But you can't give back to them, Will.

WILL   Not without a heater and some serious smelling salts, no . . .

SEAN   That's what I'm saying, Will. You'll never have that kind of relationship in a world where you're afraid to take the first step because all you're seeing are the negative things that might happen ten miles down the road.

WILL   Oh, what? You're going to take the professor's side on this?

SEAN   Don't give me your line of shit.

WILL   I didn't want the job.

SEAN   It's not about that job. I'm not saying you should work for the government. But, you could do anything you want. And there are people who work their whole lives layin' brick so their kids have a chance at the kind of opportunity you have. What do you want to do?

WILL   I didn't ask for this.

SEAN   Nobody gets what they ask for, Will. That's a cop-out.

WILL   Why is it a cop-out? I don't see anythin' wrong with layin' brick, that's somebody's home I'm buildin'. Or fixin' somebody's car, somebody's gonna get to work the next day 'cause of me. There's honor in that.

SEAN   You're right, Will. Any man who takes a forty-minute train ride so those college kids can come in in the morning and their floors will be clean and their trash cans will be empty is an honorable man.

A beat. Will says nothing.

SEAN   And when they get drunk and puke in the sink, they don't have to see it the next morning because of you. That's real work, Will. And there is honor in that. Which I'm sure is why you took the job.

A beat.

SEAN   I just want to know why you decided to sneak around at night, writing on chalkboards and lying about it.

(beat)

'Cause there's no honor in that.

Will is silent.

SEAN   Something you want to say?

Sean gets up, goes to the door and opens it.

SEAN   Why don't you come back when you have an answer for me.

WILL   What?

SEAN   If you won't answer my questions, you're wasting my time.

WILL   What?

Will loses it, slams the door shut.

WILL   Fuck you!

Sean has finally gotten to Will.

WILL   Who the fuck are you to lecture me about life? You fuckin'
              burnout! Where's your "soul mate"?!

              Sean lets this play out.

WILL   Dead! She dies and you just cash in your chips. That's a fuckin'
              cop-out!

SEAN   I been there. I played my hand.

WILL   That's right. And you fuckin' lost! And some people would have
              the sack to lose a big hand like that and still come back and ante
              up again!

SEAN   Look at me. What do you want to do?

              A beat. Will looks up.

SEAN   You and your bullshit. You got an answer for everybody. But I
              asked you a straight question and you can't give me a straight
              answer. Because you don't know.

              Sean goes to the door and opens it. Will walks out.

              CUT TO:
              INT. MAGGIORE BUILDER'S CONSTRUCTION
              SITE — DAY

              *Will and Chuckie take crowbars to a wall. This is what they do for a
              living. As they routinely hammer away, Will becomes more involved
              in his battle with the wall. Plaster and lathing fly as Will vents his
              rage. Chuckie, noticing, stops working and takes a step back, watching
              Will. Will is oblivious. . . .*

              EXT. HANRAHAN'S PACKAGE STORE — LATER

              *Will walks out carrying a brown bag. He is filthy, having just knocked
              off work.*

CUT TO:
EXT. MAGGIORE BUILDER'S CONSTRUCTION SITE —
PARKING LOT

Chuckie is sitting on the hood of his Cadillac, watching Will across the street. Chuckie is covered in grime as well. Will starts walking towards Chuckie. As he draws closer, he heaves a can of beer a good thirty yards, to Chuckie, who handles it routinely.

Will takes a seat next to Chuckie and they crack open their beers. Other workers file out of the site. They drink.

CHUCKIE   How's the woman?

WILL   Gone.

CHUCKIE   What?

WILL   She went to medical school in California.

CHUCKIE   Sorry, brother.

        (beat)

I don't know what to tell ya. You know all the girls I been with. You been with 'em too, except for Cheryl McGovern, which was a big mistake on your part, brother. . . .

WILL   Oh, I'm sure, that's why only one of us has herpes.

CHUCKIE   Some shows are worth the price of admission, partner.

This gets a small laugh from Will.

CHUCKIE   My fuckin' back is killin' me.

A passing sheet metal worker overhears this.

SHEET METAL WORKER
That's why you should'a gone to college.

WILL Fuck you.

CHUCKIE Suck my crank. Fuckin' sheet metal pussy.

    (*beat*)

    So, when are you done with those meetin's?

WILL Week after I'm twenty-one.

CHUCKIE Are they hookin' you up with a job?

WILL Yeah, sit in a room and do long division for the next fifty years.

CHUCKIE Yah, but it's better than this shit. At least you'd make some nice bank.

WILL Yeah, be a fuckin' lab rat.

CHUCKIE It's a way outta here.

WILL What do I want a way outta here for? I want to live here the rest of my life. I want to be your next door neighbor. I want to take our kids to little league together up Foley Field.

CHUCKIE Look, you're my best friend, so don't take this the wrong way, but in twenty years, if you're livin' next door to me, comin' over, watchin' the fuckin' Patriots' games and still workin' construction, I'll fuckin' kill you. And that's not a threat, that's a fact. I'll fuckin' kill you.

WILL Chuckie, what are you talkin' . . .

CHUCKIE Listen, you got somethin' that none of us have.

WILL Why is it always this? I owe it to myself? What if I don't want to?

CHUCKIE Fuck you. You owe it to me. Tomorrow I'm gonna wake up and

I'll be fifty and I'll still be doin' this. And that's all right 'cause I'm gonna make a run at it.

(beat)

But you, you're sittin' on a winning lottery ticket and you're too much of a pussy to cash it in. And that's bullshit 'cause I'd do anything to have what you got! And so would any of these guys. It'd be a fuckin' insult to us if you're still here in twenty years.

WILL   You don't know that.

CHUCKIE   Let me tell you what I do know. Every day I come by to pick you up, and we go out drinkin' or whatever and we have a few laughs. But you know what the best part of my day is? The ten seconds before I knock on the door, 'cause I let myself think I might get there, and you'd be gone. I'd knock on the door and you wouldn't be there. You just left.

A beat.

CHUCKIE   Now, I don't know much. But I know that.

James Baldwin

SONNY'S BLUES

James Baldwin (1924–1987), the great American novelist and essayist, grew up in circumstances much like those of the characters we meet in this story. The story's narrator has survived the hazards that threaten the well-being of young men in Harlem and has become a happily married high school teacher, in spite of considerable loss and hardship along the way. His younger brother, Sonny, has apparently been less fortunate.

This story raises the question of whether Sonny's exceptional musical talent, which he has cultivated under very difficult circumstances, is partly to blame for his suffering. The title, "Sonny's Blues," could refer either to the immense pain Sonny has endured or to the wonderful music he is able to create. Or does Baldwin mean to suggest that the two are inseparably interwoven? Would a life of greater safety be preferable to the creative but tortured life Sonny has led?

I read about it in the paper, in the subway, on my way to work. I read it, and I couldn't believe it, and I read it again. Then perhaps I just stared at it, at the newsprint spelling out his name, spelling out the story. I stared at it in the swinging lights of the subway car, and in the faces and bodies of the people, and in my own face, trapped in the darkness which roared outside.

It was not to be believed and I kept telling myself that, as I walked from the subway station to the high school. And at the same time I couldn't doubt it. I was scared, scared for Sonny. He became real to me again. A great block of ice got settled in my belly and kept melting there slowly all day long, while I taught my classes algebra. It was a special kind of ice. It kept melting, sending trickles of ice water all up and down my veins, but it never got less. Sometimes it hardened and seemed to expand until I felt my guts were going to come spilling out or that I was going to choke or scream. This would

James Baldwin, "Sonny's Blues," in *Going to Meet the Man* (New York: Dial Press, 1965), 103–41.

always be at a moment when I was remembering some specific thing Sonny had once said or done.

When he was about as old as the boys in my classes his face had been bright and open, there was a lot of copper in it; and he'd had wonderfully direct brown eyes, and great gentleness and privacy. I wondered what he looked like now. He had been picked up, the evening before, in a raid on an apartment downtown, for peddling and using heroin.

I couldn't believe it: but what I mean by that is that I couldn't find any room for it anywhere inside me. I had kept it outside me for a long time. I hadn't wanted to know. I had had suspicions, but I didn't name them, I kept putting them away. I told myself that Sonny was wild, but he wasn't crazy. And he'd always been a good boy, he hadn't ever turned hard or evil or disrespectful, the way kids can, so quick, so quick, especially in Harlem. I didn't want to believe that I'd ever see my brother going down, coming to nothing, all that light in his face gone out, in the condition I'd already seen so many others. Yet it had happened and here I was, talking about algebra to a lot of boys who might, every one of them for all I knew, be popping off needles every time they went to the head. Maybe it did more for them than algebra could.

I was sure that the first time Sonny had ever had horse, he couldn't have been much older than these boys were now. These boys, now, were living as we'd been living then, they were growing up with a rush and their heads bumped abruptly against the low ceiling of their actual possibilities. They were filled with rage. All they really knew were two darknesses, the darkness of their lives, which was now closing in on them, and the darkness of the movies, which had blinded them to that other darkness, and in which they now, vindictively, dreamed, at once more together than they were at any other time, and more alone.

When the last bell rang, the last class ended, I let out my breath. It seemed I'd been holding it for all that time. My clothes were wet — I may have looked as though I'd been sitting in a steam bath, all dressed up, all afternoon. I sat alone in the classroom a long time. I listened to the boys outside, downstairs, shouting and cursing and laughing. Their laughter struck me for perhaps the first time. It was not the joyous laughter which — God knows why — one associates with children. It was mocking and insular, its intent was to denigrate. It was disenchanted, and in this, also, lay the authority of their curses. Perhaps I was listening to them because I was thinking about my brother and in them I heard my brother. And myself.

One boy was whistling a tune, at once very complicated and very simple, it seemed to be pouring out of him as though he were a bird, and it sounded very cool and moving through all that harsh, bright air, only just holding its own through all those other sounds.

I stood up and walked over to the window and looked down into the courtyard. It was the beginning of the spring and the sap was rising in the boys. A teacher passed through them every now and again, quickly, as though he or she couldn't wait to get out of that courtyard, to get those boys out of their sight and off their minds. I started collecting my stuff. I thought I'd better get home and talk to Isabel.

The courtyard was almost deserted by the time I got downstairs. I saw this boy standing in the shadow of a doorway, looking just like Sonny. I almost called his name. Then I saw that it wasn't Sonny, but somebody we used to know, a boy from around our block. He'd been Sonny's friend. He'd never been mine, having been too young for me, and, anyway, I'd never liked him. And now, even though he was a grown-up man, he still hung around that block, still spent hours on the street corners, was always high and raggy. I used to run into him from time to time and he'd often work around to asking me for a quarter or fifty cents. He always had some real good excuse, too, and I always gave it to him, I don't know why.

But now, abruptly, I hated him. I couldn't stand the way he looked at me, partly like a dog, partly like a cunning child. I wanted to ask him what the hell he was doing in the school courtyard.

He sort of shuffled over to me, and he said, "I see you got the papers. So you already know about it."

"You mean about Sonny? Yes, I already know about it. How come they didn't get you?"

He grinned. It made him repulsive and it also brought to mind what he'd looked like as a kid. "I wasn't there. I stay away from them people."

"Good for you." I offered him a cigarette and I watched him through the smoke. "You come all the way down here just to tell me about Sonny?"

"That's right." He was sort of shaking his head and his eyes looked strange, as though they were about to cross. The bright sun deadened his damp dark brown skin and it made his eyes look yellow and showed up the dirt in his kinked hair. He smelled funky. I moved a little away from him and I said, "Well, thanks. But I already know about it and I got to get home."

"I'll walk you a little ways," he said. We started walking. There were a couple of kids still loitering in the courtyard and one of them said goodnight to me and looked strangely at the boy beside me.

"What're you going to do?" he asked me. "I mean, about Sonny?"

"Look. I haven't seen Sonny for over a year, I'm not sure I'm going to do anything. Anyway, what the hell *can* I do?"

"That's right," he said quickly, "ain't nothing you can do. Can't much help old Sonny no more, I guess."

It was what I was thinking and so it seemed to me he had no right to say it.

"I'm surprised at Sonny, though," he went on — he had a funny way of talking, he looked straight ahead as though he were talking to himself — "I thought Sonny was a smart boy, I thought he was too smart to get hung."

"I guess he thought so too," I said sharply, "and that's how he got hung. And now about you? You're pretty goddamn smart, I bet."

Then he looked directly at me, just for a minute. "I ain't smart," he said. "If I was smart, I'd have reached for a pistol a long time ago."

"Look. Don't tell *me* your sad story, if it was up to me, I'd give you one." Then I felt guilty — guilty, probably, for never having supposed that the poor bastard *had* a story of his own, much less a sad one, and I asked, quickly, "What's going to happen to him now?"

He didn't answer this. He was off by himself some place. "Funny thing," he said, and from his tone we might have been discussing the quickest way to get to Brooklyn, "when I saw the papers this morning, the first thing I asked myself was if I had anything to do with it. I felt sort of responsible."

I began to listen more carefully. The subway station was on the corner, just before us, and I stopped. He stopped, too. We were in front of a bar and he ducked slightly, peering in, but whoever he was looking for didn't seem to be there. The juke box was blasting away with something black and bouncy and I half watched the barmaid as she danced her way from the juke box to her place behind the bar. And I watched her face as she laughingly responded to something someone said to her, still keeping time to the music. When she smiled one saw the little girl, one sensed the doomed, still-struggling woman beneath the battered face of the semi-whore.

"I never *give* Sonny nothing," the boy said finally, "but a long time ago I come to school high and Sonny asked me how it felt." He paused, I couldn't bear to watch him, I watched the barmaid, and I listened to the music which seemed to be causing the pavement to shake. "I told him it felt great." The music stopped, the barmaid paused and watched the juke box until the music began again. "It did."

All this was carrying me some place I didn't want to go. I certainly didn't want to know how it felt. It filled everything, the people, the houses, the

music, the dark, quicksilver barmaid, with menace; and this menace was
their reality.

"What's going to happen to him now?" I asked again.

"They'll send him away some place and they'll try to cure him." He shook
his head. "Maybe he'll even think he's kicked the habit. Then they'll let him
loose" — he gestured, throwing his cigarette into the gutter. "That's all."

"What do you mean, that's *all?*"

But I knew what he meant.

"I *mean,* that's *all.*" He turned his head and looked at me, pulling down the
corners of his mouth. "Don't you know what I mean?" he asked, softly.

"How the hell *would* I know what you mean?" I almost whispered it, I don't
know why.

"That's right," he said to the air, "how would *he* know what I mean?" He
turned toward me again, patient and calm, and yet I somehow felt him shaking, shaking as though he were going to fall apart. I felt that ice in my guts
again, the dread I'd felt all afternoon; and again I watched the barmaid, moving about the bar, washing glasses, and singing. "Listen. They'll let him out
and then it'll just start all over again. That's what I mean."

"You mean — they'll let him out. And then he'll just start working his way
back in again. You mean he'll never kick the habit. Is that what you mean?"

"That's right," he said, cheerfully. "*You* see what I mean."

"Tell me," I said at last, "why does he want to die? He must want to die,
he's killing himself, why does he want to die?"

He looked at me in surprise. He licked his lips. "He don't want to die. He
wants to live. Don't nobody want to die, ever."

Then I wanted to ask him — too many things. He could not have answered, or if he had, I could not have borne the answers. I started walking.
"Well, I guess it's none of my business."

"It's going to be rough on old Sonny," he said. We reached the subway
station. "This is your station?" he asked. I nodded. I took one step down.
"Damn!" he said, suddenly. I looked up at him. He grinned again. "Damn it
if I didn't leave all my money home. You ain't got a dollar on you, have you?
Just for a couple of days, is all."

All at once something inside gave and threatened to come pouring out
of me. I didn't hate him any more. I felt that in another moment I'd start
crying like a child.

"Sure," I said. "Don't sweat." I looked in my wallet and didn't have a dollar,
I only had a five. "Here," I said. "That hold you?"

He didn't look at it — he didn't want to look at it. A terrible, closed look came over his face, as though he were keeping the number on the bill a secret from him and me. "Thanks," he said, and now he was dying to see me go. "Don't worry about Sonny. Maybe I'll write him or something."

"Sure," I said. "You do that. So long."

"Be seeing you," he said. I went on down the steps.

And I didn't write Sonny or send him anything for a long time. When I finally did, it was just after my little girl died, he wrote me back a letter which made me feel like a bastard.

Here's what he said:

Dear brother,

You don't know how much I needed to hear from you. I wanted to write you many a time but I dug how much I must have hurt you and so I didn't write. But now I feel like a man who's been trying to climb up out of some deep, real deep and funky hole and just saw the sun up there, outside. I got to get outside.

I can't tell you much about how I got here. I mean I don't know how to tell you. I guess I was afraid of something or I was trying to escape from something and you know I have never been very strong in the head (smile). I'm glad Mama and Daddy are dead and can't see what's happened to their son and I swear if I'd known what I was doing I would never have hurt you so, you and a lot of other fine people who were nice to me and who believed in me.

I don't want you to think it had anything to do with me being a musician. It's more than that. Or maybe less than that. I can't get anything straight in my head down here and I try not to think about what's going to happen to me when I get outside again. Sometime I think I'm going to flip and *never* get outside and sometime I think I'll come straight back. I tell you one thing, though, I'd rather blow my brains out than go through this again. But that's what they all say, so they tell me. If I tell you when I'm coming to New York and if you could meet me, I sure would appreciate it. Give my love to Isabel and the kids and I was sure sorry to hear about little Gracie. I wish I could be like Mama and say the Lord's will be done, but I don't know it seems to me that trouble is the one thing that never does get stopped and I don't know what good it does to blame it on the Lord. But maybe it does some good if you believe it.

Your brother,

Sonny

Then I kept in constant touch with him and I sent him whatever I could and I went to meet him when he came back to New York. When I saw him many things I thought I had forgotten came flooding back to me. This was because I had begun, finally, to wonder about Sonny, about the life that Sonny lived inside. This life, whatever it was, had made him older and thinner and it had deepened the distant stillness in which he had always moved. He looked very unlike my baby brother. Yet, when he smiled, when we shook hands, the baby brother I'd never known looked out from the depths of his private life, like an animal waiting to be coaxed into the light.

"How you been keeping?" he asked me.

"All right. And you?"

"Just fine." He was smiling all over his face. "It's good to see you again."

"It's good to see you."

The seven years' difference in our ages lay between us like a chasm: I wondered if these years would ever operate between us as a bridge. I was remembering, and it made it hard to catch my breath, that I had been there when he was born; and I had heard the first words he had ever spoken. When he started to walk, he walked from our mother straight to me. I caught him just before he fell when he took the first steps he ever took in this world.

"How's Isabel?"

"Just fine. She's dying to see you."

"And the boys?"

"They're fine, too. They're anxious to see their uncle."

"Oh, come on. You know they don't remember me."

"Are you kidding? Of course they remember you."

He grinned again. We got into a taxi. We had a lot to say to each other, far too much to know how to begin.

As the taxi began to move, I asked, "You still want to go to India?"

He laughed. "You still remember that. Hell, no. This place is Indian enough for me."

"It used to belong to them," I said.

And he laughed again. "They damn sure knew what they were doing when they got rid of it."

Years ago, when he was around fourteen, he'd been all hipped on the idea of going to India. He read books about people sitting on rocks, naked, in all kinds of weather, but mostly bad, naturally, and walking barefoot through hot coals and arriving at wisdom. I used to say that it sounded to me as though they were getting away from wisdom as fast as they could. I think he sort of looked down on me for that.

"Do you mind," he asked, "if we have the driver drive alongside the park? On the west side — I haven't seen the city in so long."

"Of course not," I said. I was afraid that I might sound as though I were humoring him, but I hoped he wouldn't take it that way.

So we drove along, between the green of the park and the stony, lifeless elegance of hotels and apartment buildings, toward the vivid, killing streets of our childhood. These streets hadn't changed, though housing projects jutted up out of them now like rocks in the middle of a boiling sea. Most of the houses in which we had grown up had vanished, as had the stores from which we had stolen, the basements in which we had first tried sex, the rooftops from which we had hurled tin cans and bricks. But houses exactly like the houses of our past yet dominated the landscape, boys exactly like the boys we once had been found themselves smothering in these houses, came down into the streets for light and air and found themselves encircled by disaster. Some escaped the trap, most didn't. Those who got out always left something of themselves behind, as some animals amputate a leg and leave it in the trap. It might be said, perhaps, that I had escaped, after all, I was a school teacher; or that Sonny had, he hadn't lived in Harlem for years. Yet, as the cab moved uptown through streets which seemed, with a rush, to darken with dark people, and as I covertly studied Sonny's face, it came to me that what we both were seeking through our separate cab windows was that part of ourselves which had been left behind. It's always at the hour of trouble and confrontation that the missing member aches.

We hit 110th Street and started rolling up Lenox Avenue. And I'd known this avenue all my life, but it seemed to me again, as it had seemed on the day I'd first heard about Sonny's trouble, filled with a hidden menace which was its very breath of life.

"We almost there," said Sonny.

"Almost." We were both too nervous to say anything more.

We live in a housing project. It hasn't been up long. A few days after it was up it seemed uninhabitably new, now, of course, it's already rundown. It looks like a parody of the good, clean, faceless life — God knows the people who live in it do their best to make it a parody. The beat-looking grass lying around isn't enough to make their lives green, the hedges will never hold out the streets, and they know it. The big windows fool no one, they aren't big enough to make space out of no space. They don't bother with the windows, they watch the TV screen instead. The playground is most popular with the children who don't play at jacks, or skip rope, or roller skate, or swing, and they can be found in it after dark. We moved in partly because it's not too far from where I teach, and partly for the kids; but it's really just like the houses in which Sonny and I grew up. The same things happen, they'll have the same things to remember. The moment Sonny and I started into the house I had the feeling that I was simply bringing him back into the danger he had almost died trying to escape.

Sonny has never been talkative. So I don't know why I was sure he'd be dying to talk to me when supper was over the first night. Everything went fine, the oldest boy remembered him, and the youngest boy liked him, and Sonny had remembered to bring something for each of them; and Isabel, who is really much nicer than I am, more open and giving, had gone to a lot of trouble about dinner and was genuinely glad to see him. And she's always been able to tease Sonny in a way that I haven't. It was nice to see her face so vivid again and to hear her laugh and watch her make Sonny laugh. She wasn't, or, anyway, she didn't seem to be, at all uneasy or embarrassed. She chatted as though there were no subject which had to be avoided and she got Sonny past his first, faint stiffness. And thank God she was there, for I was filled with that icy dread again. Everything I did seemed awkward to me, and everything I said sounded freighted with hidden meaning. I was trying to remember everything I'd heard about dope addiction and I couldn't help watching Sonny for signs. I wasn't doing it out of malice. I was trying to find out something about my brother. I was dying to hear him tell me he was safe.

"Safe!" my father grunted, whenever Mama suggested trying to move to a neighborhood which might be safer for children. "Safe, hell! Ain't no place safe for kids, nor nobody."

He always went on like this, but he wasn't, ever, really as bad as he sounded, not even on weekends, when he got drunk. As a matter of fact, he was always on the lookout for "something a little better," but he died before he found it. He died suddenly, during a drunken weekend in the middle of the war, when Sonny was fifteen. He and Sonny hadn't ever got on too well. And this was partly because Sonny was the apple of his father's eye. It was because he loved Sonny so much and was frightened for him, that he was always fighting with him. It doesn't do any good to fight with Sonny. Sonny just moves back, inside himself, where he can't be reached. But the principal reason that they never hit it off is that they were so much alike. Daddy was big and rough and loud-talking, just the opposite of Sonny, but they both had — that same privacy.

Mama tried to tell me something about this, just after Daddy died. I was home on leave from the army.

This was the last time I ever saw my mother alive. Just the same, this picture gets all mixed up in my mind with pictures I had of her when she was younger. The way I always see her is the way she used to be on a Sunday afternoon, say, when the old folks were talking after the big Sunday dinner. I always see her wearing pale blue. She'd be sitting on the sofa. And my father would be sitting in the easy chair, not far from her. And the living room would be full of church folks and relatives. There they sit, in chairs all around the living room, and the night is creeping up outside, but nobody knows it yet. You can see the darkness growing against the windowpanes and you hear the street noises every now and again, or maybe the jangling beat of a tambourine from one of the churches close by, but it's real quiet in the room. For a moment nobody's talking, but every face looks darkening, like the sky outside. And my mother rocks a little from the waist, and my father's eyes are closed. Everyone is looking at something a child can't see. For a minute they've forgotten the children. Maybe a kid is lying on the rug, half asleep. Maybe somebody's got a kid in his lap and is absent-mindedly stroking the kid's head. Maybe there's a kid, quiet and big-eyed, curled up in a big chair in the corner. The silence, the darkness coming, and the darkness in the faces frightens the child obscurely. He hopes that the hand which strokes his forehead will never stop — will never die. He hopes that there will never come a time when the old folks won't be sitting around the living room, talking about where they've come from, and what they've seen, and what's happened to them and their kinfolk.

But something deep and watchful in the child knows that this is bound to end, is already ending. In a moment someone will get up and turn on the light. Then the old folks will remember the children and they won't talk any more that day. And when light fills the room, the child is filled with darkness. He knows that every time this happens he's moved just a little closer to that darkness outside. The darkness outside is what the old folks have been talking about. It's what they've come from. It's what they endure. The child knows that they won't talk any more because if he knows too much about what's happened to *them,* he'll know too much too soon, about what's going to happen to *him.*

The last time I talked to my mother, I remember I was restless. I wanted to get out and see Isabel. We weren't married then and we had a lot to straighten out between us.

There Mama sat, in black, by the window. She was humming an old church song, *Lord, you brought me from a long ways off.* Sonny was out somewhere. Mama kept watching the streets.

"I don't know," she said, "if I'll ever see you again, after you go off from here. But I hope you'll remember the things I tried to teach you."

"Don't talk like that," I said, and smiled. "You'll be here a long time yet."

She smiled, too, but she said nothing. She was quiet for a long time. And I said, "Mama, don't you worry about nothing. I'll be writing all the time, and you be getting the checks. . . ."

"I want to talk to you about your brother," she said, suddenly. "If anything happens to me he ain't going to have nobody to look out for him."

"Mama," I said, "ain't nothing going to happen to you *or* Sonny. Sonny's all right. He's a good boy and he's got good sense."

"It ain't a question of his being a good boy," Mama said, "nor of his having good sense. It ain't only the bad ones, nor yet the dumb ones that gets sucked under." She stopped, looking at me. "Your Daddy once had a brother," she said, and she smiled in a way that made me feel she was in pain. "You didn't never know that, did you?"

"No," I said, "I never knew that," and I watched her face.

"Oh, yes," she said, "your Daddy had a brother." She looked out of the window again. "I know you never saw your Daddy cry. But *I* did — many a time, through all these years."

I asked her, "What happened to his brother? How come nobody's ever talked about him?"

This was the first time I ever saw my mother look old.

"His brother got killed," she said, "when he was just a little younger than you are now. I knew him. He was a fine boy. He was maybe a little full of the devil, but he didn't mean nobody no harm."

Then she stopped and the room was silent, exactly as it had sometimes been on those Sunday afternoons. Mama kept looking out into the streets.

"He used to have a job in the mill," she said, "and, like all young folks, he just liked to perform on Saturday nights. Saturday nights, him and your father would drift around to different places, go to dances and things like that, or just sit around with people they knew, and your father's brother would sing, he had a fine voice, and play along with himself on his guitar. Well, this particular Saturday night, him and your father was coming home from some place, and they were both a little drunk and there was a moon that night, it was bright like day. Your father's brother was feeling kind of good, and he was whistling to himself, and he had his guitar slung over his shoulder. They was coming down a hill and beneath them was a road that turned off from the highway. Well, your father's brother, being always kind of frisky, decided to run down this hill, and he did, with that guitar banging

304

and clanging behind him, and he ran across the road, and he was making water behind a tree. And your father was sort of amused at him and he was still coming down the hill, kind of slow. Then he heard a car motor and that same minute his brother stepped from behind the tree, into the road, in the moonlight. And he started to cross the road. And your father started to run down the hill, he says he don't know why. This car was full of white men. They was all drunk, and when they seen your father's brother they let out a great whoop and holler and they aimed the car straight at him. They was having fun, they just wanted to scare him, the way they do sometimes, you know. But they was drunk. And I guess the boy, being drunk, too, and scared, kind of lost his head. By the time he jumped it was too late. Your father says he heard his brother scream when the car rolled over him, and he heard the wood of that guitar when it give, and he heard them strings go flying, and he heard them white men shouting, and the car kept on a-going and it ain't stopped till this day. And, time your father got down the hill, his brother weren't nothing but blood and pulp."

Tears were gleaming on my mother's face. There wasn't anything I could say.

"He never mentioned it," she said, "because I never let him mention it before you children. Your Daddy was like a crazy man that night and for many a night thereafter. He says he never in his life seen anything as dark as that road after the lights of that car had gone away. Weren't nothing, weren't nobody on that road, just your Daddy and his brother and that busted guitar. Oh, yes. Your Daddy never did really get right again. Till the day he died he weren't sure but that every white man he saw was the man that killed his brother."

She stopped and took out her handkerchief and dried her eyes and looked at me.

"I ain't telling you all this," she said, "to make you scared or bitter or to make you hate nobody. I'm telling you this because you got a brother. And the world ain't changed."

I guess I didn't want to believe this. I guess she saw this in my face. She turned away from me, toward the window again, searching those streets.

"But I praise my Redeemer," she said at last, "that He called your Daddy home before me. I ain't saying it to throw no flowers at myself, but, I declare, it keeps me from feeling too cast down to know I helped your father get safely through this world. Your father always acted like he was the roughest, strongest man on earth. And everybody took him to be like that. But if he hadn't had *me* there — to see his tears!"

She was crying again. Still, I couldn't move. I said, "Lord, Lord, Mama, I didn't know it was like that."

"Oh, honey," she said, "there's a lot that you don't know. But you are going to find it out." She stood up from the window and came over to me. "You got to hold on to your brother," she said, "and don't let him fall, no matter what it looks like is happening to him and no matter how evil you gets with him. You going to be evil with him many a time. But don't you forget what I told you, you hear?"

"I won't forget," I said. "Don't you worry, I won't forget. I won't let nothing happen to Sonny."

My mother smiled as though she were amused at something she saw in my face. Then, "You may not be able to stop nothing from happening. But you got to let him know you's *there*."

Two days later I was married, and then I was gone. And I had a lot of things on my mind and I pretty well forgot my promise to Mama until I got shipped home on a special furlough for her funeral.

And, after the funeral, with just Sonny and me alone in the empty kitchen, I tried to find out something about him. "What do you want to do?" I asked him.

"I'm going to be a musician," he said.

For he had graduated, in the time I had been away, from dancing to the juke box to finding out who was playing what, and what they were doing with it, and he had bought himself a set of drums.

"You mean, you want to be a drummer?" I somehow had the feeling that being a drummer might be all right for other people but not for my brother Sonny.

"I don't think," he said, looking at me very gravely, "that I'll ever be a good drummer. But I think I can play a piano."

I frowned. I'd never played the role of the older brother quite so seriously before, had scarcely ever, in fact, *asked* Sonny a damn thing. I sensed myself in the presence of something I didn't really know how to handle, didn't understand. So I made my frown a little deeper as I asked: "What kind of musician do you want to be?"

He grinned. "How many kinds do you think there are?"

"Be *serious*," I said.

He laughed, throwing his head back, and then looked at me. "I *am* serious."

"Well, then, for Christ's sake, stop kidding around and answer a serious question. I mean, do you want to be a concert pianist, you want to play classical music and all that, or — or what?" Long before I finished he was laughing again. "For Christ's *sake,* Sonny!"

He sobered, but with difficulty. "I'm sorry. But you sound so — *scared!*" and he was off again.

"Well, you may think it's funny now, baby, but it's not going to be so funny when you have to make your living at it, let me tell you *that.*" I was furious because I knew he was laughing at me and I didn't know why.

"No," he said, very sober now, and afraid, perhaps, that he'd hurt me, "I don't want to be a classical pianist. That isn't what interests me. I mean" — he paused, looking hard at me, as though his eyes would help me to understand, and then gestured helplessly, as though perhaps his hand would help — "I mean, I'll have a lot of studying to do, and I'll have to study *everything,* but, I mean, I want to play *with* — jazz musicians." He stopped. "I want to play jazz," he said.

Well, the word had never before sounded as heavy, as real, as it sounded that afternoon in Sonny's mouth. I just looked at him and I was probably frowning a real frown by this time. I simply couldn't see why on earth he'd want to spend his time hanging around nightclubs, clowning around on bandstands, while people pushed each other around a dance floor. It seemed — beneath him, somehow. I had never thought about it before, had never been forced to, but I suppose I had always put jazz musicians in a class with what Daddy called "good-time people."

"Are you *serious?*"

"Hell, *yes,* I'm serious."

He looked more helpless than ever, and annoyed, and deeply hurt.

I suggested, helpfully: "You mean — like Louis Armstrong?"

His face closed as though I'd struck him. "No. I'm not talking about none of that old-time, down home crap."

"Well, look, Sonny, I'm sorry, don't get mad. I just don't altogether get it, that's all. Name somebody — you know, a jazz musician you admire."

"Bird."

"Who?"

"Bird! Charlie Parker! Don't they teach you nothing in the goddamn army?"

I lit a cigarette. I was surprised and then a little amused to discover that I was trembling. "I've been out of touch," I said. "You'll have to be patient with me. Now. Who's this Parker character?"

"He's just one of the greatest jazz musicians alive," said Sonny, sullenly, his hands in his pockets, his back to me. "Maybe *the* greatest," he added, bitterly, "that's probably why *you* never heard of him."

"All right," I said, "I'm ignorant. I'm sorry. I'll go out and buy all the cat's records right away, all right?"

"It don't," said Sonny, with dignity, "make any difference to me. I don't care what you listen to. Don't do me no favors."

I was beginning to realize that I'd never seen him so upset before. With another part of my mind I was thinking that this would probably turn out to be one of those things kids go through and that I shouldn't make it seem important by pushing it too hard. Still, I didn't think it would do any harm to ask: "Doesn't all this take a lot of time? Can you make a living at it?"

He turned back to me and half leaned, half sat, on the kitchen table. "Everything takes time," he said, "and — well, yes, sure, I can make a living at it. But what I don't seem to be able to make you understand is that it's the only thing I want to do."

"Well, Sonny," I said, gently, "you know people can't always do exactly what they *want* to do — "

"*No,* I don't know that," said Sonny, surprising me. "I think people *ought* to do what they want to do, what else are they alive for?"

"You getting to be a big boy," I said desperately, "it's time you started thinking about your future."

"I'm thinking about my future," said Sonny, grimly. "I think about it all the time."

I gave up. I decided, if he didn't change his mind, that we could always talk about it later. "In the meantime," I said, "you got to finish school." We had already decided that he'd have to move in with Isabel and her folks. I knew this wasn't the ideal arrangement because Isabel's folks are inclined to be dicty and they hadn't especially wanted Isabel to marry me. But I didn't know what else to do. "And we have to get you fixed up at Isabel's."

There was a long silence. He moved from the kitchen table to the window. "That's a terrible idea. You know it yourself."

"Do you have a *better* idea?"

He just walked up and down the kitchen for a minute. He was as tall as I was. He had started to shave. I suddenly had the feeling that I didn't know him at all.

He stopped at the kitchen table and picked up my cigarettes. Looking at me with a kind of mocking, amused defiance, he put one between his lips. "You mind?"

"You smoking already?"

He lit the cigarette and nodded, watching me through the smoke. "I just wanted to see if I'd have the courage to smoke in front of you." He grinned and blew a great cloud of smoke to the ceiling. "It was easy." He looked at my face. "Come on, now. I bet you was smoking at my age, tell the truth."

I didn't say anything but the truth was on my face, and he laughed. But now there was something very strained in his laugh. "Sure. And I bet that ain't all you was doing."

He was frightening me a little. "Cut the crap," I said. "We already decided that you was going to go and live at Isabel's. Now what's got into you all of a sudden?"

"*You* decided it," he pointed out. "I didn't decide nothing." He stopped in front of me, leaning against the stove, arms loosely folded. "Look, brother. I don't want to stay in Harlem no more, I really don't." He was very earnest. He looked at me, then over toward the kitchen window. There was something in his eyes I'd never seen before, some thoughtfulness, some worry all his own. He rubbed the muscle of one arm. "It's time I was getting out of here."

"Where do you want to *go,* Sonny?"

"I want to join the army. Or the navy, I don't care. If I say I'm old enough, they'll believe me."

Then I got mad. It was because I was so scared. "You must be crazy. You goddamn fool, what the hell do you want to go and join the *army* for?"

"I just told you. To get out of Harlem."

"Sonny, you haven't even finished *school.* And if you really want to be a musician, how do you expect to study if you're in the *army?*"

He looked at me, trapped, and in anguish. "There's ways. I might be able to work out some kind of deal. Anyway, I'll have the G.I. Bill when I come out."

"*If* you come out." We stared at each other. "Sonny, please. Be reasonable. I know the setup is far from perfect. But we got to do the best we can."

"I ain't learning nothing in school," he said. "Even when I go." He turned away from me and opened the window and threw his cigarette out into the narrow alley. I watched his back. "At least, I ain't learning nothing you'd want me to learn." He slammed the window so hard I thought the glass would fly out, and turned back to me. "And I'm sick of the stink of these garbage cans!"

"Sonny," I said, "I know how you feel. But if you don't finish school now, you're going to be sorry later that you didn't." I grabbed him by the shoulders. "And you only got another year. It ain't so bad. And I'll come back and I swear

I'll help you do *whatever* you want to do. Just try to put up with it till I come back. Will you please do that? For me?"

He didn't answer and he wouldn't look at me.

"Sonny. You hear me?"

He pulled away. "I hear you. But you never hear anything *I* say."

I didn't know what to say to that. He looked out of the window and then back at me. "OK," he said, and sighed. "I'll try."

Then I said, trying to cheer him up a little, "They got a piano at Isabel's. You can practice on it."

And as a matter of fact, it did cheer him up for a minute. "That's right," he said to himself. "I forgot that." His face relaxed a little. But the worry, the thoughtfulness, played on it still, the way shadows play on a face which is staring into the fire.

But I thought I'd never hear the end of that piano. At first, Isabel would write me, saying how nice it was that Sonny was so serious about his music and how, as soon as he came in from school, or wherever he had been when he was supposed to be at school, he went straight to that piano and stayed there until suppertime. And, after supper, he went back to that piano and stayed there until everybody went to bed. He was at the piano all day Saturday and all day Sunday. Then he bought a record player and started playing records. He'd play one record over and over again, all day long sometimes, and he'd improvise along with it on the piano. Or he'd play one section of the record, one chord, one change, one progression, then he'd do it on the piano. Then back to the record. Then back to the piano.

Well, I really don't know how they stood it. Isabel finally confessed that it wasn't like living with a person at all, it was, like living with sound. And the sound didn't make any sense to her, didn't make any sense to any of them — naturally. They began, in a way, to be afflicted by this presence that was living in their home. It was as though Sonny were some sort of god, or monster. He moved in an atmosphere which wasn't like theirs at all. They fed him and he ate, he washed himself, he walked in and out of their door; he certainly wasn't nasty or unpleasant or rude, Sonny isn't any of those things; but it was as though he were all wrapped up in some cloud, some fire, some vision all his own; and there wasn't any way to reach him.

At the same time, he wasn't really a man yet, he was still a child, and they had to watch out for him in all kinds of ways. They certainly couldn't throw him out. Neither did they dare to make a great scene about that piano because even they dimly sensed, as I sensed, from so many thousands of miles away, that Sonny was at that piano playing for his life.

But he hadn't been going to school. One day a letter came from the school board and Isabel's mother got it — there had, apparently, been other letters but Sonny had torn them up. This day, when Sonny came in, Isabel's mother showed him the letter and asked where he'd been spending his time. And she finally got it out of him that he'd been down in Greenwich Village, with musicians and other characters, in a white girl's apartment. And this scared her and she started to scream at him and what came up, once she began — though she denies it to this day — was what sacrifices they were making to give Sonny a decent home and how little he appreciated it.

Sonny didn't play the piano that day. By evening, Isabel's mother had calmed down but then there was the old man to deal with, and Isabel herself. Isabel says she did her best to be calm but she broke down and started crying. She says she just watched Sonny's face. She could tell, by watching him, what was happening with him. And what was happening was that they penetrated his cloud, they had reached him. Even if their fingers had been a thousand times more gentle than human fingers ever are, he could hardly help feeling that they had stripped him naked and were spitting on that nakedness. For he also had to see that his presence, that music, which was life or death to him, had been torture for them and that they had endured it, not at all for his sake, but only for mine. And Sonny couldn't take that. He can take it a little better today than he could then but he's still not very good at it and, frankly, I don't know anybody who is.

The silence of the next few days must have been louder than the sound of all the music ever played since time began. One morning, before she went to work, Isabel was in his room for something and she suddenly realized that all of his records were gone. And she knew for certain that he was gone. And he was. He went as far as the navy would carry him. He finally sent me a postcard from some place in Greece and that was the first I knew that Sonny was still alive. I didn't see him any more until we were both back in New York and the war had long been over.

He was a man by then, of course, but I wasn't willing to see it. He came by the house from time to time, but we fought almost every time we met. I didn't like the way he carried himself, loose and dreamlike all the time, and I didn't like his friends, and his music seemed to be merely an excuse for the life he led. It sounded just that weird and disordered.

Then we had a fight, a pretty awful fight, and I didn't see him for months. By and by I looked him up, where he was living, in a furnished room in the

Village, and I tried to make it up. But there were lots of other people in the room and Sonny just lay on his bed, and he wouldn't come downstairs with me, and he treated these other people as though they were his family and I weren't. So I got mad and then he got mad, and then I told him that he might just as well be dead as live the way he was living. Then he stood up and he told me not to worry about him any more in life, that he *was* dead as far as I was concerned. Then he pushed me to the door and the other people looked on as though nothing were happening, and he slammed the door behind me. I stood in the hallway, staring at the door. I heard somebody laugh in the room and then the tears came to my eyes. I started down the steps, whistling to keep from crying, I kept whistling to myself, *You going to need me, baby, one of these cold, rainy days.*

I read about Sonny's trouble in the spring. Little Grace died in the fall. She was a beautiful little girl. But she only lived a little over two years. She died of polio and she suffered. She had a slight fever for a couple of days, but it didn't seem like anything and we just kept her in bed. And we would certainly have called the doctor, but the fever dropped, she seemed to be all right. So we thought it had just been a cold. Then, one day, she was up, playing, Isabel was in the kitchen fixing lunch for the two boys when they'd come in from school, and she heard Grace fall down in the living room. When you have a lot of children you don't always start running when one of them falls, unless they start screaming or something. And, this time, Grace was quiet. Yet, Isabel says that when she heard that *thump* and then that silence, something happened in her to make her afraid. And she ran to the living room and there was little Grace on the floor, all twisted up, and the reason she hadn't screamed was that she couldn't get her breath. And when she did scream, it was the worst sound, Isabel says, that she'd ever heard in all her life, and she still hears it sometimes in her dreams. Isabel will sometimes wake me up with a low, moaning, strangled sound and I have to be quick to awaken her and hold her to me and where Isabel is weeping against me seems a mortal wound.

I think I may have written Sonny the very day that little Grace was buried. I was sitting in the living room in the dark, by myself, and I suddenly thought of Sonny. My trouble made his real.

One Saturday afternoon, when Sonny had been living with us, or, anyway, been in our house, for nearly two weeks, I found myself wandering aimlessly about the living room, drinking from a can of beer, and trying to work up the courage to search Sonny's room. He was out, he was usually out whenever I was home, and Isabel had taken the children to see their grandparents. Suddenly I was standing still in front of the living room window, watching Seventh Avenue. The idea of searching Sonny's room made me still. I scarcely dared to admit to myself what I'd be searching for. I didn't know what I'd do if I found it. Or if I didn't.

On the sidewalk across from me, near the entrance to a barbecue joint, some people were holding an old-fashioned revival meeting. The barbecue cook, wearing a dirty white apron, his conked hair reddish and metallic in the pale sun, and a cigarette between his lips, stood in the doorway, watching them. Kids and older people paused in their errands and stood there, along with some older men and a couple of very tough-looking women who watched everything that happened on the avenue, as though they owned it, or were maybe owned by it. Well, they were watching this, too. The revival was being carried on by three sisters in black, and a brother. All they had were their voices and their Bibles and a tambourine. The brother was testifying and while he testified two of the sisters stood together, seeming to say, amen, and the third sister walked around with the tambourine outstretched and a couple of people dropped coins into it. Then the brother's testimony ended and the sister who had been taking up the collection dumped the coins into her palm and transferred them to the pocket of her long black robe. Then she raised both hands, striking the tambourine against the air, and then against one hand, and she started to sing. And the two other sisters and the brother joined in.

It was strange, suddenly, to watch, though I had been seeing these street meetings all my life. So, of course, had everybody else down there. Yet, they paused and watched and listened and I stood still at the window. *"Tis the old ship of Zion,"* they sang, and the sister with the tambourine kept a steady, jangling beat, *"it has rescued many a thousand!"* Not a soul under the sound of their voices was hearing this song for the first time, not one of them had been rescued. Nor had they seen much in the way of rescue work being done around them. Neither did they especially believe in the holiness of the three sisters and the brother, they knew too much about them, knew where they lived, and how. The woman with the tambourine, whose voice dominated the air, whose face was bright with joy, was divided by very little from the woman who stood watching her, a cigarette between her heavy, chapped lips, her hair a cuckoo's nest, her face scarred and swollen from many beatings, and her black eyes glittering like coal. Perhaps they both knew this, which was why, when, as rarely, they addressed each other, they addressed each other as Sister. As the singing filled the air the watching, listening faces underwent a change, the eyes focusing on something within; the music seemed to soothe a poison out of them; and time seemed, nearly, to fall away from the sullen, belligerent, battered faces, as though they were fleeing back to their first condition, while dreaming of their last. The barbecue cook half shook his head and smiled, and dropped his cigarette and disappeared into his joint. A man fumbled in his pockets for change and stood holding it in his hand impatiently, as though he had just remembered a pressing appointment further up the avenue. He looked furious. Then I saw Sonny, standing on the edge of the crowd. He was carrying a wide, flat notebook with a green cover, and it made him look, from where I was standing, almost like a schoolboy. The coppery sun brought out the copper in his skin, he was very faintly smiling, standing very still. Then the singing stopped, the tambourine turned into a collection plate again. The furious man dropped in his coins and vanished, so did a couple of the women, and Sonny dropped some change in the plate, looking directly at the woman with a little smile. He started across the avenue, toward the house. He has a slow, loping walk, something like the way Harlem hipsters walk, only he's imposed on this his own half-beat. I had never really noticed it before.

I stayed at the window, both relieved and apprehensive. As Sonny disappeared from my sight, they began singing again. And they were still singing when his key turned in the lock.

"Hey," he said.

"Hey, yourself. You want some beer?"

"No. Well, maybe." But he came up to the window and stood beside me, looking out. "What a warm voice," he said.

They were singing *If I could only hear my mother pray again!*

"Yes," I said, "and she can sure beat that tambourine."

"But what a terrible song," he said, and laughed. He dropped his notebook on the sofa and disappeared into the kitchen. "Where's Isabel and the kids?"

"I think they went to see their grandparents. You hungry?"

"No." He came back into the living room with his can of beer. "You want to come some place with me tonight?"

I sensed, I don't know how, that I couldn't possibly say no. "Sure. Where?"

He sat down on the sofa and picked up his notebook and started leafing through it. "I'm going to sit in with some fellows in a joint in the Village."

"You mean, you're going to play, tonight?"

"That's right." He took a swallow of his beer and moved back to the window. He gave me a sidelong look. "If you can stand it."

"I'll try," I said.

He smiled to himself and we both watched as the meeting across the way broke up. The three sisters and the brother, heads bowed, were singing *God be with you till we meet again.* The faces around them were very quiet. Then the song ended. The small crowd dispersed. We watched the three women and the lone man walk slowly up the avenue.

"When she was singing before," said Sonny, abruptly, "her voice reminded me for a minute of what heroin feels like sometimes — when it's in your veins. It makes you feel sort of warm and cool at the same time. And distant. And — and sure." He sipped his beer, very deliberately not looking at me. I watched his face. "It makes you feel — in control. Sometimes you've got to have that feeling."

"Do you?" I sat down slowly in the easy chair.

"Sometimes." He went to the sofa and picked up his notebook again. "Some people do."

"In order," I asked, "to play?" And my voice was very ugly, full of contempt and anger.

"Well" — he looked at me with great, troubled eyes, as though, in fact, he hoped his eyes would tell me things he could never otherwise say — "they *think* so. And *if* they think so — !"

"And what do *you* think?" I asked.

He sat on the sofa and put his can of beer on the floor. "I don't know," he said, and I couldn't be sure if he were answering my question or pursuing his thoughts. His face didn't tell me. "It's not so much to *play*. It's to *stand* it, to be able to make it at all. On any level." He frowned and smiled: "In order to keep from shaking to pieces."

"But these friends of yours," I said, "they seem to shake themselves to pieces pretty goddamn fast."

"Maybe." He played with the notebook. And something told me that I should curb my tongue, that Sonny was doing his best to talk, that I should listen. "But of course you only know the ones that've gone to pieces. Some don't — or at least they haven't *yet* and that's just about all *any* of us can say." He paused. "And then there are some who just live, really, in hell, and they know it and they see what's happening and they go right on. I don't know." He sighed, dropped the notebook, folded his arms. "Some guys, you can tell from the way they play, they on something *all* the time. And you can see that, well, it makes something real for them. But of course," he picked up his beer from the floor and sipped it and put the can down again, "they *want* to, too, you've got to see that. Even some of them that say they don't — *some,* not all."

"And what about you?" I asked — I couldn't help it. "What about you? Do *you* want to?"

He stood up and walked to the window and remained silent for a long time. Then he sighed. "Me," he said. Then: "While I was downstairs before, on my way here, listening to that woman sing, it struck me all of a sudden how much suffering she must have had to go through — to sing like that. It's *repulsive* to think you have to suffer that much."

I said: "But there's no way not to suffer — is there, Sonny?"

"I believe not," he said and smiled, "but that's never stopped anyone from trying." He looked at me. "Has it?" I realized, with this mocking look, that there stood between us, forever, beyond the power of time or forgiveness, the fact that I had held silence — so long! — when he had needed human speech to help him. He turned back to the window. "No, there's no way not to suffer. But you try all kinds of ways to keep from drowning in it, to keep on top of it, and to make it seem — well, like *you.* Like you did something, all right, and now you're suffering for it. You know?" I said nothing. "Well you know," he said, impatiently, "why *do* people suffer? Maybe it's better to do something to give it a reason, *any* reason."

"But we just agreed," I said, "that there's no way not to suffer. Isn't it better, then, just to — take it?"

"But nobody just takes it," Sonny cried, "that's what I'm telling you! *Everybody* tries not to. You're just hung up on the *way* some people try — it's not *your* way!"

The hair on my face began to itch, my face felt wet. "That's not true," I said, "that's not true. I don't give a damn what other people do, I don't even care how they suffer. I just care how *you* suffer." And he looked at me. "Please believe me," I said, "I don't want to see you — die — trying not to suffer."

"I won't," he said, flatly, "die trying not to suffer. At least, not any faster than anybody else."

"But there's no need," I said, trying to laugh, "is there? in killing yourself."

I wanted to say more, but I couldn't. I wanted to talk about will power and how life could be — well, beautiful. I wanted to say that it was all within; but was it? or, rather, wasn't that exactly the trouble? And I wanted to promise that I would never fail him again. But it would all have sounded — empty words and lies.

So I made the promise to myself and prayed that I would keep it.

"It's terrible sometimes, inside," he said, "that's what's the trouble. You walk these streets, black and funky and cold, and there's not really a living ass to talk to, and there's nothing shaking, and there's no way of getting it out — that storm inside. You can't talk it and you can't make love with it, and when you finally try to get with it and play it, you realize *nobody's* listening. So *you've* got to listen. You got to find a way to listen."

And then he walked away from the window and sat on the sofa again, as though all the wind had suddenly been knocked out of him. "Sometimes you'll do *anything* to play, even cut your mother's throat." He laughed and looked at me. "Or your brother's." Then he sobered. "Or your own." Then: "Don't worry. I'm all right now and I think I'll *be* all right. But I can't forget — where I've been. I don't mean just the physical place I've been, I mean where I've *been*. And *what* I've been."

"What have you been, Sonny?" I asked.

He smiled — but sat sideways on the sofa, his elbow resting on the back, his fingers playing with his mouth and chin, not looking at me. "I've been something I didn't recognize, didn't know I could be. Didn't know anybody could be." He stopped, looking inward, looking helplessly young, looking old. "I'm not talking about it now because I feel *guilty* or anything like that — maybe it would be better if I did, I don't know. Anyway, I can't really talk about it. Not to you, not to anybody," and now he turned and faced me. "Sometimes, you know, and it was actually when I was most *out* of the world, I felt that I was in it, that I was *with* it, really, and I could play or I didn't really have to *play*, it just came out of me, it was there. And I don't know how I played, thinking about it now, but I know I did awful things, those times, sometimes, to people. Or it wasn't that I *did* anything to them — it was that they weren't real." He picked up the beer can; it was empty; he rolled it between his palms: "And other times — well, I needed a fix, I needed to find a place to lean, I needed to clear a space to *listen* — and I couldn't find it, and I — went crazy, I did terrible things to *me*, I was terrible *for* me." He began pressing the beer can between his hands, I watched the metal begin to give. It glittered, as he played with it, like a knife, and I was afraid he would cut himself, but I said nothing. "Oh well. I can never tell you. I was all by myself at the bottom of something, stinking and sweating and crying and shaking, and I smelled it, you know? *my* stink, and I thought I'd die if I couldn't get away from it and yet, all the same, I knew that everything I was doing was just locking me in with it. And I didn't know," he paused, still flattening the beer can, "I didn't know, I still *don't* know, something kept telling me that maybe it was good to smell your own stink, but I didn't think that *that* was what I'd been trying to do — and — who can stand it?" and he abruptly dropped the ruined beer can, looking at me with a small, still smile, and then rose, walking to the window as though it were the lodestone rock. I watched his face, he watched the avenue. "I couldn't tell you when Mama died — but the reason I wanted to leave Harlem so bad was to get away from drugs. And then, when I ran away, that's what I was running from — really. When I came back, nothing had changed, I hadn't changed, I was just — older." And he stopped, drumming with his fingers on the windowpane. The sun had vanished, soon darkness would fall. I watched his face. "It can come again," he said, almost as though speaking to himself. Then he turned to me. "It can come again," he repeated. "I just want you to know that."

"All right," I said, at last. "So it can come again, All right."

He smiled, but the smile was sorrowful. "I had to try to tell you," he said.

"Yes," I said. "I understand that."

"You're my brother," he said, looking straight at me, and not smiling at all.

"Yes," I repeated, "yes. I understand that."

He turned back to the window, looking out. "All that hatred down there," he said, "all that hatred and misery and love. It's a wonder it doesn't blow the avenue apart."

We went to the only nightclub on a short, dark street, downtown. We squeezed through the narrow, chattering, jam-packed bar to the entrance of the big room, where the bandstand was. And we stood there for a moment, for the lights were very dim in this room and we couldn't see. Then, "Hello, boy," said a voice and an enormous black man, much older than Sonny or myself, erupted out of all that atmospheric lighting and put an arm around Sonny's shoulder. "I been sitting right here," he said, "waiting for you."

He had a big voice, too, and heads in the darkness turned toward us.

Sonny grinned and pulled a little away, and said, "Creole, this is my brother. I told you about him."

Creole shook my hand. "I'm glad to meet you, son," he said, and it was clear that he was glad to meet me *there,* for Sonny's sake. And he smiled, "You got a real musician in *your* family," and he took his arm from Sonny's shoulder and slapped him, lightly, affectionately, with the back of his hand.

"Well. Now I've heard it all," said a voice behind us. This was another musician, and a friend of Sonny's, a coal-black, cheerful-looking man, built close to the ground. He immediately began confiding to me; at the top of his lungs, the most terrible things about Sonny, his teeth gleaming like a lighthouse and his laugh coming up out of him like the beginning of an earthquake. And it turned out that everyone at the bar knew Sonny, or almost everyone; some were musicians, working there, or nearby, or not working, some were simply hangers-on, and some were there to hear Sonny play. I was introduced to all of them and they were all very polite to me. Yet, it was clear that, for them, I was only Sonny's brother. Here, I was in Sonny's world. Or, rather: his kingdom. Here, it was not even a question that his veins bore royal blood.

They were going to play soon and Creole installed me, by myself, at a table in a dark corner. Then I watched them, Creole, and the little black man, and Sonny, and the others, while they horsed around, standing just below the bandstand. The light from the bandstand spilled just a little short of them and, watching them laughing and gesturing and moving about, I had the feeling that they, nevertheless, were being most careful not to step into that circle of light too suddenly: that if they moved into the light too suddenly, without thinking, they would perish in flame. Then, while I watched, one of them, the small, black man, moved into the light and crossed the bandstand and started fooling around with his drums. Then — being funny and being, also, extremely ceremonious — Creole took Sonny by the arm and led him to the piano. A woman's voice called Sonny's name and a few hands started clapping. And Sonny, also being funny and being ceremonious, and so touched, I think, that he could have cried, but neither hiding it nor showing it, riding it like a man, grinned, and put both hands to his heart and bowed from the waist.

Creole then went to the bass fiddle and a lean, very bright-skinned brown man jumped up on the bandstand and picked up his horn. So there they were, and the atmosphere on the bandstand and in the room began to change and tighten. Someone stepped up to the microphone and announced them. Then there were all kinds of murmurs. Some people at the bar shushed others. The waitress ran around, frantically getting in the last orders, guys and chicks got closer to each other, and the lights on the bandstand, on the quartet, turned to a kind of indigo. Then they all looked different there. Creole looked about him for the last time, as though he were making certain that all his chickens were in the coop, and then he jumped and struck the fiddle. And there they were.

All I know about music is that not many people ever really hear it. And even then, on the rare occasions when something opens within, and the music enters, what we mainly hear, or hear corroborated, are personal, private, vanishing evocations. But the man who creates the music is hearing something else, is dealing with the roar rising from the void and imposing order on it as it hits the air. What is evoked in him, then, is of another order, more terrible because it has no words, and triumphant, too, for that same reason. And his triumph, when he triumphs, is ours. I just watched Sonny's face. His face was troubled, he was working hard, but he wasn't with it. And I had the feeling that, in a way, everyone on the bandstand was waiting for him, both waiting for him and pushing him along. But as I began to watch Creole, I realized that it was Creole who held them all back. He had them on a short rein. Up there, keeping the beat with his whole body, wailing on the fiddle, with his eyes half closed, he was listening to everything, but he was listening to Sonny. He was having a dialogue with Sonny. He wanted Sonny to leave the shoreline and strike out for the deep water. He was Sonny's witness that deep water and drowning were not the same thing — he had been there, and he knew. And he wanted Sonny to know. He was waiting for Sonny to do the things on the keys which would let Creole know that Sonny was in the water.

And, while Creole listened, Sonny moved, deep within, exactly like someone in torment. I had never before thought of how awful the relationship must be between the musician and his instrument. He has to fill it, this instrument, with the breath of life, his own. He has to make it do what he wants it to do. And a piano is just a piano. It's made out of so much wood and wires and little hammers and big ones, and ivory. While there's only so much you can do with it, the only way to find this out is to try; to try and make it do everything.

And Sonny hadn't been near a piano for over a year. And he wasn't on much better terms with his life, not the life that stretched before him now. He and the piano stammered, started one way, got scared, stopped; started another way, panicked, marked time, started again; then seemed to have found a direction, panicked again, got stuck. And the face I saw on Sonny I'd never seen before. Everything had been burned out of it, and, at the same time, things usually hidden were being burned in, by the fire and fury of the battle which was occurring in him up there.

Yet, watching Creole's face as they neared the end of the first set, I had the feeling that something had happened, something I hadn't heard. Then they finished, there was scattered applause, and then, without an instant's warning, Creole started into something else, it was almost sardonic, it was *Am I Blue*. And, as though he commanded, Sonny began to play. Something began to happen. And Creole let out the reins. The dry, low, black man said something awful on the drums, Creole answered, and the drums talked back. Then the horn insisted, sweet and high, slightly detached perhaps, and Creole listened, commenting now and then, dry, and driving, beautiful and calm and old. Then they all came together again, and Sonny was part of the family again. I could tell this from his face. He seemed to have found, right there beneath his fingers, a damn brand-new piano. It seemed that he couldn't get over it. Then, for awhile, just being happy with Sonny, they seemed to be agreeing with him that brand-new pianos certainly were a gas.

Then Creole stepped forward to remind them that what they were playing was the blues. He hit something in all of them, he hit something in me, myself, and the music tightened and deepened, apprehension began to beat the air. Creole began to tell us what the blues were all about. They were not about anything very new. He and his boys up there were keeping it new, at the risk of ruin, destruction, madness, and death, in order to find new ways to make us listen. For, while the tale of how we suffer, and how we are delighted, and how we may triumph is never new, it always must be heard. There isn't any other tale to tell, it's the only light we've got in all this darkness.

And this tale, according to that face, that body, those strong hands on those strings, has another aspect in every country, and a new depth in every generation. Listen, Creole seemed to be saying, listen. Now these are Sonny's blues. He made the little black man on the drums know it, and the bright, brown man on the horn. Creole wasn't trying any longer to get Sonny in the water. He was wishing him Godspeed. Then he stepped back, very slowly, filling the air with the immense suggestion that Sonny speak for himself.

Then they all gathered around Sonny and Sonny played. Every now and again one of them seemed to say, amen. Sonny's fingers filled the air with life, his life. But that life contained so many others. And Sonny went all the way back, he really began with the spare, flat statement of the opening phrase of the song. Then he began to make it his. It was very beautiful because it wasn't hurried and it was no longer a lament. I seemed to hear with what burning he had made it his, with what burning we had yet to make it ours, how we could cease lamenting. Freedom lurked around us and I understood, at last, that he could help us to be free if we would listen, that he would never be free until we did. Yet, there was no battle in his face now. I heard what he had gone through, and would continue to go through until he came to rest in earth. He had made it his: that long line, of which we knew only Mama and Daddy. And he was giving it back, as everything must be given back, so that, passing through death, it can live forever. I saw my mother's face again, and felt, for the first time, how the stones of the road she had walked on must have bruised her feet. I saw the moonlit road where my father's brother died. And it brought something else back to me, and carried me past it, I saw my little girl again and felt Isabel's tears again, and I felt my own tears begin to rise. And I was yet aware that this was only a moment, that the world waited outside, as hungry as a tiger, and that trouble stretched above us, longer than the sky.

Then it was over. Creole and Sonny let out their breath, both soaking wet, and grinning. There was a lot of applause and some of it was real. In the dark, the girl came by and I asked her to take drinks to the bandstand. There was a long pause, while they talked up there in the indigo light and after awhile I saw the girl put a Scotch and milk on top of the piano for Sonny. He didn't seem to notice it, but just before they started playing again, he sipped from it and looked toward me, and nodded. Then he put it back on top of the piano. For me, then, as they began to play again, it glowed and shook above my brother's head like the very cup of trembling.

QUESTION THREE

With Whom and for Whom Shall I Live?

As we, the editors, prepared this revised edition of *Leading Lives That Matter*, a careful reader pointed out a discrepancy in the language we used in the original edition. The subtitle of the book is in the plural — "What We Should Do and Who We Should Be" — while the chapter titles speak in the singular, asking such questions as "To Whom Shall I Listen?" and "How Shall I Tell the Story of My Life?" "Which is it," she asked: "We or I? Do you mean to emphasize the shared character of human life and action or the personal character of the quest for meaning and significance?"

We intended to call attention to both dimensions, of course. Nonetheless, this reader's question challenged us to be more explicit in urging readers to consider how profoundly important relationships — face-to-face and in larger social groupings — are in shaping the meaning and significance of every human life. Further, the difference each of us will make depends on our relationships with others. Whom do we think our work will benefit? What persons, and what parts of the natural world, do we long to know more fully and serve more capably?

Each individual has to take his or her life seriously, of course; it is fitting that your own life matters to you personally. But if that is your only measure of significance, then your life will be destructive to yourself and others. An isolated person will miss out on the satisfactions and support that can flow from relationships with friends, family members, and larger groups of various kinds. And the contributions an isolated person might have made to the well-being of others, through work and countless other activities, will never make a difference. A life that matters is a life that matters to people beyond oneself. And so this chapter asks, "With whom and for whom shall I live?" The "I" is still there — but in the company and context created by other people, the ones with whom our lives are entwined and for whom our efforts are offered, close at hand and in the larger society.

Relationship is a matter of life and death. Without the touch and assistance of loving adults from the very moment of birth, babies die. As children grow, the character and quality of the care they receive are likely the most important factors shaping their individual development. Later, friends inspire and help one another, testing limits, figuring things out together, and providing mutual challenge and support. Sometimes, one specific friend becomes a lover and life partner as well, and a new family is born. Many people would say that the close bonds of family and friendship are the most important elements in their lives. Daughter, son; sister, brother; uncle, aunt; spouse, parent, friend — many people, probably most, would say that these are the most important roles they have played. But the irreducible human dependence on others also goes beyond personal relationships. Surrounding all of us are countless other circles of provision and influence, from the farmers, truckers, and merchants on whom we depend for sustenance to the first responders and physicians on whom we call in times of distress. Beyond these are a variety of larger social groups — neighborhoods, cities, regions, and nations; schools, religious communities, professions, and other institutions; cultural and ethnic groups; and more.

The question of individual commitment to other people takes on heightened resonance in a fluid, globalizing culture where authenticity and self-determination are highly prized. In the contemporary West, where movies and commercials depict individuals as the key loci of action, decision, choice, and satisfaction, it may seem possible to live independently. However, this sense of individual self-realization is fairly new in human history. Most cultures in the past, and many marginalized or distant cultures today, have made far less room for individual self-definition. And this is not solely because individuals had less scope of action in more traditional societies. Instead, the very concept of "the individual," as it is bandied about today, was absent.

"The Western conception of the person as a bounded, unique, more or less integrated motivational and cognitive universe, a dynamic center of awareness, emotion, judgment, and action organized into a distinctive whole and set contrastively both against other such wholes and against its social and natural background, is, however incorrigible it may seem to us, a rather peculiar idea within the context of the world's cultures," wrote the influential anthropologist Clifford Geertz in 1983. Geertz, who did extensive field studies in Java, Bali, Morocco, and elsewhere, is not at all interested in showing that some notions of the self are better or worse than others. He is interested instead in showing us how different self-conceptions are deeply embedded in different cultures. Thus, when Westerners speak or think as though leading a life that matters is an individual project, we are at best extremely shortsighted about the range of human experience over time. We are also overlooking our own deep immersion in social and cultural settings, which shape and limit even modern people far more than some contemporary notions of the self allow.

Questioning the notion that thinking itself is performed by isolated individuals (as modern philosophy has held since Descartes) has been a strong theme in philosophy across the past century. Although we are not including another excerpt by Charles Taylor in this chapter (we met Taylor on pages 59–64 above, through his explication of the vocabulary of authenticity), Taylor's work can also help prepare us to ask with whom, and for whom, we shall live. Consider the strongest case for individualism we have encountered so far in this book — the vocabulary of "authenticity." This approach to thinking and talking about what makes for a choiceworthy life proposes that there exists within each person a distinctive, original individuality. Such individuality, within the terms of this vocabulary, is a definition of who humans most truly are; further, this individuality is understood to be a good thing. As we have seen, Charles Taylor traces the emergence of this highly individual sense of self to the shifting political, economic, and cultural patterns that shaped modern culture. In the chapters of *The Ethics of Authenticity* that follow the excerpt we included in "Vocabularies," Taylor goes beyond tracing this history, however; he also scrutinizes the philosophical coherence of claiming that self-expressed individuality can ever fully describe who people are. The thoughts and actions of the individual self, Taylor argues, only make sense when placed upon wider horizons of meaning — horizons that are necessarily shared with others. Our ideas, and even our sense of self, have emerged over the course of an ongoing, sometimes silent dialogue with others — in a certain language, a certain time and place — within which we come to see that things make sense in certain ways, even if we will later challenge those ways. Taylor's argument should prompt people who think their goal is to express their own individual nature to understand the taken-for-granted but very real horizons of meaning that have led them to value some things more than others, and the opinions of certain people more than the opinions of others.

The "I" that believes itself to be an autonomous, isolated, and independent individual has failed to understand that thought, identity, and action are in fact constituted by the presence of others from whom we have absorbed patterns of meaning and senses of self that could not be established in a vacuum. In fact, we humans are social beings; we are psychologically a "we" even before we come to understand that we are also physically, morally, and spiritually a "we." When we consider our "own" identity, we should therefore acknowledge that even this refers to a plurality, not an individuality, whether we realize it or not.

The first three readings in this section explore certain physical dynamics of human relatedness. The evidence each introduces emerges from everyday life, prompting readers to consider how crucial the forms of care and community we experience throughout life are to human flourishing.

- Alasdair MacIntyre, a selection from *Dependent Rational Animals: Why Human Beings Need the Virtues*
- a poem by Kate Daniels, "Prayer for My Children"
- Malcolm Gladwell, "The Roseto Mystery"

We begin with a selection from a leading philosopher of the late twentieth and early twenty-first century, Alasdair MacIntyre. In a series of influential books, MacIntyre has argued against modern Western philosophy's absorption of individualist conceptions of the self. In the selection excerpted here, he opposes the idea that each human self is autonomous and independent and develops an account of the human that acknowledges the vulnerability and dependence every human being has experienced in infancy and will most likely experience again when ill, disabled, or aged.

Marvelously, it is often within relationships of vulnerability and dependence that we also experience our deepest joy and fulfillment — not only during illness, disability, or old age, but all our lives long. Think of spouses, for instance, or very close friends. Within such relationships, we are vulnerable even when our health is strong. We might be betrayed, or one of us might die. We know this, but even so, when we find someone right for us, we take the risk and find our lives enhanced. We come to depend on one another, ideally in ways that are mutual, though we know that unforeseen events could throw the balance off. Many people feel that they find their greatest joy in relationships like these.

As we consider with and for whom to live, we can be — and often should be — moved by delight rather than obligation and need. Indeed, delight in one another is woven into healthy human development. Even in infancy, psychologists tell us, the "social smile" of a six-to-eight-week-old baby elicits caregiving from its parents, laying the foundation for the individual development and interpersonal relationships that will come later. And part of the care good parents provide includes smiles of their own, and chuckles and hugs.

"Prayer for My Children," a poem by Kate Daniels, reflects on the connection between love and vulnerability from the perspective of a mother of young children. Although not everyone is a parent, everyone has had a parent or other primary caregiver, so this poem has wide applicability. Even so, raw, physical love like that described in this poem is rarely articulated so beautifully and powerfully. Vulnerability between parent and child, the poem suggests, runs in both directions. If asked, "with whom and for whom shall I live?," the mother in this poem might well say, "with and for my children."

Both of these pieces take very seriously a fundamental fact of human existence that modern people have been surprisingly eager to overlook: we humans are embodied beings. We have bodies and we are bodies, which both enable our emotions, thoughts, and actions and set our limits. The subsequent reading describes how a group of scientists discovered a variant of this same truth playing itself out in real life, as they investigated an unusual outbreak of good health in a small town in Pennsylvania.

Malcolm Gladwell's account of the social patterns underlying human flourishing in Roseto, Pennsylvania, introduces a term that often appears as we ponder with whom and for whom to live: "community." This word is used in many ways — some of them shallow or commonplace (the Facebook community, the campus community, and so on), but all of them shimmering with the human desire for connection. The community Gladwell describes is dense with embodied interaction — people drop in to chat, share home-cooked meals, and help the folks next door. Such face-to-face practices, Gladwell argues, are what is needed for human well-being. Yet some commentators argue that recent social trends are undermining community in this sense — and indeed, the social changes that came to Roseto within twenty years of this study erased the health advantages Rosetans had previously enjoyed. As we consider forms of belonging in this chapter, we should also reflect on how online connections shape our relationships and influence our understanding and experience of long-esteemed human goods like friendship and community.

Realizing that none of us is actually alone and acknowledging our dependence on one another are only beginning points. A next step is to figure out which people and groups rightly claim our primary affection, allegiance, and energies. We encountered some of the claimants in the previous chapter. Asking "to whom shall I listen?," we have seen "the undeclared major" struggling between what he believes his father wants for him and his own desire to take a different path, and we have watched a young Chinese American woman resisting the powerful assertions of her immigrant mother. We also had a glimpse, in the excerpt from *The Giver*, of how a tightly integrated social group can overwhelm individual choice completely — showing the possible harm in the social bonds we are considering here. In the chapter after this one, which will explore the possibility and desirability of living a "balanced" life, we will see how readily conflict can arise between the different groups to which we feel drawn or accountable. Even knowing that we live with and for others, we may find difficulty in sorting out our responses to the two tugs Jane Addams called "the family claim" and "the social claim." In the subsequent chapter, we will encounter an urgent contemporary claim that begins with awareness of our immersion in the living web of creation: the claim upon our lives that arises when we recognize our obligation to the well-being of future generations of human and other life. This profound relationship provides another context for reflection on with whom and for whom we shall live.

Irreducibly related though we humans are, and much as we desire one another's love and support, history has demonstrated again and again that our personal and social bonds are fragile and often fractured by mistrust, oppression, or violence. The readings in this chapter probe some of the situations and forces that imperil the very forms of connectedness for which we yearn. At the same time, the authors of these texts assert the importance of family, friendship, and love, helping us to glimpse how precious the bonds we share with others are.

The following set of selections shows relationships in ways that both affirm their deep value and display the forces that can strain or break them. These selections are:

- the book of Ruth
- a description of family life by a woman whose strong bonds with her parents, immigrants from India, are strained by their different cultural experiences and their attraction to different communities (Jhumpa Lahiri)
- a story of friendship between two young girls of different races (Toni Morrison)
- a letter from a soldier to his wife, written on the day before a battle he knows may end his life (Sullivan Ballou)

The book of Ruth was written down well over two thousand years ago, and it may have circulated in oral form for centuries before that. This short book from the Hebrew Bible (also in the collection Christians call the Old Testament) tells the story of a young woman — poor, widowed, a foreigner — and her mother-in-law, Naomi, who is also widowed and impoverished.

Both are homeless, and Ruth is an immigrant from a despised country; securing their safety will require Ruth to take significant risks. Forces that threaten belonging and that rupture community are strong. But this short book also contains one of the Western tradition's strongest statements of love: "Where you go, I will go; where you stay, I will stay," Ruth promises Naomi. The story ends with a grandmother holding a baby, as the women of her village circle gather around in celebration. Although the characters don't know this, readers also learn that this moment will bear good fruit for the entire nation to which these women belong. Present are several forms of relationship — and also several forces that often rupture relationship, including ethnic prejudice, national boundaries, poverty, and class distinctions.

Jhumpa Lahiri's short essay, "My Two Lives," also explores the dynamics of migration and the difficult choices living on the boundary of different cultures imposes on those trying to figure out with whom and for whom they should live. Lahiri's experience was quite different from that of the thriving Italian American residents of Roseto, Pennsylvania, who shared a single tightly knit culture. Growing up, Lahiri lived simultaneously in two contrasting cultural worlds — the world of her Bengali parents, and the world of her Rhode Island public school. She was "loyal to the old world and fluent in the new," shaped by genuine affection for each but always uncertain where she fit. As she gradually learned how to affirm both worlds, her parents negotiated the conflict of cultures in a different way, holding firmly to their Indian community and identity. As numerous families today negotiate the promise and peril of movement across national and cultural boundaries, both Lahiri's story and the book of Ruth remind us of the importance of place, family, and community in establishing identity and securing survival.

Roberta and Twyla, the leading characters in "Recitatif," meet at another cultural boundary. Toni Morrison, the Nobel Prize–winning author of *Beloved* and many other novels, explored throughout her career the African American experience and the impact of racial injustice on American lives. In this story, Morrison crafts two characters highly influenced by these realities, but she makes readers figure out the implications for themselves. At the beginning of the story, each of the two girls is so alone in the world that she is placed in an orphanage; over the course of the story, we glimpse the variety of relationships each of their lives will eventually hold. The main relationship in the story, however, is the one between the two of them. We include it here as a story of friendship, which is surely one of the most important ways in which people choose to live with and for one another. Yet this story also shows the limits and challenges of friendship. Indeed, we will need to ask, when reading the story, whether friendship is an apt name for what Twyla and Roberta share.

The action in Morrison's story plays out on a landscape shaped by the social forces of gender, race, and class. Morrison, a writer of fiction, invites readers to discern these dynamics by subtly choosing certain words and details. In the next selections, the impact of social forces on lives and relationships is displayed in a more explicit way. As a soldier writes to his wife from the battlefield, both the strength of their intimate bond and the destructive force of political and military conflict are laid bare. In this letter by Sullivan Ballou, who had enlisted in the Union army at the beginning of the Civil War, we see the intimate relationships of marriage and parenthood subordinated to and torn by the struggles of warring nations. Ballou's poignant letter reminds us forcefully of something that is also present, though sometimes less obviously so, in other selections in this chapter: personal relationships do not exist on a neutral stage, apart from the tumults and struggles of societies and nations. His letter also shows how commitments to social and political movements (here, the Union cause) also become relationships that set people's lives in certain directions. Unlike many whose families are destroyed in war, Ballou is not here a victim but a willing participant. He is choosing to live, and to die, with and for his country.

The final two selections in this chapter build on the fundamental fact of human interdependence we saw in this chapter's first three selections. They also take very seriously the challenges to human connection and flourishing we have seen in the subsequent four selections. But neither author is simply observing human behavior; instead, each one intends to challenge readers to action of a certain kind. Each author — Rev. Dr. Samuel Wells and Rev. Dr. Martin Luther King Jr. — wants to persuade readers to ask: What difference might the fact of our interdependence make as we decide what we should do and who we should be?

- "Rethinking Service," a lecture by Samuel Wells
- Selections from "The World House," a plea to build a global movement for justice and peace, by Martin Luther King Jr.

The lecture by Samuel Wells delves right into the heart of the questions addressed in this chapter. The bulk of Wells's argument, indeed, explores the two prepositions in this chapter's title, "With Whom and for Whom Shall I Live?" Wells asks readers to think deeply about the assumptions about who people are and what we most need that are embedded in those two short words. To be *with* someone carries a sense of communion and solidarity between persons, while to be *for* someone imagines one person as an agent who provides help to less fortunate others. Is it more life-giving and true to human capacities and needs to think of our service to others as something we do *for* them or as something defined by our willingness to be *with* them?

Wells's discussion recalls the tensions about individualism and community encountered earlier in this chapter. Those who think that overcoming limitations is humanity's greatest task are likely to think of themselves as independent *doers-for* — as centers of initiative and action — rather than as persons who have been and will someday again be *done-for*, as the "vulnerable, dependent animals" Alasdair MacIntyre insists all human beings fundamentally are. Reading Wells may also call to mind some features of the book of Ruth, "My Two Lives," and "Recitatif." In these stories, the yearning to overcome isolation — the desire to find friends and loved ones to be "with" — was the characters' overriding concern.

The final selection in this chapter is from *Where Do We Go from Here: Chaos or Community?*, written by Martin Luther King about a year before he was assassinated in 1968. During the civil rights movement, King often spoke of "beloved community" as a goal of the struggle for racial equality in the United States. By this he meant a community, born by nonviolent means, in which people who once saw each other as enemies would experience genuine reconciliation, living together in justice and peace not only because laws require it but because their hearts and souls have been transformed. By 1967, when this selection was written, the civil rights movement had won significant legal victories and King had begun to speak out more forthrightly about related injustices — such as economic inequality and war — that continued to oppress both his own community and other marginalized peoples around the world. He was also beginning to articulate a vision of global change leading to world peace, undergirded by justice and love.

Throughout this chapter we have seen that individual persons are necessarily related to and dependent upon one another. In King's image of the World House, this interdependence takes on a global dimension, encompassing all people and every nation. Eloquently, King establishes the fact of such interdependence, pointing by way of example to the international origins of the foods on our breakfast tables. Recognizing such connections is crucial — but his argument goes further. His point is not only that we do live together in this world but that the peoples of this world must live together rightly and well if any are to thrive at all. Poverty and war will destroy everyone, not just a few. The global situation requires humankind to work together to address the various forms of injustice that destroy the inescapable relationships all of us share. When King asked *Where Do We Go from Here: Chaos or Community?*, he was not raising an abstract dilemma. He was trying to enlist people of good will to address the world's problems by choosing community rather than chaos.

Fifty years have passed since King penned this effort to awaken his contemporaries to "the fierce urgency of *now*." Yet humankind still seems to be torn between chaos and community — between the injustices that unsettle peace in and among countries all over the world and the persistent human longing to connect in love to people of every land. When we ask with whom and for whom we shall live, our global neighbors are among those to be considered.

Alasdair MacIntyre

VULNERABILITY, DEPENDENCE, ANIMALITY

Alasdair MacIntyre is one of the leading philosophical proponents of what we have called the vocabulary of virtue. Drawing on the legacy of Aristotle, Augustine, and Thomas Aquinas, MacIntyre has argued that the self-determined independence of each person, which is assumed within the vocabulary of authenticity and which deeply influences both modern philosophy and popular culture, incorporates serious mistakes about who human beings are, what we need, and what we should hope for. In this selection, MacIntyre contends that our focus on independence and personal autonomy is misguided. Rather, we should embrace the fact that we are beings who need others; indeed, our vulnerability marks us as "human."

MacIntyre identifies some mistaken assumptions in moral philosophy as it is usually done (for example, that those who are ill, aged, or disabled are seen primarily as the objects of "our" benevolence rather than as human beings whose dependent condition, in the end, belongs to everyone, including "us"). Is MacIntyre's concern an academic dispute among philosophers, or is he making an insightful comment about an assumption that also appears in everyday life? If this assumption does indeed prevail in real-life contexts, what might change if it were relinquished? How might awareness of the "vulnerability, dependence, and animality" of ourselves and our peers reshape our sense of what we desire in the relationships and communities we treasure?

We human beings are vulnerable to many kinds of affliction and most of us are at some time afflicted by serious ills. How we cope is only in small part up to us. It is most often to others that we owe our survival, let alone our flourishing, as we encounter bodily illness and injury, inadequate nutrition, mental defect and disturbance, and human aggression and neglect. This dependence on particular others for protection and sustenance is most

From Alasdair MacIntyre, *Dependent Rational Animals: Why Human Beings Need the Virtues* (Chicago: Open Court, 1999), 1–3.

obvious in early childhood and in old age. But between these first and last stages our lives are characteristically marked by longer or shorter periods of injury, illness or other disablement and some among us are disabled for their entire lives.

These two related sets of facts, those concerning our vulnerabilities and afflictions and those concerning the extent of our dependence on particular others are so evidently of singular importance that it might seem that no account of the human condition whose authors hoped to achieve credibility could avoid giving them a central place. Yet the history of Western moral philosophy suggests otherwise. From Plato to Moore and since there are usually, with some rare exceptions, only passing references to human vulnerability and affliction and to the connections between them and our dependence on others. Some of the facts of human limitation and of our consequent need of cooperation with others are more generally acknowledged, but for the most part only then to be put on one side. And when the ill, the injured and the otherwise disabled *are* presented in the pages of moral philosophy books, it is almost always exclusively as possible subjects of benevolence by moral agents who are themselves presented as though they were continuously rational, healthy and untroubled. So we are invited, when we do think of disability, to think of "the disabled" as "them," as other than "us," as a separate class, not as ourselves as we have been, sometimes are now and may well be in the future.

Adam Smith provides us with an example. While discussing what it is that makes the "pleasures of wealth and greatness . . . strike the imagination as something grand and beautiful," he remarks that "in the languor of disease and the weariness of old age" we cease to be so impressed, for we then take note of the fact that the acquisition of wealth and greatness leaves their possessors "always as much, and sometimes more exposed than before, to anxiety, to fear and to sorrow, to disease, to danger, and to death" (*The Theory of Moral Sentiments* IV, chapter I). But to allow our attention to dwell on this is, on Smith's view, misguided.

To do so is to embrace a "splenetic philosophy," the effect of "sickness or low spirits" upon an imagination "which in pain and sorrow seems to be confined," so that we are no longer "charmed with the beauty of that accommodation which reigns in the palaces and economy of the great. . . ." The imagination of those "in better health or in better humor" fosters what may, Smith concedes, be no more than seductive illusions about the pleasures of wealth and greatness, but they are economically beneficial illusions. "It is this deception which rouses and keeps in continual motion the industry of mankind." So even someone as perceptive as Smith, when he does pause to recognize the perspectives of ill health and old age, finds reason at once to put them on one side. And in so doing Smith speaks for moral philosophy in general.

As with vulnerability and affliction, so it is correspondingly with dependence. Dependence on others is of course often recognized in a general way, usually as something that we need in order to achieve our positive goals. But an acknowledgment of anything like the full extent of that dependence and of the ways in which it stems from our vulnerability and our afflictions is generally absent. Feminist philosophers have recently done something to remedy this, not only by their understanding of the connections between blindness to and denigration of women and male attempts to ignore the facts of dependence, but also — I think here particularly of the work of Virginia Held — by their emphasis upon the importance of the mother-child relationship as a paradigm for moral relationships. Even more recently some striking philosophical work has been done on the nature of disability and on the condition of the disabled and the dependent.

Kate Daniels

PRAYER FOR MY CHILDREN

In this poem, by Kate Daniels, a mother watches her young children doing a simple task. Notice that some of the same fundamental facts about human life emphasized in the previous reading are also present here — but in a different tone and with a different purpose. Through what words does the poet communicate the *dependence* of her children? Their *animality*? Their *vulnerability*?

Reflecting on these qualities within the abstract terms of a philosophical work can help us to analyze the character of our human condition. But when depicted by a skillful poet, these qualities can also move us. Yes, vulnerability, dependence, and animality define our limits as individuals and foreshadow our mortality; but in this poem they also become sites of connection, joy, and love. In addition, the poem discloses the layered and mutual character of relatedness. Even when some of the persons involved appear at first to be the dependent and vulnerable ones (the children), the vulnerability actually runs in both directions. For whom do you think this mother is actually praying?

How might mutual dependence and vulnerability also appear within other kinds of intimate relationships? Do the first seven lines of the poem suggest that intense love overrides moral conscience — and if that is so, is that a good thing or a problem? And what do you make of the poet's emphasis on the physical character of the particular bonds she is describing? How do you think the emotional responses to this poem of a mother, a stepmother, and a father might differ? Do you find the poet's intensely embodied relationship with her children beautiful, or disturbing, or both?

....

Kate Daniels, "Prayer for My Children," in *Four Testimonies* (Baton Rouge: LSU Press, 1998), 92.

I regret nothing.
My cruelties, my betrayals
of others I once thought
I loved. All the unlived
years, the unwritten
poems, the wasted nights
spent weeping and drinking.

No, I regret nothing
because what I've lived
has led me here, to this room
with its marvelous riches,
its simple wealth —
these three heads shining
beneath the Japanese lamp, laboring
over crayons and paper.
These three who love me
exactly as I am, precisely
at the center of my ill-built being.
Who rear up eagerly when I enter,
and fall down weeping when I leave.
Whose eyes are my eyes.
Hair, my hair.
Whose bodies I cover
with kisses and blankets.
Whose first meal was my own body.
Whose last, please God, I will not live
to serve, or share.

Malcolm Gladwell

THE ROSETO MYSTERY

In this chapter, we encounter philosophical, theological, literary, and moral arguments that human beings are intrinsically "social" beings who thrive only in relationship with one another. Here Malcolm Gladwell introduces an argument of a different kind. Gladwell, a journalist who has a gift for noticing intriguing, important patterns in our culture, uses this essay to introduce his book *Outliers: The Story of Success.* The story he tells, "The Roseto Mystery," reads like a piece of imaginative literature but turns out to be an accurate account of a scientific study and its implications.

What can we learn from this study about the importance of community and relationships in lives that matter? If individual human flourishing depends fundamentally upon sharing life with others as part of a community, through what practices do Roseto's residents foster community? When and where have you seen people engaging in such practices?

I

Roseto Valfortore lies one hundred miles southeast of Rome in the Apennine foothills of the Italian province of Foggia. In the style of medieval villages, the town is organized around a large central square. Facing the square is the Palazzo Marchesale, the palace of the Saggese family, once the great landowner of those parts. An archway to one side leads to a church, the Madonna del Carmine — Our Lady of Mount Carmine. Narrow stone steps run up the hillside, flanked by closely clustered two-story stone houses with red-tile roofs.

For centuries, the *paesani* of Roseto worked in the marble quarries in the surrounding hills, or cultivated the fields in the terraced valley below, walking four and five miles down the mountain in the morning and then making

From Malcolm Gladwell, *Outliers: The Story of Success* (New York: Little, Brown, 2008), 3–11.

the long journey back up the hill at night. Life was hard. The townsfolk were barely literate and desperately poor and without much hope for economic betterment until word reached Roseto at the end of the nineteenth century of the land of opportunity across the ocean.

In January of 1882, a group of eleven Rosetans — ten men and one boy — set sail for New York. They spent their first night in America sleeping on the floor of a tavern on Mulberry Street, in Manhattan's Little Italy. Then they ventured west, eventually finding jobs in a slate quarry ninety miles west of the city near the town of Bangor, Pennsylvania. The following year, fifteen Rosetans left Italy for America, and several members of that group ended up in Bangor as well, joining their compatriots in the slate quarry. Those immigrants, in turn, sent word back to Roseto about the promise of the New World, and soon one group of Rosetans after another packed their bags and headed for Pennsylvania, until the initial stream of immigrants became a flood. In 1894 alone, some twelve hundred Rosetans applied for passports to America, leaving entire streets of their old village abandoned.

The Rosetans began buying land on a rocky hillside connected to Bangor by a steep, rutted wagon path. They built closely clustered two-story stone houses with slate roofs on narrow streets running up and down the hillside. They built a church and called it Our Lady of Mount Carmel and named the main street, on which it stood, Garibaldi Avenue, after the great hero of Italian unification. In the beginning, they called their town New Italy. But they soon changed it to Roseto, which seemed only appropriate given that almost all of them had come from the same village in Italy.

In 1896, a dynamic young priest by the name of Father Pasquale de Nisco took over at Our Lady of Mount Carmel. De Nisco set up spiritual societies and organized festivals. He encouraged the townsfolk to clear the land and plant onions, beans, potatoes, melons, and fruit trees in the long backyards behind their houses. He gave out seeds and bulbs. The town came to life. The Rosetans began raising pigs in their backyards and growing grapes for homemade wine. Schools, a park, a convent, and a cemetery were built. Small shops and bakeries and restaurants and bars opened along Garibaldi Avenue. More than a dozen factories sprang up making blouses for the garment trade. Neighboring Bangor was largely Welsh and English, and the next town over was overwhelmingly German, which meant — given the fractious relationships between the English and Germans and Italians in those years — Roseto stayed strictly for Rosetans. If you had wandered up and down the streets of Roseto in Pennsylvania in the first few decades after 1900, you would have heard only Italian, and not just any Italian but the precise southern Foggian dialect spoken back in the Italian Roseto. Roseto, Pennsylvania, was its own tiny, self-sufficient world — all but unknown by the society around it — and it might well have remained so but for a man named Stewart Wolf.

Wolf was a physician. He studied digestion and the stomach and taught in the medical school at the University of Oklahoma. He spent his summers on a farm in Pennsylvania, not far from Roseto — although that, of course, didn't mean much, since Roseto was so much in its own world that it was possible to live in the next town and never know much about it. "One of the times when we were up there for the summer — this would have been in the late nineteen fifties — I was invited to give a talk at the local medical society," Wolf said years later in an interview. "After the talk was over, one of the local doctors invited me to have a beer. And while we were having a drink, he said, 'You know, I've been practicing for seventeen years. I get patients from all over, and I rarely find anyone from Roseto under the age of sixty-five with heart disease.'"

Wolf was taken aback. This was the 1950s, years before the advent of cholesterol-lowering drugs and aggressive measures to prevent heart disease. Heart attacks were an epidemic in the United States. They were the leading cause of death in men under the age of sixty-five. It was impossible to be a doctor, common sense said, and not see heart disease.

Wolf decided to investigate. He enlisted the support of some of his students and colleagues from Oklahoma. They gathered together the death certificates from residents of the town, going back as many years as they could. They analyzed physicians' records. They took medical histories and constructed family genealogies. "We got busy," Wolf said. "We decided to do a preliminary study. We started in nineteen sixty-one. The mayor said, 'All my sisters are going to help you.' He had four sisters. He said, 'You can have the town council room.' I said, 'Where are you going to have council meetings?' He said, 'Well, we'll postpone them for a while.' The ladies would bring us lunch. We had little booths where we could take blood, do EKGs. We were there for four weeks. Then I talked with the authorities. They gave us the school for the summer. We invited the entire population of Roseto to be tested."

The results were astonishing. In Roseto, virtually no one under fifty-five had died of a heart attack or showed any signs of heart disease. For men over sixty-five, the death rate from heart disease in Roseto was roughly half that of the United States as a whole. The death rate from all causes in Roseto, in fact, was 30 to 35 percent lower than expected.

Wolf brought in a friend of his, a sociologist from Oklahoma named John Bruhn, to help him. "I hired medical students and sociology grad students as interviewers, and in Roseto we went house to house and talked to every person aged twenty-one and over," Bruhn remembers. This happened more than fifty years ago, but Bruhn still had a sense of amazement in his voice as he described what they found. "There was no suicide, no alcoholism, no drug addiction, and very little crime. They didn't have anyone on welfare. Then we looked at peptic ulcers. They didn't have any of those either. These people were dying of old age. That's it."

Wolf's profession had a name for a place like Roseto — a place that lay outside everyday experience, where the normal rules did not apply. Roseto was an outlier.

2

Wolf's first thought was that the Rosetans must have held on to some dietary practices from the Old World that left them healthier than other Americans. But he quickly realized that wasn't true. The Rosetans were cooking with lard instead of with the much healthier olive oil they had used back in Italy. Pizza in Italy was a thin crust with salt, oil, and perhaps some tomatoes, anchovies, or onions. Pizza in Pennsylvania was bread dough plus sausage, pepperoni, salami, ham, and sometimes eggs. Sweets such as biscotti and *taralli* used to be reserved for Christmas and Easter; in Roseto they were eaten year-round. When Wolf had dieticians analyze the typical Rosetan's eating habits, they found that a whopping 41 percent of their calories came from fat. Nor was this a town where people got up at dawn to do yoga and run a brisk six miles. The Pennsylvanian Rosetans smoked heavily and many were struggling with obesity.

If diet and exercise didn't explain the findings, then what about genetics? The Rosetans were a close-knit group from the same region of Italy, and Wolf's next thought was to wonder whether they were of a particularly hardy stock that protected them from disease. So he tracked down relatives of the Rosetans who were living in other parts of the United States to see if they shared the same remarkable good health as their cousins in Pennsylvania. They didn't.

He then looked at the region where the Rosetans lived. Was it possible that there was something about living in the foothills of eastern Pennsylvania that was good for their health? The two closest towns to Roseto were

Bangor, which was just down the hill, and Nazareth, a few miles away. These were both about the same size as Roseto, and both were populated with the same kind of hardworking European immigrants. Wolf combed through both towns' medical records. For men over sixty-five, the death rates from heart disease in Nazareth and Bangor were three times that of Roseto. Another dead end.

What Wolf began to realize was that the secret of Roseto wasn't diet or exercise or genes or location. *It had to be Roseto itself.* As Bruhn and Wolf walked around the town, they figured out why. They looked at how the Rosetans visited one another, stopping to chat in Italian on the street, say, or cooking for one another in their backyards. They learned about the extended family clans that underlay the town's social structure. They saw how many homes had three generations living under one roof, and how much respect grandparents commanded. They went to mass at Our Lady of Mount Carmel and saw the unifying and calming effect of the church. They counted twenty-two separate civic organizations in a town of just under two thousand people. They picked up on the particular egalitarian ethos of the community, which discouraged the wealthy from flaunting their success and helped the unsuccessful obscure their failures.

In transplanting the *paesani* culture of southern Italy to the hills of eastern Pennsylvania, the Rosetans had created a powerful, protective social structure capable of insulating them from the pressures of the modern world. The Rosetans were healthy because of where they were *from*, because of the world they had created for themselves in their tiny little town in the hills.

"I remember going to Roseto for the first time, and you'd see three-generational family meals, all the bakeries, the people walking up and down the street, sitting on their porches talking to each other, the blouse mills where the women worked during the day, while the men worked in the slate quarries," Bruhn said. "It was magical."

When Bruhn and Wolf first presented their findings to the medical community, you can imagine the kind of skepticism they faced. They went to conferences where their peers were presenting long rows of data arrayed in complex charts and referring to this kind of gene or that kind of physiological process, and they themselves were talking instead about the mysterious and magical benefits of people stopping to talk to one another on the street and of having three generations under one roof. Living a long life, the conventional wisdom at the time said, depended to a great extent on who we were — that is, our genes. It depended on the decisions we made — on what we chose to eat, and how much we chose to exercise, and how effectively we were treated by the medical system. No one was used to thinking about health in terms of *community*.

Wolf and Bruhn had to convince the medical establishment to think about health and heart attacks in an entirely new way: they had to get them to realize that they wouldn't be able to understand why someone was healthy if all they did was think about an individual's personal choices or actions in isolation. They had to look *beyond* the individual. They had to understand the culture he or she was a part of, and who their friends and families were, and what town their families came from. They had to appreciate the idea that the values of the world we inhabit and the people we surround ourselves with have a profound effect on who we are.

THE BOOK OF RUTH

This short story about family, lost and reclaimed, is one of the most beautiful pieces of literature in Tanakh, the Jewish Bible, and in the portion of the Bible Christians call the Old Testament. Across centuries of commentary, the rabbinic tradition has lifted up *chesed* (a Hebrew word meaning compassion, kindness, or faithfulness) as the main theme. *Chesed* often appears in biblical texts as an attribute of God toward God's people, but here it appears in human dealings with one another. Although the story begins in widowhood, poverty, and bitterness, Ruth and Naomi, and later Boaz, make commitments to one another that go beyond what their society requires of them. As a result, both the continuity of their family and the future of their nation (through their descendant David, who will become Israel's greatest king) are secured.

Ruth is a Moabite — a foreign woman, an immigrant, a stranger from a despised country beyond Israel's borders. Naomi is a childless widow, a woman without property, status, or power. Without Ruth's migrant labor, cleaning up the leftovers from a field, both would starve. Beginning with Ruth's choice to "cling" to her mother-in-law, notice the several choices to be in committed relationship that propel the story toward its joyful conclusion. Also notice the various social attitudes and structures that either promote or threaten the well-being of this struggling family. What forms and fruits of *chesed* do you see in this story? What dangers to personal, family, and social well-being? And where might *chesed* be emerging, or be missing, in today's world?

In the days when the judges ruled, there was a famine in the land, and a certain man of Bethlehem in Judah went to live in the country of Moab, he and his wife and two sons. The name of the man was Elimelech and the name of his wife Naomi, and the names of his two sons were Mahlon and Chilion; they were Ephrathites from Bethlehem in Judah. They went into the country of Moab and remained there. But Elimelech, the husband of

From the New Revised Standard Version of the Bible.

Naomi, died, and she was left with her two sons. These took Moabite wives; the name of one was Orpah and the name of the other Ruth. When they had lived there for about ten years, both Mahlon and Chilion also died, so that the woman was left without her two sons or her husband.

Then she started to return with her daughters-in-law from the country of Moab, for she had heard in the country of Moab that the LORD had considered for his people and given them food. So she set out from the place where she had been living, she and her two daughters-in-law, and they went on their way to go back to the land of Judah. But Naomi said to her two daughters-in-law, "Go back each of you to your mother's house. May the LORD deal kindly with you, as you have dealt with the dead and with me. The LORD grant that you may find security, each of you in the house of your husband." Then she kissed them, and they wept aloud. They said to her, "No, we will return with you to your people." But Naomi said, "Turn back, my daughters, why will you go with me? Do I still have sons in my womb that they may become your husbands? Turn back, my daughters, go your way, for I am too old to have a husband. Even if I thought there was hope for me, even if I should have a husband tonight and bear sons, would you then wait until they were grown? Would you then refrain from marrying? No, my daughters, it has been far more bitter for me than for you, because the hand of the LORD has turned against me." Then they wept aloud again. Orpah kissed her mother-in-law, but Ruth clung to her.

So she said, "See, your sister-in-law has gone back to her people and to her gods; return after your sister-in-law." But Ruth said,

> "Do not press me to leave you
>   or to turn back from following you!
> Where you go, I will go;
>   where you lodge, I will lodge;
> your people shall be my people,
>   and your God my God.
> Where you die, I will die —
>   there will I be buried.
> May the LORD do thus and so to me,
>   and more as well,
> if even death parts me from you!"

When Naomi saw that she was determined to go with her, she said no more to her.

So the two of them went on until they came to Bethlehem. When they came to Bethlehem, the whole town was stirred because of them; and the women said, "Is this Naomi?" She said to them,

> "Call me no longer Naomi,
>> call me Mara,
>> for the Almighty has dealt bitterly with me.
> I went away full,
>> but the LORD has brought me back empty;
> why call me Naomi
>> when the LORD has dealt harshly with me,
>> and the Almighty has brought calamity upon me?"

So Naomi returned together with Ruth the Moabite, her daughter-in-law, who came back with her from the country of Moab. They came to Bethlehem at the beginning of the barley harvest.

Now Naomi had a kinsman on her husband's side, a prominent rich man, of the family of Elimelech, whose name was Boaz. And Ruth the Moabite said to Naomi, "Let me go to the field and glean among the ears of grain, behind someone in whose sight I may find favor." She said to her, "Go, my daughter." So she went. She came and gleaned in the field behind the reapers. As it happened, she came to the part of the field belonging to Boaz, who was of the family of Elimelech. Just then Boaz came from Bethlehem. He said to the reapers, "The LORD be with you." They answered, "The LORD bless you." Then Boaz said to his servant who was in charge of the reapers, "To whom does this young woman belong?" The servant who was in charge of the reapers answered, "She is the Moabite who came back with Naomi from the country of Moab. She said, 'Please let me glean and gather among the sheaves behind the reapers.' So she came, and she has been on her feet from early this morning until now, without resting even for a moment."

Then Boaz said to Ruth, "Now listen, my daughter, do not go to glean in another field or leave this one, but keep close to my young women. Keep your eyes on the field that is being reaped, and follow behind them. I have ordered the young men not to bother you. If you get thirsty, go to the vessels and drink from what the young men have drawn." Then she fell prostrate, with her face to the ground, and said to him, "Why have I found favor in your sight, that you should take notice of me, when I am a foreigner?" But Boaz answered her, "All that you have done for your mother-in-law since the death of your husband has been fully told me, and how you left your father and mother and your native land and came to a people that you did not know before. May the LORD reward you for your deeds, and may you have a full reward from the LORD, the God of Israel, under whose wings you have come for refuge!" Then she said, "May I continue to find favor in your sight, my lord, for you have comforted me and spoken kindly to your servant, even though I am not one of your servants."

At mealtime Boaz said to her, "Come here, and eat some of this bread, and dip your morsel in the sour wine." So she sat beside the reapers, and he heaped up for her some parched grain. She ate until she was satisfied, and she had some left over. When she got up to glean, Boaz instructed his young men, "Let her glean even among the standing sheaves, and do not reproach her. You must also pull out some handfuls for her from the bundles, and leave them for her to glean, and do not rebuke her."

So she gleaned in the field until evening. Then she beat out what she had gleaned, and it was about an ephah of barley. She picked it up and came into the town, and her mother-in-law saw how much she had gleaned. Then she took out and gave her what was left over after she herself had been satisfied. Her mother-in-law said to her, "Where did you glean today? And where have you worked? Blessed be the man who took notice of you." So she told her mother-in-law with whom she had worked, and said, "The name of the man with whom I worked today is Boaz." Then Naomi said to her daughter-in-law, "Blessed be he by the LORD, whose kindness has not forsaken the living or the dead!" Naomi also said to her, "The man is a relative of ours, one of our nearest kin." Then Ruth the Moabite said, "He even said to me, 'Stay close by my servants, until they have finished all my harvest.'" Naomi said to Ruth, her daughter-in-law, "It is better, my daughter, that you go out with his young women, otherwise you might be bothered in another field." So she stayed close to the young women of Boaz, gleaning until the end of the barley and wheat harvests; and she lived with her mother-in-law.

Naomi her mother-in-law said to her, "My daughter, I need to seek some security for you, so that it may be well with you. Now here is our kinsman Boaz, with whose young women you have been working. See, he is winnowing barley tonight at the threshing-floor. Now wash and anoint yourself, and put on your best clothes and go down to the threshing-floor; but do not make yourself known to the man until he has finished eating and drinking. When he lies down, observe the place where he lies; then, go and uncover his feet and lie down; and he will tell you what to do." She said to her, "All that you tell me I will do."

So she went down to the threshing-floor and did just as her mother-in-law had instructed her. When Boaz had eaten and drunk, and he was in a contented mood, he went to lie down at the end of the heap of grain. Then she came stealthily and uncovered his feet, and lay down. At midnight the man was startled and turned over, and there, lying at his feet, was a woman! He said, "Who are you?" And she answered, "I am Ruth, your servant; spread your cloak over your servant, for you are next-of-kin." He said, "May you be blessed by the LORD, my daughter; this last instance of your loyalty is better than the first; you have not gone after young men, whether poor or rich. And now, my daughter, do not be afraid; I will do for you all that you ask, for all the assembly of my people know that you are a worthy woman. But now, though it is true that I am a near kinsman, there is another kinsman more closely related than I. Remain this night, and in the morning, if he will act as next-of-kin for you, good; let him do it. If he is not willing to act as next-of-kin for you, then, as the LORD lives, I will act as next-of-kin for you. Lie down until the morning."

So she lay at his feet until morning, but got up before one person could recognize another; for he said, "It must not be known that the woman came to the threshing-floor." Then he said, "Bring the cloak you are wearing and hold it out." So she held it, and he measured out six measures of barley, and put it on her back; then he went into the city. She came to her mother-in-law, who said, "How did things go with you, my daughter?" Then she told her all that the man had done for her, saying, "He gave me these six measures of barley, for he said, 'Do not go back to your mother-in-law empty-handed.'" She replied, "Wait, my daughter, until you learn how the matter turns out, for the man will not rest, but will settle the matter today."

No sooner had Boaz gone up to the gate and sat down there than the next-of-kin, of whom Boaz had spoken, came passing by. So Boaz said, "Come over, friend; sit down here." And he went over and sat down. Then Boaz took ten men of the elders of the city, and said, "Sit down here"; so they sat down. He then said to the next-of-kin, "Naomi, who has come back from the country of Moab, is selling the parcel of land that belonged to our kinsman Elimelech. So I thought I would tell you of it, and say: Buy it in the presence of those sitting here, and in the presence of the elders of my people. If you will redeem it, redeem it; but if you will not, tell me, so that I may know; for there is no one prior to you to redeem it, and I come after you." So he said, "I will redeem it." Then Boaz said, "The day you acquire the field from the hand of Naomi, you are also acquiring Ruth the Moabite, the widow of the dead man, to maintain the dead man's name on his inheritance." At this, the next-of-kin said, "I cannot redeem it for myself without damaging my own inheritance. Take my right of redemption yourself, for I cannot redeem it."

Now this was the custom in former times in Israel concerning redeeming and exchanging: to confirm a transaction, one party took off a sandal and gave it to the other; this was the manner of attesting in Israel. So when the next-of-kin said to Boaz, "Acquire it for yourself," he took off his sandal. Then Boaz said to the elders and all the people, "Today you are witnesses that I have acquired from the hand of Naomi all that belonged to Elimelech and all that belonged to Chilion and Mahlon. I have also acquired Ruth the Moabite, the wife of Mahlon, to be my wife, to maintain the dead man's name on his inheritance, in order that the name of the dead may not be cut off from his kindred and from the gate of his native place; today you are witnesses." Then all the people who were at the gate, along with the elders, said, "We are witnesses. May the LORD make the woman who is coming into your house like Rachel and Leah, who together built up the house of Israel. May you produce children in Ephrathah and bestow a name in Bethlehem; and, through the children that the LORD will give you by this young woman, may your house be like the house of Perez, whom Tamar bore to Judah."

So Boaz took Ruth and she became his wife. When they came together, the LORD made her conceive, and she bore a son. Then the women said to Naomi, "Blessed be the LORD, who has not left you this day without next-of-kin; and may his name be renowned in Israel! He shall be to you a restorer of life and a nourisher of your old age; for your daughter-in-law who loves you, who is more to you than seven sons, has borne him." Then Naomi took the child and laid him in her bosom, and became his nurse. The women of the neighborhood gave him a name, saying, "A son has been born to Naomi." They named him Obed; he became the father of Jesse, the father of David.

Now these are the descendants of Perez: Perez became the father of Hezron, Hezron of Ram, Ram of Amminadab, Amminadab of Nahshon, Nahshon of Salmon, Salmon of Boaz, Boaz of Obed, Obed of Jesse, and Jesse of David.

Jhumpa Lahiri

MY TWO LIVES

Jhumpa Lahiri is the author of a Pulitzer Prize–winning book of short stories, *Interpreter of Maladies*, and several other books. Like most of her fiction, the short essay included here delves into the cultural and emotional experience of belonging to two different cultures. While Lahiri recognizes that most Americans possess ethnic roots in other cultures, she identifies, through her own experience, special tensions in the experience of immigrant and first-generation people. As a child, she reports, she was aware of the "frequently humiliating process of immigration." How, and why, did her experience change in adulthood? Notice her artful depiction of the everyday realities that mark belonging — food, language, music, habits. How do these seemingly small markers delineate boundaries as we discern with whom and for whom we live? This short essay also subtly portrays the closeness of family ties — Lahiri's with her parents, and also with her children. How do (and how should) parents, in a culturally complicated case such as this one, guide the next generation in becoming and belonging, somehow both holding them fast and letting them go?

I have lived in the United States for almost 37 years and anticipate growing old in this country. Therefore, with the exception of my first two years in London, "Indian-American" has been a constant way to describe me. Less constant is my relationship to the term. When I was growing up in Rhode Island in the 1970s I felt neither Indian nor American. Like many immigrant offspring I felt intense pressure to be two things, loyal to the old world and fluent in the new, approved of on either side of the hyphen. Looking back, I see that this was generally the case. But my perception as a young girl was that I fell short at both ends, shuttling between two dimensions that had nothing to do with one another.

At home I followed the customs of my parents, speaking Bengali and

Jhumpa Lahiri, "My Two Lives," *Newsweek* 147, no. 10 (March 6, 2006): 43.

eating rice and dal with my fingers. These ordinary facts seemed part of a secret, utterly alien way of life, and I took pains to hide them from my American friends. For my parents, home was not our house in Rhode Island but Calcutta, where they were raised. I was aware that the things they lived for — the Nazrul songs they listened to on the reel-to-reel, the family they missed, the clothes my mother wore that were not available in any store in any mall — were at once as precious and as worthless as an outmoded currency.

I also entered a world my parents had little knowledge or control of: school, books, music, television, things that seeped in and became a fundamental aspect of who I am. I spoke English without an accent, comprehending the language in a way my parents still do not. And yet there was evidence that I was not entirely American. In addition to my distinguishing name and looks, I did not attend Sunday school, did not know how to ice-skate, and disappeared to India for months at a time. Many of these friends proudly called themselves Irish-American or Italian-American. But they were several generations removed from the frequently humiliating process of immigration, so that the ethnic roots they claimed had descended underground whereas mine were still tangled and green. According to my parents I was not American, nor would I ever be no matter how hard I tried. I felt doomed by their pronouncement, misunderstood and gradually defiant. In spite of the first lessons of arithmetic, one plus one did not equal two but zero, my conflicting selves always canceling each other out.

When I first started writing I was not conscious that my subject was the Indian-American experience. What drew me to my craft was the desire to force the two worlds I occupied to mingle on the page as I was not brave enough, or mature enough, to allow in life. My first book was published in 1999, and around then, on the cusp of a new century, the term "Indian-American" has become part of this country's vocabulary. I've heard it so often that these days, if asked about my background, I use the term myself, pleasantly surprised that I do not have to explain further. What a difference from my early life, when there was no such way to describe me, when the most I could do was to clumsily and ineffectually explain.

As I approach middle age, one plus one equals two, both in my work and in my daily existence. The traditions on either side of the hyphen dwell in me like siblings, still occasionally sparring, one outshining the other depending on the day. But like siblings they are intimately familiar with one another, forgiving and intertwined. When my husband and I were married five years ago in Calcutta we invited friends who had never been to India, and they came full of enthusiasm for a place I avoided talking about in my childhood, fearful of what people might say.

Around non-Indian friends, I no longer feel compelled to hide the fact that I speak another language. I speak Bengali to my children, even though I lack the proficiency to teach them to read or write the language. As a child I sought perfection and so denied myself the claim to any identity. As an adult I accept that a bicultural upbringing is a rich but imperfect thing.

While I am American by virtue of the fact that I was raised in this country, I am Indian thanks to the efforts of two individuals. I feel Indian not because of the time I've spent in India or because of my genetic composition but rather because of my parents' steadfast presence in my life. They live three hours from my home; I speak to them daily and see them about once a month. Everything will change once they die. They will take certain things with them — conversations in another tongue, and perceptions about the difficulties of being foreign. Without them, the back-and-forth life my family leads, both literally and figuratively, will at last approach stillness. An anchor will drop, and a line of connection will be severed.

I have always believed that I lack the authority my parents bring to being Indian. But as long as they live they protect me from feeling like an impostor. Their passing will mark not only the loss of the people who created me but the loss of a singular way of life, a singular struggle. The immigrant's journey, no matter how ultimately rewarding, is founded on departure and deprivation, but it secures for the subsequent generation a sense of arrival and advantage. I can see a day coming when my American side, lacking the counterpoint India has until now maintained, begins to gain ascendancy and weight. It is in fiction that I will continue to interpret the term "Indian-American," calculating that shifting equation, whatever answers it may yield.

Toni Morrison

RECITATIF

The fiction of Toni Morrison (1931–2019), one of America's most admired and influential authors, often explored the lives of African American women. The short story included here focuses instead on a relationship between a black woman and a white woman. We meet Roberta and Twyla (who narrates the story) when they are eight years old. A bond between them forms during the four months they share a room in a state shelter; many years later, they happen to see one another on four different occasions, during which both the strength and the strains in their connection are laid bare. How would you summarize the character of their connection? Are they, or were they, friends?

Questions of racial identity, racial justice, and interracial friendship are prominent in "Recitatif." However, Morrison's artistry creates situations that force readers to ask questions to which the story never provides final answers. For example, many readers have debated which of these two "salt and pepper" characters is white and which is black. What do you think? And within the story, Twyla and Roberta are confused about the race of a woman whose victimization they witnessed as children. Why does Maggie's race matter so much to them? By skillfully including and obscuring the descriptive details that might answer these and other questions, Morrison requires readers to be aware of the prejudices and assumptions they bring to this text. Do we also, in real life, bring such prejudices and assumptions to possible relationships with others?

My mother danced all night and Roberta's was sick. That's why we were taken to St. Bonny's. People want to put their arms around you when you tell them you were in a shelter, but it really wasn't bad. No big long room with one hundred beds like Bellevue. There were four to a room, and when

Toni Morrison, "Recitatif," in *Confirmation: An Anthology of African American Women*, ed. Imamu Amiri Baraka and Amina Baraka (New York: Quill, 1983), 243–61.

Roberta and me came, there was a shortage of state kids, so we were the only ones assigned to 406 and could go from bed to bed if we wanted to. And we wanted to, too. We changed beds every night and for the whole four months we were there we never picked one out as our own permanent bed.

It didn't start out that way. The minute I walked in and the Big Bozo introduced us, I got sick to my stomach. It was one thing to be taken out of your own bed early in the morning — it was something else to be stuck in a strange place with a girl from a whole other race. And Mary, that's my mother, she was right. Every now and then she would stop dancing long enough to tell me something important and one of the things she said was that they never washed their hair and they smelled funny. Roberta sure did. Smell funny, I mean. So when the Big Bozo (nobody ever called her Mrs. Itkin, just like nobody ever said St. Bonaventure) — when she said, "Twyla, this is Roberta. Roberta, this is Twyla. Make each other welcome." I said, "My mother won't like you putting me in here."

"Good," said Bozo. "Maybe then she'll come and take you home." How's that for mean? If Roberta had laughed I would have killed her, but she didn't. She just walked over to the window and stood with her back to us.

"Turn around," said the Bozo. "Don't be rude. Now Twyla. Roberta. When you hear a loud buzzer, that's the call for dinner. Come down to the first floor. Any fights and no movie." And then, just to make sure we knew what we would be missing, "*The Wizard of Oz.*"

Roberta must have thought I meant that my mother would be mad about my being put in the shelter. Not about rooming with her, because as soon as Bozo left she came over to me and said, "Is your mother sick too?"

"No," I said. "She just likes to dance all night."

"Oh," she nodded her head and I liked the way she understood things so fast. So for the moment it didn't matter that we looked like salt and pepper standing there and that's what the other kids called us sometimes. We were eight years old and got F's all the time. Me because I couldn't remember what I read or what the teacher said. And Roberta because she couldn't read at all and didn't even listen to the teacher. She wasn't good at anything except jacks, at which she was a killer: pow scoop pow scoop pow scoop.

We didn't like each other all that much at first, but nobody else wanted to play with us because we weren't real orphans with beautiful dead parents in the sky. We were dumped. Even the New York City Puerto Ricans and the upstate Indians ignored us. All kinds of kids were in there, black ones, white ones, even two Koreans. The food was good, though. At least I thought so. Roberta hated it and left whole pieces of things on her plate: Spam, Salisbury steak — even jello with fruit cocktail in it, and she didn't care if I ate what she wouldn't. Mary's idea of supper was popcorn and a can of Yoo-Hoo. Hot mashed potatoes and two weenies was like Thanksgiving for me.

It really wasn't bad, St. Bonny's. The big girls on the second floor pushed us around now and then. But that was all. They wore lipstick and eyebrow pencil and wobbled their knees while they watched TV. Fifteen, sixteen, even, some of them were. They were put-out girls, scared runaways most of them. Poor little girls who fought their uncles off but looked tough to us, and mean. God did they look mean. The staff tried to keep them separate from the younger children, but sometimes they caught us watching them in the orchard where they played radios and danced with each other. They'd light out after us and pull our hair or twist our arms. We were scared of them, Roberta and me, but neither of us wanted the other one to know it. So we got a good list of dirty names we could shout back when we ran from them through the orchard. I used to dream a lot and almost always the orchard was there. Two acres, four maybe, of these little apple trees. Hundreds of them. Empty and crooked like beggar women when I first came to St. Bonny's but fat with flowers when I left. I don't know why I dreamt about that orchard so much. Nothing really happened there. Nothing all that important, I mean. Just the big girls dancing and playing the radio. Roberta and me watching. Maggie fell down there once. The kitchen woman with legs like parentheses. And the big girls laughed at her. We should have helped her up, I know, but we were scared of those girls with lipstick and eyebrow pencil. Maggie couldn't talk. The kids said she had her tongue cut out, but I think she was just born that way: mute. She was old and sandy-colored and she worked in the kitchen. I don't know if she was nice or not. I just remember her legs like parentheses and how she rocked when she walked. She worked from early in the morning till two o'clock, and if she was late, if she had too much cleaning and didn't get out till two-fifteen or so, she'd cut through the orchard so she wouldn't miss her bus and have to wait another hour. She wore this really stupid little hat — a kid's hat with ear flaps — and she wasn't much taller than we were. A really awful little hat. Even for a mute, it was dumb — dressing like a kid and never saying anything at all.

"But what about if somebody tries to kill her?" I used to wonder about that. "Or what if she wants to cry? Can she cry?"

"Sure," Roberta said. "But just tears. No sounds come out."

"She can't scream?"

"Nope. Nothing."

"Can she hear?"

"I guess."

"Let's call her," I said. And we did.

"Dummy! Dummy!" She never turned her head.

"Bow legs! Bow legs!" Nothing. She just rocked on, the chin straps of her baby-boy hat swaying from side to side. I think we were wrong. I think she could hear and didn't let on. And it shames me even now to think there was somebody in there after all who heard us call her those names and couldn't tell on us.

We got along all right, Roberta and me. Changed beds every night, got F's in civics and communication skills and gym. The Bozo was disappointed in us, she said. Out of 130 of us state cases, 90 were under twelve. Almost all were real orphans with beautiful dead parents in the sky. We were the only ones dumped and the only ones with F's in three classes including gym. So we got along — what with her leaving whole pieces of things on her plate and being nice about not asking questions.

I think it was the day before Maggie fell down that we found out our mothers were coming to visit us on the same Sunday. We had been at the shelter twenty-eight days (Roberta twenty-eight and a half) and this was their first visit with us. Our mothers would come at ten o'clock in time for chapel, then lunch with us in the teachers' lounge. I thought if my dancing mother met her sick mother it might be good for her. And Roberta thought her sick mother would get a big bang out of a dancing one. We got excited about it and curled each other's hair. After breakfast we sat on the bed watching the road from the window. Roberta's socks were still wet. She washed them the night before and put them on the radiator to dry. They hadn't, but she put them on anyway because their tops were so pretty — scalloped in pink. Each of us had a purple construction-paper basket that we had made in craft class. Mine had a yellow crayon rabbit on it. Roberta's had eggs with wiggly lines of color. Inside were cellophane grass and just the jelly beans because I'd eaten the two marshmallow eggs they gave us. The Big Bozo came herself to get us. Smiling she told us we looked very nice and to come downstairs. We were so surprised by the smile we'd never seen before, neither of us moved.

"Don't you want to see your mommies?"

I stood up first and spilled the jelly beans all over the floor. Bozo's smile disappeared while we scrambled to get the candy up off the floor and put it back in the grass.

She escorted us downstairs to the first floor, where the other girls were lining up to file into the chapel. A bunch of grown-ups stood to one side.

Viewers mostly. The old biddies who wanted servants and the fags who wanted company looking for children they might want to adopt. Once in a while a grandmother. Almost never anybody young or anybody whose face wouldn't scare you in the night. Because if any of the real orphans had young relatives they wouldn't be real orphans. I saw Mary right away. She had on those green slacks I hated and hated even more now because didn't she know we were going to chapel? And that fur jacket with the pocket linings so ripped she had to pull to get her hands out of them. But her face was pretty — like always, and she smiled and waved like she was the little girl looking for her mother — not me.

I walked slowly, trying not to drop the jelly beans and hoping the paper handle would hold. I had to use my last Chiclet because by the time I finished cutting everything out, all the Elmer's was gone. I am left-handed and the scissors never worked for me. It didn't matter, though; I might just as well have chewed the gum. Mary dropped to her knees and grabbed me, mashing the basket, the jelly beans, and the grass into her ratty fur jacket.

"Twyla, baby. Twyla, baby!"

I could have killed her. Already I heard the big girls in the orchard the next time saying, "Twyyyyyla, baby!" But I couldn't stay mad at Mary while she was smiling and hugging me and smelling of Lady Esther dusting powder. I wanted to stay buried in her fur all day.

To tell the truth I forgot about Roberta. Mary and I got in line for the traipse into chapel and I was feeling proud because she looked so beautiful even in those ugly green slacks that made her behind stick out. A pretty mother on earth is better than a beautiful dead one in the sky even if she did leave you all alone to go dancing.

I felt a tap on my shoulder, turned, and saw Roberta smiling. I smiled back, but not too much lest somebody think this visit was the biggest thing that ever happened in my life. Then Roberta said, "Mother, I want you to meet my roommate, Twyla. And that's Twyla's mother."

I looked up it seemed for miles. She was big. Bigger than any man and on her chest was the biggest cross I'd ever seen. I swear it was six inches long each way. And in the crook of her arm was the biggest Bible ever made.

Mary, simple-minded as ever, grinned and tried to yank her hand out of the pocket with the raggedy lining — to shake hands, I guess. Roberta's mother looked down at me and then looked down at Mary too. She didn't say anything, just grabbed Roberta with her Bible-free hand and stepped out of line, walking quickly to the rear of it. Mary was still grinning because she's not too swift when it comes to what's really going on. Then this light bulb goes off in her head and she says "That bitch!" really loud and us almost in the chapel now. Organ music whining; the Bonny Angels singing sweetly. Everybody in the world turned around to look. And Mary would have kept it up — kept calling names if I hadn't squeezed her hand as hard as I could. That helped a little, but she still twitched and crossed and uncrossed her legs all through service. Even groaned a couple of times. Why did I think she would come there and act right? Slacks. No hat like the grandmothers and viewers, and groaning all the while. When we stood for hymns she kept her mouth shut. Wouldn't even look at the words on the page. She actually reached in her purse for a mirror to check her lipstick. All I could think of was that she really needed to be killed. The sermon lasted a year, and I knew the real orphans were looking smug again.

We were supposed to have lunch in the teachers' lounge, but Mary didn't bring anything, so we picked fur and cellophane grass off the mashed jelly beans and ate them. I could have killed her. I sneaked a look at Roberta. Her mother had brought chicken legs and ham sandwiches and oranges and a whole box of chocolate-covered grahams. Roberta drank milk from a thermos while her mother read the Bible to her.

Things are not right. The wrong food is always with the wrong people. Maybe that's why I got into waitress work later — to match up the right people with the right food. Roberta just let those chicken legs sit there, but she did bring a stack of grahams up to me later when the visit was over. I think she was sorry that her mother would not shake my mother's hand. And I liked that and I liked the fact that she didn't say a word about Mary groaning all the way through the service and not bringing any lunch.

Roberta left in May when the apple trees were heavy and white. On her last day we went to the orchard to watch the big girls smoke and dance by the radio. It didn't matter that they said, "Twyyyyyla, baby." We sat on the ground and breathed. Lady Esther. Apple blossoms. I still go soft when I smell one or the other. Roberta was going home. The big cross and the big Bible was coming to get her and she seemed sort of glad and sort of not. I thought I would die in that room of four beds without her and I knew Bozo had plans to move some other dumped kid in there with me. Roberta promised to write every day, which was really sweet of her because she couldn't read a lick so how could she write anybody. I would have drawn pictures and sent them to her but she never gave me her address. Little by little she faded. Her wet socks with the pink scalloped tops and her big serious-looking eyes — that's all I could catch when I tried to bring her to mind.

I was working behind the counter at the Howard Johnson's on the Thruway just before the Kingston exit. Not a bad job. Kind of a long ride from New-burgh, but okay once I got there. Mine was the second night shift — eleven to seven. Very light until a Greyhound checked in for breakfast around six-thirty. At that hour the sun was all the way clear of the hills behind the restaurant. The place looked better at night — more like shelter — but I loved it when the sun broke in, even if it did show all the cracks in the vinyl and the speckled floor looked dirty no matter what the mop boy did.

It was August and a bus crowd was just unloading. They would stand around a long while: going to the john, and looking at gifts and junk-for-sale machines, reluctant to sit down so soon. Even to eat. I was trying to fill the coffee pots and get them all situated on the electric burners when l saw her. She was sitting in a booth smoking a cigarette with two guys smothered in head and facial hair. Her own hair was so big and wild I could hardly see her face. But the eyes. I would know them anywhere. She had on a powder-blue halter and shorts outfit and earrings the size of bracelets. Talk about lipstick and eyebrow pencil. She made the big girls look like nuns. I couldn't get off the counter until seven o'clock, but I kept watching the booth in case they got up to leave before that. My replacement was on time for a change, so I counted and stacked my receipts as fast as I could and signed off. I walked over to the booth, smiling and wondering if she would remember me. Or even if she wanted to remember me. Maybe she didn't want to be reminded of St. Bonny's or to have anybody know she was ever there. I know I never talked about it to anybody.

I put my hands in my apron pockets and leaned against the back of the booth facing them.

"Roberta? Roberta Fisk?"

She looked up. "Yeah?"

"Twyla."

She squinted for a second and then said, "Wow."

"Remember me?"

"Sure. Hey. Wow."

"It's been a while," I said, and gave a smile to the two hairy guys.

"Yeah. Wow. You work here?"

"Yeah," I said. "I live in Newburgh."

"Newburgh? No kidding?" She laughed then a private laugh that included the guys but only the guys, and they laughed with her. What could I do but laugh too and wonder why I was standing there with my knees showing out from under that uniform. Without looking I could see the blue and white

359

triangle on my head, my hair shapeless in a net, my ankles thick in white oxfords. Nothing could have been less sheer than my stockings. There was this silence that came down right after I laughed. A silence it was her turn to fill up. With introductions, maybe, to her boyfriends or an invitation to sit down and have a Coke. Instead she lit a cigarette off the one she'd just finished and said, "We're on our way to the Coast. He's got an appointment with Hendrix." She gestured casually toward the boy next to her.

"Hendrix? Fantastic," I said. "Really fantastic. What's she doing now?"

Roberta coughed on her cigarette and the two guys rolled their eyes up at the ceiling.

"Hendrix. Jimi Hendrix, asshole. He's only the biggest — Oh, wow. Forget it."

I was dismissed without anyone saying goodbye, so I thought I would do it for her.

"How's your mother?" I asked. Her grin cracked her whole face. She swallowed. "Fine," she said. "How's yours?"

"Pretty as a picture," I said and turned away. The backs of my knees were damp. Howard Johnson's really was a dump in the sunlight.

James is as comfortable as a house slipper. He liked my cooking and I liked his big loud family. They have lived in Newburgh all of their lives and talk about it the way people do who have always known a home. His grandmother is a porch swing older than his father and when they talk about streets and avenues and buildings they call them names they no longer have. They still call the A & P Rico's because it stands on property once a mom and pop store owned by Mr. Rico. And they call the new community college Town Hall because it once was. My mother-in-law puts up jelly and cucumbers and buys butter wrapped in cloth from a dairy. James and his father talk about fishing and baseball and I can see them all together on the Hudson in a raggedy skiff. Half the population of Newburgh is on welfare now, but to my husband's family it was still some upstate paradise of a time long past. A time of ice houses and vegetable wagons, coal furnaces and children weeding gardens. When our son was born my mother-in-law gave me the crib blanket that had been hers.

But the town they remembered had changed. Something quick was in the air. Magnificent old houses, so ruined they had become shelter for squatters and rent risks, were bought and renovated. Smart IBM people moved out of their suburbs back into the city and put shutters up and herb gardens in their backyards. A brochure came in the mail announcing the opening of a Food

Emporium. Gourmet food it said — and listed items the rich IBM crowd would want. It was located in a new mall at the edge of town and I drove out to shop there one day — just to see. It was late in June. After the tulips were gone and the Queen Elizabeth roses were open everywhere. I trailed my cart along the aisle tossing in smoked oysters and Robert's sauce and things I knew would sit in my cupboard for years. Only when I found some Klondike ice cream bars did I feel less guilty about spending James's fireman's salary so foolishly. My father-in-law ate them with the same gusto little Joseph did.

Waiting in the check-out line I heard a voice say, "Twyla!"

The classical music piped over the aisles had affected me and the woman leaning toward me was dressed to kill. Diamonds on her hand, a smart white summer dress. "I'm Mrs. Benson," I said.

"Ho. Ho. The Big Bozo," she sang.

For a split second I didn't know what she was talking about. She had a bunch of asparagus and two cartons of fancy water.

"Roberta!"

"Right."

"For heaven's sake. Roberta."

"You look great," she said.

"So do you. Where are you? Here? In Newburgh?"

"Yes. Over in Annandale."

I was opening my mouth to say more when the cashier called my attention to her empty counter.

"Meet you outside." Roberta pointed her finger and went into the express line.

I placed the groceries and kept myself from glancing around to check Roberta's progress. I remembered Howard Johnson's and looking for a chance to speak only to be greeted with a stingy "wow." But she was waiting for me and her huge hair was sleek now, smooth around a small, nicely shaped head. Shoes, dress, everything lovely and summery and rich. I was dying to know what happened to her, how she got from Jimi Hendrix to Annandale, a neighborhood full of doctors and IBM executives. Easy, I thought. Everything is so easy for them. They think they own the world.

"How long," I asked her. "How long have you been here?"

"A year. I got married to a man who lives here. And you, you're married too, right? Benson, you said."

"Yeah. James Benson."

"And is he nice?"

"Oh, is he nice?"

"Well, is he?" Roberta's eyes were steady as though she really meant the question and wanted an answer.

"He's wonderful, Roberta. Wonderful."

"So you're happy."

"Very."

"That's good," she said and nodded her head. "I always hoped you'd be happy. Any kids? I know you have kids."

"One. A boy. How about you?"

"Four."

"Four?"

She laughed. "Step kids. He's a widower."

"Oh."

"Got a minute? Let's have a coffee."

I thought about the Klondikes melting and the inconvenience of going all the way to my car and putting the bags in the trunk. Served me right for buying all that stuff I didn't need. Roberta was ahead of me.

"Put them in my car. It's right here."

And then I saw the dark blue limousine. "You married a Chinaman?"

"No," she laughed. "He's the driver."

"Oh, my. If the Big Bozo could see you now."

We both giggled. Really giggled. Suddenly, in just a pulse beat, twenty years disappeared and all of it came rushing back. The big girls (whom we called gar girls — Roberta's misheard word for the evil stone faces described in a civics class) there dancing in the orchard, the ploppy mashed potatoes, the double weenies, the Spam with pineapple. We went into the coffee shop holding on to one another and I tried to think why we were glad to see each other this time and not before. Once, twelve years ago, we passed like strangers. A black girl and a white girl meeting in a Howard Johnson's on the road and having nothing to say. One in a blue and white triangle waitress hat — the other on her way to see Hendrix. Now we were behaving like sisters separated for much too long. Those four short months were nothing in time. Maybe it was the thing itself. Just being there, together. Two little girls who knew what nobody else in the world knew — how not to ask questions. How to believe what had to be believed. There was politeness in that reluctance and generosity as well. Is your mother sick too? No, she dances all night. Oh — and an understanding nod.

We sat in a booth by the window and fell into recollection like veterans.

"Did you ever learn to read?"

"Watch." She picked up the menu. "Special of the day. Cream of corn soup. Entrées. Two dots and a wriggly line. Quiche. Chef salad, scallops . . ."

I was laughing and applauding when the waitress came up.

"Remember the Easter baskets?"

"And how we tried to *introduce* them?"

"Your mother with that cross like two telephone poles."

"And yours with those tight slacks."

We laughed so loudly heads turned and made the laughter harder to suppress.

"What happened to the Jimi Hendrix date?"

Roberta made a blow-out sound with her lips.

"When he died I thought about you."

"Oh, you heard about him finally?"

"Finally. Come on, I was a small-town country waitress."

"And I was a small-town country dropout. God, were we wild. I still don't know how I got out of there alive."

"But you did."

"I did. I really did. Now I'm Mrs. Kenneth Norton."

"Sounds like a mouthful."

"It is."

"Servants and all?"

Roberta held up two fingers.

"Ow! What does he do?"

"Computers and stuff. What do I know?"

"I don't remember a hell of a lot from those days, but Lord, St. Bonny's is as clear as daylight. Remember Maggie? The day she fell down and those gar girls laughed at her?"

Roberta looked up from her salad and stared at me. "Maggie didn't fall," she said.

"Yes, she did. You remember."

"No, Twyla. They knocked her down. Those girls pushed her down and tore her clothes. In the orchard."

"I don't — that's not what happened."

"Sure it is. In the orchard. Remember how scared we were?"

"Wait a minute. I don't remember any of that."

"And Bozo was fired."

"You're crazy. She was there when I left. You left before me."

"I went back. You weren't there when they fired Bozo."

"What?"

"Twice. Once for a year when I was about ten, another for two months when I was fourteen. That's when I ran away."

"You ran away from St. Bonny's?"

"I had to. What do you want? Me dancing in that orchard?"

"Are you sure about Maggie?"

"Of course I'm sure. You've blocked it, Twyla. It happened. Those girls had behavior problems, you know."

"Didn't they, though. But why can't I remember the Maggie thing?"

"Believe me. It happened. And we were there."

"Who did you room with when you went back?" I asked her as if I would know her. The Maggie thing was troubling me.

"Creeps. They tickled themselves in the night."

My ears were itching and I wanted to go home suddenly. This was all very well but she couldn't just comb her hair, wash her face and pretend everything was hunky-dory. After the Howard Johnson's snub. And no apology. Nothing.

"Were you on dope or what that time at Howard Johnson's?" I tried to make my voice sound friendlier than I felt.

"Maybe, a little. I never did drugs much. Why?"

"I don't know; you acted sort of like you didn't want to know me then."

"Oh, Twyla, you know how it was in those days: black-white. You know how everything was."

But I didn't know. I thought it was just the opposite. Busloads of blacks and whites came into Howard Johnson's together. They roamed together then: students, musicians, lovers, protesters. You got to see everything at Howard Johnson's and blacks were very friendly with whites in those days. But sitting there with nothing on my plate but two hard tomato wedges wondering about the melting Klondikes it seemed childish remembering the slight. We went to her car, and with the help of the driver, got my stuff into my station wagon.

"We'll keep in touch this time," she said.

"Sure," I said. "Sure. Give me a call."

"I will," she said, and then just as I was sliding behind the wheel, she leaned into the window. "By the way. Your mother. Did she ever stop dancing?"

I shook my head. "No. Never."

Roberta nodded.

"And yours? Did she ever get well?"

She smiled a tiny sad smile. "No. She never did. Look, call me, okay?"

"Okay," I said, but I knew I wouldn't. Roberta had messed up my past somehow with that business about Maggie. I wouldn't forget a thing like that. Would I?

Strife came to us that fall. At least that's what the paper called it. Strife. Racial strife. The word made me think of a bird — a big shrieking bird out of 1,000,000,000 B.C. Flapping its wings and cawing. Its eye with no lid always bearing down on you. All day it screeched and at night it slept on the rooftops. It woke you in the morning and from the *Today* show to the eleven o'clock news it kept you an awful company. I couldn't figure it out from one day to the next. I knew I was supposed to feel something strong, but I didn't know what, and James wasn't any help. Joseph was on the list of kids to be transferred from the junior high school to another one at some far-out-of-the-way place and I thought it was a good thing until I heard it was a bad thing. I mean I didn't know. All the schools seemed dumps to me, and the fact that one was nicer looking didn't hold much weight. But the papers were full of it and then the kids began to get jumpy. In August, mind you. Schools weren't even open yet. I thought Joseph might be frightened to go over there, but he didn't seem scared so I forgot about it, until I found myself driving along Hudson Street out there by the school they were trying to integrate and saw a line of women marching. And who do you suppose was in line, big as life, holding a sign in front of her bigger than her mother's cross? MOTHERS HAVE RIGHTS TOO! it said.

I drove on, and then changed my mind. I circled the block, slowed down and honked my horn.

Roberta looked over and when she saw me she waved. I didn't wave back, but I didn't move either. She handed her sign to another woman and came over to where I was parked.

"Hi."

"What are you doing?"

"Picketing. What's it look like?"

"What for?"

"What do you mean, 'What for?' They want to take my kids and send them out of the neighborhood. They don't want to go."

"So what if they go to another school? My boy's being bussed too, and I don't mind. Why should you?"

"It's not about us, Twyla. Me and you. It's about our kids."

"What's more *us* than that?"

"Well, it is a free country."

"Not yet, but it will be."

"What the hell does that mean? I'm not doing anything to you."

"You really think that?"

"I know it."

"I wonder what made me think you were different."

"I wonder what made me think you were different."

"Look at them," I said. "Just look. Who do they think they are? Swarming all over the place like they own it. And now they think they can decide where my child goes to school. Look at them, Roberta. They're Bozos."

Roberta turned around and looked at the women. Almost all of them were standing still now, waiting. Some were even edging toward us. Roberta looked at me out of some refrigerator behind her eyes. "No, they're not. They're just mothers."

"And what am I? Swiss cheese?"

"I used to curl your hair."

"I hated your hands in my hair."

The women were moving. Our faces looked mean to them of course and they looked as though they could not wait to throw themselves in front of a police car, or better yet, into my car and drag me away by my ankles. Now they surrounded my car and gently, gently began to rock it. I swayed back and forth like a sideways yo-yo. Automatically I reached for Roberta, like the old days in the orchard when they saw us watching them and we had to get out of there, and if one of us fell the other pulled her up and if one of us was caught the other stayed to kick and scratch, and neither would leave the other behind. My arm shot out of the car window but no receiving hand was there. Roberta was looking at me sway from side to side in the car and her face was still. My purse slid from the car seat down under the dashboard. The four policemen who had been drinking Tab in their car finally got the message and strolled over, forcing their way through the women. Quietly, firmly they spoke. "Okay, ladies. Back in line or off the streets."

Some of them went away willingly; others had to be urged away from the car doors and the hood. Roberta didn't move. She was looking steadily at me. I was fumbling to turn on the ignition, which wouldn't catch because the gearshift was still in drive. The seats of the car were a mess because the swaying had thrown my grocery coupons all over it and my purse was sprawled on the floor.

"Maybe I am different now, Twyla. But you're not. You're the same little state kid who kicked a poor old black lady when she was down on the ground. You kicked a black lady and you have the nerve to call me a bigot."

The coupons were everywhere and the guts of my purse were bunched under the dashboard. What was she saying? Black? Maggie wasn't black.

"She wasn't black," I said.

"Like hell she wasn't, and you kicked her. We both did. You kicked a black lady who couldn't even scream."

"Liar!"

"You're the liar! Why don't you just go on home and leave us alone, huh?"

She turned away and I skidded away from the curb.

The next morning I went into the garage and cut the side out of the carton our portable TV had come in. It wasn't nearly big enough, but after a while I had a decent sign: red spray-painted letters on a white background – AND SO DO CHILDREN****. I meant just to go down to the school and tack it up somewhere so those cows on the picket line across the street could see it, but when I got there, some ten or so others had already assembled – protesting the cows across the street. Police permits and everything. I got in line and we strutted in time on our side while Roberta's group strutted on theirs. That first day we were all dignified, pretending the other side didn't exist. The second day there was name calling and finger gestures. But that was about all. People changed signs from time to time, but Roberta never did and neither did I. Actually my sign didn't make sense without Roberta's. "And so do children what?" one of the women on my side asked me. Have rights, I said, as though it was obvious.

Roberta didn't acknowledge my presence in any way and I got to thinking maybe she didn't know I was there. I began to pace myself in the line, jostling people one minute and lagging behind the next, so Roberta and I could reach the end of our respective lines at the same time and there would be a moment in our turn when we would face each other. Still, I couldn't tell whether she saw me and knew my sign was for her. The next day I went early before we were scheduled to assemble. I waited until she got there before I exposed my new creation. As soon as she hoisted her MOTHERS HAVE RIGHTS TOO I began to wave my new one, which said, HOW WOULD YOU KNOW? I know she saw that one, but I had gotten addicted now. My signs got crazier each day, and the women on my side decided that I was a kook. They couldn't make heads or tails out of my brilliant screaming posters.

I brought a painted sign in queenly red with huge black letters that said, IS YOUR MOTHER WELL? Roberta took her lunch break and didn't come back for the rest of the day or any day after. Two days later I stopped going too and couldn't have been missed because nobody understood my signs anyway.

It was a nasty six weeks. Classes were suspended and Joseph didn't go to anybody's school until October. The children – everybody's children – soon got bored with that extended vacation they thought was going to be so great. They looked at TV until their eyes flattened. I spent a couple of mornings tutoring my son, as the other mothers said we should. Twice I opened a text from last year that he had never turned in. Twice he yawned in my face. Other mothers organized living room sessions so the kids would keep up. None of the kids could concentrate so they drifted back to *The Price Is Right* and *The Brady Bunch*. When the school finally opened there were fights once or twice and some sirens roared through the streets every once in a while. There were a lot of photographers from Albany. And just when ABC was about to send up a news crew, the kids settled down like nothing in the world had happened. Joseph hung my HOW WOULD YOU KNOW? sign in his bedroom. I don't know what became of AND SO DO CHILDREN****. I think my father-in-law cleaned some fish on it. He was always puttering around in our garage. Each of his five children lived in Newburgh and he acted as though he had five extra homes.

I couldn't help looking for Roberta when Joseph graduated from high school, but I didn't see her. It didn't trouble me much what she had said to me in the car. I mean the kicking part. I know I didn't do that, I couldn't do that. But I was puzzled by her telling me Maggie was black. When I thought about it I actually couldn't be certain. She wasn't pitch-black, I knew, or I would have remembered that. What I remember was the kiddie hat, and the semicircle legs. I tried to reassure myself about the race thing for a long time until it dawned on me that the truth was already there, and Roberta knew it. I didn't kick her; I didn't join in with the gar girls and kick that lady, but I sure did want to. We watched and never tried to help her and never called for help. Maggie was my dancing mother. Deaf, I thought, and dumb. Nobody inside. Nobody who would hear you if you cried in the night. Nobody who could tell you anything important that you could use. Rocking, dancing, swaying as she walked. And when the gar girls pushed her down, and started roughhousing, I knew she wouldn't scream, couldn't — just like me — and I was glad about that.

We decided not to have a tree, because Christmas would be at my mother-in-law's house, so why have a tree at both places? Joseph was at SUNY New Paltz and we had to economize, we said. But at the last minute, I changed my mind. Nothing could be that bad. So I rushed around town looking for a tree, something small but wide. By the time I found a place, it was snowing and very late. I dawdled like it was the most important purchase in the world and the tree man was fed up with me. Finally I chose one and had it tied onto the trunk of the car. I drove away slowly because the sand trucks were not out yet and the streets could be murder at the beginning of a snowfall. Downtown the streets were wide and rather empty except for a cluster of people coming out of the Newburgh Hotel. The one hotel in town that wasn't built out of cardboard and Plexiglas. A party, probably. The men huddled in the snow were dressed in tails and the women had on furs. Shiny things glittered from underneath their coats. It made me tired to look at them. Tired, tired, tired. On the next corner was a small diner with loops and loops of paper bells in the window. I stopped the car and went in. Just for a cup of coffee and twenty minutes of peace before I went home and tried to finish everything before Christmas Eve.

"Twyla?"

There she was. In a silvery evening gown and dark fur coat. A man and another woman were with her, the man fumbling for change to put in the cigarette machine. The woman was humming and tapping on the counter with her fingernails. They all looked a little bit drunk.

"Well. It's you."

"How are you?"

I shrugged. "Pretty good. Frazzled. Christmas and all."

"Regular?" called the woman from the counter.

"Fine," Roberta called back and then, "Wait for me in the car."

She slipped into the booth beside me. "I have to tell you something, Twyla. I made up my mind if I ever saw you again, I'd tell you."

"I'd just as soon not hear anything, Roberta. It doesn't matter now, anyway."

"No," she said. "Not about that."

"Don't be long," said the woman. She carried two regulars to go and the man peeled his cigarette pack as they left.

"It's about St. Bonny's and Maggie."

"Oh, please."

"Listen to me. I really did think she was black. I didn't make that up. I really thought so. But now I can't be sure. I just remember her as old, so old. And because she couldn't talk — well, you know, I thought she was crazy. She'd been brought up in an institution like my mother was and like I thought I would be too. And you were right. We didn't kick her. It was the gar girls. Only them. But, well, I wanted to. I really wanted them to hurt her. I said we did it, too. You and me, but that's not true. And I don't want you to carry that around. It was just that I wanted to do it so bad that day — wanting to is doing it."

Her eyes were watery from the drinks she'd had, I guess. I know it's that way with me. One glass of wine and I start bawling over the littlest thing.

"We were kids, Roberta."

"Yeah. Yeah. I know, just kids."

"Eight."

"Eight."

"And lonely."

"Scared, too."

She wiped her cheeks with the heel of her hand and smiled. "Well, that's all I wanted to say."

I nodded and couldn't think of any way to fill the silence that went from the diner past the paper bells on out into the snow. It was heavy now. I thought I'd better wait for the sand trucks before starting home.

"Thanks, Roberta."

"Sure."

"Did I tell you? My mother, she never did stop dancing."

"Yes. You told me. And mine, she never got well." Roberta lifted her hands from the tabletop and covered her face with her palms. When she took them away she really was crying. "Oh shit, Twyla. Shit, shit, shit. What the hell happened to Maggie?"

Sullivan Ballou

A LETTER TO HIS WIFE, 1861

Soldiers preparing for battle, who must face the imminent possibility of their own death, have long observed the custom of writing a letter to loved ones before major engagements, to be delivered only if they die. The following selection is one such letter. Here a young officer writes to his twenty-four-year-old wife, who is at home in New England with their five-year-old and two-year-old sons. This letter, found among his belongings, opens a window that allows us to glimpse both a marriage and a life-shaping relationship with a national cause in wartime.

Ballou (March 28, 1829–July 21, 1861) met his death in the First Battle of Bull Run, one of the earliest engagements of the Civil War. Enthusiasts on both sides thought the war would be swift and easy, though in fact it ground on for nearly four more years, becoming the bloodiest war in US history. Ballou, a supporter of Lincoln who was active in Rhode Island politics and one of the first to enlist, was clear about the ideals for which he was fighting. Notice, however, his acknowledgment to his wife that his actions are also "hazarding the happiness of those I love" — her and their sons. His enlistment influenced not only what he would do and become but also their futures. How does the action of one person necessarily become related to the destinies of others, whether family members or strangers, such as, in this case, enemy troops? How does Ballou seem to understand the various relationships that he treasures — in the small circle of family and the larger circle of history — and the claims and limits of these relationships?

"'My Very Dear Wife' — the Last Letter of Major Sullivan Ballou," National Park Service, last modified February 3, 2015, https://www.nps.gov/articles/-my-very-dear-wife-the -last-letter-of-major-sullivan-ballou.htm.

July 14, 1861
Camp Clark, Washington [D.C.]

My very dear Sarah:

The indications are very strong that we shall move in a few days — perhaps tomorrow. Lest I should not be able to write you again, I feel impelled to write lines that may fall under your eye when I shall be no more.

Our movement may be one of a few days duration and full of pleasure — and it may be one of severe conflict and death to me. Not my will, but thine, O God, be done. If it is necessary that I should fall on the battlefield for my country, I am ready. I have no misgivings about, or lack of confidence in, the cause in which I am engaged, and my courage does not halt or falter. I know how strongly American Civilization now leans upon the triumph of the Government, and how great a debt we owe to those who went before us through the blood and suffering of the Revolution. And I am willing — perfectly willing — to lay down all my joys in this life, to help maintain this Government, and to pay that debt.

But, my dear wife, when I know that with my own joys I lay down nearly all of yours, and replace them in this life with cares and sorrows — when, after having eaten for long years the bitter fruit of orphanage myself, I must offer it as their only sustenance to my dear little children — is it weak or dishonorable, while the banner of my purpose floats calmly and proudly in the breeze, that my unbounded love for you, my darling wife and children, should struggle in fierce, though useless, contest with my love of country?

I cannot describe to you my feelings on this calm summer night, when two thousand men are sleeping around me, many of them enjoying the last, perhaps, before that of death — and I, suspicious that Death is creeping behind me with his fatal dart, am communing with God, my country, and thee.

I have sought most closely and diligently, and often in my breast, for a wrong motive in thus hazarding the happiness of those I loved and I could not find one. A pure love of my country and of the principles I have often advocated before the people and "the name of honor that I love more than I fear death" have called upon me, and I have obeyed.

Sarah, my love for you is deathless, it seems to bind me to you with mighty cables that nothing but Omnipotence could break; and yet my love of Country comes over me like a strong wind and bears me irresistibly on with all these chains to the battlefield.

The memories of the blissful moments I have spent with you come creeping over me, and I feel most gratified to God and to you that I have enjoyed them so long. And hard it is for me to give them up and burn to ashes the hopes of future years, when, God willing, we might still have lived and loved together, and seen our sons grow up to honorable manhood around us.

I have, I know, but few and small claims upon Divine Providence, but something whispers to me — perhaps it is the wafted prayer of my little Edgar — that I shall return to my loved ones unharmed. If I do not, my dear Sarah, never forget how much I love you, nor that, when my last breath escapes me on the battlefield, it will whisper your name.

Forgive my many faults, and the many pains I have caused you. How thoughtless and foolish I have oftentimes been! How gladly would I wash out with my tears every little spot upon your happiness, and struggle with all the misfortune of this world, to shield you and my children from harm. But I cannot. I must watch you from the spirit land and hover near you, while you buffet the storms with your precious little freight, and wait with sad patience till we meet to part no more.

But, O Sarah! If the dead can come back to this earth and flit unseen around those they loved, I shall always be near you in the garish day and in the darkest night — amidst your happiest scenes and gloomiest hours — always, always; and if there be a soft breeze upon your cheek, it shall be my breath; or the cool air fans your throbbing temple, it shall be my spirit passing by.

Sarah, do not mourn me dead; think I am gone and wait for thee, for we shall meet again.

As for my little boys, they will grow as I have done, and never know a father's love and care. Little Willie is too young to remember me long, and my blue-eyed Edgar will keep my frolics with him among the dimmest memories of his childhood. Sarah, I have unlimited confidence in your maternal care and your development of their characters. Tell my two mothers his and hers I call God's blessing upon them. O Sarah, I wait for you there! Come to me, and lead thither my children.

— Sullivan

Samuel Wells

RETHINKING SERVICE

Samuel Wells, a priest in the Church of England and an influential ethicist and theologian, is currently vicar of St. Martin-in-the-Fields, a parish in central London. Wells wrote this essay on service and what it should mean for today's students during his term as dean of the chapel at Duke University. Many students are highly aware of the needs of others and quite eager to serve, Wells noticed, and colleges and universities strive to provide opportunities for them to do so. Moreover, eagerness to serve is widespread in the larger society, where volunteers welcome the homeless, deliver meals to those who are housebound, and more, and where some professions are understood as forms of service to others. Even so, Wells suggests, those who go out to serve are often asking the wrong question. We tend to ask: "What can I do for those in need?" By contrast, Wells argues, the most important word we can use as we think about service is "with."

Wells grounds his critique of dominant notions of service in his own theological tradition. He begins with a sweeping argument about what is the essential question of human existence: mortality or isolation. How does he think modern culture's answer — that the limitations inherent in mortality are the greatest question we face as human beings — has distorted our society, character, and relationships? And how does he think our society, our character, and our approach to social problems might change if we instead agreed that isolation — our lack of communion with one another — is our greatest question? Where do you see examples of each of these approaches to others and their needs in the life of your family, community, and society?

The 1992 novel and 1996 film *The English Patient* is set in Egypt during the Second World War. A married Englishwoman, Katherine, finds herself often alone as her husband pursues a cartographical expedition. She falls in love with an impossibly exotic Hungarian nobleman, Laszlo. Count Laszlo,

Samuel Wells, "Rethinking Service," *Cresset* 76, no. 4 (Easter 2013): 6–14.

another cartographer, discovers a wondrous cave, decorated with prehistoric paintings, deep in the Sahara Desert. Laszlo and Katherine fall into a passionate affair. Katherine's husband, sensing the affair, plans a murderous revenge. He puts Katherine in the backseat of his biplane and flies toward Count Laszlo's excavation camp near the famous cave. He tries to land the plane right on Laszlo himself, but the plan catastrophically backfires. It turns out that it is Katherine's husband who dies in the crash. Laszlo, the intended target, sustains only minor injuries, but Katherine is badly hurt. We witness Laszlo carrying her slowly and lovingly to the prehistoric cave.

Now Laszlo and Katherine face an unspeakable predicament. Katherine's injuries are life-threatening. If she is going to live, Laszlo is going to need to go and find medical help. But that means going to Cairo, and Cairo is a three-day walk away. It is a dangerous journey. Even if Laszlo gets there unscathed, there may be no one he can persuade to bring help. And even if all these ifs meet happy whens, there has got to be only a small chance Katherine will still be alive when Laszlo gets back. What are they to do?

I want you to think about this predicament as the defining question of your life. Everything in our culture, and especially our institutions of higher education, orients us toward solutions, toward answers, toward ways to fix the human body, the human mind, the world's economy, the inside of a laptop, the woes of Washington, the finances of Greece, the Arab-Israeli conflict, the poverty of Somalia. *Are you ready for a problem that doesn't have an answer?* That is the question I am going to address here.

Mortality

Let us dig down to one of the biggest questions of all. What is the essential problem of human existence? I want to dig inside this question to identify the answer most people would probably give to the question. I want not just to name that answer, but to explore it in such a way that we can see how that answer shapes a number of things we do.

Here is my hypothesis. Our culture's operational assumption has long been that the central problem of human existence is mortality. From the moment we come into the world, our fundamental crisis is that we are going to die. In the words of Samuel Beckett, we "give birth astride of a grave, the light gleams an instant, then it's night once more." Given that eternity is rather extensive by anyone's measure, any limited lifespan that falls short of eternity is bound to be unsatisfactory, and three score years and ten are not inherently less adequate than a million or two: as Isaac Watts, recalling the words of 2 Peter, reminds us in his celebrated hymn, "A thousand ages, in thy sight, are like an evening gone; short as the watch that ends the night, before the rising sun." But the issue is not simply that life is limited in terms of duration. Human flourishing is circumscribed by a host of other limitations. If we simply invoke nine, we might note disability, chronic ill health, and terminal illness; poverty, hardship, and malnutrition; adverse weather, famine, and limited natural resources. It is a formidable list. We are hemmed in on all sides not just by death but by a host of other constraints.

What has changed in perhaps the last fifty or sixty years is that, at least in the West, humanity no longer feels such limitations are integral to its existence. There was a time when death and taxes named the unshiftable givens of human experience and when life was a largely Stoic matter of learning to live within the boundaries of limited human potential. Death took place in the home, most illnesses had little or no chance of a cure, and it was best to prepare oneself for a fragile existence or face hubristic disappointment or humiliation. The world's resources may have held enormous potential, but the technology and techniques for tapping that potential were still in their infancy. Those days have gone. A cascade of technological advance in fields such as medicine, transport, and information transfer has made such constraints seem absurd, rather than necessary. The human project is no longer about coming to terms with limitations and flourishing within them. It is now, almost without question, about overcoming and transcending limitations. Human contingency is to be swept aside like racist legislation during the Civil Rights Movement. It is not something we learn to live with: it is something we expect to conquer. Doing so is part of our self-assertion, our full expression, our spreading of our wings. It has more or less become the defining project of the human race.

It seems all are agreed that the key project of our species is the alleviation, overcoming, and transcendence of mortality. We achieve this by inventing new medications, discovering new dimensions of experience, reducing or reversing limitations such as blindness, breaking athletic records, and circumventing such tragedies as famine or muscular dystrophy. That is what we strive for. That is what gains outstanding individuals rewards and acclaim. That is what our society prizes most highly.

In the Middle Ages, the most celebrated moments were the discovery of precious documents from the classical period. Each one represented a reclaiming of a piece of and an avenue into a lost golden era. Today the golden moments are the transcending of another dimension of human limitation.

When we advertise our organizations we seldom still say, "Making lead pencils the same way for 150 years." Instead we say, "Testing and stretching the boundaries of knowledge: making the impossible, possible." The single notion that sums up this sense of throwing off limitations is freedom, and the term we employ to commodify freedom and give it retail value is choice. So the basic line in promoting what we do is to say that our product or service overcomes one or more of the real or perceived constraints of your daily or lifelong existence and thus gives you more choice.

Now, when an organization, such as a business or a university, wants to feel it is addressing wider human needs, and not just feathering its own nest, it encourages its members to address what it perceives as the fundamental problem of human existence. Efforts toward that end are what the church calls mission and the world calls service. Mission concerns God's hopes for the world and the church's role in bringing those hopes about. Service is the recognition that there is a lot more to the world than the activities that yield an income, and that, however much benefit many people may derive from those activities, there are a great many more who derive little or none, and whose needs, if they are to be noticed and responded to, have to be addressed in voluntary ways.

What I want to highlight right now is that *if you assume that the fundamental human problem is mortality and if the great majority of your institutional endeavor is committed to creating opportunities for people to overcome the world's limitations and their own, then it is highly likely that you will configure service and mission in corresponding terms.* You will be upholding the Millennium Development Goals. You will be providing artificial limbs for use by people in war zones who have been maimed by landmines. You will be digging wells for people in locations where there is a dearth of fresh water. When the human problem is mortality, then this is what mission and service are: they are generous acts of reducing mortality, alleviating human limitation, in ways that are not income-generating but are nonetheless life-enhancing, for both giver and receiver.

Isolation

So that is my hypothesis. Most educated people in our culture assume the fundamental human problem is mortality, specifically, and human limitation, more generally. But here is my argument. What if it turned out that the fundamental human problem was not mortality after all? What if it turned out that all along the fundamental human problem was isolation? What do I mean by this? If the fundamental human problem is isolation, then the solutions we are looking for do not lie in the laboratory or the hospital or the frontiers of human knowledge or experience. Instead the solutions lie in things we already have — most of all, in one another. What if the answer, for Laszlo, doesn't lie in walking to Cairo?

Let me explain this by asking a basic theological question. Why do Christians, to use conventional and familiar language, want people to be saved? An obvious answer might be, "Because those people are going to die, and maybe they'll go to hell, or oblivion, or nothingness," or whatever the latest term for downstairs happens to be. But if you ask, "*And what's so great about going to heaven, then?*" what kind of an answer do you get? Heaven is, I would suggest, the state of being with God and being with one another and being with the renewed creation. In other words, a heaven that is simply and only about overcoming mortality is an eternal life that is not worth having. It is not worth having because it leaves one alone forever. And being alone forever is not a description of heaven. It is a description of hell. The heaven that is worth aspiring to is a rejoining of relationship, of community, of partnership, a sense of being in the presence of another in which there is neither a folding of identities that loses their difference nor a sharpening of difference that leads to hostility, but an enjoyment of the other that evokes cherishing and relishing. The theological word for this is communion.

To explain this, I am going to describe to you three scenes that I am guessing will be familiar to all of us. And then I want to think with you about what these three scenes have in common.

The first is your relationship with the most difficult member of your family. Let's say it is your father. Christmas is coming up, but somehow you have no idea what to give him. It bothers you because deep down it feels like your inability to know what present will please your father is symbolic of your lifelong confusion about what might truly make your father happy, especially where you are concerned. So in the end you spend more than you meant to on something you do not really believe he wants, pathetically throwing money at the problem but inwardly cursing yourself because you know that what you are buying is not the answer. When Christmas comes and your father opens the present, you see in his forced smile and his half-hearted hug of thanks that you have failed yet again to do something for him that might overcome the chasm between you.

Here is a second scene. You have family or friends from out of town coming for Thanksgiving. You want everything to be perfect for them, and you exchange a flurry of emails about who is going to sleep where, and whether it is all right for them to bring the dog. You get into a frenzy of shopping and baking. You are actually a little anxious that you will forget something or burn something, so the kitchen becomes your empire, and you can't bear for someone to interrupt you, and even at Thanksgiving dinner you are mostly checking the gravy or reheating the potatoes. As you say goodbye to your guests, you hug and say, "It's such a shame we never really talked while you were here." And when they have finally left, you collapse in a heap, maybe in tears of exhaustion.

Here is a third scene. You feel there is something empty or lacking in the cozy Christmas with family and friends, and your heart is breaking for people having a tough time in the cold, in isolation, in poverty, or in grief. So you gather together presents for children of prisoners or turn all your Christmas gifts into vouchers representing your support of a house or a cow or two buffaloes for people who need the resources more than you and your friends do.

What do these scenes have in common? I want to suggest that they are based on one tiny word: it is the word "for." When we care about those for whom Christmas is a tough time, we want to do something "for" them. When we want our houseguests to enjoy their Thanksgiving visit, our impulse is to spend our whole time doing things "for" them, whether cooking dinner or constantly clearing the house or arranging activities to keep them busy. When we feel our relationship with our father is faltering, our instinct is to do something "for" him that somehow melts his heart and makes everything all right.

And those gestures of "for" matter because they sum up a whole life in which we try to make relationships better, try to make the world better, try to be better people ourselves by doing things "for" people. We praise the selflessness of those who spend their lives doing things "for" people. People still sign letters "Your obedient servant," because we want to tell each other "I'm eager to do things 'for' you." When we feel noble we hum Art Garfunkel singing "Like a bridge over troubled water, I will lay me down . . ." – presumably "for" you to walk over me without getting your dainty feet wet. When we feel romantic we put on the husky voice and turn into Bryan Adams singing, "Everything I do – I do it 'for' you."

It seems that the word that epitomizes being an admirable person, the word that sums up the spirit of Christianity, is "for." We cook "for," we buy presents "for," we offer charity "for," all to say we lay ourselves down "for." But there is a problem here. All these gestures are generous, and kind, and in some cases sacrificial and noble. They are good gestures, warm-hearted, admirable gestures. But somehow they don't go to the heart of the problem. You give your father the gift, and the chasm still lies between you. You wear yourself out in showing hospitality, but you have never actually had the conversation with your loved ones. You make fine gestures of charity, but the poor are still strangers to you. "For" is a fine word, but it does not dismantle resentment, it does not overcome misunderstanding, it does not deal with alienation, it does not overcome isolation.

Most of all, "for" is not the way God relates to us. God does not simply set the world straight for us. God does not simply shower us with good things. God does not mount up blessings upon us and then get miserable and stroppy when we open them all up and fail to be sufficiently excited or surprised or grateful. "For" is not the heart of God.

In some ways we wish it was. We would love God to make everything happy and surround us with perfect things. When we get cross with God, it is easy to feel that God is not keeping the divine side of the bargain — to do things "for" us now and forever.

But God shows us something else. God speaks a rather different word. In Matthew's gospel, the angel says to Joseph, "'Behold, the virgin shall conceive and bear a son, and they shall name him Emmanuel,' which means, 'God is with us.'" And then in John's gospel, we get the summary statement of what the Christian faith means: "The Word became flesh and lived with us." It is an unprepossessing little word, but this is the word that lies at the heart of Christmas and at the heart of the Christian faith. The word is "with."

Think back to the very beginning of all things. John's gospel says, "The Word was with God. He was in the beginning with God. Without him not one thing came into being." In other words, before anything else, there was a "with," the "with" between God and the Word, or as Christians came to call it, between the Father and the Son. "With" is the most fundamental thing about God. And then think about how Jesus concludes his ministry. His very last words in Matthew's gospel are, "Behold, I am with you always." In other words, there will never be a time when I am not "with." And at the very end of the Bible, when the book of Revelation describes the final disclosure of God's everlasting destiny, this is what the voice from heaven says: "Behold, the home of God is among mortals. He will dwell with them as their God; they will be his peoples, and God himself will be with them."

We have stumbled upon the most important word in the Bible — the word that describes the heart of God and the nature of God's purpose and destiny for us. And that word is "with." That is what God was in the very beginning;

that is what God sought to instill in the creation of all things, that is what God was looking for in making the covenant with Israel, that is what God coming among us in Jesus was all about, that is what the sending of the Holy Spirit meant, that is what our destiny in the company of God will look like. It is all in that little word "with." God's whole life and action and purpose are shaped to be "with" us.

In a lot of ways, "with" is harder than "for." You can do "for" without a conversation, without a real relationship, without a genuine shaping of your life to accommodate and incorporate the other. The reason your Christmas present for your father is doomed is not because "for" is wrong, not because there is anything bad about generosity; it is because the only solution is for you and your father to be "with" each other long enough to hear each other's stories and tease out the countless misunderstandings and hurts that have led your relationship beyond the point of being rescued by the right Christmas present. The reason why you collapse in tears when your Thanksgiving guests have gone home is because the hard work is finding out how you can share the different responsibilities and genuinely be "with" one another in the kitchen and elsewhere in ways that make a stay of several nights a joy of "with" rather than a burden of "for." What makes attempts at Christmas charity seem a little hollow is not that they are not genuine and helpful and kind but that what isolated and grieving and impoverished people usually need is not gifts or money but the faithful presence with them of someone who really cares about them as a person. It is the "with" they desperately want, and the "for" on its own (whether it is food, presents, or money) cannot make up for the lack of that "with."

But we all fear the "with," because the "with" seems to ask more of us than we can give. We would all prefer to keep charity on the level of "for," where it cannot hurt us. We all know that more families struggle over Christmas than any other time. Maybe that is because you can spend the whole year being busy and doing things "for" your family, but when there is nothing else to do but be "with" one another you realize that being "with" is harder than doing "for" — and sometimes it is just too hard. Sometimes New Year's comes as a relief as we can then go back to doing "for" and leave aside being "with" for another year.

And that is why it is glorious, almost incredible, good news that God didn't settle on "for." God said unambiguously, "I am with." Behold, my dwelling is among you. I have moved into the neighborhood. I will be "with" you always. My name is Emmanuel, God "with" us. Sure, there was an element of "for" in Jesus' life. He was "for" us when he healed and taught; he was "for" us when he died on the cross; he was "for" us when he rose from the grave and ascended to heaven. These are things that only God can do and we cannot do. But the power of these things God did "for" us lies in that they were based on his being "with" us. God has not abolished "for." But God, in becoming flesh in Jesus, has said *there will never again be a "for" that is not based on a fundamental, unalterable, everlasting, and utterly unswerving "with."* That is the good news of the incarnation.

And how do we celebrate this good news? By being "with" people in poverty and distress even when there is nothing we can do "for" them. By being "with" people in grief and sadness and loss even when there is nothing to say. By being "with" and listening to and walking with those we find most difficult rather than trying to fob them off with a gift or a face-saving gesture. By being still "with" God in silent prayer rather than rushing in our anxiety to do yet more things "for" God. By taking an appraisal of all our relationships and asking ourselves, "Does my doing 'for' arise out of a fundamental commitment to be 'with,' or is my doing 'for' driven by my profound desire to avoid the discomfort, the challenge, the patience, the loss of control involved in being 'with'?"

No one could be more tempted to retreat into doing "for" than God. God, above all, knows how exasperating, ungrateful, thoughtless, and self-destructive company we can be. Most of the time we just want God to fix it and spare us the relationship. But that is not God's way. God could have done it all alone. But God chose not to. God chose to do it "with" us, even though it cost the cross. That is the amazing news of the word "with."

The cross is usually portrayed as the ultimate moment of "for" — the definitive thing only God could do that God did do on our behalf. But let's think about the cross for a moment in the light of what we have seen about the word "with." The cross is Jesus' ultimate demonstration of being *with* us — but in the cruelest irony of all time, it is the instant Jesus finds that neither we, nor the Father, are *with* him. Remember Jesus' agonizing words, "My God, my God, why have you forsaken me?" Every aspect of being *not-with*, of being *with-out*, clusters together at the foot of the cross. Jesus experiences the reality of human sin, because sin is fundamentally living *without* God. Jesus experiences the depth of suffering, because suffering is more than anything the condition of being *without* comfort. Jesus experiences the horror of death, because death is the word we give to being *without* all things — without breath, without connectedness, without consciousness, without a body. Jesus experiences the biggest alienation of all, the state of being *without* the

Father, and thus being not-God — being, for this moment, without the *with* that is the essence of God.

Jesus gives everything that he is for the cause of being *with* us, for the cause of embracing us within the essence of God's being. He has given so much — even despite our determination to be *without* him. And yet he has given beyond our imagination, because for the sake of our being *with* the Father he has, for this moment, lost his own being *with* the Father. And the Father has longed so much to be *with* us that he has, for this moment, lost his being *with* the Son, which is the essence of his being. Here is the astonishing good news. At the central moment in history, Jesus, the incarnate Son of God, had to choose between being with the Father or being with us. And he chose us. At the same time the Father had to choose between letting the Son be with us or keeping the Son to himself. And he chose to let the Son be with us. That is the choice on which our eternal destiny depends. That is the epicenter of the Christian faith and our very definition of love.

From this moment we can see that the word "with" becomes the key to the whole story. The Holy Trinity is the perfect epitome of "with": God being with God. The incarnation of Jesus is the embodiment of "with": God being with us, being among us. The crucifixion, as we have seen, is the greatest test of God's being with us, because we see that God in Christ is so committed to being with us that Jesus will even risk his being with God to keep his commitment never to be separated from us. The resurrection is the vindication of God's being both with us and with God, and the ultimate and perpetual compatibility, and unity, of the two. Pentecost is the embodiment of that resurrection breakthrough, because in Pentecost the Holy Spirit becomes the guarantee and gift of our union with God in Christ and our union with one another in Christ's body.

Why Alleviating Mortality Heightens Isolation

So you have had my hypothesis — that our culture assumes the fundamental human problem is mortality. And you have had my argument — that the fundamental human problem is not mortality; instead, it is isolation. And I have expounded that argument by showing how in the word "with," what I call the most important word, we see the essence of what it means to be God and the essence of what it means to be human. Now, I want to show why this distinction between mortality and isolation is so important to the church's mission and the world's service.

It is not difficult to see how a philosophy based on overcoming mortality and a philosophy based on overcoming isolation can come into tension with one another. As humanity's quest to overcome mortality has gathered pace, the degree of human isolation has increased with it. For sure, enhanced transportation, telecommunications, and information technology have made it possible to communicate in ever more extensive and complex ways. But they have also facilitated lifestyles where people are in touch with conversation partners on the other side of the planet, but not with next-door neighbors; where insurance lies in investments and pensions, rather than in friendships and extended families; and where face-to-face human interaction is ceasing to become the encounter of choice for a generation who are used to having plentiful alternative ways to make themselves known to one another. The flip side of making ourselves more independent and self-sufficient is that we are simultaneously becoming more isolated and more alone.

And this brings us to the crucial point. If you see the central quest of life as being to overcome isolation rather than to overcome mortality, your notion of service and of mission will change accordingly. Service and mission that seek to overcome isolation do not look to technology to solve problems and reduce limitations. They do not assume that their own knowledge and skill are the crucial element required to change the game. Of course, if you are in the business of overcoming mortality, you are going to need plenty of knowledge and skill. But if you are in the business of overcoming isolation, then you begin to appreciate that concentrating on enhancing and promoting your own knowledge and skill may be as likely to be counterproductive as productive.

In his letter to the Ephesians, Paul cites one compelling metaphor for what Christ has done in bringing salvation. Paul says, "In his flesh he has made both groups into one and has broken down the dividing wall, that is, the hostility between us" (2:14). Paul is referring to the hostility between Jew and Gentile, but the point goes for any such degree of antagonism and alienation. Indeed, the greater the degree of isolation or antagonism, the more profound the significance of overcoming it. Thus service and mission become *recognizing those from whom one is alienated and antagonized and seeking and finding ways to be present to them.* Mission and service are not primarily using one's skills in conflict resolution to bring peace between warring parties, but instead perceiving contexts in which one is one of the warring parties and submitting oneself to a process of making peace.

The approach that sees overcoming mortality as the goal tends to approach mission and service like this. We, as outsiders to social disadvantage, and thus not, in any significant way, part of the problem, nonetheless have expert eyes to see what the problem is and ready-made solutions at hand. We will appear in the local context, deliver our solution, and then withdraw, quickly to resume our regular activities, which are not considered to have any material bearing, positive or negative, on the problem we have identified and resolved. If we have listened and learned from repeated interventions of this kind, we will have gathered that it is good to form relationships on the ground, good to involve local participants in some way, else local wisdom will be neglected and local goodwill needlessly undermined. But the point is that this local participation is never more than a means to an end. The end is never in question. The end always comes in the form of overcoming the limitations of the local environment or skill base, and the provision of technology or the enhancement of the capacity to use it.

Contrast this with the kind of mission and service that emerge from a conviction that the goal is to overcome isolation. We are not exactly sure what the problem is, but we take for granted that we are a part of it. We do not assume that the solution is to make other people more like us by ensuring that they have what we have and live as we live. We assume that we have a deficiency, and that deficiency is due to the poverty or absence of our relationship with those who have important and invigorating things to share with us, if only we could open up channels to receive those things. We may well embark on projects that seek to alleviate distress or transfer resources or develop skills. But the point of these projects is not to achieve a specific material goal: these endeavors are simply means of forming relationships from a safe common starting point. These programs are ladders that will fall away once the relationships are in place and genuine dialogue is happening. What we might call the "mortality model" insists that what is required is the introduction of new information, new technique, new technology. The "isolation model" asserts that in most cases a people or a neighborhood has everything it needs for its own redemption: what inhibits such redemption is the energy lost in isolation and wasted in antagonism.

For leaders of colleges and universities, there is a curious irony in all of this. Such leaders do more to further the overcoming of isolation by the way they run their institutions and by the way their institutions foster healthy relationships among their members and staff than their institutions do by such service projects as they undertake. Because in all the haste to provide technology and enhance technique and alleviate the limitations of climate or scarcity or skill, mortality-motivated service can often underline and even enhance the kinds of social alienation that from the isolation perspective constitutes the problem in the first place.

I once was asked to do a bit of consultancy work for a college that was seeking to expand its student service programs. I talked to the board of the service initiative. "What are you looking for in the service projects you co-ordinate?" I asked them. "We want to see *impact*," they said. "We want to see transformation. We want to *make a difference*." Try as I might I could not get the members of that board to see that not all impact is welcomed by its recipients. Not all transformation is for the better, and a lot of people in the history of the world have made a difference, but not all of those differences have been beneficial ones. The kind of service that board was talking about did not seem to be serving anyone but themselves. It did not seem to occur to them that they might be affirming and exacerbating the social divisions and inequalities that they found.

Like many professional people, they liked to use the phrase "give something back." I tried gently to point out to them that such a phrase assumed the rather problematic premise that they and the student body would inevitably and rightly spend most of their careers taking something away. I suggested that perhaps they would do better to focus on stopping taking away rather than trying to give something back. What bothered me most about the whole conversation was that here were a bunch of thoughtful, successful people, but they did not seem to be going about giving something back with the same degree of thoughtfulness to which they had given the original taking away that had made them so successful in the first place.

In conclusion, I want to return to *The English Patient*. Think again about Laszlo's choice of whether to stay beside Katherine or walk to Cairo in search of assistance. In the story, Laszlo scarcely thinks twice before he sets off on his three-day journey to find help. He has all sorts of adventures before he finally makes it back to the encampment and the ancient cave. And when he does, Katherine is very, very, very dead. Laszlo is so committed to believing that there is a solution to Katherine's agonizing plight and that he has the solution, that he overlooks the one thing needful. And that is being with Katherine. He is so concerned to solve the problem that he leaves her alone in her hour of greatest need.

I wonder whether the real reason Laszlo went to Cairo was because he could not bear to watch Katherine die. I wonder whether we fill our lives with activity and creativity and productivity because we fear that if we sit still we will go to pieces. It never occurs to any of us to think that this frenzy of programming and experiencing and sampling and trying out is madness. On the contrary, it is those that lag behind or stand outside our frenetic world that we regard as mad.

What is at the bottom of all this? Let me suggest a possible answer. Our colleges and universities are colluding with and fueling our society's attempt to construct a world that works perfectly well without love. If you have a problem, here is a host of solutions. Come to a wonderful university, and learn how to put the world to rights. Don't you wonder how much of this is like Laszlo walking to Cairo? What Katherine needed was the man she loved to be with her as she faced the near-certainty of her own impending death. But Laszlo did not, or maybe could not, give her what she needed. We are turning our world into a Laszlo society, full of products, full of gadgets, full of devices, full of techniques, full of energy, all of which make the world go round very effectively.

And the result is that we have all become Laszlo. We would all walk to Cairo rather than stay with Katherine. Wouldn't we? Yet the irony of the movie is that when Laszlo, returning to Cairo with Katherine's body, crashes another plane and is himself horribly injured, he is found and tenderly accompanied by strangers and cared for until the point of his death. He receives from strangers at the end of *his* life the patient love he was not able to give to Katherine at the end of hers.

Here lies the central choice of our lives. Are we going to give in to our society's pressure to be Laszlo? Or are we going to imitate the Christ of manger and crucifixion, the God who is with us always, even to the end of time? Are we going to love or search for solutions? That is the question at the heart of service and mission in our new century.

Martin Luther King Jr.

THE WORLD HOUSE

This selection is from the final chapter of King's last book, *Where Do We Go from Here: Chaos or Community?* During the late 1960s, after a decade of working primarily on overturning racial injustice in the United States, King was becoming increasingly outspoken in opposition to other forms of oppression as well, and was making powerful connections between the struggle for justice within his own country and the struggles for liberation taking place around the world. The ethics of resistance he had forged during the civil rights movement found fresh expression when placed in a global context, as happens in this selection. The influence on King of the two traditions that most influence *Leading Lives That Matter* — Christianity and democracy — is quite evident in this selection. King's eloquence and vision in adapting those traditions to the urgent needs of his moment in history are also evident.

Whom do you think King means when he speaks, repeatedly, of "we"?

Some years ago a famous novelist died. Among his papers was found a list of suggested plots for future stories, the most prominently underscored being this one: "A widely separated family inherits a house in which they have to live together." This is the great new problem of mankind. We have inherited a large house, a great "world house" in which we have to live together — black and white, Easterner and Westerner, Gentile and Jew, Catholic and Protestant, Muslim and Hindu — a family unduly separated in ideas, culture and interest, who, because we can never again live apart, must learn somehow to live with each other in peace.

However deeply American Negroes are caught in the struggle to be at last at home in our homeland of the United States, we cannot ignore the larger world house in which we are also dwellers. Equality with whites will not solve the problems of either whites or Negroes if it means equality in a

From Martin Luther King Jr., *Where Do We Go from Here: Chaos or Community?* (Boston: Beacon, 2010), 177–202.

world society stricken by poverty and in a universe doomed to extinction by war.

All inhabitants of the globe are now neighbors. This worldwide neighborhood has been brought into being largely as a result of the modern scientific and technological revolutions. . . .

From time immemorial men have lived by the principle that "self-preservation is the first law of life." But this is a false assumption. I would say that other-preservation is the first law of life. It is the first law of life precisely because we cannot preserve self without being concerned about preserving other selves. The universe is so structured that things go awry if men are not diligent in their cultivation of the other-regarding dimension. "I" cannot reach fulfillment without "thou." The self cannot be self without other selves. Self-concern without other-concern is like a tributary that has no outward flow to the ocean. Stagnant, still and stale, it lacks both life and freshness. Nothing would be more disastrous and out of harmony with our self-interest than for the developed nations to travel a dead-end road of inordinate selfishness. We are in the fortunate position of having our deepest sense of morality coalesce with our self-interest.

But the real reason that we must use our resources to outlaw poverty goes beyond material concerns to the quality of our mind and spirit. Deeply woven into the fiber of our religious tradition is the conviction that men are made in the image of God, and that they are souls of infinite metaphysical value. If we accept this as a profound moral fact, we cannot be content to see men hungry, to see men victimized with ill-health, when we have the means to help them. In the final analysis, the rich must not ignore the poor because both rich and poor are tied together. They entered the same mysterious gateway of human birth, into the same adventure of mortal life.

All men are interdependent. Every nation is an heir of a vast treasury of ideas and labor to which both the living and the dead of all nations have contributed. Whether we realize it or not, each of us lives eternally "in the red." We are everlasting debtors to known and unknown men and women. When we arise in the morning, we go into the bathroom where we reach for a sponge which is provided for us by a Pacific Islander. We reach for soap that is created for us by a European. Then at the table we drink coffee which is provided for us by a South American, or tea by a Chinese or cocoa by a West African. Before we leave for our jobs we are already beholden to more than half of the world.

In a real sense, all life is interrelated. The agony of the poor impoverishes the rich; the betterment of the poor enriches the rich. We are inevitably our brother's keeper because we are our brother's brother. Whatever affects one directly affects all indirectly. . . .

This call for a worldwide fellowship that lifts neighborly concern beyond one's tribe, race, class and nation is in reality a call for an all-embracing and unconditional love for all men. This often misunderstood and misinterpreted concept has now become an absolute necessity for the survival of man. When I speak of love, I am speaking of that force which all the great religions have seen as the supreme unifying principle of life. Love is the key that unlocks the door which leads to ultimate reality. This Hindu-Muslim-Christian-Jewish-Buddhist belief about ultimate reality is beautifully summed up in the First Epistle of Saint John:

> Let us love one another: for love is of God: and every one that loveth is born of God, and knoweth God. He that loveth not knoweth not God; for God is love. . . . If we love one another, God dwelleth in us, and his love is perfected in us.

Let us hope that this spirit will become the order of the day. We can no longer afford to worship the God of hate or bow before the altar of retaliation. The oceans of history are made turbulent by the ever-rising tides of hate. History is cluttered with the wreckage of nations and individuals who pursued this self-defeating path of hate. As Arnold Toynbee once said in a speech: "Love is the ultimate force that makes for the saving choice of life and good against the damning choice of death and evil. Therefore the first hope in our inventory must be the hope that love is going to have the last word."

We are now faced with the fact that tomorrow is today. We are confronted with the fierce urgency of *now*. In this unfolding conundrum of life and history there is such a thing as being too late. Procrastination is still the thief of time. Life often leaves us standing bare, naked and dejected with a lost opportunity. The "tide in the affairs of men" does not remain at the flood; it ebbs. We may cry out desperately for time to pause in her passage, but time is deaf to every plea and rushes on. Over the bleached bones and jumbled residues of numerous civilizations are written the pathetic words: "Too late." There is an invisible book of life that faithfully records our vigilance or our neglect. "The moving finger writes, and having writ moves on. . . ." We still have a choice today: nonviolent coexistence or violent coannihilation. This may well be mankind's last chance to choose between chaos and community.

Is a Balanced Life Possible and Preferable to a Life Focused Primarily on Work?

A s a college senior left the office of her premed adviser, both of them were upset. The senior had finally mustered the courage to inform the adviser that she had decided not to go to medical school, and the adviser had not taken it well. He tried unsuccessfully to get the student to change her mind: she was at the top of her class, after all, and she had always planned to be a doctor. But now, she explained, she was thinking about other life goals as well. From everything she had observed, the life of a doctor seemed all-consuming, with workweeks of sixty hours or more considered normal. She hoped someday to bear and raise children, and she was in love with a young man with whom she wanted to share her life. She wanted, she explained, a "balanced life" not so consumed by paid employment that it would take time away from family, friends, church, and community.

Her adviser was not pleased. The premed program at her college had awarded her its top summer research opportunities, assuming that she planned to stay the course, and her parents had made significant financial sacrifices to support her education as well. She had already been admitted to two top medical schools; why not continue her studies and *then* determine whether her fears were based on fact or fiction? He pointed out that she might change, that her boyfriend might abandon her, and that she might have second thoughts about children. All this was to no avail. After months of anguished reflection, this young woman knew what she did and did not want to do.

We, the editors of this book, and surely also you its readers, fully support the progress of women in the professions in recent decades, and we encourage all who feel called to embrace challenging professions to do so. Yet there is no doubt that scenes like the one just described are common on college campuses and elsewhere, as both men and women experience concerns about being overwhelmed by the demands of their jobs. Many young people have witnessed the hectic lives of their parents and other adults and have resolved not to repeat this pattern. Indeed, already in college some find that the pressures to achieve in many areas become more than they want to bear and that their efforts to juggle academic work, paid work, artistic and athletic endeavors, and friendship bring more stress than satisfaction. Later, among those who enter fast-track jobs after graduation, some grow dissatisfied and look for ways to shift gears to a different kind of employment so that they can have a more leisurely and fulfilling personal life. That said, this concern is not universal; many other people love throwing themselves completely into demanding work, or relish the experience of trying to meet multiple demands. Not everyone worries about the conflicts that probably lie ahead — but many people do.

Individual differences in physical energy, family experience, personal goals, and occupational focus surely exert great influence on decisions like the one made by the premed student. Economics also frame such decisions, which usually have significant financial consequences. But these decisions also require hard thinking and honest conversation, because what we decide reflects, at best, our convictions about what it means to lead a good life. Was this student simply fearful of taking on difficult challenges even though she might have realized, on further thought, that doing so would be worthwhile in the end? Or had she instead come to believe that a life that matters *should* be a balanced one, thinking that many of us must or should work primarily in order to live and then seek our sources of fulfillment and lasting achievement elsewhere — in family, friendship, neighborliness, and civic engagement?

The first three readings in this chapter dramatize, complicate, and extend our college senior's predicament by exploring some of the tensions between work and other commitments that often emerge in the years after graduation:

- an article on two ways of approaching a demanding job (Zuger)
- an article urging full-time work by needed professionals (Sibert)
- an essay on the tensions between one's family of origin and working to improve society (Addams)

In the first reading, Dr. Abigail Zuger describes the very different ways in which two of her interns choose to practice medicine. The interns, one male and the other female, demonstrate that struggles over how to "balance" the claims of professional life against other claims apply to both women and men — though gender is clearly involved in a complicated way. Dr. Zuger's essay suggests that the personal approaches we bring to demanding and difficult work can make a big difference for those who aspire to a balanced life. At the same time, this essay may raise questions about what may be lost when balance prevails.

Dr. Karen S. Sibert, an anesthesiologist, addresses quite forcefully the possibility that striving for "balance" can lead to loss. She says, in effect, that our premed student was wrong to continue for such a long time down a path that she eventually abandoned. She was surely right to abandon it, however! Over against those who hope to trim their medical responsibilities for the sake of other activities, Sibert declares: "If you want to be a doctor, be a doctor. You cannot have it all." Although Sibert does not use the term "vocation," her article places great emphasis on a physician's primary obligation to serve the needs of patients; she ranks the desires of individual doctors for a pleasant lifestyle much lower in priority. Those who receive a medical education — a costly investment society makes to meet a crucial public need — ought to work full time to repay the investment and do the good that only physicians can do. Given the increasing shortage of doctors and the desperate need of patients for good care, a responsible choice to be a doctor entails the sacrifice of some personal goods for the sake of a larger public good. Balance is not the point; good medical care is.

Sibert focuses her argument especially on women in her profession. For example, she displays little sympathy for a medical student who is trying to figure out which medical specialty will allow her a schedule compatible with raising children. Should Sibert not direct her criticism instead at how traditional marriage leaves most child rearing to mothers, and at hospitals and medical practices that provide little support for female staff members? Yes, she should — and she does in some of her other writing. She is herself a mother who has had to deal with the systemic difficulties women face in demanding jobs; the essay included here contains a call for better child-care provisions, and other pieces by Sibert commend various strategies for dealing with conflicts between work and family time. (We will also get a more thorough consideration of these issues in a piece later in this chapter, "Finding Time," by Heather Boushey.) Still, the distinctive claim of Sibert's piece is worth pondering alongside the various positions on "balance" we are encountering in this chapter. To repeat: Balance is not the point. Good medical care is. This claim could be applied to other professions as well. The point is good education, good construction, good ministry, good government.

What if personal satisfaction is not the only, or even the primary, factor to consider in bringing the various parts of our lives together? Here we might remember how Frederick Buechner qualified his claim that vocation is the place where "your deep gladness and the world's deep hunger meet" (see p. 181 above). When we think not only about which job we'll have but how it fits in the rest of our life, how much "gladness" should we try to grasp? For Buechner, "neither the hair shirt nor the soft berth will do" — which we might take to mean, in this context, that it is unwise either to drive yourself crazy with overwork *or* to avoid strenuous, difficult challenges altogether. People will resolve competition between the demands of service to larger groups and the desire for private satisfactions differently, of course. In lives that matter, however, both deserve consideration.

The social reform leader Jane Addams took up a similar set of questions in the essay "Filial Relations," which comes from her 1902 book *Democracy and Social Ethics*. Addams explores the competing pulls of the "social claim" — the calling to be involved in the great issues of justice in one's time — and the "family claim" — the expectation of one's parents and society that women must focus their attention on private life. Addams, a privileged white woman, was among the first American women to attain a college education, but her parents expected that she would lead a life of leisure after graduation. She desperately longed, as the poet Marge Piercy would later put it, "to be of use" (see pp. 212–13 above). After years of depression and searching, she finally found usefulness and significance and deep gladness in her pathbreaking work of service and social change in an impoverished neighborhood of Chicago. Addams's vision and example of a life that presses beyond private obligations and enjoyments to a public-spirited vision of the common good inspired many young people and also prepared the way for significant social reform. The essay below demonstrates that Addams understood that young people often have to choose what to do in the face of considerable pressure from families who disagree; the essay also acknowledges the moral validity of some aspects of familial duty. Nonetheless, Addams dared to challenge her readers to answer the summons of public service, which she saw as the higher priority.

This is not to say that reconciling appropriate familial duties and crucial societal commitments is easy, or that this tension comes only to women. Robert Reich, an economist who served as secretary of labor during the 1990s, describes a turning point in his own career. As one immersed in a very demanding but also intensely enjoyable job, Reich frequently stayed late at the office. One night, realizing he would not be home in time to tuck his young sons into bed for the fifth night in a row, he phoned to say good night. The younger of the two said that was okay but asked please to be awakened for a hug when his father got home. Reich insisted that it would be too late and that the boy needed his sleep, but his son persisted. Asked why, the boy said he just wanted to know his dad was home. "To this day, I can't explain precisely what happened to me at that moment," Reich remembers. "Yet I suddenly knew I had to leave my job."

Our disconsolate premed student, another woman who became what the student once thought she wanted to become, and the former secretary of labor all seem to conclude, in one way or another, that those who seek to lead lives that matter must sooner or later face momentous choices, variously formulated, between balanced lives on the one hand and unbalanced lives of great achievement on the other. Actually, many lyric, epic, and dramatic poets would seem to agree with this prediction. Indeed, some have sought to express and dramatize such choices from the very first instances of written literature. The following three selections span the centuries and suggest that from the very beginning of at least the Western tradition poets have represented the very dilemmas we have been considering here:

- A short lyric poem suggesting that a balanced life is impossible if one also seeks distinguished achievement (Yeats)
- A short excerpt from an epic poem, featuring part of a speech by the ancient Greek hero Achilles (Homer)
- A conversation that considers, through reflection upon dramatic poetry, the tragic character of the lives of all who seek to live morally good lives (Nussbaum and Moyers)

William Butler Yeats's poem "The Choice" explores some of the consequences of pursuing one's work with great devotion, necessarily at the expense of "perfection of the life." And this necessary choice and cost would seem to be as old as Homer's epic *The Iliad*. In the midst of that story, three of Achilles's closest friends attempt to persuade him to stop sulking and join them in the fight against the Trojans. In his response to them, Achilles reveals that his mother, the goddess Thetis, has told him that "two destinies" await him; he must choose one or the other. Those destinies were later summarized by Aristotle in the *Nicomachean Ethics*, a work we examined on pages 83–85 above. Aristotle had no doubt about which choice a human being who sought to live nobly would and should make, as Achilles finally did: "For he will choose intense pleasure for a short time over slight pleasure for a long time; a year of living finely over many years of undistinguished life; and a single fine and great action over many small actions." In our terms today, devoting oneself to a heroic life of public service or artistic/ scientific achievement would be "a single fine and great action" by contrast to a balanced life of "many small actions."

The philosopher Martha Nussbaum, drawing on her own interpretation of the Greek tragedy *Agamemnon*, argues in the next selection that all of us face small, inescapable, and tragic moments daily that force us into choices that resemble the tragic choice the ancient king Agamemnon faced: Would he sacrifice his own daughter, or would he allow his fleet never to arrive at its destination? No, Nussbaum admits, none of us are kings sailing off to the Trojan War. And no, we are not ordinarily called upon actually to sacrifice the life of one of our children. But we are finite, and we cannot be everywhere or do everything at once. So sometimes we must choose between staying at work late to finish a task and being home to tuck a child in bed, tend to a sick partner, or attend a friend's musical performance. When it comes to negotiating the competing claims of work and the rest of life, there is not that much emotional and psychological difference between Agamemnon and you and me — *if* we really care about both our work and our loved ones, and *if* we are really striving to lead lives that are both significant and good.

Must we bravely resign ourselves to living constantly in the shadow of small daily tragedies? Or do we have some ways to reinterpret or reformulate or resolve or resist what we have been thinking through here as the problem of the balanced life? The following four texts do just that, by offering fresh ways of thinking about these issues:

- An economist's analysis of workplace pressures on family life, and her recommendations for alleviating them (Boushey)
- A critique of the whole concept of a "balanced life" (Bloom)
- A poem of radical resistance to workplace constraints (Berry)
- A reflection on a religious practice, the Sabbath (Heschel)

In her interview with Bill Moyers, Martha Nussbaum notes that "there's an awful lot society can do to provide institutions that make [those tragic] conflicts arise a little less often." Many present-day economists, sociologists, and public policy experts would push that point even further, suggesting that problems involving the quest for a "balanced life" are more socially constructed than they are individually manufactured. One such economist, Heather Boushey, author of *Finding Time: The Economics of Work-Life Conflict*, develops this latter view and proposes a number of family policies that she believes will alleviate considerably the work-life conflict, in some cases eliminating it altogether.

For the ancients, the choice that Achilles faced was reserved for a tiny elite, and even today most human beings have very little choice about what kind of work they will do, under what conditions they will do it, and whether it will allow for family time. Almost always, to discuss work-life balance is to address a "first-world problem." But this issue also presents a challenge to public policy, with wider implications for all. While acknowledging, mourning, and seeking to address the economic inequality that frames many discussions of work-life balance, we would also do well to notice the longing for both personal satisfaction and meaningful work experienced by Americans of every class. As Boushey argues, public policies can help to alleviate the tragic choices great numbers of people are forced to make between these goods. We as a public have certain policy choices that isolated individuals do not have — policy choices such as those recommended by Boushey.

Another approach to this issue is to reformulate the way we think about the whole work-life conflict altogether by contesting the very concept of a "balanced life." According to Matt Bloom, a professor in the Mendoza College of Business at the University of Notre Dame, the balance metaphor is worse than inadequate; it actually tends to foster some of the psychological conflicts that it purports to describe. What counts as success within the different domains of life is hard to stipulate and harder to measure, since the goods we seek to "balance" are incommensurate. The measure of performance for a salesperson is pretty clear, but the measure of sufficient "quality time" with one's family is very difficult to specify. Moreover, according to Bloom, the balance metaphor invites us to seek an illusory perfection. No one can lead the kind of "balanced life" that the phrase itself summons to mind.

The alternative metaphors Bloom offers — portfolio, rhythm, journey — seek to capture something that seems lacking in the balance metaphor: a sense of dynamism, a sense of living a good and significant life *over time*. And indeed, some images of balance do seem static, for example, stacking a number of objects on the two sides of an antique scale. Bloom's objection to many concepts of balance calls to mind something the sociologist Robert Wuthnow wrote some years ago in a book about the changing character of work in America. We bring different expectations to what we do at different ages, Wuthnow pointed out; we take on various commitments sequentially. A snapshot of a human being's life on just one day is probably not the best way to determine whether that life is balanced or not. Perhaps the best time to take such a snapshot would be at one's funeral, as survivors begin to assess a life that is finished and can finally be seen as a whole.

Balance may, however, be a richer metaphor than Bloom realizes. As we point out in our discussion of the work of Mary Catherine Bateson in chapter 6 below, balance can also envision the kind of measured tonal structure accomplished over time in a good piece of music or the kind of equipoise maintained by a tightrope walker through all kinds of adjustments over a long high-wire walk. The metaphor of balance can, in other words, make allowances for temporality and adaptation. It can also make allowances for another deficiency identified by Bloom, namely, its tendency to overlook the fact that what might be balance for one person may not be balance for another. Balance, like the golden mean, emerges in the space between extremes, to be sure, but it also takes shape with reference to some particular point, some specific person.

And what of Bloom's complaint that the balance metaphor provokes an illusory image of perfection that will ultimately lead to frustration and disappointment? Martha Nussbaum, who has argued that some degree of failure is inescapable for those who live rightly, might say, "Yes, and why not?" Nussbaum's tragic vision may seem discouraging at first, but she actually wants to encourage you to live in such a way that "it becomes a possibility that tragedy can happen to you." To withhold oneself from a range of deep and caring attachments, to shrink back from a life that is full of worthy commitments, would be to miss what is truly important in life. For the Greeks and for Nussbaum, the suffering experienced when human beings fail to balance their multiple commitments deepens their awareness of their attachments and, in a sense, ushers them into a more expansive understanding of what it means to be human. Suffering and failure, then, are not arguments against the aspiration to lead a balanced life. Nor, for that matter, are they arguments against centering one's life around the passionate pursuit of excellence in one thing, which will surely include suffering and failure of its own.

Instead of reinterpreting work-life conflicts or seeking to remedy them or reduce their severity, one might simply resist, or reject altogether, the whole system that gave rise to them in the first place. This third response to the conundrums pondered in this chapter is powerfully articulated in Wendell Berry's poem "Manifesto: The Mad Farmer Liberation Front." Berry, an accomplished poet, essayist, novelist, and farmer, has written powerfully and influentially, across several decades and genres, about the devastation the modern economy perpetrates on the land and the human and other creatures who care for and rely on it. The alternative practices and passions commended in this "manifesto" might help Americans who think their lives are distressingly out of balance to reimagine their situation. Moreover, the "Mad Farmer" also has a good deal to contribute to the conversations taken up in question 3, "With Whom and for Whom Shall I Live?," and question 5, "What Are My Obligations to Future Human and Other Life?"

One final response to the difficulties of reconciling making a life with making a living comes in the form of a wonderful reminder: we human beings were made finally for rest, not for work. Writing about the Sabbath from within the Jewish tradition, which he lived and studied throughout his life in Europe and the United States, Rabbi Abraham Joshua Heschel develops this startling claim about human destiny with convincing clarity and beauty. And on this point, at least, the Jewish and the Greek classical traditions are akin to one another. Aristotle says very little about work, since he thought human beings were at their very best not at work but at leisure. If, in our thoughts and our practices, we attended as carefully to rest as to work, many of the difficulties this chapter outlines and analyzes might be less oppressive, and less spiritually damaging.

Abigail Zuger

DEFINING A DOCTOR

In this essay, Dr. Zuger focuses on two young doctors and their very different ways of defining the place of work in their lives. One way of putting the difference draws on terms familiar to us from other readings: one doctor "works to live" while the other "lives to work." Clearly the difference between them on this point influences how they approach their patients, a matter that may evoke concern in those of us who, though not doctors, may find ourselves in their care. Which doctor would you more likely be? Which would you rather have treating you if you were ill? Note that there is little evidence in the essay about which doctor's patients are more likely to get well. Something else is at stake here, for doctors and patients alike.

Although she depicts two physicians with different approaches, we might also imagine two teachers, two pastors, or two carpenters who come at their work differently. Dr. Zuger's account may prompt us to ponder whether a person can really be a first-rate practitioner in any demanding and potentially emotional field if his or her life is not at least somewhat unbalanced. Might such changes as emphasizing teamwork and shared responsibility make balance, or at least rest, more available, as some medical educators apparently hope? What would be the costs — to practitioners or patients — of such measures?

I had two interns to supervise that month, and the minute they sat down for our first meeting, I sensed how the month would unfold.

The man's white coat was immaculate, its pockets empty save for a sleek Palm Pilot that contained his list of patients.

The woman used a large loose-leaf notebook instead, every dog-eared page full of lists of things to do and check, consultants to call, questions to ask. Her pockets were stuffed, and whenever she sat down, little handbooks

Abigail Zuger, "Defining a Doctor," *New York Times*, November 2, 2004, D5.

of drug doses, wadded phone messages, pens, highlighters and tourniquets spilled onto the floor.

The man worked the hours legally mandated by the state, not a minute more, and sometimes considerably less. He was seldom in the hospital before 8 in the morning, and left by 5 unless he was on call. He ate a leisurely lunch every day and was never late for rounds.

The woman got to the hospital around dawn and was on the move for the rest of the day. Sometimes she went home when she was supposed to, but sometimes, if one of her patients was particularly sick, she would sign out to the covering intern and keep working, often talking to patients' relatives long into the night.

"I am now breaking the law," she would announce cheerfully to no one in particular, then trot off to do just a few final chores.

The man had a strict definition of what it meant to be a doctor. He did not, for instance, "do nurses' work" (his phrase). When one of his patients needed a specimen sent to the lab and the nurse didn't get around to it, neither did he. No matter how important the job was, no matter how hard I pressed him, he never gave in. If I spoke sternly to him, he would turn around and speak just as sternly to the nurse.

The woman did everyone's work. She would weigh her patients if necessary (nurses' work), feed them (aides' work), find salt-free pickles for them (dietitians' work) and wheel them to X-ray (transporters' work).

The man was cheerful, serene and well rested. The woman was overtired, hyperemotional and constantly late. The man was interested in his patients, but they never kept him up at night. The woman occasionally called the hospital from home to check on hers. The man played tennis on his days off. The woman read medical articles. At least, she read the beginnings; she tended to fall asleep halfway through.

I felt as if I was in a medieval morality play that month, living with two costumed symbols of opposing philosophies in medical education. The woman was working the way interns used to: total immersion seasoned with exhaustion and adrenaline. As far as she was concerned, her patients were her exclusive responsibility. The man was an intern of the new millennium. His hours and duties were delimited; he saw himself as part of a health care team, and his patients' welfare as a shared responsibility.

This new model of medical internship got some important validation in *The New England Journal of Medicine* last week, when Harvard researchers reported the effects of reducing interns' work hours to 60 per week from 80 (now the mandated national maximum). The shorter workweek required a larger staff of interns to spell one another at more frequent intervals. With shorter hours, the interns got more sleep at home, dozed off less at work and made considerably fewer bad mistakes in patient care.

Why should such an obvious finding need an elaborate controlled study to establish? Why should it generate not only two long articles in the world's most prestigious medical journal, but also three long, passionate editorials? Because the issue here is bigger than just scheduling and manpower.

The progressive shortening of residents' work hours spells nothing less than a change in the ethos of medicine itself. It means the end of Dr. Kildare, Superstar — that lone, heroic healer, omniscient, omnipotent and ever-present. It means a revolution in the complex medical hierarchy that sustained him. Willy-nilly, medicine is becoming democratized, a team sport.

We can only hope the revolution will be bloodless. Everything will have to change. Doctors will have to learn to work well with others. They will have to learn to write and speak with enough clarity and precision so that the patient's story remains accurate as care passes from hand to hand. They will have to stop saying "my patient" and begin to say "our patient" instead.

It may be, when the dust settles, that the system will be more functional, less error-prone. It may be that we will simply have substituted one set of problems for another.

We may even find that nothing much has changed. Even in the Harvard data, there was an impressive range in the hours that the interns under study worked. Some logged in over 90 hours in their 80-hour workweek. Some put in 75 instead.

Medicine has always attracted a wide spectrum of individuals, from the lazy and disaffected to the deeply committed. Even draconian scheduling policies may not change basic personality traits, or the kind of doctors that interns grow up to be.

My month with the intern of the past and the intern of the future certainly argues for the power of the individual work ethic. Try as I might, it was not within my power to modify the way either of them functioned. The woman cared too much. The man cared too little. She worked too hard, and he could not be prodded into working hard enough. They both made careless mistakes. When patients died, the man shrugged and the woman cried. If for no other reason than that one, let us hope that the medicine of the future still has room for people like her.

Karen S. Sibert

DON'T QUIT THIS DAY JOB

In the op-ed piece below, Dr. Karen Sullivan Sibert fiercely opposes doctors who give less than a full commitment to a full-time job because they are trying to lead something like a balanced life. Those who are trained as physicians owe it to society and to their patients to commit themselves fully to practicing their profession, she insists. As she notes, this view is controversial; it runs against the supposed freedom of physicians themselves to craft livable lives. Still, her concerns about patient needs, public investment, and physician shortages are serious ones. Which do you think should govern physicians' working hours: patient need or family responsibilities? What are your reasons?

Sibert wrote this essay in 2011. A few years later, she softened her views. After seeing greater stress in the lives of doctors and diminished respect and support for what they do, she found the choice of some to leave the profession or cut back on hours more understandable than she had previously maintained. In a sense, this makes physicians' situations more like those of other people, as workplaces of many kinds ask more and more of staff members, and as rewards decrease. Are the issues Siebert saw in her own profession also present in the field you may enter? To take just one example, today's teachers typically do their work with greater demands and less flexibility than was true several years ago. How onerous would a work situation for a needed professional have to be before you would disagree with Sibert's 2011 opinion that the work must come first?

Dr. Sibert is an anesthesiologist at UCLA. Before becoming a physician, she was a journalist, and she has continued to write, mostly about medicine and issues of work-life balance. Married to another anesthesiologist, she has raised four children, including a son who went to medical school.

Karen S. Sibert, "Don't Quit This Day Job," *New York Times*, June 11, 2011, WK9.

I'm a doctor and a mother of four, and I've always practiced medicine full time. When I took my board exams in 1987, female doctors were still uncommon, and we were determined to work as hard as any of the men.

Today, however, increasing numbers of doctors — mostly women — decide to work part time or leave the profession. Since 2005 the part-time physician workforce has expanded by 62 percent, according to recent survey data from the American Medical Group Association, with nearly 4 in 10 female doctors between the ages of 35 and 44 reporting in 2010 that they worked part time.

This may seem like a personal decision, but it has serious consequences for patients and the public.

Medical education is supported by federal and state tax money both at the university level — student tuition doesn't come close to covering the schools' costs — and at the teaching hospitals where residents are trained. So if doctors aren't making full use of their training, taxpayers are losing their investment. With a growing shortage of doctors in America, we can no longer afford to continue training doctors who don't spend their careers in the full-time practice of medicine.

It isn't fashionable (and certainly isn't politically correct) to criticize "work-life balance" or part-time employment options. How can anyone deny people the right to change their minds about a career path and choose to spend more time with their families? I have great respect for stay-at-home parents, and I think it's fine if journalists or chefs or lawyers choose to work part time or quit their jobs altogether. But it's different for doctors. Someone needs to take care of the patients.

The Association of American Medical Colleges estimates that, 15 years from now, with the ranks of insured patients expanding, we will face a shortage of up to 150,000 doctors. As many doctors near retirement and aging baby boomers need more and more medical care, the shortage gets worse each year.

The decline in doctors' pay is part of the problem. As we look at Medicare and Medicaid spending cuts, we need to be careful not to drive the best of the next generation away from medicine and into, say, investment banking.

But the productivity of the doctors currently practicing is also an important factor. About 30 percent of doctors in the United States are female, and women received 48 percent of the medical degrees awarded in 2010. But their productivity doesn't match that of men. In a 2006 survey by the American Medical Association and the Association of American Medical Colleges, even full-time female doctors reported working on average 4.5 fewer hours each week and seeing fewer patients than their male colleagues. The American Academy of Pediatrics estimates that 71 percent of female pediatricians take extended leave at some point — five times higher than the percentage for male pediatricians.

This gap is especially problematic because women are more likely to go into primary care fields — where the doctor shortage is most pronounced — than men are. Today 53 percent of family practice residents, 63 percent of pediatric residents and nearly 80 percent of obstetrics and gynecology residents are female. In the low-income areas that lack primary and prenatal care, there are more emergency room visits, more preventable hospitalizations and more patients who die of treatable conditions. Foreign doctors emigrate to the United States to help fill these positions, but this drains their native countries of desperately needed medical care.

If medical training were available in infinite supply, it wouldn't matter how many doctors worked part time or quit, because there would always be new graduates to fill their spots. But medical schools can only afford to accept a fraction of the students who apply.

An even tighter bottleneck exists at the level of residency training. Residents don't pay tuition; they are paid to work at teaching hospitals. Their salaries are supported by Medicare, which pays teaching hospitals about $9 billion a year for resident salaries and teaching costs as well as patient care.

In 1997, Congress imposed a cap on how many medical residencies the government could subsidize as part of the Balanced Budget Act. Last year, the Senate failed to pass an amendment to the health care bill that would have created thousands of new residency positions. Even if American medical schools could double their graduating classes, there wouldn't be additional residency positions for the new doctors. Federal and state financing to expand medical education will be hard to find in today's economic and political climate.

We often hear the argument that nurse practitioners, nurse anesthetists and physician assistants can stand in for doctors and provide cheaper care. But when critical decisions must be made, patients want a fully qualified doctor to lead the health care team.

Policy makers could encourage more doctors to stay in the profession by reforming the malpractice system to protect them from frivolous lawsuits, safeguarding their pay from further Medicare cuts and lightening the burden of bureaucratic regulations and paperwork. And in a perfect world, hospitals and clinics could keep more female doctors working full time by setting up child care centers — with long operating hours — on site.

In the meantime, we can only depend on doctors' own commitment to the profession.

Students who aspire to go to medical school should think about the consequences if they decide to work part time or leave clinical medicine. It's fair to ask them — women especially — to consider the conflicting demands that medicine and parenthood make before they accept (and deny to others) sought-after positions in medical school and residency. They must understand that medical education is a privilege, not an entitlement, and it confers a real moral obligation to serve.

I recently spoke with a college student who asked me if anesthesiology is a good field for women. She didn't want to hear that my days are unpredictable because serious operations can take a long time and emergency surgery often needs to be done at night. What she really wanted to know was if my working life was consistent with her rosy vision of limited work hours and raising children. I doubt that she welcomed my parting advice: If you want to be a doctor, be a doctor.

You can't have it all. I never took cupcakes to my children's homerooms or drove carpool, but I read a lot of bedtime stories and made it to soccer games and school plays. I've ridden roller coasters with my son, danced at my oldest daughter's wedding and rocked my first grandson to sleep. Along the way, I've worked full days and many nights, and brought a lot of very sick patients through long, difficult operations.

Patients need doctors to take care of them. Medicine shouldn't be a part-time interest to be set aside if it becomes inconvenient; it deserves to be a life's work.

Jane Addams

FILIAL RELATIONS

Jane Addams (1860–1935) was the founder of one of the first settlement houses in North America, a pioneer in the field of social work, and a political reformer and antiwar activist who was awarded the Nobel Peace Prize. She came to these accomplishments as a member of the first generation of American women to attend college, and thus as one whose educational advantages opened new doors while also raising new and perplexing questions about what to do with her life. In her autobiography, *Twenty Years at Hull House,* she depicts the eight years following her own graduation as full of illness and heartache, so intense was her desire to discover what she should do that was more important and meaningful than the travel and leisure activities her family thought appropriate. She found her vocation after recognizing that serving the urban poor — first in East London, as mentioned here, and then in Chicago, where she would spend the rest of her life — offered a way to express her "enlarged interest in life" and to participate in "the social movements around us."

Addams's dilemma was not how to balance marriage with work but rather how to balance the "social claim" — the urgent summons to be engaged in service to a world in need — with the expectations of her family of origin and their sense of the primacy of private life. In this excerpt, Addams is concerned to find a "healing compromise" among a number of claims and opportunities, each of which she acknowledges has some legitimacy. When claims conflict or compete, however, she argues that we should honor the higher claim, which to her resides with the larger life of society rather than in the family. At the same time, she advocates ways of reformulating the relationship between family and society that might both serve society well and make such choices less wrenching for individuals.

Over her decades in Hull House, Addams was a mentor to many young adults who came to Hull House seeking paths of usefulness. What summons or challenge is she offering here? How might you respond to the priorities she proposes?

....

From Jane Addams, *Democracy and Social Ethics* (New York: Macmillan, 1902; repr., Urbana, IL: University of Illinois Press, 2002), 35–47.

There are many people in every community who have not felt the "social compunction," who do not share the effort toward a higher social morality, who are even unable to sympathetically interpret it. Some of these have been shielded from the inevitable and salutary failures which the trial of new powers involve because they are content to attain standards of virtue demanded by an easy public opinion, and others of them have exhausted their moral energy in attaining to the current standard of individual and family righteousness.

Such people, who form the bulk of contented society, demand that the radical, the reformer, shall be without stain or question in his personal and family relations, and judge most harshly any deviation from the established standards. There is a certain justice in this: it expresses the inherent conservatism of the mass of men, that none of the established virtues which have been so slowly and hardly acquired shall be sacrificed for the sake of making problematic advance; that the individual, in his attempt to develop and use the new and exalted virtue, shall not fall into the easy temptation of letting the ordinary ones slip through his fingers.

This instinct to conserve the old standards, combined with a distrust of the new standard, is a constant difficulty in the way of those experiments and advances depending upon the initiative of women, both because women are the more sensitive to the individual and family claims, and because their training has tended to make them content with the response to these claims alone.

There is no doubt that, in the effort to sustain the moral energy necessary to work out a more satisfactory social relation, the individual often sacrifices the energy which should legitimately go into the fulfillment of personal and family claims, to what he considers the higher claim. . . .

The mind of each one of us reaches back to our first struggles as we emerged from self-willed childhood into a recognition of family obligations. We have all gradually learned to respond to them, and yet most of us have had at least fleeting glimpses of what it might be to disregard them and the elemental claim they make upon us. We have yielded at times to the temptation of ignoring them for selfish aims, of considering the individual and not the family convenience, and we remember with shame the self-pity which inevitably followed. But just as we have learned to adjust the personal and family claims, and to find an orderly development impossible without recognition of both, so perhaps we are called upon now to make a second adjustment between the family and the social claim, in which neither shall lose and both be ennobled.

The attempt to bring about a healing compromise in which the two shall be adjusted in proper relation is not an easy one. It is difficult to distinguish between the outward act of him who in following one legitimate claim has been led into the temporary violation of another, and the outward act of him who deliberately renounces a just claim and throws aside all obligation for the sake of his own selfish and individual development. The man, for instance, who deserts his family that he may cultivate an artistic sensibility, or acquire what he considers more fullness of life for himself, must always arouse our contempt. Breaking the marriage tie as Ibsen's "Nora" did, to obtain a larger self-development, or holding to it as George Eliot's "Romola" did, because of the larger claim of the state and society, must always remain two distinct paths. The collision of interests, each of which has a real moral basis and a right to its own place in life, is bound to be more or less tragic. It is the struggle between two claims, the destruction of either of which would bring ruin to the ethical life. Curiously enough, it is almost exactly this contradiction which is the tragedy set forth by the Greek dramatist, who asserted that the gods who watch over the sanctity of the family bond must yield to the higher claims of the gods of the state. The failure to recognize the social claim as legitimate causes the trouble; the suspicion constantly remains that woman's public efforts are merely selfish and captious, and are not directed to the general good. This suspicion will never be dissipated until parents, as well as daughters, feel the democratic impulse and recognize the social claim.

Our democracy is making inroads upon the family, the oldest of human institutions, and a claim is being advanced which in a certain sense is larger than the family claim. The claim of the state in time of war has long been recognized, so that in its name the family has given up sons and husbands and even the fathers of little children. If we can once see the claims of society in any such light, if its misery and need can be made clear and urged as an explicit claim, as the state urges its claims in the time of danger, then for the first time the daughter who desires to minister to that need will be recognized as acting conscientiously. This recognition may easily come first through the emotions, and may be admitted as a response to pity and mercy long before it is formulated and perceived by the intellect.

The family as well as the state we are all called upon to maintain as the highest institutions which the race has evolved for its safeguard and protection. But merely to preserve these institutions is not enough. There come periods of reconstruction, during which the task is laid upon a passing generation, to enlarge the function and carry forward the ideal of a long-established institution. There is no doubt that many women, consciously and unconsciously, are struggling with this task. The family, like every other element of human life, is susceptible of progress, and from epoch to epoch its tendencies and aspirations are enlarged, although its duties can never be abrogated and its obligations can never be cancelled. It is impossible to bring about the higher development by any self-assertion or breaking away of the individual will. The new growth in the plant swelling against the sheath, which at the same time imprisons and protects it, must still be the truest type of progress. The family in its entirety must be carried out into the larger life. Its various members together must recognize and acknowledge the validity of the social obligation. When this does not occur we have a most flagrant example of the ill-adjustment and misery arising when an ethical code is applied too rigorously and too conscientiously to conditions which are no longer the same as when the code was instituted, and for which it was never designed. We have all seen parental control and the family claim assert their authority in fields of effort which belong to the adult judgment of the child and pertain to activity quite outside the family life. Probably the distinctively family tragedy, of which we all catch glimpses now and then, is the assertion of this authority through all the entanglements of wounded affection and misunderstanding. We see parents and children acting from conscientious motives and with the tenderest affection, yet bringing about a misery which can scarcely be hidden.

Such glimpses remind us of that tragedy enacted centuries ago in Assisi, when the eager young noble cast his very clothing at his father's feet, dramatically renouncing his filial allegiance, and formally subjecting the narrow family claim to the wider and more universal duty. All the conflict of tragedy ensued which might have been averted, had the father recognized the higher claim, and had he been willing to subordinate and adjust his own claim to it. The father considered his son disrespectful and hard-hearted, yet we know St. Francis to have been the most tender and loving of men, responsive to all possible ties, even to those of inanimate nature. We know that by his affections he freed the frozen life of his time. The elements of tragedy lay in the narrowness of the father's mind; in his lack of comprehension and his lack of sympathy with the power which was moving his son, and which was but part of the religious revival which swept Europe from end to end in the early part of the thirteenth century; the same power which built the cathedrals of the North, and produced the saints and sages of the South. But the father's situation was nevertheless genuine; he felt his heart sore and angry, and his dignity covered with disrespect. He could not, indeed, have felt otherwise, unless he had been touched by the fire of the same revival, and lifted out of and away from the contemplation of himself and his narrower claim. It is another proof that the notion of a larger obligation can only come through the response to an enlarged interest in life and in the social movements around us. . . .

One summer the writer went from a two weeks' residence in East London, where she had become sick and bewildered by the sights and sounds encountered there, directly to Switzerland. She found the beaten routes of travel filled with young English men and women who could walk many miles a day, and who could climb peaks so inaccessible that the feats received honorable mention in Alpine journals, — a result which filled their families with joy and pride. These young people knew to a nicety the proper diet and clothing which would best contribute toward endurance. Everything was very fine about them save their motive power. The writer does not refer to the hard-worked men and women who were taking a vacation, but to the leisured young people, to whom this period was the most serious of the year, and filled with the most strenuous exertion. They did not, of course, thoroughly enjoy it, for we are too complicated to be content with mere exercise. Civilization has bound us too closely with our brethren for anyone of us to be long happy in the cultivation of mere individual force or in the accumulation of mere muscular energy.

With Whitechapel [an impoverished section of London] constantly in mind, it was difficult not to advise these young people to use some of this muscular energy of which they were so proud, in cleaning neglected alleys and paving soggy streets. Their stores of enthusiasm might stir to energy the listless men and women of East London and utilize latent social forces. The exercise would be quite as good, the need of endurance as great, the care for proper dress and food as important; but the motives for action would be turned from selfish ones into social ones. Such an appeal would doubtless be met with a certain response from the young people, but would never be countenanced by their families for an instant. . . .

Wounded affection there is sure to be, but this could be reduced to a modicum if we could preserve a sense of the relation of the individual to the family, and of the latter to society, and if we had been given a code of ethics dealing with these larger relationships, instead of a code designed to apply so exclusively to relationships obtaining only between individuals.

Doubtless the clashes and jars which we all feel most keenly are those which occur when two standards of morals, both honestly held and believed in, are brought sharply together. The awkwardness and constraint we experience when two standards of conventions and manners clash but feebly prefigure this deeper difference.

William Butler Yeats

THE CHOICE

The Irish poet William Butler Yeats (1865–1939) is widely regarded as one of the best poets of the twentieth century. The short poem below addresses the question of whether it is possible and desirable to have a balanced life by setting up a radical choice between "the life" and "the work." The poem is particularly suggestive about what consequences may attend the selection of either alternative.

As you reflect on this poem, remember that Yeats chose each word with great deliberation, pursuing, in a sense, the perfection of this particular piece of work, this poem. Why is it "the intellect" that is forced to make the choice between life and work? And what difference does it make that the choice, as Yeats puts it, is "perfection of the life, or of the work"? Is the quest for perfection — or even for highly distinguished accomplishment — essential for a life of significance? In your view, would it be acceptable to settle for less-outstanding performance if balance were thereby attainable?

> The intellect of man is forced to choose
> Perfection of the life, or of the work,
> And if it take the second must refuse
> A heavenly mansion, raging in the dark.
> When all that story's finished, what's the news?
> In luck or out the toil has left its mark:
> That old perplexity an empty purse,
> Or the day's vanity, the night's remorse.

William Butler Yeats, "The Choice," in *The Complete Poems of W. B. Yeats* (New York: Macmillan, 1933), 242.

Homer

THE ILIAD

The Iliad is a poem about the anger of Achilles. When three of his friends, including the hero of *The Odyssey*, Odysseus, beseech Achilles to join with them in battle against the Trojans, they advance several arguments to convince him that he should quiet his anger against the Greek king Agamemnon and direct it toward his enemies behind the walls of Troy. In the midst of his own counterarguments, Achilles reveals what his mother, the goddess Thetis, has told him about his future. In effect, he will be able to choose one of two destinies. He may fight and die a hero's death; or he may go home and lead a long but relatively undistinguished life. When, in *The Odyssey*, Odysseus visits the shades in Hades, he encounters the ghost of Achilles, who in effect says that he regrets having chosen the more heroic but much shorter life. In other words, even Homer seems uncertain whether a short life of splendid and memorable achievement is more noble than a longer one of modest and quickly forgotten accomplishment. Which of the two destinies do you think is the more noble? Why? To what extent does Achilles's choice resemble the dilemma faced by the premed student at the opening of this chapter?

> Mother tells me
> the immortal goddess Thetis with her glistening feet,
> that two fates bear me on the day of death.
> If I hold out here and I lay siege to Troy,
> my journey home is gone, but my glory never dies.
> If I voyage back to the fatherland I love,
> my pride, my glory dies . . .
> true, but the life that's left me will be long,
> the stroke of death will not come on me quickly.

....

From Homer, *The Iliad*, trans. Robert Fagels (New York: Viking Penguin, 1990), 265.

Martha Nussbaum

INTERVIEWED BY BILL MOYERS

Martha Nussbaum is a philosopher who teaches at the University of Chicago. In *The Fragility of Goodness: Luck and Ethics in Greek Tragedy and Philosophy* (1986), she argues that ancient Greek dramas were works of philosophy insofar as they investigated ideas that could not be presented and explored as well in any other way. The emotions that tragedies arouse, Nussbaum believes, have cognitive significance. There are some things we cannot learn without feeling our way through them.

In the conversation below, which was broadcast on public television in 1988, she shows how Aeschylus's tragedy *Agamemnon* speaks directly to questions about the balanced life. Agamemnon's unbearable but unavoidable choice between his daughter and his army, Nussbaum argues, shows how impossible it is to find easy resolutions to the dilemmas that arise when two important commitments conflict. We are all like Agamemnon, she says, in that we must daily renounce some goods for the sake of other goods, sacrificing things or people that we love for other things or people we also love. Nussbaum argues against several objections to this view, insisting that we give up efforts to deny that "tragedy" — on a small daily scale or in great matters — is a real possibility for those who "live their lives with a deep seriousness of commitment." Indeed, she claims, tragedy happens "*only* to those who seek to live well."

What does Nussbaum see as the alternatives to tragedy and the suffering it entails? What case does she make for the benefits of a life that is vulnerable to tragedy? Do you agree that "you should care about things in a way that makes it a possibility that tragedy will happen to you"?

MOYERS: You write about these ancient Greeks — Aristotle, Hecuba, Antigone, Creon — as if they were next-door neighbors. Are they really so vivid to you?

....

From Bill Moyers, *A World of Ideas* (New York: Doubleday, 1989), 449–52.

NUSSBAUM: They are. The big problems haven't changed all that much, and the Greek works face these problems head-on, with a courage and eloquence that I don't always find in modern works on moral philosophy.

MOYERS: What kinds of problems?

NUSSBAUM: Take the problem of moral conflict: In Aeschylus' *Agamemnon,* a king is trying to do his best to lead his army off to Troy. Suddenly he finds that his expedition is becalmed, and he's told that the reason is that the gods are demanding a sacrifice. He has to kill his own daughter in order to complete that expedition.

So here we have two deep and entirely legitimate commitments coming into a terrible conflict in which there's not anything the king can do that will be without wrongdoing. On the one hand, if he doesn't sacrifice his daughter, he's disobeying the gods, and his entire expedition is probably going to perish; on the other hand, he's got to kill his own daughter. Thinking about this, as the play says, with tears in his eyes, he says, "A heavy doom is disobedience, but heavy too if I shall rend my own child, the pride of my house, polluting my father's hands with streams of slaughtered maiden's blood close by the altar. Which of these is without evils?"

Often, when you care deeply about more than one thing, the very course of life will bring you round to a situation where you can't honor both of the commitments. It looks like anything you do will be wrong, perhaps even terrible, in some way.

MOYERS: Do you think it's true for the taxi driver out there on the street right now? He doesn't see himself as a King making those horrific choices. Life doesn't present itself to him that way.

NUSSBAUM: Oh, but I think it does, on a smaller basis. Just take a person who has a career and who also has children, and who has to juggle those two responsibilities every day. Nothing will guarantee that in some event you can't prevent from arising, you'll have to neglect one of those commitments and neglect something that's really ethically important because the very course of life has produced a terrible conflict.

I face this every day myself as a mother who has to juggle career and child-raising. So often, just on a very mundane level, you've got a meeting, and your child's acting in a school play, and you can't do both things. Whatever you do, you're going to be neglecting something that's really important.

MOYERS: So that's what you meant when you wrote that daycare is a modern version of an old Greek tragedy.

NUSSBAUM: If you realize that people face these conflicts, there's an awful lot society can do to provide institutions that make those conflicts arise a little less often. But no social situation, however ideal, is going to make those conflicts just go away.

MOYERS: No, but we were taught to rank obligations — you know the old term, choose priorities — and not to make of every conflict of competing goods a great moral drama.

NUSSBAUM: I think that moral philosophy has had a very bad influence here in two areas. One traditional moral view is that there are no conflicts of obligations, that that's an illogical view. Immanuel Kant and Thomas Aquinas said, in different ways, that any conflict of obligation is really only apparent, that it's a violation of logic to think that there could be a genuine conflict of this kind. I think that view is just a misdescription of what actually happens in people's lives. There is nothing illogical about saying, "I am going to care deeply about my work and my writing; I'm also going to care deeply about my family, my child." That's not illogical. That's perfectly coherent. Over the course of a life, not only can you combine these things, but they actually enrich each other and make the life of each of them better. But that doesn't prevent these terrible situations that you can't entirely foresee.

MOYERS: Is this what you meant when you wrote once that "Tragedy is trying to live well"?

NUSSBAUM: Tragedy happens *only* when you are trying to live well, because for a heedless person who doesn't have deep commitments to others Agamemnon's conflict isn't a tragedy. Somebody who's a bad person could go in and slaughter that child with equanimity or could desert all the men and let them die. But it's when you are trying to live well, and you deeply care about the things you're trying to do, that the world enters in, in a particularly painful way. It's in that struggle with recalcitrant circumstances that a lot of the value of the moral life comes in.

Now the lesson certainly is not to try to maximize conflict or to romanticize struggle and suffering, but it's rather that you should care about things in a way that makes it a possibility that tragedy will happen to you. If you hold your commitments lightly, in such a way that you can always divest yourself from one or the other of them if they conflict, then it doesn't hurt you when things go badly. But you want people to live their lives with a deep seriousness of commitment: not to adjust their desires to the way the world actually goes, but rather to try to wrest from the world the good life that they desire. And sometimes that does lead them into tragedy.

If you really feel what it is to love someone or some commitment and be bound to that, then, when a conflict arises, you will feel deep pain, and you will feel what Agamemnon felt. Even at a smaller level you will feel, "Which of these is without evils?"

MOYERS: And the good life is the life lived according to your moral values, the life that is trying to find an ethical path through the wilderness.

NUSSBAUM: It's a life that is trying to live well toward friends, toward fellow citizens, and toward one's own capabilities and their development.

MOYERS: There are so many conflicting obligations for an individual today: religion, family, friends, state, country, party, neighborhood.

NUSSBAUM: Sometimes people find this so messy that it can't be tolerated, and they retreat into some simplifying view. Either they say, "We know that obligations have to be consistent, and so if there's an apparent conflict, it's not really conflict, and all I have to do is find out which one takes precedence, and the other one just simply drops away and ceases to exert a claim on me"; or they might say, "Well, yes, it's a sort of conflict, but really we see that all values are commensurable, so that if I measure up the quantities of goodness that are here and the quantities of goodness that are over here, then all I need to do is ask myself, 'Where is there a greater quantity of goodness?' and then I go in that direction, and missing out on the other one is sort of like missing out on fifty dollars when what I'm doing is getting two hundred dollars" — and it doesn't seem very painful any more when you look at it that way.

Very often people take up some such way of looking at things because to see that they are really two altogether different things here, both of them seriously worthwhile, both of them things to which you have made a commitment in your own heart, and you can't follow both in this particular circumstance — that is very painful. What the tragedies show us is that temptation to flee into some sort of simplifying theory is a very old temptation, and it probably is going to be around as long as human beings are faced with these problems.

MOYERS: I asked you about the moral lesson, and you said what the tragedies show us. In one sense there is no lesson and no moral, is there? It's simply the revelation of life as seen through the artist, the philosopher, the sufferer, the pilgrim. There's no effort to instruct.

NUSSBAUM: But you know, sometimes just to see the complexity that's there and see it honestly without flinching and without redescribing it in the terms of some excessively simple theory — that is itself progress. It's progress for public life as well as private life, because it's only when we've done that step that we can then ask ourselves, "How can our institutions make it less likely that those conflicts will happen to people? How can we create schemes of child care, for example, that will make this tragic conflict of obligations less of a daily fact of women's lives and perhaps more of a rare and strange occurrence?"

MOYERS: Do you say, "Well, philosophy has helped me to see that this is a natural part of life, and I'll accept the stress and the strain and the conflict, and I'll walk on the tightrope with the balancing rod and hope to get to the other side"?

NUSSBAUM: Sometimes it's pretty clear which one you ought to choose, but it's very, very important to separate the question, "Which is the better choice?" from the question, "Is there any choice available to me here that's free of wrongdoing?" Agamemnon has to sacrifice his daughter because it's clear the gods are going to kill everyone, including the daughter, if he doesn't. Looked at that way, he had better make that choice. Still, he has not got the right to think that just because he's made the right choice, everything is well. In the play, he says, "May all be for the best," and the chorus says that he's mad. You don't accept an artificial, easy solution to this, but the hope would be that through that kind of pain, you understand better what your commitments are and how deep they are. That's what Aeschylus means when he says that through suffering comes a kind of learning — a grace that comes by violence from the gods.

Heather Boushey

FINDING TIME

Heather Boushey is the executive director and chief economist at the Washington Center for Equitable Growth. In this excerpt from her book *Finding Time: The Economics of Work-Life Conflict*, she emphasizes the potential efficacy of public policy to relieve the tensions arising from the conflict between making a living and making a life, between work and family (in an extended sense). Boushey argues that the modern workplace is still largely organized on the basis of social realities that began to disappear well over a half century ago. In other words, in most places in this country, businesses and professions still imagine a man spending forty to sixty hours a week at the workplace while a woman supports him domestically and cares for their children and aged relatives. Many of the work-life conflicts we have been exploring arise, she suggests, not from our own equivocations and poor choices, nor from the inherently tragic character of human life, but from atavistic social and economic practices that remain stubbornly in place even though they are completely outmoded.

Boushey advocates four sets of ideas to address four areas that require new solutions to economic problems that bear directly on work-life conflicts. Which of her ideas seem to you the most attractive and plausible? Do you agree with her that the quest for a balanced life would be much more successful if the right social and economic policies were in place?

American businesses used to have a silent partner. This partner never showed up at a board meeting or made a demand but was integral to profitability. That partner was the American Wife. She made sure the American Worker showed up for work well rested (he didn't have to wake up at 3 a.m. to feed the baby or comfort a child after a nightmare), in clean clothes (that he neither laundered nor stacked neatly in the closet), with a lunch box

From Heather Boushey, *Finding Time: The Economics of Work-Life Conflict* (Cambridge, MA: Harvard University Press, 2016), 5–11, 15–19.

packed to the brim with cold-cut sandwiches, coffee, and a home-baked cookie. She took care of all the big and small daily emergencies that might distract the American Worker from focusing 100 percent on his job while he was at work. Little Johnny got in a fight on the playground? The American Wife will be right there to talk to the school. Aunt Bea fell and broke her hip? The American Wife can spend the afternoon bringing her groceries and making her dinner. The boss is coming over for dinner? The American Wife already has the pot roast in the oven. Even if she had a job — and many American wives, like my mom, worked and had to work despite suburban cultural expectations — she was still the primary caregiver when work-life conflicts arose with her family or her employer. The presumption was that she would be the one at home.

This meant that for decades, the American Wife gave American businesses a big fat bonus. Her time at home made possible the American Worker's time at work. This unspoken yet well-understood business contract is now broken. Moreover, it doesn't look like we're going back to it anytime soon. Nor should we. American families look different today. Wives — and women more generally — work outside the home because they need to and because they want to. Families need a new contract with their employers, one that provides stability in today's world where families interact with the economy in new ways.

Today, the American Wife is a family breadwinner and a contributor to economic growth. Her economic contribution is no longer silent — it shows up in our nation's gross domestic product. A family with a working woman is not an anomaly, it's the norm — and has been for some time. While some women have always worked outside the house — newly emigrated women and women of color have historically been an integral part of the workforce compared with white or native-born women — it wasn't until the 1960s and 1970s that large numbers of white and middle-class women entered the labor force. Now women bring home at least a quarter of the earnings in more than two-thirds of families with children. In a growing number of households, women bring in half or even more of the earned income. This shift has been good for businesses and the economy. More women in the workforce means more women earning money — adding to overall demand — and using their talents to boost firms' profits. As women have increased their employment, they have ramped up their educational credentials, making them that much more valuable to businesses and the broader economy.

Working outside the home provides women with many exciting social and personal opportunities, yet the picture is not all rosy. Women are not working just to fulfill their dreams and learn new things. Many hold down a job out of sheer economic necessity. Most families would have seen their income drop precipitously over the past few decades if it were not for women going to work. Greater employment of women was a solution to the economic transformations of the past few decades that have left male earnings stagnant for nearly forty years.

While the change in employment patterns was most pronounced for white, middle-class women, all kinds of families have been transformed. Families have become more complex. People marry later – if at all – and the number of children born to unmarried mothers has risen, along with the number of women who never have children (the same is true of men, presumably, though they are not tracked so well). High rates of nonmarriage and divorce mean more blended families, with parents and stepparents, siblings and stepsiblings all under one roof or spread out across different households. In addition, the Supreme Court recently ruled that any two people – regardless of sex – have the right to marry.

Not all families have experienced the loss of the American Wife in the same way. Across the income spectrum, most families no longer have a full-time, stay-at-home caregiver. But low-income and middle-class families are more likely than those at the top to have only a single earner. Nearly 40 percent of today's families with children have a sole female breadwinner. Those families, disproportionately low-income, don't have a wife, let alone someone who can fulfill the role of the traditional American Wife. Families in the middle and at the top more often than not have two breadwinners. While there may be a wife (or two same-sex partners), she certainly isn't at home fulfilling the role of the traditional American Wife.

What is common across families is the fact that the shift from American Wife to Family (co-)Breadwinner has left a gap at home. Who's caring for the children and teaching them all they need to know? Who's tending to an aging family member who needs some extra care? Today's families report feeling insecure and pressed for time, whether they're high-achieving dual-career couples, low-income single mothers, or the middle-class families in between. For all kinds of families across the income spectrum, the dual demands of home and out-of-home work cause significant stress. The aging of our society adds a layer of people who need care, but few families have someone at home to provide it. The world of work and the needs of families always seem to be in conflict – and it's been this way for decades.

Our political process approaches this issue as a private matter or as a values issue rather than a serious economic issue. When my mother shared her frustrations with me one day in our kitchen, she gave me an insight into just how long families have been struggling. Ironically, a solution was almost enacted when my family could have used it. In 1971, both the U.S. House of Representatives and the U.S. Senate passed a bill that would have established a network of nationally funded, locally administered, comprehensive child-care centers to provide high-quality education, nutrition, and medical services. The program had a budget five times the size of today's Head Start program, which provides preschool for very low-income children. Had the bill become the law of the land, in all likelihood I would not have had the conversation with my mom that inspired this book.

A political argument about the proper role of women in society rather than serious policymaking prevented the enactment of this child-care program. At the outset, all signs were that President Richard Nixon would sign the bill into law. In his autobiography, *The Good Fight: A Life in Liberal Politics*, Walter Mondale, who was at the time a senator from Minnesota leading the fight in the Senate for the bill, talked of how Nixon's secretary of health, education, and welfare, Elliot Richardson, had "conducted several quiet meetings with [Mondale's] staff and Representative John Brademas of Indiana, the lead sponsor in the House, to find common ground." Richardson went so far as to send Mondale a letter "outlining the administration's general support to consolidate and coordinate federal child care programs" and to have Ed Zigler, from the Office of Child Development, testify in support of the legislation in 1969 hearings in front of the Subcommittee on Children and Youth. Nixon himself had come out in favor of child care, saying, "so crucial is the matter of early growth that we must make a national commitment to providing all American children an opportunity for healthful and stimulating development during the first five years of life."

Washington insiders were shocked when, on December 9, 1971, Nixon not only vetoed the bill but scathingly repudiated its aims. He said: "We cannot and will not ignore the challenge to do more for America's children in the all-important early years. But our response to this challenge must be a measured, evolutionary, painstakingly considered one, *consciously designed to cement the family in its rightful position as the keystone of our civilization*" (emphasis added). Nixon went on to say that the proposed law would be "a long leap into the dark for the United States Government and the American people."

How did Nixon and his team come to believe that a policy that would have helped tens of millions of families would do the very opposite? Nixon's speechwriter, Pat Buchanan, proudly takes credit for pushing for the veto and, specifically, for encouraging the president to include the statements portraying a federal child-care program as antifamily. Buchanan saw an active policy of providing government support for child care as the federal government's effectively encouraging women to be workers rather than supposedly traditional stay-at-home moms. (I say "supposedly" because the idealized American Wife was never a reality for many families.) In his view, the poorest mothers deserved a handout — an act of charity — because they couldn't afford to purchase child care in the market. For other families, child care wasn't so critical to their well-being that the government should step in to help.

This political setback established child care as a values issue. But left out of this cultural argument is any economic analysis. The real problem (then as now) was how to help families struggling to cope with the new economic reality that even though both Mom and Dad work — or there's just one parent — children (and the sick and the aged) still need care. It was as though the millions of families like mine where no one was at home full-time to address daily conflicts between work and family life were invisible.

Worse, it sounds like an insult. My parents certainly weren't antifamily. Even many families who wish Mom could stay at home have a hard time making that work for their bottom line. My parents needed the same things today's families need: a set of policies to allow them to be both caregivers and breadwinners. This includes child care and, increasingly, elder care, but it is by no means limited to just those areas.

The 1970s are now history, but the kind of thinking that torpedoed a promising child-care program remains, locking our society in a no-win debate. During a presidential debate in 2012 between President Barack Obama and Governor Mitt Romney, Romney answered a question about equal pay by saying, "I recognize that *if you're going to have women in the workforce* that sometimes you need to be more flexible" (emphasis added). While this gaffe got less attention than his remark that when he put his cabinet together, women's groups "brought [him and his staff] whole binders full of women" who could serve, it illustrates an ongoing tension in American politics. Too often, we are still debating "whether" or "if" women work outside the home, rather than acknowledging that most already do. The question now is how this change in the way women spend their days affects families, firms, and the economy more generally. The time has come to focus on the economic reality of this transformational shift for families and firms. . . .

Taking an economic approach allows us to see the new challenges facing firms. Changes in families affect all aspects of the economy. When employers could tap into the time and talents of their Silent Partner, the American Wife, they could assume that most of their employees didn't have regular conflicts between family care and work. This doesn't mean that conflicts never happened, but they were the exception, not the rule. Today it's the opposite. To get the most out of their workforce, employers have to find ways to address these issues. The work-life reforms I explore in this book could help businesses and families become more cost-effective than they are today.

Armed with a view that explains the full economy, not just one slice of it, I then turn to the solutions and the real-world evidence showing that they work. There are four areas where we need new solutions to the everyday economic problems facing middle-income, lower-income, and professional workers. For shorthand, I call them Here (at home), There (at work), Care, and Fair.

The first area addresses a worker's occasional need to be at home. There are days when a worker cannot be at work because he's sick, his child's sick, or he needs to take care for an ailing family member. This doesn't mean he can't hold down a job and be productive most of the time. But there will be days when he needs a little time away from work. Or maybe he needs a week to care for his mom when she breaks her hip or a few weeks to spend with his new baby. Without the security of knowing he will have a job to go back to, he either risks his paycheck or risks not meeting crucial off-the-job needs. The need to be Here (at home) cannot always come second to the need to be There (at work).

Especially for those on the middle and the bottom rungs of the income ladder, these kinds of justifiable absences from work must be paid. Otherwise, it's a nice idea, but not one that is affordable. Two ideas whose time has come are to allow workers to earn *paid sick days*, short-term leave for the occasional illness of workers or their children, and *paid family and medical leave* for at least twelve weeks for the good times, when the family welcome a new child, and the not-so-good times, when a seriously ill family member needs care. Only about two-thirds of workers have paid sick days, and the overwhelming majority do not have paid family and medical leave. Some employers and some states and cities have taken steps to change this, but we need national coverage that includes all workers, not just some of us — and everyone needs to know that they can use this leave without fear of retribution. Like our nation's longstanding rules on the minimum wage and workplace safety, paid sick days and paid family leave should be required for all employees and employers, no exceptions.

The second set of ideas covers what happens when we're at work. Work hours need to fit our lives. Some people don't get enough hours and cannot earn enough to pay their bills. Others have to cope with too many hours, or too many hours at the wrong times. Schedules are too often tilted toward the minute-by-minute demands of businesses, with little or no appreciation for the needs of workers. To rebalance this relationship, we must address overwork, underwork, and unpredictable schedules when people are There (at work).

Some employers have taken positive steps, offering their employees *flexible schedules* — be they hours that fit family life, or even telecommuting. The evidence shows that such policies benefit both firms and families, by motivating workers to be at their best at a company that cares about them and their families and by reducing turnover. But it may not be in the short-term interest of some individual firms to adopt such measures, even if doing so is good for the economy overall. That's where policies to promote flexible schedules that work for both employers and employees come in. We also need to strengthen the protections of the New Deal–era Fair Labor Standards Act by *limiting overwork* for a larger swath of workers, and putting in place greater *scheduling predictability* for workers up and down the economic ladder. These steps improve the conditions for employees when they are at work and thus boost the productivity of firms and the overall economy.

Next are solutions to the daily concern of who's caring for those who need it. Families need high-quality, affordable solutions for caring for children, the elderly, and the sick. One of the toughest choices a family makes is finding the right caregiver for a young or ill family member. We need to ensure *affordable, safe and enriching care for children and elders* for every family who needs it. Our future depends on it. Rethinking the 1971 comprehensive child-care legislation would be a good place to start, as would building on the work in cities and states today that are offering free or low-cost universal access to pre-kindergarten for all three- and four-year-olds. For elder care, we need better options both for keeping seniors at home and for long-term palliative care. Enabling families to provide the best care for their children and elderly relatives delivers intergenerational benefits to both families and society.

Finally, these work-life systems must be Fair. With both men and women in the workforce, at some point most of us need time off for family. But no one should be discriminated against because they need some flexibility to care for their loved ones. And if only some people have access to work-life policies that help them address conflicts between work and family life — and those that do are afraid to use them — then this isn't a real set of solutions. Solutions must address the challenges up and down the economic spectrum. Some ideas are now being tested in states and localities, such as prohibiting *family responsibilities discrimination*, in conjunction with existing protections such as the Americans with Disabilities Act; Title VII of the Civil Rights Act, which prohibits racial, ethnic, religious, and gender discrimination in the workplace; and the Pregnancy Discrimination Act.

Fairness also means tailoring and adjusting workplace policies to meet the needs of different breadwinners in different professions with different workplace needs. As the first half of the book documents, job quality, incomes, and access to family-friendly workplace options look different depending on where employees work. Work-life policies will not affect everyone the same way. What works for one worker may not work for another. An option to telecommute may not help a working parent whose home office has been turned into a playroom or the receptionists and line workers who must physically be at work. But better scheduling practices may be especially helpful to all these workers. Being Fair to all employees and employers means finding solutions for all families that are uniformly adhered to by everyone.

So we have a set of solutions: Here, There, Care, and Fair. We don't need one magic fix; we need policies in all four areas. And they need to cover everyone, helping all kinds of families. Paid leave, for short-term and long-term needs and when a new child comes into the family. Schedules that work for families, as well as for their employers, that are predictable and don't require too many — or too few — hours each week. High-quality, affordable care for children and the aging. This is what's fair; those who have care responsibilities are not second-class or secondary workers.

Matt Bloom

THE ILLUSIVE SEARCH FOR BALANCE

Matt Bloom teaches in the Mendoza College of Business at the University of Notre Dame. For many years he has been the principal investigator of the Wellbeing at Work Program (wellbeing.nd.edu), in which he and his team study flourishing among the helping and caring professions. The selection below is taken from the website for that program. On the basis of his own and his associates' research into the broad subject of well-being at work, Bloom argues that the "balance metaphor" is inadequate at best and destructive at worst as a way to describe a life in which work, family, and other obligations and communities are brought into a kind of harmony and equipoise within a single human life. He suggests, in other words, that the difficulties that attend efforts to lead a balanced life might arise not so much from real or imagined obstacles as from the formulation of the objective itself: the metaphor of balance is simply not helpful.

Do you find Bloom's critique of the balance metaphor compelling? Why or why not? Elsewhere, Bloom suggests some alternative metaphors for capturing the concept we have been considering: portfolio, following the beacon, journey, rhythm. What metaphors — these or others — do you think might best do justice to the widespread aspiration to lead lives that matter within several domains concurrently?

It was the first Monday after the holiday break. I was walking up the hall and spotted a colleague whom I had not seen for a few weeks. I greeted him and asked, "how was your break?" He responded, "too busy. I didn't really find any time for a break — I worked the entire time. I really need to find better balance in my life." Scenarios like this one seem to happen often, at least among the people with whom I work. His refrain — "I really need to find better balance" — is familiar to many of us. We have probably

Matt Bloom, "The Illusive Search for Balance," Well-being at Work, https://wellbeing .nd.edu/assets/169458/life_balance.pdf, 1–3.

expressed it about our own lives, but it is almost certain that we have heard many other people use it to describe themselves. We sense that something is amiss in our lives, that we are spending too much time on some things and not enough on the right things. We yearn for more hours in the day, a better allocation of our time, and an improved flow to the days and weeks that make up our lives. We want our lives to unfold in a way that feels right and so we set out on a search for balance. As hard as people try, I have yet to find anyone who feels that they have been able to find and maintain the balance they are working so hard to achieve.

The motivation at the heart of this search is important and worthy, but to be successful, I think we need a new metaphor to guide us. Both science and experience suggest that metaphors can be very helpful to us, but in my view using "balance" as a guide can actually lead us away from the better life we are searching so hard to find. I have been searching for a better metaphor and will share some of the top candidates here, metaphors that might work better, but the main theme of this article is to encourage others to jettison the balance metaphor and find one that works better. But first, I need to offer some convincing reasons to stop using balance as the principle that guides our search for a better flow to our lives.

Why Is Balance Illusive?

Hoping for perfection

Although I do think we need a better metaphor, part of making progress in our search for balance is to adjust some of our expectations. One of those is to recognize that sometimes we expect the impossible. We often hope to have a great work life, a great social life, a great recreational life, a great love life, a great. . . . Expecting greatness in the important domains of life can lead us to establish standards that our real lives will never meet. Sometimes the best jobs require us to spend periods of intense work on unfulfilling tasks. Weather or other obstacles might keep us from engaging in the activates we love. And even the best marriages have their rough spells. On a daily basis, some parts of life might not meet the standard of greatness we seek. We make it even harder on ourselves when our standard of greatness is vague. We know there must be something better out there, but cannot define specifically what that something better is. In these cases, nothing can stack up against our vague, but pervasive notion that life can be better.

Ruthless competition

We also need to recognize that competing priorities do compete, and they often compete ruthlessly. Work tells us that we *must* spend more time there, our physicians tell us we *must* exercise more, our friends signal we *must* spend more time with them, and it goes on and on. The responsibility for deciding how to allocate time and effort among these often heavy demands rests squarely on us, and no matter what we choose, one or more of those priorities will shout, "bad choice!" Another reality complicates this: the different domains of life have different measures of success. When I gather with friends at church, I do not report that I prayed an average of 4.2 times per day for an average of 10.63 minutes and that the Matt-to-God connection was successful 32.1% of the time. Likewise, I do not tell my wife that I feel the ROI on my contributions in our marriage is underperforming last year's level. Even as these different domains urge us to measure success in different ways, we are living one, single life. When I was a consultant, being busy was a measure of how important and talented you were. No one would have allowed themselves to be underworked because, we assumed, it meant you were underperforming and that you were not an important player. My family, on the other hand, wanted more of my time and they deserved it. The choice of how to allocate my time was left to me, and too often I chose poorly. For most of us, the decision about how to fit these different views of success into the one life we are living is ours alone — and we wonder how we can possibly choose right.

The goodness of work

Another challenge is that we really do care about work. Work is important to us and it constitutes an important part of our life. But in some circles, admitting this can garner criticism. I think this is particularly challenging for women. If a woman chooses career over family, she is often told that she sold out on family. If she chooses family over career, she has sold out to social pressures. And woe to the woman who tries to do both: she is criticized for trying to "have it all." But, work does not have to be a four-letter word. Science shows us that work can enrich our lives, help us find a meaningful way to use our talents, and help us grow toward our fullest potential. Work can also be stressful, frustrating and life depleting, but it can also be wonderful.

It's personal

We also need to realize that balance is personal. What constitutes balance for me as a professor at Notre Dame likely will not be balance for any of my colleagues. Likewise, what made for better balance when our children were small is not what makes for better balance now that Kim and I are empty-nesters, so we can invest more into our work. In fact, mid-life is often one of the most productive periods of life. Similarly, what constitutes the right investment in work differs from person-to-person. IF we judge our investments against those of others, we are almost certainly doomed. We have incomplete information about their other life investments, but more importantly, we are not living their life!

Balance and guilt

Lastly, we need to recognize that balance, when we do achieve it, can be a guilty pleasure. If we have it, but no one else does, we feel bad. Most of my students complicate this further. They are conscientious people of profound integrity, so when they experience balance, they tend to wonder if they are shirking their responsibilities somewhere, and so they find a place to, once again, get busy and in the process lose balance.

Jettison the Balance Metaphor

I have suggested that balance is the wrong metaphor, but why? One reason is that balance implies that we are spending exactly the right amount of time, effort, and personal resources on each important area of our life. That is, we consider our lives to be in balance when each life domain gets its rightful share of our time and attention, and all those shares match up or balance out against each other. That is very difficult even for one domain of life. It is very hard to determine how much time, energy, and effort is "correct" for work today, much less trying to balance out today's allocation for work against those needed for family, spirituality, health, and recreation. If it is difficult to determine these allocations for today, it is impossible to predict what will be the right allocations in the future. To achieve balance, we must be able to plan the future precisely, since trying to do it on-the-fly is far from effective. But, the world changes and we must often adjust to those changes. Yet, we still think we should be able to determine, with a high degree of accuracy, how much time will be enough tomorrow, next week, and maybe even next year.

We also tend to think of balance as occurring at a single point in time, but as I have mentioned, what seems like balance today might not seem like it tomorrow. And, even if we can achieve it, the changing world or our guilt will usually knock us out of balance once again.

Wendell Berry

MANIFESTO:
THE MAD FARMER LIBERATION FRONT

Wendell Berry lives on a small farm near his birthplace in Kentucky. After receiving his education and traveling in California, Europe, and New York City, he returned in his early thirties to the land and community from which he had come. There he has farmed and written for more than fifty years, creating works in many genres that advocate care and commitment to the land and to local community.

Berry's agrarian vision of what is meaningful and significant for human beings and the earth includes joyful celebrations of nature and love as well as trenchant criticisms of the social forces that work against them. The first eleven lines of the poem included here display that criticism in a few powerful images. What images of life in contemporary American society does Berry lift up, and to what larger social problems and priorities do these images point? In lines 12 and 13, the focus shifts to images that "won't compute" with the distorted way of life sketched at first. What images of meaning, significance, and goodness are presented in the remainder of the poem? In the words of the poem's title, what kind of "liberation" do these images suggest? Do you think the "farmer" who makes this "manifesto" is "mad"? Do you feel drawn to joining him in practicing resurrection?

> Love the quick profit, the annual raise,
> vacation with pay. Want more
> of everything ready-made. Be afraid
> to know your neighbors and to die.
> And you will have a window in your head.
> Not even your future will be a mystery
> any more. Your mind will be punched in a card
> and shut away in a little drawer.

Wendell Berry, "Manifesto: The Mad Farmer Liberation Front," in *The Selected Poems of Wendell Berry* (Berkeley, CA: Counterpoint, 1999), 87–88.

When they want you to buy something
they will call you. When they want you
to die for profit they will let you know.
So, friends, every day do something
that won't compute. Love the Lord.
Love the world. Work for nothing.
Take all that you have and be poor.
Love someone who does not deserve it.
Denounce the government and embrace
the flag. Hope to live in that free
republic for which it stands.
Give your approval to all you cannot
understand. Praise ignorance, for what man
has not encountered he has not destroyed.
Ask the questions that have no answers.
Invest in the millennium. Plant sequoias.
Say that your main crop is the forest
that you did not plant,
that you will not live to harvest.
Say that the leaves are harvested
When they have rotted into the mold.
Call that profit. Prophesy such returns.
Put your faith in the two inches of humus
that will build under the trees
every thousand years.
Listen to carrion — put your ear
close, and hear the faint chattering
of the songs that are to come.
Expect the end of the world. Laugh.
Laughter is immeasurable. Be joyful
though you have considered all the facts.
So long as women do not go cheap
for power, please women more than men.
Ask yourself: Will this satisfy
a woman satisfied to bear a child?
Will this disturb the sleep
of a woman near to giving birth?
Go with your love to the fields.
Lie easy in the shade. Rest your head

in her lap. Swear allegiance
to what is nighest your thoughts.
As soon as the generals and the politicos
can predict the motions of your mind,
lose it. Leave it as a sign
to mark the false trail, the way
you didn't go. Be like the fox
who makes more tracks than necessary,
some in the wrong direction.
Practice resurrection.

Abraham Joshua Heschel

THE SABBATH

Abraham Joshua Heschel (1907–1972) was born in Warsaw, Poland, and studied and taught in Germany and England before immigrating to the United States in 1940. As professor of Jewish ethics and mysticism at the Jewish Theological Seminary of America from 1945 to 1972, he was an influential and beloved teacher within the Jewish community. His books were and continue to be read and admired by many Jews, Christians, and secular intellectuals. In this passage, he considers the meaning of the Sabbath, the weekly day of rest that has been a central aspect of Jewish life for many centuries. Drawing on the history of his tradition and his belief that "the likeness of God can be found in time," he vividly portrays the holiness of this day and the urgently needed shift in perception it offers to contemporary people.

In Heschel's view, how does the Sabbath answer the question that frames this chapter of *Leading Lives That Matter*? What criticisms of the place of work in contemporary life are built into this account of Sabbath? Does Heschel manage here to address work-life issues by transcending them or transforming them?

He who wants to enter the holiness of the day must first lay down the profanity of clattering commerce, of being yoked to toil. He must go away from the screech of dissonant days, from the nervousness and fury of acquisitiveness and the betrayal in embezzling his own life. He must say farewell to manual work and learn to understand that the world has already been created and will survive without the help of man. Six days a week we wrestle with the world, wringing profit from the earth; on the Sabbath we especially care for the seed of eternity planted in the soul. The world has our hands, but our soul belongs to Someone Else. Six days a week we seek to dominate the world, on the seventh day we try to dominate the self.

From Abraham Joshua Heschel, *The Sabbath: Its Meaning for Modern Man* (New York: Farrar, Straus & Co., 1951, 1952), 13–21.

When the Romans met the Jews and noticed their strict adherence to the law of abstaining from labor on the Sabbath, their only reaction was contempt. The Sabbath is a sign of Jewish indolence, was the opinion held by Juvenal, Seneca and others.

In defense of the Sabbath, Philo, the spokesman of the Greek-speaking Jews of Alexandria, says: "On this day we are commanded to abstain from all work, not because the law inculcates slackness. . . . Its object is rather to give man relaxation from continuous and unending toil and by refreshing their bodies with a regularly calculated system of remissions to send them out renewed to their old activities. For a breathing spell enables not merely ordinary people but athletes also to collect their strength with a stronger force behind them to undertake promptly and patiently each of the tasks set before them."

Here the Sabbath is represented not in the spirit of the Bible but in the spirit of Aristotle. According to the Stagirite, "we need relaxation, because we cannot work continuously. Relaxation, then, is not an end"; it is "for the sake of activity," for the sake of gaining strength for new efforts. To the biblical mind, however, labor is the means toward an end, and the Sabbath as a day of rest, as a day of abstaining from toil, is not for the purpose of recovering one's lost strength and becoming fit for the forthcoming labor. The Sabbath is a day for the sake of life. Man is not a beast of burden, and the Sabbath is not for the purpose of enhancing the efficiency of his work. "Last in creation, first in intention," the Sabbath is "the end of the creation of heaven and earth."

The Sabbath is not for the sake of the weekdays; the weekdays are for the sake of Sabbath. It is not an interlude but the climax of living.

Three acts of God denoted the seventh day: He rested, He blessed and He hallowed the seventh day (Genesis 2:2–3). To the prohibition of labor is, therefore, added the blessing of delight and the accent of sanctity. Not only the hands of man celebrate the day, the tongue and the soul keep the Sabbath. One does not talk on it in the same manner in which one talks on weekdays. Even thinking of business or labor should be avoided.

Labor is a craft, but perfect rest is an art. It is the result of an accord of body, mind and imagination. To attain a degree of excellence in art, one must accept its discipline, one must adjure slothfulness. The seventh day is a *palace in time* which we build. It is made of soul, of joy and reticence. In its atmosphere, a discipline is a reminder of adjacency to eternity. Indeed, the splendor of the day is expressed in terms of *abstentions*, just as the mystery of God is more adequately conveyed *via negationis*, in the categories of *negative theology* which claims that we can never say what He is, we can only say what He is not. We often feel how poor the edifice would be were it built exclusively of our rituals and deeds which are so awkward and often so obtrusive. How else express glory in the presence of eternity, if not by the silence of abstaining from noisy acts? . . .

What is so luminous about a day? What is so precious to captivate the hearts? It is because the seventh day is a mine where spirit's precious metal can be found with which to construct the palace in time, a dimension in which the human is at home with the divine; a dimension in which man aspires to approach the likeness of the divine.

For where shall the likeness of God be found? There is no quality that space has in common with the essence of God. There is not enough freedom on the top of the mountain; there is not enough glory in the silence of the sea. Yet the likeness of God can be found in time, which is eternity in disguise.

The art of keeping the seventh day is the art of painting on the canvas of time the mysterious grandeur of the climax of creation: as He sanctified the seventh day, so shall we. The love of the Sabbath is the love of man for what he and God have in common. Our keeping the Sabbath day is a paraphrase of His sanctification of the seventh day.

What would be a world without Sabbath? It would be a world that knew only itself or God distorted as a thing or the abyss separating Him from the world; a world without the vision of a window in eternity that opens into time.

For all the idealization, there is no danger of the idea of the Sabbath becoming a fairy-tale. With all the romantic idealization, the Sabbath remains a concrete fact, a legal institution and a social order. There is no danger of its becoming a disembodied spirit, for the spirit of the Sabbath must always be in accord with actual deeds, with definite actions and abstentions. The real and the spiritual are one, like body and soul in a living man. It is for the law to clear the path; it is for the soul to sense the spirit.

This is what the ancient rabbis felt: the Sabbath demands all of man's attention, the service and single-minded devotion of total love. The logic of such a conception compelled them to enlarge constantly the system of laws and rules of observance. They sought to ennoble human nature and make it worthy of being in the presence of the royal day.

Yet law and love, discipline and delight, were not always fused. In their illustrious fear of desecrating the spirit of the day, the ancient rabbis established a level of observance which is within the reach of exalted souls but not infrequently beyond the grasp of ordinary men.

437

The glorification of the day, the insistence upon strict observance, did not, however, lead the rabbis to a deification of the law. "The Sabbath is given unto you, not you unto the Sabbath." The ancient rabbis knew that excessive piety may endanger the fulfillment of the essence of the law. "There is nothing more important, according to the Torah, than to preserve human life. . . . Even when there is the slightest possibility that a life may be at stake one may disregard every prohibition of the law." One must sacrifice mitzvot *for the sake of man* rather than sacrifice man "*for the sake of mitzvot.*" The purpose of the Torah is "to bring life to Israel, in this world and in the world to come."

Continuous austerity may severely dampen, yet levity would certainly obliterate the spirit of the day. One cannot modify a precious filigree with a spear or operate on a brain with a plowshare. It must always be remembered that the Sabbath is not an occasion for diversion or frivolity; not a day to shoot fireworks or to turn somersaults, but an opportunity to mend our tattered lives; to collect rather than to dissipate time. Labor without dignity is the cause of misery; rest without spirit the source of depravity. Indeed, the prohibitions have succeeded in preventing the vulgarization of the grandeur of the day. . . .

The seventh day is like a palace in time with a kingdom for all. It is not a date but an atmosphere.

It is not a different state of consciousness but a different climate; it is as if the appearance of all things somehow changed. The primary awareness is one of our being *within* the Sabbath rather than of the Sabbath being within us. We may not know whether our understanding is correct, or whether our sentiments are noble, but the air of the day surrounds us like spring which spreads over the land without our aid or notice.

"How precious is the Feast of Booths! Dwelling in the Booth, even our body is surrounded by the sanctity of the Mitzvah," said once a rabbi to his friend. Whereupon the latter remarked: "The Sabbath Day is even more than that. On the Feast you may leave the Booth for a while, whereas the Sabbath surrounds you wherever you go."

The difference between the Sabbath and all other days is not to be noticed in the physical structure of things, in their spatial dimension. Things do not change on that day. There is only a difference in the dimension of time, in the relation of the universe to God. The Sabbath preceded creation and the Sabbath completed creation; it is all of the spirit that the world can bear. . . .

Technical civilization is the product of labor, of man's exertion of power for the sake of gain, for the sake of producing goods. It begins when man, dissatisfied with what is available in nature, becomes engaged in a struggle with the forces of nature in order to enhance his safety and to increase his comfort. To use the language of the Bible, the task of civilization is to subdue the earth, to have dominion over the beast.

How proud we often are of our victories in the war with nature, proud of the multitude of instruments we have succeeded in inventing, of the abundance of commodities we have been able to produce. Yet our victories have come to resemble defeats. In spite of our triumphs, we have fallen victims to the work of our hands; it is as if the forces we had conquered have conquered us.

Is our civilization a way to disaster, as many of us are prone to believe? Is civilization essentially evil, to be rejected and condemned? The faith of the Jew is not a way out of this world, but a way of being within and above this world; not to reject but to surpass civilization. The Sabbath is the day on which we learn the art of *surpassing* Civilization.

Adam was placed in the Garden of Eden "to dress it and to keep it" (Genesis 2:15). Labor is not only the destiny of man; it is endowed with divine dignity. However, after he ate of the tree of knowledge he was condemned to toil, not only to labor. "In toil shalt thou eat . . . all the days of thy life" (Genesis 3:17). Labor is a blessing, toil is the misery of man.

The Sabbath as a day of abstaining from work is not a depreciation but an affirmation of labor, a divine exaltation of its dignity. Thou shalt abstain from labor on the seventh day is a sequel to the command: *Six days shalt thou labor, and do all thy work.*

"Six days shalt thou labor and do all thy work; but the seventh day is Sabbath unto the Lord thy God." Just as we are commanded to keep the Sabbath, we are commanded to labor. "Love work. . . ." The duty to work for six days is just as much a part of God's covenant with man as the duty to abstain from work on the seventh day.

To set apart one day a week for freedom, a day on which we would not use the instruments which have been so easily turned into weapons of destruction, a day for being with ourselves, a day of detachment from the vulgar, of independence of external obligations, a day on which we stop worshipping the idols of technical civilization, a day on which we use no money, a day of armistice in the economic struggle with our fellow men and the forces of nature — is there any institution that holds out a greater hope for man's progress than the Sabbath?

The solution of mankind's most vexing problem will not be found in renouncing technical civilization, but in attaining some degree of independence of it.

In regard to external gifts, to outward possessions, there is only one proper attitude — to have them and to be able to do without them. On the Sabbath we live, as it were, *independent of technical civilization*: we abstain primarily from any activity that aims at remaking or reshaping the things of space. Man's royal privilege to conquer nature is suspended on the seventh day.

What are the kinds of labor not to be done on the Sabbath? They are, according to the ancient rabbis, all those acts which were necessary for the construction and furnishing of the Sanctuary in the desert. The Sabbath itself is a sanctuary which we build, *a sanctuary in time.*

It is one thing to race or be driven by the vicissitudes that menace life, and another thing to stand still and to embrace the presence of an eternal moment.

The seventh day is the armistice in man's cruel struggle for existence, a truce in all conflicts, personal and social, peace between man and man, man and nature, peace within man; a day on which handling money is considered a desecration, on which man avows his independence of that which is the world's chief idol. The seventh day is the exodus from tension, the liberation of man from his own muddiness, the installation of man as a sovereign in the world of time.

What Are My Obligations to Future Human and Other Life?

Framing this question in this way signals the editors' conviction that thinking responsibly about what we should do and who we should be requires a massive change in collective consciousness. When we ask about our obligations to future human and other life, we are implying that human beings and other living things are integral parts of a common identity, all woven together in a shared web of life. A change in consciousness involves more than simply altering our views or adjusting our concepts or learning new information, though it surely includes all those things. Consciousness is in large part sheer awareness of identity, and it precedes and conditions our thoughts and actions.

Since our question about obligation to future life invites the gradual reformation of identity, we have selected a wide variety of works that awaken imagination as much as they instruct reason, and that evoke feelings as much as they unsettle habits:

- A love letter from an ethicist to his grandson
- A fable by the most influential environmental writer of the last century
- An essay that provides an actualization of the fable
- A poet's reflections on writing about nature in a time of environmental loss
- Four nature poems from the anthology *Black Nature*
- A talk by an environmental activist rooted in Native American traditions
- A Nobel Peace Prize lecture
- Excerpts from *Laudato Si'*, an encyclical letter by Pope Francis
- Two ancient Hebrew creation stories
- A creative riff on one of the Hebrew stories
- An Acoma (AA'KU) creation story
- A poem of lamentation and hope

These readings respond in different ways to the biggest change to have overtaken humanity since the first edition of *Leading Lives That Matter* appeared in 2006: the growing awareness, all over the globe, that our future is almost certainly imperiled by our past and present abuse of our planetary home. Heedless destruction of our environment has been going on for decades, even centuries, but only recently have we begun collectively to sense the scope and the consequences of the damage we have done at an increasingly accelerating pace over the last half century. In an interview with critic Paul Sika in April 2018, the filmmaker Paul Schrader, in the course of speaking about his profound film *First Reformed*, made an arresting remark. "I think we have made our choice; we have decided to trade present comfort for future survival." In other words, for Schrader, thanks to our own self-indulgence, there may not be many future generations of human beings.

Schrader's dire pronouncement echoes what many scientists, ethicists, political theorists, and economists have been saying for some time. Further, Schrader's film strongly suggests that our plight has spiritual roots as well as ecological, technological, political, and economic ones. We therefore begin the inquiry in this section by presenting a contemporary description and analysis by Christian ethicist Larry Rasmussen, whose recent book *Earth-Honoring Faith* incorporates a great deal of scientific learning. Rasmussen casts his thinking about the future of our planet in the form of a love letter to his two-year-old grandson Eduardo, whom he imagines reading the letter in 2035, when Eduardo will be eighteen. In the letter, Rasmussen addresses directly the question posed in this chapter: "What are my obligations to future human and other life?"

The vision that informs Rasmussen's love letter is planetary and epochal. However, most of us experience the phenomena that Rasmussen describes on much smaller scales of space and time. The next two readings in this section are therefore much more geographically and temporally circumscribed. The first is cast in the form of a fable and set in a small town, which, according to its author, "might easily have a thousand counterparts in America and elsewhere in the world." The fable appears at the beginning of the book that inaugurated what most environmental historians regard as the second major phase of the environmental movement in the United States. (The first phase was the so-called conservation movement of the late nineteenth and early twentieth centuries, which created wildlife refuges, wilderness areas, national forests, and the national park system.) That book is *Silent Spring*, first serialized in the *New Yorker* magazine and then published as a book during the summer of 1962. Its author, Rachel Carson, exemplifies how to meet the obligations that we owe to future life.

The next selection demonstrates that Carson's fable does indeed have a thousand counterparts. The writer Scott Russell Sanders sets his essay "Sanctuary" in Cedar Bluffs, an actual place in southern Indiana. The book in which the essay appears explores in multiple ways its author's guiding question, "How can one live a meaningful life in a world that seems broken and scattered?" Sanders's major provisional answer to that question evinces an aspect of the new consciousness that Carson had begun to arouse over a generation before. "Insofar as I have found an answer," he writes, "it has to do with understanding my place in marriage, family, and community — my place on earth, and ultimately in Creation."

Sanders had set out to Cedar Bluffs to find in nature a kind of sanctuary from the violence and the noise and the ugliness of industrial, technological society. Though he sadly discovers that there is no such escape, in his account of that small journey, he continues to some extent to think of "nature," as the Romantic poets did before him, as a source of healing and wisdom and refuge. By contrast, an entire vein of American poetry has provided a more complicated view of humanity and the natural world and has consistently offered readers incisive and often painfully revealing images that capture the often violent connections among work, the economy, technology, human beings, and the earth. African American writers often see the world through memories and feelings of oppression where conventional contrasts between nature and civilization are reconfigured, redrawn, sometimes contorted, and sometimes challenged. The experience of slavery and its legacy made the destructive power of industrial and technological "civilization" over against human and other lives palpably comprehensible long before such painful knowledge became so widely available to those who took freedom and privilege for granted.

The African American nature poetry gathered into one large anthology by the African American poet Camille T. Dungy manifests an immense treasure trove of images and ideas. Dungy not only introduces the entire volume but also contributes some of her own poetry and an autobiographical introduction to one of the "cycles" (thematically organized units) of poems in the collection. In that introduction, entitled "Writing Home," Dungy describes how her own experience of displacement and oppression shaped her as a writer. She also shows how her attitudes to the natural world became part and parcel of a much larger tradition of African American nature poetry.

No generalization can possibly do justice to that poetry's great variety, as the four poems we include here demonstrate. However, this body of poetry does feature recurrent accents and themes that distinguish it from nature poetry in the tradition of the Romantics, and that offer all readers in the midst of the present environmental crisis a number of salutary, timely, and instructive emphases. Yes, as Dungy notes, "the natural world held potential to be a source of refuge, sustenance, and uncompromised beauty" during the most difficult periods of African American history. However, the human relationship to the landscape looks and feels very different to someone writing from the perspective of a field hand, both bound to and alienated from the earth, than it does to a visitor enjoying its vistas as an escape from the city. And the proverbial contrast between nature and civilization is an entirely different matter for those driven from the land into the city than for those who, like Huck Finn, escape the grip of civilization for the freedom of unsettled territory. Had all of us paid more attention to the startling and disturbing African American images of violence of all kinds within nature — which many other poets rendered as idyllic and pastoral — we might have been made alert much sooner to the depth, the range, and the horror of the injuries some human beings have been inflicting upon human and other lives throughout history.

Indigenous or native peoples all over the world provide yet another source of wisdom about humankind's proper relationship to the rest of the natural world, as well as guidance for how best to honor our obligations to present and future life on this planet. Winona LaDuke, an environmental activist, economist, and writer who is known for her work on tribal land claims and preservation, points out in the lecture included here that on a worldwide scale "there are about five thousand indigenous nations, groups of indigenous peoples who share common language, culture, history, territory, and governmental institutions." In the course of her own efforts to re-form consciousness and to provide an account of what humans owe to the future, she develops a contrast between indigenous thinking and industrial thinking that is akin to Rasmussen's distinction between ecological civilization and industrial civilization.

The Nobel Peace Prize laureate for 2004, Wangari Maathai, represents yet another model of environmental activism. In her lecture, delivered on the occasion of receiving the prize, she described in some detail the Green Belt Movement that she had established with others in her native Kenya in 1977. The practical and symbolic center of that movement was the planting of some thirty million trees. In the re-formation of consciousness about the environment taking place in many parts of the world, trees are becoming symbols of planetary peril and obligation, especially as steadily worsening wildfires place human-created problems of climate change and faulty environmental management regularly at the forefront of public consciousness. In this context, many are coming to see that trees exhibit and exemplify the interdependence and vulnerability of all life. Works of imagination contribute mightily to this new vision. For example, trees are themselves the central characters in the Pulitzer Prize–winning novel *The Overstory*, by Richard Powers (2018), and they serve as the major point of entry into Camille Dungy's introduction to the anthology from which the African American poems in this section were taken. In featuring trees as part of a citizen education program, the Green Belt Movement developed an approach that many of us could emulate within our workplaces, our churches, our schools, and our towns and cities.

Changed consciousness and action often begin as individuals form new habits through the repetition of simple actions — like planting and caring for trees — to the point that these actions become practices that are integral to their character. In his 2015 encyclical *Laudato Si'*, Pope Francis summons the worldwide Catholic community — and people of every faith — to profound changes of consciousness and action, both individual and collective. This very important document begins with a long and searching examination of the present ecological crisis, based largely upon scientific evidence, and a review of relevant principles drawn from the Jewish and Christian traditions that can inform efforts to comprehend and respond to that crisis. The roots of environmental degradation, Pope Francis argues, have grown from the distorted way in which much of Western culture thinks about humanity and its place in the universe, and in the paradigms or patterns that have arisen from such thinking, which provide the basis for modern industrial, technological civilization and consumerist society. Only after providing this scientific, economic, ethical, and theological foundation does Pope Francis issue a call to dialogue, collective endeavor, and individual re-formation.

Three elements of Pope Francis's message coincide with the three excerpts of the letter that we include below. First, in "The Message of Each Creature in the Harmony of Creation," the pope develops an account of the interdependent character of the universe in which he includes contributions by bishops from Canada, Japan, Brazil, and elsewhere; this may be the most explicitly and persistently global portion of the letter. These several contributions underscore the message: all creatures, and beyond living creatures the sun and the moon, the planets, and the galaxies, are part of the whole. Moreover, all living creatures are sacred: "The Spirit of life dwells in every living creature and calls us to enter into relationship with him." As part of this theological description of the harmony of creation, the pope includes part of the canticle composed by his namesake, Saint Francis of Assisi (variously titled "Canticle of Brother Sun and Sister Moon" or "Canticle of the Creatures" or "Hymn to Creation"). The pope wishes to guard against what he regards as two dangerous extremes in understanding humanity's relationship to other living creatures. On the one hand, he wishes to avoid modern "anthropocentrism," the destructive view that regards the natural world as an object to be used at will by human beings. On the other hand, he wishes to avoid "biocentrism," the view that human beings are in no significant way different from other creatures. "There can be no ecology without an adequate anthropology. When the human person is considered simply one being among others, the product of chance or physical determinism, then 'our overall sense of responsibility wanes.'"

The second excerpt, "The Human Roots of the Ecological Crisis," exhibits some of the features that led Larry Rasmussen, in the letter to his grandson that began this chapter, to refer to *Laudato Si'* as "the single most powerful indictment to date of how the modern world has gone wrong." Pope Francis describes in detail what he calls the "technocratic paradigm," an aspect of modern anthropocentrism that has paradoxically "ended up prizing technical thought over reality" and "treating all of nature as an object of utility, as raw material to be hammered into useful shape." The motive that most deeply underlies this paradigm is the desire for power through manipulation and control. Technology has ceased to become an instrument and has become instead an end in itself, a mind-set, a state of consciousness. And it has come to dominate economic and political life. Since the pursuit of such control is boundless, economic and political practice depends upon endless growth. Within this mindset, the solution to the devastation created by heedless growth is simply more growth; the solution to the ills created by our manipulations is simply more manipulation. We seem trapped in an iron cage of our own making, as Max Weber once put it.

Pope Francis believes that we cannot free ourselves from this cage; our collective liberation depends upon a higher power than our own and upon the creation of communities across boundaries of religion and culture that can sustain certain habits, virtues, and practices that will lead to changes in consciousness and character. The third excerpt below, "Educating for the Covenant between Humanity and the Environment," begins to outline some of those virtues. The summons to individual and local initiative is placed upon an enormous horizon. Ecological change cannot come about without political, social, economic, and spiritual change. Problems of poverty, war, violence, inequality, oppression, and environmental catastrophe are all of a piece. Even so, we should not be daunted by the scale and complexity of the crisis. Nor should we doubt the efficacy of small efforts to change the world. The papal letter summons us to "ways of acting which directly and significantly affect the world around us, such as avoiding the use of plastic and paper, reducing water consumption, separating refuse, cooking only what can reasonably be consumed, showing care for other living beings, using public transport or carpooling, planting trees, turning off unnecessary lights, or any number of other practices." He might have added other virtues and practices like hospitality, courage, and endurance, because in the immediate future most of us will experience the environmental crisis by contending with emergency situations brought about by floods, wildfires, mud slides, earthquakes, tsunamis, and hurricanes. We will either suffer the effects of such catastrophes ourselves or minister to those who have lost homes, loved ones, jobs, and neighborhoods.

Pope Francis grounded his encyclical letter, which has become a part of Catholic social teaching, in the great creation stories that begin the book of Genesis. Very few texts that both Jews and Christians regard as sacred Scripture have received more critical attention than the first three chapters of Genesis. These two stories, like the hundreds of creation myths cherished by religious traditions around the world, form communities of faith by offering, in narrative form, answers to fundamental questions about who human beings are, how we came to be, and how we relate to the rest of the created world. And the fact that there are two stories, not one, helps to explain why the Jewish and Christian traditions not only have argued among themselves for centuries about the fundamental questions explored in these stories but also have given two-sided answers to them. It is no surprise that Pope Francis should insist that human beings are fully a part of nature but are also possessed of "unique capacities of knowledge, will, freedom, and responsibility." This interpretation of Genesis 1–3 is fully warranted by the text.

But so are other readings of Genesis that are at odds with the pope's reading and that some would say have contributed to our present perils. In 1966, for example, a medieval historian named Lynn White Jr. delivered an address to the American Academy of the Advancement of Science that was published the following year in the journal *Science*. Rarely do scholarly talks and articles generate widespread cultural conversation and controversy over many years, but White's did. Though White was himself a devout Christian, he argued that a particular strain of the Christian tradition had led to the environmental degradation that was alarming people already in 1967, thanks in part to writers like Rachel Carson. To make a long and complicated argument short, White seized upon the end of the first creation story (Gen. 1), suggesting that human beings are there portrayed as the crown of creation and placed by the Creator above and over all other creatures. As White notes, the first command given to the humans by the Creator is to "be fruitful and multiply, and fill the earth and *subdue* it; and *have dominion* over the fish of the sea and over the birds of the air and over every living thing that moves upon the earth" (Gen. 1:28, emphasis added). White's sympathizers claimed that Christians had followed this command to subdue and to dominate, that they had therefore understood all other creatures as theirs to use as they pleased, and that the relationship of dominion over the rest of creation had alienated human beings from the rest of creation in the beginning and ever afterward.

This is not the place to review the enormous body of writing in opposition to White's views. For our purposes here, three things are important. First, the continuing controversy demonstrated that White had touched a sensitive cultural nerve that has only grown more sensitive in the face of the deepening environmental crisis. Second, the two stories at the beginning of Genesis really do expose the roots of how we came to be the way we are, especially in Western culture; therefore, it is vitally important to study these texts carefully and thoroughly. Third, for as long as human beings have written down their own stories of origin, there have been both harmonies and deep conflicts among human beings, the animal world, and the vegetable world. To comprehend the character and the roots of both the harmonies and the discords, we need to study creation narratives like the ones in Genesis.

White and his critics aside, it is clear that questions of power and dominion continue to bedevil us, and that they pertain with increasing urgency to matters of the environment and how we ought properly to relate to other living beings. It should come as no surprise to learn that power dynamics have perhaps been the major theme in the seemingly endless interpretations of Genesis. That commentary has assumed many forms, from scholarly exegesis to historical analysis to midrashim, which sometimes take the form of stories to imaginatively fill in gaps in original texts. One short, contemporary, lighthearted example, written by the late science fiction writer Ursula LeGuin, focuses upon the power dynamics in Genesis — between male and female, and between humans and other animals. LeGuin concentrates upon naming as an act of dominion, separation, and classification, and she imagines the woman "unnaming" the animals that the man has named in Genesis 2:18–20a. The narrator of "She Unnames Them" is Eve, the "she" of the title. This fanciful but trenchant story raises very serious questions about the extent to which the kind of power that human beings have exercised over the rest of nature has been gendered.

The creation narratives in Genesis are only two among many from around the world. David Adams Leeming has collected and classified hundreds of these in a two-volume encyclopedia, *Creation Myths of the World*. A very large number of these myths feature a female creation figure of one kind or another. One is the creation myth included below, which, like LeGuin's riff on Genesis, features feminine characters and principles. It comes from the Acoma (AA'KU), a Pueblo people of present-day New Mexico. Though there are many variations of the story featured here throughout the several Keres-speaking people of whom the Acoma are a part, all of them feature female agents of creation. Studying this myth, and others like it, enables us to see how the relationships among humans and the rest of the world look when the creation principle is feminine.

This chapter concludes with Denise Levertov's poem "Beginners," in which glimmers of hope shine forth in a poem prompted by the untimely and unjust deaths of two environmental activists. The hope toward which Levertov points is not optimism; it is rather a force emerging from the "power that is within us if we would join our solitudes in the communion of struggle." In a sense, this poem serves as both a summary of the problems we have encountered in this chapter — "there is too much broken" — and a summons to join in a common struggle.

Virtues like hope and humility may be more important in the Anthropocene than they have been at any other time. The late historian of Christian doctrine Jaroslav Pelikan once concluded an address by revising, "in all due reverence," the apostle Paul's famous passage about the cardinal Christian virtues: "So faith, hope, and love abide," Pelikan said, "but the greatest of these is hope." Changing the emphasis in the biblical text — 1 Corinthians 13:13, where Paul identifies love as the greatest virtue — Pelikan asserted that "where there is no hope, love is a thing of the moment and faith is an idle fancy. But with hope, faith may dare to love, even amid the changes and chances of this present life." Hope instills the capacity to resist both despair and presumption; it instills strength, in the face of all the pessimistic pronouncements of our time, to maintain action in communion with others. And humility — a virtue out of keeping with the project of mastery and domination decried by Pope Francis — enables us to accept joyfully our place in the world, to heed the wisdom of others, and to participate with faith, hope, and love in the all-embracing web of life.

Thanks to the writers represented in this chapter, and also to a growing chorus of others, we may begin to grasp what it means to re-form our consciousness, and how vital that change is for the future of our planetary home. Let us begin, for time is short.

Larry Rasmussen

A LOVE LETTER FROM THE HOLOCENE
TO THE ANTHROPOCENE

Larry Rasmussen is a leader in fostering concern and wisdom about the environmental crisis in Christian ethics, often in conversation with other religious traditions. Rasmussen, the Reinhold Niebuhr Professor of Ethics at Union Theological Seminary in New York from 1986 to 2004, is best known for his books *Earth Community, Earth Ethics* (1997), which won the prestigious Grawemeyer prize, and *Earth-Honoring Faith: Religious Ethics in a New Key* (2012). His overall purpose in the more recent volume resonates with the purposes of *Leading Lives That Matter*. His book's "burning questions," Rasmussen writes, "are the questions of all ethics: How are we to live, and for what? What makes lives, any lives and all lives, go 'round so well? What is good, right, and fitting?"

In the selection below, Rasmussen ponders the epoch-making environmental changes amid which we now live — changes to which he, the editors of this volume, and other members of our generation have contributed. And he speaks to his grandson, in love, about the environmental challenges his generation will face. This letter explicitly addresses this chapter's guiding question, "What are my obligations to future human and other life?" What do you think of Rasmussen's three-part answer? Would you add additional obligations to these? What would they be? Do you think he explains to his grandson why we should owe anything at all to the future? Do you find his reasoning convincing?

Unpublished lecture by Larry L. Rasmussen, June 13, 2018.

October, 2017

Dear Eduardo,

This is a love letter. But not the usual. Of course Grandma Nyla and I, with your *abuela y abuelo* in Colombia, match doting grandparents anywhere. Our affection lacks nothing.

But this letter is unique because it's the first love letter consciously written by a grandfather who lived in one geological epoch to a grandchild living in another. No other letter in the whole history of love knowingly sends love from the late Holocene to the early Anthropocene! That's weird, but it's also important because the Anthropocene is the time of your life while the Holocene is the time of mine.

This language rings strange, at least to me. Yet probably not to you if you are reading this as a sixteen- or eighteen-year-old. Unlike me, you will experience the tumultuous changes that ride astride a new geological epoch. While human history and human experience were my main subject, earth science and planetary experience will likely be yours. So you already know from school and your smart-phone watch that Holocene means "the wholly recent" epoch — mine — while Anthropocene — yours — is "the age of the human," from the Greek *anthropos*. (God only knows why geologists all speak Greek, but they do.)

The global temperature across the last eleven thousand years, the late Holocene, varies by less than 2 degrees Celsius. This minimal difference is rare in Earth's history. It means that the geological grammar of the epoch that has hosted every human civilization to date, bar none, is climate stability, uncommon stability generating and sustaining a riot of life.

If you draw a line tracking climate across the last eleven thousand years, that line is basically straight and horizontal. My lifetime and Grandma Nyla's fall to the far right of this line, where it then takes a sudden turn and heads straight up, with further rises to come. That temperature spike is the early Anthropocene, and it's where I leave my life behind and you begin yours. You cannot know how I wish your life were not lived along that trajectory. It's climate *in*stability, eco-social uncertainty, and breathtaking extinction across the community of life.

Nonetheless, the planet is still beautiful, even beyond the singing of it, and you and I have our days together as they overlap in the great transition that will define every day of your life and the last ones of mine. Our effort together is to get from industrial to ecological civilization. However many years that takes — but surely in your lifetime — may well turn out to be, as David Grinspoon puts it, the "branching point between calamity and wisdom."

Did you know that the year you were born — 2015 — was the decisive one? It was, in three ways.

It was the warmest year on record to that point. Across the United States, 1,426 high-temperature records fell in the first days of December, when you were ten months old. We shouldn't be too surprised, since the year before, 2014, was the hottest until then, and the hottest seventeen years all occurred in the preceding twenty. In May, when you were but three months old, CO_2 passed the 400 parts per million mark for the first time in all human history. And half the climb to 400 parts per million happened after 1980 — only half my lifetime. The present 407 parts per million is the highest carbon concentration in eight hundred thousand years.

Your birth year saw unprecedented response as well. On December 12, 195 nations signed the Paris Climate Agreement — a political miracle even when everyone there knew it was only the first step and, in order to stave off runaway catastrophe, greenhouse gas emissions would have to drop to zero by 2050, when you will be thirty-five. One nation, the United States, under God and under Trump, is exiting the Paris Agreement, just as all the dour records of your birth year were being broken in your second year and will be again in your third. As I write, there are monster storms — Hurricanes Harvey, Irma, Maria, and José — and wildfires in both northern and southern California. The late afternoon temperature in late October for the first game of the World Series was 103 degrees (in LA). (A month later, on Thanksgiving Day, it had plummeted to 92.) In Barrow, Alaska, the climate-monitoring station dropped off the map. Its algorithms found the warming data so unreal, they wiped it out, cleaned the slate. The algorithms had no place for a new normal that far out of range. (The temperature was up 7.8 degrees in October and 6.9 degrees in November, while the rate of sea ice melting was faster than any in the last fifteen hundred years.) I suspect our Holocene ways are no better tuned than those algorithms. Our habits, if not our mind-set, just clean the slate and carry on as before.

The other 2015 landmark response came earlier, in June — the papal encyclical *Laudato Si'*. I'll not exegete it but only say that it is the single most powerful indictment to date of how the modern world has gone wrong. Moreover, it challenges what the Paris Agreement still enshrines — the orthodoxy of perpetual economic growth within the framework of global corporate capitalism. The encyclical dares to speak of climate-change impacts as "catastrophe" and "disaster," while the Paris accord uses the tempered language of "adverse effects," never acknowledging anything fundamentally wrong with our dominant paradigms.

The third turning point, this one all but mentioning you by name, was the filing of *Juliana et al. v. United States*. Twenty-one children and young adults, backed by Our Children's Trust, brought suit against the US government on the basis of public trust doctrine, doctrine based in the Fifth, Ninth, and Tenth Amendments, and the vesting, posterity, and nobility clauses of the US Constitution. The children's suit argues that the government holds resources such as land and water in trust for its citizens and should be considered a trustee of the atmosphere as well.

How all this turns out you will know. Right now it's wholly uncertain, and when chaos rules, "Nothing ages faster than the future," as Stanislaw Lem says. Yet even amidst uncertainty, this lawsuit is the right means for bearing my generation's moral obligation to yours. Let me say why.

But first a preface. In the latter days of the Holocene, we have become "aware of ourselves as short-lived creatures on a small planet in a long-lived galaxy of evolving stars and countless planets" (Grinspoon). This cosmology of wonder and the journey of the universe is not only sound science; it bears our collective identity. Short-lived though we be, our origins are stellar. We are stardust. The calcium in your teeth, Eduardo, the iron in your blood, and the gold of a wedding band of commitment you might someday wear are all gifts of exploding supernovae. The grace of star death funded your life. It really does take a universe to raise a child — you or all your friends.

Yet, to date, this cosmology of wonder is without translation into law or even conventional consciousness.

Still, law is powerful. It can bridge the gap between what is and what ought to be, and do so in ways that render routine human behavior constructive. It can even fashion a people, as devout Jews have known for millennia.

My prayer is that the children's lawsuit might join the cosmology of wonder and the ethic it reaches for. Since "rights" is a primary language of law, let's call this the quest for "intergenerational rights."

But is one generation ethically obligated to the next? Only if the children matter. Yet it is not that *they* matter to *us*. ("What has progeny done for me?" Robert Heilbroner once asked.) It is that *we* matter to *them*. Every generation, without any choice whatsoever, depends on those who have gone before, and depends on the earth they bequeathed. But never have the stakes been so high as now, when we are a new geological force. Anthropocene people with Holocene habits doom their children.

So what does my generation owe yours, Eduardo, or what does yours owe those who follow? Edith Weiss proposes three principles. (1) Each generation "should be required to conserve the diversity of the natural and cultural resource base" so that future generations have the means to exercise their values and solve their problems. This is the "conservation of options." (2) Each generation should also be required "to maintain the quality of the planet so that it is passed on in no worse condition than that in which it was received." This is the "conservation of quality." Lastly, (3) each generation should provide its members with "equitable rights of access to the legacy of past generations and should conserve this access for future generations." This is the "conservation of access."

These conserving principles — options, quality, and access — will take a giant step if *Juliana et al. v. United States* prevails. If it does not, like attempts must be tried even though all three essentials — options, quality, access — will be extraordinarily difficult under Anthropocene conditions. Yet that must not deter us, since law is often as much about aspiration as achievement.

I close on a related note. As a Christian ethicist, I ground obligation in a moral universe of *all* the children. "All the children" alludes to the dedication in Thomas Berry's *The Great Work: Our Way into the Future*, which addresses the children who swim in the sea and live in the soil, the children of flowers, animals, and birds as well as human children.

"All the children" translates as full-bore rights of nature, ourselves included. Its moral universe understands planetary creation as sacred, seamless, and interdependent, a single, complex, luminous ecosphere. Its moral universe also deems creation "good." *All* the children are worthy of the public trust the children's lawsuit seeks. And since no other species has lawyers, it must be *our* law for *everyone's* sake — *all* the children's.

My dear child, I must break off for now. I do so with a heavy heart because I know that, wholly against my own will, I am passing to you a bitter irony. Measured by our planetary imprint, the world I and my ancestors hand you is the most *human* of all epochs. By the same measure, it is also the most dangerous and destructive, and you will be living with that. Later I will write about the dilemma of the Anthropocene, and more joyful things, too! But for now I must sign off.

I send all my love, Grandma Nyla's, too. Te amo.

Grandpa

P.S. I have a request. If, by the time you read this as a young man, I am dead, as dead I well may be, would you join your mother's lovely voice at my memorial service? And would you sing not just any song. Rather, this one, where your living and my dying meet in a love that bridges even geological epochs.

Pues si vivimos, para Dios vivimos
Y si morimos, para Dios morimos.
Sea que vivamos o que muramos,
Somos del buen Dios, somos del buen Dios.

In all our living, we belong to God;
and in our dying, we are still with God;
So, whether living, or whether dying,
we belong to God; we belong to God.

Rachel Carson

A FABLE FOR TOMORROW

The epigraph for Rachel Carson's epochal book *Silent Spring* (1962) was drawn from another writer featured in this book, Albert Schweitzer, who had said, "Man has lost the capacity to foresee and forestall. He will end by destroying the earth." Moved by this sentiment and gifted with an ability to make scientific knowledge accessible to a broad public, Carson (1907–1964) wrote the book that launched the environmental movement as we know it today. Her animus in *Silent Spring* is directed at the widespread use of poisonous pesticides, especially DDT, in the face of scientific knowledge that had shown, in the scattered places where technical and specialized learning was published, the horrific effects of DDT exposure on all creatures, including human beings. Her book brought an immediate ban of DDT, and it added crucial impetus to a movement that resulted in the creation of the Environmental Protection Agency (1970) and the passage of the Endangered Species Act (1973). The eminent biologist E. O. Wilson, who contributed an afterword to the fortieth anniversary edition of *Silent Spring*, said that the latter act was "the most important piece of conservation legislation in the nation's history."

Carson opened *Silent Spring* with "A Fable for Tomorrow." What about her writing in that fable could have moved so many people from ignorance to scientific understanding to political action? What were your own feelings as you read it? What kinds of feeling are most likely to lead to social and political action?

There was once a town in the heart of America where all life seemed to live in harmony with its surroundings. The town lay in the midst of a checkerboard of prosperous farms, with fields of grain and hillsides of orchards where, in spring, white clouds of bloom drifted above the green fields. In autumn, oak

....

From Rachel Carson, *Silent Spring*, 40th anniversary ed. (Boston: Houghton Mifflin, 2002), 1–3.

and maple and birch set up a blaze of color that flamed and flickered across a backdrop of pines. Then foxes barked in the hills and deer silently crossed the fields, half hidden in the mists of the fall mornings.

Along the roads, laurel, viburnum and alder, great ferns and wildflowers delighted the traveler's eye through much of the year. Even in winter the roadsides were places of beauty, where countless birds came to feed on the berries and on the seed heads of the dried weeds rising about the snow. The countryside was, in fact, famous for the abundance and variety of its bird life, and when the flood of migrants was pouring through in spring and fall people traveled from great distances to observe them. Others came to fish the streams, which flowed clear and cold out of the hills and contained shady pools where trout lay So it had been from the days many years ago when the first settlers raised their houses, sank their wells, and built their barns.

Then a strange blight crept over the area and everything began to change. Some evil spell had settled on the community: mysterious maladies swept the flocks of chickens; the cattle and sheep sickened and died. Everywhere was a shadow of death. The farmers spoke of much illness among their families. In the town the doctors had become more and more puzzled by new kinds of sickness appearing among their patients. There had been several sudden and unexplained deaths, not only among adults but even among children, who would be stricken suddenly while at play and die within a few hours.

There was a strange stillness. The birds, for example — where had they gone? Many people spoke of them, puzzled and disturbed. The feeding stations in the backyards were deserted. The few birds seen anywhere were moribund; they trembled violently and could not fly. It was a spring without voices. On the mornings that had once throbbed with the dawn chorus of robins, catbirds, doves, jays, wrens, and scores of other bird voices there was now no sound; only silence lay over the fields and woods and marsh.

On the farms the hens brooded, but no chicks hatched. The farmers complained that they were unable to raise any pigs — the litters were small and the young survived only a few days. The apple trees were coming into bloom but no bees droned among the blossoms, so there was no pollination and there would be no fruit.

The roadsides, once so attractive, were now lined with browned and withered vegetation as though swept by fire. These, too, were silent, deserted by all living things. Even the streams were now lifeless. Anglers no longer visited them, for all the fish had died.

In the gutters under the eaves and between the shingles of the roofs, a white granular powder still showed a few patches; some weeks before it had fallen like snow upon the roofs and the lawns, the fields and streams.

No witchcraft, no enemy action had silenced the rebirth of new life in this stricken world. The people had done it to themselves.

This town does not actually exist, but it might easily have a thousand counterparts in America or elsewhere in the world. I know of no community that has experienced all the misfortunes I describe. Yet every one of these disasters has actually happened somewhere, and many real communities have already suffered a substantial number of them. A grim specter has crept upon us almost unnoticed, and this imagined tragedy may easily become a stark reality we all shall know.

What has already silenced the voices of spring in countless towns in America? This book is an attempt to explain.

Scott Russell Sanders

SANCTUARY

Scott Russell Sanders has lived and worked for many years in the hardwood hill country of Indiana's White River Valley. His love for the natural beauty of the region was married early to his skill as a writer, yielding many prize-winning essays and novels with environmental themes. Sanders's essays are perhaps most compelling because of their integration of the local and personal and particular with the national and global and universal. Thus, in the essay below, "Sanctuary," he moves easily from a meditation on the soothing beauty along a stream near his home to a consideration of the visible threats to that little corner of the earth to a consideration of our place on this planet to a reflection upon our responsibilities to each other and to nature itself. One key to Sanders's environmental wisdom is his steadfast refusal to consider human beings as somehow apart from or over and above nature. As other writers in this section insist, we cannot rightly gauge our obligations to future generations of planetary life unless and until we count ourselves as natural neighbors and kin to other life-forms.

How do the environmental themes in "Sanctuary" speak to both the leading question of this chapter about our obligations to future life and the leading question of the preceding section about with whom and for whom we should live? Can we really address one of the questions fully without addressing the other one as well?

Birds loose their alarm calls as I climb from the car. Beware, beware the animal that goes on two legs. My own legs are stiff from the drive that carried me out of town, through southern Indiana hills, to this nature preserve. I often visit this place called Cedar Bluffs with family or friends, idly, cheerfully, stirred by the mix of motives familiar to anyone who wearies of the human zone and hungers for the land. But this day I come alone, for I

From Scott Russell Sanders, *Writing from the Center* (Bloomington: Indiana University Press, 2002), 52–64.

need to contend with an ache deeper than weariness or hunger. This day, this midseason of my swift life, this end-time of the millennium, I need to confront despair.

It is early one June morning in a wet summer, which means the trees are lush with leaves, the waist-high grasses ripple with juice, and the meadow I must pass through on my way to the bluff will be alive with mosquitoes, chiggers, and ticks. I pull the gray wool socks up over the cuffs of my jeans, draw tight the laces on my boots, and cross the blacktop road.

As I move from the pavement onto the dirt path, I lurch to avoid stepping on a snake. The rope of muscle jerks and vanishes so quickly into the weeds I barely catch a glimpse of pale brown scales ringed by darker bands, markings that could belong to a watersnake or a copperhead. Either species would bite if pestered, but only the copperhead is venomous. My hammering heart does not care about the distinctions. I shiver. My legs seize up, and will not resume walking for a minute or so. The rush of dread feels clean, pure, old.

The fear is ancestral, a reflex that has helped keep our evolutionary string from snapping, but for me it is also personal. At the age of three or four, living on a farm in Tennessee, I stumbled into a nest of snakes and nearly died from the bites. Stabs of pain, swelling, delirium: the least flicker of a scaly body brings up the memory like a splash of nausea in the throat.

I look out over the meadow and gather myself. To my right, beyond a thicket of willows and sumac, I see the glint of Clear Creek, whose occasional floods keep this bottom land from turning to forest. The bluff rises on my left, dense with oak and maple and cedar everywhere except for a broad swath cut by the right-of-way for high-tension lines. I do not want to see the looming poles, the sagging wires, yet there they are, scrawled against the sky, higher and more potent than anything else in sight. A few turkey vultures perch on one of the crossbeams, their wings splayed to catch the early sun, like a row of black shirts hung out to dry.

My country has been at war again. The day's news is worse than any nightmare. I came to this 23-acre refuge oppressed by the frenzy of killing and burning and waste that is ravaging the planet, by the sense of my species — and myself — as monstrous. Sight of the snake has narrowed the focus of my anxiety. Beneath my love of wildness, beneath my respect for other lives, there is this primordial terror. Moving on through the meadow, my thighs stroked by the seedheads of grasses, my ears rattling with the scolding of birds, I keep checking the trail ahead.

Circles of caution spread around me as I walk. Crickets and frogs fall silent, sparrows and warblers flitter to cover, a deer grazing by the creek hoists the white flag of its tail and bounds away. Against my desire for calm, for innocence, I think of men with machine guns patrolling cities, blocking roads, stalking through woods the world over, their stares like radiation piercing everything in sight. At least some of these armed men must enjoy spreading fear, there are so many of them, and so many of them will shoot when orders are given, will shoot even when no orders are given.

In fairy tales, giants send out tremors of fright with every crashing step and thunderous breath. How far does panic spread from the sound of a chain saw, a snowmobile, an off-road motorcycle? And do the wielders of loud machines feel mighty, rousing panic wherever they go? I recall a boastful bumper sticker that shows up on local trucks:

> THOUGH I WALK THROUGH THE VALLEY OF THE SHADOW OF DEATH,
> I WILL FEAR NO EVIL,
> FOR I AM THE MEANEST SON OF A BITCH IN THE VALLEY.

Many of the same bumpers also display an even briefer summary of this popular faith:

> IN GUNS WE TRUST.

Maybe the reason we so relentlessly slaughter animals, fell trees, dam rivers, drain swamps, poison whatever thwarts us, bulldoze and batter and pave, is because we aspire to become giants, to be utterly alone and invincible in the valley, to shove death into the shadows.

Truly, I have come to Cedar Bluffs to that I might escape such thoughts for a spell. I force my attention back to the meadow, and immediately I see an electric-blue dragonfly slicing by, zig and zag, then I realize there are dozens of them, hundreds, the air shimmering with these driven flakes. I stop. A speckled orange butterfly lands near me on the yellow disk of an oxeye daisy, and I notice for the first time that the path is lined with daisies; then I notice blossoms everywhere — the fuzzy white parasols of yarrow, the creamy sacs of bladder campions, the blue trumpets of hairy beardtongues, the orange baubles of jewel weed. I draw a deep breath, and smell the rank, green luxuriance. I suddenly hear, behind the buzz of alarm cries, a glee of birds wooing mates, staking out turf, rehearsing old melodies, their voices oblivious to me.

It is a small awakening, to surface from thoughts of myself and my kind and rise up into the blooming, darting, singing world. The experience is ordinary, yet each time the waking feels fresh, as though I never quite believe that the creation keeps dancing while I sleep. As I move on, I resolve to stay alert, knowing that I will fail, knowing the resolve itself will cloud the windows of perception and shut me up once again inside the house of thoughts.

Where the trail leaves the meadow and enters the shadows of trees, a yellow plastic sign proclaims this patch of ground to be a sanctuary, and a wooden sign identifies it as being owned and managed by the Nature Conservancy. Every time I come here, I give thanks to the people who loved this place enough to salvage it from the bonfire of development, and who, instead of fencing it off for their private use, have left it open for strangers to visit. Visitors come singly, in whispering pairs, in raucous groups, sometimes dozens a day, and their feet keep the trail from grassing over, yet the land, under all that needful looking, seems undiminished.

I walk on through shadows toward the brightness of the creek. The bank is littered with massive chunks of limestone that have tumbled from the bluff. I choose a slab that juts into the stream near a riffle, where I can listen to water shooshing over rocks, and there I sit.

How long I sit I cannot say, because time lets go of me in the presence of moving water. Leaves and twigs ride the current toward me, wobble through the rapids, glide on. Minnows glimmer in the shallows. The sunlight is filled with swarming insects, gnats and midges and creatures whose names I do not know. I do know something about the rock beneath me, for I have talked with men hereabouts who quarry and carve it. I know this limestone was formed in the bed of an ocean three hundred million years ago, in an age that geologists call the Mississippian. The name pleases me, because my father was from Mississippi, and I was born beside the Mississippi River — which makes both of us kin, after a fashion, with the stone.

It is difficult, while resting on rock that is three hundred million years old, to take very seriously the little human play. It is difficult, in this vibrant place, to believe that nature is in jeopardy from anything that our species could possibly do. A fur of moss fills every hollow; green shoots rise from every crack. Seeds drifting through shafts of light flame up like sparks. Dragonflies slash through the milling insects. Behind me, the bluff hunches darkly under the shade of trees, roots gripping stone. Sycamores lean out over the creek, their trunks matted with sticks from high water. On a mud flat, raccoons have left the translucent husks of crayfish and their own dainty pawprints. Turtles bask on a snag in midstream, four of them, shell leaning against shell like a stack of saucers. The creek pours through its channel, scooping and tossing sunlight, and birds pour song into the air. How could this splendor cease? How could it even falter under our puny assault?

If you take a large enough view, of course, the creation does not appear to be in jeopardy. Nothing that we have done or that we are likely to do will upset the solar system, let alone the galaxy or universe. We are very small fry in a vast ocean. The universe revealed by science has expanded enormously since Pascal was terrified by the eternal silence of infinite spaces, since Wordsworth felt a single spirit rolling through mind and nature, even since Frost, early in our century, saw the moon as a luminary clock hung in the indifferent darkness. Within the past few decades, we have discovered that our sun is a routine star near the outer edge of the Milky Way, and the Milky Way is only one among a billionfold dusting of galaxies. Over the same period, we have uncovered deeper and deeper layers within matter itself, far below the visible surface, beyond the depths of atoms, beyond electrons and protons, beyond quarks, on diminishingly down. Everywhere we look, out far or in deep, from the clustering of galaxies to the spinning of quarks, we find an intricate order whose laws we may decipher but cannot alter.

And yet, while the great web of the cosmos appears to be invulnerable, the threads of creation that pass through our planet, through our local terrain, through our own guts, have come to seem frail, all too easily frayed or broken. The fabric of habitats, the fibers of nerves, the strands of DNA unravel. This bright thread glistening before me, the sun-dappled creek, no longer runs clear, as it did when settlers named it. The water is murky with topsoil. Mounds of dirty foam gather in the shallows. Tires and bottles and other flotsam dangle from roots exposed along the banks. Less visibly, more dangerously, the water is fouled with fertilizer, pesticides, herbicides, solvents, oil. The Indiana Department of Health announced in today's newspaper, as they have done annually for several years, that no one should eat more than half a pound of fish per week taken from Clear Creek, and that women of child-bearing age and children under eighteen should eat none at all. This particular menace comes from polychlorinated biphenyls, or PCBs, one of the many alphabet chemicals that we manufacture in haste, dump in laziness, and then regret in leisure. Every day we discover new reasons for regretting what our predecessors have done; after we are gone, our children will discover even more reasons to regret what we are doing now.

Oceans laid down this limestone over millions of years; the creek wore through the stone to carve these bluffs over thousand of years; yet we needed only a few years to poison the creek. This is no Cuyahoga River, so filthy it catches fire, no Ruhr Valley, no Love Canal, not an industrial sewer at all, but an obscure stream in the hills of southern Indiana. That we cannot safely eat the fish from this water is a sign of how far the damage has spread.

Nothing we do will unsettle the universe; everything we do affects the planet. This has always been true, but never before our own time have the effects been so rapid or so far-reaching. Some of our deadliest chemicals are now stored in the fat of penguins in Antarctica, in the eggshells of eagles nesting in Alaska, in the brains of monkeys from the Amazon. Biologists estimate that more than one hundred species of plants and animals are disappearing each *day*, the overwhelming proportion of them due to our actions. The web of life is unraveling more swiftly than at any time since the extinction of the dinosaurs, sixty-five million years ago.

Even here in the presence of water and stone I cannot forget these ruinous facts. Even here I am hounded by what I have seen — the forests cut down, the land worn out, animals flattened on roads, trash piling against fences, oil slicks in puddles, smoke sullying the air.

Grief drags me to my feet and hustles me along the trail, as though I might rush beyond reach of this knowledge. I soon come to the end of the bluff, turn away from the creek and round the point, then I climb the slope, moving so rapidly that I do not look for late-blooming columbine, I scarcely notice the lacy ferns, and by the time I emerge onto the crown of the bluff I am panting. From floodplain to summit, rising past several million years of earth's history recoded in limestone, I have seen only a gray blur.

Atop the bluff, wherever fissures open in the rock, cedars and oaks have taken root, and in their shade ferns and mosses and wild roses flourish. I pick my way among the twisted trunks until I come to a ledge that offers a view out over the valley of Clear Creek to the woods and fields beyond. Others have been attracted to this promontory, as witness the cigarette butts, the aluminum rings from beverage cans, the initials gouged into stone, the cinders from pleasure fires. Again, I sit, smelling ashes and roses, and again I lose track of time.

Two red-tailed hawks circle before me in the gulf of air, calling back and forth. After his death, my father spoke to me as a red-tailed hawk, so I listen carefully to their sharp cries. Now that I am listening, I hear the grumble of a jet, the sizzle of tires on gravel, the snort of trucks on the highway. I hear a tractor working on a nearby farm — mowing hay, I would guess, judging by the sound and season. My forearms itch from the memory of hoisting bales onto wagons.

From up here I can see the high-tension lines humping away for miles over the hills. Crews from the power company used to bush-hog the right-of-way, but now they come through every few years and spray defoliants. They sprayed here lately, and the cleared swath beneath the sagging wires is brittle brown, a sash of dead trees stretching away to the horizon. I know a man who helped perfect the poisons that were used to destroy the jungles in Vietnam, and thus to deny hiding places to the enemy. It was interesting work, the man told me, a real challenge, and patriotic besides. Without the convenience of chemicals, the first white settlers in this region killed trees by stripping away a girdle of bark around the trunks, then felled the hulks with axes and saws, then shoved the wreckage into a pile and set it afire. I suspect the settlers' impulse was not much different from that of the power company or the army — to defeat the forest, erase the shadows, annihilate everything that might oppose our will.

You would think we had cleared a broad enough space to feel secure. But so long as we imagine nature as a realm apart from us, so long as we see wildness as menacing, so long as we crave absolute safety, comfort and control, we will never be able to rest. On my way out here this morning I passed several grunting bulldozers, stacks of blazing logs, freshly scalped fields, acres of new asphalt. If we did not see this assault going on around us everywhere, every day, we would recognize it for a kind of madness.

To the east, the horizon is broken by a relay tower, a white mast bearing orange dish antennas, like a steel bouquet. I have no idea what sort of signals those antennas catch and throw. The air is laced with our messages. I awoke this morning at six to a radio news item that set me in motion toward Cedar Bluffs. President Bush, I heard, is in Rio de Janeiro today for the Earth Summit, a conference charged with protecting the environment. Although this is the largest gathering of political leaders in history, our own President has gone there reluctantly, in order to avoid bad publicity. While in Rio, he will demand the weakening of a treaty designed to slow global warming, and he alone, among over a hundred heads of state, will refuse to sign a treaty aimed at protecting the diversity of life on earth. The radio quoted a White House official who justified these dire actions by saying that the President wishes to protect jobs in America.

Hearing that, I sat up in bed and shut off the radio and felt ashamed for my country, a nation which already consumes more than a quarter of the resources used up each year on the entire planet, which produces more than a quarter of the world's pollution, which has ransacked the natural wealth of a continent in two centuries, and all of this for the sake of fewer than five percent of the world's population.

Do not read the news, Thoreau advises; read the eternities. I hear in such news, if not eternity, at least the rumbling of a glacial greed that may well be crushing everything in its path beyond the lifetime of our grandchildren, beyond the lifetime of any sentences we lay down in books, far, far into the future.

Waking to such news, I could not bear to stay within walls, within the grid of streets, and so I came out here to renew my contact with a durable sanity. You can see that I have failed. There is sanity here, and beauty, but they are giving way under the pressure of our hunger. After living for thousands of generations in tiny settlements surrounded by wilderness, over the past half century humans have reduced wilderness to a scattering of remnants surrounded by our settlements. We draw lines around these few scraps and declare them parks, preserves, sanctuaries. Yet the deed of ownership to Cedar Bluffs, the wooden signs marking the boundaries, the attitude of respect that most visitors bring here, cannot protect this place. A true sanctuary is a sacred refuge, a holy place for worship. But there are no longer any refuges from our devices and desires. We treat nothing as holy except our pleasure and ease. We worship only ourselves.

Leaning down to sniff a wild rose, I smell instead the dew-damp ashes. It is as though we have built a great bonfire, and we are heaping onto it everything we can seize — hawks and herrings, swamps and mountains, rivers and soil. If I open a book written in our time, and I do not hear the crackle of flames, I soon close it again, not because I enjoy the reminder of havoc, but because I cannot take seriously an art that ignores this holocaust. We are quick to condemn our ancestors who ignored slavery or apartheid or pogroms or the abuse of women and children. Those who follow us, and inherit from us a severely damaged world, will surely look back on our time and ask what we were doing while the earth burned.

We are all parties to the devastation. I drove to Cedar Bluffs in a gasoline-powered car. The machine on which I write these words runs on electricity carried by those high-tension lines. The choice is not between innocence and guilt; the choice is between more or less complicity. How much do we drag to the bonfire? How much do we save from the flames?

From my lookout, I follow the path on along the rim of the bluff, then steeply back down toward the meadow, where the trail completes a loop. Partway down the slope I am clambering over an outcrop when I detect a flash of movement on the stone. I flinch to a halt, thinking *snake*. Then I see it is a salamander, bright blue stripe down the back and tail, its head cocked up to stare at me. The dark eyes gleam. Its pale throat pulses with breath. After a moment it darts away into a crevice, but for that instant there was a connection between us, a dim exchange, and I felt the force of our shared life. The moment will come back to me this evening when I read a passage from Meister Eckhart:

> if you want the kernel you must break the shell. And therefore if you want to discover nature's nakedness you must destroy its symbols, and the farther you get in the nearer you come to its essence. When you come to the One that gathers all things up into itself, there you must stay.

I have come to Cedar Bluff in search of nature's nakedness, hoping to be reassured by the grace and force and fleetness of creation; and the salamander has given me a token of that inexhaustible energy.

We cannot extinguish the source. The despair that brought me here is not for nature, which will go on, but for us and our companions. We have squandered so much wealth, have fed so ravenously, and yet our appetite still grows. If we destroy ourselves, and take a million species along with us, new forms of life will arise; but that is little consolation for those who love the given world.

As I close the loop of the trail and once more draw near to the road, I think about the snake I glimpsed at the beginning of my walk, and how a sudden fear set my heart pounding. Later today, back home, I will reread the poem in which D. H. Lawrence tells of meeting a snake at the water-trough one hot noon. He admired the creature, "earth-golden from the burning bowels of the earth." He felt honored, as though he had been granted an audience with a god. But then the voices of his education spoke up, telling him to hate the snake, to kill it, and so, as it slithered into a hole, he threw a log at the departing tail.

> And immediately I regretted it,
> I thought how paltry, how vulgar, what a mean act!
> I despised myself and the voices of my accursed
>   human education.

Here on the path, now, I remember only how swiftly Lawrence's wonder tuned to contempt, his reverence to hatred.

My own education speaks in me with contradictory voices. Some of those voices tell me that the day's headlines do not belong in literature, that numbers do not mix with words, that science is opposed to art; they tell me that fathers do not return from death in the bodies of red-tailed hawks; they tell me that nature is an alien realm, a warehouse of metaphors and scenery and raw materials; they tell me there is no one holy power that gathers all things into itself, that nothing is sacred apart from our sovereign minds, because God is a fiction we have outgrown. Some of those voices tell me that I should not have followed the loop trail through Cedar Bluffs, but instead should have trampled over the ground wherever my fancy might lead; and they tell me that I should not have stayed on the loop of this narrative, but should have dashed hither and yon, demonstrating my cleverness, dazzling the reader.

I resist these falsehoods with the strength of other voices calling to me, the voices of books and teachers and friends, of my own biology, of my soul. The books I live by, the teachers I honor, and the friends I seek are ones that return me to the creation with new awareness and respect. From the confusion of urges that are coiled in my genes, I welcome those that move me to taste the world without devouring it. And what of my soul? I use that antique word for lack of a better one, to point toward the feeling inwardness that binds me to salamander and oxeye daisy and snake, the same inwardness that binds me, friend or stranger, to you.

I have stayed on the trail through Cedar Bluffs so as not to bruise the fragile ground, and I have stayed on the loop of narrative so that you who read this might walk along with me. For what we need, all of us who go on two legs, is to reimagine our place in creation. We need to enlarge our conscience so as to bear, moment by moment, a regard for the integrity and bounty of the earth. There can be no sanctuaries unless we regain a deep sense of the sacred, no refuges unless we feel a reverence for the land, for soil and stone, water and air, and for all that lives. We must find the desire, the courage, the vision to live sanely, to live considerately, and we can only do that together, calling out and listening, listening and calling out.

Camille T. Dungy

WRITING HOME

This short autobiographical sketch introduces the ninth of ten "cycles" of poems that structure the powerful collection of African American nature poetry
that Camille Dungy gathered and arranged for her anthology *Black Nature*
(2009). This cycle, entitled "Growing out of This Land," includes many poems that, like poems throughout the anthology, emerge from strong cross-
currents of feeling, memory, and imagination. Thus, what Dungy says of her
own poetry applies to the poetry of many of her poet colleagues. "When I
write poems about the land and my place in it," she confesses, "they are informed by this fact: Sometimes the landscape is of little comfort. Sometimes
I want to run far away from home. . . . My poems about nature are informed
by displacement and oppression, but they are also informed by peace, by
self-possession."

   Dungy spent the formative years of her life in southern California. Some
have said that what happens in California will sooner or later happen everywhere else. Has what Dungy describes as her own experience overtaken
you as well? In what ways? How and to what extent did Dungy's experience prepare her not only for her life as a poet but also for her life as a citizen in the late Holocene Age? Can you see why nature poetry by African
Americans might speak more directly and pertinently to humanity's present
condition on the verge of the Anthropocene Age than some other nature
poetry does?

When I was a girl-child, home was a street called Bluff View, the uppermost
block in a terraced neighborhood of Southern California houses. In the summer, when I was young and untired and forced to bed before the sun went
down, my lullaby was the view my bedroom window afforded of the hills
behind my house. Desert oak, prickly pear, eucalyptus, sage: I fell asleep

....

From Camille T. Dungy, ed., *Black Nature: Four Centuries of African American Nature
Poetry* (Athens: University of Georgia Press, 2009), 283–85.

cataloging this place. In the daytime, I would scramble over one bluff and up the hill behind it, playing teacher in the caves my neighbors and I found, scratching lessons in the chalky sand that lined the walls. We played doctor with stethoscopes fashioned from rocks and the necklaced stalks of wild mustard. We knew the contours and passages of those hills like we knew the halls and classrooms of our other, inside, school. Walking down a slope is different than walking on flat land, and each part of my legs recorded required positions until they could move as correctly up and down those bluffs as my tongue might move over the alphabet. My body memorized its place in those hills.

But even while I lived at the center of everything I knew, everything I knew erased itself. Before I entered high school, construction had begun on summit estates for our town's growing mogul class. The hilltop was leveled and two of my favorite caves lost. From my bedroom window I could now see the red tile roof of the pizza king's palacio. Less desert oak. A weaker scent of sage. When my parents bought the house on Bluff View, our backyard marked the edge of human landscaping. It was not uncommon to find tumbleweed resting in our lounge chairs, to leave wild poppies blooming along the margins of cut grass. Now the hills were asphalt and ice plant. The wild dogs we called coyotes moved down into our backyards, fighting with raccoons over scraps from overturned trash cans and preying on small pets.

Development, in California, means the building of homes, the imposition of landscaping, the digging of pools. Development in California means controlling what exists and creating something new, something only the diversion of rivers for the maintenance of reservoirs can sustain. Development in California means the mass irrigation of newly planted lawns. Houses, houses everywhere and not a wild mustard field to see. Not even the acres of organized agriculture that first moneyed the region survive. The City of Orange in Orange County kept an orange tree in a fenced area, one skinny-branched specimen saved to represent the fields for which the region was named. I grew up on a street called Bluff View in the midst of California's ambition for development. When I write poems about nature, I am writing poems about loss. I am writing poems about discovering home where home has been replaced by structures I do not want to recognize. The place I was born into no longer exists. I don't have a town I can call home. Unless language is home. Unless, when I write, what had slipped away is found.

Once, I knew the silence and wind-cry of my California hills. In California, the sky speaks with a clipped tongue. Mountains shoulder into the conversation, the ocean sighs in frustration and that frustration rolls over us, is fog. Say the sky and the sea have been arguing all night. Say the mountain blanketed itself and withdrew into silence but the sky and the sea kept at it through the night. Say it is finally morning. When the ocean rolls its wave-blue eyes and sighs, no one will believe the bright points the sky still holds onto. When I lived in California, I was at home in the language of sky and mountaintop and sea. But what my parents came to California to find began to slip away and we moved away as well.

I found myself in Iowa and believed for a long time that I had lost my home. The language of place is a slow speech to learn. Iowa is blue uninterrupted, blue talking all day and a darker blue still talking through the night. Just the waist-high tips of new corn there to listen, and they not saying anything, only nodding their young heads. A new language. I moved to Iowa and didn't write for months. When a poem finally came, it was written in a different tongue.

Now it is half my lifetime since I lived on Bluff View, and I have traveled enough and moved enough to know that home is not a place. I am thinking perhaps home is not language either. Language is too easy to lose. Perhaps home is memory.

It is years later and I am a traveler, walking. I am on public land: a park, a knoll, a meadow. I am glad to own the memories I own and through those memories to belong someplace, to have some place to belong to me. I am remembering, and I am writing a poem in my many tongues. A poem having to do with comfort; something having to do with peace. Then a dog comes growling toward me. A dog with still tail and pointed ears. A dog with fanged mouth and purposeful eyes.

The sky is quiet, and the dog is barking, and someone the dog trusts and will obey says, *Sic her, sic.*

If memory is home, I am a long way from hope. I have escaped and am running. I have to remember what has been said: I am black and female; no place is for my pleasure. How do I write a poem about the land and my place in it without these memories: the runaway with the hounds are her heels; the complaint of the poplar at the man-cry of its load; land a thing to work but not to own? How do I write a poem about the land and my place in it without remembering, without shaping my words around, the history I belong to, the history that belongs to me? The dog drags me to fields of memory where I toil from *can* see to *can't.* When I write poems about the land and my place in it, they are informed by this fact: Sometimes the landscape is of little comfort. Sometimes I want to run far away from home.

When I was a child in the hills behind the street called Bluff View, I knew no threat nor fear. Development, the advancement of possession, had not pushed coyotes from the hillside into our backyards. My poems about nature are informed by displacement and oppression, but they are also informed by peace, by self-possession. When I was a child on Bluff View, the dogs we call bloodhounds, the slave trackers' tool, were nothing I knew to remember. I was a girl-child in that kingdom of open space, and all the land I could see and name and touch was mine to love. No one, no thing possessed another, nothing was developed apart from my heart. When I was a child in the hills behind the street called Bluff View, there was no such thing as history. Sometimes my poems rest again in that quiet space, that comfort.

The dog is closer and the woman repeats her command, but it is something all together different this time: *Sit, girl. Sit.*

What place, what words, what memories should I trust? Which direction will take me home?

Paul Laurence Dunbar

THE HAUNTED OAK

Paul Laurence Dunbar (1872–1906), the son of parents born into slavery in Kentucky, grew up in Ohio. Dunbar was a prolific poet, short story writer, novelist, and playwright. By the time of his death from tuberculosis at the age of thirty-three, he had become America's premier black poet. The tragic complexities of the relationship between many African Americans and the natural world form a major theme of Dunbar's poetry. Perhaps in no other poem are they so powerfully dramatized as in the ballad "The Haunted Oak." Dunbar gives the tree, standing in for nature, a voice in his poem in order to give the many ironies of the narrative a poignantly articulate intensity. How does the poem enable the reader to understand how looking at an oak tree might be a very different experience for a son of slaves than for a son of privilege and security? How are the tree in particular and nature in general characterized in this poem?

> Pray why you are so bare, so bare,
>   Oh, bough of the old oak-tree;
> And why, when I go through the shade you throw,
>   Runs a shudder over me?
>
> My leaves were green as the best, I trow,
>   And sap ran free in my veins,
> But I saw in the moonlight dim and weird
>   A guiltless victim's pains.
>
> I bent me down to hear his sigh;
>   I shook with his gurgling moan,

From Paul Laurence Dunbar, *The Collected Poetry of Paul Laurence Dunbar*, ed. Joanne M. Braxton (Charlottesville: University of Virginia Press, 1993), 219–20.

And I trembled sore when they rode away,
    And left him here alone.

They'd charged him with the old, old crime,
    And set him fast in jail:
Oh, why does the dog howl all night long,
    And why does the night wind wail?

He prayed his prayer and he swore his oath,
    And he raised his hand to the sky;
But the beat of hoofs smote on his ear,
    And the steady tread drew nigh.

Who is it rides by night, by night,
    Over the moonlit road?
And what is the spur that keeps the pace,
    What is the galling goad?

And now they beat at the prison door,
    "Ho, keeper, do not stay!
We are friends of him whom you hold within,
    And we fain would take him away

"From those who ride fast on our heels
    With mind to do him wrong;
They have no care for his innocence,
    And the rope they bear is long."

They have fooled the jailer with lying words,
    They have fooled the man with lies;
The bolts unbar, the locks are drawn,
    And the great door open flies.

Now they have taken him from the jail,
    And hard and fast they ride,
And the leader laughs low down in his throat,
    As they halt my trunk beside.

Oh, the judge, he wore a mask of black,
    And the doctor one of white,
And the minister, with his oldest son,
    Was curiously bedight.

Oh, foolish man, why weep you now?
    'Tis but a little space,
And the time will come when these shall dread
    The mem'ry of your face.

I feel the rope against my bark,
    And the weight of him in my grain,
I feel in the throe of his final woe
    The touch of my own last pain.

And never more shall leaves come forth
    On the bough that bears the ban;
I am burned with dread, I am dried and dead,
    From the curse of a guiltless man.

And ever the judge rides by, rides by,
    And goes to hunt the deer,
And ever another rides his soul
    In the guise of a mortal fear.

And ever the man he rides me hard,
    And never a night stays he;
For I feel his curse as a haunted bough,
    On the trunk of a haunted tree.

Wanda Coleman

REQUIEM FOR A NEST

Wanda Coleman, born in Los Angeles in 1946, lived for many years below the poverty line. Her poetry, as Tony Magistrale once summarized it in *Black American Literature Forum*, illuminates "the lives of the underclass and the disenfranchised, the invisible men and women who populate America's downtown streets after dark, the asylums and waystations, the inner city hospitals and clinics." That urban sensibility, at times imbued with a desperate and despairing tone, infuses Coleman's nature poems as well. The poem below focuses on a "winged thang" of nature in the midst of a "delusionally rural" environment. To what extent do this bird's life and sensibility represent our own at the end of the Holocene Age?

the winged thang built her dream palace
amid the fine green eyes of a sheltering bough
she did not know it was urban turf
disguised as serenely delusionally rural
nor did she know the neighborhood was rife
with slant-mawed felines and those long-taloned
swoopers of prey. she was ignorant of the acidity & oil
that slowly polluted the earth, and was never
to detect the serpent coiled one strong limb below

following her nature she flitted and dove
for whatever blades twigs and mud
could be found under the humming blue
and created a hatchery for her spawn
not knowing all were doomed

From Wanda Coleman, *Ostinato Vamps* (Pittsburgh: University of Pittsburgh Press, 2003), p. 14.

Anthony E. Walton

CARRION

The poet Anthony Walton, perhaps best known for his memoir *Mississippi: An American Journey*, is especially adept at showing how language sometimes conceals as much as it reveals. This duplicitous character of words often manifests itself in nature poetry and in place-names. "Carrion" offers a powerful demonstration of the violence we do to the natural world, then concealing it under the soothing language of hackneyed place-names. How do the jarring disjunctions in this poem enable the reader to see certain truths about human beings and the natural world of which they are a part? What is the tone of this poem and the speaker's attitude toward the subject? Does it inspire contemplation or action?

    Headless deer
        at milepost 55

    something like a beaver at the bridge
    over Route 83

    smashed meat and bone beyond recognition
    on the ramp to the frontage road

    to the mall, beyond

    there the plowed under, paved
    over fields —

      Beaver Ridge,
    Houston Farms, Woodland Acres —

Anthony Walton, "Carrion," *Ecotone* 3, no. 2 (2008): 35–36.

denuded and flat farmlands dreamt
into grids of Fox
      Hills and Apple
Valley, linked and speared by channeled
clearcuts linking cities, linking

states, roads — 88, 101, 95 accumulate
and stack like suburbs
on the horizons, while

raccoons lie blankly beside
porcupines; labyrinthine mess

of intestines, hair, eyes there
or not there, glowing

reflected light every half mile

Deer Park, Beaver Ridge, Forest Glen, Indian
Ridge

Natasha Trethewey

CARPENTER BEE

The Pulitzer Prize–winning poet Natasha Trethewey has focused much of her poetry on the lives of working-class men and women and marginalized people like prostitutes. The daughter of a mixed marriage, she has sometimes found herself doubly estranged and marginalized, an experience she has captured in some of her poetry. Though her nature poetry is relatively scant compared to her social poetry, she here writes a poem about identity and the complex relationship between human and other life. The speaker of the poem comes to identify with a carpenter bee, whose life and fate are intricately and perilously connected to the speaker's. Does the speaker feel responsible for the carpenter bee's fate? Are memory and change life-giving or death-dealing in the world of the poem? Or both? How are the fates of human and other life bound up with one another in the poem?

All winter long I have passed
beneath her nest — a hole no bigger
than the tip of my thumb.

Last year, before I was here,
she burrowed into the wood
framing my porch, drilled a network

of tunnels, her round body sturdy
for the work of building, Torpid
the cold months, she now pulls herself

out into the first warm days of spring
to tread the air outside my screen door,
floating in pure sunlight, humming

From Natasha Trethewey, *Domestic Work* (Minneapolis: Graywolf Press, 2000), 56–57.

against a backdrop of green. She too
must smell the wisteria, see
— with her hundreds of eyes — purple

blossoms lacing the trees. Flower-
hopping, she draws invisible lines,
the geometry of her flight. Drunk

on nectar, she can still find her way
back; though now, she must be
confused, disoriented, doubting even

her own homing instinct — this beeline,
now, to nowhere. Today, the workmen
have come, plugged the hole — her threshold —

covered it with thick white paint, a scent
acrid and unfamiliar. She keeps hovering,
buzzing around the spot. Watching her,

I think of what I've left behind, returned to,
only to find everything changed, nothing but
my memory intact — like her eggs, still inside,

each in its separate cell — snug, ordered, certain.

Winona LaDuke

OUR HOME ON EARTH

In his essay "Sanctuary," included earlier in this chapter, Scott Russell Sanders puts our sense of place at the very center of our identities. In the following excerpt from her E. F. Schumacher Lecture, delivered at Yale University in 1993, the environmental activist Winona LaDuke puts her own sense of place at the very center of her environmental ethic. "We cannot restore our relationship to the Earth until we find our place in the world. This is our challenge today: where is home?"

LaDuke's parents came from very different backgrounds. Her father was from the Ojibwe White Earth Reservation in Minnesota, and her mother, who was of Jewish European ancestry, was from the Bronx, New York. Though LaDuke moved around a great deal, she came to claim the White Earth Reservation as her true home, and she devoted a good deal of her life to attempting to reclaim some of the two hundred fifty thousand acres the reservation lost to the State of Minnesota and to preventing other forms of depredation on Native American lands through actions such as the Dakota Access Pipeline protests. In the piece excerpted here, LaDuke develops a powerful contrast between what she calls "indigenous thinking" and "industrial thinking." What are the similarities and differences between the contrast LaDuke develops here and Rasmussen's contrast between ecological and industrial civilizations in the letter to his grandson that opens this chapter? How might the two contrasts, taken together, help us to become better environmental citizens?

Giiwedinong means "going home" in the Anishinaabeg language — it also means North, which is the place from which we come. This is a key problem that modern industrial society faces today. We cannot restore our re-

Winona LaDuke, "Our Home on Earth," *On the Commons*, May 16, 2012, https://www.onthecommons.org/magazine/our-home-earth.

lationship with the Earth until we find our place in the world. This is our challenge today: where is home?

I returned to the White Earth Reservation in Minnesota about twenty-five years ago after being raised off-reservation, which is a common circumstance for our people. White Earth is my place in the Universe. It's where the headwaters of the Mississippi and the Red Rivers are.

People of the Land

Anishinaabeg is our name for ourselves in our own language, it means "people." We are called Ojibwe, referring to "ojibige" (meaning "to write") on our birch bark scrolls. Our aboriginal territory, and where we live today, is in the northern part of five US states and the southern part of four Canadian Provinces. We are people of lakes, rivers, deep woods and lush prairies.

Now, if you look at the United States, about 4 percent of the land is held by Indian people. But if you go to Canada, about 85 percent of the population north of the fiftieth parallel is native. If you look at the whole of North America, you'll find that the majority of the population is native in about a third of the continent. Within this larger area indigenous people maintain their own ways of living and their cultural practices.

There are a number of countries in the Western Hemisphere in which native peoples are the majority of the population: in Guatemala, Ecuador, Peru, and Bolivia. In some South American countries we control as much as 22 to 40 percent of the land. Overall, the Western Hemisphere is not predominately white. Indigenous people continue their ways of living based on generations and generations of knowledge and practice on the land.

On a worldwide scale there are about five thousand indigenous nations. Nations are groups of indigenous peoples who share common language, culture, history, territory and government institutions. It is said that there are currently about five hundred million of us in the world today, depending on how you define the term indigenous. I define it as peoples who have continued their way of living for thousands of years. In 2007 the United Nations finally passed the UN Declaration of the Rights of Indigenous Peoples, recognizing our unique status in the world. Four countries opposed this: the US, Canada, New Zealand and Australia. However, New Zealand recently signed this declaration.

Indigenous peoples believe fundamentally in a state of balance. We believe that all societies and cultural practices must exist in accordance with the laws of nature in order to be sustainable. We also believe that cultural diversity is as essential as biological diversity in maintaining sustainable societies. Indigenous people have lived on Earth sustainably for thousand of years, and I suggest to you that indigenous ways of living are the only sustainable ways of living. Most indigenous ceremonies, if you look to their essence, are about the restoration of balance — they are a reaffirmation of our relationship to creation. That is our intent: to restore, and then to retain balance and honor our part in creation.

Therefore, when I harvest wild rice on our reservation, I always offer asemaa (tobacco) because when you take something, you must always give thanks to its spirit for giving itself to you. We are very careful when we harvest. Anthropologists call this reciprocity. This means that when you take, you always give. We also say that you must take only what you need and leave the rest. Because if you take more than you need, you have brought about imbalance, you have been selfish. To do this in our community is a very big disgrace. It is a violation of natural law, and it leaves you with no guarantee that you will be able to continue harvesting.

We have a word in our language which describes the practice of living in harmony with natural law: minocimaatisiiwin. This word describes how you behave as an individual in a relationship with other individuals and in relationship with the land and all things. We have tried to retain this way of living and this way of thinking in spite of all that has happened to us over the centuries. I believe we do retain most of these practices in our community, even if they are overshadowed at times by individualism.

The Clash of Indigenous and Industrial Worldviews

I would like to contrast indigenous thinking with what I call "industrial thinking," which is characterized by five key ideas that run counter to what we as native people believe.

1. Instead of believing that natural law is preeminent, industrial society believes that humans are entitled to full dominion over nature. It believes that man — and it is usually man of course — has some God-given right to all that is around him. Industrial society puts its faith in man's laws: that pollution regulations, allowable catches, etc. are sustainable.
2. In indigenous societies, we notice that much in nature is cyclical: the movement of moons, the tides, the seasons, and our bodies. Time

itself is cyclical. Instead of modeling itself on the cyclical structure of nature, industrial society is patterned on linear thinking. Industrial society strives to continually move in one direction defined by things like technology and economic growth.

3. Industrial society holds a different attitude toward what is wild as opposed to what is cultivated or "tame." In our language we have the word indinawayuuganitoog (all our relations). That is what we believe — that our relatives may have wings, fins, roots or hooves. Industrial society believes wilderness must be tamed. This is also the idea behind colonialism: that some people have the right to civilize other people.

4. Industrial society speaks in a language of inanimate nouns. Things of all kinds are not spoken of as being alive and having spirit; they are described as mere objects, commodities. When things are inanimate, "man" can take them, buy and sell them, or destroy them. Some scholars refer to this as the "commodification of the sacred."

5. The last aspect of industrial thinking is the idea of capitalism itself (which is always unpopular to question in America). The capitalist goal is to use the least labor, capital, and resources to make the most profit. The intent of capitalism is accumulation. So the capitalist's method is always to take more than is needed. With accumulation as its core, industrial society practices conspicuous consumption. Indigenous societies, on the other hand, practice what I would call "conspicuous distribution." We focus on the potlatch — the act of giving away. In fact, the more you give away, the greater your honor.

Modern industrial societies must begin to see the interlocking interests between their own ability to survive and the survival of indigenous peoples' culture. Indigenous peoples have lived sustainably on the land for thousands of years. I am absolutely sure that our societies could live without yours, but I'm not so sure that your society can continue to live without ours.

Sustainability in Action

All across the continent there are small groups of native peoples who are trying to regain control of and restore their communities.

I'll use my own people as an example. The White Earth Reservation is thirty-six by thirty-six miles square, which is about 837,000 acres. A treaty reserved it for our people in 1867 in return for relinquishing a much larger area of northern Minnesota. Out of all our territory we chose this land for its richness and diversity. There are forty-seven lakes on the reservation. There's maple sugar, there are hardwoods, and there are all the different medicine plants my people use. We have wild rice, we have deer, we have beaver, we have fish — we have every food we need. On the eastern part of the reservation there are stands of white pine; to the west is prairieland where the buffalo once roamed. Our word for prairie is mashkode (place of burned medicine) referring to the native practices of burning as a form of nurturing the soil and plants.

Our traditional forms of land use and ownership are similar to those found in community land trusts being established today. The land is owned collectively, and each family has traditional areas where it fishes and hunts. We call our concept of land ownership Anishinaabeg akiing: "the land of the people," which doesn't imply that we own our land, but that we belong on it. Unfortunately, our definition doesn't stand up well in court because this country's legal system upholds the concept of private property.

We have maintained our land by means of careful management. For example, we traditionally have "hunting bosses" and "rice chiefs," who make sure that resources are used sustainably in each region. Hunting bosses oversee rotation of trap lines, a system by which people trap in an area for two years and then move to a different area to let the land rest. Rice chiefs coordinate wild rice harvesting. The rice on each lake has its own unique taste and ripens at its own time. Traditionally, we have a "tallyman," who makes sure there are enough animals for each family in a given area. If a family can't sustain itself, the tallyman moves them to a new place where animals are more plentiful. These practices are essential to sustainability, and to maintaining what some now call the commons.

The Loss of White Earth, and How We Plan to Get It Back

Our reservation was reserved by treaty in 1867. In 1887 the Nelson Act and subsequently the General Allotment Act was passed to teach Indians the concept of private property, but also to facilitate the removal of more land from Indian Nations. The federal government divided our reservation into eighty-acre parcels of land and allotted each parcel to an individual Indian, hoping that this would somehow force us to become farmers and adopt the notion of progress — in short, to be civilized.

The allotment system was alien to our traditional concepts of land. In our society a person harvested rice in one place, trapped in another place, gathered medicines in a third place, and picked berries in a fourth. These locations depended on the ecosystem; they were not necessarily contiguous. But the government said to each Indian, "Here are your eighty acres; this is where you'll live." Then, after each Indian had received an allotment, the rest of the land was declared "surplus" and given to white people to homestead or "develop." What happened to my reservation happened to reservations all across the country.

The state of Minnesota took our pine forests away and sold them to timber companies, and then taxed us for the land that was left. When the Indians couldn't pay the taxes, the state confiscated the land. But how could these people pay taxes? In 1910, they could not even read or write English.

I'll tell you a story about how my great-grandma was cheated by a loan shark. She lived on Many-Point Lake, where she was allotted land. She had run up a bill at the local store because she was waiting until fall when she could get some money from wild rice harvesting and a payment coming from a treaty annuity. So she went to a land speculator named Lucky Waller, and she said, "I need to pay this bill." She asked to borrow fifty bucks from him until fall, and he said: "Okay, you can do that. Just sign here and I'll loan you that fifty bucks." So she signed with the thumbprint and went back to her house on Many-Point Lake. About three months later she was ready to repay him the fifty bucks, and the loan shark said: "No, you keep that money. I bought your land from you." He had purchased her eighty acres on Many-Point Lake for fifty bucks. Today that location is a Boy Scout Camp.

The White Earth Reservation lost two hundred and fifty thousand acres to the state of Minnesota because of unpaid taxes. By 1920, 99 percent of the original White Earth Reservation land was in non-Indian hands. This was done to native peoples across the country.

We have exhausted all legal recourse for getting back our land. The Federal Circuit Court ruled that to regain their land Indian people had to have filed a lawsuit within seven years of the original time of taking. Still, we believe that we must get our land back. We really do not have any other place to go. That's why we started the White Earth Land Recovery Project. Our project is like several other projects in Indian communities. We are not trying to displace people who have settled there. A third of our land is held by federal, state and county governments. That land should just be returned to us. It certainly would not displace anyone. Some of the privately held land on our reservation is held by absentee landholders — many of whom have never seen that land; they do not even know where it is. It is a commodity to them, not home. We hope to persuade them to return it to us.

Our project also works to reacquire our land. We bought some land as a site for a roundhouse, a building that holds one of our ceremonial drums. We bought back our burial grounds, which were on private land, because we believe that we should hold the land where our ancestors rest. We purchased a former elementary school, which is now the home of our new radio station and a wind turbine. In 2009, which is the 20th anniversary of our project, we had acquired 1,400 acres. We use some of this land to grow and gather sustainable products that we sell: wild rice, maple syrup and candy, berry jams, and Birch bark crafts.

Sustainable Communities, Not Sustainable Development

In conclusion, I want to say there is no such things as sustainable development. Community is the only thing in my experience that is sustainable. We all need to be involved in building communities — not solely focused on developing things. We can each do that in our own way, whether it is European-American communities or indigenous communities, by restoring a way of life that is based on the land.

The only way you can manage a commons is if you share enough cultural experiences and values so that what you take out of nature doesn't upset the natural balance — minobimaatisiiwin, as we call it. The reason native cultures have remained sustainable for all these centuries is that we are cohesive communities. A common set of values is needed to live together on the land.

Finally, I believe industrial societies continue to consume too much of the world's resources. When you need that many resources, it means constant intervention in other peoples' land and other peoples' countries. It is meaningless to talk about human rights unless you talk about consumption. In order for native communities to live and teach the world about sustainability, the dominant society must change. If modern society continues in the direction it is going, indigenous people's way of life will continue to bear the consequences.

Wangari Maathai

NOBEL PEACE PRIZE LECTURE

Planting some thirty million trees was at the heart of the women's Green Belt Movement that Kenyan Nobel laureate Wangari Maathai helped to start. These trees were themselves both the key to the health of Kenya's land and people and the symbol of the good environmental citizenship the land so needed. In her 2004 Nobel Peace Prize lecture, Maathai (1940–2011) describes a citizen education program designed to show how personal matters of identity and choice are best understood and configured as communal matters of solidarity and ecological responsibility. In keeping with a widespread African tradition, "the tree also became a symbol for peace and conflict resolution . . . and during the re-writing of the Kenyan constitution, similar trees of peace were planted in many parts of the country to promote a culture of peace." What are the similarities and differences between the way trees figure in the second Hebrew creation myth from Genesis 2 below; the tree in Paul Dunbar's ballad above, "The Haunted Oak"; and the actual trees that the Green Belt Movement planted? How might each of these different depictions of trees deepen and advance our reflections about our obligation to future human and other life?

Your Majesties
Your Royal Highnesses
Honorable Members of the Norwegian Nobel Committee
Excellencies
Ladies and Gentlemen

I stand before you and the world humbled by this recognition and uplifted by the honor of being the 2004 Nobel Peace Laureate.

As the first African woman to receive this prize, I accept it on behalf of the

Wangari Maathai, "Nobel Peace Prize Lecture" (Oslo, December 10, 2004), www.nobel prize.org/prizes/peace/2004/maathai/26050-wangari-maathai-nobel-lecture-2004/.

people of Kenya and Africa, and indeed the world. I am especially mindful of women and the girl child. I hope it will encourage them to raise their voices and take more space for leadership. I know the honor also gives a deep sense of pride to our men, both old and young. As a mother, I appreciate the inspiration this brings to the youth and urge them to use it to pursue their dreams.

Although this prize comes to me, it acknowledges the work of countless individuals and groups across the globe. They work quietly and often without recognition to protect the environment, promote democracy, defend human rights and ensure equality between women and men. By so doing, they plant seeds of peace. I know they, too, are proud today. To all who feel represented by this prize I say use it to advance your mission and meet the high expectations the world will place on us.

This honor is also for my family, friends, partners and supporters throughout the world. All of them helped shape the vision and sustain our work, which was often accomplished under hostile conditions. I am also grateful to the people of Kenya — who remained stubbornly hopeful that democracy could be realized and their environment managed sustainably. Because of this support, I am here today to accept this great honor.

I am immensely privileged to join my fellow African Peace laureates, Presidents Nelson Mandela and F. W. de Klerk, Archbishop Desmond Tutu, the late Chief Albert Luthuli, the late Anwar el-Sadat and the UN Secretary General, Kofi Annan.

I know that African people everywhere are encouraged by this news. My fellow Africans, as we embrace this recognition, let us use it to intensify our commitment to our people, to reduce conflicts and poverty and thereby improve their quality of life. Let us embrace democratic governance, protect human rights and protect our environment. I am confident that we shall rise to the occasion. I have always believed that solutions to most of our problems must come from us.

In this year's prize, the Norwegian Nobel Committee has placed the critical issue of environment and its linkage to democracy and peace before the world. For their visionary action, I am profoundly grateful. Recognizing that sustainable development, democracy and peace are indivisible is an idea whose time has come. Our work over the past 30 years has always appreciated and engaged these linkages.

My inspiration partly comes from my childhood experiences and observations of Nature in rural Kenya. It has been influenced and nurtured by the formal education I was privileged to receive in Kenya, the United States and Germany. As I was growing up, I witnessed forest being cleared and replaced by commercial plantations, which destroyed local biodiversity and the capacity of the forests to conserve water.

Excellencies, ladies and gentlemen, in 1977, when we started the Green Belt Movement, I was partly responding to needs identified by rural women, namely lack of firewood, clean drinking water, balanced diets, shelter and income.

Throughout Africa, women are the primary caretakers, holding significant responsibility for tilling the land and feeding their families. As a result, they are often the first to become aware of environmental damage as resources become scarce and incapable of sustaining their families.

The women we worked with recounted that unlike in the past, they were unable to meet their basic needs. This was due to the degradation of their immediate environment as well as the introduction of commercial farming, which replaced the growing of household food crops. But international trade controlled the price of the exports from these small-scale farmers and a reasonable and just income could not be guaranteed. I came to understand that when the environment is destroyed, plundered or mismanaged, we undermine our quality of life and that of future generations.

Tree planting became a natural choice to address some of the initial basic needs identified by women. Also, tree planting is simple, attainable and guarantees quick, successful results within a reasonable amount of time. This sustains interest and commitment.

So, together, we have planted over 30 million trees that provide fuel, food, shelter, and income to support their children's education and household needs. The activity also creates employment and improves soils and watersheds. Through their involvement, women gain some degree of power over their lives, especially their social and economic position and relevance in the family. This work continues.

Initially, the work was difficult because historically our people have been persuaded to believe that because they are poor, they lack not only capital, but also knowledge and skills to address their challenges. Instead they are conditioned to believe that solutions to their problems must come from "outside." Further, women did not realize that meeting their needs depended on their environment being healthy and well managed. They were also unaware that a degraded environment leads to a scramble for scarce resources and may culminate in poverty and even conflict. They were also unaware of the injustices of international economic arrangements.

In order to assist communities to understand these linkages, we developed a citizen education program, during which people identify their problems, the causes and possible solutions. They then make connections between their own personal actions and the problems they witness in the environment and in society. They learn that our world is confronted with a litany of woes: corruption, violence against women and children, disruption and breakdown of families, and disintegration of cultures and communities. They also identify the abuse of drugs and chemical substances, especially among young people. There are also devastating diseases that are defying cures or occurring in epidemic proportions. Of particular concern are HIV/AIDS, malaria and diseases associated with malnutrition.

On the environmental front, they are exposed to many human activities that are devastating to the environment and societies. These include widespread destruction of ecosystems, especially through deforestation, climatic instability, and contamination in the soils and waters that all contribute to excruciating poverty.

In the process, the participants discover that they must be part of the solutions. They realize their hidden potential and are empowered to overcome inertia and take action. They come to recognize that they are the primary custodians and beneficiaries of the environment that sustains them.

Entire communities also come to understand that while it is necessary to hold their governments accountable, it is equally important that in their own relationships with each other, they exemplify the leadership values they wish to see in their own leaders, namely justice, integrity and trust.

Although initially the Green Belt Movement's tree planting activities did not address issues of democracy and peace, it soon became clear that responsible governance of the environment was impossible without democratic space. Therefore, the tree became a symbol for the democratic struggle in Kenya. Citizens were mobilized to challenge widespread abuses of power, corruption and environmental mismanagement. In Nairobi's Uhuru Park, at Freedom Corner, and in many parts of the country, trees of peace were planted to demand the release of prisoners of conscience and a peaceful transition to democracy.

Through the Green Belt Movement, thousands of ordinary citizens were mobilized and empowered to take action and effect change. They learned to overcome fear and a sense of helplessness and moved to defend democratic rights.

In time, the tree also became a symbol for peace and conflict resolution, especially during ethnic conflicts in Kenya when the Green Belt Movement used peace trees to reconcile disputing communities. During the ongoing re-writing of the Kenyan constitution, similar trees of peace were planted in many parts of the country to promote a culture of peace. Using trees as a symbol of peace is in keeping with a widespread African tradition. For example, the elders of the Kikuyu carried a staff from the *thigi* tree that, when placed between two disputing sides, caused them to stop fighting and seek reconciliation. Many communities in Africa have these traditions.

Such practices are part of an extensive cultural heritage, which contributes both to the conservation of habitats and to cultures of peace. With the destruction of these cultures and the introduction of new values, local biodiversity is no longer valued or protected and as a result, it is quickly degraded and disappears. For this reason, the Green Belt Movement explores the concept of cultural biodiversity, especially with respect to indigenous seeds and medicinal plants.

As we progressively understood the causes of environmental degradation, we saw the need for good governance. Indeed, the state of any country's environment is a reflection of the kind of governance in place, and without good governance there can be no peace. Many countries, which have poor governance systems, are also likely to have conflicts and poor laws protecting the environment.

In 2002, the courage, resilience, patience and commitment of members of the Green Belt Movement, other civil society organizations, and the Kenyan public culminated in the peaceful transition to a democratic government and laid the foundation for a more stable society.

Excellencies, friends, ladies and gentlemen, it is 30 years since we started this work. Activities that devastate the environment and societies continue unabated. Today we are faced with a challenge that calls for a shift in our thinking, so that humanity stops threatening its life-support system. We are called to assist the Earth to heal her wounds and in the process heal our own — indeed, to embrace the whole creation in all its diversity, beauty and wonder. This will happen if we see the need to revive our sense of belonging to a larger family of life, with which we have shared our evolutionary process.

In the course of history, there comes a time when humanity is called to shift to a new level of consciousness, to reach a higher moral ground. A time when we have to shed our fear and give hope to each other.

That time is now.

The Norwegian Nobel Committee has challenged the world to broaden the understanding of peace: there can be no peace without equitable development; and there can be no development without sustainable management of the environment in a democratic and peaceful space. This shift is an idea whose time has come.

I call on leaders, especially in Africa, to expand democratic space and build fair and just societies that allow the creativity and energy of their citizen to flourish.

Those of us who have been privileged to receive education, skills, and experiences and even power must be role models for the next generation of leadership. In this regard, I would also like to appeal for the freedom of my fellow laureate Aung San Suu Kyi so that she can continue her work for peace and democracy for the people of Burma and the world at large.

Culture plays a central role in the political, economic and social life of communities. Indeed, culture may be the missing link in the development of Africa. Culture is dynamic and evolves over time, consciously discarding retrogressive traditions, like female genital mutilation (FGM) and embracing aspects that are good and useful.

Africans, especially, should re-discover positive aspects of their culture. In accepting them, they would give themselves a sense of belonging, identity and self-confidence.

Ladies and gentlemen, there is also a need to galvanize civil society and grassroots movements to catalyze change. I call upon governments to recognize the role of these social movements in building a critical mass of responsible citizens, who help maintain checks and balances in society. On their part, civil society should embrace not only their rights but also their responsibilities.

Further, industry and global institutions must appreciate that ensuring economic justice, equity and ecological integrity are of greater value than profits at any cost.

The extreme global inequities and prevailing consumption patterns continue at the expense of the environment and peaceful co-existence. The choice is ours.

I would like to call on young people to commit themselves to activities that contribute toward achieving their long-term dreams. They have the energy and creativity to shape a sustainable future. To the young people I say, you are a gift to your communities and indeed the world. You are our hope and our future.

The holistic approach to development, as exemplified by the Green Belt Movement, could be embraced and replicated in more parts of Africa and beyond. It is for this reason that I have established the Wangari Maathai Foundation to ensure the continuation and expansion of these activities. Although a lot has been achieved, much remains to be done.

Excellencies, ladies and gentlemen, as I conclude I reflect on my childhood experience when I would visit a stream next to our home to fetch water for my mother. I would drink water straight from the stream. Playing among the arrowroot leaves I tried in vain to pick up the strands of frogs' eggs, believing they were beads. But every time I put my little fingers under them they would break. Later, I saw thousands of tadpoles: black, energetic and wriggling through the clear water against the background of the brown earth. This is the world I inherited from my parents.

Today, over 50 years later, the stream has dried up, women walk long distances for water, which is not always clean, and children will never know what they have lost. The challenge is to restore the home of the tadpoles and give back to our children a world of beauty and wonder.

Thank you very much.

Pope Francis

LAUDATO SI'

The title of the papal encyclical letter excerpted below, *Laudato Si'* (Praise Be to You), is taken from the "Canticle of the Creatures," also known as the "Canticle to the Sun" or "The Hymn of St. Francis of Assisi." The first of the three excerpts below outlines the relationship between human beings and the rest of creation, from the vantage point of what the pope calls "the Gospel of Creation." The vision that informs this section of the letter, entitled "The Message of Each Creature in the Harmony of Creation," draws on contributions from Catholics all over the world. The second excerpt comes from chapter 3, "The Human Roots of the Ecological Crisis." In this section, Pope Francis develops a critical account of our present consciousness, which he calls the "technocratic paradigm." The third and final section moves from theological reflection and cultural analysis and critique to a call for action. Throughout the encyclical, Pope Francis emphasizes the heightened impact of environmental degradation on those who live in economic poverty.

Where and how do you see Pope Francis drawing on two of the vocabularies explored earlier in *Leading Lives That Matter*: the vocabulary of virtue and the vocabulary of vocation? Do you find yourself captivated by the technocratic paradigm? Which of the ecological virtues give shape to your character, as embodied in your own thoughts and actions?

How does the pope's theological understanding of the relation between human and other life compare and contrast to other views, such as the ones advanced by Winona LaDuke and Scott Russell Sanders? For that matter, how does his use of the canticle of St. Francis compare to what we find in the full text of that thirteenth-century hymn? Note that the part quoted by the pope ends before the following stanza: "Praise be You, my Lord, through our Sister, / Mother Earth / Who sustains and governs us, / Producing various fruits with coloured flowers and herbs."

....

From Pope Francis, *Laudato Si': On Care for Our Common Home* (Huntington, IN: Our Sunday Visitor, 2015), 58–61, 69–78, 136–40.

Might the idea that "Mother Earth . . . governs us" verge too close to the kind of biocentrism Pope Francis opposes?

The Message of Each Creature in the Harmony of Creation

84. Our insistence that each human being is an image of God should not make us overlook the fact that each creature has its own purpose. None is superfluous. The entire material universe speaks of God's love, his boundless affection for us. Soil, water, mountain: everything is, as it were, a caress of God. The history of our friendship with God is always linked to particular places which take on an intensely personal meaning; we all remember places, and revisiting those memories does us much good. Anyone who has grown up in the hills or used to sit by that spring to drink, or played outdoors in the neighborhood square; going back to these places is a chance to recover something of their true selves.

85. God has written a precious book, "whose letters are the multitude of created things present in the universe." The Canadian bishops rightly pointed out that no creature is excluded from this manifestation of God: "From panoramic vistas to the tiniest living form, nature is a constant source of wonder and awe. It is also a continuing revelation of the divine." The bishops of Japan, for their part, made a thought-provoking observation: "To sense each creature singing the hymn of its existence is to live joyfully in God's love and hope." This contemplation of creation allows us to discover in each thing a teaching which God wishes to hand on to us, since "for the believer, to contemplate creation is to hear a message, to listen to a paradoxical and silent voice." We can say that "alongside revelation properly so-called contained in sacred Scripture, there is a divine manifestation in the blaze of the sun and the fall of night." Paying attention to this manifestation, we learn to see ourselves in relation to all other creatures: "I express myself in expressing the world; in my effort to decipher the sacredness of the world, I explore my own."

86. The universe as a whole, in all its manifold relationships, shows forth the inexhaustible riches of God. Saint Thomas Aquinas wisely noted that multiplicity and variety "come from the intention of the first agent" who willed that "what was wanting to one in the representation of the divine goodness might be supplied by another," inasmuch as God's goodness "could not be represented fittingly by any one creature." Hence we need to grasp the variety of things in their multiple relationships. We understand better

the importance and meaning of each creature if we contemplate it within the entirety of God's plan. As the *Catechism* teaches: "God wills the interdependence of creatures. The sun and the moon, the cedar and the little flower, the eagle and the sparrow: the spectacle of their countless diversities and inequalities tells us that no creature is self-sufficient. Creatures exist only in dependence on each other, to complete each other, in the service of each other."

87. When we can see God reflected in all that exists, our hearts are moved to praise the Lord for all his creatures and to worship him in union with them. This sentiment finds magnificent expression in the hymn of Saint Francis of Assisi:

> Praised be you, my Lord, with all your creatures,
> especially Sir Brother Sun,
> who is the day and through whom you give us light.
> And he is beautiful and radiant with great splendor;
> and bears a likeness to you, Most High.
> Praised be you, my Lord, through Sister Moon and the stars,
> in heaven you formed them clear and precious and beautiful.
> Praised be you, my Lord, through Brother Wind,
> and through the air, cloudy and serene, and every kind of
>   weather
> through whom you give sustenance to your creatures.
> Praised be you, my Lord, through Sister Water,
> who is very useful and humble and precious and chaste.
> Praised be you, my Lord, through Brother Fire,
> through whom you light the night,
> and he is beautiful and playful and robust and strong.

88. The bishops of Brazil have pointed out that nature as a whole not only manifests God but is also a locus of his presence. The Spirit of life dwells in every living creature and calls us to enter into relationship with him. Discovering this presence leads us to cultivate the "ecological virtues." This is not to forget that there is an infinite distance between God and the things of this world, which do not possess his fullness. Otherwise, we would not be doing the creatures themselves any good either, for we would be failing to acknowledge their right and proper place. We would end up unduly demanding of them something which they, in their smallness, cannot give us. . . .

The Human Roots of the Ecological Crisis

101. It would hardly be helpful to describe symptoms without acknowledging the human origins of the ecological crisis. A certain way of understanding human life and activity has gone awry, to the serious detriment of the world around us. Should we not pause and consider this? At this stage, I propose that we focus on the dominant technocratic paradigm and the place of human beings and of human action in the world.

Technology: Creativity and Power

102. Humanity has entered a new era in which our technical prowess has brought us to a crossroads. We are the beneficiaries of two centuries of enormous waves of change: steam engines, railways, the telegraph, electricity, automobiles, airplanes, chemical industries, modern medicine, information technology and, more recently, the digital revolution, robotics, biotechnologies and nanotechnologies. It is right to rejoice in these advances and to be excited by the immense possibilities which they continue to open up before us, for "science and technology are wonderful products of God-given human creativity." The modification of nature for useful purposes has distinguished the human family from the beginning; technology itself "expresses the inner tension that impels man gradually to overcome material limitations." Technology has remedied countless evils which used to harm and limit human beings. How can we not feel gratitude and appreciation for this progress, especially in the fields of medicine, engineering and communications? How could we not acknowledge the work of many scientists and engineers who have provided alternatives to make development sustainable?

103. Technoscience, when well directed, can produce important means of improving the quality of human life, from useful domestic appliances to great transportation systems, bridges, buildings and public spaces. It can also produce art and enable men and women immersed in the material world to "leap" into the world of beauty. Who can deny the beauty of an aircraft or a skyscraper? Valuable works of art and music now make use of new technologies. So, in the beauty intended by the one who uses new technical instruments and in the contemplation of such beauty, a quantum leap occurs, resulting in a fulfillment which is uniquely human.

104. Yet it must be also recognized that nuclear energy, biotechnology, information technology, knowledge of our DNA, and many other abilities which we have acquired, have given us tremendous power. More precisely,

they have given those with the knowledge, and especially the economic resources to use them, an impressive dominance over the whole of humanity
and the entire world. Never has humanity had such power over itself, yet
nothing ensures that it will be used wisely, particularly when we consider
how it is currently being used. We need but think of the nuclear bombs
dropped in the middle of the twentieth century, or the array of technology
which Nazism, Communism and other totalitarian regimes have employed
to kill millions of people, to say nothing of the increasingly deadly arsenal of
weapons available for modern warfare. In whose hands does all this power
lie, or will it eventually end up? It is extremely risky for a small part of
humanity to have it.

105. There is a tendency to believe that every increase in power means
"an increase of 'progress' itself," an advance in "security, usefulness, welfare
and vigor . . . an assimilation of new values into the stream of culture," as
if reality, goodness and truth automatically flow from technological and
economic power as such. The fact is that "contemporary man has not been
trained to use power well," because our immense technological development
has not been accompanied by a development in human responsibility, values
and conscience. Each age tends to have only a meager awareness of its own
limitations. It is possible that we do not grasp the gravity of the challenges
now before us. "The risk is growing day by day that man will not use his
power as he should"; in effect, "power is never considered in terms of the
responsibility of choice which is inherent in freedom" since its "only norms
are taken from alleged necessity, from either utility or security." But human beings are not completely autonomous. Our freedom fades when it is
handed over to the blind forces of the unconscious, of immediate needs, of
self-interest, and of violence. In this sense, we stand naked and exposed in
the face of our ever-increasing power, lacking the wherewithal to control
it. We have certain superficial mechanisms, but we cannot claim to have a
sound ethics, a culture and spirituality genuinely capable of setting limits
and teaching clear-minded self-restraint.

The Globalization of the Technocratic Paradigm

106. The basic problem goes even deeper: it is the way that humanity has
taken up technology and its development *according to an undifferentiated
and one-dimensional paradigm.* This paradigm exalts the concept of a subject
who, using logical and rational procedures, progressively approaches and
gains control over an external object. This subject makes every effort to

establish the scientific and experimental method, which in itself is already a technique of possession, mastery and transformation. It is as if the subject were to find itself in the presence of something formless, completely open to manipulation. Men and women have constantly intervened in nature, but for a long time this meant being in tune with and respecting the possibilities offered by the things themselves. It was a matter of receiving what nature itself allowed, as if from its own hand. Now, by contrast, we are the ones to lay our hands on things, attempting to extract everything possible from them while frequently ignoring or forgetting the reality in front of us. Human beings and material objects no longer extend a friendly hand to one another; the relationship has become confrontational. This has made it easy to accept the idea of infinite or unlimited growth, which proves so attractive to economists, financiers and experts in technology. It is based on the lie that there is an infinite supply of the earth's goods, and this leads to the planet being squeezed dry beyond every limit. It is the false notion that "an infinite quantity of energy and resources are available, that it is possible to renew them quickly, and that the negative effects of the exploitation of the natural order can be easily absorbed."

107. It can be said that many problems of today's world stem from the tendency, at times unconscious, to make the method and aims of science and technology an epistemological paradigm which shapes the lives of individuals and the workings of society. The effects of imposing this model on reality as a whole, human and social, are seen in the deterioration of the environment, but this is just one sign of the reductionism which affects every aspect of human and social life. We have to accept that technological products are not neutral, for they create a framework which ends up conditioning lifestyles and shaping social possibilities along the lines dictated by the interest of certain powerful groups. Decisions which may seem purely instrumental are in reality decisions about the kind of society we want to build.

108. The idea of promoting a different cultural paradigm and employing technology as a mere instrument is nowadays inconceivable. The technological paradigm has become so dominant that it would be difficult to do without its resources and even more difficult to utilize them without being dominated by their internal logic. It has become countercultural to choose a lifestyle whose goals are even partly independent of technology, of its costs and its power to globalize and make us all the same. Technology tends to absorb everything into its ironclad logic, and those who are surrounded with technology "know full well that it moves forward in the final analysis neither for profit nor for the well-being of the human race," that "in the most radical

sense of the term power is its motive — a lordship over all." As a result, "man seizes hold of the naked elements of both nature and human nature." Our capacity to make decisions, a more genuine freedom and the space for each one's alternative creativity are diminished.

109. The technocratic paradigm also tends to dominate economic and political life. The economy accepts every advance in technology with a view to profit, without concern for its potentially negative impact on human beings. Finance overwhelms the real economy. The lessons of the global financial crisis have not been assimilated, and we are learning all too slowly the lessons of environmental deterioration. Some circles maintain that current economics and technology will solve all environmental problems, and argue, in popular and non-technical terms, that the problems of global hunger and poverty will be resolved simply by market growth. They are less concerned with certain economic theories, which today scarcely anybody dares defend, than with their actual operation in the functioning of the economy. They may not affirm such theories with words, but nonetheless support them with their deeds by showing no interest in more balanced levels of production, a better distribution of wealth, concern for the environment and the rights of future generations. Their behavior shows that for them, maximizing profits is enough. Yet by itself the market cannot guarantee integral human development and social inclusion. At the same time, we have "a sort of 'superdevelopment' of a wasteful and consumerist kind which forms an unacceptable contrast with the ongoing situations of dehumanizing deprivation," while we are all too slow in developing economic institutions and social initiatives which can give the poor regular access to basic resources. We fail to see the deepest roots of our present failures, which have to do with the direction, goals, meaning and social implications of technological and economic growth.

110. The specialization which belongs to technology makes it difficult to see the larger picture. The fragmentation of knowledge proves helpful for concrete applications, and yet it often leads to a loss of appreciation for the whole, for the relationships between things, and for the broader horizon, which then becomes irrelevant. This very fact makes it hard to find adequate ways of solving the more complex problems of today's world, particularly those regarding the environment and the poor; these problems cannot be dealt with from a single perspective or from a single set of interests. A science which would offer solutions to the great issues would necessarily have to take into account the data generated by other fields of knowledge, including philosophy and social ethics; but this is a difficult

habit to acquire today. Nor are there genuine ethical horizons to which one can appeal. Life gradually becomes a surrender to situations conditioned by technology, itself viewed as the principal key to the meaning of existence. In the concrete situation confronting us, there are a number of symptoms which point to what is wrong, such as environmental degradation, anxiety, a loss of the purpose of life and of community living. Once more we see that "realities are more important than ideas."

111. Ecological culture cannot be reduced to a series of urgent and partial responses to the immediate problems of pollution, environmental decay and the depletion of natural resources. There needs to be a distinctive way of looking at things, a way of thinking, policies, an educational program, a lifestyle and a spirituality which together generate resistance to the assault of the technocratic paradigm. Otherwise, even the best ecological initiatives can find themselves caught up in the same globalized logic. To seek only a technical remedy to each environmental problem which comes up is to separate what is in reality interconnected and to mask the true and deepest problems of the global system.

112. Yet we can once more broaden our vision. We have the freedom needed to limit and direct technology; we can put it at the service of another type of progress, one which is healthier, more human, more social, more integral. Liberation from the dominant technocratic paradigm does in fact happen sometimes, for example, when cooperatives of small producers adopt less polluting means of production, and opt for a non-consumerist model of life, recreation and community. Or when technology is directed primarily to resolving people's concrete problems, truly helping them live with more dignity and less suffering. Or indeed when the desire to create and contemplate beauty manages to overcome reductionism through a kind of salvation which occurs in beauty and in those who behold it. An authentic humanity, calling for a new synthesis, seems to dwell in the midst of our technological culture, almost unnoticed, like a mist seeping gently beneath a closed door. Will the promise last, in spite of everything, with all that is authentic rising up in stubborn resistance?

113. There is also the fact that people no longer seem to believe in a happy future; they no longer have blind trust in a better tomorrow based on the present state of the world and our technical abilities. There is a growing awareness that scientific and technological progress cannot be equated with the progress of humanity and history, a growing sense that the way to a better future lies elsewhere. This is not to reject the possibilities which technology continues to offer us. But humanity has changed profoundly, and the

accumulation of constant novelties exalts a superficiality which pulls us in one direction. It becomes difficult to pause and recover depth in life. If architecture reflects the spirit of an age, our megastructures and drab apartment blocks express the spirit of globalized technology, where a constant flood of new products coexists with a tedious monotony. Let us refuse to resign ourselves to this, and continue to wonder about the purpose and meaning of everything. Otherwise we would simply legitimate the present situation and need new forms of escapism to help us endure the emptiness.

114. All of this shows the urgent need for us to move forward in a bold cultural revolution. Science and technology are not neutral; from the beginning to the end of a process, various intentions and possibilities are in play and can take on distinct shapes. Nobody is suggesting a return to the Stone Age, but we do need to slow down and look at reality in a different way, to appropriate the positive and sustainable progress which has been made, but also to recover the values and the great goals swept away by our unrestrained delusions of grandeur. . . .

Educating for the Covenant between Humanity and the Environment

209. An awareness of the gravity of today's cultural and ecological crisis must be translated into new habits. Many people know that our current progress and the mere amassing of things and pleasures are not enough to give meaning and joy to the human heart, yet they feel unable to give up what the market sets before them. In those countries which should be making the greatest changes in consumer habits, young people have a new ecological sensitivity and a generous spirit, and some of them are making admirable efforts to protect the environment. At the same time, they have grown up in a milieu of extreme consumerism and affluence which makes it difficult to develop other habits. We are faced with an educational challenge.

210. Environmental education has broadened its goals. Whereas in the beginning it was mainly centered on scientific information, consciousness-raising and the prevention of environmental risks, it tends now to include a critique of the "myths" of modernity grounded in a utilitarian mindset (individualism, unlimited progress, competition, consumerism, the unregulated market). It seeks also to restore the various levels of ecological equilibrium, establishing harmony within ourselves, with others, with nature and other living creatures, and with God. Environmental education should facilitate making the leap towards the transcendent which gives ecological ethics its

504

deepest meaning. It needs educators capable of developing an ethics of ecology, and helping people, through effective pedagogy, to grow in solidarity, responsibility and compassionate care.

211. Yet this education, aimed at creating an "ecological citizenship," is at times limited to providing information, and fails to instill good habits. The existence of laws and regulations is insufficient in the long run to curb bad conduct, even when effective means of enforcement are present. If the laws are to bring about significant, long-lasting effects, the majority of the members of society must be adequately motivated to accept them, and personally transformed to respond. Only by cultivating sound virtues will people be able to make a selfless ecological commitment. A person who can afford to spend and consume more but regularly uses less heating and wears warmer clothes, shows the kind of convictions and attitudes which help to protect the environment. There is a nobility in the duty to care for creation through little daily actions, and it is wonderful how education can bring about real changes in lifestyle. Education in environmental responsibility can encourage ways of acting which directly and significantly affect the world around us, such as avoiding the use of plastic and paper, reducing water consumption, separating refuse, cooking only what can be reasonably consumed, showing care for other living beings, using public transport or carpooling, planting trees, turning off unnecessary lights, or any number of other practices. All of these reflect a generous and worthy creativity which brings out the best in human beings. Reusing something instead of immediately discarding it, when done for the right reasons, can be an act of love which expresses our own dignity.

212. We must not think that these efforts are not going to change the world. They benefit society, often unbeknown to us, they call forth a goodness which, albeit unseen, inevitably tends to spread. Furthermore, such actions can restore our sense of self-esteem; they can enable us to live more fully and to feel that life on earth is worthwhile.

213. Ecological education can take place in a variety of settings: at school, in families, in the media, in catechesis and elsewhere. Good education plants seeds when we are young, and these continue to bear fruit throughout life. Here, though, I would stress the great importance of the family, which is "the place in which life — the gift of God — can be properly welcomed and protected against the many attacks to which it is exposed, and can develop in accordance with what constitutes authentic human growth. In the face of the so-called culture of death, the family is the heart of the culture of life." In the family we first learn how to show love and respect for life; we are

taught the proper use of things, order and cleanliness, respect for the local ecosystem and care for all creatures. In the family we receive an integral education, which enables us to grow harmoniously in personal maturity. In the family we learn to ask without demanding, to say "thank you" as an expression of genuine gratitude for what we have been given, to control our aggressivity and greed, and to ask forgiveness when we have caused harm. These simple gestures of heartfelt courtesy help to create a culture of shared life and respect for our surroundings.

214. Political institutions and various other social groups are also entrusted with helping to raise people's awareness. So too is the Church. All Christian communities have an important role to play in ecological education. It is my hope that our seminaries and houses of formation will provide an education in responsible simplicity of life, in grateful contemplation of God's world, and in concern for the needs of the poor and the protection of the environment. Because the stakes are so high, we need institutions empowered to impose penalties for damage inflicted on the environment. But we also need the personal qualities of self-control and willingness to learn from one another.

215. In this regard, "the relationship between a good aesthetic education and the maintenance of a healthy environment cannot be overlooked." By learning to see and appreciate beauty, we learn to reject self-interested pragmatism. If someone has not learned to stop and admire something beautiful, we should not be surprised if he or she treats everything as an object to be used and abused without scruple. If we want to bring about deep change, we need to realize that certain mindsets really do influence our behavior. Our efforts at education will be inadequate and ineffectual unless we strive to promote a new way of thinking about human beings, life, society and our relationship with nature. Otherwise, the paradigm of consumerism will continue to advance, with the help of the media and the highly effective workings of the market.

GENESIS 1–3

The first three chapters of the first book of the Hebrew and Christian Scriptures present two very different stories of the creation of the world and the origins of humanity. The first story (1:1–2:4b) was written long after the second story (2:4b–25), so the story in chapter 1 is first in the order of presentation but second in the order of composition. Both stories present a kind of philosophical anthropology in mythical terms. In other words, they explore and explicate, through how the story is told, fundamental matters of human identity, human origins, and humankind's relationship to the divine, to other animals, and to the rest of creation. Therefore, figuring out what Genesis says about these matters, the same matters that have governed this entire chapter, requires the close reading of both accounts.

The differences between the two accounts and the significance of those differences are excellent points of entry into the study of this text. For example, compare the roles of human beings relative to the rest of the natural world in the two stories. What are the differences between subduing and dominating on the one hand and tilling and keeping on the other? What are we to make of the order of creation in the two stories, especially of the fact that humans are created last in the first story and first in the second one? Human beings would seem to be commanded to dominate the animals in the first creation account, but if so, why are humans given only plants for food? Would humans be natural vegetarians in the first account? The original state of creation in the second account changes profoundly in chapter 3. How are the humans, the rest of the animal world, and the vegetable world implicated in this change, and who or what is primarily responsible for it? Is the change for the better or for the worse? Are all the elements of creation equally cursed? Why or why not?

··

From the New Revised Standard Version.

1 In the beginning when God created the heavens and the earth, ² the earth was a formless void and darkness covered the face of the deep, while a wind from God swept over the face of the waters. ³ Then God said, "Let there be light"; and there was light. ⁴ And God saw that the light was good; and God separated the light from the darkness. ⁵ God called the light Day, and the darkness he called Night. And there was evening and there was morning, the first day.

⁶ And God said, "Let there be a dome in the midst of the waters, and let it separate the waters from the waters." ⁷ So God made the dome and separated the waters that were under the dome from the waters that were above the dome. And it was so. ⁸ God called the dome Sky. And there was evening and there was morning, the second day.

⁹ And God said, "Let the waters under the sky be gathered together into one place, and let the dry land appear." And it was so. ¹⁰ God called the dry land Earth, and the waters that were gathered together he called Seas. And God saw that it was good. ¹¹ Then God said, "Let the earth put forth vegetation: plants yielding seed, and fruit trees of every kind on earth that bear fruit with the seed in it." And it was so. ¹² The earth brought forth vegetation: plants yielding seed of every kind, and trees of every kind bearing fruit with the seed in it. And God saw that it was good. ¹³ And there was evening and there was morning, the third day.

¹⁴ And God said, "Let there be lights in the dome of the sky to separate the day from the night; and let them be for signs and for seasons and for days and years, ¹⁵ and let them be lights in the dome of the sky to give light upon the earth." And it was so. ¹⁶ God made the two great lights — the greater light to rule the day and the lesser light to rule the night — and the stars. ¹⁷ God set them in the dome of the sky to give light upon the earth, ¹⁸ to rule over the day and over the night, and to separate the light from the darkness. And God saw that it was good. ¹⁹ And there was evening and there was morning, the fourth day.

²⁰ And God said, "Let the waters bring forth swarms of living creatures, and let birds fly above the earth across the dome of the sky." ²¹ So God created the great sea monsters and every living creature that moves, of every kind, with which the waters swarm, and every winged bird of every kind. And God saw that it was good. ²² God blessed them, saying, "Be fruitful and multiply and fill the waters in the seas, and let birds multiply on the earth." ²³ And there was evening and there was morning, the fifth day.

²⁴ And God said, "Let the earth bring forth living creatures of every kind: cattle and creeping things and wild animals of the earth of every kind." And

it was so. ²⁵ God made the wild animals of the earth of every kind, and the cattle of every kind, and everything that creeps upon the ground of every kind. And God saw that it was good.

²⁶ Then God said, "Let us make humankind in our image, according to our likeness; and let them have dominion over the fish of the sea, and over the birds of the air, and over the cattle, and over all the wild animals of the earth, and over every creeping thing that creeps upon the earth."

> ²⁷ So God created humankind in his image,
> in the image of God he created them;
> male and female he created them.

²⁸ God blessed them, and God said to them, "Be fruitful and multiply, and fill the earth and subdue it; and have dominion over the fish of the sea and over the birds of the air and over every living thing that moves upon the earth." ²⁹ God said, "See, I have given you every plant yielding seed that is upon the face of all the earth, and every tree with seed in its fruit; you shall have them for food. ³⁰ And to every beast of the earth, and to every bird of the air, and to everything that creeps on the earth, everything that has the breath of life, I have given every green plant for food." And it was so. ³¹ God saw everything that he had made, and indeed, it was very good. And there was evening and there was morning, the sixth day.

2 Thus the heavens and the earth were finished, and all their multitude. ² And on the seventh day God finished the work that he had done, and he rested on the seventh day from all the work that he had done. ³ So God blessed the seventh day and hallowed it, because on it God rested from all the work that he had done in creation.

⁴ These are the generations of the heavens and the earth when they were created.

In the day that the LORD God made the earth and the heavens, ⁵ when no plant of the field was yet in the earth and no herb of the field had yet sprung up — for the LORD God had not caused it to rain upon the earth, and there was no one to till the ground; ⁶ but a stream would rise from the earth, and water the whole face of the ground — ⁷ then the LORD God formed man from the dust of the ground, and breathed into his nostrils the breath of life; and the man became a living being. ⁸ And the LORD God planted a garden in Eden, in the east; and there he put the man whom he had formed. ⁹ Out of the ground the LORD God made to grow every tree that is pleasant to the sight and good for food, the tree of life also in the midst of the garden, and the tree of the knowledge of good and evil.

¹⁰ A river flows out of Eden to water the garden, and from there it divides and becomes four branches. ¹¹ The name of the first is Pishon; it is the one that flows around the whole land of Havilah, where there is gold; ¹² and the gold of that land is good; bdellium and onyx stone are there. ¹³ The name of the second river is Gihon; it is the one that flows around the whole land of Cush. ¹⁴ The name of the third river is Tigris, which flows east of Assyria. And the fourth river is the Euphrates.

¹⁵ The LORD God took the man and put him in the garden of Eden to till it and keep it. ¹⁶ And the LORD God commanded the man, "You may freely eat of every tree of the garden; ¹⁷ but of the tree of the knowledge of good and evil you shall not eat, for in the day that you eat of it you shall die."

¹⁸ Then the LORD God said, "It is not good that the man should be alone; I will make him a helper as his partner." ¹⁹ So out of the ground the LORD God formed every animal of the field and every bird of the air, and brought them to the man to see what he would call them; and whatever the man called every living creature, that was its name. ²⁰ The man gave names to all cattle, and to the birds of the air, and to every animal of the field; but for the man there was not found a helper as his partner. ²¹ So the LORD God caused a deep sleep to fall upon the man, and he slept; then he took one of his ribs and closed up its place with flesh. ²² And the rib that the LORD God had taken from the man he made into a woman and brought her to the man. ²³ Then the man said,

> "This at last is bone of my bones
>> and flesh of my flesh;
> this one shall be called Woman,
>> for out of Man this one was taken."

²⁴ Therefore a man leaves his father and his mother and clings to his wife, and they become one flesh. ²⁵ And the man and his wife were both naked, and were not ashamed.

3 Now the serpent was more crafty than any other wild animal that the LORD God had made. He said to the woman, "Did God say, 'You shall not eat from any tree in the garden'?" ² The woman said to the serpent, "We may eat of the fruit of the trees in the garden; ³ but God said, 'You shall not eat of the fruit of the tree that is in the middle of the garden, nor shall you touch it, or you shall die.'" ⁴ But the serpent said to the woman, "You will not die; ⁵ for God knows that when you eat of it your eyes will be opened, and you will be like God, knowing good and evil." ⁶ So when the woman saw that the tree was good for food, and that it was a delight to the eyes, and that the tree was to be desired to make one wise, she took of its fruit and ate; and she also gave some to her husband, who was with her, and he ate. ⁷ Then the eyes of both were opened, and they knew that they were naked; and they sewed fig leaves together and made loincloths for themselves.

⁸ They heard the sound of the Lord God walking in the garden at the time of the evening breeze, and the man and his wife hid themselves from the presence of the Lord God among the trees of the garden. ⁹ But the Lord God called to the man, and said to him, "Where are you?" ¹⁰ He said, "I heard the sound of you in the garden, and I was afraid, because I was naked; and I hid myself." ¹¹ He said, "Who told you that you were naked? Have you eaten from the tree of which I commanded you not to eat?" ¹² The man said, "The woman whom you gave to be with me, she gave me fruit from the tree, and I ate." ¹³ Then the Lord God said to the woman, "What is this that you have done?" The woman said, "The serpent tricked me, and I ate." ¹⁴ The Lord God said to the serpent,

> "Because you have done this,
>   cursed are you among all animals
>   and among all wild creatures;
> upon your belly you shall go,
>   and dust you shall eat
>   all the days of your life.
> ¹⁵ I will put enmity between you and the woman,
>   and between your offspring and hers;
> he will strike your head,
>   and you will strike his heel."

¹⁶ To the woman he said,

> "I will greatly increase your pangs in childbearing;
>   in pain you shall bring forth children,
> yet your desire shall be for your husband,
>   and he shall rule over you."

¹⁷ And to the man he said,

"Because you have listened to the voice of your wife,
> and have eaten of the tree
about which I commanded you,
> 'You shall not eat of it,'
cursed is the ground because of you;
> in toil you shall eat of it all the days of your life;
> [18] thorns and thistles it shall bring forth for you;
> and you shall eat the plants of the field.
[19] By the sweat of your face
> you shall eat bread
until you return to the ground,
> for out of it you were taken;
you are dust,
> and to dust you shall return."

[20] The man named his wife Eve, because she was the mother of all living. [21] And the LORD God made garments of skins for the man and for his wife, and clothed them.

[22] Then the LORD God said, "See, the man has become like one of us, knowing good and evil; and now, he might reach out his hand and take also from the tree of life, and eat, and live forever" — [23] therefore the LORD God sent him forth from the garden of Eden, to till the ground from which he was taken. [24] He drove out the man; and at the east of the garden of Eden he placed the cherubim, and a sword flaming and turning to guard the way to the tree of life.

Ursula K. LeGuin

SHE UNNAMES THEM

Ursula LeGuin (1929–2018) is known primarily for her works of science
fiction and fantasy. The same playfulness that suffuses many of her more
famous works informs this short piece of fiction, which plays upon part of
the ancient Hebrew story of creation we encountered in the previous section.
That story's passage on the naming of the animals (Gen. 2:19–20a) inspired
extended commentary by Jewish rabbis, Christian Bible scholars, and major
philosophers like Martin Heidegger. The attention it has received highlights
one of the central issues explored in this section, namely, humankind's relationship to the rest of the animals. After all, the naming of the animals
in Genesis 2 is undertaken in the context of the quest to find a companion
suitable for the first human. And the animals, like the human, are formed
from the ground. So the "ground" of kinship, if you will, is very deep.

But there is also the question of all that is involved in the very act of naming, and "She Unnames Them" brings all this complexity into profound relief.
For Eve, the narrator of this story, just what is involved in naming? And by
unnaming the animals, what is Eve saying about her own relationship to
them? Do you think the Eve of this piece or the earth creature (a.k.a. Adam)
of the Genesis story is closer to a right understanding of what obligation we
have to human and other life?

Most of them accepted namelessness with the perfect indifference with
which they had so long accepted and ignored their names. Whales and
dolphins, seals and sea otters consented with particular grace and alacrity,
sliding into anonymity as into their element. A faction of yaks, however,
protested. They said that "yak" sounded right, and that almost everyone
who knew they existed called them that. Unlike the ubiquitous creatures
such as rats and fleas, who had been called by hundreds or thousands of different names since Babel, the yaks could truly say, they said, that they had

Ursula K. LeGuin, "She Unnames Them," *New Yorker* (January 21, 1985), 27.

a *name*. They discussed the matter all summer. The councils of the elderly females finally agreed that though the name might be useful to others it was so redundant from the yak point of view that they never spoke it themselves and hence might as well dispense with it. After they presented the argument in this light to their bulls, a full consensus was delayed only by the onset of severe early blizzards. Soon after the beginning of the thaw, their agreement was reached and the designation "yak" was returned to the donor.

Among the domestic animals, few horses had cared what anybody called them since the failure of Dean Swift's attempt to name them from their own vocabulary. Cattle, sheep, swine, asses, mules, and goats, along with chickens, geese, and turkeys, all agreed enthusiastically to give their names back to the people to whom — as they put it — they belonged.

A couple of problems did come up with pets. The cats, of course, steadfastly denied ever having had any name other than those self-given, unspoken, ineffably personal names which, as the poet named Eliot said, they spend long hours daily contemplating — though none of the contemplators has ever admitted that what they contemplate is their names and some onlookers have wondered if the object of that meditative gaze might not in fact be the Perfect, or Platonic, Mouse. In any case, it is a moot point now. It was with the dogs, and with some parrots, lovebirds, ravens, and mynahs, that the trouble arose. These verbally talented individuals insisted that their names were important to them, and flatly refused to part with them. But as soon as they understood that the issue was precisely one of individual choice, and that anybody who wanted to be called Rover, or Froufrou, or Polly, or even Birdie in the personal sense, was perfectly free to do so, not one of them had the least objection to parting with the lowercase (or, as regards German creatures, uppercase) generic appellations "poodle," "parrot," "dog," or "bird," and all the Linnaean qualifiers that had trailed along behind them for two hundred years like tin cans tied to a tail.

The insects parted with their names in vast clouds and swarms of ephemeral syllables buzzing and stinging and humming and flitting and crawling and tunneling away.

As for the fish of the sea, their names dispersed from them in silence throughout the ocean like faint, dark blurs of cuttlefish ink, and drifted off on the currents without a trace.

None were left now to unname, and yet how close I felt to them when I saw one of them swim or fly or trot or crawl across my way or over my skin, or stalk me in the night, or go along beside me for a while in the day. They seemed far closer than when their names had stood between myself and them like a clear barrier: so close that my fear of them and their fear of me became one same fear. And the attraction that many of us felt, the desire to smell one another's smells, feel or rub or caress one another's scales or skin or feathers or fur, taste one another's blood or flesh, keep one another warm — that attraction was now all one with the fear, and the hunter could not be told from the hunted, nor the eater from the food.

This was more or less the effect I had been after. It was somewhat more powerful than I had anticipated, but I could not now, in all conscience, make an exception for myself. I resolutely put anxiety away, went to Adam, and said, "You and your father lent me this — gave it to me, actually. It's been really useful, but it doesn't exactly seem to fit very well lately. But thanks very much! It's really been very useful."

It is hard to give back a gift without sounding peevish or ungrateful, and I didn't want to leave him with that impression of me. He was not paying much attention, as it happened, and said only, "Put it down over there, O.K.?" and went on with what he was doing.

One of my reasons for doing what I did was that talk was getting us nowhere, but all the same I felt a little let down. I had been prepared to defend my decision. And I thought that perhaps when he did notice he might be upset and want to talk. I put some things away and fiddled around a little, but he continued to do what he was doing and to take no notice of anything else. At last I said, "Well, goodbye, dear. I hope the garden key turns up."

He was fitting parts together, and said, without looking around, "O.K., fine, dear. When's dinner?"

"I'm not sure," I said. "I'm going now. With the — " I hesitated, and finally said, "With them, you know," and went on out. In fact, I had only just then realized how hard it would have been to explain myself. I could not chatter away as I used to do, taking it all for granted. My words now must be as slow, as new, as single, as tentative as the steps I took going down the path away from the house, between the dark-branched, tall dancers motionless against the winter shining.

ACOMA CREATION STORY

The Acoma people are Native Americans who are part of the Pueblo people of present-day New Mexico. Their larger family includes several peoples in the region, all of whom speak the Keres language. They are among those Winona LaDuke refers to as "indigenous people." Though they were "Christianized" during the Spanish occupation of the North American Southwest in the sixteenth century, they retained many of their original beliefs, myths, and ceremonies. David Leeming, in his encyclopedia of creation myths, has classified the Acoma story as a "myth of emergence," meaning that the emphasis in the story is upon the emergence of human beings. In the Acoma myth, the two primordial human beings are sisters, who emerge gradually from the womb-like underworld into the light of the present world through the help of animals. The sisters then complete the creation by planting seeds and breathing life into the animals they have brought with them from the underworld. How would you characterize the implied relationship between the sisters and the rest of creation? What part do animals play in the narrative? What is the significance of the fact that the leading characters in the story are female? Are the sisters divine, human, or a combination of both? To what extent are they similar to and different from the earth creature formed from the ground in Genesis 2?

In the beginning two sister-spirits were born somewhere in the darkness of the underground. Living in constant darkness they grew slowly and knew one another only by touch. For some time they were fed by a female spirit named Tsichtinako (Thinking Woman) who taught them language. When she thought the twins were ready, Tsichtinako gave the sisters baskets containing seeds for all the plants and models of all the animals that would be in the next world. Tsichtinako said the baskets were from their father and

From David Adams Leeming, ed., *Creation Myths of the World: An Encyclopedia*, vol. 1, 2nd ed. (Santa Barbara, CA: ABC-CLIO, 2010), 33.

that they were to be carried to the light of the upper world. She helped the sisters find the seeds of four trees in the baskets, and these seeds the sisters planted in the dark. After a long time the trees sprouted and one — a pine — grew sufficiently to break a small hole through the earth above and let in some light. With Tsichtinako's help, the girls found the model of the badger, to whom they gave the gift of life and whom they instructed to dig around the hole so it would become bigger. They cautioned the animal not to enter into the world of light, and he obeyed. As a reward he was promised eventual happiness in the upper world. Next the sisters found the model of the locust in the baskets. After they gave him life, they asked him to smooth the opening above but warned him not to enter the world of light. When he returned after doing his job he admitted he had indeed passed through the hole. "What was it like up there?" the sisters asked. "Flat," he answered. Locust was told that for having done his work he could accompany the spirits to the upper world but that for his disobedience he would live in the ground and would have to die and be reborn each year. Then it was time for the sister-spirits to emerge. Instructed by Tsichtinako, they took the baskets, Badger, and Locust, climbed the pine tree to the hole above, and broke through into the upper world. There they stood waiting until the sun appeared in what Tsichtinako had told them was the east. They had also learned the other three directions from her, as well as a prayer to the sun, which they now recited, and the song of creation, which they sang for the first time.

Tsichtinako revealed that she had been sent to be the sisters' constant guide by the creator, Uchtsiti, who had made the world from a clot of his blood. The sisters were to complete the creation by giving life to the things in the baskets. This they did by planting the seeds and breathing life into the animals, but when the first night came the sisters were afraid and called on Tsichtinako, who explained that the dark time was for sleep and that the sun would return.

The creation was duly completed by the sisters, who took the names Iatiku (Life-Bringer) and Nautsiti (Full Basket).

Denise Levertov

BEGINNERS

Denise Levertov (1911–1997) was born and raised in England, but she moved to the United States when she was twenty-five and remained there until her death. Levertov had great poetic range in genre and theme, and she was drawn to the most difficult and painful subjects — war, loneliness, loss, and grief. Thus many of her poems, like "Beginners," blend a tone of melancholy with a note of hope. Because she was not formally schooled, her poetry is generally free from the arcane allusions and elliptical expressions that render much of twentieth-century poetry inaccessible. Here she sets forth in simple and direct diction one of the truths that has permeated much of this section: "But we have only begun to love the earth," where "we" refers presumably to the dominant, majority culture in this country, not to the many marginalized voices we have encountered in this chapter. Do you think the "we" in this poem becomes more and more inclusive as the poem proceeds, thereby enacting what it prescribes? Or do you think that the poem laments various divisions among us that must be healed before we can together heal the wounds that many of us have inflicted upon nature?

Levertov dedicated this poem to the memory of two activists who had recently died, Karen Silkwood and Eliot Gralla. Silkwood died in a mysterious car crash while driving to meet a *New York Times* reporter about unsafe conditions in the nuclear power plant where she worked. Her story is told in the film *Silkwood* (1983), with Meryl Streep as the title character.

> *"From too much love of living,*
> *Hope and desire set free,*
> *Even the weariest river*
> *Winds somewhere to the sea — "*

But we have only begun
to love the earth.

....

From Denise Levertov, *Selected Poems* (New York: New Directions Books, 2002), 137–38.

We have only begun
to imagine the fulness of life.

How could we tire of hope?
— so much is in bud.

How can desire fail?
— we have only begun

to imagine justice and mercy,
only begun to envision

how it might be
to live as siblings with beast and flower,
not as oppressors.

Surely our river
cannot already be hastening
into the sea of nonbeing?

Surely it cannot
drag, in the silt,
all that is innocent?
Not yet, not yet —
there is too much broken
that must be mended,

too much hurt we have done to each other
that cannot yet be forgiven.

We have only begun to know
the power that is in us if we would join
our solitudes in the communion of struggle.

So much is unfolding that must
complete its gesture,

so much is in bud.

How Shall I Tell the Story of My Life?

The first reading featured in this chapter, Robert Frost's "The Road Not Taken," surely numbers among the five or ten most familiar and beloved poems in all of American literature. Most people, including some famous writers who have used phrases from the poem as titles for their books, believe that the poem is about life's major choices and their consequences. For them, the whole poem reduces to its last two lines: "I took the [road] less traveled by / And that has made all the difference."

Several readings in the previous sections of this anthology go far to explain why Americans, of all people, would be disposed to read Frost's poem this way. As Charles Taylor has argued (see pages 59–64 above), Americans may value free choice above almost everything else. Indeed, many citizens believe that choice by itself confers significance upon the object of choice. Russell Muirhead taught us in chapter 1 that a complete account of "just work" in a democratic society should provide for an element of choice. We believe that our work is "just" in part because we have chosen to do it. We've read about the reasons for choosing one kind of life over another one, and about whom we should heed when making decisions. Leading a life that matters surely involves making good choices.

Though these deep and legitimate concerns about the place of free choice in our lives may explain why "The Road Not Taken" has been "taken" to be about choice, the poem is not mainly about choice at all. It instead explores the shape of the stories we tell to ourselves and others about ourselves over the course of our lives. The poem is also about how and why these stories change. The poem teaches us that there are two things of roughly equal importance in determining the quality of the lives we lead: the choices we make and what we make of those choices. Our interpretations of what we have chosen to do and of what has happened to us often take the form of stories, and these narratives in turn constitute our inner sense of ourselves, which includes feelings of meaning, purpose, and significance. To put this a bit differently, our imagination is just as important as our reason in shaping our identities and in making for lives of significance and substance. The widespread misreading of "The Road Not Taken" may indicate that as a people we do not rightly appreciate the importance of the imagination in shaping our efforts to lead lives that matter.

When we come to Frost's poem with these latter ideas in our minds, we notice right away that the whole poem consists of two very different stories of the "same" event. The first story is relatively long (the first fifteen lines) and quite indecisive about whether the two roads encountered on an autumn morning differ from one another at all, and concludes by a resolution to keep one of the roads for some other time. The second story is much shorter (the final three lines) and much more resolute about the differences between the two roads, and concludes by a resolution to take the one "less traveled." The speaker tells the first story soon after the event and then imagines how he will tell the story differently "ages and ages hence." The speaker knows that his perspective on life will change over time and that he will be a different kind of person in old age than he was when he first came upon the two roads. He (or she) even knows how he will be different: he'll be surer in his judgments and more dramatic in narrating certain particular choices in his life. Memory, the thread of continuity in his identity, will serve to some extent his sense of himself even as the changing shape of his life's story will serve to change his sense of the significance of his past. One choice will have made "all the difference," and his literally "self"-serving memory will move him to claim that he once chose a "less traveled" way, even though he was not at all clear about this matter in the immediate aftermath of the moment of choice.

Like the speaker in this poem, all of us revise our own life stories all the time. Unlike the speaker in the poem, many of us are not as aware of this as we should be. Sometimes we revise our stories depending on our audience. Would not most of us tell the story of an embarrassing experience somewhat differently to our parents, our siblings, our lovers, or our employers? But we undertake our work of revision more often for the sake of our primary audience, ourselves. The readings that follow "The Road Not Taken" will help us to understand the complexities and the vital importance of this constant process of "composing our lives." Three of them are from creative artists who make their living telling stories, and two are by social scientists who study the importance of the stories we fashion for ourselves to our identities and personalities. The last reading reminds us that, just as we cannot fully control those things that we remember and shape into our stories, we cannot fully control how others will remember us, and that what the living remember — or fail to remember — about those who have died may influence their own sense of what constitutes a life that matters. The readings are as follows:

- Mary Catherine Bateson, "Composing a Life Story"
- Julia Alvarez, "First Muse"
- Wendell Berry, from the novel *Jayber Crow*
- Alice Walker, "Saving the Life That Is Your Own"
- Dan P. McAdams, "A Life Story Made in America"
- Michael T. Kaufman, "Robert McG. Thomas, 60, Chronicler of Unsung Lives"

Mary Catherine Bateson has lived most of her life on the boundary between creative writing and social science. She is an anthropologist who has told true stories about the lives of other people. In her essay below, which is based on her book *Composing a Life,* she shows why we should attend as much to what we make of our choices as we do to the choices we make. Learning to become more imaginative and resourceful in composing our own pasts can enable us to lead more significant lives in the future. We can discover that what appear to be sudden ruptures in our lives really connect at a deeper level to skills and interests that we have always had, thereby helping us draw upon our past selves in facing some new challenge that has suddenly come upon us. Someone, for example, might have been a teacher in New Orleans for many years prior to Hurricane Katrina, only to find herself living with relatives in Boise, Idaho, where the only job available to her is in the development office of a local hospital. If she can understand development work as a kind of education, she might discover more continuity than discontinuity between work as a high school English teacher and work attempting to enlist community support for a new health-care facility. This discovery might in turn enable her to become a very effective fund-raiser. Her success, in this case, would be directly linked to her imaginative capacity to shape a story of continuity from what first seemed to her a broken and disconnected narrative.

Bateson's essay uses three senses of the word "compose," drawn from the three arts of painting, music, and creative writing, to explicate the complexities involved in shaping the narratives of our lives. This work of composition touches upon all the topics and questions raised so far in this anthology. For example, if we think of composing our life as a painter composes on a canvas, we will attend with great care to achieving balance and harmony among the several elements in our lives. Balance, in this view, consists less of walking a tightrope to give equal attention to our work, our home, and our community so that we do not tumble, and more of creatively imagining the ways in which the parts of our lives might constitute a whole, might complement one another, and might be assigned our own special proportions to produce a distinctive life of harmony and integrity. If, on the other hand, we view our life as a musical composition, a tonal structure unfolding over time, we are apt to look for harmonies over the course of our life rather than expecting perfect harmony at each and every moment.

Bateson knows that when we compose our lives as a creative writer might, we invariably choose from a repertoire of plots, characters, and themes that we inherit from our culture. We are reminded here of Russell Muirhead's discussion of how our choice of work is both free and constrained. We may be free to choose from a menu of possible jobs, but we did not create the menu. Just so with the stories that we fashion about ourselves. We are free to plot our narratives as comedies or tragedies, but we did not invent comedy and tragedy. We absorb from our culture without realizing it a host of narrative possibilities from the films we see, the books we read, and the stories we hear other people tell about themselves. The shape that we give at any moment to our own life's story will therefore resemble the shape of other people's stories, some of them "real" and others "fictional." Part of the work of coming to know ourselves involves our ability to choose, from a repertoire of characters and plots, those that most truly capture who we are and what we can reasonably aspire to become.

The power of literature to help readers make sense of their life stories figures in each of the next three selections. In "First Muse," Julia Alvarez remembers how a certain story, which she read again and again in a treasured book as a young girl, provided a plot that made sense of her experience and laid the foundations of her character and her vocation. *The Thousand and One Nights*, a gift from a beloved aunt who was the only "reader" the young Julia knew, carried truth and relevance that the stories she encountered in school did not. Alvarez's account should remind us that not all the plots we are offered as we grow up prove to be life giving. Some stories, Alvarez suggests, limit our possibilities and imaginations. Other stories can "save you."

The excerpt from Wendell Berry's novel *Jayber Crow* shows us the title character as he interrupts the telling of his own life's story to consider the shape of that story. While Alvarez sees a strong continuity between her childhood reading and her adult work as a writer, Jayber finds it difficult to detect a strong plotline. As he ponders his lifelong journey, he draws on images from works of literature he treasured as a student. Though he admires the plots and the central characters in some of these books and even wishes that his own story could credibly be told in their terms, he realizes that some of the narratives drawn from this repertoire don't quite fit him. Even so, framing Jayber's reflections on how to tell his life story in terms drawn from great works of literature allows Berry to disclose to readers the profundity of Jayber's serious effort to discern the shape of his life's narrative and to commend such an effort to us as well.

Alice Walker, the eminent novelist and essayist, places the story of a key moment in her own professional and personal development into the context of a wider concern. Artists need models, she insists, forerunners whose creativity and commitment convey companionship and courage in the midst of the arduous, solitary work of making art. Bateson also used art making as an image for coming to terms with who we are and how our lives are shaped. However, Bateson assumed that each of us could find ready materials for the art of life composition in the available repertoire of forms and stories. Speaking for herself while also drawing on the experience of Vincent van Gogh, Walker lifts up contexts in which the resources that are needed most are not available. Van Gogh felt that he had no models as an artist. And Walker realized that the models she desired — the African American women writers who had gone before her — were hidden from view. Discovering her literary foremother, Zora Neale Hurston, opens the floodgates of Walker's creativity, enabling her to tell stories from her own family in a way that was previously impossible. Knowing the story and the books of Zora, Alice becomes equipped to tell her own story. Have you likewise been inspired by the stories of specific other people to try to tell your story in a new way?

Dan P. McAdams, a personality psychologist at Northwestern University, has spent much of his life studying "good" people. And he has discerned a complex connection between such people and the kind of stories they tell about their lives. By "good" people, McAdams means "generative" people, to use the more technical and precise vocabulary of his discipline. Such people are for the most part virtuous, in Aristotle's sense, but they also show an unusual amount of interest in and devotion to the welfare of the next generation. So, in the terms of this anthology, their lives are meaningful, virtuous, *and* significant. These people really do make a difference in the world. And the majority of them have a tendency to tell their life stories in a particular way, according to a particular kind of plot. McAdams calls these stories "narratives of redemption."

The connection between the "goodness" of these people and the shape of their stories is not a causal one exactly. Generative people do not become good because they see their life stories as narratives of redemption, nor do they tell such stories because they are good. Instead, a tendency to discern "redemption" in their own stories and in the larger story of the world of which they are a part is very frequently, though not always, an important mark of a generative personality. Identity and story are linked here, but more in terms of a revealing statistical correlation than in terms of a causal sequence.

In this sense, discerning redemptive patterns is part of what it means to lead a significant life. Some Christian theologians would resonate with McAdams's findings, because they sense that the Christian life at its best includes the ability to discover and interpret redemption in the world and to participate in the great story of redemption embodied in the life and death of Jesus of Nazareth. McAdams's research does not suggest, however, that the disposition to interpret one's life as a narrative of redemption is a distinctively Christian phenomenon. Though many of the generative people McAdams studied are religious, a large number are not. And among the religious, not all are Christian. Some international reactions to his work, however, have made him suspect a different correlation: a correlation with nationality based on the possibility that, compared to Europeans, Americans may be unusually disposed to see their life stories in redemptive terms. In other words, like the idea of vocation, the idea of redemption has extended its provenance well beyond religious communities, lying at the intersection of religious and democratic traditions.

The last reading in this chapter reminds us that, however important the stories we fashion about our lives, the final versions, the ones that will largely determine how we will be remembered in this world, will be written by others, whether in newspaper obituaries or in stories told around the Thanksgiving table years after we have died. What stories will come to define us in the minds of others? The obituary of Robert McG. Thomas, himself a writer of obituaries, reminds us that someday each of us will be the subject, not the author, of a life story. Even for people who expect to live for many more years, drafting updated versions of our own obituaries from time to time can be an intriguing spiritual exercise. What might stand out to others who observe us? And what do we think should stand out? The truth of our lives may lie somewhere in between.

Robert Frost

THE ROAD NOT TAKEN

As we noted in the introduction to "Two Tramps in Mud Time" (see pp. 208–9 above), another of Frost's poems, the deceptive simplicity of much of his work has tempted readers to offer interpretations that are superficial at best and altogether mistaken at worst. To avoid such interpretations here, compare the two accounts of the "same" event that exist within the poem. We indicated some of the differences between the two stories a few pages earlier.

This poem helps us understand the process by which we revise our own life stories. So we need to ask what kind of person the speaker is, based on the kind of story he tells and the way he tells it in lines 1–15. For example, he seems constantly to second-guess himself and his judgments. How else would you characterize him?

When the speaker imagines what he *will* be saying about the same event many years later, he offers an account interrupted by a sigh (that dash at the end of line 18). Is this a sigh of regret or of resignation or of fatigue? The feat the speaker accomplishes is quite remarkable. To see how and why this is so, think of the story you would now tell about why you made a certain decision — for example, about why you chose to attend one college rather than another one. Now imagine how you will tell that story "ages and ages hence." Now compare the two. What does that comparison teach you about how you expect to develop over time?

> Two roads diverged in a yellow wood,
> And sorry I could not travel both
> And be one traveler, long I stood
> And looked down one as far as I could
> To where it bent in the undergrowth;   5

Robert Frost, "The Road Not Taken," in *Collected Poems of Robert Frost* (New York: Holt, 1930), 131.

Then took the other, as just as fair,
And having perhaps the better claim,
Because it was grassy and wanted wear;
Though as for that the passing there
Had worn them really about the same,   10

And both that morning equally lay
In leaves no step had trodden black.
Oh, I kept the first for another day!
Yet knowing how way leads on to way,
I doubted if I should ever come back.   15

I shall be telling this with a sigh
Somewhere ages and ages hence:
Two roads diverged in a wood, and I —
I took the one less traveled by,
And that has made all the difference.   20

Mary Catherine Bateson

COMPOSING A LIFE STORY

Mary Catherine Bateson is a writer and anthropologist who has spent many years studying how human beings grow and change over time. One of her best-known books, *Composing a Life* (1989) is a comparative biographical study of five very different, creative women. In observing their lives and listening to their life stories, in remembering the lives of her famous parents, Gregory Bateson and Margaret Mead, and in thinking about the different ways she had thought about her own life, she came to think of life as a kind of improvisational art form. The essay below is about the importance of our imaginative ability to compose our lives in multiple and resourceful ways. It suggests that if we become skilled in telling stories to ourselves about ourselves, we will be more likely to lead actual lives that matter, more likely to discover and maintain a constancy of purpose beneath a surface of many changes, more likely to achieve some kind of balance among our sometimes competing obligations, even more likely to learn from the generation before us and to teach the generation following. In other words, the capacity to "compose" our lives affects all the several aspects of our identities and our life's work that we have thus far considered.

Bateson also suggests that though there is always a good deal of invention in our life compositions, there is some discovery as well. Moreover, we do not very often invent new plotlines; we typically absorb them from our culture. When you think of the shape of your own life, do you adopt one of the story lines Bateson mentions — for example, a conversion narrative? Finally, do we live our lives first and then retrospectively compose them, or do we first compose them and seek to live according to the plotline we have constructed or chosen from the repertoire offered to us by our culture?

From Mary Catherine Bateson, *Willing to Learn: Passages of Personal Discovery* (Hanover, NH: Steerforth, 2004), 66–74.

There are three meanings that "composing a life," as a phrase, has to me. Two of those meanings compare living to different arts, in that I see the way people live their lives as, in itself, an artistic process. An artist takes ingredients that may seem incompatible, and organizes them into a whole that is not only workable, but finally pleasing and true, even beautiful. As you get up in the morning, as you make decisions, as you spend money, make friends, make commitments, you are creating a piece of art called: your life. The word *compose* helps me look at two aspects of that process.

Very often in the visual arts, you put together components to find a way that they fit together and balance each other in space. You make a visual composition of form and color. One thing that you do in composing a life is to put together disparate elements that need to be in some kind of balance, like a still life with tools, fruit, and musical instruments. This sense of balance is something that women have been especially aware of in recent years because they cannot solve the problem of composing the different elements of their lives simply by making them separate, as men have.

Of course, less and less are men able to compartmentalize their lives. For a long time it was possible for men to think in terms of a line between the public and the private. A man would go to the workplace, and then, at a certain point, he would switch that part of the day off and go home to a world where the atmosphere was different. He could switch gears from one aspect of his life to the other.

But it hasn't been possible for women to separate their commitments in quite the same way. It is one thing in the traditional nuclear family for the husband to go to the office and stop thinking about his family during the day because he has left his wife in charge. It is quite a different thing for both parents to go off and feel that they can completely forget what is happening with the family. Many women have the sense that the combining of different areas in their lives is a problem that is with them all the time.

What this has meant is that women have lived their lives experiencing multiple simultaneous demands from multiple directions. Increasingly men are also living that way. So thinking about how people manage this is becoming more and more important. One way to approach the situation is to think of how a painter composes a painting: by synchronously putting elements together and finding a pattern in how they fit.

But of course *compose* has another meaning in music. Music is an art in which you create something that happens *over time* that goes through various transitions. Examining your life in this way, you have to look at the change that occurs within a lifetime — discontinuities, transitions, and the growth of various sorts — and the artistic unity, like that of a symphony with very different movements, that can characterize a life.

In addition to these two meanings of composing a life — one that relates to the visual arts and the other that relates to music — I want to emphasize a third meaning, one that has to do with the ways in which you compose your own *versions* of your life. I'm referring to the stories you make about your life, the stories you tell first to yourself and then to other people, the stories you use as lenses for interpreting experience as it comes along. What I want to say is that you can play with, compose, multiple versions of a life.

There are advantages in having access to multiple versions of your life story. I am not referring to a true version versus a false version, or to one that works in a given therapeutic context as opposed to others, or to one that will sell to *People* magazine as opposed to ones that won't. I am referring to the freedom that comes not only from owning your memory and your life story but also from knowing that you make creative choices in how you look at your life.

In the postmodern environment in which we live, it is easy to say that no version is fixed, no version is completely true. I want to push beyond that awareness and encourage you to think about the creative responsibility involved in the fact that there are different ways to tell your stories. It's not that one is true and another is not true. It's a matter of emphasis and context. For example, one of the things that people do at meetings is to introduce themselves. I was at a conference recently where, in the course of two days, I introduced myself three times in different breakout groups. One person who had been there all three times came up to me and said, "You know, you said something completely different every time." Of course I did. The contexts were different.

Imagine the choices you have in saying things about yourself and about other people. These are real choices, but they are made in the presence of a set of conventions. Think of a self-introduction as a literary genre. There are things you include and things you don't. Those decisions are related to who you're talking to and where you are, as well as who you're talking about.

You can do the same with versions of your life history. For instance, most people can tell a version that emphasizes the continuities in their lives to make a single story that goes in a clear direction. But the same people can also tell their life stories as if they were following on this statement: "After lots of surprises and choices, or interruptions and disappointments, I have arrived someplace I could never have anticipated." Every one of us has a preference for one of these versions, but if we try, we can produce both. My guess is that there are a lot of people reading this who think of themselves as growing and developing and moving on smoothly. That's part of the intellectual context many of us are in. But some of us experience our lives as discontinuous, interrupted processes.

For example, one version of my life story goes like this: I already thought of myself as a writer when I was in high school, and there hasn't been a year since college that I haven't published something. Now I spend half the year writing full-time and half the year writing and teaching. Many of my students are future writers.

That's one version of me. The other version goes like this: I planned in high school to be a poet. But I gave up writing poetry in college. The only writing I did for years was academic publish-or-perish writing. When I became unemployed because of the Iranian revolution, shortly after my mother died, I dealt with unemployment by starting to write a memoir. I suddenly found that I could write nonfiction. Now I'm considering switching again and writing a novel.

Both of these are true stories. But they are very different stories. One person told me there had been so much discontinuity in her life that it wasn't hard to think of a discontinuous version, but it was painful to tell it. I think that's a problem many people have. Because our society has preferred continuous versions of stories, discontinuities seem to indicate that something is wrong with you. A discontinuous story becomes a very difficult story to claim.

I would say that the most important effect of my recent book *Composing a Life* has been to give people who feel that they've been bumped from one thing to another, with no thread of continuity, a way of positively interpreting their experience. You might be uncomfortable with your life if it has been like *The Perils of Pauline,* yet many of us have lives like that. One strategy for working with that kind of life is to make a story that *interprets change as continuity.* One of my favorites was someone who said, "My life is like surfing, with one wave coming after another." He unified his whole life with that single simile.

The choice you make affects what you can do next. Often people use the choice of emphasizing either continuity or discontinuity as a way of preparing for the next step. They interpret the present in a way that helps them construct a particular future. . . .

When I started *Composing a Life,* the issue I wanted to explore was discontinuity. Part of my interest was based on two events in my own life. One was that I had just gone through the experience of losing, in a rather painful way, a job I cared about. I had been forced to change jobs before, because of my husband changing jobs, and I had had to adapt to that situation. So what I set out to do was to look at a group of women who had been through a lot of transitions and who were able to cope with the changes. I was asking the question "How on earth does one survive this kind of interruption?"

The other circumstance that made me focus on the issue of discontinuity had to do with my experiences in Iran. At the time of the Iranian revolution, my husband and I had been living and working there for seven years. We, and a great many of our friends, had to make fresh starts; many Iranians became refugees. The way they interpreted their situation was absolutely critical to their adjustment. I could see very clearly, among them, that there were those who came into the refugee situation with a sense that they had skills and adaptive patterns they could transfer to the new situation. They were emphasizing continuity. Other people came into the refugee situation feeling that their lives had ended and they had to start from zero. You could see that the choices people made about how to interpret the continuities and discontinuities in their lives had great implications for the way they approached the future.

Much of coping with discontinuity has to do with discovering threads of continuity. You cannot adjust to change unless you can recognize some analogy between your old situation and your new situation. Without that analogy you cannot transfer learning. You cannot apply skills. If you can recognize a problem that you've solved before, in however different a guise, you have a much greater chance of solving that problem in the new situation. That recognition is critical to the transfer of learning.

It can be very difficult to recognize the ways in which one situation or event in your life is linked to others. When I was working on my memoir of my parents, *With a Daughter's Eye,* I found an example of this in my father's life. Some of you may know my father, Gregory Bateson, as a great anthropologist, a great thinker. But in the middle of his life, he went through a difficult period that lasted for some time. From year to year he didn't know whether he would have a salary, whether there would be anything to live on.

His career at that time must have seemed totally discontinuous. First he was a biologist. Then he got interested in anthropology and went to New Guinea. He made a couple of field trips that he never wrote up. Then to Bali. During World War II he wrote an analysis of propaganda films and worked in psychological warfare. Then he did a study of communication in psychotherapy. Then he worked on alcoholism and schizophrenia, and then on dolphins and octopuses. Somehow he turned into a philosopher.

One of the things that I realized while I was putting together the memoir is that only when he drew together a group of his articles — all written in very different contexts for very different audiences, with apparently different subject matter — to put them into the book called *Steps to an Ecology of Mind* did it become clear to him that he had been working on the same kind of question all his life: The continuous thread through all of his work was an interest in the relationships between ideas.

The interruptions that forced him to change his research focus were absolutely critical to pushing him up the ladder of logical types, so that ultimately he could see continuity at a very abstract level. His insight, his understanding of what he had been working on all his life, was a result of a sometimes desperate search for a continuity beyond the discontinuities. So even when I was working on the memoir, I was picking at this question of continuity and discontinuity, and examining the incredible gains that can come from reconstruing a life history by combining both interpretations.

Of course, in composing any life story, there is a considerable weight of cultural pressure. Narratives have canonical forms. One of the stories that we, as a culture, respond to is the story in which the hero's or heroine's end is contained in the beginning. . . .

One of my favorite examples is a story from the life of St. Teresa of Avila, a Counter-Reformation saint. When she was a child, part of Spain was still controlled by the Moors: part of the country was Catholic, and part was Muslim. When she was ten or so, she set out, with her younger brother, for the territory controlled by the Moors in order to be martyred and go to heaven. This becomes an appropriate story to prefigure a life of self-sacrifice and dedication to God. Many biographies and autobiographies have this pattern. . . .

Another popular form is one that we can think of as the conversion narrative. It's a simple plot. Lives that in reality have a lot of zigzags in them get reconstructed into before-and-after narratives with one major discontinuity. One very interesting example is the *Confessions of St. Augustine,* which tells the story of his life before and after his conversion to Christianity. The narrative structure requires that he depict himself before conversion as a terrible sinner, that he devalue all he did before he was converted, and that he dredge up sins to talk about so he can describe a total turnaround. . . .

A more complicated conversion story is *The Autobiography of Malcolm X.* Much of the book tells of how Malcolm X, who had been a small-time crook, was converted in prison to the Nation of Islam, Elijah Muhammad's American Black Muslim movement. About two-thirds of the book is written as a conventional conversion narrative: "I was deep in sin and then I was saved by Elijah Muhammad."

But then another big discontinuity occurs. Malcolm X becomes disillusioned with the corruption within the Nation of Islam and isolated by the politics around Elijah Muhammad. He separates from them, making a pilgrimage to Mecca and converting to orthodox Islam, and starts his own Muslim organization in the United States. So in this book you have the image of somebody who developed an interpretation of his life to support the validity of one particular message of salvation and then had to flip over into another one. It's an extraordinarily interesting and unusual story because the conversion happens not once but twice.

One very common example of the uses of the conversion story shows up in Twelve-Step programs. Twelve-Step programs essentially convey the message that if you can construe your life in such a way as to support a turnaround, we will help you construct a new life. But you have to define yourself, as St. Augustine had to define himself, as a sinner, or as Malcolm X had to define himself for his second conversion, as having been duped. An emphasis on a turnaround becomes the condition for moving on to the next stage.

The conversion narrative can be a very empowering way of telling your story, because it allows you to make a fresh start. The more continuous story, in which the end is prefigured in the beginning, is powerful in different ways. But what I want to emphasize are the advantages of choosing a particular interpretation at a particular time, and the even greater advantage of using *multiple* interpretations.

The availability of multiple interpretations of a life story is particularly important in how the generations communicate with each other. When we, as parents, talk to our children about our lives, there is a great temptation to edit out the discontinuities, to reshape our histories so that they look more coherent than they are. But when we tell stories to our children with the zigzags edited out, it causes problems for many of those children. A lot of young people have great difficulty committing themselves to a relationship or to a career because of the feeling that once they do, they're trapped for a long, long time. They feel they've got to get on the right "track" because, after all, this is a long and terrifying commitment. I think it is very liberating for college students when an older person says to them, "Your first job after college need not be the beginning of an ascending curve that's going to take you through your life. It can be a zigzag. You might be doing something different in five years." That's something young people need to hear: that the continuous story, where the whole of a person's life is prefigured very early on, is often a cultural creation, not a reflection of life as it is really lived.

The ways in which we interpret our life stories have a great effect on how our children come to define their own identities. An example of this occurred in my own life when my daughter was about to become a teenager. She said to me, "Gee, Mom, it must be awfully hard on you and Daddy that I'm not interested in any of the things you're interested in." I said, "What do you mean?" She said, "Well, you're professors. You write books about social science. I'm an actress. I care about theater." I said a secret prayer because it was clearly a very tricky moment. Maybe she needed to believe in that discontinuity. Maybe it was worrying her and she needed to get away from that discontinuity.

But what I said to her was "Well, to be a social scientist, to be an anthropologist, you have to be a good observer of human behavior. You have to try and understand how people think and why they behave as they do. It strikes me that that's pretty important for a good actor." She has been telling that story ever since because it gave her permission to pursue what she deeply wanted to pursue without feeling she was betraying me and her father. But it also gave her permission to use anything she might pick up from us by giving her a way of construing the cross-generational relationship as a continuity. . . .

Julia Alvarez

FIRST MUSE

Children hear many stories while growing up, false and true, limiting and liberating, boring and exciting. They hear stories from family members and teachers, on the playground and on the screen. And they read stories in books. Occasionally a certain story sets a child's imagination free, and she comes to understand herself and her world as full of possibility. This is what happened to the writer Julia Alvarez during her childhood in the Dominican Republic. Many of Alvarez's own novels and stories, written decades after she moved with her family to the United States at the age of ten, explore the experience of growing up with one foot in each of two cultures.

This same sense of deep identification and liberating perspective on the world can also come to readers later in life. Has a certain book captured and empowered you, either as a child or as an adult, in a way similar to what Alvarez experienced? If so, try to trace the connections between your world and the world of that book, as Alvarez does in this passage. Do you ever look to reading in the hope that such connections – and hence insights – might emerge? To what extent do books continue to be important storytellers for you, in this age when stories are told so frequently and vividly on the screens of cineplexes, televisions, and computers? Can we learn anything from the excerpt below about the special power of books to help us to tell our own life stories?

Once upon a time, I lived in another country and in another language under a cruel dictatorship, which my father was plotting to overthrow. But what I remember is not the cruel dictator, not the disappearances, not my parents' nervous voices behind closed doors, but the storybook that helped me get though the long, dull school days that were my understanding of what dictatorships made children do.

....

From Julia Alvarez, *Something to Declare: Essays* (Chapel Hill, NC: Algonquin Books of Chapel Hill, 1998), 133–38.

I lay on my stomach under my bed, a six-, seven-, eight-, nine-, ten-year-old-girl — this went on for a long time, as long times do during childhood. With the bedskirt providing a perfect cover, I felt as if I had actually been transported to a silken tent in a faraway country with nothing but my wits to keep me alive. The storybook I was reading was one that my maiden aunt Tití, the only reader I knew, had given me. *The Thousand and One Nights*, it was called, and on its cover sat a young girl with a veil over her long, dark hair and beside her, reclining on one elbow and listening to what she was saying, was a young man with a turban on his head. What I like about this young girl was that unlike the fair princesses in the other storybooks, Scheherazade could have been a Dominican girl: dark-haired, almond-eyed, with color in her skin.

This book was the only voluntary reading I did, for I was a poor student and poorly behaved. In fact, if you want to know the truth, the reason I was hiding under the bed early in the morning instead of reading my book openly on top of my bed was to avoid having to go to school that day.

Every morning after breakfast my mother and aunts rounded up my sisters and cousins for the drive to school. There was a crowd of us — three cars were needed — and by the time one car was filled up and on its way, the aunts weren't quite sure who was already gone and who was left to transport. So, if I slipped away from my sisters and cousins, and hightailed it to my bedroom, and threw myself under the bed, and stayed there, quietly reading my book of stories, it would not be until midday, when the school crowd returned for a la comida del mediodía, that my mother realized that I had played hooky again right under her very nose.

Why did I do this? School was deadly. I thought I would surely die of boredom sitting on the hard chair listening to Mrs. Brown talk about the pilgrims or *i* before *e* or George Washington cutting down a cherry tree. We were attending the Carol Morgan School because my parents had decided that we should learn English and get "an American education" rather than a Dominican one. To this day, they claim this choice made our transition to the United States so much easier. But how could they have known back then that we would be going into exile in a few years?

So what I was learning in school had nothing to do with the lush, tropical, and dangerous world around me. We were living in a dictatorship, complete with spies, late-night disappearances, torture, and death. What, indeed, did this world have to do with the capital of Alabama and Dick and Jane and a big red bouncing ball? And what on earth was apple pie? Was it anything at all like a pastel de tamarindo? No wonder I shut the doors to my attention and refused to do my homework. My education was a colonialist one: not imposed from the outside but from within my own family. I was to learn the culture, tongue, manners of the powerful country to our north that had set our dictator in place and kept him there for thirty-one years. Maybe my parents did know what they were doing.

And maybe, I, sensing the unspoken world of intrigue and danger around me, where El Jefe ruled supreme, found kinship with the girl on the cover of my storybook.

Certainly she had more to say to me than Dick and Jane.

I AM SCHEHERAZADE, she would always begin. *I am a girl stuck in a king-dom that doesn't think females are very important.*

Why, that's just like me, I'd pipe up. It's always the boy cousins who are asked what they want to do with their lives. Girls are told we are going to be wives and mothers. If we're asked at all, it's usually how many children we want and whom we might want to marry.

But even though I am a girl, Scheherazade went on, *I am ambitious and clever and I've found ways of getting around the restraints put upon me.*

Why, that's just like me, I put in. Here I am, hiding under this bed in the middle of a school day, doing what I please. And I've found other ways of getting around things as well. I can learn any poem by heart if I hear it read out loud a few times. When company comes, Mami dresses me up in my first communion dress and takes me out to recite in front of everyone. They reward me with pesetas and sometimes a whole peso. I've already told Mami that when I grow up, I'll go ahead and have those half-dozen babies I'm supposed to have, but I'm also going to become a famous actress who gets to travel around the world and do whatever she wants —

Very recently, I had a shock, Scheherazade interrupted. (Pobrecita, she could hardly get a word in edgewise!) *I found out that I am living in a country where our cruel sultan is killing all my girlfriends. First he marries them, then the next day he kills them. I've been racking my brains, trying to figure out a way to stop all this killing, and I think I've finally got a plan.*

Far off in the direction of the palacio nacional, a siren sounded. I wasn't sure what it meant. Sometimes the siren meant a "resignation," with the retiree appearing in the papers a few days later in a black-outlined box with a crucifix and "Que descanse en paz" above a blurry photo of his face. Some-times the siren meant our jefe, Rafael Leonidas Trujillo, was going out, and so the streets had to be cleared. I am sure that siren also meant other things my parents were afraid to tell me.

What I am going to do, Scheherazade confided, *is marry the sultan, and then, before he can kill me the next morning, I'm going to tell him a story.*

That worked for me, I said, nodding at her bright-eyed face on the cover.

Many, many times I had escaped punishment with a story. Just last week, Mami came rushing to find out who had broken my grandmother's blue crystal ball that sat on a pedestal under the tamarind tree. Of course, it seemed pretty obvious to her when she found my cousin Ique and me holding rakes, but I set her straight. I told Mami that the reason we were holding rakes was that we had just chased off the man who had broken the ball.

"And what man would that be?" my mother asked, eyes narrowed.

Hmm, I thought. What man would that be? I knew my parents were afraid of the guardia who periodically came on the property searching for an acquaintance or just asking for un regalito to buy their cigarillos. So, I explained that the man we had chased off was a guardia whom we had caught snooping around the property.

That sent a volley of terrified looks among the adults who had followed my mother outside at the sound of breaking glass. How was I supposed to know that my father and uncles had joined the underground and were plotting the overthrow of the dictator? That my parents' seeming compliance was all show. That guardia on the grounds meant my family's participation had been uncovered. The adults went off in a cold sweat to a private conference behind locked doors while Ique and I were left to enjoy the tamarinds we had knocked down with our rakes.

I finally talk my father into going along with my plan, Scheherazade continued, *and so after my first night with the sultan, just as the sun is coming up, I say to the sultan, Oh, sultan, would you like to hear one of my wonderful stories? And the sultan shrugs, sure, go ahead —*

Just then, the bedskirt was lifted up. My mother's face peered angrily at me. "So, this is where you are. Come out this instant!" I crept out slowly, hunching my shoulders as if to take up less space on this earth. My mother shook me by the arm. "You better have a good explanation as to what you're doing under that bed instead of at school with your sisters."

Her yanking shook the book out of my hands. It fell, face up, on the floor. Scheherazade gazed up at me with an eager look in her eye, as if to say, "Go ahead, girl. Think up something!"

So, early on, I learned that stories could save you. That stories could weave a spell even over powerful adults and get them off your case and on to other things like talking politics behind closed doors or making a tamarind pastel in the kitchen.

Wendell Berry

JAYBER CROW

Wendell Berry is a poet, essayist, and novelist who lives on a small, working farm in Kentucky. We have already encountered him in a text in question 4, "Manifesto: The Mad Farmer Liberation Front."In the short passage below from his novel *Jayber Crow,* which is about the life of a barber in a Kentucky hamlet, Berry raises important questions about the relationship between our actual lives and the stories we might be tempted to tell ourselves about them. Mary Catherine Bateson makes a powerful case for our lives as improvisational art forms, but to what extent should we be free to improvise? Every life story omits some details and exaggerates others, selects some incidents as crucial and tries to diminish the importance of embarrassing moments. But to what extent should we be constrained by faithfulness to the record?

Here, Jayber Crow finds himself wishing that his life had been plotted one way rather than another. But he seems constrained by what he actually did or failed to do, by what actually happened to him and by what he made of those events at the time, to tell his life's story in a way that is perhaps less coherent and admirable than he would hope. Bateson shows us how important it is to be resourceful in formulating our life's stories. To what extent is it also important that we be truthful? What does "truthfulness" mean in the context of our autobiographies?

Jayber seems to settle at times for mystery over clarity, for trust in providence over rational plot resolution. But this interpretation itself has precedents, and Jayber knows it. The story of a life told as a series of accidents that seem best represented as a sometimes confused and confusing pilgrimage, often marked by ironic twists and turns, resembles one of the great stories that Bateson alludes to in her essay. St. Augustine, in his *Confessions,* composed his own life as a sometimes ironic pilgrimage suffused throughout with a "feeling that he had been led." Note that the first sentences of the selection refer to Dante's *Divine Comedy,* which begins in the Dark Wood of Error, and John Bunyan's *Pilgrim's Progress,* which follows the King's Highway.

From Wendell Berry, *Jayber Crow* (Washington, DC: Counterpoint, 2000), 133.

If you could do it, I suppose, it would be a good idea to live your life in a straight line — starting, say, in the Dark Wood of Error, and proceeding by logical steps through Hell and Purgatory and into Heaven. Or you could take the King's Highway past appropriately named dangers, toils, and snares, and finally cross the River of Death and enter the Celestial City. But that is not the way I have done it, so far. I am a pilgrim, but my pilgrimage has been wandering and unmarked. Often what has looked like a straight line to me has been a circle or a doubling back. I have been in the Dark Wood of Error any number of times. I have known something of Hell, Purgatory, and Heaven, but not always in that order. The names of many snares and dangers have been made known to me, but I have seen them only in looking back. Often I have not known where I was going until I was already there. I have had my share of desires and goals, but my life has come to me or I have gone to it mainly by way of mistakes and surprises. Often I have received better than I have deserved. Often my fairest hopes have rested on bad mistakes. I am an ignorant pilgrim, crossing a dark valley. And yet for a long time, looking back, I have been unable to shake off the feeling that I have been led — make of that what you will.

Alice Walker

SAVING THE LIFE THAT IS YOUR OWN

We tell our life stories by drawing on our culture's repertoire of plots, Mary Catherine Bateson has argued. Both Julia Alvarez and Jayber Crow (as animated by Wendell Berry) apparently did this, seeking reflections of their own struggles in stories written by others. The author of the next selection points out that sometimes the available repertoire is deficient. Early in her career as a writer, Alice Walker confronted the fact that the stories she needed most to lead the life that most mattered to her — becoming a writer — were not available to her. In this selection from the book *In Search of Our Mothers' Gardens*, she recounts the need she felt and the joyful discovery she made: other African American women writers had indeed existed, and they had left behind work that was beautiful and profound, even though mostly forgotten. Walker's discovery enabled her to craft a story from her own family into a literary work that turned out, in the end, also to incorporate the insights of the forebear she had been seeking, as well as her own contemporary perspective. Walker would later work to make the life stories and writings of her literary ancestors known. Zora Neale Hurston, who figures prominently in the selection below, is now recognized as one of America's greatest writers; her best-known work is the short novel *Their Eyes Were Watching God*.

The excerpt below is the story of how Walker became the storyteller she is. She found a "model." Sadly, the first part of her essay concludes, another artist, Vincent van Gogh, did not. Although Walker emphasizes the need for models who share her race and gender, she honors the intense need of a European man as well and seems to find connections between their aspirations. Do you have the "models" you need? Who are they? If models are lacking, where might you seek them?

Walker is the author of *The Color Purple* and many other novels, stories, poems, and essays.

....

From Alice Walker, *In Search of Our Mothers' Gardens* (New York: Harcourt Brace Jovanovich, 1983), 3–13.

There is a letter Vincent Van Gogh wrote to Emily Bernard that is very meaningful to me. A year before he wrote the letter, Van Gogh had had a fight with his domineering friend Gauguin, left his company, and cut off, in desperation and anguish, his own ear. The letter was written in Saint-Remy, in the South of France, from a mental institution to which Van Gogh had voluntarily committed himself.

I imagine Van Gogh sitting at a rough desk too small for him, looking out at the lovely Southern light, and occasionally glancing critically next to him at his own paintings of the landscape he loved so much. The date of the letter is December 1889. Van Gogh wrote:

> However hateful painting may be, and however cumbersome the times we are living in, if anyone who has chosen this handicraft pursues it zealously, he is a man of duty, sound and faithful.
>
> Society makes our existence wretchedly difficult at times, hence our impotence and the imprecation of our work.
>
> . . . I myself am suffering under an absolute lack of models.
>
> But on the other hand, there are beautiful spots here. I have just done five size 30 canvasses, olive trees. And the reason I am staying on here is that my health is improving a great deal.
>
> What I am doing is hard, dry, but that is because I am trying to gather new strength by doing some rough work, and I'm afraid abstractions would make me soft.

Six months later, Van Gogh — whose health was "improving a great deal" — committed suicide. He had sold one painting during his lifetime. Three times was his work noticed in the press. But these are just details.

The real Vincent Van Gogh is the man who has "just done five size 30 canvasses, olive trees." To me, in context, one of the most moving and revealing descriptions of how a real artist thinks. And the knowledge that when he spoke of "suffering under an absolute lack of models" he spoke of that lack in terms of both the intensity of his commitment and the quality and singularity of his work, which was frequently ridiculed in his day.

The absence of models, in literature as in life, to say nothing of painting, is an occupational hazard for the artist, simply because models in art, in behavior, in growth of spirit and intellect — even if rejected — enrich and enlarge one's view of existence. Deadlier still, to the artist who lacks models, is the curse of ridicule, the bringing to bear on an artist's best work, especially his or her most original, most strikingly deviant, only a fund of ignorance and the presumption that, as an artist's critic, one's judgment is free of the restrictions imposed by prejudice, and is well informed, indeed, about all the art in the world that really matters.

What is always needed in the appreciation of art, or life, is the larger perspective. Connections made, or at least attempted, where none existed before, the straining to encompass in one's glance at the varied world the common thread, the unifying theme through immense diversity, a fearlessness of growth, of search, of looking that enlarges the private and the public world. And yet, in our particular society, it is the narrowed and narrowing view of life that often wins. . . .

I have often been asked why, in my own life and work, I have felt such a desperate need to know and assimilate the experiences of earlier black women writers, most of them unheard of by you and by me, until quite recently; why I felt a need to study them and to teach them.

I don't recall the exact moment I set out to explore the works of black women, mainly those in the past, and certainly, in the beginning, I had no desire to teach them. Teaching being for me, at that time, less rewarding than star-gazing on a frigid night. My discovery of them — most of them out of print, abandoned, discredited, maligned, nearly lost — came about, as many things of values do, almost by accident. As it turned out — and this should not have surprised me — I found I was in need of something that only one of them could provide.

Mindful that throughout my four years at a prestigious black and then a prestigious white college I had heard not one word about early black women writers, one of my first tasks was simply to determine whether they had existed. After this, I could breathe easier, with more assurance about the profession I myself had chosen.

But the incident that started my search began several years ago: I sat down at my desk one day, in a room of my own, with key and lock, and began preparations for a story about voodoo, a subject that had always fascinated me. Many of the elements of this story I had gathered from a story my mother several times told me. She had gone, during the Depression, into town to apply for some government surplus food at the local commissary, and had been turned down, in a particularly humiliating way, by the white woman in charge.

My mother always told this story with a most curious expression on her face. She automatically raised her head higher than ever — it was always high — and there was a look of righteousness, a kind of holy *heat* coming from her eyes. She said she had lived to see this same white woman grow old and senile and so badly crippled she had to get about on *two* sticks.

To her, this was clearly the working of God, who, as in the old spiritual, ". . . may not come when you want him, but he's right on time!" To me, hearing the story for about the fiftieth time, something else was discernible: the possibilities of the story, for fiction.

What, I asked myself, would have happened if, after the crippled old lady died, it was discovered that someone, my mother perhaps (who would have been mortified at the thought, Christian that she is), had voodooed her?

Then, my thoughts sweeping me away into the world of hexes and conjurings of centuries past, I wondered how a larger story could be created out of my mother's story; one that would be true to the magnitude of her humiliation and grief, and to the white woman's lack of sensitivity and compassion.

My third quandary was: How could I find out all I needed to know in order to write a story that used *authentic* black witchcraft?

Which brings me back, almost, to the day I became really interested in black women writers. I say "almost" because one other thing, from my childhood, made the choice of black magic a logical and irresistible one for my story. Aside from my mother's several stories about root doctors she had heard of or known, there was the story I had often heard about my "crazy" Walker aunt.

Many years ago, when my aunt was a meek and obedient girl growing up in a strict, conventionally religious house in the rural South, she had suddenly thrown off her meekness and had run away from home, escorted by a rogue of a man permanently attached elsewhere.

When she was returned home by her father, she was declared quite mad. In the backwoods South at the turn of the century, "madness" of this sort was cured not by psychiatry but by powders and by spells. (Once can see Scott Joplin's *Treemonisha* to understand the role voodoo played among black people of that period.) My aunt's madness was treated by the community conjurer, who promised, and delivered, the desired results. His treatment was a bag of white powder, bought for fifty cents, and sprinkled on the ground around her house, with some of it sewed, I believe, into the bodice of her nightgown.

So when I sat down to write my story about voodoo, my crazy Walker aunt was definitely on my mind.

But she had experienced her temporary craziness so long ago that her story had all the excitement of a might-have-been. I needed, instead of family memories, some hard facts about the *craft* of voodoo, as practiced by Southern blacks in the nineteenth century. (It never once, fortunately, occurred to me that voodoo was not worthy of the interest I had in it, or was too ridiculous to study seriously.)

I began reading all I could find on the subject of "The Negro and His Folkways and Superstitions." There were Botkin and Puckett and others, all white, most racist. How was I to believe anything they wrote, since at least one of them, Puckett, was capable of wondering, in his book, if "The Negro" had a large enough brain?

Well, I thought, where are the *black* collectors of folklore? Where is the *black* anthropologist? Where is the *black* person who took the time to travel the back roads of the South and collect the information I need: how to cure heart trouble, treat dropsy, hex somebody to death, lock bowels, cause joints to swell, eyes to fall out, and so on. Where was this black person?

And that is when I first saw, in a *footnote* to the white voices of authority, the name Zora Neale Hurston.

Folklorist, novelist, anthropologist, serious student of voodoo, also all-around black woman, with guts enough to take a slide rule and measure random black heads in Harlem; not to prove their inferiority, but to prove that whatever their size, shape, or present condition of servitude, those heads contained all the intelligence anyone could use to get through this world.

Zora Hurston, who went to Barnard to learn how to study what she really wanted to learn: the ways of her own people, and what ancient rituals, customs, and beliefs had made them unique.

Zora, of the sandy-colored hair and the daredevil eyes, a girl who escaped poverty and parental neglect by hard work and a sharp eye for the main chance.

Zora, who left the South only to return to look at it again. Who went to root doctors from Florida to Louisiana and said, "Here I am. I want to learn your trade."

Zora, who had collected all the black folklore I could ever use.

That Zora.

And having found *that Zora* (like a golden key to a storehouse of varied treasure), I was hooked.

What I had discovered, of course, was a model. A model, who, as it happened, provided more than voodoo for my story, more than one of the greatest novels America had produced — though, being America, it did not realize this. She had provided, as if she knew someday I would come along wandering in the wilderness, a nearly complete record of her life. And though her life sprouted an occasional wart, I am eternally grateful for that life, warts and all.

It is not irrelevant, nor is it bragging (except perhaps to gloat a little on the happy relatedness of Zora, my mother, and me), to mention here that the story I wrote, called "The Revenge of Hannah Kemhuff," based on my mother's experiences during the Depression, and on Zora Hurston's folklore collection of the 1920s, and on my own response to both out of a contemporary existence, was immediately published and was later selected, by a reputable collector of short stories, as one of the *Best Short Stories of 1974*.

I mention it because this story might never have been written, because the very bases of its structure, authentic black folklore, viewed from a black perspective, might have been lost.

Had it been lost, my mother's story would have had no historical underpinning, none I could trust, anyway. I would not have written the story, which I enjoyed writing as much as I've enjoyed writing anything else in my life, had I not known that Zora had already done a thorough job of preparing the ground over which I was then moving.

In that story I gathered up the historical and psychological threads of the life my ancestors lived, and in the writing of it I felt joy and strength and my own continuity. I had that wonderful feeling writers get sometimes, not very often, of being *with* a great many people, ancient spirits, all very happy to see me consulting and acknowledging them, and eager to let me know, through the joy of their presence, that, indeed, I am not alone.

Dan P. McAdams

A LIFE STORY MADE IN AMERICA

Personality psychologist Dan McAdams, a professor at Northwestern University, adds one very important narrative form to the cultural repertoire of stories Mary Catherine Bateson describes in her essay and from which we may choose in composing our own lives. In this essay, drawn from the prologue of his book *The Redemptive Self* (2005), McAdams summarizes findings that are especially pertinent to our concerns about leading lives that matter.

McAdams has spent many years studying Americans who are leading lives that matter according to almost every standard we have encountered in the other readings. They are people of good character who have "made a positive difference" in the world. And if they are Americans, they are much more disposed than others anywhere to construe their lives in redemptive terms, to cast the stories they tell themselves about themselves in a particular narrative form.

Why are people of noble character who do make a difference in the world so drawn to narratives of redemption when they talk about their lives? Does McAdams think such an affinity is always a salutary thing? In other words, does a tendency to think of your life in redemptive terms make you a better person? Two features of redemptive narratives are an early conviction that one has been specially blessed and that others have suffered. Do those who have been specially blessed in fact have an obligation to serve those who have not been similarly fortunate? Why or why not?

Beginning September 11, 2001, William Langewiesche spent 9 months at the site of the World Trade Center disaster. He observed and interviewed firefighters, construction workers, engineers, police officers, and paid volunteers who cleared the debris and dug through the rubble in search of survivors.

From Dan P. McAdams, *The Redemptive Self: Stories Americans Live By* (New York: Oxford University Press, 2005), 3–14.

"Within hours of the collapse [of the towers], as rescuers rushed in and re-sources were marshaled," Langewiesche later wrote, "the disaster was smoth-ered in an exuberant and *distinctively American* embrace." The workers were convinced that something good would rise from the carnage. "Despite the apocalyptic nature of the scene," Langewiesche suggested, "the response was unhesitant and almost childishly optimistic: *it was simply understood* that you would find survivors, and then that you would find the dead, and that this would help their families to get on with their lives, and that your resources were unlimited, and that you would work night and day to clean up the mess, and that this would allow the world's greatest city to rebuild quickly, and maybe even to make itself into something better than before."

Put differently, it was simply understood that there would be *redemp-tion*.

An "exuberant" and "distinctively American" response, "unhesitant," al-most childish. The workers were convinced that the death and the destruc-tion of September 11 would give way to new life, new growth, new power, and a new reality that, in some fundamental sense, would prove better than what came before. Their faith reflected the hopes of many American citi-zens — men and women who had never known a foreign attack on American soil but who felt deep in their bones that bad things, even things this bad, ultimately lead to good outcomes, that suffering is ultimately redeemed.

Maybe there *is* something childish (and presumptuous) about this re-sponse, this expectation that we will be delivered from our pain and suf-fering no matter what, that we will overcome in the long run, that we will rise from the depths of the present, that things will get better and that we will eventually grow and find fulfillment in the world. But I am not talking here about the naïveté of children. I am talking instead about mature men and women who, like many of the workers at the World Trade Center site, are committed to making a positive difference in the world. I am talking about productive and caring, socially responsible, hardworking adults who try to pay their bills and their taxes, try to provide for their families, and try to make something good out of their lives, even as they fail and get dis-tracted along the way. I am talking about the kinds of people who support the institutions that are necessary to create and sustain what the sociolo-gist Robert Bellah calls a "good society." Let us imagine that these are the people whom the framers of the U.S. Constitution had in mind when they identified the ultimate authors of their document as "we the people." For the framers, we the people aimed to "form a more perfect union, establish justice, insure domestic tranquility, provide for the common defense, promote the general welfare, and secure the blessings of liberty to ourselves and our posterity."

From a psychological standpoint, who *are* "we the people"? What are we like? In considering this question, I turn first to the eminent psychoanalyst Erik H. Erikson, who, during much of the second half of the 20th century, wrote provocatively about mental health, maturity, and the human life span. Erikson depicted we the people as those members of a society who have worked though the psychological dilemmas of childhood, adolescence, and the very early years of adulthood and who have committed themselves to patterns of love and work aimed at leaving a positive legacy for the future. The Constitution suggests that we the people should strive to assure justice, peace, security, and freedom not just for us today — but also for our posterity, our children and our children's children. The good society must work to promote the well-being of future generations. Erikson claimed that responsible and mature men and women — especially in their middle-adult years — should do the same. Erikson even had a word for this. He called it *generativity*.

Generativity is the adult's concern for and commitment to promoting the welfare and development of future generations. The most obvious and natural expression of generativity is the care that parents provide for their children. But generativity can be expressed in many other ways, too, including teaching, mentoring, leadership, and even citizenship. Generative adults seek to give something back to society. They work to make their world a better place, not just for themselves but for future generations, as well. They try to take the long view. Whether they consciously think about it this way or not, generative adults work for the good of posterity. A good society depends on the generative efforts of adults. For this reason (among others), Erikson believed that generativity was more than simply a psychological standard for adult mental health. He also saw it as the prime virtue of adulthood.

Different people have different virtues. Some people are more honest than others. Some may be more courageous, faithful, or self-disciplined. And so it is with generativity, as Erikson well knew. Most adults are moderately generative on the average, focusing most of their generative inclinations on their families. A few adults show virtually no generativity in their lives. And some, on the other end of the spectrum, are extraordinarily generative in many different ways. Think of them as generativity superstars.

For many years now, I have been studying the superstars. Who are the especially generative people in our society? What are their lives like? In the summer of 2000, I was presenting some of this research at a scientific conference in the Netherlands when I received a comment from a woman in the audience that eventually gave birth to this book. The main point of my talk was that highly generative adults tend to tell a certain kind of story about their lives, a story that emphasizes the themes of suffering, redemption, and personal destiny. The comment I received went something like this: "Professor McAdams, this is very interesting, but these life stories you describe, they seem so, well, *American*." Initially, I heard this as a criticism of the work. After all, I had been assuming that my findings applied to very generative adults *in general*, regardless of their backgrounds. To say the life stories I described all sounded very "American" was to suggest that my research findings were too limited, that they were not "generalizable," as we social scientists often say.

After thinking longer about the woman's comment, however, I came to realize two things. First, she was probably right, at least in part. My results about Americans might *not* generalize completely to other societies. Second, I think I like the fact that she may have been right. Her comment suggests an important insight: The life stories of highly generative American adults may reveal as much about American society and culture as they do about the generative adults themselves. It is as if these well-meaning American people who dedicate their lives to promoting the well-being of the next generation are walking embodiments of some of the most cherished (and contested) ideas in our American heritage. Their lives personify and proclaim the stories that we all — we Americans — might like to tell about our own lives, stories that we indeed *do* often tell, though perhaps with less conviction, consistency, and gusto. The stories they live and tell are our stories, too — made in America.

What is the story that highly generative American adults tell? Everybody has a unique life story to tell. But if you listen to many life stories, as I and my students have over the past 20 years, you begin to recognize some common patterns. The pattern that I will focus on in this book is the one that tends to distinguish the life stories told by highly generative American adults from those told by less generative American adults. Research findings suggest that highly generative American adults are statistically more likely than their less generative counterparts to make sense of their own lives through an idealized story script that emphasizes, among other themes, the power of human redemption. In the most general sense, redemption is *a deliverance from suffering to a better world*. Religious conceptions of redemption imagine it as a divine intervention or sacred process, and the better world may mean heaven, a state of grace, or some other transcendent status. The general idea of redemption can be found in all of the world's major religions and many cultural traditions.

It is important to realize, however, that redemption carries many secular meanings that have nothing to do with religion. Everyday talk is filled with redemptive metaphors. People often speak of "putting the past behind" them in order to move away from something negative to a positive future. Adages such as "every dark cloud has a silver lining," "it's always darkest before the dawn," and "no pain, no gain" suggest that suffering in life can often lead to growth or fulfillment. "When life gives you lemons, make lemonade," we are told. Try to transform the negative into some kind of positive. We all know expressions like these, and we can all probably find a few instances in our own lives when this general idea seemed to take hold. Furthermore, we are encouraged to think about our lives in redemptive terms. As just one example, many high school counselors in the United States today strongly urge their college-bound seniors to write personal essays that document the ways they have overcome adversity. College admissions officers appear to value these redemptive accounts quite highly, sometimes even assigning extra points to an applicant's file for especially compelling stories of resilience, recovery, defying the odds, and the like.

When they take stock of their own lives, highly generative American adults tent to *narrate* them around the theme of redemption. They are more likely than the rest of us to see redemptive patterns in their lives. Almost everybody can find some kind of redemption in his or her life story. But progress is very common in these stories. The protagonist gives birth to many things and people, cares for them and provides for their well-being, and eventually lets them go so that they can move forward in life with the generative blessings they have received. One highly generative adult put it this way: "When I die, I guess the chemicals in my body, well, they'll go to fertilize some plants, you know, some ears of corn, and the good deeds I do will live through my children and through the people I love."

In sum, then, here is the general script of the life story I have described: *I learn in childhood that I have a special gift. At the same time, I see (and am moved by) suffering and injustice in my world. As a result, I come to believe that my personal destiny is to have some positive impact on others. In adolescence I internalize a belief system that sustains my commitment to improving the world. I will never abandon these core beliefs. Over the course of my adult life, I struggle to reconcile my strong needs for power and independence with my equally strong needs for love and community. Bad things happen to me, but good outcomes often follow. My suffering is usually redeemed, as I continue to progress, to learn, to improve. Looking to the future, I expect the things I have generated will continue to grow and flourish, even in a dangerous world.*

Do you see your life this way? Is this the kind of story you might tell if asked to tell the story of your life? Some people will say that their life fits the pattern pretty closely; others will claim that there is no resemblance at all. Most likely, though, there are parts of this story that seem like yours and others that do not. Highly generative American adults tend, on average, to construct life stories that resemble, sometimes quite closely, the pattern I have described. Like many of us, but perhaps a little more strongly than most of us, they tell life stories that affirm the power of human redemption. What does this life story mean? Why does this kind of redemptive story appear so often in the lives of very generative American adults? What is so great about this story? And what is wrong with it?

My central goal in this book is to explore the psychological and cultural meaning of redemptive stories in American lives. The great American novelist Robert Penn Warren has written that to be an American is not a matter of blood or birth; it is a matter of an idea. That idea is large and "contains multitudes," as Walt Whitman wrote, but at the heart of it are stories that Americans have traditionally told about themselves and about their nation. Highly generative American adults tell life stories that unconsciously re-work deep and vexing issues in our cultural heritage. These same stories, furthermore, address thorny new problems we face as Americans living at the dawn of the 21st century. As I move back and forth in this book between psychology and American culture, I will affirm and defend six key points. Taken together, these six points make up my book's essential argument:

1. Generativity is the central psychological and moral challenge adults face, especially in their 30s, 40s, and 50s.

2. Generative adults tend to see their lives as redemptive stories that emphasize related themes such as early advantage, the suffering of others, moral clarity, the conflict between power and love, and leaving a legacy of growth.

3. Redemptive life stories promote psychological health and maturity, and they provide narrative guidelines for living a responsible and caring life.

4. Redemptive life stories reflect and rework such quintessentially American ideas as *manifest destiny, the chosen people,* and the ambivalence Americans have traditionally felt about our most cherished of all values — freedom. Expressions of these themes can be found not

only in the life stories of highly generative American adults, but also in a wide range of American cultural texts, from Puritan conversion stories and the Gettysburg Address to contemporary self-help books and *People* magazine. And, indeed, you do not have to be a generativity superstar to see your life in redemptive terms. Many Americans see their lives this way, to some extent. The story, like our lives, is made in America.

5. Redemptive life stories in America are profoundly shaped by two American peculiarities: (a) that this is one of the most religious industrialized societies in the world and (b) that this society has been torn asunder, from its inception, by the issue of race. Some of the most redemptive texts in the American tradition may be found in the African American heritage and in the life stories of highly generative Black adults.

6. For all their psychological and moral strength, redemptive life stories sometimes fail, and they may reveal dangerous shortcomings and blind spots in Americans' understandings of themselves and the world. After all, is it not presumptuous to expect deliverance from all suffering? Is it not an affront to those who have suffered the greatest calamities and heartaches to expect, even to suggest, that things will turn out nice and happy in the end? In this sense, there may indeed be something "almost childish" about the redemptive self — something a bit too naïve and Pollyanna for a world where tragedy often seems more common and compelling than redemption. And is it not arrogant to imagine one's life as the full manifestation of an inner destiny? You can sometimes detect an entitled, "true believer" quality in the life stories of many highly generative American adults — an assuredness regarding the goodness and the power of the individual self that may seem off-putting and can sometimes prove destructive. We will see, then, that redemptive narratives sometimes condone and reinforce social isolation and a kind of psychological *American exceptionalism*. Redemptive narratives may support, intentionally or unconsciously, a naïve optimism about the world, excessive moral fervor, and self-righteous aggression, even war, in the service of self-centered ends. The rhetoric of redemption makes it easy for us Americans to see ourselves as superior to the rest of the world and to identify our enemies as the "axis of evil." While redemptive life narratives affirm hope and human progress, therefore, we must also face up to the dark side of American redemption.

Twenty years ago, the sociologist Robert Bellah and his colleagues published an influential book, *Habits of the Heart*, that examined the ways Americans have traditionally talked about their strivings for personal fulfillment and interpersonal community. In the 18th and 19th centuries, figures like Thomas Jefferson and Abraham Lincoln personified uniquely American character types, the authors argued, who inspired Americans to live good lives. These types no longer work for us, however. *Habits of the Heart* showed that Americans today have a difficult time finding an appropriate language to express desires for living together in harmony, helping each other, and committing themselves to meaningful long-term life projects beyond the self. It is not so much that we are selfish people as that we are incapable of expressing the desires we do have to go beyond self-interest. Bellah and is colleagues challenged their readers to imagine new character types that might inspire future generations of Americans to live caring and productive lives.

From a psychological standpoint, the authors of *Habits of the Heart* may have been asking for too much. Research in personality and developmental psychology suggests that most people are too complex to fit into the kind of neat character types that Bellah ascribed to American heroes like Jefferson and Lincoln. Human lives are messy and filled with contradictions. Each person shows a wide range of different traits; different traits get expressed in different situations; people change in important ways over time. Nonetheless, Bellah and his colleagues were definitely onto something important in focusing so much attention on how Americans talk about their lives. When people talk about their lives, they tell *stories*. It is through stories that we often learn the greatest lessons for our lives — lessons about success and failure, good and evil, what makes a life worth living, and what makes a society good. It is through stories, furthermore, that we define who we are. Stories provide us with our identities.

Highly generative American adults may not fit neatly into any single character type, but they do seem to have a type of *story* to tell about life. The redemptive stories that highly generative American adults tell recapture some of the ideas espoused in moral character types from long ago, but they also speak in the very contemporary language of 21st century America. Redemptive stories provide images, scenes, plots, and themes that we might wish to borrow and rework into our own lives. I will never be just like my most admired hero from history or the movies, or my most beloved high school coach. But I may borrow pieces of their stories and work them into my own. . . .

My research is part of an emerging movement in the social sciences called the *narrative study of lives*. The central idea in this movement is that human lives are cultural texts that can be interpreted as stories. People create stories to make sense of their lives. These evolving stories — or *narrative identities* — provide our lives with some semblance of meaning, unity, and purpose. Along with our dispositional traits and our motives and goals, internalized life stories make up important aspects of our personality. Our stories are implicated in determining what we do and how we make sense of what we do. As a *narrative psychologist*, I systematically analyze the texts of people's life stories to obtain a better understanding of both the people who tell the stories and the culture within which those stories (and those people) are born. "We tell ourselves stories in order to live," writes the American essayist Joan Didion. By examining life stories, we may learn more about how Americans live, and how we might live better.

Michael T. Kaufman

ROBERT McG. THOMAS, 60, CHRONICLER OF UNSUNG LIVES

The value, perhaps even the virtue, of the stories that we tell about ourselves during our lifetimes derives in part from their serviceability: such stories help us to recollect our identity and purpose, thereby encouraging us to lead lives that matter. But this cannot be the virtue of a good obituary, since the subject of the obituary is no longer living. It would seem that the virtue of a good obituary is its "truthfulness," its capacity to be faithful to the actual life of its subject. When truthful, an obituary serves not only the one who has died but also those who remain, who may glimpse something about the meaning and significance of a life — and possibly, by extension, of their own lives — even in a short article.

The reading below is most unusual; it is an obituary of a writer of obituaries. The colleague writing this obituary writer's obituary expresses admiration for the skill and insight of the deceased, who was gifted in discerning the "telling details" that illuminated a life's shape and significance. What telling detail — what moment, what choice, what habit — might someone writing your obituary find especially noteworthy? How might this detail fit, or not fit, into the more encompassing story of your life? After pondering those questions for a while, revisit "The Road Not Taken." Did you really know, at the time of that moment or choice, that something significant was happening? How has the story you now tell about that moment or choice been fashioned by a later version of yourself? And how might this story be serviceable as you seek to lead a life that matters?

Robert McG. Thomas Jr., a reporter for *The New York Times* who extended the possibilities of the conventional obituary form, shaking the dust from one of the most neglected areas of daily journalism, died on Thursday at

Michael T. Kaufman, "Robert McG. Thomas, 60, Chronicler of Unsung Lives," *New York Times*, January 8, 2000.

his family's summer home in Rehoboth Beach, Del. He was 60 and also had a home in Manhattan.

The cause was abdominal cancer, said his wife, Joan.

Mr. Thomas began writing obituaries full time in 1995 after serving as a police reporter, a rewrite man, a society news reporter and a sports writer. He developed a fresh approach to the genre, looking for telling details to illuminate lives that might otherwise have been overlooked or underreported.

Mr. Thomas saw himself as the sympathetic stranger at the wake listening to the friends and survivors of the deceased, alert for the moment when one of them would tell a memorable tale that could never have made its way into *Who's Who* or a resume but that just happened to define a life.

In 1995, when *The Times* proposed him for a Pulitzer Prize in the category of spot news, the nomination began: "Every week, readers write to *The New York Times* to say they were moved to tears or laughter by an obituary of someone they hadn't known until that morning's paper. Invariably, the obituary is the work of Robert McG. Thomas Jr., who hadn't known the subject, either, until the assignment landed on his desk a few hours before deadline."

The gallery of portraits that Mr. Thomas compiled covered an impressive range. Among them were Howard C. Fox, "the Chicago clothier and sometime big-band trumpeter who claimed credit for creating and naming the zoot suit with the reet pleat, the reave sleeve, the ripe stripe, the stuff cuff and the drape shape that was the stage rage during the boogie-woogie rhyme time of the early 1940's," and Russell Colley, a mechanical engineer who became "the Calvin Klein of space" and was known to a generation of astronauts as the "father of the space suit." There were Rose Hamburger, a 105-year-old racing handicapper; Marion Tinsley, a checker champion unbeaten by man or machine, and a vivacious woman who started out as a showgirl and ended up a princess ("Honeychile Wilder is dead, and if the '21' Club is not in actual mourning, it is because the venerable former speakeasy on West 52nd Street was closed for vacation last week when word got around that one of its most memorable former patrons had died on Aug. 11 at Memorial Sloan-Kettering Cancer Center").

Mr. Thomas, a tall man with wavy hair who spoke in a voice soft with traces of his native Tennessee, was an extremely gregarious and social man. Last week he officiated at the annual New Year's Eve party he first started giving at the family home in Shelbyville 32 years ago. About 5 percent of the town's 12,000 people attended, and Mr. Thomas, wearing a blue silk shirt with embroidered sun and moon that he bought for the occasion, cheered his guests and the new century. As in past years, he expressed hopes that the fireworks he had ordered would not set fire to the Presbyterian church across the road.

He was fond of writing about people who became legendary as a result of a single exploit, like Douglas Corrigan, who took off from New York in a tiny overloaded plane bound for California (he said) in 1938 and landed in Dublin some 28 hours later. He became an instant hero, forever to be known as Wrong Way Corrigan, but in his obituary, Mr. Thomas went beyond recapitulation to suggest that Mr. Corrigan was more cunning than befuddled. He wrote:

"Although he continued to claim with a more or less straight face that he had simply made a wrong turn and been led astray by a faulty compass, the story was far from convincing, especially to the American aviation authorities who had rejected his repeated requests to make just such a flight because his modified 1929 Curtiss-Robin monoplane was judged unworthy."

In a similar vein, he wrote of Johnny Sylvester, who died in 1990, 64 years after he came to fame as a bedridden boy who inspired Babe Ruth. Here is how Mr. Thomas began his obituary, which was included in "The Last Word: The New York Times Book of Obituaries and Farewells" (William Morrow): "There are those who will tell you that little Johnny Sylvester was never that sick and certainly not dying. They will tell you that Babe Ruth never promised to hit a home run for him in Game 4 of the 1926 World Series, and that the three home runs that the Babe did hit in that game in no way saved the 11-year-old youngster's life.

"Any representations to the contrary, these people will tell you, were simply embellishments of a trivial incident by an oversentimental press in a hypersentimental age.

"Such people are known as cynics."

There was something mythic, too, about Sylvia Weinberger, Mr. Thomas wrote, "who used a sprinkling of matzoh meal, a pinch of salt and a dollop of schmaltzmanship to turn chopped liver into a commercial success."

Robert McGill Thomas Jr. was born and grew up in Shelbyville, Tenn., where chopped liver is rare and schmaltz is not part of the vernacular. He spent his 15th year cheering for a distant relative, Senator Estes Kefauver, as Kefauver ran for vice president on the Democratic ticket with Adlai E. Stevenson. Three years later Mr. Thomas went to Yale, where he worked on the student newspaper and flunked out as a result of a decision, he said, "to major in New York rather than anything academic."

After joining *The Times* as a copyboy in 1959, Mr. Thomas spent the next four decades in a variety of reporting assignments, often prowling police stations and working the phones in the late hours to produce fast-breaking stories. With his fondness for anomalies, Mr. Thomas might have described his own journalistic career as more circuitous than meteoric.

Always regarded as a stylish writer by his colleagues, he sometimes ran into career turbulence because of an acknowledged tendency to carry things like sentences, paragraphs, ideas and enthusiasms further than at least some editors preferred. Indeed, he went beyond acknowledging this trait to defending it. "Of course I go too far," he used to say. "But unless you go too far how are you ever going to find out how far you can go?"

All of this may explain the sympathy he showed in his obituaries of underachievers and late bloomers.

There was certainly no sense of superiority in his account of the life choice made by Steven Slepack, a man who gave up a promising career in marine biology to become Professor Bendeasy, "the man in the beribboned tuxedo jacket who delighted a generation of schoolchildren by twisting balloons into animals in Central Park." He described a character actor named Jack Weston as "the quintessential New Yorker, which is to say he was born in Cleveland and lived in Los Angeles for 18 years, hating every minute of it he wasn't actually in front of the camera."

In writing about Anton Rosenberg, a painter and jazz musician, Mr. Thomas said he "embodied the Greenwich Village hipster ideal of 1950's cool to such a laid-back degree and with such determined detachment that he never amounted to much of anything."

For some admirers, for whom Mr. Thomas's work came to be known as "McG's," a favorite was his obituary of Edward Lowe, which revealed how Mr. Lowe, a sawdust merchant from Cassopolis, Mich., found a new use for some kiln-dried granulated clay he had been selling as a sop for grease spills in industrial plants and created a million-dollar market for the product he named and marketed as Kitty Litter.

Mr. Thomas provided the antecedent action to the tale in a second paragraph that established the historical significance of Mr. Lowe's achievement: "Cats have been domesticated since ancient Egypt, but until a fateful January day in 1947, those who kept them indoors full time paid a heavy price. For all their vaunted obsession with paw-licking cleanliness, cats, whose constitutions were adapted for arid desert climes, make such an efficient use of water that they produce a highly concentrated urine that is one of the most noxious effluences of the animal kingdom. Boxes filled with sand, sawdust or wood shavings provided a measure of relief from the resulting stench, but not enough to make cats particularly welcome in discriminating homes."

One of his admirers was Joseph Epstein, the literary essayist. "I have noted an interesting general-assignment obituary writer with the somewhat overloaded name of Robert McG. Thomas Jr., who occasionally gets beyond the facts and the rigid formula of the obit to touch on — of all things to find in *The New York Times* — a deeper truth," Mr. Epstein wrote.

"Thus Thomas on one Fred Rosenstiel, 'who spent his life planting gardens to brighten the lives of his fellow New Yorkers, and to alleviate an abiding sadness in his heart. . . .' The sadness, we learn later in the obituary, derived from Mr. Rosenstiel's inability to 'forgive himself for surviving the Holocaust.' A fine touch."

In addition to his wife, Mr. Thomas is survived by their twin sons, Andrew, of Lewes, Del., and David, of Manhattan; a sister, Carey Gates Thomas Hines of Birmingham, Ala., and two grandchildren.

EPILOGUE

n the funeral scene early in *The Death of Ivan Ilych,* one of Ivan Ilych's associates looks at him lying in his casket. He notices the expression on the dead man's face, which showed that "what was necessary" had been "accomplished rightly": the body had been "rightly" prepared for burial by the professionals charged with that responsibility. But beneath the proprieties, "there was in that expression a reproach and a warning to the living." We readers are among the living who must reckon with the expression on Ivan Ilych's face. What, we should wonder as we read Leo Tolstoy's great story, do the life and death of the main character say to us about what it means to live a life that matters?

Answering this question carefully will require us to revisit in a serious and enlightening way most of the issues raised in this anthology. *Leading Lives That Matter* has demonstrated time and time again that the question of what it means to lead a significant and choiceworthy life needs to be explored from many vantage points within thickly described contexts. We learned in the vocabularies section of this book that people in our society have different ways of speaking and thinking about what makes for a life that matters. We then considered a variety of readings about several of the concerns that are part of the larger inquiry into what a significant and meaningful life might look like, including especially the complicated relationship between what we do to earn a living and who we are as human beings. Often, we made better progress in this investigation when we focused upon particular characters in well-defined situations, such as the young Albert Schweitzer as he was deciding to become a jungle doctor or the singer Thea Kronborg, the character in Willa Cather's novel who was trying to figure out whether she should continue her musical career. When we examined and compared short sketches of whole lives under the "exemplarist"vocabulary, we were able to focus and clarify our own thinking about how and why we ourselves might choose one kind of life over another one.

More often than not, however, we wanted to know more about a particular life before we could pass judgment on it. What options did the person

565

really have available to her? What was the person like in all areas of life, not just the one portrayed? What really motivated someone to act as he did? What kinds of advice was he receiving? What support did he receive from family and friends? What were the social or religious norms that had shaped him? Thanks to the genius of Leo Tolstoy, the story of Ivan Ilych, if we read it closely, can answer all these questions and more. We can take the measure of the man's life both as he lived it and as he interpreted it retrospectively just before his death. And though the work is quite short compared to the ones for which Tolstoy is best known, *War and Peace* (1865–1869) and *Anna Karenina* (1873–1877), we will grow to feel as we read that we have access to Ivan Ilych's entire life, that nothing that we need to understand this man, his living, and his dying has been omitted.

Curiously, the novella both begins and ends with the death of Ivan Ilych, or, to be more precise, it begins with a funeral notice and a subsequent dramatization of how his family and friends respond to his death, and it closes with the death itself, dramatizing how Ivan Ilych responds to his own dying. By beginning with the funeral, Tolstoy allows us to examine Ivan Ilych's society before we meet the man himself. This enables us to determine how much he was himself the product of that society, how much his own character, aspirations, and values were those of his family, his friends, and his professional associates. *Leading Lives That Matter* has been organized in a similar way, attending first to the ways various voices within our own culture think and speak about matters of life and death. Readers should therefore be especially attentive in the first part of the novella to what the characters say about their own lives and Ivan Ilych's, and what this discloses about how they think about what matters in a human life.

The second and third parts of the work tell the story of Ivan Ilych's life within the two domains that have most often occupied us in this anthology — work and family. At the very beginning, the narrator characterizes Ivan Ilych as "intelligent, polished, lively, and agreeable," and soon after as "capable, cheerful, good-natured, and sociable." These attributes certainly seem admirable, but how are they different from the adjectives Aristotle would have used to describe a human being of good character — "wise," "temperate," "just," "courageous," and "generous"? We should consider the main character in his two primary settings and ask what kind of a lawyer and judge, and what kind of a husband and father, he was. How did he understand the relationship between love and work, or between home and the office? We can study this relationship by examining how he went about purchasing and furnishing his home. We must wonder, too, about which was more important and significant to him, professional ambition or familial intimacy. Consider, for example, that the narrator tells us about the death of one of his children almost in passing, yet Ivan Ilych's "hardest year" involved a professional setback, not a personal loss.

The fourth part of the novella begins with the onset of the main character's illness and then traces his reaction to it. At first, he seems to deal with his disease similarly to how he dealt with the rest of his life. But a subtle process of discovery and reversal begins to take place. For example, when he becomes a patient, the ministrations and the demeanor of the doctors remind him of his own behavior toward those who came before him on the bench. Indeed, the nature of professional work constitutes one of the minor themes of the novella, giving us a chance to review the relationship between what we do for a living and who we are. Does this man's story suggest that Russell Muirhead was right? Has Ivan Ilych's work formed his character or at least reinforced some aspects of his personality while diminishing others? And if so, has this process ennobled him? And how might he see the relationship between professional and personal identity playing out in the character of his own doctors?

Ivan Ilych grows to regard one person with larger and larger measures of gratitude, admiration, and affection: the butler's young assistant, Gerasim. As a way of comparing a vocation to a job, we might compare the way the doctors and lawyers in the book work with the way Gerasim works. Gerasim, in the judgment of both the narrator and Ivan Ilych, seems to be living rightly and truly. But what exactly about his character, the manner in which he carries out his tasks, and the nature of his relationship to Ivan Ilych makes him a positive example of living a human life worthy of choice and admiration? The people around him are certainly better educated, more "successful," and more solidly established in the world. What does Gerasim know that they do not?

From the beginning of the fifth section of the novella through most of the rest of the story, Ivan Ilych's growing conviction that he is dying leads him to ask these very questions. And he reviews and revises, over and over again, his own life and directs similar questions to himself. Soon he is tormented by them. "Maybe I did not live as I ought to have done," it suddenly occurs to him. "But how could that be, when I did everything properly?" This question is part of a dialogue that goes on within him almost to the point of his death. One of the voices is clearly his own, but where does the other one come from? And, especially, what did Ivan Ilych lack that Gerasim had?

On what basis does Ivan Ilych come to believe that his life has been a failure? At times he seems to speak in the vocabulary of authenticity. He says he lived a "false life" as opposed to a "true one." His most pleasant memories, his *only* pleasant memories, seem to be those of his childhood. And he seems to resemble exactly the kind of people Charles Taylor says have "missed the point of their lives" (see pp. 59–64 above). At other times one of the voices within him seems to speak the vocabulary of virtue. He seems to believe that he failed to live "rightly" according to certain standards and in accordance with certain virtues. He also engages in exemplarist moral thinking, in that his increasing admiration of Gerasim's life provokes his own deep reflection on what matters most. At still other times he seems to think in the vocabulary of vocation. Like Dietrich Bonhoeffer, he comes to realize that he should have challenged the socially prescribed boundaries of his duties as a lawyer and judge. Having objectified death as an *"It"* that he cannot escape, he seems at times also to be looking for another "it," the one thing that would have given his life significance and substance. But what was it? This is his question, as it remains ours.

No one can read the ending of this story without wondering whether and how it is a credible "narrative of redemption," to use Dan McAdams's phrase from chapter 6. Can a life that has been almost entirely "false" or "wrong" or "unreal" be redeemed by a certain kind of death? If so, how? Our answers to these questions will depend on how we regard Ivan Ilych's last feelings and acts toward his wife and young son, and on how we interpret his seeming "denial of death" at the end, compared to his earlier efforts to deny *It*. They will depend most importantly upon what exactly about his life we think required "redemption." Was it something missing that needed to be acquired, something lost that needed to be restored, or something sinful that needed to be forgiven? And what of death itself? Was death something that happened to Ivan Ilych, or was it the last act of his life?

The Death of Ivan Ilych was the first piece of fiction that Tolstoy wrote after his conversion to a rather idiosyncratic form of Christianity. He had himself been rather dissolute and self-indulgent in his early life, and he had for a time been convinced that human life and destiny were totally determined by impersonal historical forces. Most critics have argued that the power of *The Death of Ivan Ilych* derives in part from tensions within the story between Tolstoy's Christian and non-Christian self. Whatever the case may be, Tolstoy was in many ways very much like his exact contemporary, William James, and also like Albert Schweitzer. (Indeed, both James and Schweitzer mention Tolstoy in the selections included in this book.) These three all belonged a century ago, as most of us do today, to several sometimes conflicting traditions of human thought, religious as well as secular.

For Tolstoy, some of these conflicts were at one and the same time a source of terrible agony and wonderful genius. As one of the most astute students of his life and work, Isaiah Berlin, has written, Tolstoy "had the eyes of a fox and the heart of a hedgehog." Like a fox, he saw the many and various and irreconcilable ways of living in the world, the endlessly diverse ways that human beings have chosen to lead lives of substance and significance. With artistic skill unmatched among novelists, he faithfully dramatized these many ways to truth. But like a hedgehog, he longed his whole life for *one* truth that would unify human experience and that might provide a clear and compelling answer for everyone about how they should live. His torment came from the fact that his gifts and his longings were often deeply at odds. His vocation was to represent in nearly inexhaustible detail many lives in such a way that his readers could gain greater clarity about the issues that mattered so deeply to him. The same spirit and purpose have guided this anthology, so it is altogether fitting that it should end with a work by the great Russian master.

Leo Tolstoy

THE DEATH OF IVAN ILYCH

i

During an interval in the Melvinski trial in the large building of the Law Courts, the members and public prosecutor met in Ivan Egorovich Shebek's private room, where the conversation turned on the celebrated Krasovski case. Fëdor Vasilievich warmly maintained that it was not subject to their jurisdiction, Ivan Egorovich maintained the contrary, while Peter Ivanovich, not having entered into the discussion at the start, took no part in it but looked through the *Gazette* which had just been handed in.

"Gentlemen," he said, "Ivan Ilych has died!"

"You don't say so!"

"Here, read it yourself," replied Peter Ivanovich, handing Fëdor Vasilievich the paper still damp from the press. Surrounded by a black border were the words: "Praskovya Fëdorovna Golovina, with profound sorrow, informs relatives and friends of the demise of her beloved husband Ivan Ilych Golovin, Member of the Court of Justice, which occurred on February the 4th of this year 1882. The funeral will take place on Friday at one o'clock in the afternoon."

Ivan Ilych had been a colleague of the gentlemen present and was liked by them all. He had been ill for some weeks with an illness said to be incurable. His post had been kept open for him, but there had been conjectures that in case of his death Alexeev might receive his appointment, and that either Vinnikov or Shtabel would succeed Alexeev. So on receiving the news of Ivan Ilych's death the first thought of each of the gentlemen in that private room was of the changes and promotions it might occasion among themselves or their acquaintances.

"I shall be sure to get Shtabel's place or Vinnikov's," thought Fëdor

From Leo Tolstoy, *The Death of Ivan Ilych and Other Stories*, trans. Aylmer Maude (New York: Signet Classic, 2003), 93–152.

Vasilievich. "I was promised that long ago, and the promotion means an extra eight hundred rubles a year for me besides the allowance."

"Now I must apply for my brother-in-law's transfer from Kaluga," thought Peter Ivanovich. "My wife will be very glad, and then she won't be able to say that I never do anything for her relations."

"I thought he would never leave his bed again," said Peter Ivanovich aloud. "It's very sad."

"But what really was the matter with him?"

"The doctors couldn't say — at least they could, but each of them said something different. When last I saw him I thought he was getting better."

"And I haven't been to see him since the holidays. I always meant to go."

"Had he any property?"

"I think his wife had a little — but something quite trifling."

"We shall have to go to see her, but they live so terribly far away."

"Far away from you, you mean. Everything's far away from your place."

"You see, he never can forgive my living on the other side of the river," said Peter Ivanovich, smiling at Shebek. Then, still talking of the distances between different parts of the city, they returned to the Court.

Besides considerations as to the possible transfers and promotions likely to result from Ivan Ilych's death, the mere fact of the death of a near acquaintance aroused, as usual, in all who heard of it the complacent feeling that "it is he who is dead and not I."

Each one thought or felt, "Well, he's dead but I'm alive!" But the more intimate of Ivan Ilych's acquaintances, his so-called friends, could not help thinking also that they would now have to fulfil the very tiresome demands of propriety by attending the funeral service and paying a visit of condolence to the widow.

Fëdor Vasilievich and Peter Ivanovich had been his nearest acquaintances. Peter Ivanovich had studied law with Ivan Ilych and had considered himself to be under obligations to him.

Having told his wife at dinner-time of Ivan Ilych's death and of his conjecture that it might be possible to get her brother transferred to their circuit, Peter Ivanovich sacrificed his usual nap, put on his evening clothes, and drove to Ivan Ilych's house.

At the entrance stood a carriage and two cabs. Leaning against the wall in the hall downstairs near the cloak-stand was a coffin-lid covered with cloth of gold, ornamented with gold cord and tassels, that had been polished up with metal powder. Two ladies in black were taking off their fur cloaks. Peter Ivanovich recognized one of them as Ivan Ilych's sister, but the other was a stranger to him. His colleague Schwartz was just coming downstairs, but on seeing Peter Ivanovich enter he stopped and winked at him, as if to say: "Ivan Ilych has made a mess of things — not like you and me."

Schwartz's face, with his Piccadilly whiskers and his slim figure in evening dress, had as usual an air of elegant solemnity which contrasted with the playfulness of his character and had a special piquancy here, or so it seemed to Peter Ivanovich.

Peter Ivanovich allowed the ladies to precede him and slowly followed them upstairs. Schwartz did not come down but remained where he was, and Peter Ivanovich understood that he wanted to arrange where they should play bridge that evening. The ladies went upstairs to the widow's room, and Schwartz with seriously compressed lips but a playful look in his eyes, indicated by a twist of his eyebrows the room to the right where the body lay.

Peter Ivanovich, like everyone else on such occasions, entered feeling uncertain what he would have to do. All he knew was that at such times it is always safe to cross oneself. But he was not quite sure whether one should make obeisances while doing so. He therefore adopted a middle course. On entering the room he began crossing himself and made a slight movement resembling a bow. At the same time, as far as the motion of his head and arm allowed, he surveyed the room. Two young men — apparently nephews, one of whom was a high-school pupil — were leaving the room, crossing themselves as they did so. An old woman was standing motionless, and a lady with strangely arched eyebrows was saying something to her in a whisper. A vigorous, resolute Church Reader, in a frock-coat, was reading something in a loud voice with an expression that precluded any contradiction. The butler's assistant, Gerasim, stepping lightly in front of Peter Ivanovich, was strewing something on the floor. Noticing this, Peter Ivanovich was immediately aware of a faint odor of a decomposing body.

The last time he had called on Ivan Ilych, Peter Ivanovich had seen Gerasim in the study. Ivan Ilych had been particularly fond of him and he was performing the duty of a sick nurse.

Peter Ivanovich continued to make the sign of the cross slightly inclining his head in an intermediate direction between the coffin, the Reader, and the icons on the table in a corner of the room. Afterwards, when it seemed to him that this movement of his arm in crossing himself had gone on too long, he stopped and began to look at the corpse.

The dead man lay, as dead men always lie, in a specially heavy way, his rigid limbs sunk in the soft cushions of the coffin, with the head forever bowed on the pillow. His yellow waxen brow with bald patches over his sunken temples was thrust up in the way peculiar to the dead, the protruding nose seeming to press on the upper lip. He was much changed and had grown even thinner since Peter Ivanovich had last seen him, but, as is always the case with the dead, his face was handsomer and above all more dignified than when he was alive. The expression on the face said that what was necessary had been accomplished, and accomplished rightly. Besides this there was in that expression a reproach and a warning to the living. This warning seemed to Peter Ivanovich out of place, or at least not applicable to him. He felt a certain discomfort and so he hurriedly crossed himself once more and turned and went out of the door — too hurriedly and too regardless of propriety, as he himself was aware.

Schwartz was waiting for him in the adjoining room with legs spread wide apart and both hands toying with his top-hat behind his back. The mere sight of that playful, well-groomed, and elegant figure refreshed Peter Ivanovich. He felt that Schwartz was above all these happenings and would not surrender to any depressing influences. His very look said that this incident of a church service for Ivan Ilych could not be a sufficient reason for infringing the order of the session — in other words, that it would certainly not prevent his unwrapping a new pack of cards and shuffling them that evening while a footman placed four fresh candles on the table: in fact, that there was no reason for supposing that this incident would hinder their spending the evening agreeably. Indeed he said this in a whisper as Peter Ivanovich passed him, proposing that they should meet for a game at Fëdor Vasilievich's. But apparently Peter Ivanovich was not destined to play bridge that evening. Praskovya Fëdorovna (a short, fat woman who despite all efforts to the contrary had continued to broaden steadily from her shoulders downwards and who had the same extraordinarily arched eyebrows as the lady who had been standing by the coffin), dressed all in black, her head covered with lace, came out of her own room with some other ladies, conducted them to the room where the dead body lay, and said: "The service will begin immediately. Please go in."

Schwartz, making an indefinite bow, stood still, evidently neither accepting nor declining this invitation. Praskovya Fëdorovna, recognizing Peter Ivanovich, sighed, went close up to him, took his hand, and said: "I know you were a true friend to Ivan Ilych . . ." and looked at him awaiting some suitable response. And Peter Ivanovich knew that, just as it had been the right thing to cross himself in that room, so what he had to do here was to press her hand, sigh, and say, "Believe me. . . ." So he did all this and as he did it felt that the desired result had been achieved: that both he and she were touched.

"Come with me. I want to speak to you before it begins," said the widow. "Give me your arm."

Peter Ivanovich gave her his arm and they went to the inner rooms, passing Schwartz, who winked at Peter Ivanovich compassionately.

"That does for our bridge! Don't object if we find another player. Perhaps you can cut in when you do escape," said his playful look.

Peter Ivanovich sighed still more deeply and despondently, and Praskovya Fëdorovna pressed his arm gratefully. When they reached the drawing-room, upholstered in pink cretonne and lighted by a dim lamp, they sat down at the table — she on a sofa and Peter Ivanovich on a low pouffe, the springs of which yielded spasmodically under his weight. Praskovya Fëdorovna had been on the point of warning him to take another seat, but felt that such a warning was out of keeping with her present condition and so changed her mind. As he sat down on the pouffe Peter Ivanovich recalled how Ivan Ilych had arranged this room and had consulted him regarding this pink cretonne with green leaves. The whole room was full of furniture and knick-knacks, and on her way to the sofa the lace of the widow's black shawl caught on the carved edge of the table. Peter Ivanovich rose to detach it, and the springs of the pouffe, relieved of his weight, rose also and gave him a push. The widow began detaching her shawl herself, and Peter Ivanovich again sat down, suppressing the rebellious springs of the pouffe under him. But the widow had not quite freed herself and Peter Ivanovich got up again, and again the pouffe rebelled and even creaked. When this was all over she took out a clean cambric handkerchief and began to weep. The episode with the shawl and the struggle with the pouffe had cooled Peter Ivanovich's emotions and he sat there with a sullen look on his face. This awkward situation was interrupted by Sokolov, Ivan Ilych's butler, who came to report that the plot in the cemetery that Praskovya Fëdorovna had chosen would cost two hundred rubles. She stopped weeping and, looking at Peter Ivanovich with the air of a victim, remarked in French that it was very hard for her. Peter Ivanovich made a silent gesture signifying his full conviction that it must indeed be so.

"Please smoke," she said in a magnanimous yet crushed voice, and turned to discuss with Sokolov the price of the plot for the grave.

Peter Ivanovich while lighting his cigarette heard her inquiring very circumstantially into the prices of different plots in the cemetery and finally decide which she would take. When that was done she gave instructions about engaging the choir. Sokolov then left the room.

"I look after everything myself," she told Peter Ivanovich, shifting the albums that lay on the table; and noticing that the table was endangered by his cigarette-ash, she immediately passed him an ash-tray, saying as she did so: "I consider it an affectation to say that my grief prevents my attending to practical affairs. On the contrary, if anything can — I won't say console me, but — distract me, it is seeing to everything concerning him." She again took out her handkerchief as if preparing to cry, but suddenly, as if mastering her feeling, she shook herself and began to speak calmly. "But there is something I want to talk to you about."

Peter Ivanovich bowed, keeping control of the springs of the pouffe, which immediately began quivering under him.

"He suffered terribly the last few days."

"Did he?" said Peter Ivanovich.

"Oh, terribly! He screamed unceasingly, not for minutes but for hours. For the last three days he screamed incessantly. It was unendurable. I cannot understand how I bore it; you could hear him three rooms off. Oh, what I have suffered!"

"Is it possible that he was conscious all that time?" asked Peter Ivanovich.

"Yes," she whispered. "To the last moment. He took leave of us a quarter of an hour before he died, and asked us to take Volodya away."

The thought of the sufferings of this man he had known so intimately, first as a merry little boy, then as a school-mate, and later as a grown-up colleague, suddenly struck Peter Ivanovich with horror, despite an unpleasant consciousness of his own and this woman's dissimulation. He again saw that brow, and that nose pressing down on the lip, and felt afraid for himself.

"Three days of frightful suffering and then death! Why, that might suddenly, at any time, happen to me," he thought, and for a moment felt terrified. But — he did not himself know how — the customary reflection at once occurred to him that this had happened to Ivan Ilych and not to him, and that it should not and could not happen to him, and that to think that it could would be yielding to depression which he ought not to do, as Schwartz's expression plainly showed. After which reflection Peter Ivanovich felt reassured, and began to ask with interest about the details of Ivan Ilych's death, as though death was an accident natural to Ivan Ilych but certainly not to himself.

After many details of the really dreadful physical sufferings Ivan Ilych had endured (which details he learnt only from the effect those sufferings had produced on Praskovya Fëdorovna's nerves) the widow apparently found it necessary to get to business.

"Oh, Peter Ivanovich, how hard it is! How terribly, terribly hard!" and she again began to weep.

Peter Ivanovich sighed and waited for her to finish blowing her nose. When she had done so he said, "Believe me . . ." and she again began talking and brought out what was evidently her chief concern with him — namely, to question him as to how she could obtain a grant of money from the government on the occasion of her husband's death. She made it appear that she was asking Peter Ivanovich's advice about her pension, but he soon saw that she already knew about that to the minutest detail, more even than he did himself. She knew how much could be got out of the government in consequence of her husband's death, but wanted to find out whether she could not possibly extract something more. Peter Ivanovich tried to think of some means of doing so, but after reflecting for a while and, out of propriety, condemning the government for its niggardliness, he said he thought that nothing more could be got. Then she sighed and evidently began to devise means of getting rid of her visitor. Noticing this, he put out his cigarette, rose, pressed her hand, and went out into the ante-room.

In the dining-room where the clock stood that Ivan Ilych had liked so much and had bought at an antique shop, Peter Ivanovich met a priest and a few acquaintances who had come to attend the service, and he recognized Ivan Ilych's daughter, a handsome young woman. She was in black and her slim figure appeared slimmer than ever. She had a gloomy, determined, almost angry expression, and bowed to Peter Ivanovich as though he were in some way to blame. Behind her, with the same offended look, stood a wealthy young man, an examining magistrate, whom Peter Ivanovich also knew and who was her fiancé, as he had heard. He bowed mournfully to them and was about to pass into the death-chamber, when from under the stairs appeared the figure of Ivan Ilych's schoolboy son, who was extremely like his father. He seemed a little Ivan Ilych, such as Peter Ivanovich remembered when they studied law together. His tear-stained eyes had in them the look that is seen in the eyes of boys of thirteen or fourteen who are not pure-minded. When he saw Peter Ivanovich he scowled morosely and shamefacedly. Peter Ivanovich nodded to him and entered the death-chamber. The service began: candles, groans, incense, tears, and sobs. Peter Ivanovich stood looking gloomily down at his feet. He did not look once at the dead man, did not yield to any depressing influence, and was one of the first to leave the room. There was no one in the anteroom, but Gerasim darted out of the dead man's room, rummaged with his strong hands among the fur coats to find Peter Ivanovich's and helped him on with it.

"Well, friend Gerasim," said Peter Ivanovich, so as to say something. "It's a sad affair, isn't it?"

"It's God's will. We shall all come to it some day," said Gerasim, displaying his teeth — the even, white teeth of a healthy peasant — and, like a man in the thick of urgent work, he briskly opened the front door, called the coachman, helped Peter Ivanovich into the sledge, and sprang back to the porch as if in readiness for what he had to do next.

Peter Ivanovich found the fresh air particularly pleasant after the smell of incense, the dead body, and carbolic acid. "Where to, sir?" asked the coachman.

"It's not too late even now. . . . I'll call round on Fëdor Vasilievich."

He accordingly drove there and found them just finishing the first rubber, so that it was quite convenient for him to cut in.

ii

Ivan Ilych's life had been most simple and most ordinary and therefore most terrible.

He had been a member of the Court of Justice, and died at the age of forty-five. His father had been an official who after serving in various ministries and departments in Petersburg had made the sort of career which brings men to positions from which by reason of their long service they cannot be dismissed, though they are obviously unfit to hold any responsible position, and for whom therefore posts are specially created, which though fictitious carry salaries of from six to ten thousand rubles that are not fictitious, and in receipt of which they live on to a great age.

Such was the Privy Councillor and superfluous member of various superfluous institutions, Ilya Epimovich Golovin.

He had three sons, of whom Ivan Ilych was the second. The eldest son was following in his father's footsteps only in another department, and was already approaching that stage in the service at which a similar sinecure would be reached. The third son was a failure. He had ruined his prospects in a number of positions and was now serving in the railway department. His father and brothers, and still more their wives, not merely disliked meeting him, but avoided remembering his existence unless compelled to do so. His sister had married Baron Greff, a Petersburg official of her father's type. Ivan Ilych was *le phénix de la famille* as people said. He was neither as cold and formal as his elder brother nor as wild as the younger, but was a happy mean between them — an intelligent, polished, lively and agreeable man. He had studied with his younger brother at the School of Law, but the latter had failed to complete the course and was expelled when he was in the fifth class. Ivan Ilych finished the course well. Even when he was at the School of Law he was just what he remained for the rest of his life: a capable, cheerful, good-natured, and sociable man, though strict in the fulfilment of what he considered to be his duty: and he considered his duty to be what was so considered by those in authority. Neither as a boy nor as a man was he a toady, but from early youth was by nature attracted to people of high station as a fly is drawn to the light, assimilating their ways and views of life and establishing friendly relations with them. All the enthusiasms of childhood and youth passed without leaving much trace on him; he succumbed to sensuality, to vanity, and latterly among the highest classes to liberalism, but always within limits which his instinct unfailingly indicated to him as correct.

At school he had done things which had formerly seemed to him very horrid and made him feel disgusted with himself when he did them; but when later on he saw that such actions were done by people of good position and that they did not regard them as wrong, he was able not exactly to regard them as right, but to forget about them entirely or not be at all troubled at remembering them.

Having graduated from the School of Law and qualified for the tenth rank of the civil service, and having received money from his father for his equipment, Ivan Ilych ordered himself clothes at Scharmer's, the fashionable tailor, hung a medallion inscribed *respice finem* on his watch-chain, took leave of his professor and the prince who was patron of the school, had a farewell dinner with his comrades at Donon's first-class restaurant, and with his new and fashionable portmanteau, linen, clothes, shaving and other toilet appliances, and a traveling rug, all purchased at the best shops, he set off for one of the provinces where, through his father's influence, he had been attached to the Governor as an official for special service.

In the province Ivan Ilych soon arranged as easy and agreeable a position for himself as he had had at the School of Law. He performed his official tasks, made his career, and at the same time amused himself pleasantly and decorously. Occasionally he paid official visits to country districts, where he behaved with dignity both to his superiors and inferiors, and performed the duties entrusted to him, which related chiefly to the sectarians, with an exactness and incorruptible honesty of which he could not but feel proud.

In official matters, despite his youth and taste for frivolous gaiety, he was exceedingly reserved, punctilious, and even severe; but in society he was often amusing and witty, and always good-natured, correct in his manner, and *bon enfant,* as the governor and his wife — with whom he was like one of the family — used to say of him.

In the province he had an affair with a lady who made advances to the elegant young lawyer, and there was also a milliner; and there were carousals with aides-de-camp who visited the district, and after-supper visits to a certain outlying street of doubtful reputation; and there was too some obsequiousness to his chief and even to his chief's wife, but all this was done with such a tone of good breeding that no hard names could be applied to it. It all came under the heading of the French saying: *"Il faut que jeunesse se passe."* [*"Youth must have its fling."*] It was all done with clean hands, in clean linen, with French phrases, and above all among people of the best society and consequently with the approval of people of rank.

So Ivan Ilych served for five years and then came a change in his official life. The new and reformed judicial institutions were introduced, and new men were needed. Ivan Ilych became such a new man. He was offered the post of examining magistrate, and he accepted it though the post was in another province and obliged him to give up the connections he had formed and to make new ones. His friends met to give him a send-off; they had a group-photograph taken and presented him with a silver cigarette-case, and he set off to his new post.

As examining magistrate Ivan Ilych was just as *comme il faut* and decorous a man, inspiring general respect and capable of separating his official duties from his private life, as he had been when acting as an official on special service. His duties now as examining magistrate were far more interesting and attractive than before. In his former position it had been pleasant to wear an undress uniform made by Scharmer, and to pass through the crowd of petitioners and officials who were timorously awaiting an audience with the governor, and who envied him as with free and easy gait he went straight into his chief's private room to have a cup of tea and a cigarette with him. But not many people had then been directly dependent on him — only police officials and the sectarians when he went on special missions — and he liked to treat them politely, almost as comrades, as if he were letting them feel that he who had the power to crush them was treating them in this simple, friendly way. There were then but few such people. But now, as an examining magistrate, Ivan Ilych felt that everyone without exception, even the most important and self-satisfied, was in his power, and that he need only write a few words on a sheet of paper with a certain heading, and this or that important, self-satisfied person would be brought before him in the role of an accused person or a witness, and if he did not choose to allow him to sit down, would have to stand before him and answer his questions. Ivan Ilych never abused his power; he tried on the contrary to soften its expression, but the consciousness of it and of the possibility of softening its effect, supplied the chief interest and attraction of his office. In his work itself, especially in his examinations, he very soon acquired a method of eliminating all considerations irrelevant to the legal aspect of the case, and reducing even the most complicated case to a form in which it would be presented on paper only in its externals, completely excluding his personal opinion of the matter, while above all observing every prescribed formality. The work was new and Ivan Ilych was one of the first men to apply the new Code of 1864 [a judicial reform following the emancipation of the serfs in 1861].

On taking up the post of examining magistrate in a new town, he made new acquaintances and connections, placed himself on a new footing, and assumed a somewhat different tone. He took up an attitude of rather dignified aloofness towards the provincial authorities, but picked out the best circle of legal gentlemen and wealthy gentry living in the town and assumed a tone of slight dissatisfaction with the government, of moderate liberalism, and of enlightened citizenship. At the same time, without at all altering the elegance of his toilet, he ceased shaving his chin and allowed his beard to grow as it pleased.

Ivan Ilych settled down very pleasantly in this new town. The society there, which inclined towards opposition to the Governor, was friendly, his salary was larger, and he began to play *vint* [a form of bridge], which he found added not a little to the pleasure of life, for he had a capacity for cards, played good-humoredly, and calculated rapidly and astutely, so that he usually won.

After living there for two years he met his future wife, Praskovya Fëdorovna Mikhel, who was the most attractive, clever, and brilliant girl of the set in which he moved, and among other amusements and relaxations from his labors as examining magistrate, Ivan Ilych established light and playful relations with her.

While he had been an official on special service he had been accustomed to dance, but now as an examining magistrate it was exceptional for him to do so. If he danced now, he did it as if to show that though he served under the reformed order of things, and had reached the fifth official rank, yet when it came to dancing he could do it better than most people. So at the end of an evening he sometimes danced with Praskovya Fëdorovna, and it was chiefly during these dances that he captivated her. She fell in love with him. Ivan Ilych had at first no definite intention of marrying, but when the girl fell in love with him he said to himself: "Really, why shouldn't I marry?"

Praskovya Fëdorovna came of a good family, was not bad looking, and had some little property. Ivan Ilych might have aspired to a more brilliant match, but even this was good. He had his salary, and she, he hoped, would have an equal income. She was well connected, and was a sweet, pretty, and thoroughly correct young woman. To say that Ivan Ilych married because he fell in love with Praskovya Fëdorovna and found that she sympathized with his views of life would be as incorrect as to say that he married because his social circle approved of the match. He was swayed by both these considerations: the marriage gave him personal satisfaction, and at the same time it was considered the right thing by the most highly placed of his associates.

So Ivan Ilych got married.

The preparations for marriage and the beginning of married life, with its conjugal caresses, the new furniture, new crockery, and new linen, were very pleasant until his wife became pregnant — so that Ivan Ilych had begun to think that marriage would not impair the easy, agreeable, gay and always decorous character of his life, approved of by society and regarded by himself as natural, but would even improve it. But from the first months of his wife's pregnancy, something new, unpleasant, depressing, and unseemly, and from which there was no way of escape, unexpectedly showed itself.

His wife, without any reason — *de gaieté de cœur* as Ivan Ilych expressed it to himself — began to disturb the pleasure and propriety of their life. She began to be jealous without any cause, expected him to devote his whole attention to her, found fault with everything, and made coarse and ill-mannered scenes.

At first Ivan Ilych hoped to escape from the unpleasantness of this state of affairs by the same easy and decorous relation to life that had served him heretofore: he tried to ignore his wife's disagreeable moods, continued to live in his usual easy and pleasant way, invited friends to his house for a game of cards, and also tried going out to his club or spending his evenings with friends. But one day his wife began upbraiding him so vigorously, using such coarse words, and continued to abuse him every time he did not fulfil her demands, so resolutely and with such evident determination not to give way till he submitted — that is, till he stayed at home and was bored just as she was — that he became alarmed. He now realized that matrimony — at any rate with Praskovya Fëdorovna — was not always conducive to the pleasures and amenities of life, but on the contrary often infringed both comfort and propriety, and that he must therefore entrench himself against such infringement. And Ivan Ilych began to seek for means of doing so. His official duties were the one thing that imposed upon Praskovya Fëdorovna, and by means of his official work and the duties attached to it he began struggling with his wife to secure his own independence.

With the birth of their child, the attempts to feed it and the various failures in doing so, and with the real and imaginary illnesses of mother and child, in which Ivan Ilych's sympathy was demanded but about which he understood nothing, the need of securing for himself an existence outside his family life became still more imperative.

As his wife grew more irritable and exacting and Ivan Ilych transferred the center of gravity of his life more and more to his official work, so did he grow to like his work better and became more ambitious than before.

Very soon, within a year of his wedding, Ivan Ilych had realized that marriage, though it may add some comforts to life, is in fact a very intricate and difficult affair towards which in order to perform one's duty, that is, to lead a decorous life approved of by society, one must adopt a definite attitude just as towards one's official duties.

And Ivan Ilych evolved such an attitude towards married life. He only required of it those conveniences — dinner at home, housewife, and bed — which it could give him, and above all that propriety of external forms required by public opinion. For the rest he looked for lighthearted pleasure and propriety, and was very thankful when he found them, but if he met with antagonism and querulousness he at once retired into his separate fenced-off world of official duties, where he found satisfaction.

Ivan Ilych was esteemed a good official, and after three years was made Assistant Public Prosecutor. His new duties, their importance, the possibility of indicting and imprisoning anyone he chose, the publicity his speeches received, and the success he had in all these things, made his work still more attractive.

More children came. His wife became more and more querulous and ill-tempered, but the attitude Ivan Ilych had adopted towards his home life rendered him almost impervious to her grumbling.

After seven years' service in that town he was transferred to another province as Public Prosecutor. They moved, but were short of money and his wife did not like the place they moved to. Though the salary was higher the cost of living was greater, besides which two of their children died and family life became still more unpleasant for him.

Praskovya Fëdorovna blamed her husband for every inconvenience they encountered in their new home. Most of the conversations between husband and wife, especially as to the children's education, led to topics which recalled former disputes, and those disputes were apt to flare up again at any moment. There remained only those rare periods of amorousness which still came to them at times but did not last long. These were islets at which they anchored for a while and then again set out upon that ocean of veiled hostility which showed itself in their aloofness from one another. This aloofness might have grieved Ivan Ilych had he considered that it ought not to exist, but he now regarded the position as normal, and even made it the goal at which he aimed in family life. His aim was to free himself more and more from those unpleasantnesses and to give them a semblance of harmlessness and propriety. He attained this by spending less and less time with his family, and when obliged to be at home he tried to safeguard his position by the presence of outsiders. The chief thing however was that he had his official duties. The whole interest of his life now centered in the official world and that interest absorbed him. The consciousness of his power, being able to ruin anybody he wished to ruin, the importance, even the external dignity of his entry into court, or meetings with his subordinates, his success with superiors and inferiors, and above all his masterly handling of cases, of which he was conscious — all this gave him pleasure and filled his life, together with chats with his colleagues, dinners, and bridge. So that on the whole Ivan Ilych's life continued to flow as he considered it should do — pleasantly and properly.

So things continued for another seven years. His eldest daughter was already sixteen, another child had died, and only one son was left, a schoolboy and a subject of dissension. Ivan Ilych wanted to put him in the School of Law, but to spite him Praskovya Fëdorovna entered him at the High School. The daughter had been educated at home and had turned out well: the boy did not learn badly either.

iii

So Ivan Ilych lived for seventeen years after his marriage. He was already a Public Prosecutor of long standing, and had declined several proposed transfers while awaiting a more desirable post, when an unanticipated and unpleasant occurrence quite upset the peaceful course of his life. He was expecting to be offered the post of presiding judge in a University town, but Happe somehow came to the front and obtained the appointment instead. Ivan Ilych became irritable, reproached Happe, and quarrelled both with him and with his immediate superiors — who became colder to him and again passed him over when other appointments were made.

This was in 1880, the hardest year of Ivan Ilych's life. It was then that it became evident on the one hand that his salary was insufficient for them to live on, and on the other that he had been forgotten, and not only this, but that what was for him the greatest and most cruel injustice appeared to others a quite ordinary occurrence. Even his father did not consider it his duty to help him. Ivan Ilych felt himself abandoned by everyone, and that they regarded his position with a salary of 3,500 rubles as quite normal and even fortunate. He alone knew that with the consciousness of the injustices done him, with his wife's incessant nagging, and with the debts he had contracted by living beyond his means, his position was far from normal.

In order to save money that summer he obtained leave of absence and went with his wife to live in the country at her brother's place.

In the country, without his work, he experienced *ennui* for the first time in his life, and not only *ennui* but intolerable depression, and he decided that it was impossible to go on living like that, and that it was necessary to take energetic measures.

Having passed a sleepless night pacing up and down the veranda, he decided to go to Petersburg and bestir himself, in order to punish those who had failed to appreciate him and to get transferred to another ministry.

Next day, despite many protests from his wife and her brother, he started for Petersburg with the sole object of obtaining a post with a salary of five thousand rubles a year. He was no longer bent on any particular department, or tendency, or kind of activity. All he now wanted was an appointment to another post with a salary of five thousand rubles, either in the administration, in the banks, with the railways, in one of the Empress Marya's Institutions, or even in the customs — but it had to carry with it a salary of five thousand rubles and be in a ministry other than that in which they had failed to appreciate him.

And this quest of Ivan Ilych's was crowned with remarkable and unexpected success. At Kursk an acquaintance of his, F. I. Ilyin, got into the first-class carriage, sat down beside Ivan Ilych, and told him of a telegram just received by the Governor of Kursk announcing that a change was about to take place in the ministry: Peter Ivanovich was to be superseded by Ivan Semënovich.

The proposed change, apart from its significance for Russia, had a special significance for Ivan Ilych, because by bringing forward a new man, Peter Petrovich, and consequently his friend Zachar Ivanovich, it was highly favorable for Ivan Ilych, since Zachar Ivanovich was a friend and colleague of his.

In Moscow this news was confirmed, and on reaching Petersburg Ivan Ilych found Zachar Ivanovich and received a definite promise of an appointment in his former department of Justice.

A week later he telegraphed to his wife: "Zachar in Miller's place. I shall receive appointment on presentation of report."

Thanks to this change of personnel, Ivan Ilych had unexpectedly obtained an appointment in his former ministry which placed him two stages above his former colleagues besides giving him five thousand rubles salary and three thousand five hundred rubles for expenses connected with his removal. All his ill humor towards his former enemies and the whole department vanished, and Ivan Ilych was completely happy.

He returned to the country more cheerful and contented than he had been for a long time. Praskovya Fëdorovna also cheered up and a truce was arranged between them. Ivan Ilych told of how he had been fêted by everybody in Petersburg, how all those who had been his enemies were put to shame and now fawned on him, how envious they were of his appointment, and how much everybody in Petersburg had liked him.

Praskovya Fëdorovna listened to all this and appeared to believe it. She did not contradict anything, but only made plans for their life in the town to which they were going. Ivan Ilych saw with delight that these plans were his plans, that he and his wife agreed, and that, after a stumble, his life was regaining its due and natural character of pleasant lightheartedness and decorum.

Ivan Ilych had come back for a short time only, for he had to take up his new duties on the 10th of September. Moreover, he needed time to settle into the new place, to move all his belongings from the province, and to buy and order many additional things: in a word, to make such arrangements as he had resolved on, which were almost exactly what Praskovya Fëdorovna too had decided on.

Now that everything had happened so fortunately, and that he and his wife were at one in their aims and moreover saw so little of one another, they got on together better than they had done since the first years of marriage. Ivan Ilych had thought of taking his family away with him at once, but the insistence of his wife's brother and her sister-in-law, who had suddenly become particularly amiable and friendly to him and his family, induced him to depart alone.

So he departed, and the cheerful state of mind induced by his success and by the harmony between his wife and himself, the one intensifying the other, did not leave him. He found a delightful house, just the thing both he and his wife had dreamt of. Spacious, lofty reception rooms in the old style, a convenient and dignified study, rooms for his wife and daughter, a study for his son — it might have been specially built for them. Ivan Ilych himself superintended the arrangements, chose the wallpapers, supplemented the furniture (preferably with antiques which he considered particularly *comme il faut*), and supervised the upholstering. Everything progressed and progressed and approached the ideal he had set himself: even when things were only half completed they exceeded his expectations. He saw what a refined and elegant character, free from vulgarity, it would all have when it was ready. On falling asleep he pictured to himself how the reception-room would look. Looking at the yet unfinished drawing-room he could see the fireplace, the screen, the what-not, the little chairs dotted here and there, the dishes and plates on the walls, and the bronzes, as they would be when everything was in place. He was pleased by the thought of how his wife and daughter, who shared his taste in this matter, would be impressed by it. They were certainly not expecting as much. He had been particularly successful in finding, and buying cheaply, antiques which gave a particularly aristocratic character to the whole place. But in his letters he intentionally understated everything in order to be able to surprise them. All this so absorbed him that his new duties — though he liked his official work — interested him less than he had expected. Sometimes he even had moments of absent-mindedness during the Court Sessions, and would consider whether he should have straight or curved cornices for his curtains. He was so interested in it all that he often did things himself, rearranging the furniture, or rehanging the curtains. Once when mounting a stepladder to show the upholsterer, who did not understand, how he wanted the hangings draped, he made a false step and slipped, but being a strong and agile man he clung on and only knocked his side against the knob of the window frame. The bruised place was painful but the pain soon passed, and he felt particularly bright and well just then. He wrote: "I feel fifteen years younger." He thought he would have everything ready by September, but it dragged on till mid-October. But the result was charming not only in his eyes but to everyone who saw it.

In reality it was just what is usually seen in the houses of people of moderate means who want to appear rich, and therefore succeed only in resembling others like themselves: there were damasks, dark wood, plants, rugs, and dull and polished bronzes — all the things people of a certain class have in order to resemble other people of that class. His house was so like the others that it would never have been noticed, but to him it all seemed to be quite exceptional. He was very happy when he met his family at the station and brought them to the newly furnished house all lit up, where a footman in a white tie opened the door into the hall decorated with plants, and when they went on into the drawing-room, and the study uttering exclamations of delight. He conducted them everywhere, drank in their praises eagerly, and beamed with pleasure. At tea that evening, when Praskovya Fëdorovna among other things asked him about his fall, he laughed and showed them how he had gone flying and had frightened the upholsterer.

"It's a good thing I'm a bit of an athlete. Another man might have been killed, but I merely knocked myself, just here; it hurts when it's touched, but it's passing off already — it's only a bruise."

So they began living in their new home — in which, as always happens, when they got thoroughly settled in they found they were just one room short — and with the increased income, which as always was just a little (some five hundred rubles) too little, but it was all very nice.

Things went particularly well at first, before everything was finally arranged and while something had still to be done: this thing bought, that thing ordered, another thing moved, and something else adjusted. Though there were some disputes between husband and wife, they were both so well satisfied and had so much to do that it all passed off without any serious quarrels. When nothing was left to arrange it became rather dull and something seemed to be lacking, but they were then making acquaintances, forming habits, and life was growing fuller.

Ivan Ilych spent his mornings at the law court and came home to dinner, and at first he was generally in a good humor, though he occasionally became irritable just on account of his house. (Every spot on the tablecloth or the upholstery, and every broken window-blind string, irritated him. He had devoted so much trouble to arranging it all that every disturbance of it distressed him.) But on the whole his life ran its course as he believed life should do: easily, pleasantly, and decorously.

He got up at nine, drank his coffee, read the paper, and then put on his undress uniform and went to the law courts. There the harness in which he worked had already been stretched to fit him and he donned it without a hitch: petitioners, inquiries at the chancery, the chancery itself, and the sittings public and administrative. In all this the thing was to exclude everything fresh and vital, which always disturbs the regular course of official business, and to admit only official relations with people, and then only on official grounds. A man would come, for instance, wanting some information. Ivan Ilych, as one in whose sphere the matter did not lie, would have nothing to do with him: but if the man had some business with him in his official capacity, something that could be expressed on officially stamped paper, he would do everything, positively everything he could within the limits of such relations, and in doing so would maintain the semblance of friendly human relations, that is, would observe the courtesies of life. As soon as the official relations ended, so did everything else. Ivan Ilych possessed this capacity to separate his real life from the official side of affairs and not mix the two, in the highest degree, and by long practice and natural aptitude had brought it to such a pitch that sometimes, in the manner of a virtuoso, he would even allow himself to let the human and official relations mingle. He let himself do this just because he felt that he could at any time he chose resume the strictly official attitude again and drop the human relation. And he did it all easily, pleasantly, correctly, and even artistically. In the intervals between the sessions he smoked, drank tea, chatted a little about politics, a little about general topics, a little about cards, but most of all about official appointments. Tired, but with the feelings of a virtuoso — one of the first violins who has played his part in an orchestra with precision — he would return home to find that his wife and daughter had been out paying calls, or had a visitor, and that his son had been to school, had done his homework with his tutor, and was duly learning what is taught at High Schools. Everything was as it should be. After dinner, if they had no visitors, Ivan Ilych sometimes read a book that was being much discussed at the time, and in the evening settled down to work, that is, read official papers, compared the depositions of witnesses, and noted paragraphs of the Code applying to them. This was neither dull nor amusing. It was dull when he might have been playing bridge, but if no bridge was available it was at any rate better than doing nothing or sitting with his wife. Ivan Ilych's chief pleasure was giving little dinners to which he invited men and women of good social position, and just as his drawing-room resembled all other drawing-rooms so did his enjoyable little parties resemble all other such parties.

Once they even gave a dance. Ivan Ilych enjoyed it and everything went off well, except that it led to a violent quarrel with his wife about the cakes and sweets. Praskovya Fëdorovna had made her own plans, but Ivan Ilych insisted on getting everything from an expensive confectioner and ordered too many cakes, and the quarrel occurred because some of those cakes were left over and the confectioner's bill came to forty-five rubles. It was a great and disagreeable quarrel. Praskovya Fëdorovna called him "a fool and an imbecile," and he clutched at his head and made angry allusions to divorce.

But the dance itself had been enjoyable. The best people were there, and Ivan Ilych had danced with Princess Trufonova, a sister of the distinguished founder of the Society "Bear my Burden."

The pleasures connected with his work were pleasures of ambition; his social pleasures were those of vanity; but Ivan Ilych's greatest pleasure was playing bridge. He acknowledged that whatever disagreeable incident happened in his life, the pleasure that beamed like a ray of light above everything else was to sit down to bridge with good players, not noisy partners, and of course to four-handed bridge (with five players it was annoying to have to stand out, though one pretended not to mind), to play a clever and serious game (when the cards allowed it) and then to have supper and drink a glass of wine. After a game of bridge, especially if he had won a little (to win a large sum was unpleasant), Ivan Ilych went to bed in specially good humor.

So they lived. They formed a circle of acquaintances among the best people and were visited by people of importance and by young folk. In their views as to their acquaintances, husband, wife and daughter were entirely agreed, and tacitly and unanimously kept at arm's length and shook off the various shabby friends and relations who, with much show of affection, gushed into the drawing-room with its Japanese plates on the walls. Soon these shabby friends ceased to obtrude themselves and only the best people remained in the Golovins' set.

Young men made up to Lisa, and Petrishchev, an examining magistrate and Dmitri Ivanovich Petrishchev's son and sole heir, began to be so attentive to her that Ivan Ilych had already spoken to Praskovya Fëdorovna about it, and considered whether they should not arrange a party for them, or get up some private theatricals.

So they lived, and all went well, without change, and life flowed pleasantly.

iv

They were all in good health. It could not be called ill health if Ivan Ilych sometimes said that he had a queer taste in his mouth and felt some discomfort in his left side.

But this discomfort increased and, though not exactly painful, grew into a sense of pressure in his side accompanied by ill humor. And his irritability became worse and worse and began to mar the agreeable, easy, and correct life that had established itself in the Golovin family. Quarrels between husband and wife became more and more frequent, and soon the ease and amenity disappeared and even the decorum was barely maintained. Scenes again became frequent, and very few of those islets remained on which husband and wife could meet without an explosion. Praskovya Fëdorovna now had good reason to say that her husband's temper was trying. With characteristic exaggeration she said he had always had a dreadful temper, and that it had needed all her good nature to put up with it for twenty years. It was true that now the quarrels were started by him. His bursts of temper always came just before dinner, often just as he began to eat his soup. Sometimes he noticed that a plate or dish was chipped, or the food was not right, or his son put his elbow on the table, or his daughter's hair was not done as he liked it, and for all this he blamed Praskovya Fëdorovna. At first she retorted and said disagreeable things to him, but once or twice he fell into such a rage at the beginning of dinner that she realized it was due to some physical derangement brought on by taking food, and so she restrained herself and did not answer, but only hurried to get the dinner over. She regarded this self-restraint as highly praiseworthy. Having come to the conclusion that her husband had a dreadful temper and made her life miserable, she began to feel sorry for herself, and the more she pitied herself the more she hated her husband. She began to wish he would die; yet she did not want him to die because then his salary would cease. And this irritated her against him still more. She considered herself dreadfully unhappy just because not even his death could save her, and though she concealed her exasperation, that hidden exasperation of hers increased his irritation also.

After one scene in which Ivan Ilych had been particularly unfair and after which he had said in explanation that he certainly was irritable but that it was due to his not being well, she said that if he was ill it should be attended to, and insisted on his going to see a celebrated doctor.

He went. Everything took place as he had expected and as it always does. There was the usual waiting and the important air assumed by the doctor, with which he was so familiar (resembling that which he himself assumed in court), and the sounding and listening, and the questions which called for answers that were foregone conclusions and were evidently unnecessary, and the look of importance which implied that "if only you put yourself in our hands we will arrange everything — we know indubitably how it has to be done, always in the same way for everybody alike." It was all just as it was in the law courts. The doctor put on just the same air towards him as he himself put on towards an accused person.

The doctor said that so-and-so indicated that there was so-and-so inside the patient, but if the investigation of so-and-so did not confirm this, then he must assume that and that. If he assumed that and that, then . . . and so on. To Ivan Ilych only one question was important: was his case serious or not? But the doctor ignored that inappropriate question. From his point of view it was not the one under consideration, the real question was to decide between a floating kidney, chronic catarrh, or appendicitis. It was not a question of Ivan Ilych's life or death, but one between a floating kidney and appendicitis. And that question the doctor solved brilliantly, as it seemed to Ivan Ilych, in favor of the appendix, with the reservation that should an examination of the urine give fresh indications the matter would be reconsidered. All this was just what Ivan Ilych had himself brilliantly accomplished a thousand times in dealing with men on trial. The doctor summed up just as brilliantly, looking over his spectacles triumphantly and even gaily at the accused. From the doctor's summing up Ivan Ilych concluded that things were bad, but that for the doctor, and perhaps for everybody else, it was a matter of indifference, though for him it was bad. And this conclusion struck him painfully, arousing in him a great feeling of pity for himself and of bitterness towards the doctor's indifference to a matter of such importance.

He said nothing of this, but rose, placed the doctor's fee on the table, and remarked with a sigh: "We sick people probably often put inappropriate questions. But tell me, in general, is this complaint dangerous, or not? . . ."

The doctor looked at him sternly over his spectacles with one eye, as if to say: "Prisoner, if you will not keep to the questions put to you, I shall be obliged to have you removed from the court."

"I have already told you what I consider necessary and proper. The analysis may show something more." And the doctor bowed.

Ivan Ilych went out slowly, seated himself disconsolately in his sledge, and drove home. All the way home he was going over what the doctor had said, trying to translate those complicated, obscure, scientific phrases into plain language and find in them an answer to the question: "Is my condition bad? Is it very bad? Or is there as yet nothing much wrong?" And it seemed to him that the meaning of what the doctor had said was that it was very bad. Everything in the streets seemed depressing. The cabmen, the houses, the passers-by, and the shops were dismal. His ache, this dull gnawing ache that never ceased for a moment, seemed to have acquired a new and more serious significance from the doctor's dubious remarks. Ivan Ilych now watched it with a new and oppressive feeling.

He reached home and began to tell his wife about it. She listened, but in the middle of his account his daughter came in with her hat on, ready to go out with her mother. She sat down reluctantly to listen to this tedious story, but could not stand it long, and her mother too did not hear him to the end.

"Well, I am very glad," she said. "Mind now to take your medicine regularly. Give me the prescription and I'll send Gerasim to the chemist's." And she went to get ready to go out.

While she was in the room Ivan Ilych had hardly taken time to breathe, but he sighed deeply when she left it.

"Well," he thought, "perhaps it isn't so bad after all."

He began taking his medicine and following the doctor's directions, which had been altered after the examination of the urine. But then it happened that there was a contradiction between the indications drawn from the examination of the urine and the symptoms that showed themselves. It turned out that what was happening differed from what the doctor had told him, and that he had either forgotten, or blundered, or hidden something from him. He could not, however, be blamed for that, and Ivan Ilych still obeyed his orders implicitly and at first derived some comfort from doing so.

From the time of his visit to the doctor, Ivan Ilych's chief occupation was the exact fulfilment of the doctor's instructions regarding hygiene and the taking of medicine, and the observation of his pain and his excretions. His chief interests came to be people's ailments and people's health. When sickness, deaths, or recoveries were mentioned in his presence, especially when the illness resembled his own, he listened with agitation which he tried to hide, asked questions, and applied what he heard to his own case.

The pain did not grow less, but Ivan Ilych made efforts to force himself to think that he was better. And he could do this so long as nothing agitated him. But as soon as he had any unpleasantness with his wife, any lack of success in his official work, or held bad cards at bridge, he was at once acutely sensible of his disease. He had formerly borne such mischances, hoping soon to adjust what was wrong, to master it and attain success, or make a grand slam. But now every mischance upset him and plunged him into despair. He would say to himself: "There now, just as I was beginning to get better and the medicine had begun to take effect, comes this accursed misfortune, or unpleasantness. . . ." And he was furious with the mishap, or with the people who were causing the unpleasantness and killing him, for he felt that this fury was killing him but could not restrain it. One would have thought that it should have been clear to him that this exasperation with circumstances and people aggravated his illness, and that he ought therefore to ignore unpleasant occurrences. But he drew the very opposite conclusion: he said that he needed peace, and he watched for everything that might disturb it and became irritable at the slightest infringement of it. His condition was rendered worse by the fact that he read medical books and consulted doctors. The progress of his disease was so gradual that he could deceive himself when comparing one day with another — the difference was so slight. But when he consulted the doctors it seemed to him that he was getting worse, and even very rapidly. Yet despite this he was continually consulting them.

That month he went to see another celebrity, who told him almost the same as the first had done but put his questions rather differently, and the interview with this celebrity only increased Ivan Ilych's doubts and fears. A friend of a friend of his, a very good doctor, diagnosed his illness again quite differently from the others, and though he predicted recovery, his questions and suppositions bewildered Ivan Ilych still more and increased his doubts. A homoeopathist diagnosed the disease in yet another way, and prescribed medicine which Ivan Ilych took secretly for a week. But after a week, not feeling any improvement and having lost confidence both in the former doctor's treatment and in this one's, he became still more despondent. One day a lady acquaintance mentioned a cure effected by a wonder-working icon. Ivan Ilych caught himself listening attentively and beginning to believe that it had occurred. This incident alarmed him. "Has my mind really weakened to such an extent?" he asked himself. "Nonsense! It's all rubbish. I mustn't give way to nervous fears but having chosen a doctor must keep strictly to his treatment. That is what I will do. Now it's all settled. I won't think about it, but will follow the treatment seriously till summer, and then we shall see. From now there must be no more of this wavering!" This was easy to say but impossible to carry out. The pain in his side oppressed him and seemed to grow worse and more incessant, while the taste in his mouth grew stranger and stranger. It seemed to him that his breath had a disgusting smell, and he was conscious of a loss of appetite and strength. There was no deceiving himself: something terrible, new, and more important than anything before in his life, was taking place within him of which he alone was aware. Those about him did not understand or would not understand it, but thought everything in the world was going on as usual. That tormented Ivan Ilych more than anything. He saw that his household, especially his wife and daughter who were in a perfect whirl of visiting, did not understand anything of it and were annoyed that he was so depressed and so exacting, as if he were to blame for it. Though they tried to disguise it he saw that he was an obstacle in their path, and that his wife had adopted a definite line in regard to his illness and kept to it regardless of anything he said or did. Her attitude was this: "You know," she would say to her friends, "Ivan Ilych can't do as other people do, and keep to the treatment prescribed for him. One day he'll take his drops and keep strictly to his diet and go to bed in good time, but the next day unless I watch him he'll suddenly forget his medicine, eat sturgeon — which is forbidden — and sit up playing cards till one o'clock in the morning."

"Oh, come, when was that?" Ivan Ilych would ask in vexation. "Only once at Peter Ivanovich's."

"And yesterday with Shebek."

"Well, even if I hadn't stayed up, this pain would have kept me awake."

"Be that as it may you'll never get well like that, but will always make us wretched."

Praskovya Fëdorovna's attitude to Ivan Ilych's illness, as she expressed it both to others and to him, was that it was his own fault and was another of the annoyances he caused her. Ivan Ilych felt that this opinion escaped her involuntarily — but that did not make it easier for him.

At the law courts too, Ivan Ilych noticed, or thought he noticed, a strange attitude towards himself. It sometimes seemed to him that people were watching him inquisitively as a man whose place might soon be vacant. Then again, his friends would suddenly begin to chaff him in a friendly way about his low spirits, as if the awful, horrible, and unheard-of-thing that was going on within him, incessantly gnawing at him and irresistibly drawing him away, was a very agreeable subject for jests. Schwartz in particular irritated him by his jocularity, vivacity, and *savoir-faire,* which reminded him of what he himself had been ten years ago.

Friends came to make up a set and they sat down to cards. They dealt, bending the new cards to soften them, and he sorted the diamonds in his hand and found he had seven. His partner said "No trumps" and supported him with two diamonds. What more could be wished for? It ought to be jolly and lively. They would make a grand slam. But suddenly Ivan Ilych was conscious of that gnawing pain, that taste in his mouth, and it seemed ridiculous that in such circumstances he should be pleased to make a grand slam.

He looked at his partner Mikhail Mikhaylovich, who rapped the table with his strong hand and instead of snatching up the tricks pushed the cards courteously and indulgently towards Ivan Ilych that he might have the pleasure of gathering them up without the trouble of stretching out his hand for them. "Does he think I am too weak to stretch out my arm?" thought Ivan Ilych, and forgetting what he was doing he over-trumped his partner, missing the grand slam by three tricks. And what was most awful of all was that he saw how upset Mikhail Mikhaylovich was about it but did not himself care. And it was dreadful to realize why he did not care.

They all saw that he was suffering, and said: "We can stop if you are tired. Take a rest." Lie down? No, he was not at all tired, and he finished the rubber. All were gloomy and silent. Ivan Ilych felt that he had diffused this gloom over them and could not dispel it. They had supper and went away, and Ivan Ilych was left alone with the consciousness that his life was poisoned and was poisoning the lives of others, and that this poison did not weaken but penetrated more and more deeply into his whole being.

With this consciousness, and with physical pain besides the terror, he must go to bed, often to lie awake the greater part of the night. Next morning he had to get up again, dress, go to the law courts, speak, and write; or if he did not go out, spend at home those twenty-four hours a day each of which was a torture. And he had to live thus all alone on the brink of an abyss, with no one who understood or pitied him.

v

So one month passed and then another. Just before the New Year his brother-in-law came to town and stayed at their house. Ivan Ilych was at the law courts and Praskovya Fëdorovna had gone shopping. When Ivan Ilych came home and entered his study he found his brother-in-law there — a healthy, florid man — unpacking his portmanteau himself. He raised his head on hearing Ivan Ilych's footsteps and looked up at him for a moment without a word. That stare told Ivan Ilych everything. His brother-in-law opened his mouth to utter an exclamation of surprise but checked himself, and that action confirmed it all.

"I have changed, eh?"

"Yes, there is a change."

And after that, try as he would to get his brother-in-law to return to the subject of his looks, the latter would say nothing about it. Praskovya Fëdorovna came home and her brother went out to her. Ivan Ilych locked the door and began to examine himself in the glass, first full face, then in profile. He took up a portrait of himself taken with his wife, and compared it with what he saw in the glass. The change in him was immense. Then he bared his arms to the elbow, looked at them, drew the sleeves down again, sat down on an ottoman, and grew blacker than night.

"No, no, this won't do!" he said to himself, and jumped up, went to the table, took up some law papers and began to read them, but could not continue. He unlocked the door and went into the reception-room. The door leading to the drawing-room was shut. He approached it on tiptoe and listened.

"No, you are exaggerating!" Praskovya Fëdorovna was saying.

"Exaggerating! Don't you see it? Why, he's a dead man! Look at his eyes — there's no light in them. But what is it that is wrong with him?"

"No one knows. Nikolaevich [that was another doctor] said something, but I don't know what. And Leshchetitsky [this was the celebrated specialist] said quite the contrary. . . ."

Ivan Ilych walked away, went to his own room, lay down, and began musing: "The kidney, a floating kidney." He recalled all the doctors had told him of how it detached itself and swayed about. And by an effort of imagination he tried to catch that kidney and arrest it and support it. So little was needed for this, it seemed to him. "No, I'll go to see Peter Ivanovich again." [That was the friend whose friend was a doctor.] He rang, ordered the carriage, and got ready to go.

"Where are you going, Jean?" asked his wife, with a specially sad and exceptionally kind look.

This exceptionally kind look irritated him. He looked morosely at her.

"I must go to see Peter Ivanovich."

He went to see Peter Ivanovich, and together they went to see his friend, the doctor. He was in, and Ivan Ilych had a long talk with him.

Reviewing the anatomical and physiological details of what in the doctor's opinion was going on inside him, he understood it all.

There was something, a small thing, in the vermiform appendix. It might all come right. Only stimulate the energy of one organ and check the activity of another, then absorption would take place and everything would come right. He got home rather late for dinner, ate his dinner, and conversed cheerfully, but could not for a long time bring himself to go back to work in his room. At last, however, he went to his study and did what was necessary, but the consciousness that he had put something aside — an important, intimate matter which he would revert to when his work was done — never left him. When he had finished his work he remembered that this intimate matter was the thought of his vermiform appendix. But he did not give himself up to it, and went to the drawing-room for tea. There were callers there, including the examining magistrate who was a desirable match for his daughter, and they were conversing, playing the piano, and singing. Ivan Ilych, as Praskovya Fëdorovna remarked, spent that evening more cheerfully than usual, but he never for a moment forgot that he had postponed the important matter of the appendix. At eleven o'clock he said good-night and went to his bedroom. Since his illness he had slept alone in a small room next to his study. He undressed and took up a novel by Zola, but instead of reading it he fell into thought, and in his imagination that desired improvement in the vermiform appendix occurred. There was the absorption and evacuation and the re-establishment of normal activity. "Yes, that's it!" he said to himself. "One need only assist nature, that's all." He remembered his medicine, rose, took it, and lay down on his back watching for the beneficent action of the medicine and for it to lessen the pain. "I need only take it regularly and avoid all injurious influences. I am already feeling better, much better." He began touching his side: it was not painful to the touch. "There, I really don't feel it. It's much better already." He put out the light and turned on his side.... "The appendix is getting better, absorption is occurring." Suddenly he felt the old, familiar, dull, gnawing pain, stubborn and serious. There was the same familiar loathsome taste in his mouth. His heart sank and he felt dazed. "My God! My God!" he muttered. "Again, again! and it will never cease." And suddenly the matter presented itself in a quite different aspect. "Vermiform appendix! Kidney!" he said to himself. "It's not a question of appendix or kidney, but of life and . . . death. Yes, life was there and now it is going, going and I cannot stop it. Yes. Why deceive myself? Isn't it obvious to everyone but me that I'm dying, and that it's only a question of weeks, days . . . it may happen this moment. There was light and now there is darkness. I was here and now I'm going there! Where?" A chill came over him, his breathing ceased, and he felt only the throbbing of his heart.

"When I am not, what will there be? There will be nothing. Then where shall I be when I am no more? Can this be dying? No, I don't want to!" He jumped up and tried to light the candle, felt for it with trembling hands, dropped candle and candlestick on the floor, and fell back on his pillow.

"What's the use? It makes no difference," he said to himself, staring with wide-open eyes into the darkness. "Death. Yes, death. And none of them know or wish to know it, and they have no pity for me. Now they are playing." (He heard through the door the distant sound of a song and its accompaniment.) "It's all the same to them, but they will die too! Fools! I first, and they later, but it will be the same for them. And now they are merry . . . the beasts!"

Anger choked him and he was agonizingly, unbearably miserable. "It is impossible that all men have been doomed to suffer this awful horror!" He raised himself.

"Something must be wrong. I must calm myself — must think it all over from the beginning." And he again began thinking. "Yes, the beginning of my illness: I knocked my side, but I was still quite well that day and the next. It hurt a little, then rather more. I saw the doctors, then followed despondency and anguish, more doctors, and I drew nearer to the abyss. My strength grew less and I kept coming nearer and nearer, and now I have wasted away and there is no light in my eyes. I think of the appendix — but this is death! I think of mending the appendix, and all the while here is death! Can it really be death?" Again terror seized him and he gasped for breath. He leant down and began feeling for the matches, pressing with his elbow on the stand beside the bed. It was in his way and hurt him, he grew furious with it, pressed on it still harder, and upset it. Breathless and in despair he fell on his back, expecting death to come immediately.

Meanwhile the visitors were leaving. Praskovya Fëdorovna was seeing them off. She heard something fall and came in.

"What has happened?"

"Nothing. I knocked it over accidentally."

She went out and returned with a candle. He lay there panting heavily, like a man who has run a thousand yards, and stared upwards at her with a fixed look.

"What is it, Jean?"

"No . . . o . . . thing. I upset it." ("Why speak of it? She won't understand," he thought.)

And in truth she did not understand. She picked up the stand, lit his candle, and hurried away to see another visitor off. When she came back he still lay on his back, looking upwards.

"What is it? Do you feel worse?"

"Yes."

She shook her head and sat down.

"Do you know, Jean, I think we must ask Leshchetitsky to come and see you here."

This meant calling in the famous specialist, regardless of expense. He smiled malignantly and said "No." She remained a little longer and then went up to him and kissed his forehead.

While she was kissing him he hated her from the bottom of his soul and with difficulty refrained from pushing her away.

"Good-night. Please God you'll sleep."

"Yes."

vi

Ivan Ilych saw that he was dying, and he was in continual despair.

In the depth of his heart he knew he was dying, but not only was he not accustomed to the thought, he simply did not and could not grasp it.

The syllogism he had learnt from Kiezewetter's Logic: "Caius is a man, men are mortal, therefore Caius is mortal," had always seemed to him correct as applied to Caius, but certainly not as applied to himself. That Caius — man in the abstract — was mortal, was perfectly correct, but he was not Caius, not an abstract man, but a creature quite, quite separate from all others. He had been little Vanya, with a mamma and a papa, with Mitya and Volodya, with the toys, a coachman and a nurse, afterwards with Katenka and with all the joys, griefs, and delights of childhood, boyhood, and youth. What did Caius know of the smell of that striped leather ball Vanya had been so fond of? Had Caius kissed his mother's hand like that, and did the silk of her dress rustle so for Caius? Had he rioted like that at school when the pastry was bad? Had Caius been in love like that? Could Caius preside at a session as he did? "Caius really was mortal, and it was right for him to die; but for me, little Vanya, Ivan Ilych, with all my thoughts and emotions, it's altogether a different matter. It cannot be that I ought to die. That would be too terrible."

Such was his feeling.

"If I had to die like Caius I should have known it was so. An inner voice would have told me so, but there was nothing of the sort in me and I and all my friends felt that our case was quite different from that of Caius. And now here it is!" he said to himself. "It can't be. It's impossible! But here it is. How is this? How is one to understand it?"

He could not understand it, and tried to drive this false, incorrect, morbid thought away and to replace it by other proper and healthy thoughts. But that thought, and not the thought only but the reality itself, seemed to come and confront him.

And to replace that thought, he called up a succession of others, hoping to find in them some support. He tried to get back into the former current of thoughts that had once screened the thought of death from him. But strange to say, all that had formerly shut off, hidden, and destroyed his consciousness of death, no longer had that effect. Ivan Ilych now spent most of his time in attempting to re-establish that old current. He would say to himself: "I will take up my duties again — after all I used to live by them." And banishing all doubts he would go to the law courts, enter into conversation with his colleagues, and sit carelessly as was his wont, scanning the crowd with a thoughtful look and leaning both his emaciated arms on the arms of his oak chair; bending over as usual to a colleague and drawing his papers nearer he would interchange whispers with him, and then suddenly raising his eyes and sitting erect would pronounce certain words and open the proceedings. But suddenly in the midst of those proceedings the pain in his side, regardless of the stage the proceedings had reached, would begin its own gnawing work. Ivan Ilych would turn his attention to it and try to drive the thought of it away, but without success. *It* would come and stand before him and look at him, and he would be petrified and the light would die out of his eyes, and he would again begin asking himself whether *It* alone was true. And his colleagues and subordinates would see with surprise and distress that he, the brilliant and subtle judge, was becoming confused and making mistakes. He would shake himself, try to pull himself together, manage somehow to bring the sitting to a close, and return home with the sorrowful consciousness that his judicial labors could not as formerly hide from him what he wanted them to hide, and could not deliver him from *It*. And what was worst of all was that *It* drew his attention to itself not in order to make him take some action but only that he should look at *It*, look it straight in the face: look at it and without doing anything, suffer inexpressibly.

And to save himself from this condition Ivan Ilych looked for consolations — new screens — and new screens were found and for a while seemed to save him, but then they immediately fell to pieces or rather became transparent, as if *It* penetrated them and nothing could veil *It*.

In these latter days he would go into the drawing-room he had arranged — that drawing-room where he had fallen and for the sake of which (how bitterly ridiculous it seemed) he had sacrificed his life — for he knew that his illness originated with that knock. He would enter and see that something had scratched the polished table. He would look for the cause of this and find that it was the bronze ornamentation of an album that had got bent. He would take up the expensive album which he had lovingly arranged, and feel vexed with his daughter and her friends for their untidiness — for the album was torn here and there and some of the photographs turned upside down. He would put it carefully in order and bend the ornamentation back into position. Then it would occur to him to place all those things in another corner of the room, near the plants. He could call the footman, but his daughter or wife would come to help him. They would not agree, and his wife would contradict him, and he would dispute and grow angry. But that was all right, for then he did not think about *It*. *It* was invisible.

But then, when he was moving something himself, his wife would say: "Let the servants do it. You will hurt yourself again." And suddenly *It* would flash through the screen and he would see it. It was just a flash, and he hoped it would disappear, but he would involuntarily pay attention to his side. "It sits there as before, gnawing just the same!" And he could no longer forget *It,* but could distinctly see *It* looking at him from behind the flowers. "What is it all for?"

"It really is so! I lost my life over that curtain as I might have done when storming a fort. Is that possible? How terrible and how stupid. It can't be true! It can't, but it is."

He would go to his study, lie down, and again be alone with *It:* face to face with *It.* And nothing could be done with *It* except to look at it and shudder.

vii

How it happened it is impossible to say because it came about step by step, unnoticed, but in the third month of Ivan Ilych's illness, his wife, his daughter, his son, his acquaintances, the doctors, the servants, and above all he himself, were aware that the whole interest he had for other people was whether he would soon vacate his place, and at last release the living from the discomfort caused by his presence and be himself released from his sufferings.

He slept less and less. He was given opium and hypodermic injections of morphine, but this did not relieve him. The dull depression he experienced in a somnolent condition at first gave him a little relief, but only as something new, afterwards it became as distressing as the pain itself or even more so.

Special foods were prepared for him by the doctors' orders, but all those foods became increasingly distasteful and disgusting to him.

For his excretions also special arrangements had to be made, and this was a torment to him every time — a torment from the uncleanliness, the unseemliness, and the smell, and from knowing that another person had to take part in it.

But just through this most unpleasant matter, Ivan Ilych obtained comfort. Gerasim, the butler's young assistant, always came in to carry the things out. Gerasim was a clean, fresh peasant lad, grown stout on town food and always cheerful and bright. At first the sight of him, in his clean Russian peasant costume, engaged in that disgusting task embarrassed Ivan Ilych.

Once when he got up from the commode too weak to draw up his trousers, he dropped into a soft armchair and looked with horror at his bare, enfeebled thighs with the muscles so sharply marked on them.

Gerasim with a firm light tread, his heavy boots emitting a pleasant smell of tar and fresh winter air, came in wearing a clean Hessian apron, the sleeves of his print shirt tucked up over his strong bare young arms; and refraining from looking at his sick master out of consideration for his feelings, and restraining the joy of life that beamed from his face, he went up to the commode.

"Gerasim!" said Ivan Ilych in a weak voice.

Gerasim started, evidently afraid he might have committed some blunder, and with a rapid movement turned his fresh, kind, simple young face which just showed the first downy signs of a beard.

"Yes, sir?"

"That must be very unpleasant for you. You must forgive me. I am helpless."

"Oh, why, sir," and Gerasim's eyes beamed and he showed his glistening white teeth, "what's a little trouble? It's a case of illness with you, sir."

And his deft strong hands did their accustomed task, and he went out of the room stepping lightly. Five minutes later he as lightly returned.

Ivan Ilych was still sitting in the same position in the armchair.

"Gerasim," he said when the latter had replaced the freshly-washed utensil. "Please come here and help me." Gerasim went up to him. "Lift me up. It is hard for me to get up, and I have sent Dmitri away."

Gerasim went up to him, grasped his master with his strong arms deftly but gently, in the same way that he stepped — lifted him, supported him with one hand, and with the other drew up his trousers and would have set him down again, but Ivan Ilych asked to be led to the sofa. Gerasim, without an effort and without apparent pressure, led him, almost lifting him, to the sofa and placed him on it.

"Thank you. How easily and well you do it all!"

Gerasim smiled again and turned to leave the room. But Ivan Ilych felt his presence such a comfort that he did not want to let him go.

"One thing more, please move up that chair. No, the other one — under my feet. It is easier for me when my feet are raised."

Gerasim brought the chair, set it down gently in place, and raised Ivan Ilych's legs on to it. It seemed to Ivan Ilych that he felt better while Gerasim was holding up his legs.

"It's better when my legs are higher," he said. "Place that cushion under them."

Gerasim did so. He again lifted the legs and placed them, and again Ivan Ilych felt better while Gerasim held his legs. When he set them down Ivan Ilych fancied he felt worse.

"Gerasim," he said. "Are you busy now?"

"Not at all, sir," said Gerasim, who had learnt from the townsfolk how to speak to gentlefolk.

"What have you still to do?"

"What have I to do? I've done everything except chopping the logs for tomorrow."

"Then hold my legs up a bit higher, can you?"

"Of course I can. Why not?" And Gerasim raised his master's legs higher and Ivan Ilych thought that in that position he did not feel any pain at all.

"And how about the logs?"

"Don't trouble about that, sir. There's plenty of time."

Ivan Ilych told Gerasim to sit down and hold his legs, and began to talk to him. And strange to say it seemed to him that he felt better while Gerasim held his legs up.

After that Ivan Ilych would sometimes call Gerasim and get him to hold his legs on his shoulders, and he liked talking to him. Gerasim did it all easily, willingly, simply, and with a good nature that touched Ivan Ilych. Health, strength, and vitality in other people were offensive to him, but Gerasim's strength and vitality did not mortify but soothed him.

What tormented Ivan Ilych most was the deception, the lie, which for some reason they all accepted, that he was not dying but was simply ill, and that he only need keep quiet and undergo a treatment and then something very good would result. He however knew that do what they would nothing would come of it, only still more agonizing suffering and death. This deception tortured him — their not wishing to admit what they all knew and what he knew, but wanting to lie to him concerning his terrible condition, and wishing and forcing him to participate in that lie. Those lies — lies enacted over him on the eve of his death and destined to degrade this awful, solemn act to the level of their visitings, their curtains, their sturgeon for dinner — were a terrible agony for Ivan Ilych. And strangely enough, many times when they were going through their antics over him he had been within a hairbreadth of calling out to them: "Stop lying! You know and I know that I am dying. Then at least stop lying about it!" But he had never had the spirit to do it. The awful, terrible act of his dying was, he could see, reduced by those about him to the level of a casual, unpleasant, and almost indecorous incident (as if someone entered a drawing-room diffusing an unpleasant odor) and this was done by that very decorum which he had served all his life long. He saw that no one felt for him, because no one even wished to grasp his position. Only Gerasim recognized it and pitied him. And so Ivan Ilych felt at ease only with him. He felt comforted when Gerasim supported his legs (sometimes all night long) and refused to go to bed, saying: "Don't you worry, Ivan Ilych. I'll get sleep enough later on," or when he suddenly became familiar and exclaimed: "If you weren't sick it would be another matter, but as it is, why should I grudge a little trouble?" Gerasim alone did not lie; everything showed that he alone understood the facts of the case and did not consider it necessary to disguise them, but simply felt sorry for his emaciated and enfeebled master. Once when Ivan Ilych was sending him away he even said straight out: "We shall all of us die, so why should I grudge a little trouble?" — expressing the fact that he did not think his work burdensome, because he was doing it for a dying man and hoped someone would do the same for him when his time came.

Apart from this lying, or because of it, what most tormented Ivan Ilych was that no one pitied him as he wished to be pitied. At certain moments after prolonged suffering he wished most of all (though he would have been ashamed to confess it) for someone to pity him as a sick child is pitied. He longed to be petted and comforted. He knew he was an important functionary, that he had a beard turning grey, and that therefore what he longed for was impossible, but still he longed for it. And in Gerasim's attitude towards him there was something akin to what he wished for, and so that attitude comforted him. Ivan Ilych wanted to weep, wanted to be petted and cried over, and then his colleague Shebek would come, and instead of weeping and being petted, Ivan Ilych would assume a serious, severe, and profound air, and by force of habit would express his opinion on a decision of the Court of Cassation and would stubbornly insist on that view. This falsity around him and within him did more than anything else to poison his last days.

viii

It was morning. He knew it was morning because Gerasim had gone, and Peter the footman had come and put out the candles, drawn back one of the curtains, and begun quietly to tidy up. Whether it was morning or evening, Friday or Sunday, made no difference, it was all just the same: the gnawing, unmitigated, agonizing pain, never ceasing for an instant, the consciousness of life inexorably waning but not yet extinguished, the approach of that ever dreaded and hateful Death which was the only reality, and always the same falsity. What were days, weeks, hours, in such a case?

"Will you have some tea, sir?"

"He wants things to be regular, and wishes the gentlefolk to drink tea in the morning," thought Ivan Ilych, and only said "No."

"Wouldn't you like to move onto the sofa, sir?"

"He wants to tidy up the room, and I'm in the way. I am uncleanliness and disorder," he thought, and said only:

"No, leave me alone."

The man went on bustling about. Ivan Ilych stretched out his hand. Peter came up, ready to help.

"What is it, sir?"

"My watch."

Peter took the watch which was close at hand and gave it to his master.

"Half-past eight. Are they up?"

"No, sir, except Vladimir Ivanich" (the son) "who has gone to school. Praskovya Fëdorovna ordered me to wake her if you asked for her. Shall I do so?"

"No, there's no need to." "Perhaps I'd better have some tea," he thought, and added aloud: "Yes, bring me some tea."

Peter went to the door, but Ivan Ilych dreaded being left alone. "How can I keep him here? Oh yes, my medicine." "Peter, give me my medicine." "Why not? Perhaps it may still do me some good." He took a spoonful and swallowed it. "No, it won't help. It's all tomfoolery, all deception," he decided as soon as he became aware of the familiar, sickly, hopeless taste: "No, I can't believe in it any longer. But the pain, why this pain? If it would only cease just for a moment!" And he moaned. Peter turned towards him. "It's all right. Go and fetch me some tea."

Peter went out. Left alone Ivan Ilych groaned not so much with pain, terrible though that was, as from mental anguish. Always and for ever the same, always these endless days and nights. If only it would come quicker! If only *what* would come quicker? Death, darkness? . . . No, no! Anything rather than death!

When Peter returned with the tea on a tray, Ivan Ilych stared at him for a time in perplexity, not realizing who and what he was. Peter was disconcerted by that look and his embarrassment brought Ivan Ilych to himself.

"Oh, tea! All right, put it down. Only help me to wash and put on a clean shirt."

And Ivan Ilych began to wash. With pauses for rest, he washed his hands and then his face, cleaned his teeth, brushed his hair, and looked in the glass. He was terrified by what he saw, especially by the limp way in which his hair clung to his pallid forehead.

While his shirt was being changed he knew that he would be still more frightened at the sight of his body, so he avoided looking at it. Finally he was ready. He drew on a dressing-gown, wrapped himself in a plaid, and sat down in the armchair to take his tea. For a moment he felt refreshed, but as soon as he began to drink the tea he was again aware of the same taste, and the pain also returned. He finished it with an effort, and then lay down stretching out his legs, and dismissed Peter.

Always the same. Now a spark of hope flashes up, then a sea of despair rages, and always pain; always pain, always despair, and always the same. When alone he had a dreadful and distressing desire to call someone, but he knew beforehand that with others present it would be still worse. "Another dose of morphine — to lose consciousness. I will tell him, the doctor, that he must think of something else. It's impossible, impossible, to go on like this."

An hour and another pass like that. But now there is a ring at the door bell. Perhaps it's the doctor? It is. He comes in fresh, hearty, plump, and cheerful, with that look on his face that seems to say: "There now, you're in a panic about something, but we'll arrange it all for you directly!" The doctor knows this expression is out of place here, but he has put it on once for all and can't take it off — like a man who has put on a frock-coat in the morning to pay a round of calls.

The doctor rubs his hands vigorously and reassuringly.

"Brr! How cold it is! There's such a sharp frost; just let me warm myself!" he says, as if it were only a matter of waiting till he was warm, and then he would put everything right.

"Well now, how are you?"

Ivan Ilych feels that the doctor would like to say: "Well, how are our affairs?" but that even he feels that this would not do, and says instead: "What sort of a night have you had?"

Ivan Ilych looks at him as much as to say: "Are you really never ashamed of lying?" But the doctor does not wish to understand this question, and Ivan Ilych says: "Just as terrible as ever. The pain never leaves me and never subsides. If only something . . ."

"Yes, you sick people are always like that. . . . There, now I think I am warm enough. Even Praskovya Fëdorovna, who is so particular, could find no fault with my temperature. Well, now I can say good-morning," and the doctor presses his patient's hand.

Then, dropping his former playfulness, he begins with a most serious face to examine the patient, feeling his pulse and taking his temperature, and then begins the sounding and auscultation.

Ivan Ilych knows quite well and definitely that all this is nonsense and pure deception, but when the doctor, getting down on his knee, leans over him, putting his ear first higher then lower, and performs various gymnastic movements over him with a significant expression on his face, Ivan Ilych submits to it all as he used to submit to the speeches of the lawyers, though he knew very well that they were all lying and why they were lying.

The doctor, kneeling on the sofa, is still sounding him when Praskovya Fëdorovna's silk dress rustles at the door and she is heard scolding Peter for not having let her know of the doctor's arrival.

She comes in, kisses her husband, and at once proceeds to prove that she has been up a long time already, and only owing to a misunderstanding failed to be there when the doctor arrived.

Ivan Ilych looks at her, scans her all over, sets against her the whiteness and plumpness and cleanness of her hands and neck, the gloss of her hair, and the sparkle of her vivacious eyes. He hates her with his whole soul. And the thrill of hatred he feels for her makes him suffer from her touch.

Her attitude towards him and his disease is still the same. Just as the doctor had adopted a certain relation to his patient which he could not abandon, so had she formed one towards him — that he was not doing something he ought to do and was himself to blame, and that she reproached him lovingly for this — and she could not now change that attitude.

"You see he doesn't listen to me and doesn't take his medicine at the proper time. And above all he lies in a position that is no doubt bad for him — with his legs up."

She described how he made Gerasim hold his legs up.

The doctor smiled with a contemptuous affability that said: "What's to be done? These sick people do have foolish fancies of that kind, but we must forgive them."

When the examination was over the doctor looked at his watch, and then Praskovya Fëdorovna announced to Ivan Ilych that it was of course as he pleased, but she had sent today for a celebrated specialist who would examine him and have a consultation with Michael Danilovich (their regular doctor).

"Please don't raise any objections. I am doing this for my own sake," she said ironically, letting it be felt that she was doing it all for his sake and only said this to leave him no right to refuse. He remained silent, knitting his brows. He felt that he was so surrounded and involved in a mesh of falsity that it was hard to unravel anything.

Everything she did for him was entirely for her own sake, and she told him she was doing for herself what she actually was doing for herself, as if that was so incredible that he must understand the opposite.

At half-past eleven the celebrated specialist arrived. Again the sounding began and the significant conversations in his presence and in another room, about the kidneys and the appendix, and the questions and answers, with such an air of importance that again, instead of the real question of life and death which now alone confronted him, the question arose of the kidney and appendix which were not behaving as they ought to and would now be attacked by Michael Danilovich and the specialist and forced to amend their ways.

The celebrated specialist took leave of him with a serious though not hopeless look, and in reply to the timid question Ivan Ilych, with eyes glistening with fear and hope, put to him as to whether there was a chance of recovery, said that he could not vouch for it but there was a possibility. The look of hope with which Ivan Ilych watched the doctor out was so pathetic that Praskovya Fëdorovna, seeing it, even wept as she left the room to hand the doctor his fee.

The gleam of hope kindled by the doctor's encouragement did not last long. The same room, the same pictures, curtains, wall-paper, medicine bottles, were all there, and the same aching suffering body, and Ivan Ilych began to moan. They gave him a subcutaneous injection and he sank into oblivion.

It was twilight when he came to. They brought him his dinner and he swallowed some beef tea with difficulty, and then everything was the same again and night was coming on.

After dinner, at seven o'clock, Praskovya Fëdorovna came into the room in evening dress, her full bosom pushed up by her corset, and with traces of powder on her face. She had reminded him in the morning that they were going to the theatre. Sarah Bernhardt was visiting the town and they had a box, which he had insisted on their taking. Now he had forgotten about it and her toilet offended him, but he concealed his vexation when he remembered that he had himself insisted on their securing a box and going because it would be an instructive and aesthetic pleasure for the children.

Praskovya Fëdorovna came in, self-satisfied but yet with a rather guilty air. She sat down and asked how he was, but, as he saw, only for the sake of asking and not in order to learn about it, knowing that there was nothing to learn — and then went on to what she really wanted to say: that she would not on any account have gone but that the box had been taken and Helen and their daughter were going, as well as Petrishchev (the examining magistrate, their daughter's fiancé) and that it was out of the question to let them go alone; but that she would have much preferred to sit with him for a while; and he must be sure to follow the doctor's orders while she was away.

"Oh, and Fëdor Petrovich" (the fiancé) "would like to come in. May he? And Lisa?"

"All right."

Their daughter came in in full evening dress, her fresh young flesh exposed (making a show of that very flesh which in his own case caused so much suffering), strong, healthy, evidently in love, and impatient with illness, suffering, and death, because they interfered with her happiness.

Fëdor Petrovich came in too, in evening dress, his hair curled *à la Capoul,* a tight stiff collar round his long sinewy neck, an enormous white shirt-front and narrow black trousers tightly stretched over his strong thighs. He had one white glove tightly drawn on, and was holding his opera hat in his hand.

Following him the schoolboy crept in unnoticed, in a new uniform; poor little fellow, and wearing gloves. Terribly dark shadows showed under his eyes, the meaning of which Ivan Ilych knew well.

His son had always seemed pathetic to him, and now it was dreadful to see the boy's frightened look of pity. It seemed to Ivan Ilych that Vasya was the only one besides Gerasim who understood and pitied him.

They all sat down and again asked how he was. A silence followed: Lisa asked her mother about the opera-glasses, and there was an altercation between mother and daughter as to who had taken them and where they had been put. This occasioned some unpleasantness.

Fëdor Petrovich inquired of Ivan Ilych whether he had ever seen Sarah Bernhardt. Ivan Ilych did not at first catch the question, but then replied: "No, have you seen her before?"

"Yes, in *Adrienne Lecouvreur.*"

Praskovya Fëdorovna mentioned some roles in which Sarah Bernhardt was particularly good. Her daughter disagreed. Conversation sprang up as to the elegance and realism of her acting — the sort of conversation that is always repeated and is always the same.

In the midst of the conversation Fëdor Petrovich glanced at Ivan Ilych and became silent. The others also looked at him and grew silent. Ivan Ilych was staring with glittering eyes straight before him, evidently indignant with them. This had to be rectified, but it was impossible to do so. The silence had to be broken, but for a time no one dared to break it and they all became afraid that the conventional deception would suddenly become obvious and the truth become plain to all. Lisa was the first to pluck up courage and break that silence, but by trying to hide what everybody was feeling, she betrayed it.

"Well, if we are going it's time to start," she said, looking at her watch, a present from her father, and with a faint and significant smile at Fëdor Petrovich relating to something known only to them. She got up with a rustle of her dress.

They all rose, said good-night, and went away.

When they had gone it seemed to Ivan Ilych that he felt better; the falsity had gone with them. But the pain remained — that same pain and that same fear that made everything monotonously alike, nothing harder and nothing easier. Everything was worse.

Again minute followed minute and hour followed hour. Everything remained the same and there was no cessation. And the inevitable end of it all became more and more terrible.

"Yes, send Gerasim here," he replied to a question Peter asked.

ix

His wife returned late at night. She came in on tiptoe, but he heard her, opened his eyes, and made haste to close them again. She wished to send Gerasim away and to sit with him herself, but he opened his eyes and said: "No, go away."

"Are you in great pain?"

"Always the same."

"Take some opium."

He agreed and took some. She went away.

Till about three in the morning he was in a state of stupefied misery. It seemed to him that he and his pain were being thrust into a narrow, deep black sack, but though they were pushed further and further in they could not be pushed to the bottom. And this, terrible enough in itself, was accompanied by suffering. He was frightened yet wanted to fall through the sack, he struggled but yet co-operated. And suddenly he broke through, fell, and regained consciousness. Gerasim was sitting at the foot of the bed dozing quietly and patiently, while he himself lay with his emaciated stockinged legs resting on Gerasim's shoulders; the same shaded candle was there and the same unceasing pain.

"Go away, Gerasim," he whispered.

"It's all right, sir. I'll stay awhile."

"No. Go away."

He removed his legs from Gerasim's shoulders, turned sideways onto his arm, and felt sorry for himself. He only waited till Gerasim had gone into the next room and then restrained himself no longer but wept like a child. He wept on account of his helplessness, his terrible loneliness, the cruelty of man, the cruelty of God, and the absence of God.

"Why hast Thou done all this? Why hast Thou brought me here? Why, why dost Thou torment me so terribly?"

He did not expect an answer and yet wept because there was no answer and could be none. The pain again grew more acute, but he did not stir and did not call. He said to himself: "Go on! Strike me! But what is it for? What have I done to Thee? What is it for?"

Then he grew quiet and not only ceased weeping but even held his breath and became all attention. It was as though he were listening not to an audible voice but to the voice of his soul, to the current of thoughts arising within him.

"What is it you want?" was the first clear conception capable of expression in words, that he heard.

"What do you want? What do you want?" he repeated to himself.

"What do I want? To live and not to suffer," he answered. And again he listened with such concentrated attention that even his pain did not distract him.

"To live? How?" asked his inner voice.

"Why, to live as I used to — well and pleasantly."

"As you lived before, well and pleasantly?" the voice repeated.

And in imagination he began to recall the best moments of his pleasant life. But strange to say none of those best moments of his pleasant life now seemed at all what they had then seemed — none of them except the first recollections of childhood. There, in childhood, there had been something really pleasant with which it would be possible to live if it could return. But the child who had experienced that happiness existed no longer, it was like a reminiscence of somebody else.

As soon as the period began which had produced the present Ivan Ilych, all that had then seemed joys now melted before his sight and turned into something trivial and often nasty.

And the further he departed from childhood and the nearer he came to the present the more worthless and doubtful were the joys. This began with the School of Law. A little that was really good was still found there — there was lightheartedness, friendship, and hope. But in the upper classes there had already been fewer of such good moments. Then during the first years of his official career, when he was in the service of the Governor, some pleasant moments again occurred: they were the memories of love for a woman. Then all became confused and there was still less of what was good; later on again there was still less that was good, and the further he went the less there was. His marriage, a mere accident, then the disenchantment that followed it, his wife's bad breath and the sensuality and hypocrisy: then that deadly official life and those preoccupations about money, a year of it, and two, and ten, and twenty, and always the same thing. And the longer it lasted the more deadly it became. "It is as if I had been going downhill while I imagined I was going up. And that is really what it was. I was going up in public opinion, but to the same extent life was ebbing away from me. And now it is all done and there is only death."

"Then what does it mean? Why? It can't be that life is so senseless and horrible. But if it really has been so horrible and senseless, why must I die and die in agony? There is something wrong!"

"Maybe I did not live as I ought to have done," it suddenly occurred to him. "But how could that be, when I did everything properly?" he replied, and immediately dismissed from his mind this, the sole solution of all the riddles of life and death, as something quite impossible.

"Then what do you want now? To live? Live how? Live as you lived in the law courts when the usher proclaimed 'The judge is coming!' The judge is coming, the judge!" he repeated to himself. "Here he is, the judge. But I am not guilty!" he exclaimed angrily. "What is it for?" And he ceased crying, but turning his face to the wall continued to ponder on the same question: Why, and for what purpose is there all this horror? But however much he pondered he found no answer. And whenever the thought occurred to him, as it often did, that it all resulted from his not having lived as he ought to have done, he at once recalled the correctness of his whole life and dismissed so strange an idea.

x

Another fortnight passed. Ivan Ilych now no longer left his sofa. He would not lie in bed but lay on the sofa, facing the wall nearly all the time. He suffered ever the same unceasing agonies and in his loneliness pondered always on the same insoluble question: "What is this? Can it be that it is Death?" And the inner voice answered: "Yes, it is Death."

"Why these sufferings?" And the voice answered, "For no reason — they just are so." Beyond and besides this there was nothing.

From the very beginning of his illness, ever since he had first been to see the doctor, Ivan Ilych's life had been divided between two contrary and alternating moods: now it was despair and the expectation of this uncomprehended and terrible death, and now hope and an intently interested observation of the functioning of his organs. Now before his eyes there was only a kidney or an intestine that temporarily evaded its duty, and now only that incomprehensible and dreadful death from which it was impossible to escape.

These two states of mind had alternated from the very beginning of his illness, but the further it progressed the more doubtful and fantastic became the conception of the kidney, and the more real the sense of impending death.

He had but to call to mind what he had been three months before and what he was now, to call to mind with what regularity he had been going downhill, for every possibility of hope to be shattered.

Latterly during that loneliness in which he found himself as he lay facing the back of the sofa, a loneliness in the midst of a populous town and surrounded by numerous acquaintances and relations but that yet could not have been more complete anywhere — either at the bottom of the sea or under the earth — during that terrible loneliness Ivan Ilych had lived only in memories of the past. Pictures of his past rose before him one after another. They always began with what was nearest in time and then went back to what was most remote — to his childhood — and rested there. If he thought of the stewed prunes that had been offered him that day, his mind went back to the raw shrivelled French plums of his childhood, their peculiar flavor and the flow of saliva when he sucked their stones, and along with the memory of that taste came a whole series of memories of those days: his nurse, his brother, and their toys. "No, I mustn't think of that. . . . It is too painful," Ivan Ilych said to himself, and brought himself back to the present — to the button on the back of the sofa and the creases in its morocco. "Morocco is expensive, but it does not wear well: there had been a quarrel about it. It was a different kind of quarrel and a different kind of morocco that time when we tore father's portfolio and were punished, and mamma brought us some tarts. . . ." And again his thoughts dwelt on his childhood, and again it was painful and he tried to banish them and fix his mind on something else.

Then again together with that chain of memories another series passed through his mind — of how his illness had progressed and grown worse. There also the further back he looked the more life there had been. There had been more of what was good in life and more of life itself. The two merged together. "Just as the pain went on getting worse and worse, so my life grew worse and worse," he thought. "There is one bright spot there at the back, at the beginning of life, and afterwards all becomes blacker and blacker and proceeds more and more rapidly — in inverse ratio to the square of the distance from death," thought Ivan Ilych. And the example of a stone falling downwards with increasing velocity entered his mind. Life, a series of increasing sufferings, flies further and further towards its end — the most terrible suffering. "I am flying. . . ." He shuddered, shifted himself, and tried to resist, but was already aware that resistance was impossible, and again with eyes weary of gazing but unable to cease seeing what was before them, he stared at the back of the sofa and waited — awaiting that dreadful fall and shock and destruction.

"Resistance is impossible!" he said to himself. "If I could only understand what it is all for! But that too is impossible. An explanation would be possible if it could be said that I have not lived as I ought to. But it is impossible to say that," and he remembered all the legality, correctitude, and propriety of his life. "That at any rate can certainly not be admitted," he thought, and his lips smiled ironically as if someone could see that smile and be taken in by it. "There is no explanation! Agony, death. . . . What for?"

xi

Another two weeks went by in this way and during that fortnight an event occurred that Ivan Ilych and his wife had desired. Petrishchev formally proposed. It happened in the evening. The next day Praskovya Fëdorovna came into her husband's room considering how best to inform him of it, but that very night there had been a fresh change for the worse in his condition. She found him still lying on the sofa but in a different position. He lay on his back, groaning and staring fixedly straight in front of him.

She began to remind him of his medicines, but he turned his eyes towards her with such a look that she did not finish what she was saying; so great an animosity, to her in particular, did that look express.

"For Christ's sake let me die in peace!" he said.

She would have gone away, but just then their daughter came in and went up to say good morning. He looked at her as he had done at his wife, and in reply to her inquiry about his health said dryly that he would soon free them all of himself. They were both silent and after sitting with him for a while went away.

"Is it our fault?" Lisa said to her mother. "It's as if we were to blame! I am sorry for papa, but why should we be tortured?"

The doctor came at his usual time. Ivan Ilych answered "Yes" and "No," never taking his angry eyes from him, and at last said: "You know you can do nothing for me, so leave me alone."

"We can ease your sufferings."

"You can't even do that. Let me be."

The doctor went into the drawing-room and told Praskovya Fëdorovna that the case was very serious and that the only resource left was opium to allay her husband's sufferings, which must be terrible.

It was true, as the doctor said, that Ivan Ilych's physical sufferings were terrible, but worse than the physical sufferings were his mental sufferings, which were his chief torture.

His mental sufferings were due to the fact that that night, as he looked at Gerasim's sleepy, good-natured face with its prominent cheek-bones, the question suddenly occurred to him: "What if my whole life has really been wrong?"

It occurred to him that what had appeared perfectly impossible before, namely that he had not spent his life as he should have done, might after all be true. It occurred to him that his scarcely perceptible attempts to struggle against what was considered good by the most highly placed people, those scarcely noticeable impulses which he had immediately suppressed, might have been the real thing, and all the rest false. And his professional duties and the whole arrangement of his life and of his family, and all his social and official interests, might all have been false. He tried to defend all those things to himself and suddenly felt the weakness of what he was defending. There was nothing to defend.

"But if that is so," he said to himself, "and I am leaving this life with the consciousness that I have lost all that was given me and it is impossible to rectify it — what then?"

He lay on his back and began to pass his life in review in quite a new way. In the morning when he saw first his footman, then his wife, then his daughter, and then the doctor, their every word and movement confirmed to him the awful truth that had been revealed to him during the night. In them he saw himself — all that for which he had lived — and saw clearly that it was not real at all, but a terrible and huge deception which had hidden both life and death. This consciousness intensified his physical suffering tenfold. He groaned and tossed about, and pulled at his clothing which choked and stifled him. And he hated them on that account.

He was given a large dose of opium and became unconscious, but at noon his sufferings began again. He drove everybody away and tossed from side to side.

His wife came to him and said:

"Jean, my dear, do this for me. It can't do any harm and often helps. Healthy people often do it."

He opened his eyes wide.

"What? Take communion? Why? It's unnecessary! However. . . ."

She began to cry.

"Yes, do, my dear. I'll send for our priest. He is such a nice man."

"All right. Very well," he muttered.

When the priest came and heard his confession, Ivan Ilych was softened and seemed to feel a relief from his doubts and consequently from his sufferings, and for a moment there came a ray of hope. He again began to think of the vermiform appendix and the possibility of correcting it. He received the sacrament with tears in his eyes.

When they laid him down again afterwards he felt a moment's ease, and the hope that he might live awoke in him again. He began to think of the operation that had been suggested to him. "To live! I want to live!" he said to himself.

His wife came in to congratulate him after his communion, and when uttering the usual conventional words she added:

"You feel better, don't you?"

Without looking at her he said "Yes."

Her dress, her figure, the expression of her face, the tone of her voice, all revealed the same thing. "This is wrong, it is not as it should be. All you have lived for and still live for is falsehood and deception, hiding life and death from you." And as soon as he admitted that thought, his hatred and his agonizing physical suffering again sprang up, and with that suffering a consciousness of the unavoidable, approaching end. And to this was added a new sensation of grinding shooting pain and a feeling of suffocation.

The expression of his face when he uttered that "yes" was dreadful. Having uttered it, he looked her straight in the eyes, turned on his face with a rapidity extraordinary in his weak state and shouted:

"Go away! Go away and leave me alone!"

xii

From that moment the screaming began that continued for three days, and was so terrible that one could not hear it through two closed doors without horror. At the moment he answered his wife he realized that he was lost, that there was no return, that the end had come, the very end, and his doubts were still unsolved and remained doubts.

"Oh! Oh! Oh!" he cried in various intonations. He had begun by screaming, "I won't!" and continued screaming on the letter *O*.

For three whole days, during which time did not exist for him, he struggled in that black sack into which he was being thrust by an invisible, resistless force. He struggled as a man condemned to death struggles in the hands of the executioner, knowing that he cannot save himself. And every moment he felt that despite all his efforts he was drawing nearer and nearer to what terrified him. He felt that his agony was due to his being thrust into that black hole and still more to his not being able to get right into it. He was hindered from getting into it by his conviction that his life had been a good one. That very justification of his life held him fast and prevented his moving forward, and it caused him most torment of all.

Suddenly some force struck him in the chest and side, making it still harder to breathe, and he fell through the hole and there at the bottom was a light. What had happened to him was like the sensation one sometimes experiences in a railway carriage when one thinks one is going backwards while one is really going forwards and suddenly becomes aware of the real direction.

"Yes, it was all not the right thing," he said to himself, "but that's no matter. It can be done. But what *is* the right thing?" he asked himself, and suddenly grew quiet.

This occurred at the end of the third day, two hours before his death. Just then his schoolboy son had crept softly in and gone up to the bedside. The dying man was still screaming desperately and waving his arms. His hand fell on the boy's head, and the boy caught it, pressed it to his lips, and began to cry.

At that very moment Ivan Ilych fell through and caught sight of the light, and it was revealed to him that though his life had not been what it should have been, this could still be rectified. He asked himself, "What *is* the right thing?" and grew still, listening. Then he felt that someone was kissing his hand. He opened his eyes, looked at his son, and felt sorry for him. His wife came up to him and he glanced at her. She was gazing at him open-mouthed, with undried tears on her nose and cheek and a despairing look on her face. He felt sorry for her too.

"Yes, I am making them wretched," he thought. "They are sorry, but it will be better for them when I die." He wished to say this but had not the strength to utter it. "Besides, why speak? I must act," he thought. With a look at his wife he indicated his son and said: "Take him away . . . sorry for him . . . sorry for you too. . . ." He tried to add, "forgive me," but said "forgo" and waved his hand, knowing that He whose understanding mattered would understand.

And suddenly it grew clear to him that what had been oppressing him and would not leave him was all dropping away at once from two sides, from ten sides, and from all sides. He was sorry for them, he must act so as not to hurt them: release them and free himself from these sufferings.

"How good and how simple!" he thought. "And the pain?" he asked himself. "What has become of it? Where are you, pain?"

He turned his attention to it.

"Yes, here it is. Well, what of it? Let the pain be."

"And death . . . where is it?"

He sought his former accustomed fear of death and did not find it. "Where is it? What death?" There was no fear because there was no death.

In place of death there was light.

"So that's what it is!" he suddenly exclaimed aloud. "What joy!"

To him all this happened in a single instant, and the meaning of that instant did not change. For those present his agony continued for another two hours. Something rattled in his throat, his emaciated body twitched, then the gasping and rattle became less and less frequent.

"It is finished!" said someone near him.

He heard these words and repeated them in his soul.

"Death is finished," he said to himself. "It is no more!"

He drew in a breath, stopped in the midst of a sigh, stretched out, and died.

ACKNOWLEDGMENTS

Excerpt from "First Muse" from *Something to Declare* by Julia Alvarez. Published by Plume, an imprint of Penguin Random House, and originally in hardcover by Algonquin Books of Chapel Hill. First published under the title "One of a Thousand Scheherezades" in *Mirror, Mirror: Women Writers Explore the Fairy Tales That Have Changed Their Lives*, Anchor Books/Doubleday, 1998. © 1998 by Julia Alvarez. By permission of Susan Bergholz Literary Services, New York, NY, and Lamy, NM. All rights reserved.

Excerpt from *Nicomachean Ethics* by Aristotle. Translated by Terence Irwin, 2nd edition, Indianapolis: Hackett Publishing Company, 1999. Reprinted by permission of Hackett Publishing Company Inc. All rights reserved.

Excerpt from *The Way of Life: A Theology of Christian Vocation* by Gary D. Badcock. © 1998 by Gary D. Badcock. By permission of Wm. B. Eerdmans Publishing Co.

"Sonny's Blues" by James Baldwin, originally published in the *Partisan Review*. Collected in *Going to Meet the Man*, published by Vintage Books. © 1957 by James Baldwin. Reprinted by arrangement with the James Baldwin Estate.

"Composing a Life Story" from *Willing to Learn: Passages of Personal Discovery* by Mary Catherine Bateson. © 2004 by Mary Catherine Bateson. Used by permission of the author.

Excerpt from *Jaber Crow* by Wendell Berry. © 2000 by Wendell Berry. Reprinted by permission of Counterpoint Press.

"Manifesto: The Mad Farmer Liberation Front" by Wendell Berry from *Selected Poems of Wendell Berry*. © 1988 by Wendell Berry. Reprinted by permission of Counterpoint Press.

"No-Self or Not-Self" from *Noble Strategy* by Thanissaro Bhikkhu. © 1999 by Abhayagiri Buddhist Monastery. Reprinted with permission.

Excerpt from "The Illusive Search for Balance" from *Well-Being at Work* by Matt Bloom. © 2011 by Matt Bloom. Reprinted by permission of the author.

Excerpts from *Ethics* by Dietrich Bonhoeffer. Translated from the German by Neville Horton Smith. © 1955 by SCM Press and by Macmillan Publishing

Company. Reprinted by permission of Hymns Ancient & Modern Ltd and of Scribner, a division of Simon & Schuster Inc. All rights reserved.

Excerpt from *Finding Time: The Economics of Work-Life Conflict* by Heather Boushey, Cambridge, Mass.: Harvard University Press. © 2016 by Heather Boushey.

"A Moral Bucket List" by David Brooks from *The New York Times*. © 2015 The New York Times. All rights Reserved. Used under license. www.nytimes.com.

"Vocation" from *Wishful Thinking: A Theological ABC* by Frederick Buechner. © 1973 by Frederick Buechner. Reprinted by permission of HarperCollins Publishers.

"Vocation as Grace" by Will D. Campbell, in *Callings!*, edited by James Y. Holloway and Will D. Campbell. ©1974 by Paulist Press (Deus Books). Reprinted by permission of Will D. Campbell.

"A Fable for Tomorrow" from *Silent Spring* by Rachel Carson. © 1962 by Rachel L. Carson, renewed 1990 by Roger Christie. Reprinted by permission of Houghton Mifflin Harcourt Publishing Company and Frances Collin, Trustee. All rights reserved. Unauthorized redistribution of this text is expressly forbidden.

"Requiem for a Nest," fourteen lines from *Ostinato Vamps: Poems* by Wanda Coleman. © 2003. Reprinted by permission of the University of Pittsburgh Press.

Excerpt from *Good Will Hunting* by Matt Damon & Ben Affleck, as originally published by Faber and Faber Ltd., 1998.

"Prayer for My Children" from *Four Testimonies: Poems* by Kate Daniels, as originally published by LSU Press, 1998. Reprinted by permission of Kate Daniels.

Excerpts from *Therese* by Dorothy Day, Templegate Publishing, 1960. Reprinted by permission of Templegate Publishers.

"A Roofer" from *Callings* by Carl Dennis. © 2010 by Carl Dennis. Used by permission of Penguin Books, an imprint of Penguin Publishing Group, a division of Penguin Random House LLC. All rights reserved.

Excerpt from *Glittering Vices* by Rebecca Konyndyk DeYoung. © 2009. Used by permission of Brazos, a division of Baker Publishing Group.

"Writing Home" from *Black Nature* by Camille T. Dungy. © 2009. The University of Georgia. Reprinted with permission.

"The Last Hours" from *Different Hours* by Stephen Dunn. © 2000 by Stephen Dunn. Used by permission of W. W. Norton & Company, Inc.

Excerpt from *The Iliad* by Homer, translated by Robert Fagles. Translation © 1990 by Robert Fagles. Used by permission of Viking Books, an imprint of Penguin Publishing Group, a division of Penguin Random House LLC. All rights reserved.

Encyclical Letter *Laudato Si'* of the Holy Father Francis on Care for Our Common

Home, May 24, 2015. © 2015 by Libreria Editrice Vaticana. Reprinted with permission of Libreria Editrice Vaticana.

"Two Tramps in Mud Time" by Robert Frost from the book *The Poetry of Robert Frost*, edited by Edward Connery Lathem. © 1969 by Henry Holt and Company. © 1936 by Robert Frost. © 1964 by Lesley Frost Ballantine. Utilized by permission of Henry Holt and Company. All rights reserved.

Excerpt from *The Little Virtues* by Natalia Ginsburg. Reprinted by permission of Arcade Publishing, an imprint of Skyhorse Publishing, Inc.

Excerpt from *Outliers: The Story of Success* by Malcolm Gladwell. © 2008, 2011. Reprinted by permission of Little, Brown and Company, an imprint of Hachette Book Group, Inc.

"I Hear Them . . . Calling (And I Know What It Means)" by Vincent Harding, in *Callings!*, edited by James Y. Holloway and Will D. Campbell. © 1974 by Paulist Press (Deus Books). Reprinted by permission of Vincent Harding.

"Making the Match: Career Choice" from *The Fabric of This World* by Lee Hardy. © 1990. Reprinted by permission of Wm. B. Eerdmans Publishing Company.

Excerpts from "A Palace in Time" and "Beyond Civilization" from *The Sabbath: Its Meaning for Modern Man* by Abraham Joshua Heschel. © 1979 by Sylvia Heschel. Reprinted by permission of Farrar, Straus and Giroux.

Excerpts from *The Remains of the Day* by Kazuo Ishiguro. © 1988 by Kazuo Ishiguro. Used by permission of Alfred A. Knopf, an imprint of the Knopf Doubleday Publishing Group, a division of Penguin Random House LLC; Faber and Faber Ltd.; and Vintage Canada/Alfred A. Knopf Canada, a division of Penguin Random House Canada, Limited. All rights reserved.

Excerpt from *Beginning Our Day*, vol 1, by Ajahn Karunadhammo. © 2015 by Abhayagiri Buddist Monastery. Reprinted with permission.

Excerpt from "Robert McG. Thomas, 60, Chronicler of Unsung Lives" by Michael T. Kaufman from *The New York Times*. © 2000 by The New York Times. All rights Reserved. Used under license. www.nytimes.com.

Excerpts from "The World House" in *Where Do We Go from Here: Chaos of Community?* Reprinted by arrangement with The Heirs to the Estate of Martin Luther King Jr., c/o Writers House as agent for the proprietor New York, NY. © 1967 by Dr. Martin Luther King, Jr. © renewed 1995 by Coretta Scott King.

"Our Home on Earth" by Winona LaDuke, originally published by *On the Commons*, May 16, 2012. http://onthecommons.org/magazine/our-home-earth. Published with author's permission.

Excerpt from "My Two Lives" by Jhumpa Lahiri, *Newsweek*. © 2006 by Newsweek Media Group. All rights reserved. Used under license. www.newsweek.com.

"She Unnames Them" by Ursula K. LeGuin. © 1985 by Ursula K. LeGuin. First appeared in *The New Yorker* in 1985, reprinted in *Buffalo Gals and Other Animal Presences* by Ursula K. Le Guin. Reprinted by permission of Curtis Brown Ltd.

"Acoma Creation Myth" from *Creation Myths of the World: An Encyclopedia*, vol. 1, 1994, by David Leeming. Republished with permission of ABC-CLIO Inc. and conveyed through Copyright Clearance Center Inc.

"Annunciation" by Denise Levertov from *A Door in the Hive*, © 1989 by Denise Levertov, and from *New Selected Poems* by Denise Levertov (2003). Reprinted by permission of New Directions Publishing Corp. and Bloodaxe Books. www.bloodaxebooks.com.

"Beginners" by Denise Levertov from *Candles in Babylon*, © 1982 by Denise Levertov, and from *New Selected Poems* by Denise Levertov (2003). Reprinted by permission of New Directions Publishing Corp. and Bloodaxe Books. www.bloodaxebooks.com.

"Learning in War Time" from *The Weight of Glory* by C. S. Lewis. © 1949 by C. S. Lewis Pte. Ltd. Reprinted with permission.

Excerpt from *The Giver* by Lois Lowry. © 1993 by Lois Lowry. Reprinted by permission of Houghton Mifflin Harcourt Publishing Company. All rights reserved.

Wangari Maathai–Nobel Lecture. © 2004 by The Nobel Foundation. Used with permission.

"Vulnerability, Dependence, Animality" from *Dependent Rational Animals: Why Human Beings Need the Virtues* by Alasdair C. MacIntyre. © 1999 by Carus Publishing Company. Reproduced with permission.

"The Greatest: How Muhammad Ali Won Me Over" by Gordon Marino (July 8, 2016). © 2016 by Commonweal Foundation. Reprinted with permission. For more information, visit www.commonwealmagazine.org.

Excerpt from *The Redemptive Self* by Dan McAdams. © 2005 by Dan P. McAdams. Reproduced with permission of Oxford Publishing Limited through PLSclear.

"Friendship and Vocation" in *Friendship, A Study in Theological Ethics* by Gilbert C. Meilaender. © 1981 by University of Notre Dame Press. Used with permission.

Excerpt from *The Sayings of Mencius*, translated by James R. Ware. Translation © 1960 by James R. Ware. Used by permission of Berkley, an imprint of Penguin Publishing Group, a division of Penguin Random House LLC. All rights reserved.

"False Counselor" by Madeline Miller. TLS / News Licensing. October 10, 2018. Reprinted with permission.

"Recitatif" from *Confirmation: An Anthology of African American Women* by Toni

ACKNOWLEDGMENTS

"Saving the Life That Is Your Own: The Importance of Models in the Artist's Life" from *In Search of Our Mothers' Gardens: Womanist Prose* by Alice Walker. © 1973 by Alice Walker. Reprinted by permission of Houghton Mifflin Harcourt Publishing Company and The Joy Harris Literary Agency Inc. All rights reserved.

"Carrion" by Anthony Walton. Used with permission of Anthony Walton.

Excerpt from *Chuang Tzu: Basic Writings*, edited by Burton Watson. © 1964 by Columbia University Press. Reprinted with permission of the publisher.

Excerpt from *Hsun Tzu: Basic Writings*, edited by Burton Watson. © 1963, 1996 by Columbia University Press. Reprinted with permission of the publisher.

"The Undeclared Major" from *A Gravestone of Wheat*. © 1989 by Will Weaver. Originally published by Simon & Schuster. Used by permission of Will Weaver.

"Rethinking Service" by Samuel Wells. © 2013 by *The Cresset*. Reprinted with permission.

Excerpt from *Exemplarist Moral Theory* by Linda Zagzebski. © 2017 by Oxford Publishing Limited. Reproduced with permission of Oxford Publishing Limited through PLSclear.

"Defining a Doctor with a Tear, a Shrug, and a Schedule" by Abigail Zuger from *The New York Times*. © 2004 by The New York Times. All rights reserved. Used under license. www.nytimes.com.

Genesis 1–3 and Book of Ruth, New Revised Standard Version Bible. © 1989 by National Council of the Churches of Christ in the United States of America. Used by permission. All rights reserved worldwide.

INDEX

"Acoma Creation Story," 449, 516–17
Addams, Jane, 328, 394, 407–11
admiration, 6, 11
  and exemplarity, 52–53, 119–20, 121,
    129, 132, 138, 143, 146, 193, 567, 568
advice, 6, 229–34
  and community, 31–39, 107, 229, 235,
    258–67, 277–84, 285
  and conscience, 232, 254–57
  and parents' expectations, 235–41,
    242–52
  and religious tradition, 232, 254–57
  and teachers, 16–30, 160–61, 229,
    230, 406
Aeschylus, 414–18
Affleck, Ben, 285–93
Agamemnon (Aeschylus), 396, 414–18
Ali, Muhammad, 43, 53, 138–42
Alvarez, Julia, 524, 537–40, 543
"The Ancient People" (Cather), 233,
  268–76
"Annunciation" (Levertov), 149–52
Anthony, P. D., 206
Aquinas, Thomas, 49, 86, 91, 173
Aristotle, 51, 205, 395
  on ethics, 53, 54, 119
  on happiness, 83–85, 168–69
  on leisure, 399, 436
  on virtue, 48, 49, 86, 88, 89–90, 97,
    108, 110, 525, 566
  on wisdom, 120–21

authenticity, 6, 45, 46–48, 567–68
  and identity, 59–64, 229, 324–25, 333
  and true self, 65–71, 76–78, 79–80
  and vocation, 194, 199, 218–27
  and women's rights, 72–75

Badcock, Gary, 55, 164–70, 177, 285
balanced lives, 391–99
  contesting metaphor of, 397–98,
    427–31
  and heroism, 413
  and rest, 435–40
  and tragedy, 414–18
  and women, 404–6, 408–11, 419–24
  and work, 398–99, 400–402, 404–6,
    412, 419–26
Baldwin, James, 233, 294–322
Ballou, Sullivan, 330, 371–73
Barth, Karl, 158, 159, 207
Bateson, Gregory, 533–34
Bateson, Mary Catherine, 397, 523–24,
  525, 529–36, 541, 543, 549
"Beginners" (Levertov), 449, 518–19
Bellah, Robert, 550, 556
Berry, Wendell, 398–99, 432–34, 524,
  525, 541–42
Bhikkhu, Thanissaro, 47–48, 76–78
Bloom, Matt, 397–98, 427–31
Bonhoeffer, Dietrich, 55, 176–79, 182,
  568
Book of Ruth, 328–29, 331, 344–49

Boushey, Heather, 396–97, 419–26

Brooks, David, 50, 102–7

Brooks, Phillips, 25–26

Buechner, Frederick, 55–56, 180–81, 258, 393–94

Calvin, John, 161, 204, 207

Campbell, Will, 56, 182–83

"Carpenter Bee" (Trethewey), 480–81

"Carrion" (Walton), 478–79

Carson, Rachel, 443, 448, 457–59

Cather, Willa, 233, 268–76, 565

character
    formation of, 50–51, 87–91, 97–101, 103–7, 110–13
    judgments about, 43, 47, 48–49, 566
    and significant life, 11, 26–28, 549
    and virtue, 6, 83–85, 128
    and work, 184–85, 189, 192, 195–98, 214, 216–17, 567

Chautauqua, 16–18, 19, 28

choice
    and balanced life, 395–96, 407–11, 412, 414–18
    and freedom, 13, 150–52, 214–15, 233, 327–28, 377, 521
    and identity, 46, 47, 59–64, 229, 231
    and just work, 195–98, 524
    and life stories, 521–26, 527–28, 529–36
    vocational, 153–63, 164–70, 235–41, 277–84, 396–97

"The Choice" (Yeats), 395, 412

"Choosing" (Badcock), 164–70

Chuang Tzu, 56, 184–85

Coleman, Wanda, 477

community, 89, 125–27
    and advice, 231, 232–33, 235–41

and balanced life, 407–11, 432–34, 523–24

and environment, 484–88

and health, 338–43

and human flourishing, 326, 327–28, 378–83, 388–90, 488

and identity, 59–64, 69–71, 329, 443, 489

religious, 134–36

and significant life, 14–15, 331–32, 338–43

and vocation, 31–39, 154, 155, 157, 182–83, 203, 258–67, 285

"Composing a Life Story" (Bateson), 523–24, 529–36

Confucius, 51, 108, 109, 119, 122, 127–28

Damon, Matt, 285–93

Daniels, Kate, 326–27, 336–37

Day, Dorothy, 53, 105, 129–37

The Death of Ivan Ilych (Tolstoy), 7, 565, 566–69, 570–618

"Defining a Doctor" (Zuger), 400–402

democracy, 388, 409, 490, 492
    and just work, 190, 195–98
    and secular traditions, 3, 15, 16–30

"Democracy and the Value of Work" (Muirhead), 195–98

Dennis, Carl, 216–17

dependence, 333–37
    vs. autonomy, 73–75, 160
    on others, 61, 182, 324, 326–27, 330, 331–32, 498

DeYoung, Rebecca Konyndyk, 49, 51–52, 86–91

"Don't Quit This Day Job" (Sibert), 403–6

Dunbar, Paul Laurence, 33, 474–76, 489

Dungy, Camille T., 443–44, 445, 470–73
Dunn, Stephen, 214–15

Eisenhower, Dwight David, 11–12, 104
Eliot, George, 106, 409
environmental crisis, 441–50, 451–59, 464–69, 482, 489, 496
 and democracy, 489–95
 and education, 504–6
 human roots of, 499–504
Erikson, Erik H., 551
The Ethics of Authenticity (Taylor), 59–64, 325
exemplarity, 6, 43–44, 45, 51–53, 119–28, 149, 193, 565–66, 568
 of heroes, 123–24, 143–46
 of sages, 120–21, 127–28
 of saints, 92–93, 94, 125–27, 131–37, 153
"Explorations of True Self" (Parker), 65–71
"A Fable for Tomorrow" (Carson), 442–43, 457–59
"False Counsellor" (Miller), 53, 143–46
family
 and motherhood, 336–37
 parental expectations, 33, 160, 214–15, 231–32, 235–41, 242–52
 vs. social claim, 328, 394, 407–11
 and vocational choice, 166–68
 and work, 391–99, 403–6, 419–26, 429–30
"Filial Relations" (Addams), 394, 407–11
"Finding Time" (Boushey), 393, 396–97, 417–26
"First Muse" (Alvarez), 524, 537–40
Francis (pope), 445–47, 496–506

Francis of Assissi, 410, 446, 496, 498
freedom
 and authenticity, 61–62, 72–75, 78
 and choice, 13, 156–57, 192, 196, 377, 500, 503
 and life stories, 531–33, 554–55
 and responsibility, 176–79, 447
friendship, 329–30, 353–70
 Aristotle on, 48, 54, 205
 and balanced lives, 391–92
 and identity, 229
 and virtue, 89
 and vocation, 7, 126–27, 192, 204, 233, 235–41, 280–81, 285, 290–93
 See also human interdependence
"Friendship and Vocation" (Meilaender), 204–7
Frost, Robert, 191, 208–11, 234, 464, 521–22, 527–28

Genesis 1–3, 439, 447–49, 507–12, 513
Ginzburg, Natalia, 50, 97–101, 102
The Giver (Lowry), 232–33, 258–67, 327–28
Gladwell, Malcolm, 327, 338–43
"Glittering Vices" (DeYoung), 49, 51, 86–91
Good Will Hunting (Affleck and Damon), 233, 285–93

Habits of the Heart (Bellah), 556
"A Handful of Dates" (Salih), 232, 253–57
happiness
 Aristotle on, 48, 83–85, 168–69
 of individuals, 73, 74
 and love, 95
Harding, Vincent, 12, 13–15, 31–39, 229
Hardy, Lee, 55, 153–63, 164, 176–77

"The Haunted Oak" (Dunbar), 474–76, 489
health, 339–43
heroes, heroism, 16, 18–19, 282
  and exemplarity, 52, 53, 90–91, 119, 120, 121, 122, 123–24, 143–46
  of ordinary lives, 19–26, 28
  and significant life, 395, 413
Heschel, Abraham Joshua, 191, 399, 435–40
Homer, 53, 143–46, 395, 413
Horne, James, 165
Hsun Tzu, 51, 108, 110–13, 119
human interdependence, 323–32, 338–43, 344–49, 374–87, 388–90, 445, 498. *See also* community; friendship
Hurston, Zora Neale, 525, 543, 547–48

ideals
  defined, 26–27
  fighting for, 371
  and fitting work, 196–98
  moral, 90–91
  and significant life, 16, 17–19, 25, 28–30, 47, 61–64, 107, 284
identity
  and authenticity, 47, 65–71
  and community, 59–64, 229, 231–32, 325, 329, 343, 350–52
  and life stories, 521–22, 526, 556–57
  and vocation, 1–2, 6, 164–68, 184–85, 218–27
  and work, 1–2, 6, 189–94, 195–98, 205–7, 212–13, 214–15, 216–17, 567
The Iliad (Homer), 144, 145, 146, 395, 413
"The Illusive Search for Balance" (Bloom), 427–31

"Improving Yourself" (Hsun Tzu), 110–13
individualism, 6, 48, 60–62, 333
  and community, 70, 324–25, 331–32
  and women's rights, 73–75
"I Resolve to Become a Jungle Doctor" (Schweitzer), 233, 277–84
Ishiguro, Kazuo, 193–94, 218–27
isolation, 374, 378–83, 384–87
  overcoming, 344–49, 350–52, 353–70
  of soul, 73

James, Henry, Sr., 12–13
James, William, 12–13, 15, 16–30, 229, 568
Jayber Crow (Berry), 524–25, 541–42, 543
Jones, Edith (Wharton), 51, 114–15

Karunadhammo, Ajahn, 48, 79–80
Kaufman, Michael T., 558–62
King, Martin Luther, Jr., 14, 36, 91, 330, 331–32, 388–90

LaDuke, Winona, 444, 482–88, 516
Lahiri, Jhumpa, 329, 350–52
"The Last Hours" (Dunn), 214–15
Laudato Si' (Pope Francis), 445–47, 453–54, 496–506
"Learning in War-Time" (Lewis), 171–75
LeGuin, Ursula, 448–49, 513–15
"A Letter to His Wife, 1861" (Ballou), 371–73
Levertov, Denise, 54, 149–52, 449, 518–19
Lewis, C. S., 55, 171–75
life stories
  composing, 522–24, 529–36, 543–48

continuity/discontinuity of, 530–34
and conversion narratives, 534–35
final versions of, 558–62
and generativity, 525–26, 551, 554,
556–57
literature and, 524–25, 537–40, 542
multiple interpretations of, 535–36
redemption narratives, 525–26, 549,
552–55, 568
revision of, 527–28
"A Life Story Made in America"
(McAdams), 525–26, 549–57
The Little Virtues (Ginzburg), 50,
97–101
"A Love Letter from the Holocene to
the Anthropocene" (Rasmussen),
451–55
Lowry, Lois, 232–33, 258–67
Luther, Martin, 54, 55, 207

Maathai, Wangari, 444–45, 489–95
MacIntyre, Alasdair, 88, 326, 331,
333–35
Malcolm X, 38, 534–35
"Manifesto: The Mad Farmer Liberation Front" (Berry), 398–99, 432–34
Marino, Gordon, 53, 138–42
McAdams, Dan P., 525–26, 549–57,
568
Meilaender, Gilbert, 191, 192, 204–7
Mencius, 51, 108–9, 110, 119, 184
Miller, Madeline, 53, 143–46
"The Moral Bucket List" (Brooks), 50,
102–7
moral formation, 49–53, 83, 86–91,
102–7, 110–13
and authenticity, 60–62
of children, 97–101
and conflict, 415–18

and the environment, 504–6
and exemplarity, 119–46
Morrison, Toni, 329–30, 353–70
mortality, 175, 336, 374, 375–77, 378,
383–87, 456, 558, 565–69
Muirhead, Russell, 190, 192, 195–98,
199, 258, 521, 524, 567
"My Two Lives" (Lahiri), 329, 331,
350–52

natural world/nature
African American relationship to,
472–73, 474–76
humanity and, 51, 108–9, 443–44,
445–49, 450, 454, 457–59, 460,
466–67, 470–71, 478–79, 480–81,
497–98, 507, 509–10, 511–12, 513–15,
518–19
human responsibilities to, 460, 466,
467
indigenous people's relationship to,
444, 483–87
views of, 466, 468–69
Nesse, Rudolph, 68–69
Nicomachean Ethics (Aristotle), 83–85,
395
"Nobel Peace Prize Lecture" (Maathai),
489–95
"No-Self or Not-Self" (Bhikkhu),
76–78
Nussbaum, Martha, 396, 398, 414–18

Odysseus, 143–46, 413
"On Love" (Pieper), 92–96
"Our Home on Earth" (LaDuke),
482–88

Parker, Palmer, 47, 65–71, 79, 108
"Patience" (Jones), 51, 114–15

Perkins, Frances, 105–6

Perkins, William, 54–55, 204, 205

Pieper, Josef, 50, 86, 92–96, 149

Piercy, Margaret, 191–92, 212–13, 394

"The Place of Responsibility" (Bonhoeffer), 55, 177–79

poverty, 25–26, 389–90
  and environmental degradation, 491–92, 496, 502

"Prayer for My Children" (Daniels), 326–27, 336–37

Rasmussen, Larry, 442, 444, 446, 451–55, 482

reason
  and authenticity, 62–63
  and formation of identity, 85, 521–22

"Recitatif" (Morrison), 329–30, 331, 353–70

Reich, Robert, 394–95

The Remains of the Day (Ishiguro), 193–94, 218–27

"Requiem for a Nest" (Coleman), 477

"Rethinking Service" (Wells), 330–31, 374–87

"The Road Not Taken" (Frost), 521–22, 527–28, 558

"Robert McG. Thomas, 60, Chronicler of Unsung Lives" (Kaufman), 526, 558–62

"Roofer" (Dennis), 216–17

"The Roseto Mystery" (Gladwell), 327, 338–43

Rousseau, Jean-Jacques, 61, 65

"The Sabbath" (Heschel), 435–40

sage, 52–53, 119, 120–21, 122, 127–28

saint, 52–53, 119, 120, 122, 125–27, 131–37

Salih, Tayeb, 253–57

"Sanctuary" (Sanders), 443, 460–69, 482

Sanders, Scott Russell, 443, 460–69, 482

"Saving the Life That Is Your Own" (Walker), 543–48

Sayers, Dorothy, 190–91, 199–203, 204, 205, 212

Sayings (Mencius), 51, 108–9

Schrader, Paul, 442

Schweitzer, Albert, 233, 277–84, 457, 565, 568

secularism, 67–68, 69

self, selfhood, true self, 47, 65–71
  and Buddhist thought, 47–48, 76–78, 79–80
  moralism and, 67, 68–71
  and the other, 389, 556
  redemptive, 555
  solitude of, 47, 73–75

service, 331, 374–87

"She Unnames Them" (LeGuin), 448–49, 513–15

Sibert, Karen S., 393, 403–6

significant lives, 3–7, 16–30
  and balance, 392–99, 432–34
  and character, 48–49, 50
  and choice, 521, 523
  and community, 14–15, 31, 33–39, 182–83, 327–28, 338–43
  vs. good life, 11–12, 396
  and life stories, 529, 558
  and meaning of *Death of Ivan Ilych*, 565–69
  and relationship to others, 323–24, 326–27, 328–30, 331, 344–49, 371–73
  and work, 193, 203, 204, 216–17

Smith, Adam, 334–35

Socha, Leopold, 123–24
"Solitude of Self" (Stanton), 47, 72–75
"Sonny's Blues" (Baldwin), 233, 234,
    294–322
Stalin, Joseph, 11
Stanton, Elizabeth Cady, 47, 48, 72–75
Stevenson, Robert Louis, 22–23

talent
    and genius, 120, 233–34, 285–93,
        294–322
    and vocation, 106, 154–55, 157–58,
        161, 172–73, 230, 429
Tan, Amy, 232, 242–52
Taylor, Charles, 46, 54, 59–64, 72, 76,
    229, 230, 325, 521, 568
technology, 499–504
Teresa of Avila, 130, 137, 534
Teresa of Calcutta, 91, 92, 93, 94, 153
Therese (Day), 130–37
Therese of Lisieux, 53, 129–37
"This Is Who I Am" (Karunadhammo),
    48, 79–80
time, 419–26, 435–40
"To Be of Use" (Piercy), 191–92, 212–13,
    394
Tolstoy, Leo, 7, 20, 21–23, 25, 27, 28,
    565, 566, 568–69, 570–618
Trethewey, Natasha, 480–81
"Two Kinds" (Tan), 232, 242–53
"Two Tramps in Mud Time" (Frost),
    191, 208–11, 234, 527

"The Undecided Major" (Weaver),
    231–32, 235–41, 327

Van Gogh, Vincent, 525, 543, 544
Vanier, Jean, 125–27
virtue, 6, 45, 48–51, 193, 568

and character, 6, 87–91, 102–7, 108–9
contrasted to exemplarity, 52–53
and generosity, 97, 98–101
and happiness, 83–85
and love, 92–96
and patience, 114–15
vocation
    and balanced life, 393–94, 400–402,
        404–6
    and community, 182–83, 231–32,
        258–67
    definition of, 100–101, 180–81
    and identity, 1–2, 6, 45, 101, 105–6,
        189–90
    religious tradition and, 2–3, 6,
        172–75
    responsibility and, 55, 176–79
    and retreat, 268–76
    and students, 171–75
    vocabulary of, 53–56, 149–52, 193,
        568
    and vocational choice, 7, 13, 31–39,
        154–63, 164–70, 171–75, 230, 235–41
    work and, 200, 202–3, 205–7, 209–11
"Vocation" (Buechner), 55–56, 180–81
"Vocation as Grace" (Campbell), 31,
    182–83
vulnerability, 326–27, 333–37
"Vulnerability, Dependence, Animality"
    (MacIntyre), 333–35

Walker, Alice, 525, 543–48
Walton, Anthony E., 478–79
Weaver, Will, 231, 235–41
Wells, Samuel, 194, 330–31, 374–87
White, Lynn, Jr., 447–48
"Why Exemplarism?" (Zagzebski),
    119–28

"Why Work?" (Sayers), 190–91, 199–203

women

authenticity and women's rights, 72–75

and balanced life, 391, 392–94, 404, 406, 407–11, 429

and changing nature of work, 419–26

and composing life stories, 529, 530, 543, 544–48

and the environment, 490, 491, 495

and talent, 268–76

work

and identity, 189, 192–94, 195–96, 197–98, 199–203, 216–17, 218–27, 567

and justice, 195–98

views of, 190–92, 196, 204, 205–7, 208–11, 212–13, 521

"Work, Life, and Vocational Choice" (Hardy), 153–63

"The World House" (King), 331–32, 388–90

"Writing Home" (Dungy), 443–44, 470–73

Wyckoff, Walter, 23–25

Yeats, William Butler, 395, 412

Zagzebski, Linda, 52, 119–28, 138, 143

Zuger, Abigail, 392–93, 400–402